The
Interpersonal
Communication
Book

The Interpersonal Communication Book

SEVENTH EDITION

JOSEPH A. DeVITO

Hunter College of the City University of New York

HarperCollins*CollegePublishers*

Acquisitions Editor: Cynthia Biron
Developmental Editor: Dawn Groundwater
Project Editor: Thomas R. Farrell
Cover Designer: Mary McDonnell
Cover Illustration: Tina Vey
Photo Researcher: Carol Parden
Desktop Administrator: LaToya Wigfall
Manufacturing Administrator: Alexandra Odulax
Electronic Page Makeup: RR Donnelley Barbados
Printer and Binder: RR Donnelley & Sons Company
Cover Printer: The Lehigh Press, Inc.

For permission to use copyrighted material, grateful acknowledgment is made to the copyright holders on page C1, which is hereby made part of this copyright page.

The Interpersonal Communication Book, Seventh Edition
Copyright © 1995 by Joseph A. DeVito

Library of Congress Cataloging-in-Publication Data

DeVito, Joseph A.
  The interpersonal communication book / Joseph A. DeVito. – 7th
ed.
    p. cm.
  Includes bibliographical references and index.
  ISBN 0-673-99177-6
  1. Interpersonal communication.   I. Title.
BF637.C45D49 1995   94-5005
302.2—dc20   CIP
  95 96 97 9 8 7 6 5 4 3 2

To my brother, Louis,
who taught me the values of hard work and fun living

Contents in Brief

Contents in Detail

CONTENTS IN DETAIL **XV**

Preface

It is an honor to write a preface to a text that has proven so popular with students and teachers alike. The many revisions have enabled me to perfect a presentation of interpersonal communication that keeps pace with the rapid research advances in the field and that meets the ever-changing needs of today's students.

This seventh edition builds on the most positively received aspects of past editions while updating and improving the text in several important ways.

The philosophical foundation of the text continues to be the notion of choice. Choice is central to interpersonal communication because the speaker, listener, and communication analyst are constantly confronted with choice points at every stage of the communication process. The text provides readers with worthwhile options in a wide variety of interpersonal situations and discusses the theory, research, and evidence bearing on these communication choices. As a result, after completing this text, the reader should be better equipped to make more reasoned, reasonable, and effective communication decisions.

THE TEXT

This text is a complete learning package that provides students with the opportunity to learn about the research and theory in interpersonal communication and to practice the skills necessary for effective interpersonal interaction.

The unit divisions of the previous editions have been retained. Students continue to favor their brief length and their clear and limited focus, making them easier to read and review. As in the previous edition, the units are grouped into three parts: Preliminaries, Messages, and Relationships.

Each unit opens with **Unit Topics** and **Unit Objectives,** which identify the major topics to be considered in the unit and the behaviors that readers should be able to demonstrate after finishing the unit. The objectives also highlight the most pertinent principles and skills to be presented. The **Summary: Unit in Brief** charts at the end of each unit recap the major concepts discussed. Questions for **Thinking Critically** about the topics of each unit raise significant issues concerning both the theory and research and the skills and applications of interpersonal communication. The tenth and final question in each of these sections focuses on discovering/researching a variety of questions in interpersonal communication and relationships.

Experiential Vehicles follow each unit; these exercises reinforce the concepts discussed and help the student to internalize the principles of the unit.

Two glossaries are included in this edition. First, there is a **Glossary of Interpersonal Concepts,** a detailed glossary of the terms used in the text. Second, there is a

Glossary of Interpersonal Communication Skills, which presents the skills in brief form. This glossary replaces the "Skills in Brief" sections formerly at the end of each part. They are here alphabetized for easy access. These statements of skills may be used in a variety of ways: to help identify areas of weakness, to help sharpen skills by applying them to more complex situations, and to serve as discussion probes or stimuli for class discussion. They are also useful as a handy summary for review and self-testing.

THE SEVENTH EDITION

Among the major improvements in this seventh edition are these:

1. **Cultural aspects** are now integrated throughout the text; the material formerly covered in a separate unit on culture, as well as a wealth of new material, is here spread throughout the text, for example:
   - principles of intercultural communication—contexting and individual versus collective orientation (Unit 2)
   - cultural sensitivity as a skill of interpersonal competence (Unit 6)
   - nonverbals that can create problems around the world (Unit 13)
   - cultural differences in silence (Unit 13)
   - cultural maxims of conversation (Unit 15)
   - conversational taboos around the world (Unit 15)
   - cultural differences in self-disclosure (Unit 8)
   - racism, sexism, and heterosexism (Unit 11)
   - ethnocentrism (Unit 12)
   - gender differences (discussed throughout)

2. Like many textbooks, this one, too, reflects an increased emphasis on **critical thinking.** Additional questions and numerous specific sections throughout the text focus on critical thinking as it relates to interpersonal communication, for example: perception (Unit 3), listening (Unit 4), effectiveness (Unit 6), language barriers (Unit 12), and nonverbal communication (Units 10, 13, and 14).

3. **Research coverage** has been greatly increased in this edition. Recent research findings now support just about every topic considered and reflect the changes that have taken place in the field of interpersonal communication over the last ten years. This research emphasis is also reflected in the end-of-unit questions, which focus on seeking answers to a wide variety of questions, and in the research component of the ancillary *Studying Communication* (explained below under "Ancillaries").

4. A new unit, **Dysfunctional Relationships and Interpersonal Communication (Unit 22),** has been added; it introduces verbally abusive and addictive relationships and the problem of sexual harassment. For too long we have focused almost exclusively on positive relationships and have ignored the destructive and unhealthy ones—a situation that has only contributed to our collective ignorance.

5. The units devoted to the **self** have been expanded from two to three and now cover self-concept, self-awareness, and self-esteem (Unit 7); self-disclosure (now a complete unit—Unit 8); and apprehension and assertiveness (Unit 9).

6. A new unit, **Relationship Maintenance and Repair (Unit 19),** has been added and reflects the growing research interest in this important area. As a result, each of the major relationship processes receives parallel treatment:

- Unit 17. Relationship Development and Involvement
- Unit 18. Relationship Deterioration and Dissolution
- Unit 19. Relationship Maintenance and Repair

7. The two units on friendship and love have been recast into one unit, **Friends and Lovers (Unit 23).** This organization helps to emphasize the similarities and differences between the two relationships, to eliminate redundancies in the previous two-unit approach, and to increase the content and research coverage.

8. Questions for **Thinking Critically** about the contents of the unit have been expanded and are now more oriented toward questioning research and theory, evaluating principles and suggestions, and synthesizing material covered in the unit.

9. The **self-tests,** so popular in the previous edition, have been expanded. This edition now contains 22 self-tests. New topics include verbal aggressiveness, argumentativeness, addictive relationships, confirmation, verbally abusive relationships, and conversational satisfaction.

10. **Other material** has been added, expanded, or substantially revised, most notably:

- four special-interest boxes appear in this edition: The Art of Facilitating Self-Disclosure (Unit 8), Stage Talk (Unit 16), Sexual Harassment (Unit 22), and Loving and Communication (Unit 23)
- expansion of listening into a five-step process (Unit 4)
- theories about space and the factors influencing spatial distances (Unit 14)
- clearer focus on assertiveness as a *communication* behavior (Unit 9)
- expansion of the model of relationships to include repair (Unit 16)
- increased coverage of theories in Units 17, 18, and 19
- opening lines (Unit 17)
- friendship and romantic rules (Unit 18)
- popular myths about conflict and what to do before and after the conflict (Unit 21)
- integration of the unproductive and productive conflict strategies (Unit 21)
- new relationship strategies, for example, reconciliation (Unit 19), compliance resisting (Unit 20), and maintenance (Unit 19)
- cultural differences in context and individualism versus collectivism (Unit 2)
- verbal aggressiveness and argumentativeness as approaches to conflict (Unit 21)
- self-esteem and self-concept (Unit 7)
- communicating with people with disabilities (Unit 6) and with the grief stricken (Unit 11)

THE INTERACTIVE COMPONENT

In this edition, I have increased efforts to make the text even more interactive than it was in the previous edition. Some examples of this emphasis are:

- **22 self-tests** that ask students to assess their communication behaviors or beliefs (with instructions for analyzing their own responses so they can see how their behaviors compare with those of other groups). The 22 self-tests are integrated throughout the book.
- **questions for thinking critically** about the contents of each unit, as well as questions included in all photo captions, that prompt students to analyze their own

interpersonal communication patterns and objectives.

- **questions** interspersed with many of the text discussions that ask students to pause and consider their own assumptions about interpersonal communication.
- **dialogues** that invite analysis and discussion; many are new to this edition (for example, those in Units 6, 8, and 15).
- **54 experiential vehicles**—13 are new to this edition—that provide opportunities for active work with the concepts discussed in the text.

ANCILLARIES

A variety of ancillaries are available with this textbook.

STUDYING COMMUNICATION

A new booklet—**Studying Communication**—is packaged with this edition. This booklet introduces the student to the field of communication and to the way research is conducted—topics that we have too long neglected. In addition, it contains a variety of practical suggestions for helping the student get the most out of the course and the text and covers, for example, how to read a textbook, how to take a test, and how to write a paper in communication.

THE INTERPERSONAL CHALLENGE 2

The Interpersonal Challenge 2 is keyed to this seventh edition. In addition to the question categories of Self-Perception, Ethical Dilemmas, and Interpersonal Relationships (present in the first edition), a new category has been added: Intercultural Communication. Further, the game has been extensively revised; it will play more smoothly and prove more involving. The directions have been revised and simplified.

INSTRUCTOR'S MANUAL/TEST BANK

The *Instructor's Manual,* by Thomas Veenendall, of Montclair State College, covers additional class exercises and experiences, suggestions for using the text's Experiential Vehicles, suggestions for teaching the course, additional references, transparency masters that highlight essential terms and principles, and a test bank organized by unit. The test bank is also available on computer disks (TestMaster). Both items are available from the publisher. Contact your local HarperCollins sales representative.

INTERPERSONAL COMMUNICATION VIDEOS

Videos cover topics that range from conflict resolution to love and relationships. Since new videos are frequently added to the library, contact your local HarperCollins sales representative for details.

ACKNOWLEDGMENTS

I would like to express my appreciation to the many specialists who carefully reviewed the previous edition and assisted me in this revision:

Leonard Barchak, McNeese State University
Ernest Bartow, Bucks County Community College
Jerry Ferguson, South Dakota State University
David Fusani, Erie Community College
Jane Goodale, Ashland Community College
Donna R. Hall, Texas Christian University
Michael Hecht, Arizona State University
Christine Hirsch, Western Michigan University
Virginia Katz, University of Minnesota
Robert E. Looney, Prestonburg Community College
Terri Main, Kings River Community College
Paul Mongeau, Miami University
Michelle Neaton, Lakewood Community College
George B. Ray, Cleveland State University
Helen Sands, University of Southern Indiana
Kristi A. Schaller, Indiana University
Ted Spencer, University of Maryland
Laurel Vartabedian, Amarillo College
Dennis Weeden, Concordia University (WI)
Jerry Windsor, Central Missouri State University
Deanna Womack, Stonehill College

In addition, I wish to thank the many people who reviewed earlier editions and whose reviews continue to prove valuable with each revision. Thank you, H. Ablomowicz, A. Abrams, Ronald Bassett, Charles Berger, Bernard Brommel, Marquita Byrd, Matt Campbell, Sumitra Chakrapani, James Chesebro, Ronald Coleman, Mark Comadena, Dan Crary, Hal Dalrymple, John Daly, Sue DeWine, Robert Dick, Susan Doyle, Steve Duck, Paul Feingold, Mary Anne Fitzpatrick, Fran Franklin, Rex Gaskill, Elizabeth Graham, James Hasenauer, Katherine Hawkins, Michael Hecht, Randy Hirokawa, Thomas Jewell, James Johnston, Marilyn Kelly, Lynne Kelly, Catherine Konsky, Cheris Kramarae, Thomas Mader, Janet McKenney, Sandra Metts, Bert Miller, Larry Miller, Carolyn Offutt, Jeff Ringer, Leonard Robuck, Charles Rossiter, William Schenck-Hamlin, Stuart Sigman, Alan Sillars, Dennis Smith, Ralph Smith, Ted Spencer, Jim Towns, Laurel Vartabedian, Ralph Webb, Paul Westbrook, Ethel Wilcox, W. Gill Woodall, and Christopher Zahn.

As always, the staff at HarperCollins helped greatly. I especially want to thank Cynthia Biron, the new acquisitions editor for communication; Dawn Groundwater, developmental editor; Thomas Farrell, project editor; and Nancy Hitchner, copy editor. All did admirable work in transforming the text from manuscript to book. I am in their debt.

JOSEPH A. DEVITO

A Visual Guide To:

THE INTERPERSONAL COMMUNICATION BOOK

Seventh Edition

Joseph A. DeVito
Hunter College of the City University of New York

ISBN 0-673-99177-6

Now in its seventh edition, this market leader continues to provide a perfect balance of up-to-the-minute coverage of research and theories in interpersonal communication and the practical applications students need for effective interaction. Since choice is central to interpersonal communication, the text helps students select the best option at every stage of the communication process by providing them with a worthwhile variety of interpersonal situations, and by discussing the theory, research, and evidence bearing on these choices. As a result, students are better equipped to make more informed and effective communication decisions. Organized around twenty-four concise units, the preliminaries, messages, and relationships of interpersonal communication are explored.

PART THREE   INTERPERSONAL RELATIONSHIPS

Sexual Harassment

Sexual harassment is not a single act but rather a series of communicative acts that come to characterize a relationship; therefore, it is useful to place sexual harassment in the context of dysfunctional relationships.

WHAT IS SEXUAL HARASSMENT?

Ellen Bravo and Ellen Cassedy (1992) define sexual harassment as "bothering someone in a sexual way. The harasser offers sexual attention to someone who didn't ask for it and doesn't welcome it. The unwelcome behavior might or might not involve touching. It could just as well be spoken words, graphics, gestures or even looks (not any look—but the kind of leer or stare that says, 'I want to undress you.'"

Other researchers say "sexual harassment refers to conduct, typically experienced as offensive in nature, in which unwanted sexual advances are made in the context of a relationship of unequal power or authority. The victims are subjected to verbal comments of a sexual nature, unconsented touching and requests for sexual favors" (Friedman, Boumil, and Taylor 1992).

Attorneys note that under the law "sexual harassment is any unwelcome sexual advance or conduct on the job that creates an intimidating, hostile or offensive working environment" (Petrocelli and Repa 1992).

The Equal Employment Opportunity Commission (EEOC) has defined sexual harassment as follows:

Unwelcome sexual advances, requests for sexual favors and other verbal or physical conduct of a sexual nature constitute sexual harassment when (1) submission to such conduct is made either explicitly or implicitly a term or condition of an individual's employment, (2) submission to or rejection of such conduct by an individual is used as the basis for employment decisions affecting such individual, or (3) such conduct has the purpose or ... interfering with ...

NEW SPECIAL INTEREST BOXES

New to this seventh edition are four specialty boxed items which focus on informative and topical areas of interest in interpersonal communication. Each of the four boxes— "Facilitating Self-Disclosure" in Unit 8, "Stage Talk" in Unit 16, "Sexual Harassment" in Unit 22, and "Loving Communication" in Unit 23—give additional perspectives on the unit topics.

This unit incorporates the latest findings regarding turning points in relationships, the major complaints of couples, the repair phase of relationships, non-traditional relationships, and new relationship surveys.

UNIT 19

Relationship Maintenance and Repair

UNIT TOPICS

Relationship Maintenance
Reasons for Maintaining Relationships
Maintenance Behaviors
Interpersonal Maintenance and Rules
What the Theories Say About Maintenance
Relationship Repair
General Relationship Repair Strategies
Solo Relationship Repair

UNIT 22

Dysfunctional Relationships and Interpersonal Communication

UNIT TOPICS

Verbally Abusive Relationships
The Characteristics and Effects of Verbal Abuse
Problems in Recognizing and Combating Verbal Abuse
Dealing with Verbal Abuse
Addictive Relationships
Dealing with Addictive Relationships

This unit on dysfunctional relationships introduces material on verbally abusive and addictive relationships and the problems of sexual harassment. A more balanced coverage between positive and unhealthy relationships is thus presented.

Objectives identify the major topics students should study in each unit and the behaviors they should be able to demonstrate after completing each section. Objectives also highlight the most pertinent principles and skills that will be covered in the unit.

PART THREE   INTERPERSONAL RELATIONSHIPS

UNIT OBJECTIVES

AFTER COMPLETING THIS UNIT, YOU SHOULD BE ABLE TO:

1. Define *family* and *primary relationship*
2. Identify five characteristics common to all primary relationships
3. Define and distinguish among *traditionals, independents,* and *separates*
4. Explain the four communication patterns that
characterize primary relationships
5. Describe the five suggestions for improving communication within the primary relationship and the family

All of us are now or were at one time part of a family. Some of our experiences have been pleasant and positive and are recalled with considerable pleasure. Other experiences have been unpleasant and negative and are recalled only with considerable pain. Part of the reason for this lies in the interpersonal communication patterns that operate within the family. This unit is designed to provide a better understanding of these patterns as well as insight into how family interactions can be made more effective, more productive, and more pleasant.

PRIMARY RELATIONSHIPS AND FAMILIES: NATURE AND CHARACTERISTICS

If you had to define "family," you would probably note that a family consists of a husband, a wife, and one or more children. When pressed, you might add that some of these families also consist of other relatives-in-law, brothers and sisters, grandparents, aunts and uncles, and so on. But there are other types of relationships that are, to its own members, "families."

One obvious example is the family with one parent. Statistics from 1991 indicate that out of 67 million households in the United States, 52.5 million are headed by two adults, 11.7 million by a woman, and 3.0 million by a man (Johnson 1994).

Another obvious example is people living together in an exclusive relationship who are not married. For the most part, these cohabitants live as if they were married: there is an exclusive sexual commitment; there may be children; there are shared financial responsibilities, shared time, and shared space; and so on. These relationships mirror traditional marriages, except that in marriage the union is recognized by a religious body, [and in a relationship of cohabitants it generally is not. In their compre]hensive [*Couples*] (1983), the sociologists Philip Blumstein and Pepper [Schwartz report that altho]ugh cohabiting couples represent only about 2 percent to 3.8

PART ONE   INTERPERSONAL COMMUNICATION PRELIMINARIES

SUMMARY: UNIT IN BRIEF

Axioms	Implications
Transactional: Interpersonal communication is a process, an ongoing event, in which the elements are interdependent.	Communication is constantly occurring; do not look for clear-cut beginnings or endings. All communication elements are always changing; do not look for sameness. Look, too, for mutual interaction among elements.
Inevitability: When in an interactional situation, you cannot *not* communicate.	Seek to control as many aspects of your behavior as possible; seek out nonobvious messages.
Irreversibility and Unrepeatability: You cannot *uncommunicate* or repeat exactly a specific message.	Beware of messages you may later wish to take back—for example, conflict and commitment messages.
Culture-specific: Communication rules and principles vary from one culture to another.	Beware of assuming that the other person is following the same rules and principles you are.
Adjustment: Communication depends on participants sharing the same system of signals and meaning.	Expand common areas, and learn each other's system of signals to increase interpersonal effectiveness; share your own system of signals with significant others.
Punctuation: Everyone separates communication sequences into stimuli and responses on the basis of his or her own perspective.	View punctuation as arbitrary, and adopt the other's point of view to increase empathy and understanding.
Symmetrical and complementary relationships: Interpersonal interactions may stimulate similar or different behavior patterns, and relationships may be described as basically symmetrical or complementary.	Develop an awareness of symmetrical and complementary relationships. Avoid clinging rigidly to behavioral patterns that are no longer useful and mirroring another's destructive behaviors.
Content and relationship dimensions: All communications refer both to content and to the relationships between the participants.	Seek out and respond to relationship messages as well as content messages.

THINKING CRITICALLY ABOUT THE AXIOMS OF INTERPERSONAL
COMMUNICATION

principle

Unit in Brief Summaries, at the ends of each unit, review the major concepts covered. All Summaries are arranged into tables which enables the reader to see the entire unit as a whole and to better appreciate the relationship among the specific topics.

touching members of your sex), total the scores for items 1, 3, 4, 6, 9, 12, 13, 16, and 18.
3. To obtain your opposite-sex touch avoidance score (the extent to which you avoid touching members of the opposite sex), total the scores for items 2, 5, 7, 8, 10, 14, 15, and 17.
4. To obtain your total touch avoidance score, add the subtotals from steps 2 and 3.

The higher the score, the higher the touch avoidance—that is, the greater your tendency to avoid touch. In studies by Andersen and Leibowitz (1978), who constructed this test, average opposite-sex touch avoidance scores were 12.9 for males and 14.85 for females. Average same-sex touch avoidance scores were 26.43 for males and 21.70 for females.

The cultural differences in nonverbal communication discussed here center on touch. In what other areas of nonverbal communication covered in this unit might cultural differences be important?

INTERCULTURAL PHOTO PROGRAM

A culturally sensitive photo program heightens the focus on intercultural issues in communication and increases students' awareness of culture and interpersonal communication.

---

need to be frank and spontaneous when talking with a close friend about your feelings, but you may not want to be so open when talking with your grandmother about the dinner she prepared that you disliked.

CULTURAL SENSITIVITY

In applying the skills for interpersonal effectiveness, be sensitive to the cultural differences among people. What may prove effective for upper-income people working in the IBM subculture of Boston or New York may prove ineffective for lower-income people working as fruit pickers in Florida or California. What works in Japan may not work in Mexico. The direct eye contact that signals intimacy in most of the United States may be considered rude or too intrusive in Hispanic and other cultures. The empathy that most Americans welcome may be uncomfortable for the average Korean (Yun 1976). The specific skills discussed below are considered generally effective in the United States and among most people living in the United States. Do note, however, that these skills and the ways in which we use them verbally or nonverbally are specific to the general U.S. culture.

Here are some suggestions for communicating cultural sensitivity.

- Be careful not to ignore differences between yourself and people who are culturally different from you. When you assume similarities and ignore differences, you implicitly communicate to others that your ways are the right ways and that their ways are not important to you. Talking about religion provides a good example. So often people assume that the beliefs of their religion (concerning, for example, redemption, penance, marriage and divorce, abortion, or the value of good deeds)—perhaps because these beliefs are so fundamental to their way of thinking—are held by everyone.
- Be careful not to ignore differences among the culturally different group. When you ignore these differences, you are stereotyping; that is, you are assuming that all persons covered by the same label (in this case, a national or racial label) are the same.
- Be careful not to ignore differences in meaning, even when using the same words. Consider, for example, the differences in meaning of such words as "woman" for an American and a Saudi Arabian, "religion" for a born-again Christian and an atheist, and "lunch" for a Chinese rice farmer and a Wall Street executive. Moreover, in the case of nonverbal messages, the potential differences seem even greater. To an American, holding up two fingers to make a V signifies victory. For certain South Americans, however, it is an obscene gesture.

INTERCULTURAL MATERIAL INTEGRATED THROUGHOUT

The text's increased emphasis on intercultural issues includes research and theory on intercultural communication and discussion questions that emphasize intercultural thinking to a greater extent.

- What are the major consequences of verbal abuse for children? For teens? For adult women? For adult men?
- What verbal and nonverbal messages constitute sexual harassment? How do these messages vary from one culture to another?
- What happens to a person's self-esteem when he or she is in an addictive relationship?

EXPERIENTIAL VEHICLES

22.1 RESPONDING TO VERBAL ABUSE

Here are a few specific instances of verbal abuse that call for some response. How would you respond?

1. *Your friend* frequently belittles anything you say, do, or try to do. Comments such as "You can't be serious about that" or "That's just plain stupid" or "You won't be able to do that" have become so debilitating that you decide to tell him or her to stop.
2. *Your mother* criticizes the way you dress: "You always dress like a slob, like you just got out of bed. Why don't you dress like your brother?" You know your mother loves you, but her behavior makes you feel inadequate.
3. *Your boyfriend (or girlfriend)* constantly interrupts you, never allowing you to finish a thought. When you object, s/he says s/he knows you so well, s/he knows just what you're going to say. You're tired of this and want it to stop.
4. *Your boss* is a blamer; whenever things go wrong, the boss blames you for not following the rules, reading the directions, or exercising caution. This constant blaming undermines your confidence, and you want it to stop.

22.2 ADDICTIVE RELATIONSHIPS

Here are a few letters to our fictional advice columnists. For each letter, describe the situation in terms of addiction and offer any advice you think might prove useful, based on the principles discussed in this unit and throughout the text. What explanations other than addiction might be reasonable?

an about to be married. My fiancé, I'll call him Tom, insists that I
millionaire and wants me to assume my role in the community,
and the like. I really was looking forward to teaching (I just grad-
…its), but I'm wondering whether …
simply

THINKING CRITICALLY ABOUT APPREHENSION AND ASSERTIVENESS

1. In what communication situations are you most apprehensive? Why do you suppose this is so?
2. Can you create a hierarchy of at least ten behaviors that vary in terms of your level of apprehension? Begin with behavior 1, identifying a situation in which you have little to no apprehension, and then work up to behavior 10, identifying a situation in which you have great apprehension. What distinguishes the situations with low numbers from situations with high numbers?
3. What do you think has contributed to your current level of communication apprehension? For example, can you identify early childhood influences? Will you be apprehensive? What can you do about it at this point?
4. In what communication situations are you likely to be evaluated during the next 12 months? Will you be apprehensive? What can you do about it at this point?
5. Read the following Dear Abby letter. Do the sentiments in this letter suggest any changes in your behaviors in dealing with shy people?

DEAR ABBY: Thank you for printing the letter from the teenage girl who was struggling with shyness.

I, too, am a very shy and quiet person. I've been this way all my life. I can't tell you how many people have said, "You sure are quiet." I can't imagine anyone going up to a person and saying, "You sure have a big mouth!"

I would like to reassure everyone that I know I am quiet, but I am a very well-adjusted, happy person who enjoys being quiet. I am quiet because I have nothing to say, and I don't want to fill the quietness with empty chatter. I would find it quite exhausting to make small talk, or worse yet, try to be the life of the party, or the center of attention.

In the past, I have tried to talk more and be more outgoing so people would like me better, but it did not become me . . . it was not natural.

It has taken me years to like myself just the way I am. I have many friends who like me just the way I am, so to the others who are disturbed by my quietness and shy personality, please leave me alone. Please don't try to make me feel that there is something wrong with me because I am different from you who feel compelled to talk all the time.

Abby, if you print this—and I hope you do—you will be doing an enormous favor to all the shy, quiet people who read your column. There are more of us than you could possibly imagine

—QUIET IN ATLANTA

CRITICAL THINKING

The seventh edition has been updated to include even more emphasis on critical thinking by including more analytical questions. Numerous specific sections throughout the text focus on critical thinking as it relates to interpersonal communication. Questions included in photo captions also prompt students to analyze their own interpersonal communication patterns.

EXPERIENTIAL VEHICLES

Of the fifty-four experiential vehicles in the text, thirteen are entirely new to this edition. These vehicles provide students with opportunities for actively working with the concepts discussed in the text.

GRAPHIC COMMUNICATION MODELS

Full-color communication models and tables provide students with detailed illustrations of unit theories and concepts.

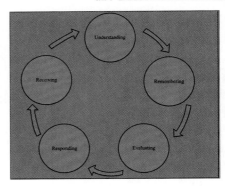

Figure 4.2
A five-stage model of listening. This five-step model draws on a variety of previous models that listening researchers have developed (for example, Barker 1990; Steil, Barker, and Watson 1983; Brownell 1987; Alessandra 1986).

mother is ill, the effective listener remembers this and inquires about Joe's mother's health later in the week.

What you remember is actually not what was said but what you think (or remember) was said. Memory for speech is not reproductive; you don't simply reproduce in your memory what the speaker said. Rather, memory is *reconstructive;* you actually reconstruct the messages you hear into a system that makes sense to you.

To illustrate this important concept, try to memorize the list of 12 words presented below (Glucksberg and Danks 1975). Don't worry about the order of the words. Only the number remembered counts. Take about 20 seconds to memorize as many words as possible. Don't read any further until you have tried to memorize the list of words.

Word List

BED	DREAM	COMFORT
REST	AWAKE	SOUND
	NIGHT	SLUMBER
	EAT	SNORE

he book and write down as many of the words from this list as you can
ead any further until you have tested your own memory.

TEST YOURSELF

HOW SATISFACTORY IS YOUR CONVERSATION?*

INSTRUCTIONS:
Respond to each of the following statements by recording the number that best represents your feelings. Use this scale:

1 = strongly agree
2 = moderately agree
3 = slightly agree
4 = neutral
5 = slightly disagree
6 = moderately disagree
7 = strongly disagree

_____ 1. The other person let me know that I was communicating effectively.
_____ 2. Nothing was accomplished.
_____ 3. I would like to have another conversation like this one.
_____ 4. The other person genuinely wanted to get to know me.
_____ 5. I was very *dis*satisfied with the conversation.
_____ 6. I felt that during the conversation I was able to present myself as I wanted the other person to view me.
_____ 7. I was very satisfied with the conversation.
_____ 8. The other person expressed a lot of interest in what I had to say.
_____ 9. I did NOT enjoy the conversation.
_____ 10. The other person did NOT provide support for what he/she was saying.
_____ 11. I felt I could talk about anything with the other person.
_____ 12. We each got to say what we wanted.
_____ 13. I felt that we could laugh easily together.
_____ 14. The conversation flowed smoothly.
_____ 15. The other person frequently said things which added little to the conversation.
_____ 16. We talked about something I was NOT interested in.

SCORING
1. Add the scores for items 1, 3, 4, 6, 7, 8, 11, 12, 13, and 14.
2. Rever_____ for items 2, 5, 9, 10, 15, and 16 such that 7 _____ disagree)
_____ as 2, 5 h

SELF-TESTS

Twenty-two self-tests ask students to assess their own communication behavior or beliefs, with instructions for analyzing their own responses. The self-tests promote active involvement with the text material and help personalize the concepts and principles discussesd.

IN-TEXT DIALOGUES

These dialogues encourage students to analyze interpersonal communication situations and apply their critical thinking skills.

SALLY: Come on, Mom.
[Frank exits; Tommy turns on the TV.]

In Act I, Tommy's father, mother, and sister illustrate the typical failure to help another person share feelings. Although Tommy gave enough signals—throwing books down on the coffee table, saying nothing, staring into space—nobody showed any real concern, and nobody encouraged him to talk about what was on his mind. Note, too, that even though the father was aware that Tommy was disturbed, he directed his question to Millie instead of Tommy. Moreover, in his comment, Frank expressed a negative evaluation ("What's wrong with him?"). Even if Tommy had wanted to talk about his feelings, the father effectively closed the door to any empathic communication.

Note also that the few comments addressed to Tommy (for example, the father's "You got a girl, Tommy?" and the mother's "You don't want to come with us, do you?") fail to consider Tommy's *present* feelings. The father's comment is intimidating and seems more a reference to his own macho image than a question about Tommy. The mother's comment is negative and, in effect, asks Tommy not to join them.

But the most damaging part of this interaction occurs when father, mother, and sister not only ignore Tommy's feelings and problems but also express concern for someone else—sister for Jack, father for Joe, and mother for Grandma. Their comments tell Tommy that he is not worth their time and energy but that others are. When both the father and mother ignore Sally's put-downs of Tommy (normal as they may be among young children), they reinforce the idea that Tommy is unworthy. In their silence, they communicate agreement. In the language of transactional analysis, they tell Tommy that he is not OK but that these others are OK.

ACT II. *The Success*
[Frank, Millie, and Sally are sitting together. Tommy enters the living room, throws his books down on the coffee table, then goes to the refrigerator.]

FRANK: [Calling into the kitchen] Hey, Tommy, what's up? You look pretty angry.
TOMMY: It's nothing. Just school.
SALLY: ... t weird, Dad.
... "weird" like the mad scientist in the old movies?
... now what I mean—he's different.
... at's something else. That's great. I'm glad Tommy is different.
... doesn't need another clone, and Tommy is certainly no clone.
... d it's not easy being unique. Right ...

TOMMY: No. You want to go bowling.
FRANK: I can bowl anytime. After all, what's another 200 game? It's hardly a challenge. Come on. How about we take a drive to the lake and take a swim—just the two of us. And I'd like to hear about what's going on in school.
TOMMY: OK, let's go. I need to put on my trunks. You know, I can swim four lengths without stopping.
FRANK: Four lengths? Well, I've got to see that. Get those trunks on and we're out of here.
SALLY: Mom, let's go-o-o-o.
MILLIE: OK. OK. OK. But I have to call Grandma first to see if she's all right.
FRANK: Let me say hello, too.
MILLIE: [To Tommy and Sally] Do you two want to talk to Grandma?
SALLY: Of course. I've got to tell her about this great new guy at school.
MILLIE: Oh, I want to hear about this, too. Well, we'll have plenty of time to talk in the car.
TOMMY: Hey, Mom, I gotta tell Grandma about my new bike. So let me talk first so Dad and I can get to the lake.

[Later, Tommy and Frank in car]

FRANK: [Puts arm on Tommy's shoulder] School got you down?
TOMMY: It's this new teacher. What a pain. I can't understand what he's talking about. Maybe I'm just stupid.
FRANK: What don't you understand?
TOMMY: I don't know. He calls it pregeometry. What's pregeometry?

Note that the interaction in Act II is drastically different from the interaction in Act I and illustrates how you can help someone self-disclose. Notice that Tommy's feelings are addressed immediately and directly by his father. Frank shows concern for Tommy's feelings by asking him about them and then about school. He shows that he cares for Tommy by defending him. For example, he turns Sally's negative comment into a positive one ("weird" becomes "unique") and also gives up bowling to be with Tommy. He continues to show caring and concern by putting Tommy first—ahead of his bowling and ahead of his friends Bill and Joe.

Frank further helps Tommy to disclose by being nonevaluative. Instead of asking Tommy indirectly, "What's wrong with him?" he talks to Tommy directly and asks about his feelings, using the information Tommy has already revealed ("School got you down?"). This is a good example of active listening (see Unit 4).

Thi... ... introductory; it merely sets the stage f... ... lf-dis-

The
Interpersonal
Communication
Book

Part

ONE

Interpersonal Communication Preliminaries

1. UNIVERSALS OF INTERPERSONAL COMMUNICATION
2. AXIOMS OF INTERPERSONAL COMMUNICATION
3. PERCEPTION IN INTERPERSONAL COMMUNICATION
4. LISTENING IN INTERPERSONAL COMMUNICATION
5. ETHICS IN INTERPERSONAL COMMUNICATION
6. EFFECTIVENESS IN INTERPERSONAL COMMUNICATION
7. THE SELF IN INTERPERSONAL COMMUNICATION
8. SELF-DISCLOSURE
9. APPREHENSION AND ASSERTIVENESS

APPROACHING INTERPERSONAL COMMUNICATION

In approaching your study of interpersonal communication, keep the following in mind:

- The study of interpersonal communication involves both research and theory on the one hand and applications and skills on the other. Seek both to increase your understanding of the theory and to improve your skills.
- Effective interpersonal communicators are not born effective; rather, effectiveness comes through learning and experience. Whatever your present level of skills, you can improve your effectiveness by applying the principles discussed here.
- The theories and research in interpersonal communication do not provide all the answers; fortunately, a vigorous research program is under way, and our understanding is growing rapidly.
- The principles and skills discussed throughout this book relate directly to your everyday interactions. Personalize what you are learning; identify examples from your own interactions that illustrate the ideas considered here.
- Interpersonal communication—like other disciplines—has its own vocabulary. The new vocabulary will help you highlight significant ideas and think more clearly about your own interpersonal communications.

UNIT 1

Universals of Interpersonal Communication

UNIT OBJECTIVES

AFTER COMPLETING THIS UNIT, YOU SHOULD BE ABLE TO:

1. Define *interpersonal communication* using a dyadic (relational) and a developmental definition
2. Diagram the model of interpersonal communication presented in this unit and label its parts
3. Define the following elements of interpersonal communication: *source-receiver, encoding-decoding, competence, message, channel, noise, feedback, feedforward,* Context *content, effect,* and *ethics*
4. Explain the purposes of interpersonal communication

Interpersonal communication is something you do every day:

* making friends
* asking for a date
* applying for a job
* responding to a compliment
* being an empathic listener
* giving instructions to new workers
* persuading a friend to go bowling
* developing new relationships
* maintaining and repairing relationships
* dissolving relationships

Understanding these interactions is an essential part of a liberal education. Much as an educated person must know world geography and history or science and mathematics, you need to know the how, why, and what of people communication. It is simply a significant part of the world. Moreover, interpersonal communication is an extremely practical art, and your effectiveness as a friend, relationship partner, co-worker, or manager will depend on your interpersonal communication abilities.

Understanding the theory and research in interpersonal communication and mastering its skills go hand in hand. The more you know about interpersonal communication, the more insight you will gain about what works and what does not work. This greater knowledge will increase your abilities to apply the principles to unique situations. The more skills you have within your arsenal of communication strategies, the greater will be your options for communicating in any situation. Also, because of these added options, the likelihood is greater that you will be successful.

Realize, too, that interpersonal communication skills are essential to your own empowerment. The ability to communicate successfully in interpersonal situations gives you the power to achieve your goals—to make friends, to establish and maintain successful relationships, to climb the organizational ladder, to adjust to new and different situations, to interact effectively with people from cultures different from your own, and so on. So important is this ability that the U.S. Department of Labor identifies interpersonal skills as one of the five essential skills for a nation and an individual to be economically competitive *(New York Times,* 3 July 1991, A17).

In this book, the emphasis is on your understanding of interpersonal communication: its theories and research and its practical skills. These two sides, the theory-research and the skills, of interpersonal communication are considered together as we progress through the elements of interpersonal communication, the ways verbal and nonverbal messages operate in interpersonal encounters, and the ways relationships develop and are maintained, repaired, and even dissolved.

As a preface to getting started in interpersonal communication, examine your assumptions about it by taking the self-test.

TEST YOURSELF

WHAT DO YOU BELIEVE ABOUT INTERPERSONAL COMMUNICATION?

INSTRUCTIONS
Respond to each of the following statements with *true* if you believe the statement is usually true or *false* if you believe the statement is usually false.

_____ 1. The more you communicate, the better at it you will be.

_____ 2. Opening lines such as "Hello, how are you?" or "Fine weather today" or "Have you got a light?" serve no useful interpersonal purpose.

_____ 3. In your interpersonal communications, a good guide to follow is to be as open, empathic, and supportive as you can be.

_____ 4. When verbal and nonverbal messages contradict each other, people believe the verbal message.

_____ 5. The best guide to follow when communicating with people from other cultures is to ignore the differences and treat the other person just as you'd treat members of your own culture.

_____ 6. It is better to reveal your feelings than to keep them bottled up.

_____ 7. Effective interpersonal communicators do not rely on "power tactics."

_____ 8. Fear of speaking is detrimental and must be eliminated.

_____ 9. When there is conflict, your relationship is in trouble.

_____ 10. Couples who communicate a great deal are more likely to stay together than couples who communicate significantly less.

SCORING
All ten statements are false. As you read this book, you'll discover not only why these statements are false but also the problems that can arise if you act on these misconceptions.

A Dyadic (Relational) Definition of Interpersonal Communication

In a dyadic or relational definition, **interpersonal communication** is communication that takes place between two persons who have an established relationship; the people are in some way "connected." Interpersonal communication would thus include what takes place between a son and his father, an employer and employee, two sisters, a teacher and a student, two lovers, two friends, and so on.

You could argue that it is impossible to have dyadic (two-person) communication that is not interpersonal. Invariably, there is some relationship between two people who are interacting. Even the stranger who asks directions of a neighborhood resident has an identifiable relationship with the resident as soon as the first message is sent. This interpersonal (but non-intimate) relationship will then influence how the two individuals interact with each other.

Dyadic Primacy

Even when you have triads (groups of three people), dyads (two-person relationships) are still primary; dyads are always central to interpersonal relationships (Wilmot 1987). Consider, for example, the following situation: Al and Bob (a dyad) have been roommates for their first two years of college. Expenses have increased, and so they ask Carl to join them and become a third roommate. Now a triad exists. But the original dyad has not gone away; in fact, now there are three dyads: Al and Bob, Al and Carl, and Bob and Carl. Al and Bob are ballplayers and interact a lot about sports. Al and Carl are both studying communication and talk about their classes. Bob and Carl belong to the same religious club and frequently discuss the club's activities. At times, of course, all three interact, but even then the topic of conversation will determine who talks primarily to whom. If the topic is sports, Al and Bob will primarily address each other; Carl will be a kind of outsider. When the topic is classes, Bob is the outsider.

You can observe **dyadic primacy** in almost every large group (Wilmot 1987). If you examine families, workers in a factory, neighbors in an apartment house, or students in class, for example, you will find that each large group breaks down, at some times, into a series of dyads. The specific dyad formed naturally depends on the situation, and dyads will probably change over time. As in the case of Al, Bob, and Carl, different dyads will form, depending on the nature of the interaction.

Dyadic Coalitions

A **dyadic coalition** is a two-person relationship formed for achieving a mutually desired benefit or goal (Wilmot 1987). In groups larger than two, dyadic coalitions are frequently formed. Coalitions—whether in the family, among friends, or at work—may be productive or unproductive. Two workers may form a coalition to develop a program for improving worker morale. Two teachers may undertake research together. The result of these coalitions will benefit not only the individuals involved but also, eventually, all members of the group.

At other times, coalitions are unproductive. The grandparent who develops a coalition with the grandchild against the child's parent may cause all sorts of family difficulties; parental resentment and jealousy, as well as guilt for the child, are just a few possibilities. A husband or a wife, especially during marital difficulties, may form a coalition with one of their children. This often results in alienating the left-out spouse and preventing the child from benefiting from a close relationship with that parent.

DYADIC CONSCIOUSNESS

In addition to what you do and say, your interpersonal relationships depend on what you think about your relationship. As your relationship develops, a **dyadic consciousness** emerges; you begin to see yourself as part of a pair, a team, a couple. It is almost as if a third party enters the picture. No longer is it just you and the other person; it is now you, the other person, and the relationship. As the relationship becomes more involved, this third party takes on greater importance. Often individuals sacrifice their own desires or needs for the well-being of "the relationship."

A DEVELOPMENTAL DEFINITION OF INTERPERSONAL COMMUNICATION

In the developmental approach, communications are viewed as existing on a continuum ranging from impersonal at one end to intimate at the other. Interpersonal communication is distinguished from impersonal communication by three factors (Miller 1978).

PSYCHOLOGICAL DATA

In interpersonal interactions, people base their predictions about each other on psychological data—that is, the ways in which a person differs from the members of his or her group. In impersonal encounters, people respond to each other chiefly as members of the class or group to which each belongs. For example, initially you respond to a particular college professor as you respond to college professors in general. Similarly, the college professor responds to you as he or she responds to students generally. As your relationship becomes more personal, however, both of you begin to respond to each other not as members of groups but as unique individuals. Put differently, in impersonal encounters, the social or cultural role of the person governs your interaction, while in personal or interpersonal encounters, the psychological uniqueness of the person tells you how to interact.

This general move from social data to psychological data is true in the United States and in most European cultures. In many Asian and African cultures, however, the individual's group membership is always important; it never recedes into the background. Thus, in these cultures, one's group membership (one's social data)—even in the closest intimate relationships—is always important, often more important than one's individual or psychological characteristics (Moghaddam, Taylor, and Wright 1993).

EXPLANATORY KNOWLEDGE

Interactions are based on knowledge that advances from description through prediction to explanation as your relationship moves to greater intimacy. In impersonal relationships,

Do men and women behave similarly in regard to dyadic primacy, coalitions, and consciousness? For example, do men and women development dyadic consciousness at the same time in the development of a relationship? Do they define it in the same way? Do they have different expectations on the basis of dyadic consciousness? Are men and women equally likely to form dyads? To form dyadic coalitions?

you can do little more than **describe** a person or a person's way of communicating. As you get to know someone a bit better, you can **predict** his or her behavior. If you get to know the person well, you'll become able to **explain** the behavior. The college professor, in an impersonal relationship, may be able to describe, say, your lateness and perhaps also predict that you will be five minutes late to class each Friday. In an interpersonal situation, however, the professor can go beyond these levels to explain the behavior—in this case, give reasons why you are late.

PERSONALLY ESTABLISHED RULES

In impersonal situations, the rules of interaction are set down by social norms. Students and professors behave toward one another—in impersonal situations—according to the social norms established by their culture and society. However, as the relationship between student and professor becomes interpersonal, the social rules no longer regulate the interaction. Student and professor begin to establish rules of their own largely because they begin to see each other as unique individuals rather than merely as members of a particular social group.

These three characteristics vary in degree. You respond to each other on the basis of psychological data *to some degree*. You base your predictions of another's behavior *to some degree* on your explanatory knowledge. And you interact on the basis of mutually established rules rather than socially established rules *to some degree.* As already noted, a developmental approach to communication implies a continuum ranging from highly impersonal to highly intimate. Interpersonal communication occupies a broad area on this continuum, although each person might draw its boundaries differently.

These two approaches to interpersonal communication—the dyadic and the developmental—are not as separate as they may at first appear. Both help explain what interpersonal communication is, each giving a different perspective to this important form of human behavior. The developmental definition emphasizes the types of interactions that are most significant to people—the more intimate types of relationships that make a substantial difference in your life. The dyadic or relational definition presents an extremely broad view of interpersonal communication while emphasizing that the interactants are—in some ways, at least—connected. An additional perspective on interpersonal communication may be gained by looking at the major divisions or areas of the field as identified in Table 1.1.

THE ELEMENTS OF INTERPERSONAL COMMUNICATION

In looking at the elements of interpersonal communication, we have many time-honored sources on which to draw. One of the most popular analyses was presented by the political scientist Harold Lasswell, who viewed communication as concerned with five basic questions:

Who
Says what
In what channel
To whom
With what effect

This view of communication is relatively linear; it implies that communication begins at one end and moves through discrete steps to the other end. Such linear views of communication are much too limiting, however, because they ignore its circular nature and fail to note that each person in the communication act simultaneously sends and receives messages. These factors need to be reflected in all views of communication.

The model presented in Figure 1.1 is a more accurate reflection of interpersonal communication. Each one of the concepts discussed here may be thought of as a **universal,** in that it is present in all interpersonal communication acts.

SOURCE-RECEIVER

Interpersonal communication involves at least two persons. Each person formulates and sends messages (source functions) and also perceives and comprehends messages (receiver functions). The hyphenated term **source-receiver** emphasizes that both functions are performed by each individual in interpersonal communication.

Who you are, what you know, what you believe, what you value, what you want, what you have been told, what your attitudes are, and so on all influence what you say,

Table 1.1

The Areas of Interpersonal Communication and Relationships*

GENERAL AREA	SELECTED TOPICS	RELATED ACADEMIC AREAS
Interpersonal interaction	Characteristics of effectiveness Conversational processes Self-disclosure Listening actively Nonverbal messages in conversation	Psychology Education Linguistics
Health communication: communication between health professional and patient	Talking about AIDS Increasing doctor-patient effectiveness Communication and aging Therapeutic communication	Medicine Psychology Counseling
Family communication: communication within the family system	Power in the family Dysfunctional families Family conflict Heterosexual and homosexual families Parent-child communication	Sociology Psychology Family studies
Intercultural communication: communication among members of different races, nationalities, religions, genders, and generations	Cross-generational communication Male-female communication Black-Hispanic-Asian-Caucasian communication Prejudice and stereotypes in communication Barriers to intercultural communication	Anthropology Sociology Cultural studies
Business and organizational communication: communication among workers in an organizational environment	Interviewing strategies Sexual harassment Upward and downward communication Increasing managerial effectiveness Leadership in business	Business Management Public relations
Social and personal relationships: communication in close relationships, such as friendship and love	Relationship development Relationship breakdown Repairing relationships Gender differences in relationships Increasing intimacy Verbal abuse	Psychology Sociology Anthropology

*This is not intended as a formal typology of the field but rather as a guide for identifying some of the important areas under the general topic of interpersonal communication and relationships. The six areas of interpersonal communication are not independent but interact and overlap. For example, interpersonal interaction is a part of all the other areas; similarly, intercultural communication can exist in any of the other areas. The related academic areas suggest the close ties among fields of study.

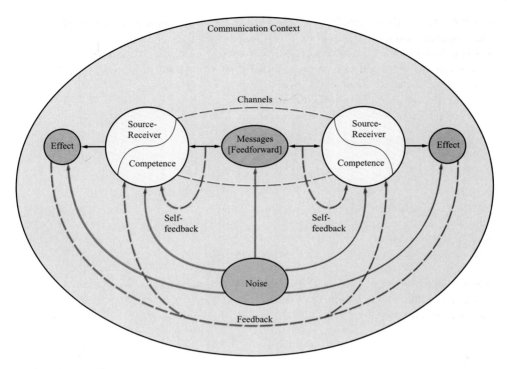

Figure 1.1
A model of some universals of interpersonal communication.

how you say it, what messages you receive, and how you receive them. Each person is unique; each person's communications are unique.

Encoding-Decoding

Encoding refers to the act of producing messages—for example, speaking or writing. **Decoding** refers to the act of understanding messages. By sending your ideas via sound waves, you are putting these ideas into a code, hence *en*coding. By translating sound waves into ideas, you are taking them out of a code, hence *de*coding. Thus, speakers and writers are called **encoders,** and listeners and readers **decoders.** The hyphenated term **encoding-decoding** is used to emphasize that the two activities are performed in combination by each participant. For interpersonal communication to occur, messages must be encoded and decoded. For example, when a parent talks to a child whose eyes are closed and whose ears are covered by stereo headphones, interpersonal communication does not occur because the messages, verbal and nonverbal, are not being received.

Competence

Your ability to communicate effectively is your *interpersonal competence* (Spitzberg and Cupach 1989). For example, your competence includes the knowledge that in certain contexts and with certain listeners one topic is appropriate and another is not. Knowledge about the rules of nonverbal behavior—for example, the appropriateness of touching, vocal volume, and physical closeness—is also part of your competence. In short, interpersonal competence includes knowing how to adjust your communications according to the context of the interaction, the person with whom you are interacting, and a host of other factors discussed throughout this text.

You learn communication competence much as you learn to eat with a knife and fork—by observing others, by explicit instruction, by trial and error, and so on. Some have learned better than others, though, and these people are generally the ones you find interesting and comfortable to talk to. They seem to know what to do and how and when to do it.

Recent research has found a positive relationship between interpersonal competence on the one hand and success in college (Rubin and Graham 1988) and job satisfaction (Wertz, Sorenson, and Heeren 1988) on the other. So much of college and professional life depends on communication competence—from meeting and interacting with other students, teachers, or colleagues; to asking and answering questions; to presenting information or argument. Other researchers have found that interpersonally competent people suffer less from anxiety, depression, and loneliness (Spitzberg and Cupach 1989). Interpersonal competence enables you to develop and maintain meaningful relationships, which help reduce anxiety and depression that may come from fear of not having friendships and love relationships.

One of the major goals of this text and your course is to explain the nature of interpersonal competence to improve your own skills. By improving your competence, you will have a greater number of options available to you. It is much like learning vocabulary: the more words you know, the more ways you have for expressing yourself. This interdependence of theory and skills goes like this:

Knowledge of interpersonal communication

leads to
↓

Greater interpersonal competence

leads to
↓

Greater number of available choices or options for interacting

leads to
↓

Greater likelihood of interpersonal effectiveness

Culture and Competence   Competence is specific to a given culture. The principles of effective communication vary from one culture to another; what proves effective in one culture may prove ineffective in another. For example, in the United States corporate executives get down to business during the first several minutes of a meeting. In Japan, business executives interact socially for an extended period and try to find out something about each other. Thus, the communication principle influenced by U.S. culture would advise participants to get down to the meeting's agenda during the first five minutes. The principle influenced by Japanese culture would advise participants to avoid dealing with business until everyone has socialized sufficiently and feels well enough acquainted to begin negotiations.

Note that neither principle is right and neither is wrong. Each is effective within its own culture, and each is ineffective outside its own culture. When specific interpersonal communication advice is given in this book, it is from the perspective of the general U.S. culture, though with clear recognition that "general U.S. culture" is in great part multicultural (cf. Shuter 1990). Significant cultural differences in communication practices and principles are also incorporated throughout this text.

MESSAGES

In interpersonal communication, messages—signals that serve as stimuli for a receiver—must be sent and received. Messages may be auditory (hearing), visual (seeing), tactile (touching), olfactory (smelling), gustatory (tasting), or any combination. Note that interpersonal communication does not have to be oral; you communicate by gesture or touch, for example, as well as by sound.

The clothes you wear communicate to others and, in fact, to yourself as well. The way you walk communicates, as does the way you shake hands, cock your head, comb your hair, sit, smile, or frown. These signals are your interpersonal communication messages.

Interpersonal communication need not occur face-to-face. It can take place by telephone, through prison cell walls, or through videophone hookup. Increasingly, it is taking place over computer networks, such as America On-Line, Compuserve, Prodigy, Genie, and the vast number of specialized computer networks uniting people with similar interests. In "chat mode," for example, the screen is split, with your messages in one half of the screen and the incoming messages in the other half. Note, too, that messages need not be intentionally sent. You also communicate through a slip of the tongue, a lingering body odor, or a nervous twitch.

You can create messages to talk about the world, people, and events as well as to talk about other messages. Messages that are about other messages are called **metamessages** and represent a fairly large number of your everyday messages. Note how the following expressions refer to other messages: "Do you understand?" "Did I say that right?" "What did you say?" "Is it fair to say that. . . ?" "I want to be honest." "That's not logical." Two particularly important types of metamessages are feedback and feedforward.

Feedback   Throughout the interpersonal communication process, you exchange **feedback**—messages sent back to the speaker concerning reactions to what is said (Clement and Frandsen 1976). Feedback tells the speaker what effect he or she is having on listeners. On the basis of this feedback, the speaker may adjust, modify, strengthen, deemphasize, or change the content or form of the messages.

Feedback may come from yourself or from others. In the diagram of the universals of communication (Figure 1.1), the arrows from source-receiver to effect and from one source-receiver to the other source-receiver go in both directions to illustrate the notion of feedback. When you send a message—say, in speaking to another person—you also hear yourself. That is, you get feedback from your own messages: you hear what you say, you feel the way you move, you see what you write.

In addition to this self-feedback, you get feedback from others. This feedback can take many forms. A frown or a smile, a yea or a nay, a pat on the back or a punch in the mouth are all types of feedback.

Feedback can be looked upon in terms of four important dimensions: positive-negative, immediate-delayed; low monitoring–high monitoring, and critical-supportive. To use feedback effectively, then, you need to make educated choices along these dimensions.

Positive-Negative.   Feedback may be positive—as when you compliment or pat someone on the back for a good job—or negative—as when you criticize what the speaker has said or done or when you make some negative reaction gesturally. Positive feedback tells the speaker that he or she is on the right track and should continue communicating in essentially the same way. Negative feedback tells the speaker that something is wrong and that some adjustment should be made. Thus, for example, a puzzled look from the listener may suggest that the speaker clarify a term or explain a concept in greater detail.

Immediate-Delayed.   Generally, the most effective feedback is that which is most immediate. In interpersonal situations, feedback is most often sent immediately after the message is received. Feedback, like reinforcement, loses its effectiveness with time. The longer you wait to praise or punish, for example, the less effect the praise or punishment will have.

In other communication situations, however, the feedback may be delayed. Instructor evaluation questionnaires completed at the end of the course provide feedback long after the class began. When you applaud or ask questions of a public speaker, the feedback is delayed. In interview situations, the feedback may come weeks afterward. In media situations, some feedback comes immediately through, for example, Nielsen ratings, and other feedback comes much later through viewing and buying patterns.

Low Monitoring–High Monitoring.   Feedback varies from the spontaneous and totally honest reaction (low-monitored feedback) to the carefully constructed response designed to serve a specific purpose (high-monitored feedback). In most interpersonal situations, you probably give feedback spontaneously; you allow your responses to show without any monitoring. At other times, however, you may be more guarded, as when your boss asks you how you like your job or when your grandfather asks what you think of his new motorcycle outfit.

Critical-Supportive.   Critical feedback is evaluative; it's judgmental. When you give critical feedback (whether positive or negative), you judge another's performance, as in, for example, evaluating a speech or coaching someone learning a new skill. Feedback can also be supportive, as when you console another, simply encourage the other to talk, or affirm another's self-definition.

Feedforward   **Feedforward** is information you provide before sending your primary messages (Richards 1951). Feedforward reveals something about the messages to come.

Examples of feedforward include the preface or table of contents of a book, the opening paragraph of a chapter, movie previews, magazine covers, and introductions in public speeches. Feedforward has four major functions: (1) to open the channels of communication, (2) to preview the message, (3) to disclaim, and (4) to altercast.

To Open the Channels of Communication. In his influential essay "The Problem of Meaning in Primitive Languages," the anthropologist Bronislaw Malinowski (1923) coined the phrase *phatic communion* to refer to messages that open the channels of communication rather than communicate information. Phatic communion is a perfect example of feedforward. It is information that tells us that the normal, expected, and accepted rules of interaction will be in effect. It tells us another person is willing to communicate.

Phatic messages are essential in initiating interactions, especially with strangers. The famous "opening line" ("Have you got a match?" or "Haven't we met before?") is a clear example of phatic communion. When such phatic messages do not precede an initial interaction, we sense that something is wrong and may conclude that the speaker lacks the basic skills of communication.

To Preview the Message. Feedforward messages frequently preview other messages. They do so in a variety of ways. Feedforward may, for example, preview the content ("I'm afraid I have bad news for you"), the importance ("Listen to this before you make a move"), the form or style ("I'll tell you all the gory details"), and the positive or negative quality of subsequent messages ("You're not going to like this, but here's what I heard").

To Disclaim. The **disclaimer** is a statement that aims to ensure that your message will be understood and will not reflect negatively on you. Disclaimers, which try to persuade the listener to hear your message as you wish it to be heard, are discussed in greater depth in Unit 15.

To Altercast. Feedforward is often used to place the receiver in a specific role and to request that the receiver respond to you in terms of this assumed role. This process, known as **altercasting,** asks the receiver to approach your message from a particular role or even as someone else (Weinstein and Deutschberger 1963; McLaughlin 1984). For example, you might ask a friend, "As an advertising executive, what would you think of corrective advertising?" This question casts your friend in the role of advertising executive (rather than parent, Democrat, or Baptist, for example). It asks your friend to answer from a particular perspective.

We might also ask people to assume roles quite foreign to them. Here are a few examples:

- If you were the author of this book, how would you explain the feedforward process?
- If money were no object, which car would you buy?
- What would you do if you were her father?
- If you won the lottery, what changes would you make in your life?

CHANNEL

The communication **channel** is the medium through which messages pass. The channel acts as a bridge connecting source and receiver. Communication rarely takes place over only one channel; two, three, or four channels are normally used simultaneously. For example, in face-to-face interaction, you speak and listen (vocal-auditory channel), but you also gesture and receive signals visually (gestural-visual channel), and you emit odors and smell those of others (chemical-olfactory channel). Often you touch one another, and this touching also communicates (cutaneous-tactile channel).

Another way to think about channels is to consider them as the means of communication: for example, face-to-face contact, telephone, electronic and traditional mail, film, television, radio, smoke signal, fax, or telegraph.

NOISE

Noise enters into all communication systems, no matter how well designed or technically sophisticated. **Noise** is anything that distorts or interferes with message reception. It is present in a communication system to the extent that the message received differs from the message sent. Three main types of noise are physical, psychological, and semantic.

Physical noise interferes with the physical transmission of the signal or message. Sunglasses, the screech of a passing car, the hum of a computer, a speaker's lisp, or a bad phone connection may all be viewed as physical noise because they interfere physically with the transmission of signals from one person to another.

Psychological noise refers to any form of psychological interference that can lead to distortions in the reception and processing of information. This type of noise includes biases and prejudices held by senders and receivers. Closed-mindedness is perhaps the classic example of psychological noise.

Semantic noise occurs when the receiver does not decode the meanings intended by the sender. An extreme form of semantic noise occurs between people speaking different languages. A more common form is created when you use jargon or technical and complex terms not understood by your listener, or when the listener assigns meanings different from those you intend (as would frequently be the case with ambiguous or highly emotional terms, as in racist, sexist, or heterosexist talk, discussed in Unit 11).

Noise is inevitable; all communication contains noise of some kind. And while you cannot eliminate it completely, you can reduce noise and its effects. Making your language more precise, acquiring the skills for sending and receiving nonverbal messages, and improving your perceptual, listening, and feedback skills are just a few of the ways in which you can effectively combat the effects of noise.

CONTEXT

Communication always takes place in a **context,** the environment in which communication occurs and which exerts influence on the form and content of the communication. At times this context is not obvious or intrusive; it seems so natural that it is ignored, like

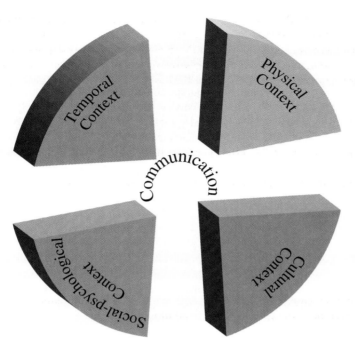

Figure 1.2
The influence of context on the communication process.

background music. At other times the context dominates, and the ways in which it restricts or stimulates our communications are obvious. Compare, for example, the differences among communicating in a funeral home, in a football stadium, in a quiet restaurant, and at a rock concert. The context of communication has at least four dimensions: physical, temporal, social-psychological, and cultural, all of which interact and influence each other (see Figure 1.2).

The **physical dimension** is the tangible or concrete environment in which communication takes place—the room, hallway, or park, the boardroom or the family dinner table. The **temporal dimension** refers not only to the time of day and moment in history but also to where a particular message fits into the sequence of communication events. For example, a joke about illness told immediately after the disclosure of a friend's sickness will be received differently than the same joke told in response to a series of similar jokes.

The **social-psychological dimension** includes, for example, status relationships among the participants, roles and games that people play, norms of the society or group, and the friendliness, formality, or gravity of the situation.

Communication also takes place in a **cultural context.** The implications of this simple observation are enormous for interpersonal communication. When people from different cultures interact, they may each follow different rules of communication, rules that are often unknown to the other participants. This can result in confusion, unintentional insult, inaccurate judgments, and a host of other miscommunications. Similarly, communication strategies or techniques that prove satisfying to members of one culture may prove disturbing or offensive to members of another.

EFFECTS

Every communication act has **effects,** which may be felt by one person or both. When communication affects the environment or context, it does so through people. The effects of communication, then, are first felt by people and are always personal. Even when effects cannot be observed (which may be most of the time), it is assumed that for every interpersonal communication act there are effects, somewhat as "for every action there is a reaction."

ETHICS

Because communication has consequences, interpersonal communication also involves **ethics,** the rightness or wrongness of a communication act. The ethical dimension of communication is further complicated by the fact that it is so closely interwoven with each person's own philosophy of life that it is difficult to propose universal guidelines. Notwithstanding this difficulty, ethics is included as a universal of interpersonal communication (see Unit 5). The choices you make concerning communication are guided by ethical considerations as well as by effectiveness, satisfaction, or other factors.

PURPOSES OF INTERPERSONAL COMMUNICATION

Interpersonal communication may serve a variety of purposes. A purpose need not be conscious at the time of the interpersonal encounter; nor is it necessarily the intended reason for the encounter. "Purposes" may be conscious or subconscious, intentional or unintentional.

TO LEARN

Interpersonal communication enables you to better understand the external world—the world of objects, events, and other people. Although a great deal of information comes from the media, you probably discuss and ultimately "learn" or internalize information through interpersonal interactions. In fact, your beliefs, attitudes, and values are probably influenced more by interpersonal encounters than by the media or even formal education.

Most important, however, interpersonal communication helps you learn about yourself. By talking about yourself with others, you gain valuable feedback on your feelings, thoughts, and behaviors. Through these communications, you also learn how you appear to others—who likes you, who dislikes you, and why.

To Relate

One of the greatest needs people have is to establish and maintain close relationships. You want to feel loved and liked, and in turn you want to love and like others. Such relationships help to alleviate loneliness and depression, enable you to share and heighten your pleasures, and generally make you feel more positive about yourself.

To Influence

Very likely, you influence the attitudes and behaviors of others in your interpersonal encounters. You may wish them to vote a particular way, try a new diet, buy a new book, listen to a record, see a movie, take a specific course, think in a particular way, believe that something is true or false, or value some idea—the list is endless. A good deal of your time is probably spent in interpersonal persuasion.

To Play

Play includes all activities of which pleasure is the primary or exclusive goal. Talking with friends about your weekend activities, discussing sports or dates, telling stories and jokes, and, in general, just passing the time serve this function. Far from frivolous, this purpose is an extremely important one. It gives your activities a necessary balance and your mind a needed break from all the seriousness around us. Everyone has an inner child, and that child needs time to play.

To Help

Therapists of various kinds serve a helping function professionally by offering guidance through interpersonal interaction. But everyone does this in everyday interactions: you console a friend who has broken off a love affair, counsel another student about courses to take, or offer advice to a colleague about work. Success in accomplishing this helping function, professionally or otherwise, depends on your knowledge and skill in interpersonal communication.

The purposes of interpersonal communication can also be viewed from two other perspectives (see Table 1.2). First, purposes may be seen as motives for engaging in interpersonal communication. That is, you engage in interpersonal communication to satisfy your need for knowledge or to form relationships. Second, these purposes may be viewed in terms of the results you want to achieve. That is, you engage in interpersonal communication to increase your knowledge of yourself and others or to exert influence or power over others.

Interpersonal communication is usually motivated by a combination of factors and has a combination of results or effects. Any interpersonal interaction, then, serves a unique combination of purposes, is motivated by a unique combination of factors, and can produce a unique combination of results.

Table 1.2
Why You Engage in Interpersonal Communication

PURPOSES	MOTIVATIONS	RESULTS
To learn: to acquire knowledge of oneself, others, and the world; to acquire skills	Need to know, to acquire knowledge, to learn	Increased knowledge of oneself, others, and the world; skill acquisition
To relate: to establish and maintain interpersonal relationships	Need to form relationships, to relate to others, to interact	Relationship formation and maintenance, friendships, love relationships
To influence: to control, to manipulate, to direct	Need to control, to influence, to lead, to gain compliance, to secure agreement	Influence, power, control, compliance, agreement
To play: to escape from work, to enjoy oneself	Need for diversion, for pleasure, for sensory gratification	Enjoyment, pleasure, satisfaction, gratification
To help: to minister to the needs of others, to console	Need to console, to help, to befriend, to feel needed, to gain satisfaction	Guidance, direction, attitude and behavior adjustment

SUMMARY: UNIT IN BRIEF

Definitions of Interpersonal Communication	Elements of Interpersonal Communication	Purposes of Interpersonal Communication
Dyadic (Relational): communication between two or a few connected individuals	**Source-receiver:** the sender-and-receiver of messages	**To learn** about self, others, and the world
Developmental: two-person communication based on psychological data, explanatory knowledge, and personally established rules	**Encoding-decoding:** the act of putting meaning into verbal and nonverbal messages and deriving meaning from such messages	**To relate** to others and to form relationships
	Competence: the knowledge of and ability to use appropriately one's communication system	**To influence** or control the attitudes and behaviors of others
	Messages: the signals that serve as stimuli for a receiver; metamessages are messages that refer to other messages	**To play** or enjoy oneself
	Feedback messages: messages that are sent back by the receiver to the source in response to other messages	**To help** others
	Feedforward messages: messages that preface other messages and ask that the listener approach future messages in a certain way	
	Channel: the medium through which messages pass	
	Noise: the physical, psychological, or semantic interference that distorts a message	
	Context: the physical, social-psychological, temporal, and cultural dimensions in which the communication act takes place	
	Effects: the consequences of communication	
	Ethics: the moral dimension of communication	

THINKING CRITICALLY ABOUT THE UNIVERSALS OF INTERPERSONAL COMMUNICATION

1. In what ways would interpersonal communication between two persons from the same culture and two persons from widely different cultures differ? In what ways would they be the same?
2. What kinds of feedforward can you find in this book? Are these feedforward messages helpful to you as you read the text?
3. What types of interpersonal communications would you consider unethical? Why? What ethical principles do you think should govern interpersonal communication?
4. How would you describe your relationship with your best friend or romantic partner in terms of the three characteristics of interpersonal communication noted in the developmental definition: predictions are based on psychological data, interactions are based on explanatory knowledge, and interactions are based on personally established rules? How does this relationship differ from, for example, the relationship you have with one of your college instructors?
5. Can you identify any primary dyads in your extended family? What functions do these dyads serve?
6. What dyadic coalitions are you currently a member of? Why were these coalitions formed? Have they served productive purposes?
7. Do you talk to your instructor differently than you talk to your friends? Can you identify ten differences?
8. Can you identify how you used each of the five purposes of interpersonal communication in the last four hours?
9. What characters in television sitcoms or dramas do you feel demonstrate superior interpersonal competence? What characters demonstrate obvious interpersonal incompetence?
10. How would you go about answering such questions as the following? (See the "Researching Communication" section in *Studying Communication* for guidance on these research questions.)

    • Are interpersonal communication skills related to relationship success? To occupational success?
    • Are competent communications less anxious?
    • How does the physical context influence communication?
    • How is effective teaching related to the use of feedback and feedforward?

EXPERIENTIAL VEHICLES

1.1 MODELING SOME UNIVERSALS OF INTERPERSONAL COMMUNICATION

Review the section on the elements of interpersonal communication (pp. 10–18) and construct an original visual representation of the process of interpersonal communication. In constructing this model, be careful that you do not fall into the trap of visualizing interpersonal communication as a linear or simple left-to-right, static process. Remember that all elements are interrelated and interdependent.

When everyone has completed the model, form groups of five or six, pool your insights, and construct one improved model of communication. After this is completed, each group should share its model with the entire class.

You may wish to consider some or all of the following questions:

1. Why is it important to speak of a source-receiver rather than a source and a receiver? Why is it important to speak of encoding-decoding rather than encoding and decoding?
2. Most models of communication do not include the concept of competence. Does this concept help to clarify the nature of interpersonal communication? If so, in what ways?
3. Some theorists have argued that it is not necessary to consider feedback as a distinct element. They argue that it is just another message that does not differ in any essential way from "regular" messages. Do you think that the concept of feedback as distinct from "regular" messages helps in understanding the nature of interpersonal communication? If so, in what ways? What about feedforward?
4. Could your model also serve as a model of *intra*personal communication?
5. What elements or concepts other than those noted above might be added to the model? Why would they help us to understand interpersonal communication?

1.2 METAPHORICALLY SPEAKING

Metaphors—figures of speech in which one concept is used in place of another—are powerful tools for gaining different perspectives on a concept. Explain interpersonal communication in terms of these metaphors:

1. A seesaw
2. A ball game
3. A flower
4. Ice skates
5. A microscope
6. A television sitcom
7. A work of art
8. A long book
9. A rubber band
10. A software program

UNIT 2

Axioms of Interpersonal Communication

UNIT OBJECTIVES

AFTER COMPLETING THIS UNIT, YOU SHOULD BE ABLE TO:

1. Explain the transactional nature of interpersonal communication
2. Explain why communi-cation is inevitable
3. Explain the irreversibility and unrepeatability of interpersonal communication
4. Explain how communi-cation is culture-specific and the major implications of culture in interpersonal communication
5. Explain why interpersonal communication involves a process of adjustment
6. Explain punctuation in interpersonal communication
7. Distinguish between symmetrical and complemen-tary relationships
8. Distinguish between the content and relationship dimensions of interpersonal communication

In this unit, we continue to explore the special nature of interpersonal communication by identifying some of its axioms or principles. These axioms are largely the work of the transactional researchers Paul Watzlawick, Janet Helmick Beavin, and Don D. Jackson, presented in their landmark *Pragmatics of Human Communication* (1967; also see Watzlawick 1977, 1978). Together with the concepts already presented (Unit 1), these axioms complete our characterization of what interpersonal communication is and how it works.

These axioms, although significant in terms of explaining theory, also have very practical applications. They provide insight into such day-to-day issues as the following:

- Why disagreements so often center on trivial matters and yet seem so difficult to resolve
- Why you will never be able to mind read—to know exactly what another person is thinking
- How communication expresses power relationships
- Why you and your partner often see the causes of arguments quite differently

INTERPERSONAL COMMUNICATION IS A TRANSACTIONAL PROCESS

A transactional perspective views interpersonal communication as (1) a process (2) whose elements are *inter*dependent.

INTERPERSONAL COMMUNICATION IS A PROCESS

Interpersonal communication is a process. It is not static; it is ongoing. Everything involved in interpersonal communication is in a state of flux: you are changing, the people you communicate with are changing, and your environment is changing. Sometimes these changes go unnoticed, and sometimes they intrude in obvious ways. But they are always occurring.

The interpersonal communication process is best described as a circular and continuous one. When you view communication as the transmitting of messages from speaker to listener, you imply that the process begins with the speaker and ends with the listener. This is a linear view. In fact, interpersonal communication is a circular process in which each person serves simultaneously as a speaker *and* a listener, an actor *and* a reactor.

Consider a "simple" interpersonal act: you meet and talk with another person. Because it is convenient, you may say that this interaction began when you started to speak or when you and the other person first saw each other. However, that analysis is too simplistic because what each of you says and how each of you responds depend on factors that developed at some unidentifiable earlier time: for example, your self-confidence, your previous experience, your fears, your competencies, your expectations, your needs, and hundreds of other factors.

ELEMENTS ARE INTERDEPENDENT

The elements in interpersonal communication are *inter*dependent. Each element—each part of interpersonal communication—is intimately connected to the other parts and to the whole. For example, there can be no source without a receiver; there can be no message without a source; there can be no feedback without a receiver. Because of interdependency, a change in any one element causes changes in the others. For example, you are talking with a group of fellow students about a recent examination, and your teacher joins the group. This change in participants will lead to other changes—perhaps in the content of what you say, perhaps in the manner in which you express it. But regardless of what change is introduced, other changes result.

COMMUNICATION IS INEVITABLE

Often communication is thought of as intentional, purposeful, and consciously motivated. In many instances it is. But in other instances you are communicating even though you might not think you are or might not even want to communicate. Consider, for example, the student sitting in the back of the room with an "expressionless" face, perhaps staring out the window. Although the student might say that she or he is not communicating with the teacher, the teacher may derive any of a variety of messages from this behavior—for example, the student lacks interest, is bored, or is worried about something. In any event, the teacher is receiving messages even though the student might not intend to communicate. In an interactional situation, all behavior is potentially communication. That is, any aspect of your behavior may communicate if the other person gives it message value. On the other hand, if the behavior (for example, the student's looking out the window) goes unnoticed, then no communication would have taken place (Watzlawick, Beavin, and Jackson 1967; Motley 1990a, 1990b; Bavelas 1990; Beach 1990).

The axiom of inevitability has created lots of controversy (Motley 1990a, 1990b; Bavelas 1990; Beach, 1990). Some assumed that this axiom meant that all behavior communicates; therefore, you cannot not communicate since you cannot not behave. But, the original intention of this axiom was that all behavior *in an interactional situation* communicates; therefore, if you are interacting with another person, all your behavior communicates something. A more reasoned view is that, in general, communication in an interactional situation is inevitable, because you are always behaving; but the behavior must be perceived in some way by some other person for this behavior to be considered communication. What arguments could you advance to support or refute any of these notions?

Further, when in an interactional situation, your responses all have potential message value. For example, if you notice someone winking at you, you must respond in some way. Even if you do not respond openly, that lack of response is itself a response and it communicates (assuming it is perceived by the other person).

COMMUNICATION IS IRREVERSIBLE AND UNREPEATABLE

The processes of some systems can be reversed. For example, you can turn water into ice and then reverse the process by melting the ice. Moreover, you can repeat this reversal of ice and water for as long as you wish. Other systems, however, are irreversible. In these systems, the process can move in only one direction; it cannot go back again. For example, you can turn grapes into wine, but you cannot reverse the process and turn the wine back into grapes.

Interpersonal communication is irreversible. What you have communicated remains communicated; you cannot *un*communicate. Although you may try to qualify, negate, or somehow reduce the effects of your message, once it has been sent and received the message itself cannot be reversed.

In interpersonal interactions (especially in conflict), you need to be especially careful that you do not say things you may wish to withdraw later. Similarly, commitment messages, such as "I love you," must be monitored lest you commit yourself to a position you may be uncomfortable with later.

In addition to being irreversible, interpersonal communication is also unrepeatable. The reason is simple: everyone and everything are constantly changing. As a result, you can never recapture the exact same situation, frame of mind, or relationship dynamics that defined a previous interpersonal act. For example, you can never repeat the experience of meeting a particular person for the first time, comforting a grieving friend on the death of his or her mother, or resolving a specific conflict.

You can, of course, try again, as when you say, "I'm sorry I came off so forward; can we try again?" But notice that even when you say this, you do not erase the initial impression. Instead, you try to counteract the initial (and perhaps negative) impression by going through the motions once more. In doing so, you try to create a more positive impression, which you hope will lessen the original negative effect.

COMMUNICATION IS CULTURE-SPECIFIC

The ways in which cultures differ in terms of their (1) orientation (whether individual or collective) and (2) context (whether high or low) have a significant impact on interpersonal communication (Gudykunst 1991; Hall and Hall 1987).

INDIVIDUAL AND COLLECTIVE ORIENTATION

This aspect of culture refers to the extent to which the individual's goals and desires or the group's goals and desires are given greater importance. Individual and collective tendencies are not mutually exclusive; it is not "all or nothing" but rather a matter of emphasis. Thus, you may, for example, compete with other members of your basketball team for the most baskets or the most valuable player award. At the same time, however, you will—in a game—act in a way that benefits the group. In actual practice, both individual and collective tendencies help each player and the team as a whole achieve their respective goals.

At times, however, these tendencies may come into conflict. For example, do you shoot for the basket and try to raise your individual score, or do you pass the ball to another player who is better positioned to score the basket and thus benefit your team?

In an individualistic culture, you are responsible for yourself and perhaps your immediate family; in a collectivist culture, you are responsible for the entire group. Success, in an individualistic culture, is measured by the extent to which you surpass other members of your group; you would take pride in standing out from the crowd. Furthermore, your heroes—in the media, for example—are likely to be those who are unique and who stand apart. In a collectivist culture, success is measured by your contribution to the achievements of the group as a whole; you would take pride in your similarity to other members of your group. Your heroes, in contrast to those of someone in an individualistic culture, are more likely to be team players who do not stand out from the rest of the group's members.

In an individualistic culture, you are responsible to your own conscience, and responsibility is largely an individual matter. In a collectivist culture, you are responsible to the rules of the social group, and responsibility for an accomplishment or a failure is shared by all members.

Competition is promoted in individualistic cultures, whereas cooperation is promoted in collectivist cultures. Not surprisingly, research shows that in the United States and Canada (individualistic cultures) people work harder when working individually. But, in China (a collectivist culture) people work harder in groups than when on their own (Latané, Williams, and Harkins 1979, Gabrenya, Wang, and Latané 1985, Moghaddam, Taylor, and Wright 1993).

Distinctions between in-group members and out-group members are extremely important in collectivist cultures. In individualistic cultures, which prize a person's distinctive qualities, the in-group versus out-group distinction is likely to be less important.

HIGH- AND LOW-CONTEXT CULTURES

A high-context culture is one in which much of the information in communication is contained in the context or in the person—for example, information that is shared through previous communications, through assumptions that participants hold about each other, and through shared experiences. The information is not explicitly stated in the verbal message.

A low-context culture is one in which most information is explicitly stated in the verbal message, as well as in formal transactions in written (contract) form.

To appreciate the distinction between high and low context, consider giving directions ("Where's the voter registration center?") to someone who knows the neighborhood and to a newcomer to your city. In the case of someone who knows the neighborhood (a high-context situation), you can assume that the person is familiar with the local landmarks. So you can give directions such as "next to the laundromat on Main Street" or "at the corner of Albany and Elm." To the newcomer (a low-context situation), you cannot assume that the person shares any information with you. So you would have to use only those directions that even a stranger would understand: for example, "make a left at the next stop sign" or "go two blocks and then turn right."

High-context cultures are also collectivist cultures (Gudykunst, Ting-Toomey, and Chua 1988). These cultures (Japanese, Arabic, Latin American, Thai, Korean, Apache, and Mexican are examples) place great emphasis on personal relationships and oral agreements (Victor 1992).

Low-context cultures are also individualistic cultures. These cultures (U.S., German, Swedish, and Norwegian are examples) place less emphasis on personal relationships and more emphasis on written, explicit explanation—for example, on the written contracts in business transactions.

In low-context cultures, such as the culture of the United States, relationships come to resemble high-context interactions as they become more intimate. The more you and your partner know about each other, the less you have to make verbally explicit. Truman Capote once defined love as "never having to finish your sentences," which is an apt description of high-context relationships. Because you know the other person so well, you can make some pretty good guesses as to what the person will say.

How would you describe the culture in which you were raised in terms of high context and low context? Have you ever encountered communication difficulties as a result of differences in context?

Members of high-context cultures spend lots of time getting to know each other before any important transactions take place. Because of this prior personal knowledge, a great deal of information is shared and therefore does not have to be explicitly stated. Members of low-context cultures spend a great deal less time getting to know each other and hence do not have that shared knowledge. As a result, much has to be stated explicitly. In high-context cultures, members rely more on nonverbal cues in reducing uncertainty (Sanders, Wiseman, and Matz 1991).

To the members of high-context cultures, what is assumed is a vital part of the communication transaction. Silence, for example, is highly valued (Basso 1972). To low-context cultures' members, what is omitted creates ambiguity; this ambiguity is to be eliminated by explicit and direct communication (Gudykunst 1983).

When the difference between high and low context is not grasped, misunderstandings can easily result. For example, the directness characteristic of the low-context culture may prove insulting, insensitive, or unnecessary to a member of a high-context culture. Conversely, to a low-context culture's members, someone from a high-context culture may appear vague, underhanded, or dishonest in his or her reluctance to be explicit or to engage in communication that members of a low-context culture would consider open and direct.

Another frequent source of misunderstanding that can be traced to the distinction between high- and low-context cultures is face-saving (Hall and Hall 1987). High-context cultures place a great deal more emphasis on face-saving. For example, they are more likely to avoid argument for fear of causing others to lose face, whereas members of low-context cultures (with their individualistic orientation) will use argument to win a point. Similarly, in high-context cultures, criticism should only take place in private to enable the person to save face. Low-context cultures may not make this public-private distinction.

People in high-context cultures are reluctant to say no for fear of giving offense and causing the person to lose face. So, for example, it is necessary to determine when the Japanese executive's yes means yes and when it means no. The difference is not in the words used but in the way they are used. It is easy to see how the low-context individual may interpret this reluctance to be direct—to say no when someone means no—as a weakness or as an unwillingness to confront reality.

A summary of these differences as they relate to interpersonal communication is presented in Table 2.1. As you read this table, consider which statements you agree with and which you disagree with and how these beliefs influence your communications.

INTERPERSONAL COMMUNICATION IS A PROCESS OF ADJUSTMENT

Interpersonal communication can take place only to the extent that the parties communicating share the same system of symbols. This is obvious when dealing with speakers of two different languages. Your communication with another person will be hindered to the extent that your language systems differ. This principle takes on particular relevance

Table 2.1 **Some Cultural Differences***	
INDIVIDUAL (LOW-CONTEXT) CULTURES	COLLECTIVE (HIGH-CONTEXT) CULTURES
Your goals are most important.	The group's goals are most important.
You are responsible for yourself and to your own conscience.	You are responsible for the entire group and to the group's values and rules.
Success depends on your surpassing others; competition is emphasized.	Success depends on your contribution to the group; cooperation is emphasized.
Clear distinction is made between leaders and members.	Little distinction is made between leaders and members; leadership is normally shared.
In-group versus out-group distinctions have little importance.	In-group versus out-group distinctions have great importance.
Information is made explicit; little is left unstated.	Information is often left implicit, and much is often omitted from an explicit statement.
Personal relationships are less important; hence, little time is spent getting to know each other in meetings.	Personal relationships are extremely important; hence, much time is spent getting to know each other in meetings.
Directness is valued; face-saving is seldom considered.	Indirectness is valued; face-saving is a major consideration.

*This table is based on the work of Hall and Hall (1987; Hall 1983) and the commentaries by Gudykunst (1991) and Victor (1992).

when you realize that no two persons share identical symbol systems. Parents and children, for example, not only have very different vocabularies but also, even more important, have different meanings for some of the terms they have in common. Different cultures and social groups, even when they share a common language, often have greatly differing nonverbal communication systems. To the extent that these systems differ, communication will not take place.

Part of the art of interpersonal communication is learning the other person's signals, how they are used, and what they mean. People in close relationships—either as intimate friends or as romantic partners—realize that learning the other person's signals takes a long time and, often, great patience. If you want to understand what another person means—by a smile, by saying "I love you," by arguing about trivial matters, by self-deprecating comments—you have to learn their system of signals. Furthermore, you have to share your own system of signals with others so that they can better understand you. Although some people may know what you mean by your silence or by your avoidance of eye contact, others may not. You cannot expect others to decode your behaviors accurately without help.

COMMUNICATION IS A SERIES OF PUNCTUATED EVENTS

Communication events are continuous transactions. There is no clear-cut beginning and no clear-cut end. As participants in or observers of the communication act, you segment this continuous stream of communication into smaller pieces. You label some of these pieces causes or stimuli and others effects or responses.

Consider an example: A couple is at a party. The husband is flirting with another woman, and the wife is drinking. Both are scowling at each other and are obviously in a deep nonverbal argument. In later recalling the situation, the husband might observe that the wife drank, so he flirted with the sober woman. The more she drank, the more he flirted. The only reason for his behavior (he says) was his anger over her drinking. Notice that he sees his behavior as a response to her behavior. In recalling the same incident, the wife might say that she drank when he started flirting. The more he flirted, the more she drank. She had no intention of drinking until he started flirting. To her, his behavior was the stimulus and hers was the response; he caused her behavior. Thus, the husband sees the sequence as going from drinking to flirting, and the wife sees it as going from flirting to drinking. This example is depicted visually in Figure 2.1.

Figure 2.1(A) shows the actual sequence of events as a continuous series of actions with no specific beginning or end. Each action (drinking and flirting) stimulates another action, but no initial cause is identified. Figure 2.1(B) shows the same sequence of events as seen by the wife. She sees the sequence as beginning with the husband's flirting and her drinking behavior as a response to that stimulus. Figure 2.1(C) shows the same sequence of events from the husband's point of view. He sees the sequence as beginning with the wife's drinking and his flirting as a response to that stimulus.

This tendency to divide communication transactions into sequences of stimuli and responses is referred to as **punctuation** (Watzlawick, Beavin, and Jackson 1967). Everyone punctuates the continuous sequences of events into stimuli and responses for convenience. Moreover, as the example of the husband and wife illustrates, punctuation usually is done in ways that benefit the person and are consistent with his or her self-image.

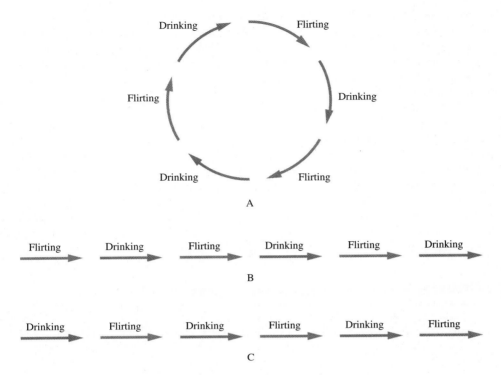

Figure 2.1
Punctuation and the sequence of events.

Understanding how another person interprets a situation, how he or she punctuates, is a crucial step in interpersonal understanding. It is also essential in achieving empathy (feeling what the other person is feeling). In all communication encounters, but especially in conflicts, try to see how others punctuate the situation.

RELATIONSHIPS MAY BE VIEWED AS SYMMETRICAL OR COMPLEMENTARY

Interpersonal relationships can be described as either symmetrical or complementary (Bateson 1972; Watzlawick, Beavin, and Jackson 1967). In a **symmetrical** relationship, the two individuals mirror each other's behavior (Bateson 1972). If one member nags, the other member responds in kind. If one member is passionate, the other member is passionate. If one member expresses jealousy, the other member also expresses jealousy. If one member is passive, so is the other. The relationship is one of equality, with the emphasis on minimizing the differences between the two individuals.

Note, however, the problems that can arise in this type of relationship. Consider the situation of a couple in which both members are very aggressive. The aggressiveness of one person fosters aggressiveness in the other, which fosters increased aggressiveness in the first individual. As this cycle escalates, the aggressiveness can no longer be contained, and the relationship is consumed by the aggression.

In a **complementary** relationship, the two individuals engage in different behaviors. The behavior of one serves as the stimulus for the other's complementary behavior. In complementary relationships, the differences between the parties are maximized. The people occupy different positions, one superior and the other inferior, one passive and the other active, one strong and the other weak. At times, cultures establish such relationships—for example, the complementary relationship between teacher and student or between employer and employee.

A problem in complementary relationships, familiar to many college students, is created by extreme rigidity. Whereas the complementary relationship between a nurturing and protective mother and a dependent child is at one time vital, that same relationship becomes a handicap to further development when the child is older. The change so essential to growth is not allowed to occur.

An interesting perspective on complementary and symmetrical relationships can be gained by looking at the ways in which these patterns combine to exert control in an interpersonal relationship (Rogers-Millar and Millar 1979; Millar and Rogers 1987; Rogers and Farace 1975). Nine patterns are identified; three deal with symmetry (similar-type messages), two deal with complementarity (opposite-type messages), and four are transitional (neither similar- nor opposite-type messages).

In **competitive symmetry,** each person tries to exert control over the other (symbolized by an upward arrow↑). Each communicates one-up messages (messages that attempt to control the behaviors of the other person):

PAT: Do it now.↑
CHRIS: I'll do it when I'm good and ready; otherwise, do it yourself.↑

In **submissive symmetry,** each person communicates submission (symbolized by a downward arrow ↓); the messages are one-down (messages that indicate submission to what the other person wants):

PAT: What do you want for dinner?↓
CHRIS: Whatever you'd like is fine with me.↓

In **neutralized symmetry,** each person communicates similarly. However (as symbolized by a horizonal arrow →), neither person communicates competitively (one-up) or submissively (one-down):

PAT: Jackie needs new shoes.→
CHRIS: And a new jacket.→

In **complementarity,** one person communicates the desire to control (one-up), and the other person communicates submission (one-down):

PAT: Here, honey, do it this way.↑
CHRIS: Oh, that's great; you're so clever.↓

In another type of **complementarity**—the reverse of the pattern above—the submissive message (one-down) comes first and is followed by a controlling (one-up) message:

PAT: I need suggestions for teaching this new course.↓
CHRIS: Oh, that's easy; I've taught that course for years.↑

Transition patterns do not involve stating the opposite of the previous message; communicators do not respond to a competitive message with submission or to a submissive message with competition. There are four possible transition patterns:

1. A competitive message (one-up) is responded to without either another competitive message or a submissive message:

   PAT: I want to go to the movies. ↑
   CHRIS: There certainly are a lot of choices this weekend. →

2. A submissive message (one-down) is responded to without either another submissive message or a competitive message:

   PAT: I'm just helpless with tools. ↓
   CHRIS: Lots of people have difficulty using a router. →

3. A transition message (one-across) is responded to with a competitive (one-up) message:

   PAT: We can do the job many different ways. →
   CHRIS: Well, here's the right way. ↑

4. A transition message (one-across) is responded to with a submissive (one-down) message:

   PAT: We can do the job many different ways. →
   CHRIS: Whatever way you do it is fine. ↓

In thinking about these patterns, consider your own friendship, love, and family relationships:

- How rigid or flexible are these patterns? For example, do you and your friend share control and submission, or does one of you exercise control and the other respond with submission?
- Can you identify a relationship you have that makes use of one major pattern? What part do you play? Are you comfortable with this pattern?
- Can you identify a general pattern that you use in many or most of your relationships? How satisfied are you with this customary pattern of expression?
- Can you identify relationships you have that began with one pattern of communication and shifted over the years to another pattern? What happened?
- Do these patterns have anything to do with the degree of relationship satisfaction you experience? For example, do you derive greater satisfaction from a relationship that relies on one pattern than you do from a relationship that relies on another pattern?

COMMUNICATIONS HAVE CONTENT AND RELATIONSHIP DIMENSIONS

Communications usually refer to the real world, to something external to both speaker and listener. At the same time, they refer to the relationship between the parties. For example, a judge may say to a lawyer, "See me in my chambers immediately." This simple message has both a content aspect, which refers to the behavioral response expected (namely, that the lawyer will see the judge immediately), and a relationship aspect, which says something about the relationship between the judge and the lawyer and, as a result of this relationship, how the communication is to be dealt with. Even the use of the simple command shows that there is a status difference between the two parties. This difference can perhaps be seen most clearly if you imagine the command being made by the lawyer to the judge. Such a communication appears awkward and out of place because it violates the normal relationship between judge and lawyer.

In any two communications, the content dimension may be the same, but the relationship aspect may be different, or the relationship aspect may be the same and the content dimension different. For example, the judge could say to the lawyer, "You had better see me immediately" or "May I please see you as soon as possible?" In both cases, the content is essentially the same; that is, the message about the expected behavioral response is the same. But the relationship dimension is quite different. The first communication signifies a very definite superior-inferior relationship, whereas the second signals a more equal relationship and shows respect for the lawyer.

Similarly, at times the content may be different but the relationship is essentially the same. For example, a daughter might say to her parents, "May I go away this weekend?" or "May I use the car tonight?" The content of the two questions is clearly very different, but the relationship dimension is essentially the same. It clearly reflects a superior-inferior relationship in which permission to do certain things must be secured.

IMPLICATIONS OF CONTENT AND RELATIONSHIP DIMENSIONS

The major implications of these content and relationship dimensions center on conflict and its effective resolution. Many problems between people result from failure to recognize the distinction between the content and the relationship dimensions of communication. For example, consider the couple arguing over the fact that Pat made plans to study with friends during the weekend without first asking Chris if that would be all right. Probably both would agree that to study over the weekend is the right decision. Thus, the argument is not primarily concerned with the content level. It centers on the relationship level; Chris expected to be consulted about plans for the weekend. Pat, in not doing so, rejected this definition of their relationship. Similar situations occur when one member of a couple buys something, makes dinner plans, or invites a guest to dinner without first asking the other person. Even though the other person might have agreed with the decision, the couple argue because of the message communicated on the relationship level.

Let me give you a personal example. My mother came to stay for a week at a summer place I had. On the first day, she swept the kitchen floor six times, although I repeatedly said that it did not need sweeping, that I would be tracking in dirt and mud from outside, and that all her effort was just wasted. But she persisted, saying that the floor was dirty and should be swept. On the content level, we were talking about the value of sweeping the kitchen floor, but on the relationship level we were talking about something quite different: we were each saying, "This is my house." When I realized this (although, I confess, only after considerable argument), I stopped complaining about sweeping a floor that did not need sweeping. Not surprisingly, she stopped sweeping.

Consider the following interchange:

Dialogue	Comments
HE: I'm going bowling tomorrow. The guys at the plant are starting a team.	*He focuses on the content and ignores any relationship implications of the message.*
SHE: Why can't we ever do anything together?	*She responds primarily on a relationship level, ignores the content implications of the message, and expresses her displeasure at being ignored in his decision.*
HE: We can do something together anytime; tomorrow's the day they're organizing the team.	*Again, he focuses almost exclusively on the content.*

This example reflects research findings that men generally focus more on the content while women focus more on the relationship dimensions of communication. Once you recognize this difference, you may be better able to remove a potential barrier to communication between the sexes by being sensitive to the orientation of the opposite sex. Here is essentially the same situation but with the added sensitivity:

Dialogue	Comments
HE: The guys at the plant are organizing a bowling team. I'd sure like to be on the team. Would it be a problem if I went to the organizational meeting tomorrow?	*Although focused on content, he is aware of the relationship dimensions of his message and includes both in his comments—by acknowledging their partnership, asking if there would be a problem, and expressing his desire rather than his decision.*
SHE: That sounds great, but I was hoping we could do something together.	*She focuses on the relationship dimension but also acknowledges his content orientation. Note, too, that she does not respond as though she has to defend her emphasis on relationship aspects.*
HE: How about your meeting me at Pizza Hut, and we can have dinner after the organizational meeting?	*He responds to the relationship aspect—without abandoning his desire to join the bowling team—and incorporates it into his communications.*
SHE: That sounds great. I'm dying for pizza.	*She responds to both messages, approving of his joining the team and their dinner date.*

Arguments over the content dimension are relatively easy to resolve. Generally, you can look up something in a book or ask someone what actually took place. It is relatively easy to verify disputed facts. Arguments on the relationship level, however, are much more difficult to resolve, in part because you may not recognize that the argument is in fact a relational one. Once you realize that, you can approach the dispute appropriately and deal with it directly.

SUMMARY: UNIT IN BRIEF

Axioms	Implications
Transactional: Interpersonal communication is a process, an ongoing event, in which the elements are interdependent.	Communication is constantly occurring; do not look for clear-cut beginnings or endings. All communication elements are always changing; do not look for sameness. Look, too, for mutual interaction among elements.
Inevitability: When in an interactional situation, you cannot *not* communicate.	Seek to control as many aspects of your behavior as possible; seek out nonobvious messages.
Irreversibility and Unrepeatability: You cannot *un*communicate or repeat exactly a specific message.	Beware of messages you may later wish to take back—for example, conflict and commitment messages.
Culture-specific: Communication rules and principles vary from one culture to another.	Beware of assuming that the other person is following the same rules and principles you are.
Adjustment: Communication depends on participants sharing the same system of signals and meaning.	Expand common areas, and learn each other's system of signals to increase interpersonal effectiveness; share your own system of signals with significant others.
Punctuation: Everyone separates communication sequences into stimuli and responses on the basis of his or her own perspective.	View punctuation as arbitrary, and adopt the other's point of view to increase empathy and understanding.
Symmetrical and complementary relationships: Interpersonal interactions may stimulate similar or different behavior patterns, and relationships may be described as basically symmetrical or complementary.	Develop an awareness of symmetrical and complementary relationships. Avoid clinging rigidly to behavioral patterns that are no longer useful and mirroring another's destructive behaviors.
Content and relationship dimensions: All communications refer both to content and to the relationships between the participants.	Seek out and respond to relationship messages as well as content messages.

THINKING CRITICALLY ABOUT THE AXIOMS OF INTERPERSONAL COMMUNICATION

1. What implications are there to the principle of transactionalism for your everyday communications with your friends and family?
2. What implications does the principle that communication is inevitable have for you today?

3. How does the principle of inevitability operate in the classroom? In your home? On your job?

4. For what types of messages—in addition to messages of conflict and commitment, noted in the text—is it especially important to remember that communication is irreversible? Why is it important to recognize that communication is unrepeatable? What problems can arise when this is not recognized?

5. How would you describe your culture in terms of individual and collective orientation and high and low context? Has a failure to recognize cultural orientation or context ever caused any interpersonal misunderstandings?

6. What practical insights does the principle of adjustment offer? Put differently, what problems would arise in communication if the influence of adjustment was not recognized?

7. How do you punctuate the events leading up to your successes and your failures? Has punctuation ever been used against you? Have you ever used punctuation against someone else? What effects did this have?

8. Examine one of your interpersonal relationships. Can you describe it as symmetrical or complementary? For example, is it a relationship defined by the differences between the two of you or by your similarities? Is there equality between you, or is one of you superior and the other subordinate? Are you dependent on each other or independent? Is the power and decision making shared, or is one person in control? Do you have other relationships that adhere to a different pattern? Which do you find most satisfying? Why?

9. Have you had an argument that focused on relationship rather than content issues? How did the argument develop? At what point did you recognize that it was a relationship (rather than a content) argument? How was it resolved?

10. How would you go about finding answers to the following questions:

    • Are the students in your class who are in symmetrical relationships happier than those who are in complementary relationships?

    • Will persons from high-context cultures adapt more easily to a low-context culture than persons from low-context cultures would adapt to a high-context culture?

    • Will persons from cultures with the same context orientation (either high or low) develop stronger and more lasting relationships than will persons from cultures with different context orientations?

    • Will knowledge of these axioms of interpersonal communication have any impact on the number of conflicts a couple has? On the speed with which the conflicts are resolved?

EXPERIENTIAL VEHICLES

2.1 WHAT'S HAPPENING?

In the introduction to this unit, it was noted that the axioms of interpersonal communication would provide insight into a number of practical issues. How would you use the axioms to describe what is happening in each of the following situations? Three qualifications need to be identified before beginning this exercise. First, these scenarios are extremely brief and are written only as aids to stimulate you to think more concretely about the axioms. Second, the objective is not to select the one correct axiom (each scenario can probably be elucidated by reference to several axioms) but to make use of an opportunity to think about the axioms in reference to specific situations. Third, the objective is to describe what is going on, not to solve the problem.

1. A couple, together for 20 years, argues constantly about the seemingly most insignificant things—who takes the dog out, who does the shopping, who decides where to go to dinner, and so on. It has gotten to the point where they rarely have a day without argument and both are seriously considering a separation.
2. In teaching interpersonal communication skills, Professor Jones frequently asks students to role play effective and ineffective communication patterns and offers criticism after each session. Although most students respond well to this instructional technique, Mariz has difficulty and has frequently left the class in tears.
3. Pat has sought the assistance of a family therapist: the problem is simple—whatever Pat says, Chris says the opposite. If Pat wants to eat Chinese, Chris wants to eat Italian; if Pat wants Italian, Chris wants Chinese. And on and on. The problem is made worse by the fact that Chris has to get what Chris wants; Pat's wishes are invariably dismissed.
4. Jim is fiercely competitive and strives always to outdo his colleagues, who are generally team players. Jim's supervisor has threatened to let him go if he doesn't learn to work more effectively as a team player rather than as an individual.
5. Tanya and her grandmother can't seem to agree on what Tanya should do or not do. Tanya, for example, wants to go away for the weekend with her friends from college. But her grandmother fears she will come back pregnant and refuses to allow her to go.
6. In the heat of a big argument, Harry said he didn't want to see Peggy's family ever again. "They don't like me, and I don't like them," he said. Peggy reciprocated and said she felt the same way about his family. Now, weeks later, there remains a great deal of tension between them, especially when they find themselves with one or both families.
7. Grace and Mark are engaged to be married and are currently senior executives at a large advertising agency. Recently, Grace made a presentation, which was not received positively by the other members of the team. Grace feels that Tom—in not defending her proposal—created a negative attitude and actually encouraged others to reject her ideas. Tom says that he felt he could not defend her proposal because others in the room would have believed his defense was motivated by their relationship and not by his positive evaluation of her proposal. He concluded it was best to say nothing.
8. After having too many drinks, Carl slobberingly asks Diane for a date. Understandably, Diane refuses. Later in the week and on several occasions after that, Carl repeats his request for a date but is turned down each time.
9. Margo has just taken over as vice president in charge of sales for a manufacturing company. Margo is extremely organized and refuses to waste time on nonessentials. In her staff meetings, she is business only. Several top sales representatives have requested to be assigned to other VPs. Their reason: they feel she works them too hard and doesn't care about them as people.
10. Joe, a police detective, can't understand what happened: "All I did was introduce myself, and they refused to talk to me."

11. Simka has been denied promotion by management, which claims that she was not self-motivating and didn't do her job as effectively as she might have. Simka says that management never gave her the right kinds of projects to work on.

12. Junko supervises 12 designers who complain that they never know what she really wants. She always seems to like what they have done, but then the designs never get final approval. They have asked Junko for feedback, but all she says is that everything is good.

2.2 ANALYZING AN INTERACTION

The axioms of human communication discussed in this unit should prove useful in analyzing any communication interaction. To help you understand these principles better and to provide some practice in applying them to a real-life situation, the following interaction is presented. Read it carefully, and analyze each of the axioms of communication identified following the interaction.

An Interpersonal Transaction

MARGARET: mother, housewife, junior high school history teacher; 41 years old
FRED: father, gas station attendant; 46 years old
DIANE: daughter, receptionist in an art gallery; 22 years old
STEPHEN: son, college freshman; 18 years old

> *Margaret is in the kitchen finishing preparing dinner—lamb chops, Fred's favorite, though she does not much care for them. Diane is going through some CDs. Stephen is reading one of his textbooks. Fred comes in from work and throws his jacket over the couch; it falls to the floor.*

FRED: [*Bored but angry, looking at Stephen*] What did you do with the car last night? It stunk like hell. And you left all your damn school papers all over the back seat.

STEPHEN: [*As if expecting the angry remarks*] What did I do now?

FRED: You stunk up the car with your damn pot or whatever you kids smoke, and you left the car looking like hell. Can't you hear?
[*Stephen says nothing; goes back to looking at his book but without really reading.*]

MARGARET: Dinner's almost ready. Come on. Wash up and sit down.
[*At dinner*]

DIANE: Mom, I'm going to go to the shore for the weekend with some friends from work.

MARGARET: OK. When will you be leaving?

DIANE: Friday afternoon, right after work.

FRED: Like hell you're going. No more going to the shore with that group.

MARGARET: Fred, they're nice people. Why shouldn't she go?

FRED: Because I said so, OK? Finished. Closed.

DIANE: [*Mumbling*] I'm 22 years old and he gives me problems. You make me feel like a kid, like some stupid little kid.

FRED: Get married and then you can tell your husband what to do.

DIANE: I wish I could.

STEPHEN: But nobody'll ask her.

MARGARET: Why should she get married? She's got a good life—good job, nice friends, good home. Listen, I was talking with Elizabeth and Cara this morning, and they both feel they've just wasted their lives. They raised a family and what have they got? They got *nothing.* [*To Diane*] And don't think sex is so great either; it isn't, believe me.

FRED: Well, they're idiots.

MARGARET: [*Snidely*] They're idiots? Yeah, I guess they are.

DIANE: Joanne's getting married.

MARGARET: Who's Joanne?

STEPHEN: That creature who lives with that guy Michael.

FRED: Watch your mouth, wiseass. Don't be disrespectful to your mother or I'll teach you how to act right.

MARGARET: Well, how do you like the dinner?
[*Prolonged silence*]

DIANE: Do you think I should be in the wedding party if Joanne asks me? I think she will; we always said we'd be in each other's wedding.

MARGARET: Sure, why not. It'll be nice.

FRED: I'm not going to no wedding, no matter who's in it.

STEPHEN: Me neither.

DIANE: I hope you'll both feel that way when I get married.

STEPHEN: By then I'll be too old to remember I got a sister.

MARGARET: How's school, Stephen?

STEPHEN: I hate it. It's so big. Nobody knows anyone. You sit in these big lecture halls and listen to some creep talk. I really feel lonely and isolated, like nobody knows I'm alive.

FRED: Listen to that college-talk garbage. Get yourself a woman and you won't feel lonely, instead of hanging out with those pothead faggots.
[*Diane looks to Margaret, giving a sigh as if to say, "Here we go again."*]

MARGARET: [*To Diane, in whisper*] I know.

DIANE: Mom? Do you think I'm getting fat?

STEPHEN: Yes.

FRED: Just don't get fat in the stomach or you'll get thrown out of here.

MARGARET: No, I don't notice it.

DIANE: Well, I just thought I might be.

STEPHEN: [*Pushing his plate away*] I'm finished; I'm going out.

FRED: Sit down and finish your damn supper. You think I work all day for you to throw the food away? You wanna go smoke your dope?

STEPHEN: No. I just want to get away from you—forever.

MARGARET: You mean we both work all day; it's just that I earn a lot more than you do.

FRED: No, I mean I work and you baby-sit.

MARGARET: Teaching junior high school history isn't baby-sitting.

FRED: What the hell is it then? You don't teach them anything.

MARGARET: [*To Diane*] You see? You're better off single. I should've stayed single. Instead . . . Oh, well. I was young and stupid. It was my own fault for getting involved with a loser. Just don't you make the same mistake.

FRED: [*To Stephen*] Go ahead. Leave the table. Leave the house. Who cares what you do?

Analyze the Transaction

1. **Communication is transactional.**
    a. How is the process nature of communication illustrated in this interaction? For example, why is it impossible to identify specific beginnings and specific endings for any of the varied interactions? Are there instances in which individual characters attempt to deny the process nature of interpersonal interaction?
    b. Can you illustrate how the messages of the different characters are interdependent?

2. **Communication is inevitable.**
    a. Do the characters communicate significant messages, even though they may attempt not to communicate?
    b. In what ways do the characters communicate simply by their physical presence or by the role they occupy in the family?
    c. What attempts do the characters make not to communicate? Why do these attempts fail?

3. **Communication is irreversible and unrepeatable.**
    a. Are any messages being communicated that you think the characters will later wish they had not communicated? Why do you think so?
    b. Do any of the characters try to reverse the communication process—that is, to "uncommunicate"?
    c. What evidence can you offer to illustrate that communication is unrepeatable?

4. **Communication is culture-specific.**
    a. How would you describe this family as an intercultural group?
    b. Are some of the participants more individually oriented than others? Do some seem to act on the basis of a high- or a low-context orientation?

5. **Communication is a process of adjustment.**
    a. Can any of the failures to communicate be traced to the lack of adjustment?
    b. Throughout the interaction, how do the characters adjust to one another?
    c. What suggestions would you offer this family for increasing their abilities to adjust to one another?

6. **Communication sequences are punctuated for processing.**
    a. Select any two characters and indicate how they differ in their punctuation of any specific sequence of events. Do the characters realize that they are each punctuating differently?
    b. What problems might a failure to recognize the arbitrary nature of punctuation create?

7. **Communication involves symmetrical and complementary transactions.**
   a. What type of relationship do you suppose exists between Fred and Margaret? Between Fred and Diane? Between Fred and Stephen? Between Diane and Stephen? Between Margaret and Stephen?
   b. Can any instances of inappropriate complementarity be found? Inappropriate symmetry? What problems might these cause this particular family?
   c. Can you find any of the nine patterns of interaction identified here: symmetry (competitive, submissive, or neutralized); complementarity (one-up followed by one-down or one-down followed by one-up messages); and transitions (one-up plus one-across, one-down plus one-across, one-across plus one-up, and one-across plus one-down)? What added insights does this analysis provide?

8. **Communication involves both content and relationship dimensions.**
   a. How does each of the characters deal with the self-definitions of the other characters? For example, how does Fred deal with the self-definition of Margaret? How does Margaret deal with the self-definition of Fred?
   b. Are any problems caused by failure to recognize the distinction between the content and the relationship levels of communication?
   c. Select one topic of conversation and identify both the content and the relationship messages communicated.

   As an alternative to analyzing this interaction, the entire class may watch a situation comedy show, television drama, or film and explore the communication axioms in these presentations. The questions used in this exercise should prove useful in formulating parallel questions for the television program or film. Another way of approaching this topic is for all students to watch the same television programs for an entire evening, with groups of students focusing on the operation of different axioms. Thus, one group would focus on examples and illustrations of the impossibility of not communicating, another group would focus on the content and relationship dimensions of messages, and so on. Each group can then report its findings and insights to the entire class.

UNIT 3

Perception in Interpersonal Communication

UNIT OBJECTIVES

AFTER COMPLETING THIS UNIT, YOU SHOULD BE ABLE TO:

1. Define *interpersonal perception* and explain its major stages
2. Explain the process of attribution and the criteria used in making causal judgments
3. Define and explain the relevance in interpersonal perception of the following: *implicit personality theory, self-* *fulfilling prophecy, perceptual accentuation, primacy-recency, consistency,* and *stereotype*
4. Identify the major strategies for reducing uncertainty about another person
5. Identify at least five guidelines for increasing accuracy in interpersonal perception

---

Perception is the process by which you become aware of objects, events, and, especially, people through your senses: sight, smell, taste, touch, and hearing. Perception is an active, not a passive process. Your perceptions result from what exists in the outside world *and* from your own experiences, desires, needs and wants, loves and hatreds.

[handwritten: your experience with funerals etc can be the basis for the way you react to someone in that type of situation]

THE PERCEPTION PROCESS

Perception occurs in three stages, which are continuous and blend into one another (see Figure 3.1).

SENSORY STIMULATION OCCURS

At this first stage, your sense organs are stimulated—you hear the Rolling Stones' new recording, you see a friend, you smell someone's perfume, you taste a juicy orange, you feel another's sweaty palm.

Naturally, you do not perceive everything; rather, you engage in **selective perception,** a general term that includes selective attention and selective exposure. In **selective attention,** you attend to those things that you anticipate will fulfill your needs or will prove enjoyable. For example, when daydreaming in class, you do not hear what the teacher is saying until your name is called. Your selective attention mechanism focuses your senses on your name.

In **selective exposure,** you expose yourself to people or messages that will confirm your existing beliefs, that will contribute to your objectives, or that will prove satisfying in some way. For example, after you buy a car, you are more apt to read and listen

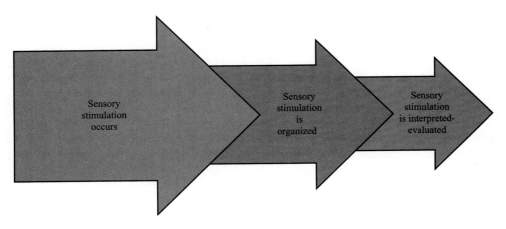

Figure 3.1
The three stages in the perception process.

to advertisements for the car you just bought because these messages tell you that you made the right decision. At the same time, you would avoid advertisements for the cars that you considered but eventually rejected because these messages would tell you that you made the wrong decision.

You are also more likely to perceive stimuli that are greater in **intensity** than surrounding stimuli and those that have **novelty** value (Lahey 1989). For example, television commercials normally play at a greater intensity than regular programming to ensure that you take special notice. You are also more likely to notice the co-worker who dresses in a novel way than you are to notice the one who dresses like everyone else. You will quickly perceive someone who shows up in class wearing a tuxedo or at a formal party in shorts.

An obvious implication here is that you perceive only a very small portion of what you could perceive. Just as there are limits on how far you can see, there are also limits on the quantity of stimulation you can take in at any given time.

SENSORY STIMULATION IS ORGANIZED

At the second stage, you organize the sensory stimulations according to certain principles. For example, according to the principle of **proximity,** you perceive as a group persons who are physically close together. You see them as having something in common. For example, you probably perceive family members or members of a club as having similar attitudes, values, and beliefs. According to the principle of **resemblance,** you group people who are similar in appearance and distinguish them from those who are dissimilar. For example, you might perceive members of the same race to have similar values and opinions. You might perceive people who dress similarly (for example, business executives in their gray suits) to be similar in attitudes or behaviors.

Be aware, of course, that neither of these principles will necessarily yield accurate information. Such information should serve only as hypotheses or possibilities that need to be investigated further, not as true conclusions that should be acted upon.

SENSORY STIMULATION IS INTERPRETED-EVALUATED

The third step in the perceptual process is interpretation-evaluation (hyphenated because the two processes cannot be separated). This step is inevitably subjective; your interpretations-evaluations are greatly influenced by your experiences, needs, wants, values, beliefs about the way things are or should be, expectations, physical and emotional state, and so on. Obviously, there is much room here for disagreement. Although we may all be exposed to the same external stimulus, the way we interpret-evaluate (and organize) it will differ from person to person and from one time to another for the same person.

Notice that who you are—your own personality characteristics; your present feelings; your physiological well-being; your prior history; your cultural attitudes, beliefs, and values; and just about everything else about you—will influence the way you interpret and evaluate what you sense. When your child is being particularly difficult, your interpretation and evaluation of that behavior will vary, depending on, for example, whether you just got home from a hard day at work and are trying to get your term paper done or whether you are on the phone and eager for an excuse to get off.

PERCEPTIONS ABOUT PERCEPTIONS AND PERCEPTION CHECKING

In addition to your perception of another's behaviors (verbal or nonverbal), you can also perceive what you think another person is feeling or thinking (Laing, Phillipson, and Lee 1966; Littlejohn 1992). You can, for example, perceive Pat kissing Chris. This is a simple, relatively direct perception of some behavior. But you can also sense (or perceive)—on the basis of the kiss—that Pat loves Chris. Notice the difference: you have observed the kiss but have not observed the love. (Of course, you could continue in this vein and, from your conclusion that Pat loves Chris, conclude that Pat no longer loves Terry. That is, you can always formulate a conclusion on the basis of a previous conclusion. The process is unending.)

The important point to see here is that when your perceptions are based on something observable (here, the kiss), you have a greater chance of being accurate when you describe this kiss or even when you interpret and evaluate it. As you move further away from your actual observation, however, your chances of being accurate decrease—when, for example, you try to describe or evaluate the love. Generally, when you draw conclusions on the basis of what you think someone is thinking as a result of the behavior, you have a greater chance of making errors than when you stick to conclusions about what you observe yourself.

The ability to read another person's perceptions accurately is a skill not easily found. There are so many factors that can get in the way of an accurate interpretation that it is almost always best to engage in **perception checking.**

In its most basic form, perception checking consists of two steps:

1. Describe (in tentative terms) what you think is happening. Try to do this as descriptively (not evaluatively) as you can.
   - You seem depressed. You say you feel fine about the breakup, but you don't seem happy.
   - You don't seem to want to go out this evening.
   - You seemed disturbed when he said. . . .
   - You sound upset with my plans.

2. Ask the other person for confirmation. Do be careful that your request for confirmation does not sound as though you already know the answer. So avoid phrasing your questions defensively. Avoid saying, for example, "You really don't want to go out, do you; I knew you didn't when you turned on that lousy television." Instead, ask for confirmation in as supportive a way as possible: "Would you rather watch TV?"
   - Are you really okay about the breakup?
   - Do you feel like going out, or would you rather stay home?
   - Are you disturbed?
   - Did my plans upset you?

As these examples illustrate, the goal of perception checking is not to prove that your initial perception is correct but to explore further the thoughts and feelings of the other person.

With this simple technique, you lessen your chances of misinterpreting another's feelings. At the same time, you give the other person an opportunity to elaborate on his or her thoughts and feelings. Similar purposes are served and similar techniques are used in "active listening," discussed in Unit 4.

Before reading about the specific processes that you use in perceiving other people, examine your own perception strategies by taking the self-test, "How Accurate Are You at People Perception?"

ATTRIBUTION

Think about each of the following situations:

1. A woman is begging in the street.
2. A store owner kills a thief.
3. A father abandons his children.

To what do you attribute the causes of these situations? Did the begging, killing, and abandonment result from something within the person or from within the situation? The way you would answer these questions is neatly explained in **attribution theory.** Attribution theory explains the process you go through in trying to understand your own and others' behaviors, particularly the reasons or motivations for these behaviors.

Attribution helps you to make sense of what you perceive, of what is going on in your world (Zanden 1984). It helps you to impose order and logic and to better understand the possible causes of the behaviors you observe.

Attribution also helps you to make predictions about what will happen, what others are likely or unlikely to do. If you can be reasonably sure that Pat gave money out of a desire to help the poor (that is, you can attribute the behavior to a desire to help), then you can make predictions about Pat's future behaviors that are more likely to be correct than predictions made without this initial attribution to guide you.

INTERNAL AND EXTERNAL JUDGMENTS

In your attempt to discover the causes of another's behavior, your first step is to determine whether the individual or some outside factor is responsible. That is, you must first determine whether the cause is **internal** (for example, due to some personality trait) or **external** (for example, due to some situational factor). Internal and external are the two

---

TEST YOURSELF

HOW ACCURATE ARE YOU AT PEOPLE PERCEPTION?

INSTRUCTIONS
Respond to each of the following statements with *true* if the statement is usually or generally accurate in describing your behavior or *false* if the statement is usually or generally inaccurate in describing your behavior.

_____ 1. I base most of my impressions of people on the first few minutes of our meeting.

_____ 2. When I know some things about another person, I can fill in what I don't know.

_____ 3. I make predictions about people's behaviors that generally prove to be true.

_____ 4. I have clear ideas of what people of different national, racial, and religious groups are really like.

_____ 5. I generally attribute people's attitudes and behaviors to their most obvious physical or psychological characteristic.

_____ 6. I avoid making assumptions about what is going on in someone else's head on the basis of the person's behaviors.

_____ 7. I pay special attention to behaviors of people that might contradict my initial impressions.

_____ 8. On the basis of my observations of people, I formulate guesses (that I am willing to revise) about them rather than firmly held conclusions.

_____ 9. I reserve making judgments about people until I learn a great deal about them and see them in a variety of situations.

_____ 10. After I formulate an initial impression, I check my perceptions by, for example, asking questions or by gathering more evidence.

SCORING
This brief perception test is designed to raise issues considered in this chapter. The first six questions refer to the tendencies to make judgments of others on the basis of first impressions (question 1), implicit personality theories (question 2), self-fulfilling prophecies (question 3), stereotypes (question 4), attribution (question 5), and mind reading (question 6). Ideally, you would have answered *false* to these six questions. (The tendencies they refer to are covered in the sections titled "Attribution" and "Perceptual Processes.") Questions 7 through 10 refer to specific guidelines for increasing accuracy in people perception: being especially alert to contradictory cues (question 7), formulating hypotheses rather than conclusions (question 8), delaying any conclusions until sufficient evidence is in (question 9), and using perception checking (question 10). Ideally, you would have answered *true* to these four questions.

---

kinds of causality with which attribution theory is concerned. Note that your assessment of someone's behavior as internally or externally motivated will greatly influence your evaluation of that person. If you judge people's cooperative behavior as internally caused (that is, as motivated by their personality), you are more apt to form a positive evaluation of them and, eventually, to like them. In contrast, if you judge that very same behavior to be externally caused (the watchful eye of the boss is forcing someone to behave coopera-tively, for example), you are more apt to form a negative evaluation and, eventually, to dislike the person (because he or she is not "really" or "genuinely" cooperative).

Consider another example. You look at a teacher's grade book and observe that ten Fs were assigned in cultural anthropology. In an attempt to discover what this reveals about the teacher, you first have to discover whether the teacher was in fact responsible for the assignment of the ten Fs or whether the grading could be attributed to external fac-tors. Let's say you discover that the examinations on which the grades were based had been made up by a faculty committee, which also set the standards for passing or failing. In this case, you could not attribute any particular motives to this individual teacher because the behavior was not internally caused.

On the other hand, let's assume the following: this teacher made up the examina-tion without any assistance, no departmental or university standards were used, and the teacher made up a personal set of standards for passing and failing. Now you would be more apt (though perhaps not fully justified) to attribute the ten Fs to internal causes. You would be strengthened in your beliefs that there was something within this teacher, some personality characteristic, for example, that led to this behavior if you discovered that (1) no other teacher in anthropology gave nearly as many Fs, (2) this particular teacher fre-quently gives Fs in cultural anthropology, and (3) this teacher frequently gives Fs in other courses as well. These three bits of added information would lead you to conclude that there was something within this teacher that motivated the behavior. In forming such causal judgments, which you make every day, you use three principles: (1) consensus, (2) consistency, and (3) distinctiveness.

Consensus: Similarity to Others   When you focus on the principle of **consensus,** you ask essentially, "Do other people react or behave in the same way as the person on whom I am focusing?" That is, is the person acting in accordance with the consensus? If the answer is no, you are more likely to attribute the behavior to some internal cause. In the previous example, you were strengthened in your belief that something internal caused the Fs to be given when you learned that other teachers did not do this; that is, there was low consensus. When only one person acts contrary to the norm, you are more likely to at-tribute that person's behavior to internal motivation. If all teachers gave many Fs (that is, if there was high consensus), you would be more likely to look for causality outside the in-dividual teacher; you might conclude that the anthropology department uses a particular curve in determining grades or that the students were not very bright—or any other reason external to the specific teacher.

Consistency: Similarity Over Time   When you focus on the principle of **consis-tency,** you ask if this person repeatedly behaves in the same way in similar situations. If the answer is yes, there is high consistency, and you are likely to attribute the behavior to internal motivation. The fact that this teacher frequently gives Fs in cultural anthropology leads you to attribute the cause to the teacher rather than to outside sources. If, on the other hand, there was low consistency—that is, if this teacher rarely gives Fs—you would be more likely to look for reasons external to the teacher. You might consider, for example, the possibility that this specific class was not very bright or that the department required the teacher to start giving out Fs, and so on. That is, you would look for causes external to the teacher.

Distinctiveness: Similarity in Different Situations   When you focus on the principle of **distinctiveness,** you ask if this person reacts in similar ways in different situations. If the answer is yes, there is low distinctiveness, and you are likely to conclude that the behavior has an internal cause. The fact that the teacher reacted the same way (gave lots of Fs) in different situations (other courses) led you to conclude that this particular class was not distinctive and that the motivation for the behavior could not be found in a unique situation. You further concluded that this behavior must be due to the teacher's inner motivation. Consider the alternative: if this teacher gave all high grades and no Fs in other courses (that is, if the cultural anthropology class situation was highly distinctive), you would conclude that the motivation for the failures was to be found in sources outside the teacher and for reasons unique to this class. A summary of all three factors, with a specific example, is presented in Table 3.1.

Let's return to the three examples with which we opened this discussion of attribution as a way of summarizing the principles of consensus, consistency, and distinctiveness. Generally, you would consider the three example actions—begging, killing, and abandonment—to result from something inherent in the begging woman, the store owner, and the father if other people behaved differently in situations similar to these (low consensus), if these people had engaged in these behaviors in the past (high consistency), and if these people behaved similarly in other situations (low distinctiveness). Under these conditions, you would conclude that the persons bear the responsibility for their behaviors.

Alternatively, you would consider these actions to have resulted from something external to the persons if many other people reacted the same way in similar situations (high consensus), if these people had never behaved in this way before (low consistency), and if these people never engaged in these behaviors in different situations (high distinctiveness). Under these conditions, you could conclude that these actions resulted from factors over which these people had little or no control and that, therefore, they may not be personally responsible.

Table 3.1

A Summary of Consensus, Consistency, and Distinctiveness in Causal Attribution

Situation: A student is heard complaining about a grade received in a philosophy course. On what basis will you conclude whether this behavior is internally or externally caused?

INTERNALLY CAUSED[a]	EXTERNALLY CAUSED[b]
1. No one else complained. (low consensus)	1. Many others have complained. (high consensus)
2. Student has complained in this course in the past. (high consistency)	2. Student has never complained in this course in the past. (low consistency)
3. Student has complained to other teachers in other courses. (low distinctiveness)	3. Student has never complained to other teachers. (high distinctiveness)

[a]That is, the person is responsible: for example, the student is a complainer.
[b]That is, the situation brings about the behavior: for example, unfair tests lead the student to complain.

CONTROLLABILITY AND STABILITY JUDGMENTS

Researchers have pointed to additional factors that play a part in attribution. The most relevant to interpersonal communication are controllability and stability (Weiner 1985).

Controllability: Was the Person in Control of the Behavior?   Let's say your friend is an hour late for a dinner appointment (cf. Weiner et al. 1987). How would you feel about the following two possible excuses?

> Excuse 1: I was reading this book, and I just couldn't put it down. I had to find out who the killer was.
>
> Excuse 2: I was stuck on the subway for two hours; a water main broke, killing all the electricity.

It's very likely you would resent the first and accept the second excuse. The first excuse says that the reason for the lateness was controllable: your friend chose to be late by completing the novel. You therefore hold your friend responsible for wasting your time and for a lack of consideration. The second excuse says that the reason was uncontrollable: you cannot hold your friend responsible for the subway breakdown or for the lateness. Generally, excuses involving uncontrollable factors are more effective than those involving controllable factors. You may wish to test this observation against your own experience in making or receiving excuses.

Stability: How Changeable or Unchangeable Is the Behavior?   Let's say you are in a public speaking class, and you get an F on your first speech. How do you think you would perform in the rest of the course if you were told and believed either of the following:

> Belief 1: Public speaking is an ability that you either have or don't have. Practice and dedication will result in very little improvement if you don't have what it takes to be an effective public speaker.
>
> Belief 2: Most people do poorly on their first speech. Public speaking is like riding a bicycle: no one can do it well in the beginning. With the right practice, however, you can become very proficient, either as a cyclist or as a public speaker.

Belief 1 says that your poor public speaking behavior was due to stable factors, factors that would not change over time. Belief 2, however, points to unstable factors (for example, lack of practice and experience), factors that will change over time. Generally, if you believe that your poor behavior (in anything from typing to being a relational partner) is produced by stable factors, you will not try to improve and may develop a defeatist attitude. If, in contrast, you believe that your poor behavior is produced by unstable factors, you will be more willing to exert effort to improve.

BEWARE THE SELF-SERVING BIAS

The self-serving bias leads us to take credit for the positive and to deny responsibility for the negative. Thus, you are more apt to attribute your own negative behaviors to situational or external factors. For example, after getting a D on an exam, you are more likely

One of the great tragedies of our time is homelessness. Part of the difficulty that homeless people must face is how they are seen by others. What are your perceptions of homeless people? What are they based on? In terms of attribution theory, do your perceptions attribute homelessness to internal or external factors? To controllable or uncontrollable factors? To stable or unstable factors? How might these attributions influence the way you treat and respond to homeless people on a day-to-day basis?

to attribute it to the difficulty or unfairness of the test. However, you are likely to attribute your positive behaviors to internal factors. For example, after getting an A on an exam, you are more likely to attribute it to ability or hard work (Bernstein, Stephan, and Davis 1979).

Although the self-serving bias may distort attributions, it has at least one benefit: it helps protect self-esteem. Our self-esteem is enhanced by this tendency to attribute negative behaviors to outside and uncontrollable forces and positive behaviors to internal and controllable forces.

PERCEPTUAL PROCESSES

Several processes influence what you perceive and what you fail to perceive. These processes help to explain why you make some predictions and not others and also help you impose order on the enormous amount of data that impinges on your senses. They enable you to simplify and categorize the vast amount of information around you. Note, however, that each of these six processes presents potential barriers to accurate perception. In some cases, they lead to oversimplification or distortion of information.

IMPLICIT PERSONALITY THEORY

Each person has a subconscious or implicit system of rules that says which characteristics of an individual go with other characteristics. This principle is well illustrated in the poem "Mister Cory," by Edward Arlington Robinson, in which the onlookers see certain characteristics of Mister Cory and then fill in the rest on the basis of their implicit or unstated personality theories.

> *Whenever Richard Cory went down town,*
> *We people on the pavement looked at him:*
> *He was a gentleman from sole to crown,*
> *Clean flavored, and imperially slim.*
>
> *And he was always quietly arrayed,*
> *And he was always human when he talked;*
> *But still he fluttered pulses when he said,*
> *"Good-morning," and he glittered when he walked.*
>
> *And he was rich—yes, richer than a king—*
> *And admirably schooled in every grace:*
> *In fine, we thought that he was everything*
> *To make us wish that we were in his place.*
>
> *So on we walked, and waited for the light,*
> *And went without the meat, and cursed the bread;*
> *And Richard Cory, one calm summer night,*
> *Went home and put a bullet through his head.*

Like the people observing Mister Cory, we, too, are often wrong when we use these theories to fill in missing parts about a person. Consider, for example, the following brief statements. Note the word in parentheses that you think best completes each sentence:

Carlo is energetic, eager, and (intelligent, stupid).
Kim is bold, defiant, and (extroverted, introverted).
Joe is bright, lively, and (thin, fat).
Ava is attractive, intelligent, and (likable, unlikable).
Susan is cheerful, positive, and (attractive, unattractive).
Angel is handsome, tall, and (flabby, muscular).

Certain of the words seem right and others seem wrong. What makes some seem right is your **implicit personality theory,** the system of rules that tells you which characteristics go with which other characteristics. Your theory may, for example, have told you that a person who is energetic and eager is also intelligent, not stupid, although there is no logical reason why a stupid person could not be energetic and eager.

The widely documented **halo effect** is a function of the implicit personality theory (Dion, Berscheid, and Walster 1972; Riggio 1987). If you believe a person has some positive qualities, you are likely to infer that she or he also possesses other positive qualities. There is also a **reverse halo effect:** if you know a person possesses several negative qualities, you are more likely to infer that the person also has other negative qualities.

Thinking Critically About Implicit Personality Theories   Apply implicit personality theories carefully and critically so as to avoid:

- perceiving qualities in an individual that your theory tells you should be present when they actually are not. For example, you see "goodwill" in a friend's "charitable" acts when a tax deduction may have been the "real" motive.
- ignoring or distorting qualities that do not conform to your theory but that are actually present in the individual. For example, you may ignore negative qualities in your friends that you would easily perceive in your enemies.

THE SELF-FULFILLING PROPHECY

A **self-fulfilling prophecy** occurs when you make a prediction that comes true because you act on it as if it were true (Merton 1957). There are four basic steps in the self-fulfilling prophecy:

1. You make a prediction or formulate a belief about a person or a situation. For example, you predict that Pat is awkward in interpersonal encounters.
2. You act toward that person or situation as if that prediction or belief were true. For example, you act as if Pat were awkward.
3. Because you act as if the belief were true, it becomes true. For example, because of the way you act toward Pat, Pat becomes tense and awkward.
4. You observe *your* effect on the person or the resulting situation, and what you see strengthens your beliefs. For example, you observe Pat's awkwardness, and this reinforces your belief that Pat is in fact awkward.

If you expect people to act in a certain way or if you make a prediction about a situation, your predictions will frequently come true because of self-fulfilling prophecy. Consider, for example, people who enter a group situation convinced that the other members will dislike them. Almost invariably they are proved right; the other members do dislike them. What they may be doing is acting in a way that encourages a negative response. Such people fulfill their own prophecies.

A widely known example of the self-fulfilling prophecy is the **Pygmalion effect.** In one study, teachers were told that certain pupils were expected to do exceptionally well, that they were late bloomers. The names of these students were actually selected at random by the experimenters. The results, however, were not random. The students whose names were given to the teachers actually performed at a higher level than the others. In fact, these students' IQ scores even improved more than did the other students'. The teachers' expectations probably prompted them to give extra attention to the selected students, thereby positively affecting their performance (Rosenthal and Jacobson 1968; Insel and Jacobson 1975).

The self-fulfilling prophecy is similar to the **law of expectations,** which states that your behaviors will be largely determined by your expectations (Kelley 1979). If you have negative expectations ("We're going to have a fight when I get home late tonight" or "This dinner party is going to be a disaster"), your behavior will assist in making these negative expectations come true. If you have positive expectations ("This blind date is going to be the best yet" or "This semester I'm going to make some really good friends"), your behavior will assist in making these positive expectations come true.

Thinking Critically About Self-Fulfilling Prophecies   Self-fulfilling prophecies can short-circuit critical thinking and:

- influence another's behavior so that it conforms to your prophecy.
- lead you to see what you predicted rather than what is really there (for example, to perceive yourself as a failure because you have predicted it rather than because of any actual failures).

PERCEPTUAL ACCENTUATION

When poor and rich children were shown pictures of coins and later asked to estimate their size, the poor children's size estimates were much greater than the rich children's. Similarly, hungry people perceive food objects and food terms at lower recognition thresholds (needing fewer physical cues) than do people who are not hungry.

This process, called **perceptual accentuation,** leads you to see what you expect and want to see. You see people you like as better looking than those you do not like. You see people you like as smarter than those you do not like. You magnify or accentuate that which will satisfy your needs and wants: the thirsty person sees a mirage of water; the sexually deprived person sees a mirage of sexual satisfaction.

Thinking Critically About Perceptual Accentuation   The tendency to perceive what you want or need can lead you to:

- distort your perceptions of reality, perceive what you need or want to perceive rather than what is really there, and fail to perceive what you do not want to perceive. For example, you may not perceive signs of impending problems because you focus on what you want to perceive.
- filter out or distort information that might damage or threaten your self-image and thus make self-improvement extremely difficult.
- perceive in others the negative qualities you see in yourself, a defense mechanism known as projection.
- perceive and remember positive qualities more than negative ones (a phenomenon referred to as the **Pollyanna effect**) and thus distort your perceptions of others.
- perceive certain behaviors as indicative that someone likes you simply because you want to be liked. For example, general politeness and friendly behavior used as a persuasive strategy (say, by a salesperson) are frequently seen as indicating a genuine personal liking.

PRIMACY-RECENCY

Assume for a moment that you are enrolled in a course in which half the classes are extremely dull and half extremely exciting. At the end of the semester, you evaluate the course and the instructor. Would your evaluation be more favorable if the dull classes occurred in the first half of the semester and the exciting classes in the second? Would it be more favorable if the order were reversed? If what comes first exerts the most influence, this is a **primacy effect.** If what comes last (or most recently) exerts the most influence, this is a **recency effect.**

In the classic study on the effects of primacy-recency in interpersonal perception, Solomon Asch (1946) read a list of descriptive adjectives to a group of students and found that the effects of order were significant. A person described as "intelligent, industrious, impulsive, critical, stubborn, and envious" was evaluated more positively than a person described as "envious, stubborn, critical, impulsive, industrious, and intelligent." There is a tendency to use early information to get a general idea about a person and to use later information to make this impression more specific. The obvious practical implication of primacy-recency is this: the first impression you make is likely to be the most important. It is through this that others will filter additional information in formulating a picture of how they perceive you.

Thinking Critically About Primacy and Recency   The tendency to give greater weight to early information and to interpret later information in light of early impressions can distort your critical thinking and lead you to:

- formulate a total picture of an individual on the basis of initial impressions that may not be typical or accurate (for example, judging a job applicant as generally nervous when he or she may simply be showing normal nervousness at being interviewed for a much-needed job).
- discount or distort subsequent perceptions so as not to disrupt your initial impression. For example, you may fail to see signs of deceit in someone you like because of your early impressions.

CONSISTENCY

The tendency to maintain balance among perceptions or attitudes is called **consistency.** You expect certain things to go together and other things not to go together. On a purely intuitive basis, for example, respond to the following sentences by noting your *expected* response:

1. I expect a person I like to (like, dislike) me.
2. I expect a person I dislike to (like, dislike) me.
3. I expect my friend to (like, dislike) my friend.
4. I expect my friend to (like, dislike) my enemy.
5. I expect my enemy to (like, dislike) my friend.
6. I expect my enemy to (like, dislike) my enemy.

According to most consistency theories, your expectations would be as follows: You would expect a person you liked to like you (1) and one you disliked to dislike you (2).

You would expect a friend to like a friend (3) and to dislike an enemy (4). You would expect your enemy to dislike your friend (5) and to like your other enemy (6). All these expectations are intuitively satisfying.

Further, you would expect someone you liked to possess characteristics you like or admire. And you would expect your enemies not to possess characteristics you like or admire. Conversely, you would expect people you liked to lack unpleasant characteristics and those you disliked to possess unpleasant characteristics.

Thinking Critically About Consistency   Uncritically assuming that an individual is consistent can lead you to:

- ignore or distort your perceptions of behaviors that are inconsistent with your picture of the whole person. For example, you may misinterpret Karla's unhappiness because your image of Karla is "happy, controlled, and contented."
- see certain behaviors as positive if you interpreted other behaviors positively (the halo effect) or as negative if you interpreted other behaviors negatively (the reverse halo effect).

STEREOTYPING

One of the most common shortcuts in interpersonal perception is stereotyping. A sociological or psychological **stereotype** is a fixed impression of a group of people. We all have attitudinal stereotypes—of national, religious, sexual, or racial groups, or perhaps of criminals, prostitutes, teachers, or plumbers. If you have these fixed impressions, you will, upon meeting a member of a particular group, often see that person primarily as a member of that group and apply to him or her all the characteristics you assign to that group. If you meet someone who is a prostitute, for example, there is a host of characteristics for prostitutes that you may apply to this one person. To complicate matters further, you will often see in this person's behavior the manifestation of characteristics that you would not see if you did not know that this person was a prostitute. Stereotypes distort accurate perception. They prevent you from seeing an individual as an individual rather than as a member of a group.

Thinking Critically About Stereotyping   The tendency to group people and to respond to individuals primarily as members of groups can lead you to:

- perceive an individual as possessing those qualities (usually negative) that you believe characterize his or her group (for example, all Venusians are smart) and, therefore, fail to appreciate the multifaceted nature of all individuals and groups.
- ignore each person's unique characteristics and, therefore, fail to benefit from the special contributions each individual can bring to an encounter.

INCREASING ACCURACY IN INTERPERSONAL PERCEPTION

Successful interpersonal communication depends largely on the accuracy of your interpersonal perception. You can increase this accuracy by (1) employing strategies for reducing uncertainty and (2) following some suggested guidelines.

In describing these women, how might you err in using each of the six perceptual processes discussed in this unit? That is, how might you misjudge these women with your implicit personality theories, self-fulfilling prophecies, perceptual accentuation, primacy-recency, consistency, and stereotyping?

UNCERTAINTY REDUCTION STRATEGIES

Interpersonal communication involves a gradual process of reducing uncertainty about each other. With each interaction, we learn more about each other and gradually come to know each other on a more meaningful level. The three main strategies for achieving this reduction in uncertainty are passive, active, and interactive (Berger and Bradac 1982).

Passive Strategies   When you observe another person without his or her knowledge, you are using **passive strategies.** Usually, you can learn more about people while observing them engaged in an active task, preferably interacting with others in social (and informal) situations. In such informal situations, people are less apt to monitor their behaviors and are more likely to reveal their true selves.

Active Strategies   When you actively seek out information about someone in any way other than direct interaction with the person, you are using **active strategies.** For example, you can ask others about the person: "What is she like?" "Does he work out?" "Does she date guys younger than she is?" You can also manipulate the situation in such a way that you observe the person in more specific and more revealing contexts. Employment interviews, theatrical auditions, and student teaching are some of the ways in which the situation can be manipulated to observe how the person might act and react and hence to reduce uncertainty about the person.

Interactive Strategies   When you interact with the individual, you are using **interactive strategies.** For example, you can ask questions: "Do you enjoy sports?" "What did you think of that computer science course?" "What would you do if you got fired?" You also gain knowledge of another by disclosing information about yourself. Your self-disclosure creates a relaxed environment that encourages subsequent disclosures from the person about whom you wish to learn more.

You probably use these strategies all the time to learn about each other. Unfortunately, many people feel that they know a person well enough after employing only passive strategies. But all three types of strategy are useful; employing all three will strengthen the accuracy of your perceptions.

GUIDELINES FOR INCREASING ACCURACY IN INTERPERSONAL PERCEPTION

In addition to perception checking, thinking critically about the perceptual processes discussed earlier, and employing all three uncertainty reduction strategies, consider the following suggestions.

Recognize Your Role in Perception   Your emotional and physiological state will influence the meaning you give to your perceptions. The sight of raw clams may be physically upsetting when you have a stomachache but mouthwatering when you are hungry.

Formulate Hypotheses   On the basis of your observations of behaviors, formulate hypotheses to test against additional information and evidence rather than drawing conclusions you then look to confirm. **Delay formulating conclusions** until you have had a chance to process a wide variety of cues.

Look for a Variety of Cues   Look for a variety of cues pointing in the same direction. The more cues pointing to the same conclusion, the more likely it is that your conclusion will be correct. **Be especially alert to contradictory cues,** cues that refute your initial hypotheses. It is relatively easy to perceive cues that confirm your hypotheses but more difficult to acknowledge contradictory evidence.

Avoid Mind Reading   Regardless of how many behaviors you observe and how carefully you examine them, you can only *guess* what is going on in someone's mind. A person's motives are not open to outside inspection; you can only make assumptions based on overt behaviors. Substitute perception checking ("Did you realize that my birthday was Thursday?") for **mind reading** ("You forgot my birthday because you don't really love me").

Beware of Your Own Biases   Know when your perceptual evaluations are unduly influenced by your own biases: for example, perceiving only the positive in people you like and only the negative in people you do not like.

Seek Validation   Compare your perceptions with those of others. Do others see things in the same way you do? If not, ask yourself if your perceptions may be in some way distorted.

SUMMARY: UNIT IN BRIEF

Definitions	Processes		Accuracy
Perception: the process by which you become aware of objects and events in the external world. Perception occurs in three stages: (1) occurrence of sensory stimulation, (2) organization of sensory stimulation, and (3) interpretation-evaluation of sensory stimulation.	**Implicit personality theory:** expectations that certain characteristics go with certain other characteristics. **Self-fulfilling prophecy:** predictions that influence behaviors. **Perceptual accentuation:** tendency to perceive what you expect to perceive.	**Primacy-recency:** tendency for first impressions (primacy) to influence later perceptions (recency). **Consistency:** tendency for perception to be influenced by your expectation of consistent or balanced behaviors. **Stereotyping:** tendency for fixed impressions about a group to influence your perceptions of individual members.	**Uncertainty reduction strategies:** **passive strategies:** observation of others without their awareness. **active strategies:** actively seeking out information about others without interpersonal interaction with them. **interactive strategies:** interacting with others to learn more about them.
Attribution: the process through which you try to understand the behaviors of others (and your own, in **self-attribution**), particularly the reasons or motivations for these behaviors.	**Consensus:** the degree to which a person's behavior conforms to the norm. **Consistency:** the degree to which the same behavior occurs in other, similar situations. **Distinctiveness:** the degree to which the same behavior occurs in different situations. **Internal motivation** is attributed in cases of low consensus, high consistency, and low distinctiveness.	**External motivation** is attributed in cases of high consensus, low consistency, and high distinctiveness. **Controllability:** the extent to which the person is in control of his or her behavior. **Stability:** the extent to which the behavior is due to stable, unchanging factors or to unstable, changing factors.	**To increase accuracy in interpersonal perception:** Use perception checking. Recognize your role in perception. Formulate hypotheses, not conclusions. Look for a variety of cues, especially contradictory cues. Avoid mind reading. Beware of your own biases. Seek validation for your perceptions.

THINKING CRITICALLY ABOUT INTERPERSONAL PERCEPTION

1. What is your implicit personality theory for
   a.   the bright, dedicated, and aggressive college professor?
   b.   the out-of-work, dirty, and homeless man on the street?
   c.   the stylish, wealthy, and sophisticated penthouse owner?
2. How does the theory that certain personality characteristics go with other personality characteristics influence your perception of people? How do the implicit personality theories of others influence their perceptions of you?

3. Have you ever experienced or witnessed the Pygmalion effect? What were the circumstances?

4. Does perceptual accentuation influence the dating behavior of your peers?

5. What role do your first impressions play in perceiving people? Have you ever been wrong? Do others form impressions of you based on an initial interaction? Have these people ever been wrong? What might you do to make your first impressions more accurate?

6. What kinds of stereotypes do others apply to you? How accurate are they? On what are they based?

7. Can you explain, with the concepts of attribution—especially controllability and stability but also consensus, consistency, and distinctiveness—the attitudes that many people have about the homeless? About drug addicts or alcoholics? About successful politicians, scientists, or millionaires?

8. Which single guideline for increasing accuracy in interpersonal perception do you think is the most important? Which one do you violate most often?

9. Can you recall a recent example of selective attention or selective exposure? How did it happen? What purposes did it serve?

10. How would you go about answering such questions as the following?

   • Is the tendency to judge by first impressions universal? That is, do all cultures judge people very quickly?

   • What other characteristics do people with lots of stereotypes possess? In what ways are people with lots of stereotypes different from people with few stereotypes?

   • Are children more accurate than adults as judges of people? Is perceptual accuracy a function of age?

EXPERIENTIAL VEHICLES

3.1 CAUSAL ATTRIBUTION

For each of the following examples, indicate whether you think the behavior of the individual was due to internal causes (for example, personality characteristics or personal motives) or external causes (for example, the particular situation one is in, the demands of others who might be in positions of authority, or the behaviors of others). The behavior in question appears in italics.

1. *Ted has just quit his job.* No one else we know has quit that job. Ted has quit a number of jobs in the last five years and has in fact quit this same job once before.

2. *Mary has just failed her chemistry test.* A number of other students (in fact, some 40 percent of the class) also failed the test. Mary has never failed a chemistry test before and, in fact, has never failed any other test in her life.

3. *Liz tasted the wine, rejected it, and complained to the server.* No one else in the place seemed to complain about the wine. Liz has complained about the wine before and has frequently complained that her food was seasoned incorrectly, that the coffee was not hot enough, and so on.

Consensus / No Consistency

Consensus / No consistency

No Consensus / No Consistency

No Consistency

4. *Russell took the children to the zoo.* Russell works for the board of education in a small town, and taking the children on trips is one of his major functions. All people previously in the job have taken the children to the zoo. Russell has never taken any other children to the zoo.

5. *John ran from the dog.* A number of other people also ran from this dog. I was surprised to see John do this because he has never run from other animals before and never from this particular dog.

6. *Donna received all As on her film projects.* In fact, everyone in the class got As. This was the first A that Donna has ever received in film—in fact, it is the first A she has ever received in any course.

After you have responded to all six examples, identify the information contained in the brief behavioral descriptions that enabled you to make judgments concerning (1) consensus, (2) consistency, and (3) distinctiveness. What combination of these three principles would lead you to conclude that the behavior was internally motivated? What combination would lead you to conclude that the behavior was externally motivated?

3.2 TALKING ABOUT OTHERS

This exercise is designed to reinforce an understanding of the processes of perception. Read the following dialogue and identify the operation of each of the six processes of perception.

PAT: All I had to do was to spend two seconds with him to know he's an idiot. I said I went to Graceland, and he asked what that was. Can you believe it? Graceland! The more I got to know him, the more I realized how stupid he was. A real loser; I mean, really.

CHRIS: Yeah, I know what you mean. Well, he is a jock, you know.

PAT: Jocks! The worst. And I bet I can guess who he goes out with. I'll bet it's Lucy.

CHRIS: Why do you say that?

PAT: Well, I figure that the two people I dislike would like each other. And I figure you must dislike them, too.

CHRIS: For sure.

PAT: By the way, have you ever met Marie? She's a computer science major, so you know she's bright. And attractive—really attractive.

CHRIS: Yes, I went out of my way to meet her, because she sounded like she'd be a nice person to know.

PAT: You're right. I knew she'd be nice as soon as I saw her.

CHRIS: We talked at yesterday's meeting. She's really complex, you know. I mean really complex. Really.

PAT: Whenever I think of Marie, I think of the time she helped that homeless man. There was this homeless guy—real dirty—and he fell, running across the street. Well, Marie ran right into the street and picked this guy up and practically carried him to the other side.

CHRIS: And you know what I think of when I think of Lucy? The time she refused to visit her grandmother in the hospital. Remember? She said she had too many other things to do.

PAT: I remember that—a real selfish egomaniac. I mean really.

UNIT 4

Listening in Interpersonal Communication

UNIT OBJECTIVES

AFTER COMPLETING THIS UNIT, YOU SHOULD BE ABLE TO:

1. Define *listening* and its five stages
2. Define and distinguish among *participatory* and *passive listening, empathic* and *objective listening,* *nonjudgmental* and *critical listening,* and *surface* and *depth listening*
3. Define *active listening* and identify its major functions and techniques

There is little doubt that you listen a great deal. Upon awakening, you listen to the radio. On the way to work, you listen to friends, to people around you, and perhaps to screeching cars, singing birds, or falling rain. In school, you listen to teachers and to other students. You arrive home and again listen to your family and friends. Perhaps you then listen to CDs, tapes, radio, or television. All in all, you spend a good part of your waking day listening.

In fact, if you were to measure importance in terms of time spent, listening would be your most important communication activity because it engages most of your communication time. A glance at Figure 4.1, which diagrams the results of two studies, confirms this point. Note that in both studies, one (Rankin 1929) using adults as subjects (A) and one (Barker et al. 1980) using college students (B), listening occupied more time than any other communication activity. The results of other studies, using people in business, for example, further confirm the importance of listening.

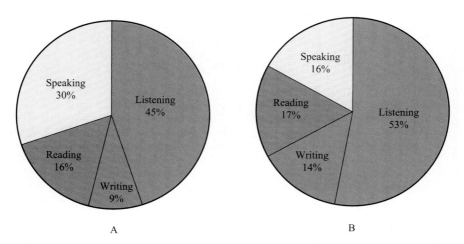

A   B

Figure 4.1
The time spent in listening.

Another way to gauge the importance of listening is to examine the purposes that listening serves and the many benefits that you can derive from listening more effectively. Listening serves the same purposes already noted for interpersonal communication: to learn, to relate, to influence, to play, and to help. These purposes and a variety of benefits that accrue to the effective listener are summarized in Table 4.1.

Table 4.1
Purposes and Benefits of Effective Listening

PURPOSES AND BENEFITS	EXAMPLES
Learn: acquire knowledge of others, the world, and yourself and profit from the insights of others who have learned or seen what you have not	Listening to Peter about his travels to Cuba will help you understand more about Peter as well as about life in a communist country.
avoid difficulties by hearing and being able to respond to warnings before problems develop or escalate and become impossible to control	Listening to student reactions (instead of responding with "Students just don't want to work hard") will help the teacher plan more effective and relevant classes and be better able to respond to students' real needs and concerns.
make reasoned and reasonable choices by acquiring information relevant to decisions you'll make in business or professional life	Listening to the difficulties your sales staff has (instead of responding with "You're just not trying hard enough") may help you design a more effective advertising campaign or offer more pertinent sales training.
Relate: form and maintain friendships and love relationships on the basis of social acceptance and popularity because people come to like those who are attentive and supportive	Others will increase their liking for you once they feel you have genuine concern for them, a concern that is readily communicated through attentive and supportive listening.
Influence: have an effect on the attitudes and behaviors of others because people are more likely to respect and follow those whom they feel have listened to and understood them	Workers are more likely to follow your advice once they feel you have truly listened to and heard their points of view, concerns, and insights.
Play: know when to suspend critical and evaluative thinking and when simply to engage in passive and accepting listening	Listening to the stories, jokes, and anecdotes of co-workers will allow you to gain a more comfortable balance between the world of work and the world of play and perhaps to see humor in a world of seriousness.
Help: be able to assist other people because you hear more, empathize more, and come to understand others more deeply	Listening to your child's complaints about her teacher (instead of responding with "Now what did you do wrong?") will put you in a better position to help your child cope with school and with her teacher.

That you listen a great deal of the time, then, can hardly be denied. Whether you listen effectively and efficiently, however, is another matter. In actual practice, most people are relatively poor listeners, and their listening behavior could be much improved. Given the amount of time spent listening, such improvement seems well worth the required effort. And it does take effort.

Before reading about the principles and techniques of listening, examine your own listening habits by taking the self-test "How Good a Listener Are You?"

TEST YOURSELF

HOW GOOD A LISTENER ARE YOU?

INSTRUCTIONS
Respond to each question according to the following scale:

1 = always
2 = frequently
3 = sometimes
4 = seldom
5 = never

_____ 1. I think about my own performance during an interaction; as a result, I miss some of what the speaker has said.

_____ 2. I allow my mind to wander away from what the speaker is talking about.

_____ 3. I try to simplify messages I hear by omitting details.

_____ 4. I focus on a particular detail of what the speaker is saying instead of on the general meanings the speaker wishes to communicate.

_____ 5. I allow my attitudes toward the topic or speaker to influence my evaluation of the message.

_____ 6. I hear what I expect to hear instead of what is actually being said.

_____ 7. I listen passively, letting the speaker do the work while I relax.

_____ 8. I listen to what others say, but I don't feel what they are feeling.

_____ 9. I evaluate what the speaker is saying before I fully understand the meanings intended.

_____ 10. I listen to the literal meanings that a speaker communicates but do not look for hidden or underlying meanings.

SCORING
All the statements describe ineffective listening tendencies. High scores, therefore, reflect effective listening and low scores reflect ineffective listening. If you scored significantly higher than 30, then you probably have better-than-average listening skills. Scores significantly below 30 represent lower-than-average listening skills. Regardless of your score, however, you can significantly improve your listening skills. Each of the statements in this listening test refers to an obstacle or effectiveness principle discussed in this unit.

THE LISTENING PROCESS

Listening is not the same as hearing. Hearing is a physiological process that occurs when you are in the vicinity of vibrations in the air and these vibrations impinge on your eardrum. Hearing is basically a passive process that occurs without any attention or effort on your part. Listening is different.

Listening can be described as a series of five steps: receiving, understanding, remembering, evaluating, and responding (Figure 4.2). Note that the listening process is a circular one. The responses of one person serve as the stimuli for the other person, whose responses in turn serve as the stimuli for the first person, and so on.

RECEIVING

Listening begins with receiving the messages the speaker sends. The messages are both verbal and nonverbal; they consist of words as well as gestures, facial expressions, and variations in volume and rate, for example.

At this stage, you note not only what is said (verbally and nonverbally) but also what is omitted. You receive, for example, your friend's summary of good deeds as well as the omission of all the broken promises.

In receiving, try to:

- focus your attention on the speaker's verbal and nonverbal messages, on what is said and on what is not said.
- avoid distractions in the environment.
- focus your attention on the speaker rather than on what you will say next.
- maintain your role as listener and avoid interrupting.

UNDERSTANDING

Understanding, the stage at which you learn what the speaker means, includes the thoughts that are expressed and the emotional tone that accompanies these thoughts.

In understanding, try to:

- relate the new information the speaker is giving to what you already know.
- see the speaker's messages from the speaker's point of view; avoid judging the message until you fully understand it as the speaker intended it.
- ask questions for clarification, if necessary; ask for additional details or examples if they are needed.
- rephrase (paraphrase) the speaker's ideas in your own words.

REMEMBERING

Messages that you receive and understand need to be retained at least for some period. In some small-group and public speaking situations, you can augment your memory by taking notes or by taping the messages. In most interpersonal communication situations, however, note taking would be considered inappropriate, although you often do write down a telephone number, an appointment, or directions.

For example, when Susan says she is planning to buy a new car, the effective listener remembers this and at later meetings asks her about the car. When Joe says his

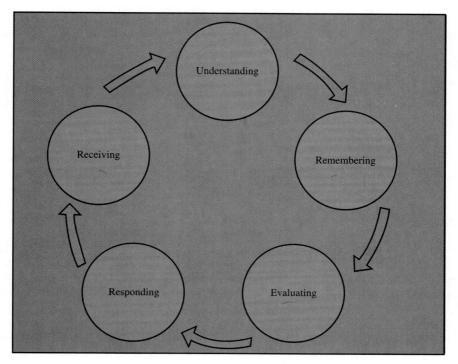

Figure 4.2
A five-stage model of listening. This five-step model draws on a variety of previous models
that listening researchers have developed (for example, Barker 1990; Steil, Barker, and
Watson 1983; Brownell 1987; Alessandra 1986).

mother is ill, the effective listener remembers this and inquires about Joe's mother's
health later in the week.

What you remember is actually not what was said but what you think (or remember) was said. Memory for speech is not reproductive; you don't simply reproduce in
your memory what the speaker said. Rather, memory is *reconstructive;* you actually
reconstruct the messages you hear into a system that makes sense to you.

To illustrate this important concept, try to memorize the list of 12 words presented
below (Glucksberg and Danks 1975). Don't worry about the order of the words. Only the
number remembered counts. Take about 20 seconds to memorize as many words as possible. Don't read any further until you have tried to memorize the list of words.

BED	DREAM	COMFORT
REST	AWAKE	SOUND
AWAKE	NIGHT	SLUMBER
TIRED	EAT	SNORE

Now close the book and write down as many of the words from this list as you can
remember. Don't read any further until you have tested your own memory.

If you are like my own students, you not only remembered a good number of the words on the list, but you also "remembered" at least one word that was not on the list: "sleep." You did not simply reproduce the list; you reconstructed it. In this case, you gave the list meaning, and part of that meaning included the word "sleep." It frequently happens that messages are reconstructed into a meaningful whole (that is, meaningful to you as a listener), and in the process you remember a distorted version of what was said.

In remembering, try to:

- identify the central ideas and the major support advanced.
- summarize the message in a more easily retained form, but be careful not to ignore crucial details or qualifications.
- repeat names and key concepts to yourself or, if appropriate, aloud.

EVALUATING

Evaluating consists of judging the messages in some way. At times, you may try to evaluate the speaker's underlying intentions or motives. Often this evaluation process goes on without much conscious awareness. For example, Elaine tells you that she is up for a promotion and is really excited about it. You may then try to judge her intention. Does she want you to use your influence with the company president? Is she preoccupied with the promotion and so tells everyone? Is she looking for a compliment?

In other situations, your evaluation is more in the nature of critical analysis. For example, in listening to proposals advanced in a business meeting, you might ask: Are they practical? Will they increase productivity? What's the evidence? Is there contradictory evidence?

In evaluating, try to:

- resist evaluation until you fully understand the speaker's point of view.
- assume that the speaker is a person of goodwill, and give the speaker the benefit of any doubt by asking for clarification on positions to which you feel you might object.
- distinguish facts from inferences (see Unit 12), opinions, and personal interpretations by the speaker.
- identify any biases, self-interests, or prejudices that may lead the speaker to slant unfairly what is presented.

RESPONDING

Responding occurs in two phases: (1) responses you make while the speaker is talking and (2) responses you make after the speaker has stopped talking. These responses are feedback—information that you send back to the speaker; this information tells the speaker how you feel and what you think about his or her messages (Unit 15). Responses made while the speaker is talking should be supportive and should acknowledge that you are listening to the speaker. These responses include what nonverbal researchers call **back-channeling cues,** such as "I see," "yes," "uh-huh," and similar signals that let the speaker know you are listening.

Responses made after the speaker has stopped talking are generally more elaborate and might include expressing empathy ("I know how you must feel"), asking for clarification ("Do you mean that this new health plan is to replace the old one?"), challenging ("I think your evidence is weak here"), and agreeing ("You're absolutely right on this; I'll support your proposal").

In responding, try to:

* be supportive of the speaker throughout the speaker's talk by using and varying your back-channeling cues; using only one back-channeling cue—for example, saying "uh-huh" throughout—will make it appear that you are not listening but are merely on automatic pilot.
* express support for the speaker in your final responses (especially).
* be honest; the speaker has a right to expect honest responses, even if they express disagreement.
* own your responses; state your thoughts and feelings as your own, and use I-messages (for example, say "I think the new proposal will entail greater expense than you outlined" rather than "Everyone will object to the plan for costing too much").

EFFECTIVE LISTENING

Because you listen for different purposes, the principles of effective listening should vary from one situation to another. The following four dimensions of listening illustrate the appropriateness of different listening modes for different communication situations.

PARTICIPATORY AND PASSIVE LISTENING

The general key to effective listening in interpersonal situations is active participation. Perhaps the best preparation for participatory listening is to *act* (physically and mentally) like a participant. For many people, this may be the most abused rule of effective listening. Recall, for example, how your body almost automatically reacts to important news: almost immediately, you assume an upright posture, cock your head to the speaker, and remain relatively still and quiet. You do this almost reflexively because this is the way you listen most effectively. Even more important than this physical alertness is mental alertness. As a listener, participate in the communication interaction as an equal partner with the speaker, as one who is emotionally and intellectually ready to engage in the sharing of meaning.

Effective participatory listening is expressive. Let the listener know that you are participating in the communication interaction. Nonverbally, maintain eye contact, focus your concentration on the speaker rather than on others present, and express your feelings facially. Verbally, ask appropriate questions, signal understanding with "I see" or "yes," and express agreement or disagreement as appropriate.

Passive listening, however, is not without merit, and some recognition of its value is warranted. Passive listening—listening without talking or directing the speaker in any obvious way—is a powerful means of communicating acceptance. Passive listening allows the speaker to develop his or her thoughts and ideas in the presence of another person who accepts but does not evaluate, who supports but does not intrude. By listening passively, you provide a supportive and receptive environment. Once that has been established, you may wish to participate in a more active way, verbally and nonverbally.

In regulating participatory and passive listening, keep the following guidelines in mind:

- Work at listening. Listening is hard work, so be prepared to participate actively. Unaided, people are likely to follow the law of least effort and to do whatever is easiest and requires the smallest amount of energy. This tendency needs to be combatted. Avoid, too, "the entertainment syndrome," the expectation to be amused by a speaker (Floyd 1985).
- Combat sources of "noise" as much as possible. Remove distractions or other interferences (newspapers, magazines, stereos) so that your listening task will have less competition.
- Avoid preoccupation with yourself or with external issues. Avoid focusing on your own performance in the interaction or on rehearsing your responses. Avoid, too, focusing on matters that are irrelevant to the interaction—for example, what you did Saturday night or your plans for this evening.
- Use the thought-speech time differential effectively. Because you can process information faster than the average rate of speech, there is often a time lag. Use this time to summarize the speaker's thoughts, formulate questions, and draw connections between what the speaker says and what you already know.
- Assume there is value in what the speaker is saying. Resist assuming that what you have to say is more valuable than the speaker's remarks.

EMPATHIC AND OBJECTIVE LISTENING

If you want to understand what a person means and what a person is feeling, you need to listen empathically. To empathize with others is to feel with them, to see the world as they see it, to feel what they feel.

Popular students, for example, might intellectually understand why an unpopular student feels depressed, but that will not enable them to understand emotionally the feelings of depression. To gain that understanding, they must put themselves in the position of the unpopular student, role-play a bit, and begin to feel that student's feelings and think his or her thoughts. Then the popular students will be in a better position to understand, to genuinely empathize. (See Unit 6 for specific suggestions for developing and communicating empathy).

Although empathic listening is the preferred response in most communication situations, there are times when you need to go beyond empathy and measure the meanings and feelings against some objective reality. It is important to listen to a friend tell you how the entire world hates him or her and to understand how your friend feels and why. But then you need to look a bit more objectively at your friend and at the world and perhaps see the paranoia or self-hatred at work. Sometimes you have to put your empathic responses aside and listen with objectivity and detachment.

In adjusting your empathic and objective listening focus, keep the following recommendations in mind:

- See the sequence of events as punctuated from the speaker's point of view, and see how this can influence what the speaker says and does.
- View the speaker as an equal. To encourage openness and empathy, try to eliminate any physical or psychological barriers to equality; for example, step from

behind the large desk separating you from your employees. Avoid interrupting, a sign that you feel what you have to say is more important.

- Seek to understand both thoughts and feelings. Do not consider your listening task finished until you have understood what the speaker is feeling as well as thinking.
- Avoid "offensive listening," the tendency to listen to bits and pieces of information that will help you attack the speaker or find fault with something the speaker has said.
- Avoid *sharpening,* the situation in which you highlight or emphasize one or two aspects of the message and ignore other aspects.
- Beware of the "friend-or-foe" factor that may lead you to distort messages because of your attitudes toward another person. For example, if you think Freddy is stupid, then it will take added effort to listen objectively to Freddy's messages and to hear anything that is clear or insightful.

NONJUDGMENTAL AND CRITICAL LISTENING

Effective listening is both nonjudgmental and critical. It involves listening with an open mind with a view toward understanding. And it involves listening critically with a view toward making some kind of evaluation or judgment. Clearly, you should first listen for understanding while suspending judgment. Only after you have fully understood the messages should you evaluate or judge. Listening with an open mind is extremely difficult. It is not easy, for example, to listen to arguments against some cherished belief or to criticisms of something you value highly.

Supplement open-minded listening with critical listening. Listening with an open mind will help you better understand the messages; listening with a critical mind will help you better analyze and evaluate the messages. This is especially true in college. It's a lot easier to listen to a teacher and take down what is said than to evaluate and critically analyze what is said. Yet teachers (and textbook authors) have biases, too; at times consciously and at times unconsciously, these biases creep into scholarly discussions. Identify and bring these biases to the surface. The vast majority of teachers will appreciate critical responses. They demonstrate that someone is listening, and they often stimulate further examination of ideas.

In adjusting your nonjudgmental and critical listening, focus on the following guidelines:

- Keep an open mind. Delay evaluation until you have fully understood the intent and the content of the message being communicated.
- Avoid distorting messages through oversimplication or leveling—the tendency to eliminate details and to simplify complex messages so that they are easier to remember. Also avoid filtering out unpleasant or undesirable messages; you may miss the very information you need to change your assumptions or your behaviors.
- Recognize your own biases; everyone has them. They may interfere with accurate listening and cause you to distort message reception through the process of *assimilation,* the tendency to interpret what you hear or think you hear according to your own biases, prejudices, and expectations. For example, are your ethnic, national, or religious biases preventing you from appreciating a speaker's point

of view? Biases may also lead to *sharpening,* the tendency for a particular item of information to take on increased importance because it confirms your stereotypes or prejudices.

* Avoid uncritical listening when evaluations and judgments are called for.

SURFACE AND DEPTH LISTENING

In Shakespeare's *Julius Caesar,* Marc Antony, delivering Caesar's funeral oration, says: "I come to bury Caesar, not to praise him. . . . The evil that men do lives after them. . . . The good is oft interred with their bones." And later: "For Brutus is an honorable man. . . . So are they all, all honorable men." But Antony, as you know, did come to praise Caesar and to convince the crowd that Brutus was not an honorable man. He came to incite the crowd to avenge the death of Caesar.

In most messages, there is an obvious meaning that a literal reading of the words and sentences reveals. But there is often another level of meaning. Sometimes, as in *Julius Caesar,* it is the opposite of the expressed literal meaning; sometimes it seems totally unrelated. In reality, few messages have only one level of meaning. Most function on two or three levels at the same time. Consider some of these frequently heard messages: a friend asks you how you like his new haircut. Another friend asks you how you like her painting. On one level, the meaning is clear: do you like the haircut? Do you like the painting? But it is reasonable to assume that on another level, perhaps a more important level, your friends are asking you to say something positive about them—about his appearance, about her artistic ability. The parent who seems at first to be complaining about working hard at the office or in the home may be asking for appreciation. The child who talks about the unfairness of the other children in the playground may be asking for some expression of caring. To appreciate these other meanings, you need to engage in depth listening.

When listening interpersonally, be particularly sensitive to different levels of meaning. If you respond only to the surface-level communication (the literal meaning), you will miss the opportunity to make meaningful contact with the other person's feelings and real needs. Suppose you say to your parent, "You're always complaining. I bet you really love working so hard." You may be failing to answer a very real call for understanding and appreciation.

In regulating your surface and depth listening, consider the following guidelines:

* Focus on both verbal and nonverbal messages. Recognize both consistent and inconsistent "packages" of messages and take these cues as guides to the meaning the speaker is trying to communicate. Ask questions when in doubt. Listen also to what is omitted.
* Listen for both content and relational messages. The student who constantly challenges the teacher is on one level communicating disagreement over content; the student is debating the issues. However, on another level—the relationship level—the student may well be voicing objections to the instructor's authority or authoritarianism. If the instructor is to deal effectively with the student, he or she must listen and respond to both types of messages.
* Make special note of statements that refer to the speaker. Remember that people inevitably talk about themselves—from their own point of view, colored by their needs and desires, and influenced by their own experiences.

- Do not disregard the literal (surface) meaning of interpersonal messages in your attempt to uncover the more hidden (deep) meanings. If you do, you will quickly find that your listening problems disappear: no one will talk to you anymore. Balance your attention between the surface and the underlying meanings. Respond to the various levels of meaning in the messages of others as you would like others to respond to yours—sensitively but not obsessively, readily but not overambitiously.

ACTIVE LISTENING

Active listening is one of the most important communication skills you can learn (Gordon 1975). Consider the following brief comment and some possible responses:

APHRODITE: That creep gave me a C on the paper. I really worked on that project, and all I get is a lousy C.

APOLLO: That's not so bad; most people got around the same grade. I got a C, too.

ATHENA: So what? This is your last semester. Who cares about grades anyway?

ACHILLES: You should be pleased with a C. Peggy and Michael both failed, and John and Judy got Ds.

DIANA: You got a C on that paper you were working on for the last three weeks? You sound really angry and hurt.

All four listeners are probably eager to make Aphrodite feel better, but they go about it in very different ways and, you can be sure, with very different outcomes. The first three listeners give fairly typical responses. Apollo and Athena both try to minimize the significance of a C grade, a common response to someone who has expressed displeasure or disappointment. Usually, it is also inappropriate. Although well-intentioned, this response does little to promote meaningful communication and understanding. Achilles tries to give the C grade a more positive meaning. Note, however, that all three listeners also say a great deal more: that Aphrodite should not be feeling unhappy, that these feelings are not legitimate. These responses deny the validity of these feelings and put Aphrodite in the position of having to defend them.

Diana, however, is different. Diana uses **active listening,** a process of sending back to the speaker what the listener thinks the speaker meant, both literally and emotionally.

Active listening does not mean simply repeating the speaker's exact words. It is rather a process of putting into some meaningful whole your understanding of the speaker's total message—the verbal and the nonverbal, the content and the feelings.

PURPOSES OF ACTIVE LISTENING

Active listening serves a number of important purposes. First, it helps you **check how accurately you have understood what the speaker said and meant.** By reflecting back what you perceive to be the speaker's meaning, you give the speaker an opportunity to confirm, clarify, or amend your perceptions. In this way, future messages have a better chance of being relevant and purposeful.

Second, through active listening, you **express acceptance of the speaker's feelings.** Note that in the sample responses given, the first three listeners challenge the speaker; they refuse to give the expressed feelings legitimacy. The active listener accepts the speaker. The speaker's feelings are not challenged; rather, they are echoed in a sympathetic and empathic manner. Note, too, that in the first three responses, the feelings of the speaker are denied without ever actually being identified. Diana, however, not only accepts these feelings but also identifies them explicitly, again allowing the opportunity for correction.

Interestingly enough, when confronted by a person in distress, those listeners who try to solve the person's problem or who veer off the issue by engaging in "chitchat" come away significantly more depressed than those listeners who show acceptance of the distressed person's problems or who use supportive listening techniques (Notarius and Herrick 1988).

Third, in active listening you **prompt the speaker to further explore his or her feelings and thoughts.** The active listening response gives the speaker the opportunity to elaborate on these feelings without having to defend them. Active listening sets the stage for meaningful dialogue, a dialogue of mutual understanding. In stimulating this further exploration, active listening also encourages the speaker to resolve his or her own conflicts.

TECHNIQUES OF ACTIVE LISTENING

Three techniques will help you master active listening. At first, these principles may seem awkward and unnatural. With practice, however, they will flow and blend into a meaningful and effective dialogue.

Paraphrase the Speaker's Meaning   State in your own words what you think the speaker meant. This paraphrase helps to ensure understanding because the speaker can correct or modify your restatement. It also communicates your interest and your attention. Everyone wants to feel attended to, especially when angry or depressed. The active listening paraphrase confirms this.

When you paraphrase the speaker's meanings, you give the speaker a kind of green light to go into more detail, to elaborate. Thus, when you echo the thought about the C grade, the speaker can elaborate on why that grade was important. Make your paraphrases objective; be careful not to lead the speaker in the direction you think best. Also, be careful that you do not maximize or minimize the speaker's emotions; try to echo these feelings as accurately as you can.

Express Understanding of the Speaker's Feelings   In addition to paraphrasing the content, echo the feelings you believe the speaker expressed or implied. This enables you to check your perception of the speaker's feelings and provides the speaker with the opportunity to see his or her feelings more objectively. Consider this dialogue:

> **PAT:** That creep demoted me. He told me I wasn't an effective manager. I can't believe he did that, after all I've done for this company.

When was the last time you needed someone to be an active listener? What happened? When was the last time you served as an active listener for someone? Might either of these interactions have been improved by the three principles discussed here?

CHRIS: I can understand your anger. You've been manager for three or four months now, haven't you?

PAT: A little over three months. I know I was on trial, but I thought I was doing a good job.

CHRIS: Can you get another trial?

PAT: Yes, he said I could try again in a few months. But I feel like a failure.

CHRIS: I know what you mean. It's not a pleasant feeling. What else did he say?

PAT: He said I had trouble getting the paperwork done on time.

CHRIS: You've been late filing the reports?

PAT: A few times.

CHRIS: Is there a way to delegate the paperwork?

PAT: No, but I think I know now what needs to be done.

CHRIS: You sound as though you're ready to give that manager's position another try.

PAT: Yes, I think I am, and I'm going to let him know that I intend to apply in the next few months.

Even in this brief interaction, Pat has moved from unproductive anger with the supervisor as well as a feeling of failure to a determination to correct an unpleasant situation. Note, too, that Chris merely echoed these feelings and expressed understanding of them.

Expressing understanding is especially helpful when someone is angry, hurt, or depressed. Hearing these feelings objectively and seeing them from a less impassioned perspective will help in dealing effectively with them.

Most of us hold back our feelings until we are certain that others will be accepting. We need to hear statements such as "I understand" and "I see how you feel." When we feel that our emotions are accepted, we then feel free to go into more detail. Active listening provides the speaker with this important opportunity.

Ask Questions   Ask questions to make sure that you understand the speaker's thoughts and feelings and to secure additional helpful information. Design your questions to provide just enough stimulation and support for the speaker to express the thoughts and feelings he or she wants to express. Avoid questions that pry into irrelevant areas or that challenge the speaker in any way.

SUMMARY: UNIT IN BRIEF

Definitions	Functions and Purposes	Techniques and Guidelines
Listening: an active process of receiving, understanding, remembering, evaluating, and responding to communications.	To learn, relate, influence, play, help	Participatory-passive Empathic-objective Nonjudgmental-critical Surface-depth
Active listening: a process of sending back to the speaker what you think the speaker meant in content and in feeling.	To enable the listener to check on the accuracy of her or his understanding To express acceptance of the speaker's feelings To stimulate the speaker to explore further feelings and thoughts	Paraphrase Express understanding Ask questions

THINKING CRITICALLY ABOUT LISTENING IN INTERPERSONAL COMMUNICATION

1. Are you satisfied with the level of listening that others give you? How might you go about increasing their level?
2. With which of the five stages of the listening process do you have the most difficulty? The least difficulty?
3. What purpose does your listening serve most of the time? Do you listen for a reason in addition to the five noted here?
4. In what types of listening situations are you at your best? At your worst?
5. How effective a listener are you? Are you satisfied with this? How might you improve your listening effectiveness?
6. In which situations or with which people do you have the greatest difficulty listening nonjudgmentally? The greatest difficulty listening empathically? Why?
7. Might listening "in depth" get you into trouble? What principle or suggestion would you offer to combat this possibility?
8. How would you describe the ideal listener?

9. Which of the four responses given to Aphrodite would you be most likely to give? Why? In what types of situations do you engage in active listening? Does it serve useful functions? In what situations might active listening be counterproductive?

10. How would you go about answering the following questions?

   • Is listening efficiency influenced by the sex of the speaker and listener? For example, is listening more efficient when speaker and listener are the same sex or opposite sexes?
   • Of what value is listening competency in business and industry?
   • Do male and female voices differ in their ability to command attention?
   • Do male and female voices differ in credibility?

EXPERIENTIAL VEHICLES

4.1 SEQUENTIAL COMMUNICATION

This exercise is designed to illustrate some of the processes involved in what might be called "sequential communication"—communication that is passed on from one individual to another.

The first subject is read a statement once, twice, or even three times; the subject should feel comfortable that he or she has grasped it fully. The second subject then enters the room and listens carefully to the first subject's restatement of the communication. The second subject then repeats it to the third subject, and so on, until all subjects have restated the communication. The last restatement and the original are then compared on the basis of the processes listed below.

Members of the class not serving as subjects should record the changes made in the various restatements. Special attention should be given to the following basic processes in sequential communication:

1. *Omissions.* What kinds of information are omitted? At what point in the chain of communication are such omissions introduced? Do the omissions follow any pattern?

2. *Additions.* What kinds of information are added? When? Can patterns be discerned here, or are the additions totally random?

3. *Distortions.* What kinds of information are distorted? When? Are there any patterns? Can the distortions be classified in any way? Are the distortions in the direction of increased simplicity? Increased complexity? Can the sources of or reasons for the distortions be identified?

A verbal communication that works well comes from William Haney (1981).

> *Every year at State University, the eagles in front of the Psi Gamma fraternity house were mysteriously sprayed during the night. Whenever this happened, it cost the Psi Gams from $75 to $100 to have the eagles cleaned. The Psi Gams complained to officials and were promised by the president that if ever any students were caught painting the eagles, they would be expelled from school.*

4.2 PRACTICING ACTIVE LISTENING

For each of the situations described below, supply at least one appropriate active listening response.

1. Your friend Karla has been married for the last three years and has two small children, one two years old and one six months. Karla has been having an affair with a colleague at work. Her husband discovered this and is now suing for divorce. She confides this to you and says, *I really don't know what I'm going to do. I may lose the kids. I could never support myself and live the way we do now. I sure love that BMW. I wish these last two months had never happened and that I had never started up with Taylor.*

2. Your boss, Ruth, has been an especially hard supervisor to work for. On several occasions, she filed negative evaluation reports on you and other members of your department. This has prevented you and others from getting merit raises in at least three instances. She is a perfectionist who doesn't understand that people make mistakes. During lunch, she comes over to your table and tells you that she has been fired and has to clean out her desk by 3 p.m. She says, *I can't believe they did this to me; I was the best supervisor they had. Our production level was always the highest in the company. They're idiots. Now I don't know what I'm going to do. Where will I get another job?*

3. Your colleague at work has been selling company secrets for the last two years (that you know of). What he does is claim that he has to work late, so he gets to stay in the office after everyone else leaves. He then accesses files that are normally confidential, prints them, and sells them to competing companies. These files have included proprietary client lists, proposed company decisions, and personnel records for various members of the company. He has now been caught and comes to you, saying, *What am I going to do? They're putting it into my personnel record; I'll never get another job in this field. Old Smith is even talking about taking legal action. I could go to jail. That would kill me and my family. What can I do?*

4. Your mother has been having a difficult time at work. She was recently passed up for promotion and has received one of the lowest merit raises given in the company. She says, *I'm not sure what I did wrong. I do my work, mind my own business, don't take my sick days like everyone else. How could they give that promotion to Manuela, who's only been with the company for two years? I've given them seven years. Maybe I should just quit and try to find something else.*

5. Your friend is bemoaning the lack of suitable partners and the difficulties involved in forming long-lasting and productive relationships. Your friend is worried about the *future and the possibility of never forming a meaningful relationship. I feel bad that I may never meet someone I can love and who will love me. I'm worried that I'm going to be alone the rest of this rotten life.*

UNIT 5

Ethics in Interpersonal Communication

Unit Objectives

After completing this unit, you should be able to:

1. Explain the ethical dimension of interpersonal communication
2. Explain the ethical implications of lying, using fear and emotional tactics, censoring messages and interactions, and gossiping

---

Before reading about ethics in interpersonal communication, read the following dialogue. It raises questions about the four ethical issues discussed in this unit: lying, using fear and emotional appeals, censoring interactions, and revealing secrets. Individually, in small groups, or with the entire class, consider what you feel would be ethical or unethical behavior in each case.

FRANK:	father
LAURA:	mother
BARBARA:	daughter
JEFF:	son
ALEX:	son

Frank, Barbara, Jeff, and Alex are sitting in the living room.

FRANK: Look. I don't want anything said to your mother about this. Do you hear me? Not one word.

ALEX: Pop, I really think she should know.

BARBARA: She has a right to know. She has more of a right to know than anyone else.

JEFF: Yeah. I agree. You can't keep this from her. You have no right.

FRANK: I don't give a damn what you kids think. I want her to continue thinking that everything is the way it was. The first one to open their trap is going to have my foot in it.

ALEX: OK, but I don't like it.

JEFF: OK.

BARBARA: I think it stinks but OK.

Assuming that all remain true to their promise, are all four guilty of lying by omission? Are all four equally guilty? Would your answer be different if:

- Frank had just learned he was going to die in the next six months, Laura was in poor health, and Frank feared that the shock might kill her?
- one of the children found Frank with a girlfriend, whom he has been seeing romantically for years?
- Frank got a large pay raise or pay cut?
- Frank was plotting to commit suicide because he had an incurable illness?

Is the behavior of Barbara, Alex, and Jeff unethical because they agree to act against their conscience? Would your answer to this question depend on the age of the children?

[*Exit Jeff; enter Laura*]

LAURA: Barbara, I can't believe what you're telling me. Of the three of you kids, you were the last one I would think would want to marry someone of another race and religion. After all I did for you? I can't believe you're going to do this to me. I'll never be able to face the rest of the family. You're destroying everything. You're throwing away everything we tried to do for you. I just want to die. Your father is going to have a heart attack.

FRANK: Listen. You marry that creep and we're through. You'll never be allowed in this house again. Don't ever call; don't ever write. You marry this guy and you have no family. And your kids will have no grandparents. We will never ever ever see you again. To us, you'll be dead.

ALEX: And I'm going to get the guys together and knock that guy's teeth out if I ever see him around here.

FRANK: Now, Alex, I don't think that's going to be necessary.

Are these parents and brother ethical in their use of emotional and fear appeals? Is Frank's threat ethical? Is Alex's physical threat (and Frank's implicit agreement with it) any different ethically from the emotional or interpersonal threats? What (if anything) would you have to know to answer this question? For example, would your answer be different if:

- Laura was honestly expressing her feelings?
- Laura was using this appeal merely as a persuasive strategy to keep Barbara from marrying outside her race and religion?
- Frank thought that this type of appeal was the only one that would keep Barbara from marrying this man and that she would—later in life—be grateful to him?
- the issue centered on Barbara's intention to change her own religion and join a religious cult?
- Barbara was 18 years old?
- Barbara was 55 years old (and never married but always wanted to be)?

[*Exit Barbara*]

FRANK: Listen, Alex. I hear you've been hanging out with the Franklin brothers. I want that stopped. I don't want you hanging around with—hell, I don't want you even seeing—the Franklins. Even from a distance. They're bad news.

LAURA: He's right, Alex. Stay away from them from now on.

FRANK: Don't act like a know-it-all. You listen to your mother.

LAURA: You hear us, Alex? Do you?

FRANK: We mean it, Alex. We want you to stay far away from those guys.

Are these parents justified in trying to censor interactions between their son and others they consider undesirable? Would you need additional information about the Franklins to make your decision? How would you answer if:

- The Franklin brothers were drug dealers and were trying to persuade Alex to run drugs for them?
- The Franklin brothers had AIDS?
- The Franklin brothers were of a different race or religion?
- Alex was mentally retarded or 11 years old or on parole?

[*Exit Alex; Enter Jeff*]

JEFF: Listen, everyone. Kim told me something today that I want to tell you. I promised her I wouldn't tell anyone but I just have to tell you.

LAURA: Well, maybe you shouldn't. I mean, if you promised Kim, maybe you shouldn't tell us.

JEFF: No, no, I really want to—I have to.

FRANK: Your mother's right. If you promised to keep a secret, then keep it. You'll be the better person for it.

JEFF: Well, if you all promise to keep it a secret, it'll be OK.

Would it be wrong for Jeff to reveal the secret? Would your answer depend on the kind of secret? If so, what would you have to know about the secret to answer this question? What would you answer if the secret was that:

- Kim broke up with her boyfriend yesterday for the third time this month (and they are both 14 years old)?
- Kim, who has been having mental problems, plans to kill her father?
- Kim, 17 years old, plans to commit suicide?
- Kim is heavily into drugs?

Would your answer be different if:

- Kim was 4 and Jeff was 5?
- Kim was 4 and Jeff was 32?
- Kim and Jeff were both 19?
- If the family members kept the secret confidential?

All interpersonal interactions have an ethical dimension (cf. Jaksa and Pritchard 1994; Johannesen 1990). Interpersonal interactions, therefore, must be viewed not only in terms of effective-ineffective or satisfactory-unsatisfactory but also in terms of right-wrong, moral-immoral.

The purpose of this unit is to present a variety of issues that have ethical implications to help you develop your own ethical system. At the conclusion of the discussion of each of these issues is a series of questions you may wish to ponder. As a preface to these discussions, consider the notion of choice and how it may aid our understanding of the ethics of interpersonal communication.

INTERPERSONAL ETHICS AND CHOICE

The major determinant of whether communications are ethical or unethical can be found in the notion of choice. The underlying assumption is that people have a right to make their own choices. Interpersonal communications are ethical to the extent that they facilitate a person's freedom of choice by presenting that person with accurate information. Communications are unethical to the extent that they interfere with the individual's freedom of choice by preventing the person from securing information relevant to the choices he or she will make. Unethical communications, therefore, are those that force a person (1) to make choices he or she would not normally make or (2) to decline to make choices he or she would normally make or both. The ethical communicator provides others with the kind of information that is helpful in making their own choices.

You have the right to information about yourself that others possess and that influences the choices you will make. Thus, for example, you have the right to face your accusers, to know the witnesses who will be called to testify against you, to see your credit ratings, and to know what Social Security benefits you will receive.

At the same time that you have the right to information bearing on your own choices, you also have the obligation to reveal information that you possess that bears on the choices of your society. Thus, for example, you have an obligation to identify wrongdoing that you witness, to identify someone in a police lineup, to notify the police of criminal activity, and to testify at a trial when you possess pertinent information. This information is essential for society to accomplish its purposes and to make its legitimate choices.

Similarly, the information presented must be accurate; obviously, reasonable choices depend on accuracy of information. Doubtful information must be presented with qualifications, whether it concerns a crime that you witnessed or things you have heard about others.

At the same time that you have these obligations to communicate information, you also have the right to remain silent; you have a right to privacy, to withhold information that has no bearing on the matter at hand. Thus, for example, a man's or woman's previous relationship history, affectional orientation, or religion is usually irrelevant to the person's ability to function as a doctor or police officer, for example, and may thus be kept private in most job-related situations. If these issues become relevant—say, the person is about to enter a new relationship—then there may be an obligation to reveal previous relationships, affectional orientation, or religion, for example.

In a court, of course, you have the right to refuse to incriminate yourself, to reveal information about yourself that could be used against you. But you do not have the right to refuse to reveal information about the criminal activities of others. Priests, psychiatrists, and lawyers, for example, are often exempt from this general rule if the information was revealed in confession or if the "criminal" was a patient or client.

In this ethic based on choice, however, there are a few qualifications that may restrict your freedom. The ethic assumes that persons are of an age and mental condition that allows free choice to be reasonably executed and that the choices they make do not prevent others from doing likewise. A child 5 or 6 years old is not ready to make certain choices, so someone else must make them. Similarly, some people with mental disabilities need others to make certain decisions for them.

The circumstances under which you are living also can restrict free choice. For example, persons in the military will at times have to give up free choice and eat hamburger rather than steak, wear uniforms rather than jeans, and march rather than stay in bed. By entering the armed forces, one waives, at least partially, the right to make one's own choices. Furthermore, the choices made must not prevent others from making their legitimate choices. You cannot permit a thief to steal, because in granting that freedom you would be imposing on the rights of potential victims.

These, then, are some of the qualifications that must be considered in any theory of choice. Admittedly, it is not always easy to determine when people possess the mental ability to make their own decisions or when one person's choice actually interferes with the choices or rights of another. These are the vagaries we must contend with in any theory concerned with the morality of human behavior.

LYING

According to the *Random House Dictionary,* a lie is "a false statement made with deliberate intent to deceive; a falsehood; something intended or serving to convey a false impression" (cf. Bok 1978). Lying may be both overt and covert. Although it usually involves overt statements, lying may also be committed by omission. When you omit something relevant, leading others to draw incorrect inferences, you are lying just as surely as if you had stated an untruth. Most of us can appreciate this by recalling times in our youth when our parents, suspicious of what had gone on the previous night, asked us what had happened. Many of us probably recited all the innocent events and omitted what our parents really wanted to know. We were lying, and we knew it.

Similarly, although most lies are verbal, some are nonverbal; in fact, most lies involve at least some nonverbal elements. The innocent facial expression—despite the commission of some wrong—and the knowing nod instead of the honest expression of ignorance are common examples of nonverbal lying (O'Hair, Cody, and McLaughlin 1981). Lies may range from the "white lie" and truth stretching to lies that form the basis of infidelity in a relationship, libel, and perjury.

LYING AND ETHICS

Lying or otherwise hiding the truth is unethical because it prevents another person from learning about possible alternative choices. Consider the situation in which a patient has six months to live. Is it ethical for the doctor or family members to tell the patient that he or she is doing fine? Applying our notion of choice, we would have to conclude that it is not. In not telling the patient the truth, these people are making choices for him or her. They are in effect preventing the patient from living these last six months as he or she might want to, given the knowledge of imminent death. Similarly, parents who keep the truth about their child's adoption secret after the child has grown up are denying the child the right to make choices he or she might wish to make. Such choices might, for example, concern finding the biological parents or recognizing a different ethnic or religious heritage.

To lie about your infidelity would be unethical because it prevents your partner from making choices that might otherwise be made. Falsely saying "I love you," misrepresenting your abilities in a job interview, even lying about the cleaning power of a detergent are all examples of preventing people from making choices that they might make if they knew your real feelings, your true abilities, or the real power of the detergent.

If you misrepresent or hide certain facts, you prevent others from making choices they have a right to make. If you take the position that you've manipulated the truth for another's own good, you are in effect saying that you—and not they—have the right to make the choice.

People may, of course, give up their right to hear all the information that concerns them. A patient may make it known that he or she does not want to know when death will occur. Marital partners may make an agreement not to disclose their affairs. When this is the case, there is no lying, no deceit, and hence no unethical behavior in withholding such information.

WHY WE LIE

There are probably as many reasons for lying as there are lies; each situation is different, and each seems to be governed by a different reason or set of reasons. Research finds that people like to achieve one of the following rewards (Camden, Motley, and Wilson 1984):

- *Basic needs:* lies told to gain or retain objects that fulfill basic needs (for example, money or material possessions)
- *Affiliation:* lies told to increase desired affiliations or decrease undesired affiliations (for example, lies told to prolong desirable social interactions, to avoid interpersonal conflicts, to avoid granting some request, or to avoid prolonged interaction); lies told to gain or maintain conversational control during interpersonal interaction (for example, lies told to avoid certain self-disclosures or to manipulate the conversation in a desired direction)
- *Self-esteem:* lies told to protect or increase one's own self-esteem, that of the person with whom one is interacting, or some third party (for example, lies told to increase one's perceived competence or social desirability)
- *Self-gratification:* lies told for personal satisfaction (for example, for the sake of humor or to exaggerate a desired effect)

Generally, people lie to gain some reward for themselves, although some lies are motivated by the desire to benefit another. From an analysis of 322 lies, one study found that 75.8 percent benefited the liar, 21.7 percent benefited the other interactant, and 2.5 percent benefited some third party (Camden, Motley, and Wilson 1984).

In the kind of close relationships focused on in this text, lying centers on four elements: the partner, the deceiver or teller, the relationship, or the issue (see Table 5.1, Metts 1989).

CAN A "LIE" NOT BE A LIE?

Consider the person who arrives wearing a new outfit, looking pretty awful. The person asks you what you think of the new look. There seem to be several options. First, you can say something ambiguous, such as that it sure is different—even unique—something quite unlike anything you have ever seen before. Second, you might, in a burst of total candor, say it is the worst outfit you have ever seen. Third, you might say that the outfit is highly becoming, even attractive, and suits the person very well. The first response, although technically and literally evasive and noncommittal, actually leads the other person to conclude the opposite of what you mean; this is lying. The second response is truthful but insensitive and cruel. And the third is dishonest. Although at the time you make the comment it may seem kind, on future occasions (if, for example, the person were to dress this way for an important job interview or date), it could turn out to be the cruelest of all responses.

Table 5.1 Lying in Close Relationships	
FOCUS AND MOTIVATION	EXAMPLES
Partner-focused reasons claim that the partner's attitudes or behaviors motivated the lying.	"I knew he would be terribly hurt if I told him." "I felt she couldn't take the truth at the time; she was under so much stress."
Teller-focused reasons claim that the teller's desire to protect his or her image motivated the lying.	"If I told him I had money, I would never get it back." "If she found out, she would make life miserable for us."
Relationship-focused reasons claim that the desire to maintain a stable relationship motivated the lying.	"I was afraid it would start a fight." "I think he would have just broken up with me."
Issue-focused reasons claim that the privateness or insignificance of the issue motivated the lying.	"I never told her about my 'fling' because it was only a one-night stand." "It was my mistake and not really any of his business."

If your primary concern is the person asking the question, you must consider what is really being sought. If the question asks you to evaluate the new outfit, you should focus on this and give your honest opinion in as kind and responsive (but truthful) a manner as possible. Thus, instead of saying, "It makes you look old and sickly," you can more appropriately say, "I think you would look much better in something different, something more colorful." If, however, the question about the outfit is a way to get positive stroking, you should address that and provide the kind of positive response the person is seeking. Here is one of the many instances in which specific content is not important; the psychological need of the person is the primary concern, and it is this that you want to address. You are therefore not lying when you say, for example, "You look good," because the real question asked you to say something positive, and you have done so with your compliment.

Ethical?

- Is it ever ethical to lie? If so, under what conditions? Under what conditions is lying unethical? Is it ethical to lie, for example, at an interview, in response to an unlawful (say, a racist or sexist) question?
- Are there conditions under which the *failure* to lie would be unethical?
- Is it ethical to lie in order to achieve some "greater good"? For example, would it be ethical to lie to save a person's life? To help a person out of a severe depression? To achieve a deserved promotion?

How is the U.S. military's policy of "don't ask, don't tell" in regard to gays and lesbians in the military a reflection of the attitude of the general society? Does this attitude have a counterpart in racist and sexist policies of some organizations and institution?

- Is it ethical for adults to tell children fables (for example, about Santa Claus and the tooth fairy) and have them believe the stories as truth?
- What ethical guidelines would you propose for lying?

FEAR AND EMOTIONAL APPEALS

One of the most widely discussed ethical issues in communication is the legitimacy of appeals based on fear and emotion. Although this topic is frequently focused on public and mass communication situations, it is even more applicable to interpersonal encounters.

Consider the mother who does not want her teenage son or daughter of 18 or 19 to move out of the house. Depending on her ingenuity, the mother might focus on instilling fear in the teenager for his or her own well-being ("Who'll care for you? You won't eat right. You'll get sick") or, more frequently, for the mother's well-being. The caricature of a mother having a heart attack at the first sign of a child's leaving is probably played out every day, in various forms, throughout the world. But whether a heart attack or some other gross difficulty is invoked, the appeal is built on fear. Obviously, few children want to be the cause of their mother's suffering. It is interesting to note that in our culture the father is not permitted to use his own suffering as an argument. Rather, his task is to show the children how much their actions will hurt their mother. Some parents are quite adept at using fear appeals and will do so to discourage anything from smoking to premarital sex to interracial dating. The list is endless.

Similar issues are raised when we consider the use of emotional appeals in attempting to change attitudes, beliefs, and behaviors. The case of a real estate broker appealing to your desire for status, a friend who wants a favor appealing to your desire for social approval, and a salesperson appealing to your desire for sexual rewards are all familiar examples. The question they all raise is simply, "Is this type of appeal justified?"

Many arguments can be advanced on both sides of the issue. The "everyone is doing it" argument is perhaps the most familiar, but it does not address the question of whether such appeals are justified. Another argument is that because people are composites of logic and emotion, effective appeals must be based in part on emotions. Again, however, this does not answer the question of whether emotional appeals are ethical; it merely states that they are effective.

Fear, Emotion, and Choice

The question of fear and emotional appeals is not as easy to fit into the issue of freedom of choice as is lying. The reason is that it is difficult to determine at what point the use of fear or emotion prevents certain choices from being exercised. Furthermore, we must recognize that both parties have the right to free choice. Some people might argue that the parents of the teenager who wishes to leave home are unethical when they force the teenager to choose between leaving home and hurting them on the one hand and staying home and pleasing them on the other. To many this would not be *free* choice. Similarly, a group that withdraws social support from an individual unless he or she does as they wish may be charged with unethically limiting the individual's freedom of choice. Although it is true that the teenager and the deviant group member are physically free to do as they wish, they may be emotionally and psychologically pressured to the point where they are not free in any meaningful sense.

On the other hand, it might be argued that the teenager's parents also have rights and that they have the specific right to display their emotional pain should the child wish to leave home. Similarly, it might be argued that the group members have the right to withdraw their social support from an individual if they so wish.

It is not easy to preserve the freedom of choice for both sides of a conflict and at the same time not allow one side to unduly restrict the other's freedoms. Part of the difficulty is due to the fact that we are on the outside looking in rather than actually participating in the conflict. It seems that the parents have the right to show their hurt if this is their honest emotional response to the child's leaving home. However, if this display is a technique designed to instill guilt in the child and to prevent the child from exercising certain options, their behavior must be judged unethical. Similarly, group members have a right to withdraw their support if they decide that they no longer wish to associate with an individual because of deviant behavior. However, if they are withdrawing social support to "force" the individual to conform and consequently limit the individual's freedom of choice to certain options, the group members are behaving unethically. In these situations, it is only the participants (the parents and the group members, in these examples) who can decide if they are acting ethically or unethically, because only they can know their true motives.

Ethical?

- Is it ethical for parents to use fear appeals to dissuade their teenage children from engaging in sexual relationships?
- Is it ethical to feign crying in order to win an argument and get your way?
- Is it ethical to use fear appeals to prevent sexually transmitted diseases? Is it ethical to use the same appeals if the motive is to sell condoms?
- What ethical guidelines would you propose for the use of fear and emotional appeals?

CENSORING MESSAGES AND INTERACTIONS

Throughout your life, the messages you receive are censored. When you were very young, your parents censored certain television programs, magazines, and movies—perhaps even records—that they thought inappropriate, usually because they were either too sexually explicit or too violent. Currently, the appropriateness or legitimacy of advertising certain products on television, most notably condoms, is being debated. Many would have this material censored.

Similarly, when we were young, our parents may have encouraged us to play with certain children and not to play with others. Sometimes these decisions were based on the character of the other children. Sometimes they were based on the racial, religious, or national background of the would-be friends. Today, the most obvious instances in which interactions are prevented are those involving interracial marriage and homosexual relations. These prohibitions prevent certain people from interacting in the manner in which they choose. If an interracial couple wish to marry, they must be careful in choosing where the ceremony is performed and where they will settle. Interracial couples run into difficulty finding housing, employment, and, most significantly, acceptance into a community. Gay men and lesbians encounter the same difficulty, and consequently many are forced to live "straight" lives—at least on the surface.

If, for example, you run a business, should you have the right to refuse someone a job because he or she is married to an individual of another race or has an affectional orientation different from yours? And if you do have the right to choose your employees on the basis of such preferences, do you still retain the rights to protection by the law that the society as a whole has granted to everyone?

Lesbians and gay men are currently prevented from holding jobs as teachers, police officers, and fire fighters in many states. These discriminatory laws are not terribly effective, but this is not the issue. The relative ineffectiveness of such prohibitions should not blind us to the social realities that these laws incorporate. What should be considered is that the gay man or lesbian cannot work under their own identity but only if they mask themselves as heterosexuals. The military policy of "don't ask, don't tell" is a perfect example of how the society as a whole forces certain of its citizens to hide their true selves. Is society ethical when it requires such concealment of identity?

Ethical?

- Is it ethical to try to persuade your friends to avoid interacting with Tom and Lisa because you think they are immoral? Because you are jealous of them? Because you know they are plotting to commit a series of robberies, and you don't want your friends implicated? Because you feel they will have a bad influence on your friends?
- Is it ethical for a group to ostracize a person on the basis of sex? Race? Religion? Affectional orientation? Physical condition? Financial condition? Drug behavior? Criminal connections?
- Is it ethical for a child to turn in his or her parents to the police for alcohol abuse? For smoking marijuana? For using cocaine? For child abuse?
- Is it ethical to forcibly prevent a friend who has had too much to drink (in your opinion) from driving? To forcibly prevent a friend from riding in a car driven by someone who has just smoked marijuana?
- What ethical guidelines would you propose for the censorship of interactions?

GOSSIPING

There can be no doubt that we spend a great deal of time gossiping. According to the *Random House Dictionary,* gossip is "idle talk or rumor, especially about the personal or private affairs of others." It occurs when two people talk about a third party and profit in some way—for example, to hear more gossip, gain social status or control, have fun, or cement social bonds (Rosnow 1977, Miller and Wilcox 1986). Gossip is an inevitable part of our daily interactions, and to advise anyone to refrain from gossiping would be absurd—no one would listen, and if they did, it would eliminate one of the most frequently employed and enjoyed forms of communication. Clearly, we are not going to stop talking about the personal and private affairs of others. And, let us be equally clear, others are not going to stop talking about our personal and private affairs. Few of us would actually want others to do so; it would be testimony that our lives were too dull and that our friends and associates were indifferent to our feelings, thoughts, and behaviors.

Nevertheless, gossip does create serious problems when not managed fairly, and we need to direct our attention to this management. When we tell someone something about our feelings for some third party, we normally expect that the conversation will be held in confidence; we do not expect it to be relayed to others, especially not to the individual discussed. If we had wanted it relayed, we probably would have done so ourselves. When such a conversation is relayed without our knowledge or approval, we feel, and rightly so, that our confidence has been betrayed. Consider the following fairly typical incident: You're talking with a friend and mention that a mutual friend, Leslie, should really devote more attention to dressing properly. You also note that you would like to invite Leslie to your home to meet your parents, but Leslie's constant use of vulgar language might embarrass your parents and make the evening difficult. Surely, this is not a savage attack on Leslie and may even have been said with a certain degree of kindness. But consider what happens when your "friend" tells Leslie that you said Leslie doesn't know how to dress and is embarrassing because of a filthy mouth.

The effect of such an exchange is to create hostility toward all—toward you for making the original observations and toward the person for repeating them. The person

How do you feel about being the subject of gossip? What would you like people to say about you in their gossiping? What would you particularly dislike?

talked about is probably going to act in a less friendly manner or perhaps respond in kind by repeating personal conversations to others. The net result is that the situation snowballs until what may have been an innocent remark becomes the cause of a broken friendship.

Quite often, the person who repeats such remarks is, perhaps subconsciously, seeking to create friction between the two individuals. This motivation is usually recognized, sooner or later, by all parties involved. To claim, as some people do, that they had no idea that you did not want anything repeated is absurd. It is usually obvious from the context what should and should not be held in confidence. We have little trouble deciding when we've said something in confidence, and it is not unreasonable to expect others to be equally discerning.

GOSSIP AND ETHICS

Gossip also has an ethical dimension. In some instances gossip is immoral. In *Secrets* (1983), Sissela Bok identifies three kinds of gossip that she considers unethical. First, it is unethical to reveal information that you have promised to keep secret. In situations in which that is impossible (Bok offers the example of a teenager who confides a suicide plan), the information should be revealed only to those required to know it and not to the world at large.

Second, gossip is unethical when we know it to be false and pass it on nevertheless. When we try to deceive our listeners by spreading gossip we know to be false, our communications are unethical.

Third, gossip is unethical when it invades the privacy to which everyone has a right. Invasive gossip is especially unethical when the gossip can hurt the individual involved. These conditions are not easy to identify in any given instance, but they do provide us with excellent starting points for asking ourselves whether or not a discussion of another person is ethical.

Adopt a principle of confidentiality. A good one to begin with is this: keep confidential all private conversations about third parties. Messages that begin with "He said . . . " or "She thinks that you . . . " should be automatically suspect as potential violators of confidentiality. Remember, too, the principle of irreversibility—you cannot take messages back; once you say something, you cannot "uncommunicate" it.

Ethical?

- Under what conditions would revealing another person's secrets be ethical? Under what conditions would this be unethical? Are there times when the failure to reveal such secrets would be unethical?
- You are in a conversation and observe the following: Ricky and Lyn are discussing Terry. Ricky makes a number of statements about Terry that you know to be false. Is it ethical for you to say nothing? Does it matter whether these statements about Terry are positive or negative?
- Is it ethical for you to observe someone (without his or her knowledge) and report your observations to others? For example, would it be ethical to observe your communication professor on a date with a student or smoking marijuana and then report these observations back to your classmates?
- What ethical guidelines would you propose for revealing secrets?

Lying, using emotional and fear appeals, censoring messages and preventing interactions, and gossiping are not the only interpersonal issues that have an ethical dimension. But they should make you begin to consider the ethical dimensions of interpersonal communication and encourage you to develop your own system of interpersonal communication ethics.

SUMMARY: UNIT IN BRIEF		
Definition	**Ethical Communications**	**Unethical Communications**
Communication ethics: the moral principles governing communication; the right-wrong, moral-immoral dimension of communication	Communications that facilitate a person's freedom of choice by presenting accurate information (verbal or nonverbal) on which to base such choices	Communications that interfere with a person's freedom of choice by preventing the securing of information relevant to the choices to be made, for example: • lying • extreme fear and emotional appeal • censoring messages and interactions • gossiping

THINKING CRITICALLY ABOUT ETHICS IN INTERPERSONAL COMMUNICATION

1. How do you feel when someone lies to you? Does it depend on the type of lie? Does it depend on the reason for the lie? Does it depend on the person who tells the lie?
2. Under what conditions, if any, do you think that people should lie? That is, are there any situations in which the ethical or moral choice is to lie?
3. What television commercials or print advertisements use fear or emotional appeals? Are these appeals ethical? Are they effective?
4. Would you seek to censor any interactions of your romantic partner? Which types? Why?
5. In what types of gossip do you enjoy participating? What types make you uncomfortable? Why?
6. What is the single most popular topic of gossip among you and your friends?
7. Oscar Wilde once noted, "There is only one thing in the world worse than being talked about, and that is not being talked about." What do you think of this statement?
8. What is your ethical obligation if you see your best friend's spouse in a romantic liaison with another person? If you see two students cheating on an examination?
9. What is the single most important ethical principle by which you live?
10. How would you go about finding answers to the following questions?
    • Do satisfied couples have ethical systems that are more similar than those of dissatisfied couples?
    • How do other cultures view "ethical" and "unethical" communications?
    • Why do people gossip? How accurate is gossip?

EXPERIENTIAL VEHICLES

5.1 SOME ETHICAL ISSUES

This exercise is designed to raise only a few of the many possible questions about the ethics of interpersonal communication and to encourage you to think in concrete terms about some of the relevant issues. The purpose is not to persuade you to adopt a particular point of view but rather to prompt you to formulate your own.

The exercise consists of several cases, each of which raises a somewhat different ethical question. This exercise will probably work best if you respond to each of the cases individually and then discuss your decisions and their implications in groups of five or six or with the class as a whole.

The Right to Date? A teacher and a student have been dating for the past few months. Although the student was once in this teacher's class—where they met—they no longer have an academic connection. The school administrators have objected to this relationship and have affirmed that the teacher must break it off or leave the school. The teacher and student both claim that they have a right to make their own personal decisions and that their dating has nothing whatsoever to do with the fact that one is a teacher and one is a student at the same school. How do you feel about this situation? Would your feelings be influenced by the ages of the student and the teacher? For example, would it matter if the teacher were younger than the student? Significantly older than the student? Would the sex of the teacher and student matter?

Affirmative Action? A new faculty position in the communication department has become available, and ten candidates have applied. The candidates have been ranked from 1 (the most highly qualified) down to 10 (the least qualified) in order of merit based on their teaching experience, teaching ability, publications, and service to their previous colleges and communities. The slate of candidates is then submitted to a committee, of which you are a member, for final selection. Of this seven-person committee, three people argue for Candidate No. 1. Three other people argue for Candidate No. 4; they argue that there are too few women on the faculty and that because Candidate No. 4 is the highest-ranked woman, she should be offered the job. How would you vote? Would your vote be different if the highest-ranked woman was No. 2? If the highest-ranked woman was No. 10?

Freedom of Communication? A college committee on AIDS education has secured a number of educational materials that it wishes to make available to students and teachers for classroom use. These materials include explicit safe-sex videos and articles. The committee plans to set up TV monitors to show these videos in various public places around campus; the articles are to be distributed at similar sites. The committee also plans to have a vendor install condom dispensers in the men's and women's rest rooms. A parents' group has objected, arguing that it is not the school's place to distribute materials or information that may be in conflict with their religious or family values. How do you feel about these issues? If these issues were submitted to a vote, where would you stand?

What arguments would you use to support your position? Would you feel the same way if it were a high school? A junior high school? An elementary school?

Friendship Obligations? You have been friends with Pat ever since elementary school. Last year, Pat became engaged to Chris. Last night, you saw Chris in a romantic encounter with a stranger. You do not want to interfere with the relationship between Pat and Chris, yet you wonder if you have an obligation to Pat to reveal what you have learned. Do you?

5.2 THE ETHICS OF ANSWERING QUESTIONS

Here are questions that others might ask you; all the questions request information that you are presumed to have. For each question, there are extenuating circumstances that may militate against your responding fully or even truthfully. Consider each question and the mitigating circumstances (these are noted as the **Thoughts** you are thinking as you consider your possible answer). How do you respond?

Question [A friend asks your opinion] How do I look?
Thought *You look terrible, but I don't want to hurt your feelings.*

Question [A romantic partner asks] Do you love me?
Thought *I don't want to commit myself, but I don't want to end the relationship, either. I want to allow the relationship to progress further before making any commitment.*

Question [An interviewer says] You seem a bit old for this type of job. How old are you?
Thought *I am old for this job, but I need it anyway. Further, it's really illegal for the interviewer to ask my age. I don't want to turn the interviewer off, because I really need this job. Yet I don't want to reveal my age either.*

Question [A 15-year-old asks] Was I adopted? Who are my real parents?
Thought *Yes, you were adopted, but I fear that you will look for your biological parents and will be hurt when you find that they are drug dealers and murderers.*

UNIT 6

Effectiveness in Interpersonal Communication

AFTER COMPLETING THIS UNIT, YOU SHOULD BE ABLE TO:

1. Explain the concept of effectiveness in interpersonal communication
2. Explain mindfulness, flexibility, cultural sensitivity, and metacommunicational ability as they apply to interpersonal effectiveness
3. Define *openness, empathy, supportiveness, positiveness,* and *equality* as they relate to interpersonal communication effectiveness
4. Define *confidence, immediacy, interaction management, expressiveness,* and *other-orientation* as they relate to interpersonal communication effectiveness

---

Your interpersonal communication, like any of your behaviors, can vary from extremely effective to extremely ineffective. Still, no interpersonal encounter is ever a total failure or a total success; each could have been worse and each could have been better.

Interpersonal skills exist on two levels. On the specific level, there are the skills of being open or empathic, for example. These skills help you express your openness and empathy when you wish. On a higher level—a metaskill level—there are skills for regulating the specific skills. These metaskills—for example, flexibility and cultural sensitivity—help you regulate your openness and empathy as the specific situation warrants. For example, in being open or empathic, you need to do so with flexibility and with sensitivity to the specific cultural context. Both types of skills are essential to interpersonal effectiveness.

The skills identified here were derived from research conducted primarily over the last 25 years by a large number of interpersonal communication researchers. Table 6.1 identifies just a few of the many models of effectiveness available. Although the models differ, there is also much similarity. Note that all researchers agree that interpersonal effectiveness consists not of one single quality but of several qualities that must work together. Note also that the models are a mixture of specific qualities (openness, empathy) and more general qualities, such as flexibility and appropriateness. These general qualities (what we identify as metaskills or skills about skills) oversee or regulate the application of the specific qualities. For example, in being open or empathic, you need to do so with flexibility and appropriateness to the specific situation in which you find yourself.

SKILLS ABOUT SKILLS

Four metaskills will help you regulate your use of the more specific skills: mindfulness, flexibility, cultural sensitivity, and metacommunication.

Table 6.1
Competency Models[1]

THE INTERPERSONAL COMMUNICATION BOOK	GIBB (1961)	HART & BURKS (1972)	BOCHNER & KELLY (1974)	WEIMANN (1977)	SPITZBERG & HECHT (1984)	RUBIN & NEVINS (1988)
Skills about skills: mindfulness, flexibility, cultural sensitivity, metacommunication Openness Empathy Supportiveness Positiveness Equality Confidence Immediacy Interaction management Expressiveness Other-orientation	Description rather than evaluation Problem orientation rather than control Spontaneity rather than strategy Empathy rather than neutrality Equality rather than superiority Provisionalism rather than certainty	Acceptance of personal complexity Flexibility Interaction consciousness Appreciation of the communicability of ideas Tolerance of different ways to communicate	Empathy Descriptiveness Owning feelings Self-disclosure Behavioral flexibility	Affiliation-support Social relaxation Empathy Behavioral flexibility Interaction management	Absence of social anxiety Immediacy Interaction management Expressiveness Other-orientation	Self-disclosure Empathy Social relaxation Assertiveness Interaction management Altercentrism (other-orientation) Expressiveness Supportiveness Immediacy Environmental control

[1]The characteristics of effectiveness identified in this unit and in the table under *The Interpersonal Communication Book* come primarily from the research of Bochner and Kelly (1974) and from Spitzberg and Hecht (1984) but also make use of the insights of Rubin and Nevins (1988), Weimann (1977), Gibb (1963), Hart and Burks (1972) and Hart, Carlson, and Eadie (1980). In interpersonal communication research, a distinction is often drawn between competence and effectiveness. Along with Spitzberg and Cupach (1989), I use the terms interchangeably. "In general terms," note these researchers, "interpersonal competence typically is defined as the ability of a person to interact effectively with other people."

MINDFULNESS

After you have learned a skill or rule, you may have a tendency to apply it without thinking, or "mindlessly"—without, for example, considering the novel aspects of a situation. For instance, after learning the skills of active listening, many will use them in response to all situations. Some of these responses will be appropriate, but others will prove inappropriate and ineffective. In interpersonal and even in small-group communication (Elmes and Gemmill 1990), apply the skills **mindfully** (Langer 1989).

Langer (1989) offers several suggestions for increasing mindfulness:

* Create and re-create categories. See an object, event, or person as belonging to a wide variety of categories. Avoid storing in memory an image of a person, for example, with only one specific label; it will be difficult to recategorize the image later.
* Be open to new information, even if it contradicts your most firmly held stereotypes.
* Be open to different points of view. This will help you avoid the tendency to blame outside forces for your negative behaviors ("that test was unfair") and internal forces for the negative behaviors of others ("Pat didn't study," "Pat isn't very bright"). Be willing to see your own and others' behaviors from a variety of perspectives.
* Beware of relying too heavily on first impressions, what is sometimes called "premature cognitive commitment" (Chanowitz and Langer 1981, Langer 1989). Treat your first impressions as tentative, as hypotheses.

FLEXIBILITY

Respond to each of the following statements according to the following scale:

A = almost always true
B = frequently true
C = sometimes true
D = infrequently true
E = almost never true

_____ 1. People should be frank and spontaneous in conversation.

_____ 2. When angry, a person should say nothing rather than say something he or she will be sorry for later.

_____ 3. When talking to your friends, you should adjust your remarks to suit them.

_____ 4. It is better to speak your gut feelings than to beat around the bush.

_____ 5. If people would open up to each other the world would be better off.

The preferred answer to all five of these statements, taken from research on rhetorical sensitivity, is C, and this underscores the importance of flexibility (Hart and Burks 1972; Hart, Carlson, and Eadie 1980) in all interpersonal encounters. Although we provide general principles for effective interpersonal communication, be flexible when applying them, and be sensitive to the unique factors of every situation. Thus, you may need to be frank and spontaneous when talking with a close friend about your feelings, but you may not want to be so open when talking with your grandmother about the dinner she prepared that you disliked.

CULTURAL SENSITIVITY

In applying the skills for interpersonal effectiveness, be sensitive to the cultural differences among people. What may prove effective for upper-income people working in the IBM subculture of Boston or New York may prove ineffective for lower-income people working as fruit pickers in Florida or California. What works in Japan may not work in Mexico. The direct eye contact that signals immediacy in most of the United States may be considered rude or too intrusive in Hispanic and other cultures. The empathy that most Americans welcome may be uncomfortable for the average Korean (Yun 1976). The specific skills discussed below are considered generally effective in the United States and among most people living in the United States. Do note, however, that these skills and the ways in which we use them verbally or nonverbally are specific to the general U.S. culture.

Here are suggestions for communicating cultural sensitivity (Barna 1985; Ruben 1985).

- Be careful not to ignore differences between yourself and people who are culturally different from you. When you assume similarities and ignore differences, you implicitly communicate to others that your ways are the right ways and that their ways are not important to you. Talk about religion provides a good example. So often people assume that the beliefs of their religion (concerning, for example, redemption, penance, marriage and divorce, abortion, or the value of good deeds)—perhaps because these beliefs are so fundamental to their way of thinking—are held by everyone.
- Be careful not to ignore differences among the culturally different group. When you ignore these differences, you are stereotyping; that is, you are assuming that all persons covered by the same label (in this case, a national or racial label) are the same.
- Be careful not to ignore differences in meaning, even when using the same words. Consider, for example, the differences in meaning of such words as "woman" for an American and a Saudi Arabian, "religion" for a born-again Christian and an atheist, and "lunch" for a Chinese rice farmer and a Wall Street executive. Moreover, in the case of nonverbal messages, the potential differences seem even greater. To an American, holding up two fingers to make a V signifies victory. For certain South Americans, however, it is an obscene gesture.
- Avoid violating cultural rules and customs. Each culture has its own rules for communication that identify what is and what is not appropriate. Thus, for example, in U.S. culture you would call a person three or four days in advance if you wished to make a date. In certain Asian cultures, you might call the person's parents weeks or even months in advance. In some cultures, people show respect by avoiding direct eye contact, whereas in others this same eye avoidance would signal lack of interest. A good example of a series of rules for an extremely large and important culture that many people do not know appears in the accompany-

---

Ten Commandments for Communicating With People With Disabilities

1. Speak directly rather than through a companion or sign language interpreter who may be present.

2. Offer to shake hands when introduced. People with limited hand use or an artificial limb can usually shake hands and offering the left hand is an acceptable greeting.

3. Always identify yourself and others who may be with you when meeting someone with a visual impairment. When conversing in a group, remember to identify the person to whom you are speaking.

4. If you offer assistance, wait until the offer is accepted. Then listen or ask for instructions.

5. Treat adults as adults. Address people who have disabilities by their first names only when extending that same familiarity to all others. Never patronize people in wheelchairs by patting them on the head or shoulder.

6. Do not lean against or hang on someone's wheelchair. Bear in mind that disabled people treat their chairs as extensions of their bodies.

7. Listen attentively when talking with people who have difficulty speaking and wait for them to finish. If necessary, ask short questions that require short answers, a nod or shake of the head. Never pretend to understand if you are having difficulty doing so. Instead repeat what you have understood and allow the person to respond.

8. Place yourself at eye level when speaking with someone in a wheelchair or on crutches.

9. Tap a hearing-impaired person on the shoulder or wave your hand to get his or her attention. Look directly at the person and speak clearly, slowly and expressively to establish if the person can read your lips. If so, try to face the light source and keep hands, cigarettes and food away from your mouth when speaking.

10. Relax. Don't be embarrassed if you happen to use common expressions such as "See you later," or "Did you hear about this?" that seem to relate to a person's disability.

Source: United Cerebral Palsy Associations, Inc.
"Ten Commandments for Communicating with People with Disabilities," *The New York Times,* June 7,1992. Copyright © 1992 by the New York Times. Reprinted by permissions.

---

ing "Ten Commandments for Communicating with People with Disabilities." Have you seen any violations of these suggestions? Were you explicitly taught any of these principles?

• Be careful not to evaluate differences negatively. Consider, for example, the simple act of spitting (LaBarre 1964). In the United States, men are (stereotypically) not supposed to show emotions and display affection; nor are men expected to rely on intuition rather than logic. In Iran, however, men are expected to show emotion and to rely on intuition. Iranian women, in contrast, are expected to be practical and logical rather than intuitive (Hall 1959).

Effectiveness in intercultural communication requires that we be (Kim 1991):

• *open* to new ideas and to differences among people
• *flexible* in ways of communicating and in adapting to the communications of the culturally different
• *tolerant* of other attitudes, values, and ways of doing things
• *creative* in seeking varied ways to communicate

These qualities—along with some knowledge of the other culture and the general skills of effectiveness—"should enable a person to approach each intercultural encounter with the psychological posture of an interested learner . . . and to strive for the communication outcomes that are as effective as possible under a given set of relational and situational constraints" (Kim 1991).

METACOMMUNICATIONAL ABILITY

Much of our talk concerns people, objects, and events in the world. But we also talk about our talk. We **metacommunicate;** that is, we communicate about our communication. Our interpersonal effectiveness often hinges on this ability to metacommunicate. Let's say that someone says something positive but in a negative way; for example, the person says, "Yes, I think you did . . . a good job," but shows no enthusiasm and avoids eye contact. You are faced with several alternatives. You may respond to the message as positive or as negative.

A third alternative, however, is to talk about the message and say something like, "I'm not sure I understand whether you're pleased or displeased with what I did. You said you were pleased, but I detect dissatisfaction in your voice. Am I wrong?" In this way, you may avoid lots of misunderstandings.

Here are a few suggestions for increasing your metacommunicational effectiveness:

* *Give clear feedforward.* This will help the other person get a general picture of the message that will follow; feedforward provides a kind of schema that makes information processing and learning easier.
* *Confront contradictory or inconsistent messages.* At the same time, explain messages of your own that may appear inconsistent to your listener.
* *Explain the feelings that go with the thoughts.* Often people communicate only the thinking part of their message, with the result that listeners are not able to appreciate the other parts of the meaning.
* *Paraphrase your own complex messages.* Similarly, to check on your understanding of another's message, paraphrase what you think the other person means and ask whether you are accurate.
* *Ask questions.* If you have doubts about another's meaning, don't assume; instead, ask.
* *Talk about your talk only to gain an understanding of the other person's thoughts and feelings.* Avoid substituting talk about talk for talk about a specific problem.

As the characteristics of interpersonal effectiveness are reviewed, be mindful, flexible, and culturally sensitive, and remember that you can talk about your talk to further clarify meaning.

A HUMANISTIC MODEL OF INTERPERSONAL EFFECTIVENESS

In the humanistic (sometimes referred to metaphorically as "soft") approach to interpersonal effectiveness presented here—an approach that draws on the early theorizing of a number of researchers (see Table 6.1)—five general qualities are considered: openness, empathy, supportiveness, positiveness, and equality. In general, these qualities foster meaningful, honest, and satisfying interactions. This approach begins with the qualities that philosophers and humanists feel define superior human relationships, and from these generalizations it derives specific behaviors that should characterize effective interpersonal communication.

OPENNESS

Openness refers to at least three aspects of interpersonal communication. First, it refers to your willingness to self-disclose—to reveal information about yourself that might normally be kept hidden—provided that such disclosure is appropriate (see Unit 8). Openness shown by only one person is usually insufficient. For interpersonal communication to be effective, it must be, as Barbara Montgomery (1981) observes, **bilateral:** "the exchange of personal, private information must be reciprocal."

Second, openness refers to a willingness to react honestly to the messages of others. Silent, uncritical, and immovable psychiatrists may be of some help in a clinical situation, but they are generally boring conversationalists. Usually we want people to react openly to what we say, and we feel we have a right to expect this. We demonstrate openness by responding spontaneously and without subterfuge to the communications and the feedback of others.

Third, openness refers to the "owning" of feelings and thoughts. To be open in this sense is to acknowledge that the feelings and thoughts we express are ours and that we bear the responsibility for them; we do not try to shift the responsibility for our feelings to others. For example, consider these comments:

1. Your behavior was grossly inconsiderate.
2. Everyone thought your behavior was grossly inconsiderate.
3. I was really disturbed when you told my father he was an old man.

Comments 1 and 2 do not demonstrate ownership of feelings. In comment 1, the speaker accuses the listener of being inconsiderate without assuming any responsibility for the judgment. In comment 2, the speaker assigns responsibility to the convenient but vague "everyone" and again assumes none of the responsibility. In comment 3, however, we see a drastic difference. Note that here the speaker is taking responsibility for his or her own feelings ("*I* was really disturbed").

When we own our messages, we use I-messages instead of you-messages. Instead of saying, "You make me feel so stupid when you ask what everyone else thinks but don't ask my opinion," the person who owns his or her feelings says, "I feel stupid when you ask everyone else what they think but don't ask me." When we own our feelings and thoughts—when we use I-messages—we say, in effect, "This is how *I* feel," "This is how *I* see the situation," and "This is what *I* think," with the *I* always emphasized. Instead of saying, "This discussion is useless," one would say, "*I'm* bored by this discussion," "*I* want to talk more about myself," or any other such statement that includes a reference to the fact that *I* am making an evaluation and not describing objective reality. By doing so, we make it explicit that our feelings result from the interaction between what is going on outside our skin (what others say, for example) and what is going on inside our skin (our preconceptions, attitudes, and prejudices, for example).

EMPATHY

Perhaps the most difficult communication quality to achieve is the ability to empathize with another person. The term **empathy** was derived from Greek to translate the German word *Einfuhlung,* meaning "feeling with." To **empathize** with someone is to feel as that person feels, to experience what the other is experiencing from that person's point of view without losing your own identity. To **sympathize,** in contrast, is to feel *for* the person—to feel sorry for the person, for example. To empathize is to feel *as* the person feels, to walk in the same shoes, to feel the same feelings in the same way. Empathy, then, enables you to understand, emotionally as well as intellectually, what another person is experiencing.

Of course, empathy will mean little if you do not communicate this empathic understanding to the other person. For example, consider these responses made to a friend who is being expelled from college:

1. Getting thrown out of college isn't the worst thing in the world. You can always go part-time and eventually get back full-time. So cheer up and smile. You've got a great smile, you know.
2. I can feel what you're going through. I got thrown out of college, too, and I, too, felt like a failure.

Both responses are well-intentioned; both people are trying to respond appropriately and sensitively to a friend. In statement 1, however, the speaker fails to empathize. In fact, the speaker makes no attempt to feel or even acknowledge what the friend is feeling. In statement 2, the speaker tries to understand, to share the friend's feelings, and to communicate this shared feeling.

Achieving Empathy   Should you wish to achieve empathy, your first step is to avoid evaluating the other person's behaviors. If you evaluate them as right or wrong, good or bad, you will see the behaviors through these labels and will fail to see a great deal more that might not be consistent with them. Therefore, resist the temptation to evaluate, to judge, to interpret, to criticize. Focus, instead, on understanding.

Second, learn as much as you can about the other person's desires, experiences, abilities, fears, and so on. The more you know about a person, the more you will be able to see what that person sees and feel what that person feels. Try to understand the reasons and the motivations for the person's feelings.

Third, try to experience emotionally what the other person is feeling from his or her point of view. Playing the role of the other person in your mind (or even out loud) can help you see the world a little more as the other person does.

Communicating Empathy   Most people find it easier to communicate empathy in response to a person's positive statements (Heiskell and Rychiak 1986). So perhaps we have to exert special effort to communicate empathy for negative statements. We can do so both nonverbally and verbally. Here are a few suggestions for communicating empathy nonverbally:

- Express your active involvement with the other person through appropriate facial expressions and gestures.
- Focus your concentration; maintain eye contact, an attentive body posture, and physical closeness.
- Use touch if and as appropriate.

Jerry Authier and Kay Gustafson (1982) suggest several useful methods for communicating empathy verbally.

- Reflect back to the speaker the feelings (and their intensity) that you think are being experienced to help you to check on the accuracy of your perceptions and to show your desire to understand the speaker's feelings.

- Make tentative statements about what you think the person is feeling: for example, "I get the impression you're angry with your father" or "I hear anger in your voice."
- Use your own relevant self-disclosures to communicate your understanding of and involvement in what the other is experiencing.
- Address mixed messages in order to foster more open and honest communication, as in the following interaction:

ROBIN: How did you do on the exam?
KATHY: Oh, fine. I got a B. [*Looks down and sighs; speech is unusually slow.*]
ROBIN: You said you did fine, but the way you said it tells me it's not fine. You seem disappointed.

SUPPORTIVENESS

Supportiveness, a concept that owes much to the work of Jack Gibb (1961), is fostered by your being (1) descriptive rather than evaluative and (2) provisional rather than certain.

Descriptiveness   Consider the following sentence sets:

1A.   I can't wait to meet him.
1B.   He sure is great looking.
1C.   His hair is black and his eyes are green.

2A.   I'm sure glad we went on strike for this contract.
2B.   That contract was ideal for labor but will cripple management.
2C.   Workers got a 12 percent raise, more than at any other plant.

Note that the A and C sentences are descriptive. The A sentences describe one's own feelings; the C sentences describe the situation, the "reality." The B sentences, however—which are similar in form to the others—are evaluative. These sentences express the speaker's judgment or evaluation of a person or situation.

An atmosphere that is descriptive rather than evaluative leads to supportiveness. When we perceive a communication as being a request for information or a description of some event, we generally do not perceive it as threatening. We are not being challenged and have no need to defend ourselves. However, a communication that is judgmental or evaluative often leads us to become defensive, to back off, to erect some kind of barrier between ourselves and the evaluator.

This does not mean that all evaluative communications elicit a defensive response. People often respond to positive evaluations without defensiveness. Even here, however, note that if someone has the power, the knowledge, or the "right" to evaluate us in any way (even positively), it may lead us to feel uneasy and possibly defensive, perhaps anticipating that the next evaluation may not be as favorable.

In a similar way, negative evaluations do not always elicit a defensive response. The would-be actor who wants to improve technique often welcomes negative evaluations. Similarly, many students welcome negative evaluations when they feel they are constructive and lead to improvement in their ability, for example, to communicate or to operate a computer program. Generally, however, an evaluative atmosphere leads people to become more defensive than would a descriptive atmosphere.

In being descriptive, Toni Brougher (1982) advises that you do the following:

* Describe what happened ("I lost the promotion").
* Describe how you feel ("I feel miserable," "I feel I've failed").
* Explain how this relates to the other person ("Would you mind if we went into the city tonight? I need to forget the job and everything about it").

Further, Brougher advises that you:

* avoid accusations or blame ("Those Martians, they always stick together;" "I should have stayed with my old job and not listened to your brother's lousy advice").
* avoid negative evaluative terms ("Didn't your sister look *horrible* in that red dress?")
* avoid "preaching" ("Why can't you ever cook steak the way I like it?" "Why don't you learn something about word processing before you open your mouth?").

Provisionalism   Being **provisional** means having a tentative, open-minded attitude and a willingness both to hear opposing points of view and to change one's position if warranted. Such provisionalism, rather than unwavering certainty, helps to create a supportive atmosphere. Compare these two observations:

1. It's obvious. She just doesn't know the first thing about caring for a relationship. She's so egocentric.
2. It seems to me that she is having trouble in her relationship. Maybe she's too caught up in herself.

Note that sentence 1 claims certainty; it is definite and provides for no other possibility. Sentence 2 expresses essentially the same thought but with a tentativeness, a provisionalism. It is relatively difficult to say anything in response to sentence 1; it appears that everything that needs to be said has already been said. Sentence 2, however, invites comment, involvement, further discussion.

People who "know everything" and who always have a definite answer to any question are rarely appreciated. Such people are set in their ways and seem to tolerate no differences. They have arguments ready for any possible alternative attitude or belief. After a very short time, we become defensive with such people, and we hold back our own opinions rather than subject them to attack. But we open up with people who take a more provisional position, who are willing to change their minds when reasonable arguments are presented. With such people we feel equal.

POSITIVENESS

You can communicate positiveness in interpersonal communication in at least two ways: (1) stating positive attitudes and (2) complimenting the person with whom you interact.

Attitudes   **Attitudinal positiveness** in interpersonal communication refers to a positive regard for oneself, for the other person, and for the general communication situation. Your feelings (whether positive or negative) become clear during conversation and greatly influence the satisfaction (or dissatisfaction) you derive from the interaction. Negative feelings usually make communication more difficult and can contribute to its eventual breakdown.

Positiveness is seen most clearly in the way you phrase statements. Consider these two sets of sentences:

1A. I wish you wouldn't handle me so roughly.
1B. I really enjoy it when you're especially gentle.

2A. You look horrible in stripes.
2B. You look your best, I think, in solid colors.

The A sentences are negative; they are critical and will almost surely encourage an argument. The B sentences, in contrast, express the speaker's thought clearly but are phrased positively and should encourage cooperative responses.

Compliments Another aspect of positiveness is **stroking*** or **complimenting,** behavior that acknowledges the existence, and in fact the importance, of the other person; it is the antithesis of indifference. When you stroke someone, you acknowledge him or her as a person, as a significant human being. Stroking may be verbal, as in "I like you" or "I enjoy being with you," or nonverbal, such as a smile or a pat on the back.

Many people structure interpersonal encounters almost solely for the purpose of getting positively stroked. People may buy new clothes to get complimented, compliment associates so that the associates compliment back, do favors for people to receive thanks, associate with certain people because they are generous with their compliments, and so on. Some people even enter relationships because they hold the promise of frequent positive stroking.

EQUALITY

Equality is a peculiar characteristic. In any situation, there is probably some inequality. One person will be smarter, richer, better looking, or more athletic. No two people are absolutely equal in all respects. Despite this inequality, interpersonal communication is generally considered more effective when the atmosphere is one of equality, at least in the United States. (In other cultures—in Japan, for example—where status differences greatly influence interpersonal interactions, this presumption of equality would not hold.)

Compare these examples:

1A. When will you learn to phone for reservations? Must I do everything?
1B. One of us should phone for reservations. Do you want me to do it, or do you want to do it?

2A. When the hell are you going to fix this wallpaper? It's coming down on my head!
2B. This wallpaper is coming down on my head. How about we stay home tonight and try to fix it together?

In both examples, the A sentences lack equality; one person demands compliance and the other is ordered to do something. Questions such as these encourage defensiveness, resentment, and hostility. They provoke arguments rather than solve problems. In the B

---

* In the literature of transactional analysis, stroking may be positive (as described here) or negative. Both types of stroking acknowledge the importance of the person. Here, however, the term is used in its more popular usage as a positive expression.

sentences, there is equality—an explicitly stated desire to work together to address a specific problem. As a general rule, requests (especially courteous ones) communicate equality; demands (especially discourteous ones) communicate superiority.

In an interpersonal relationship characterized by equality, disagreement and conflict are seen as attempts to understand inevitable differences rather than as opportunities to put down the other person. Disagreements are viewed as ways of solving problems rather than of winning points, getting one's way, or proving oneself superior to the other. Equality does not require that you accept and approve of all the other person's behaviors. Some behaviors are self-destructive or have negative consequences for others, and these may, of course, be challenged—again, out of concern for the other person and for the relationship.

If you wish to communicate equality, the following suggestions should prove useful:

- Avoid "should" and "ought" statements that signal an unequal relationship. For example, avoid statements such as "You really should call your mother more often" or "You should learn to speak up." These statements put the listener in a one-down position (see Unit 2).

- Avoid interrupting; it signals that what you have to say is more important than what the other person is saying.

- Acknowledge the other person's contributions before you express your own. Expressions such as "I see," "I understand," or "That's right" communicate that what the other person has said has been received and understood.

- Avoid correcting or amending another's messages. Limit expressions such as "I think what you're trying to say is . . . " or "That's not exactly right; actually, what happened was. . . ." Statements such as these signal an unequal relationship and often embarrass or "put down" the other person.

A PRAGMATIC MODEL OF INTERPERSONAL EFFECTIVENESS

A pragmatic or behavioral (sometimes referred to metaphorically as "hard") approach to interpersonal effectiveness focuses on specific behaviors that a speaker or listener should use to gain his or her desired outcome. This model, too, offers five qualities of effectiveness: confidence, immediacy, interaction management, expressiveness, and other-orientation (Spitzberg and Hecht 1984; Spitzberg and Cupach 1989). This approach derives from the more recent pragmatic approach to communication articulated by such writers as Paul Watzlawick (Watzlawick, Beavin, and Jackson 1967; Watzlawick 1977), William Lederer (1984), Don Jackson (Lederer and Jackson 1968), and others (see Spitzberg and Cupach 1989). This approach starts from specific skills that research finds to be effective in interpersonal communication, then groups these specific skills into general classes of behavior (for example, interaction management skills, other-orientation skills).

CONFIDENCE

The effective communicator has social **confidence**; any anxiety that is present is not readily perceived by others. There is instead an ease with the other person and with the communication situation generally. Everyone has some communication apprehension or shyness (see Unit 9), but the effective interpersonal communicator controls it so that it is not a source of discomfort and does not interfere with communication.

The socially confident communicator is relaxed (not rigid), flexible (not locked into one or two vocal ranges or body movements), and controlled (not shaky or awkward). Researchers find that a relaxed posture communicates a sense of control, superior status, and power (Spitzberg and Cupach 1984, 1989). Tenseness, rigidity, and discomfort, on the other hand, signal a lack of self-control, which in turn signals an inability to control one's environment or other people and gives an impression of being under the power and control of an outside force or another person.

After analyzing the results of a series of five studies, Amerigo Farina concluded (Jones et al. 1984, 48): "Whether male or female, ex-mental patient, or average person, a nervous and tense individual was disliked and unequivocally rejected by the workers. The consistency and strength of these findings are noteworthy, and we believe they are in keeping with most people's intuition."

Here are a few additional suggestions for communicating confidence:

- Take the initiative in introducing yourself to others and in introducing topics of conversation. Taking the initiative will help you communicate confidence and control over the situation.
- Use open-ended questions to involve the other person in the interaction (as opposed to questions that merely ask for a yes or no answer).
- Use "you-statements"—statements that refer directly to the other person, such as "Do you agree?" or "How do you feel about that?"—to signal your personal attention to the speaker. This particular feature, incidentally, has been shown to increase men's attractiveness to women.

IMMEDIACY

Immediacy refers to the joining of the speaker and listener, the creation of a sense of togetherness, of oneness. The communicator demonstrating immediacy conveys a sense of interest and attention, a liking for and an attraction to the other person. People respond to language that is immediate more favorably than to language that is not. Immediacy joins speaker and listener; nonimmediacy separates them.

Nonverbally, you can communicate immediacy in several ways:

- Maintain appropriate eye contact and limit looking around at others.
- Maintain a physical closeness that suggests psychological closeness.
- Use a direct and open body posture by, for example, arranging your body to keep others further away.
- Smile and otherwise express your interest in and concern about the other person.

Likewise, you can communicate immediacy verbally in a variety of ways:

- Use the other person's name: for example, say, "Joe, what do you think?" instead of "What do you think?" Say "I like that, Mary" instead of "I like that."
- Focus on the other person's remarks. Make the speaker know that you heard and understood what was said, and give the speaker feedback. For example, use questions that ask for clarification or elaboration ("Do you think the same thing is true of baseball?"). Also, refer to the speaker's previous remarks ("Vermont does

How many nonverbal cues can you find in this photo that might reveal the effective application of any of the ten principles of effective interpersonal communication? Can you find any cues that might reveal their ineffective application?

sound like a great vacation spot").
- Reinforce, reward, or compliment the other person. Make use of such expressions as "I like your new outfit" or "Your comments were really to the point."
- Use self-references in your evaluative statements rather than depersonalizing them. Say, for example, "I think your report is great" rather than "Your report is great" or "Everyone likes your report."

INTERACTION MANAGEMENT

The effective communicator controls the interaction to the satisfaction of both parties. In effective **interaction management,** neither person feels ignored or on stage; each contributes to the total communication exchange. Maintaining your role as speaker or listener and passing the opportunity to speak back and forth—through appropriate eye movements, vocal expressions, and body and facial gestures—are interaction management skills. Similarly, keeping the conversation fluent without long and awkward pauses is a sign of effective interaction management. For example, it has been found that patients are less satisfied with their interaction with their doctor when the silence between their comments and the doctor's response is overly long (Rowland-Morin and Carroll 1990).

The effective interaction manager presents verbal and nonverbal messages that are consistent and reinforce one another. Contradictory signals—for example, a nonverbal message that contradicts the verbal message—are rarely in evidence. It is relevant to note here that women generally use more positive or pleasant nonverbal expressions than men. For example, they smile more, nod in agreement more, and more openly verbalize positive feelings. When expressing anger or power, however, many (though surely not all) women continue using these positive nonverbal signals, which dilute the verbally expressed anger or power. The net result, according to Jacqueline Shannon (1987), is that we see such women as being uncomfortable with strong negative emotions and expressions of power, and we are therefore less likely to believe them or to feel threatened by them.

Self-Monitoring   Integrally related to interpersonal interaction management is **self-monitoring,** the manipulation of the image you present to others in your interpersonal interactions (Snyder 1986). High self-monitors carefully adjust their behaviors according to the feedback they get from others. They manipulate their interpersonal interactions to give the most effective impression and to produce the desired effect. Low self-monitors, in contrast, are not concerned with the image they present. Rather, they communicate their thoughts and feelings openly, without trying to manipulate the impressions they create. Most of us lie somewhere between the two extremes. (You may wish at this point to take the brief self-test developed by Mark Snyder [1986], "Are You a High Self-Monitor?")

When high and low self-monitors are compared, several interesting differences emerge. For example, high self-monitors are more apt to take charge of a situation, more sensitive to the deceptive techniques of others, and better able to detect self-monitoring or impression management techniques being used by others. High self-monitors prefer to interact with low self-monitors. By interacting with low self-monitors, high self-monitors are better able to assume positions of influence and power. They also seem better able to present their true selves than are low self-monitors. For example, if an innocent person is charged with a crime, to use the example cited by Snyder (1986), a high self-monitor would be able to present his or her innocence more effectively than would a low self-monitor.

A careful reading of the research and theory on self-monitoring, openness, and self-disclosure (a topic reviewed in detail in Unit 8) supports the conclusion that we increase our effectiveness if we are selectively self-disclosing, selectively open, and selectively self-monitoring. To be totally open, to disclose everything to everyone, to ignore the feedback of others, and to refuse to engage in any self-monitoring seem effective. The opposite extreme is equally ineffective and should likewise be avoided.

There are no easy answers to such questions as "To what degree should we be open?" "How much and to whom should we self-disclose?" and "To what extent should we self-monitor our communications?" Fortunately, however, there are competencies we can develop to guide us and enable us to function more effectively interpersonally. It is to the development of this competence that much of the study of interpersonal communication is directed.

EXPRESSIVENESS

Expressiveness refers to the skill of communicating genuine involvement in the interpersonal interaction. Similar to openness in its emphasis on involvement, expressiveness includes, for example, taking responsibility for your thoughts and feelings, encouraging

TEST YOURSELF

ARE YOU A HIGH SELF-MONITOR?*

INSTRUCTIONS

The following statements concern personal reactions to a number of different situations. No two statements are exactly alike, so consider each statement carefully before answering. If a statement is true or mostly true as applied to you, write *T*. If a statement is false or not usually true as applied to you, write *F*.

_____ 1. I find it hard to imitate the behavior of other people.

_____ 2. At parties and social gatherings, I do not attempt to do or say things that others will like.

_____ 3. I can only argue for ideas which I already believe.

_____ 4. I can make impromptu speeches even on topics about which I have almost no information.

_____ 5. I guess I put on a show to impress or entertain people.

_____ 6. I would probably make a good actor.

_____ 7. In a group of people I am rarely the center of attention.

_____ 8. In different situations and with different people, I often act like very different persons.

_____ 9. I am not particularly good at making other people like me.

_____ 10. I'm not always the person I appear to be.

_____ 11. I would not change my opinions (or the way I do things) in order to please someone or win their favor.

_____ 12. I have considered being an entertainer.

_____ 13. I have never been good at games like charades or improvisational acting.

_____ 14. I have trouble changing my behavior to suit different people and different situations.

_____ 15. At a party I let others keep the jokes and stories going.

_____ 16. I feel a bit awkward in company and do not show up quite as well as I should.

_____ 17. I can look anyone in the eye and tell a lie with a straight face (if for a right end).

_____ 18. I may deceive people by being friendly when I really dislike them.

SCORING

Give yourself one point for each *true (T)* response you gave to questions 4, 5, 6, 8, 10, 12, 17, and 18, and give yourself one point for each *false (F)* response you gave to questions 1, 2, 3, 7, 9, 11, 13, 14, 15, and 16. According to research (Gangestad and Synder 1985; Snyder 1987), scores may be interpreted roughly as follows:

> 13 or higher = very high self-monitoring
> 11–12 = high self-monitoring
> 8–10 = low self-monitoring
> 0–7 = very low self-monitoring

expressiveness or openness in others, and providing appropriate feedback. In conflict situations (see Unit 20), expressiveness involves fighting actively, stating disagreement directly, and using I-messages rather than fighting passively, withdrawing from the encounter, or attributing responsibility to others.

Expressiveness may be communicated in a wide variety of ways. Here are a few guidelines:

- Practice active listening by paraphrasing, expressing understanding of the thoughts and feelings of the other person, and asking relevant questions (as explained in Unit 4, "Listening in Interpersonal Communication").
- Avoid cliches and trite expressions that signal a lack of personal involvement and originality.
- Address mixed messages—messages (verbal or nonverbal) that are communicated simultaneously but that contradict each other. Similarly, address messages that seem somehow unrealistic to you (for example, statements claiming that failing a course doesn't mean anything).
- Use I-messages to signal personal involvement and a willingness to share your feelings. Instead of saying, "You never give me a chance to make any decisions," say, "I want to contribute to the decisions that affect both of us."

Nonverbally, you communicate expressiveness by using appropriate variations in vocal rate, pitch, volume, and rhythm to convey involvement and interest and by allowing your facial muscles to reflect this inner involvement. The appropriate use of gestures also communicates involvement. Too few gestures signal uninterest, while too many may communicate discomfort, uneasiness, and awkwardness.

OTHER-ORIENTATION

Many people are self-oriented; they focus almost exclusively on themselves. In interpersonal interaction, this takes the form of doing most if not all of the talking, talking about themselves, their experiences, their interests, and their desires, without paying any attention to verbal and nonverbal feedback from others. **Other-orientation** is the opposite; it is the ability to adapt to the other person during the interpersonal encounter. It involves communicating attentiveness and interest in the other person and in what is being said.

You communicate other-orientation nonverbally through focused eye contact, smiles, nods, leaning toward the other person, and appropriate facial expression. Verbally, you communicate other-orientation in several ways:

- Ask the other person for suggestions and opinions. Statements such as "How do you feel about it?" or "What do you think?" go a long way toward focusing the communication on the other person.
- Acknowledge the presence and the importance of the other person. (See the discussion of confirmation and disconfirmation in Unit 11, "Verbal Messages: Principles and Pitfalls.")
- Ask the other person for clarification as appropriate. This will ensure that you understand what the other person is saying from that person's point of view.
- Express agreement when appropriate. Comments such as "You're right" or "That's interesting" help to focus the interaction on the other person.
- Grant the other person permission to express feelings. You can do this by talking

about your own feelings or perhaps by noting how difficult it is to talk about feelings. Statements such as "I feel especially depressed when I'm alone" or "I know how difficult it is to talk openly about feelings for our parents" open up the topic of feelings and give the necessary permission for such a discussion.

Other-orientation demonstrates consideration and respect—for example, asking if it's all right to dump your troubles on someone before doing so, or asking if your phone call comes at an inopportune time before launching into your conversation. Other-orientation involves acknowledging others' feelings as legitimate: "I can understand why you're so angry; I would be, too."

These qualities of interpersonal effectiveness (both the specific skills and the more general skills about skills) are mentioned throughout the text. These qualities should serve as general headings under which the additional and more detailed discussions that follow may be subsumed.

SUMMARY: UNIT IN BRIEF

Skills About Skills	Humanistic Model of Effectiveness	Pragmatic Model of Effectiveness
Mindfulness: Be mindful in applying these principles of effectiveness (for example, be aware of what is or is not appropriate in a situation).	**Openness:** self-disclosure regulation; honest reactions to others; owning one's thoughts and feelings	**Confidence:** comfortable, at-ease feeling; control of shyness
Flexibility: Be flexible in applying the principles; each situation requires a slightly different set of interpersonal behaviors.	**Empathy:** feeling as the other feels	**Immediacy:** a sense of contact and togetherness; a feeling of interest and liking
Cultural sensitivity: Take care not to ignore differences between self and other, differences within the group, or differences in meaning.	**Supportiveness:** Descriptions and provisionalism encourage a supportive atmosphere.	**Interaction management:** control of interaction to the satisfaction of both parties; managing conversational turns, fluency, and message consistency; self-monitoring as appropriate
Metacommunication: Use your metacommunicational (communicating about communicating) ability to ensure understanding of the other person's thoughts and feelings.	**Positiveness:** expression of positive attitudes toward self, other, and situation; stroking to acknowledge and reinforce the other person	**Expressiveness:** genuine involvement in speaking and listening, expressed verbally and nonverbally
	Equality: recognition that both parties are important; an equal sharing of the several communication functions	**Other-orientation:** attentiveness, interest, and concern for the other

THINKING CRITICALLY ABOUT EFFECTIVENESS IN INTERPERSONAL COMMUNICATION

1. Research tells us that men are much more reluctant to be open than women. Why do you think this is so? Is this changing? Is this true in all cultures?
2. After reviewing the research on the empathic and listening abilities of men and women, Pearson, Turner, and Todd-Mancillas (1992) conclude: "Men and women do not differ as much as conventional wisdom would have us believe. In many instances, she thinks like a man, and he thinks like a woman because they both think alike." Does your experience support or contradict this observation?
3. In what situations do you think empathic responses would be inappropriate?
4. What do you do to get stroked? Is it effective?
5. In what types of situations do you display confidence? In what situations are you lacking in confidence? What distinguishes the two types of situations?
6. What type of self-monitor are you? In what situations are you most likely to self-monitor your behaviors? In what situations are you least likely to self-monitor?
7. Can you identify a specific instance in which one of the qualities identified here figured prominently?
8. Can you identify other qualities that you would add to the list given in this unit? What specific behaviors would help you communicate these qualities?
9. Which of the qualities of effectiveness discussed here do you consider most important? Why?
10. How would you go about seeking answers to the following questions?

   - Are people who demonstrate the qualities of effective interpersonal communication better liked and more persuasive than those who do not?
   - Is immediacy important in health communication?
   - What role does other-orientation play in first dates and the impressions that people form of their first dates?

EXPERIENTIAL VEHICLES

6.1 THE SKILLS OF EFFECTIVENESS

The skills of interpersonal communication identified in this unit are applicable to a wide variety of situations. Their relative importance, however, will vary with the interpersonal situation or context. For each of the following situations, identify the one interpersonal skill from this unit that you feel is most relevant, and explain why you feel it is especially relevant.

1. A college teacher lecturing to a class of 300 students in interpersonal communication
2. Parents talking with their fifth grader after being told by the teacher that their child doesn't get along well with other students and frequently gets into fights with them
3. A recent college graduate applying for a job with a conservative banking company
4. A real estate agent trying to sell a house to a young couple
5. A teenager telling his or her parents of plans to join a religious cult
6. A factory worker who has been with the company for 15 months asking for a raise

7. A high school junior who is enrolled in a new school and doesn't know any other students
8. A young couple experiencing their first major argument
9. A lawyer—defending an accused murderer—presenting opening remarks to the jury
10. A doctor telling a patient who recently suffered a heart attack that drastic changes in lifestyle must be made
11. A single parent answering her young son's questions about why he doesn't have a father as his friends do
12. A family therapist explaining to parents the need for open communication
13. An employer explaining to workers why there will be no raises this year
14. A social worker trying to get a homeless person to enter a municipal shelter
15. A political candidate explaining to voters that no illegal campaign contributions were received and that the opposing candidate's charges are groundless

6.2 ASSESSING A COUPLE'S INTERPERSONAL EFFECTIVENESS

Here is a test for measuring effectiveness in interpersonal communication. It covers the ten qualities discussed in this unit. Complete this test yourself, and have someone with whom you interact frequently (a close friend, a romantic partner, a sibling, your parent or child) also complete it for herself or himself.

Indicate the degree to which each of the following statements is true of your general interpersonal communications. Use this scale:

1 = always or almost always true
2 = frequently true
3 = sometimes true
4 = rarely true
5 = never or almost never true

_____ 1. In my communications, I am willing to reveal myself to others.

_____ 2. When communicating, I can feel what the other person is feeling.

_____ 3. In my interpersonal interactions, I describe rather than evaluate, and I state my views tentatively rather than with certainty.

_____ 4. I express positive attitudes toward the other person; for example, I compliment the person I communicate with.

_____ 5. I look upon the other person and myself as essentially equal partners in the communication act.

_____ 6. I am confident and communicate this confidence in my interpersonal interactions.

_____ 7. I communicate a sense of togetherness, of oneness, with my listener.

_____ 8. I manage the interpersonal communication situation to both my own and the other person's satisfaction.

_____ 9. I communicate my involvement in the interpersonal interaction.

_____10. I adapt to the needs of the other person (rather than only considering my own needs) during the interpersonal interaction.

The effectiveness concepts were discussed in this unit in the same order as the questions here: (1) openness, (2) empathy, (3) supportiveness, (4) positiveness, (5) equality, (6) confidence, (7) immediacy, (8) interaction management, (9) expressiveness, and (10) other-orientation.

After both of you have completed the test:

- Discuss each of the test items and try to identify examples from *your* past interactions in which you used or failed to use the principle.
- Share your feelings about the role of each principle in *your* interpersonal relationships in general and in this relationship in particular.

UNIT 7

The Self in Interpersonal Communication

AFTER COMPLETING THIS UNIT, YOU SHOULD BE ABLE TO:

1. Define *self-concept* and explain how it develops
2. Explain the Johari window and define the *open, blind, hidden,* and *unknown selves*

3. Explain how self-awareness can be increased
4. Define *self-esteem* and explain how it might be raised

Who you are and how you see yourself influence the way you communicate with others and the way others communicate with you. Your self-concept, self-awareness, and self-esteem all play a significant role in your interpersonal interactions.

SELF-CONCEPT

You no doubt have an image of who you are; this is your self-concept. It consists of your feelings and thoughts about your strengths and weaknesses, your abilities and limitations. Your self-concept develops from at least three sources: (1) the image of you that others have and that they reveal to you, (2) the comparisons you make between yourself and others, and (3) the way you interpret and evaluate your own thoughts and behaviors.

OTHERS' IMAGES OF YOU

If you wished to see the way your hair looked, you would likely look in a mirror. But what would you do if you wanted to see how friendly or how assertive you are? According to Charles Horton Cooley's (1922) concept of the *looking-glass self,* you would look at the image of yourself that others reveal to you through the way they treat you and react to you.

You would look especially to those who are most significant in your life—to your *significant others.* As a child, you would look to your parents and then to your teachers. As an adult, you might look to your friends, romantic partners, and colleagues at work. If these significant others think highly of you, you will see this positive image of yourself reflected in their behaviors; if they think little of you, you will see a more negative image. These reflections that you see in others help you define your self-concept.

SOCIAL COMPARISONS

Another way you develop your self-concept is by comparing yourself with others. When you want to gain insight into who you are and how effective or competent you are, you probably look to your peers. For example, after an examination you probably want to know how you performed relative to the other students in your class. If you play on a baseball team, it's important to know your batting average in comparison with the batting average of others on the team. Absolute scores on the exam or knowledge of your batting average may be helpful in telling you something about your performance, but you gain an additional perspective when you see your score in comparison with the scores of your peers.

Your Own Interpretations and Evaluations

Much in the way others form images of you based on what you do, you also react to your own behavior; you interpret and evaluate it. These interpretations and evaluations help to form your self-concept. For example, let us say you believe that lying is wrong. If you lie, you will evaluate this behavior in terms of your internalized beliefs about lying. You will thus react negatively to your own behavior. You may, for example, experience guilt if your behavior contradicts your beliefs. In contrast, let's say you pulled someone out of a burning building at great personal risk. You would probably evaluate this behavior positively; you would feel good about this behavior and, as a result, about yourself.

Self-Awareness

Your self-awareness represents the extent to which you know yourself. Understanding how your self-concept develops is one way to increase your self-awareness: the more you understand about the reasons why you view yourself as you do, the more you will understand who you are. Additional insight is gained by looking at self-awareness through the Johari model of the self.

The Four Selves

Self-awareness is neatly explained by the model of the four selves (the Johari window). This model, presented in Figure 7.1, is divided into four basic areas, or quadrants, each of which represents a somewhat different self.

Note that a change in one area of the self brings about a change in the other areas. Visualize this model as representing your self. The entire model is of constant size, but each section can vary, from very small to very large. As one section becomes smaller, one or more of the others grow larger. Similarly, as one section grows, one or more of the others must get smaller. For example, if you enlarge your open self, this shrinks your hidden self. Further, this revelation or disclosure may in turn lead to a decrease in the size of your blind self if other people reveal insights that they have gained about you but that you have not known.

The Johari model emphasizes that the several aspects of the self are not separate pieces but are interactive parts of a whole. Each part is dependent on each other part. Like that of interpersonal communication, this model of the self is a transactional one.

Two models of the self, presented in Figure 7.2, illustrate how the relative sizes of the four selves depend on the particular interpersonal situation. In Figure 7.2 (left), let's assume you are with a friend to whom you have opened up a great deal. Consequently, your open self is large and your hidden self is small. In Figure 7.2 (right), you might be

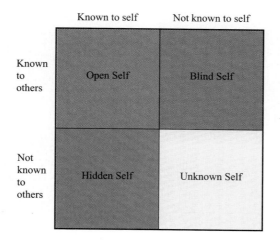

Figure 7.1
The Johari window. The name Johari was derived from the first names of the two people who developed the model, Joseph Luft and Harry Ingham. [*Source:* From *Group Processes: An Introduction to Group Dynamics* by Joseph Luft, 1984, p. 60. Reprinted by permission Mayfield Publishing Company, Mountain View, CA.]

with a new employer whom you do not know very well and with whom you are still a bit uncomfortable. Thus, your open self is relatively small and your hidden self is large.

The Open Self   The **open self** represents all the information, behaviors, attitudes, feelings, desires, motivations, and ideas that are known to yourself and to others. The type of information included here might range from your name, skin color, and sex to your age, political and religious affiliations, and batting average. Each person's open self varies in size, depending on the situation and the individuals the person is interacting with. Some people, for example, make you feel comfortable and supported; to them, you open yourself wide, but to others you may prefer to leave most of yourself closed.

Communication depends on the degree to which you open yourself to others and to yourself (Luft 1970). If you do not allow other people to know you (thus keeping your open self small), communication between you and others becomes difficult, if not impossible. You can communicate meaningfully only to the extent that you know others and yourself. To improve communication, work first on enlarging the open self.

The Blind Self   The **blind self** represents all the things about yourself that others know but of which you are ignorant. These may vary from the relatively insignificant habit of saying "You know," rubbing your nose when you get angry, or having a peculiar body odor, to things as significant as defense mechanisms, fight strategies, or repressed experiences.

Some people have a very large blind self and seem totally oblivious of their faults and sometimes (though not as often) of their virtues. Others seem overly anxious to have a small blind self. They seek therapy at every turn and join every self-help group. Some are even convinced that they know everything there is to know about themselves, that they have reduced the blind self to zero. Most of us lie between these extremes.

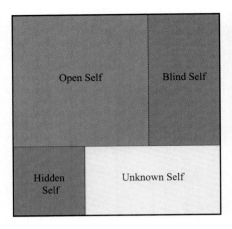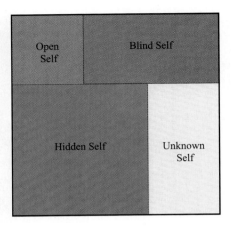

Figure 7.2
Two models of the four selves.

Although communication and interpersonal relations are generally enhanced as the blind self becomes smaller, do not assume that people should therefore be forced to see themselves as you see them, because this may cause serious trauma. Such a revelation might trigger a breakdown in defenses; it might force people to admit their own jealousy or prejudice when they are not psychologically ready to deal with such information. Such revelations are best dealt with cautiously or under the guidance of trained professionals.

The Hidden Self   The **hidden self** contains all that you know of yourself and of others that you keep secret. In any interaction, this area includes everything you do not want to reveal, whether it is relevant or irrelevant to the conversation.

At the extremes, we have the overdisclosers and the underdisclosers. The overdisclosers tell all. They keep nothing hidden about themselves or others. They tell you their marital difficulties, their children's problems, their financial status, and just about everything else. The underdisclosers tell nothing. They talk about you but not about themselves.

The problem with these extremes is that individuals do not distinguish between those who should and those who shouldn't be privy to such information. They also do not distinguish among the various types of information that should or should not be disclosed. The vast majority of people, however, keep certain things hidden and disclose others; they make disclosures to some people and not to others. They are *selective* disclosers.

The Unknown Self   The **unknown self** represents truths about yourself that neither you nor others know. The existence of this self is inferred from a number of sources. Sometimes it is revealed through temporary changes brought about by drugs or through special experimental conditions, such as hypnosis or sensory deprivation. Sometimes this area is revealed by certain projective tests or dreams. Mostly, however, it is revealed by the fact that you are constantly learning things about yourself that you didn't know before (things that were previously in the unknown self).

Although you cannot easily manipulate this area, recognize that it does exist and that there are things about yourself and about others that you do not know and may never know.

INCREASING SELF-AWARENESS

You can increase your self-awareness in a number of ways. Here are a few.

Ask Yourself About Yourself   One way to ask yourself about yourself is to take an informal "Who am I?" test (Bugental and Zelen 1950). Take a piece of paper, head it "Who Am I?" and write 10, 15, or 20 times "I am. . . ." Then complete each of the sentences. Try not to give only positive or socially acceptable responses; just respond with what comes to mind first. Second, take another piece of paper and divide it into two columns. Head one column "Strengths" and the other column "Weaknesses." Fill in each column as quickly as possible. Third, using these first two "tests" as a base, take a third piece of paper, head it "Self-Improvement Goals," and complete the statement "I want to improve my . . . " as many times as you can in, say, five minutes.

One way to grow in self-awareness is to listen to what others say to and about you. How well do you listen to this? Are there certain issues about yourself that you are more open to than others? Check your perceptions with those who know you well. Ask them if you listen openly and if you are more open to some issues than to others.

Further, remember that you are constantly changing; consequently, these self-perceptions and goals also change rapidly, often in drastic ways. Update them frequently.

Listen to Others   You can learn a lot about yourself by seeing yourself as others do. Conveniently, others are constantly giving you the very feedback you need to increase self-awareness. In every interpersonal interaction, people comment on you in some way—on what you do, what you say, how you look. Sometimes these comments are explicit; most often they are "hidden" in the way in which others look at you, in what they talk about, in their interest in what you say. Pay close attention to this kind of information (both verbal and nonverbal) and use it to increase your own self-awareness.

Actively Seek Information About Yourself   Actively seek out information to reduce your blind self. You need not be so obvious as to say, "Tell me about myself" or "What do you think of me?" But you can use everyday situations to gain self-information: "Do you think I was assertive enough when asking for the raise?" or "Do you think I'd be thought too forward if I invited myself for dinner?" Do not, of course, seek this information constantly; your friends would surely and quickly find others with whom to interact. But you can make use of some situations—perhaps those in which you are particularly unsure of what to do or how you appear—to reduce your blind self and increase self-awareness.

See Your Different Selves   Each of your friends and relatives views you differently; to each you are a somewhat different person. Yet you are really *all* of these. Practice seeing yourself as do the people with whom you interact. For starters, visualize how you are seen by your mother, your father, your teachers, your best friend, the stranger you sat next to on the bus, your employer, your neighbor's child. Because you are, in fact, a composite of all these views, it is important that you periodically see yourself through the eyes of others. The experience will give you new and valuable perspectives on yourself.

Increase Your Open Self   When you increase your open self and reveal yourself to others, you also reveal yourself to yourself. At the very least, you bring into clearer focus what you may have buried within. As you discuss yourself, you may see connections that you had previously missed, and with the aid of feedback from others you may gain still more insight. Also, by increasing the open self, you increase the likelihood that a meaningful and intimate dialogue will develop; through such interactions you best get to know yourself. Do, however, consider the risks involved in such self-disclosures (discussed in Unit 8).

SELF-ESTEEM

How much do you like yourself? How valuable a person do you think you are? How competent do you think you are? The answers to these questions reflect your self-esteem, the value you place on yourself.

Self-esteem is very important because success breeds success. When you feel good about yourself—about who you are and what you are capable of doing—you will perform better. When you think like a success, you are more likely to act like a success. When you think you're a failure, you're more likely to act like a failure. Increasing self-esteem will, therefore, help you to function more effectively in school, in interpersonal relationships, and in careers. Here are a few suggestions for increasing self-esteem.

ATTACK YOUR SELF-DESTRUCTIVE BELIEFS

Self-destructive beliefs are those that damage your self-esteem and prevent you from building meaningful and productive relationships. They may be about yourself ("I'm not creative"; "I'm boring"), your world ("The world is an unhappy place"; "People are out to get me"), and your relationships ("All the good people are already in relationships"; "If I ever fall in love, I know I'll be hurt"). Identifying these beliefs will help you to examine them critically and to see that they are both illogical and self-defeating.

Another way of looking at self-destructive beliefs is to identify what Pamela Butler (1981) calls "drivers"—unrealistic beliefs that may motivate you to act in ways that are self-defeating. Butler identifies five such drivers: be perfect, hurry up, be strong, please others, and try hard.

The drive to **be perfect** impels you to try to perform at unrealistically high levels in just about everything you do. Whether it is directed toward work, school, athletics, or appearance, this drive tells you that anything short of perfection is unacceptable and that you are to blame for any imperfections—imperfections that by any other standard would be considered quite normal.)

The drive to **hurry up** compels you to do things quickly, to do more than can be reasonably expected in any given amount of time. This drive is at the foundation of what has come to be called "Type A" behavior (Friedman and Rosenman 1974), the personality that is always impatient, always rushing. (As an aside, it might be noted that appearing rushed is one of the ways in which powerlessness is communicated. People with power do not rush; they don't have to. The ones who hurry are the people who are being judged by others, whose job or promotion depends on others).

The drive to **be strong** tells you that weakness and any of the more vulnerable emotions, such as sadness, compassion, or loneliness, are wrong. This driver is seen in the stereotypical man, but it is also becoming more prevalent among women as well who are not permitted to cry, ask for help, or have unfulfilled needs.

The drive to **please others** leads you to seek approval from others. Pleasing yourself is secondary, and self-pleasure is to come from pleasing others. The logic is that if you gain the approval of others, then you are a worthy and deserving person; if others disapprove of you, then you must be worthless and undeserving.

The drive to **try hard** makes you take on more responsibilities than anyone can be expected to handle. This driver leads you to accept tasks that would be impossible for any normal person to manage, yet you take them on without any concern for your own limits (physical or emotional).

Instead of helping you become successful, these drivers almost ensure your failure. Because they foster unrealistically high standards, they make it impossible for you to accomplish the very things you feel are essential for approval by others and by yourself.

Recognizing that you may have internalized such drivers is a first step toward eliminating them. A second step involves recognizing that these drivers are in fact unrealistic and self-defeating. The psychotherapist Albert Ellis (1988; Ellis and Harper 1975) and other cognitive therapists (for example, Beck 1988) would argue that you can accomplish this by understanding why these drivers are unrealistic and substituting more realistic ones. For example, following Ellis, you might try replacing an unrealistic driver to please others (always and in everything you do) with a more realistic belief that it would be nice if others were pleased with you but it certainly isn't essential. A third step is giving yourself permission to fail, to be less than perfect, to be normal.

Do recognize that it is the *unrealistic* nature of these drivers that creates problems. Certainly, trying hard and being strong are not unhealthy when they are realistic. It is only when they become absolute—when you try to be everything to everyone—that they become impossible to achieve and create problems.

ENGAGE IN SELF-AFFIRMATION

Remind yourself of your successes. There are enough people around who will remind you of your failures. Focus, too, on your good acts, your good deeds. Focus on your positive qualities, your strengths, your virtues. Focus on the good relationships you have with friends and relatives.

The way you talk to yourself about yourself influences what you think of yourself. If you talk positively about yourself, you will come to feel more positive about yourself. If you tell yourself that you are a success, that others like you, that you will succeed on the next test, and that you will be welcomed when asking for a date, you will soon come to feel positive about yourself. Table 7.1 presents a useful list of self-affirming phrases. Reading over the list is sure to stimulate your own self-affirmations.

SEEK OUT NOURISHING PEOPLE

The psychologist Carl Rogers drew a distinction between noxious and nourishing people. Noxious people criticize and find fault with just about everything. Nourishing people, on the other hand, are positive. They are optimists. Most important, they reward you, they stroke you, they make you feel good about yourself. Seek out these people.

WORK ON PROJECTS THAT WILL RESULT IN SUCCESS

Some people want to fail, or so it seems. Often, they select projects that will result in failure. Perhaps the projects are too large or too difficult. In any event, they are impossible. Instead, select projects that will result in success. Each success helps build self-esteem. Each success makes the next success a little easier.

When a project does fail, recognize that this does not mean that you are a failure (see Experiential Vehicle 12.1). Everyone fails somewhere along the line. Failure is something that happens; it is not something inside you. Further, your failing once does not mean that you will fail the next time. So put failure in perspective. Do not make it an excuse for not trying again.

Table 7.1

Self-Affirming Phrases

I am beautiful, capable, and lovable.

I am a lovable and worthy person.

I appreciate and love myself!

The love I give to others I also can offer to myself.

I can live a nurturing, exciting, and creative life.

I am creating the experience of love in my life.

My love comes from me.

I am capable and willing to handle my fears as they come up one at a time.

I always do my best.

I am acceptable and I am open to new forms of being acknowledged.

I can accept the past and welcome the future.

I deserve to feel good.

I am learning to see the beauty of my life.

I am all I need to be.

I am creative, loving, and nurturing.

I find my life satisfying and rewarding.

I can learn to accept and love everyone unconditionally—including myself.

I can ask for what I want with love in my heart.

I am the source of my security and self-esteem.

I always have abundance.

I am a powerful, creative being who now chooses to love, nurture, and heal himself or herself.

Where I am now is perfect for my growth.

I can let others love me the way I am.

There is nothing I have to do to feel loved.

I am open to new forms of loving relationships.

I am open to new forms of being acknowledged.

I deserve to be healthy.

I love my brothers and sisters unconditionally.

I can shine my light gently every moment of every day.

I bring others out.

I love myself when I want to feel loved.

I can forgive myself.

I can learn how to care for my body in a loving and gentle manner.

I am learning to flow joyfully in the present moment.

I can accept imperfection.

My love flows freely to one and all.

I am a worthwhile person and there is a place for me.

I am lovable because I'm here.

I can feel good doing the things I'm skilled at.

I am learning to support myself with love.

I release the past and now choose a life of love and fulfillment.

I don't have to be sick to get nurtured.

I am worthy of a loving relationship.

My world is safe and friendly.

I can be gentle with myself.

I can feel supported even when I don't meet my models of perfection.

My guilt doesn't help anyone.

I am learning to get in touch with my feelings.

I can accept praise and attention at any time.

I have the right to live as I want.

What somebody else does and says means nothing about me.

SUMMARY: UNIT IN BRIEF

Self-Concept	Self-Awareness	Self-Esteem
Self-concept is the image you have of who you are. **Sources of self-concept:** • others' images of you • social comparisons • your own interpretations and evaluations	**Self-awareness** is your knowledge of yourself; the extent to which you know who you are. **The four selves:** *Open self:* information known to self and others *Blind self:* information known only to others *Hidden self:* information known only to self *Unknown self:* information known to neither self nor others **Increasing self-awareness:** • Ask yourself about yourself. • Listen to others. • Actively seek information about yourself. • See your different selves. • Increase your open self.	**Self-esteem** is the value you place on yourself; your perceived self-worth. **Increasing self-esteem:** • Attack your self-destructive beliefs. • Engage in self-affirmation. • Seek out nourishing people. • Work on projects that will result in success.

THINKING CRITICALLY ABOUT THE SELF IN INTERPERSONAL COMMUNICATION

1. What is your self-concept? How satisfied are you with it? Are you convinced that you can develop a more positive self-concept? What do you intend to do about it?
2. Are there sources of self-concept other than the three mentioned in this unit? How would you describe their operation?
3. How would you draw your Johari window to show yourself when interacting with your parents? With your friends? With your college instructors?
4. How well do you feel you know yourself? Poll a few people and see how well they feel they know themselves. If the people you poll are like some students, you will find very few people who say they have low self-awareness. How do you explain this? Is everyone exceptionally self-aware?
5. What specific steps do you intend to take to increase your own self-awareness?
6. How would you describe your self-esteem? How satisfied are you with it?
7. How might you apply the principles for increasing your own self-esteem to increasing the self-esteem of a friend, lover, or family member?

8. Do men and women differ in self-awareness or self-esteem? How would you go about finding the answer to this question?

9. Let's say you think that self-awareness contributes significantly to a person's self-esteem. That is, you believe a person's high self-awareness will lead that person to develop high positive self-esteem. How would you go about testing this hypothesis? You may find it helpful to refer to the "Researching Communication" section in *Studying Communication,* the booklet that accompanies this text.

10. How would you go about finding answers to such questions as the following?

   • Are self-awareness and self-esteem positively related (as self-awareness increases, so does self-esteem, and as self-awareness decreases, so does self-esteem)?
   • Do people with high self-esteem have types of friends that are different from those of people with low self-esteem?
   • Can the repetition of self-affirming phrases raise a person's self-esteem?

EXPERIENTIAL VEHICLES

7.1 THE SOURCES OF SELF-CONCEPT

Directions Your self-concept develops from other people's images of you, from your social comparisons, and from your interpretations and evaluations of your own thoughts and behaviors. Examine your self-concept, and try to identify how you developed the views you have. In the columns headed "Others' Images," "Social Comparison," and "Self-Evaluations" on p.134 indicate the approximate percentage of influence each of these three sources may have had in the ten areas listed in column 1. Adding across from left to right, each line should total 100 percent.

Analysis After you have filled in percentages for all ten items, consider the following questions:

1. Whose images of you have had the greatest influence on your self-concept? Do these sources contribute more to a positive or to a negative self-concept?

2. With whom and with what types of people do you compare yourself? Do certain people contribute positively, whereas others contribute negatively?

3. How would you describe your self-evaluations? Do your positive or your negative experiences influence you more? Why?

4. Are you able to identify any other sources that have contributed to your self-concept?

5. Are you satisfied with your self-concept? What suggestions might you derive from this unit to help you develop a more positive, healthier, and more helpful self-concept?

7.2 PERCEIVING MY SELVES

The purpose of this Experiential Vehicle is to allow us to better understand how we perceive ourselves, how others perceive us, and how we would like to perceive ourselves. In

My Self-Concept Concerning My:	Others' Images	Social Comparisons	Self-Evaluations
Academic abilities	%	%	%
Potential job success			
Romantic talents			
Physical attractiveness			
Present happiness			
Athletic abilities			
Communication abilities			
Potential for professional success			
Moral values			
Sensitivity to others; ability to empathize			

some instances and for some people, these three perceptions will be the same; in most cases and for most people, however, they will be different.

Following this brief introduction are nine lists of items (animals, birds, colors, communications media, dogs, drinks, music, transportation, and sports). Read over each list carefully, attempting to look past the purely physical characteristics of the objects to their "personalities" or "psychological meanings."

Instructions

1. For each of the nine lists, indicate the one item that best represents how you perceive yourself—not your physical self, but your psychological and philosophical self. Mark these items *MM* (Myself to Me).
2. In each of the nine lists, select the one item that best represents how you feel others perceive you. By "others" is meant acquaintances—neither passing strangers nor close friends, but people you meet and talk with for some time—for example, people in this class. Mark these items *MO* (Myself to Others).
3. In each of the nine lists, select the one item that best represents how you would like to be. Put differently, what items would your ideal self select? Mark these items *MI* (Myself as Ideal).

After all nine lists are marked three times, discuss your choices in groups of five or six in any way you feel is meaningful. Your objective is to get a better perspective on how your self-perception compares with both the perceptions of you by others and your own ideal perception. In discussions, you should try to state as clearly as possible why you selected the items you did and specifically what each selected item means to you at this time. You should also welcome any suggestions from the group members as to why they think you selected the items you did. You might also wish to integrate consideration of some or all of the following questions into your discussion:

1. How different are the items marked *MM* from those marked *MO*? Why do you suppose this is so? Which is the more positive? Why?
2. How different are the items marked *MM* from those marked *MI*? Why do you suppose this is so?
3. What do the number of differences between the items marked *MM* and the items marked *MI* mean for personal happiness?
4. How accurate were you in the items you marked *MO*? Ask members of the group which items they would have selected for you.
5. Which of the three perceptions (*MM, MO, MI*) is easiest to respond to? Which are you surest of?
6. Would you show these forms to your best same-sex friend? Your best opposite-sex friend? Your parents? Your children? Explain.

Animals
_____ bear
_____ deer
_____ fox
_____ lion
_____ monkey
_____ rabbit
_____ turtle

Birds
_____ chicken
_____ eagle
_____ ostrich
_____ owl
_____ parrot
_____ swan
_____ turkey

Colors
_____ black
_____ blue
_____ gray
_____ pink
_____ red
_____ white
_____ yellow

Communications Media
_____ book
_____ film
_____ fourth-class mail
_____ radio
_____ special delivery
_____ telephone
_____ television

Dogs
_____ boxer
_____ Doberman
_____ greyhound
_____ husky
_____ mutt
_____ poodle
_____ St. Bernard

Drinks
_____ beer
_____ champagne
_____ milk
_____ prune juice
_____ water
_____ wine
_____ hot chocolate

Sports
_____ auto racing
_____ baseball
_____ boxing
_____ bullfighting
_____ chess
_____ ice skating
_____ tennis

Transportation
_____ bicycle
_____ jet plane
_____ horse and wagon
_____ motorcycle
_____ Rolls-Royce
_____ van
_____ Volkswagen

Music
_____ rap
_____ country/western
_____ folk
_____ jazz
_____ opera
_____ popular
_____ rock

7.3 I'D PREFER TO BE

This exercise should enable members of the class to get to know each other better and at the same time get to know themselves better. The questions asked here should encourage each individual to think about and increase awareness of one or more facets of her or his thoughts or behaviors.

"I'd Prefer to Be" is played in a group of four to six. First, individuals rank each of the three traits in the 15 groupings listed, using 1 for the most preferred and 3 for the least preferred choice. Then, after the traits are ranked by individuals, the group considers each category, with each member giving her or his rank order.

Members may refuse to reveal their rankings for any category by saying "I pass." The group is not permitted to question the reasons for any member's passing. When a member reveals rankings for a category, the group members may ask questions relevant to that category. These questions may be asked after any individual member's response or may be reserved until all members have given their rankings for a particular category.

"I'd Prefer to Be"

1. _____ intelligent
   _____ wealthy
   _____ physically attractive

2. _____ a movie star
   _____ a senator
   _____ a successful businessperson

3. _____ blind
   _____ deaf
   _____ mute

4. _____ on an average date
   _____ reading an average book
   _____ watching average television

5. _____ loved
   _____ feared
   _____ respected

6. _____ bisexual
   _____ heterosexual
   _____ homosexual

7. _____ applying for a job by letter
   _____ applying by face-to-face interview
   _____ applying by telephone interview

8. _____ adventurous
   _____scientific
   _____ creative

9. _____ successful in social life
   _____ successful in family life
   _____ successful in business life

10. _____ a traitor to my friend
    _____ a traitor to my country
    _____ a traitor to myself

11. _____ angry
    _____ guilty
    _____ fearful

12. _____ introverted
    _____ extroverted
    _____ ambiverted

13. _____ the loved
    _____ the lover
    _____ the good friend

14. _____ a leader
    _____ a follower
    _____ a loner

15. _____ more open, more disclosive
    _____ more flexible, more willing to try new things
    _____ more supportive, more giving of myself

Areas for Discussion

1. What are the reasons for the individual choices? Note that the reasons for the least-preferred choice may often be as important as, or even more important than, the reasons for the most-preferred choice.
2. What is the homogeneity or heterogeneity of the group as a whole? Do the members evidence relatively similar choices or wide differences? What does this mean in terms of the members' ability to communicate with each other?
3. Do the members accept or reject the choices of other members? Are some members disturbed by the choices other members made? If so, why? Are some apathetic? Why? Did hearing the choices of one or more members make you want to get to know them better?
4. Did any of the choices make you aware of your own or others' preferences you were not aware of before?
5. Are members reluctant to share their preferences with the group? Why?

UNIT 8

Self-Disclosure

UNIT OBJECTIVES

AFTER COMPLETING THIS UNIT, YOU SHOULD BE ABLE TO:

1. Define *self-disclosure* and the factors that influence it
2. Identify the rewards and dangers of self-disclosure
3. Explain the guidelines for self-disclosing and for responding to the disclosures of others.

One of the most important forms of interpersonal communication that you could engage in is talking about yourself, or self-disclosure. **Self-disclosure** refers to your communicating information about yourself to another person. Because self-disclosure is a type of communication, overt statements about yourself as well as slips of the tongue, unconscious nonverbal movements, and written or public confessions would all be classified as self-disclosing communications. Self-disclosure may also involve your reactions to the feelings of others: for example, when you tell your friend that you are sorry she was fired.

Although self-disclosure may occur as a single message—for example, you tell a stranger on a train that you are thinking about getting a divorce—it is best viewed as a *developing* process in which information is exchanged between people in a relationship over the period of their relationship (Spencer 1993, 1994). Seen as a developing process, we can then appreciate how it changes as the relationship changes, for example, from initial contact through involvement to intimacy and then perhaps to deterioration or dissolution. We can also appreciate how self-disclosure will differ depending on the type of relationship you have with another person, for example, whether the other person is, say, your friend, parent, child, or counselor.

Self-disclosure may involve information that you communicate to others freely or that you normally keep hidden. It may supply information ("I earn $45,000) or reveal feelings ("I'm feeling very depressed").

Self-disclosure involves at least one other individual; it cannot be an *intra*personal communication act. To qualify as self-disclosure, the information must be received and understood by another individual. As you can appreciate, self-disclosure can vary from the relatively insignificant ("I'm a Sagittarius") to the highly revealing and deeply personal ("I'm currently in an abusive relationship" or "I'm almost always depressed"). The remaining discussion of this important concept will be more meaningful if you first take the accompanying self-disclosure test.

FACTORS INFLUENCING SELF-DISCLOSURE

Self-disclosure occurs more readily under certain circumstances than others. A few of the more significant factors influencing self-disclosure are identified here.

THE DISCLOSURES OF OTHERS

Generally, self-disclosure is reciprocal. In any interaction, it is more likely to occur if the other person has previously self-disclosed. This is the **dyadic effect**—what one person in a dyad does, the other does in response. The dyadic effect in self-disclosure takes a kind of spiral form, with each self-disclosure prompting an additional self-disclosure by the other person, which in turn prompts still more self-disclosure, and so on. It's interesting to note that disclosures made in response to the disclosures of others are generally more intimate than those that are not the result of the dyadic effect (Berg and Archer 1983).

This dyadic effect is not universal across cultures. For example, while Americans are likely to follow the dyadic effect and reciprocate with explicit, verbal self-disclosure, Koreans do not (Won-Doornink 1985).

AUDIENCE SIZE

Perhaps because of the many fears about revealing oneself, self-disclosure is more likely to occur in small groups than in large ones. Dyads are perhaps the most common settings. A dyad seems more suitable to self-disclosure because it is easier to deal with one person's reactions and responses than with those of several people. In a dyad, you can attend quite carefully to the responses and, on the basis of support or lack of support, monitor further disclosures, continuing if the situation is supportive and stopping if it is not.

TOPIC

Certain topics are more likely to be disclosed than others. For example, you would more likely disclose information about your job or hobbies than information about your sex life or financial situation. Self-disclosures about money (for example, the amount of money you owe), personality (for example, the things you feel guilty about), and body (for example, your feelings of sexual adequacy) are less common than self-disclosures about tastes and interests, attitudes and opinions, and work (Jourard 1968, 1971a). Clearly, the topics of money, personality, and body are closely related to your self-concept, and such disclosures are therefore potentially more threatening than are disclosures about tastes in clothing, views on religion, or pressures at work.

VALENCE

The valence, or positive or negative quality, of a self-disclosure is also significant. Positive self-disclosures are more common than negative self-disclosures and are often made to nonintimates as well as to intimates. In some cultures—for example, Mexican—there is a strong emphasis on discussing all matters in a positive mode, and this undoubtedly influences the way Mexicans approach self-disclosure as well. Negative self-disclosures, in contrast, are usually made to close intimates and then only after considerable time has elapsed in a relationship. This pattern is consistent with evidence that self-disclosure and trust are related positively (Wheeless and Grotz 1977).

You develop a greater attraction for those who engage in positive self-disclosure than for those who engage in negative self-disclosure. This is particularly significant in the early stages of a relationship. Negative self-disclosures to a stranger or even a casual acquaintance are perceived as inappropriate, no doubt because they violate the culture's norms for such communications. This suggests a warning: if your aim is to be perceived as attractive, consider curtailing negative self-disclosures, at least in the early stages of a relationship.

GENDER

Most research shows that women disclose more than men but that men and women make negative disclosures about equally (Naifeh and Smith 1984). More specifically, women disclose more than men about their previous romantic relationships, their feelings about their closest same-sex friends, their greatest fears, and what they do not like about their partners (Sprecher 1987). Women also seem to increase the depth of their self-disclosures as the relationship becomes more intimate, while men seem not to change their self-disclosure levels. Another difference is that women self-disclose more to members of the extended family than do men (Komarovsky 1964; Argyle and Henderson 1985; Moghaddam, Taylor, and Wright 1993).

Men and women give different reasons for avoiding self-disclosure (Rosenfeld 1979), but they hold the main reason in common: "If I disclose, I might project an image I do not want to project." In a society in which image is so important—in which one's image is often the basis for success or failure—this reason is expected. Other reasons for avoiding self-disclosure, however, are unique to men or women. For men, the following reasons are reported: "If I self-disclose, I might give information that makes me appear inconsistent"; "If I self-disclose, I might lose control over the other person"; and "Self-disclosure might threaten relationships I have with people other than close acquaintances." Lawrence Rosenfeld (1979) sums up males' reasons for self-disclosure avoidance: "If I disclose to you, I might project an image I do not want to project, which could make me look bad and cause me to lose control over you. This might go so far as to affect relationships I have with people other than you." The men's principal objective in avoiding self-disclosure is to maintain control.

In addition to fearing an unfavorable image, women avoid self-disclosure for the following reasons: "Self-disclosure would give the other person information that he or she might use against me at some time," "Self-disclosure is a sign of some emotional disturbance," and "Self-disclosure might hurt our relationship." The general reason women avoid self-disclosure, says Rosenfeld, is that "if I disclose to you, I might project an image I do not want to project, such as my being emotionally ill, which you might use against me and which might hurt our relationship." The women's principal objective for avoiding self-disclosure is "to avoid personal hurt and problems with the relationship."

RECEIVER RELATIONSHIP

Your relationship with the person to whom you self-disclose influences the frequency and the likelihood of your self-disclosure (Derlega and Berg 1987). Most studies find that you disclose more often to people who are close to you—your spouse, family, and close friends. In many Latin cultures, for example, in which the extended family is especially close, this tendency may well be heightened. Some studies find that you disclose most to persons you like and least to persons you dislike, regardless of how close they are to you. Thus, you may disclose to a well-liked teacher who is not particularly close and yet not disclose to a brother or sister whom you dislike.

You are more apt to disclose to people you see as accepting, understanding, warm, and supportive. Generally, of course, these are people you are close to and like. Some studies claim that a lasting relationship increases the likelihood of self-disclosure, whereas others find that self-disclosure is heightened in temporary relationships—for example, between "strangers on a train" (Thibaut and Kelley 1959).

Male college students are more likely to disclose to a close friend than to either parent. Female college students disclose about equally to their mothers and to their best friends, but they do not disclose very much to their fathers or boyfriends.

As might be expected, husbands and wives self-disclose to each other more than they do to any other person or group of persons. Marital status, at least for men, even affects self-disclosure to friends. Married men disclose significantly less to friends than do unmarried men (Tschann 1988). The marital status of women, however, does not affect the amount of their self-disclosure to friends. One possible reason for this gender difference, as Jeanne Tschann (1988) observes, may be that women "place a higher value on personal relationships than men do, with the result that women continue friendships even when basic intimacy needs are being met by a spouse, while married men allow friendships to atrophy."

REWARDS OF SELF-DISCLOSURE

The obvious question when the topic of self-disclosure arises is "Why?" Why should anyone self-disclose to anyone else? What is it about this type of communication that merits its being singled out and discussed at length? Actually, research shows clearly that the benefits are many. Self-disclosure influences how many friends you have and whether people think you are psychologically stable or maladjusted; it also affects your general level of happiness and satisfaction, your level of self-awareness, your psychological and physiological health, and your general effectiveness in interpersonal relationships (Chaikin and Derlega 1974; Derlega, Margulis, and Winstead 1987), as well as the extent to which counselors are liked by their clients (VandeCreek and Angstadt 1985). Let's look at a few of these benefits in more detail.

KNOWLEDGE OF SELF

By self-disclosing, you gain a new perspective on yourself, a deeper understanding of your own behavior. After a thorough review of the self-disclosure and mental-adjustment literature, Paul Cozby (1973), concluded that "persons with positive mental health . . . are characterized by high disclosure to a few significant others and medium disclosure to others in the social environment. Individuals who are poorly adjusted . . . are characterized by either high or low self-disclosure to virtually everyone in the social environment." It is selective self-disclosure, or self-disclosure in moderation, then, that seems to characterize the well-adjusted personality (Bochner 1984).

ABILITY TO COPE

An improved ability to deal with your problems, especially guilt, frequently comes through self-disclosure (Cherry 1991). One of the great fears many people have is that they will not be accepted because of some deep, dark secret; because of something they have done; or because of some feeling or attitude they may have. We feel that these things might be the basis for rejection, so we develop guilt. By self-disclosing such feelings and being supported rather than rejected, we are better prepared to deal with the guilt and perhaps reduce or even eliminate it. Even self-acceptance is difficult without self-disclosure. We accept ourselves largely through the eyes of others. If we feel that others will reject us, we are apt to reject ourselves as well.

COMMUNICATION EFFECTIVENESS

Self-disclosure can improve communication effectiveness. Because you understand another's messages largely to the extent that you understand the person, you can better understand what a person means if you know that person well. You can tell what certain nuances mean, know when that person is joking, know when sarcasm is prompted by fear and when it comes from resentment, and so on. Self-disclosure is an essential condition for getting to know and for feeling comfortable with another individual. You might study a person's behavior or even live with a person for years, but if that person were never to self-disclose, you would be far from an understanding of that individual as a complete person.

MEANINGFULNESS OF RELATIONSHIPS

Self-disclosure helps you achieve a closer relationship with the person to whom you self-disclose (Schmidt and Cornelius 1987). Couples who engage in significant self-disclosure are found to remain together longer than couples who do not (Sprecher 1987) and couples who self-disclose honestly have higher marital satisfaction (Dickson-Markman 1984). And progressive self-disclosure among couples, along with appropriate responding to the disclosures of the other person, significantly increases the chances of relationship development (Falk and Wagner 1985).

If a meaningful relationship is to be established and maintained, then self-disclosure seems essential. There are, it is true, relationships that last for as long as 30 or 40 years without self-disclosure. Many couples would fall into this category, as would colleagues working in the same office or factory, or people living in the same neighborhood or apartment house. Without self-disclosure, however, these relationships are probably not as meaningful as they might be. By self-disclosing, you are in effect saying to other

What differences do you find between the self-disclosures of men and women? What cultural differences do you find?

individuals that you trust them, that you respect them, that you care enough about them and your relationship to reveal yourself to them.

Interestingly enough, your affection for your partner increases when you self-disclose. Men, but not women, also increase their affection for their partner when the partner self-discloses. This finding seems to reinforce the notion that women do not respond positively to the disclosures of men (Sprecher 1987).

Physiological Health

People who self-disclose are less vulnerable to illness (Pennebacker 1991). Self-disclosure seems to protect the body from the damaging stresses that accompany nondisclosure. For example, bereavement over the death of someone very close is linked to physical illness for those who bear it alone and in silence but is unrelated to any physical problems for those who share their grief with others. Similarly, women who have suffered sexual trauma experience a variety of illnesses (among them headaches and stomach problems). Women who keep these experiences to themselves, however, suffer much more than those who talk with others about these traumas.

Dangers of Self-Disclosure: Risks Ahead

As is usually the case, when the potential rewards are great so are the risks. Self-disclosure is no exception; the risks can be personal, relational, and professional and can be considerable. Weigh these potential risks carefully before engaging in significant self-disclosure.

Personal Risks

If you self-disclose aspects of your life that are greatly at variance with the values of those to whom you disclose, you may be met by rejection from even the closest friends and family members. Men and women who disclose that they have AIDS, for example, may find their friends and family no longer wanting to be quite as close as before.

Relational Risks

Even in close and long-lasting relationships, self-disclosure can cause problems. "Uncensored candor," notes the interpersonal researcher Arthur Bochner (1984), "is a bad idea." Total self-disclosure may prove threatening to a relationship by causing a decrease in mutual attraction, trust, or any of the bonds holding the individuals together. Self-disclosures concerning infidelity, romantic fantasies, past indiscretions or crimes, lies, or hidden weaknesses and fears could easily have such negative effects.

Professional Risks

The extensive media coverage of the gays and lesbians in the military who are coming out in protest of the "don't ask, don't tell" policy amply illustrates the professional dangers that self-disclosure may entail. Openly gay and lesbian military personnel, as well as those in education, fire departments and law enforcement, or health care agencies—to cite just a few examples—may find themselves confined to desk jobs, prevented from further advancement, or even charged with criminal behavior and fired. Similarly, politicians who disclose that they have been seeing a psychiatrist may later face loss of party and voter support. Teachers who disclose former or current drug use or cohabitation with students may find themselves denied tenure, teaching at undesirable hours, and eventually falling victim to "budget cuts." Further, teachers or students who, in the supportive atmosphere of their interpersonal communication course, disclose details about their sex life or financial condition or reveal self-doubts, anxieties, and fantasies may find some less-than-sympathetic listeners later using that information against them.

In making your choice between disclosing and not disclosing, keep in mind—in addition to the advantages and dangers already noted—the irreversible nature of communication, discussed in Unit 2. Regardless of how many times you may try to qualify something or "take it back," once you have said something you cannot withdraw it. You cannot erase the conclusions and inferences listeners have made on the basis of your disclosures. This is not to suggest that you therefore refrain from self-disclosing, but only to suggest that it is especially important to recognize the irreversible nature of communication.

SELF-DISCLOSURE GUIDELINES

Because self-disclosure is so important and so delicate a matter, guidelines are offered here for (1) deciding whether and how to self-disclose and (2) responding to the disclosures of others.

GUIDELINES FOR MAKING SELF-DISCLOSURES

In addition to weighing the potential rewards and dangers of self-disclosure already discussed, consider the following guidelines; they will help raise the right questions before you make what must be *your* decision.

Consider the Motivation for the Self-Disclosure   Self-disclosure should be motivated by a concern for the relationship, for the others involved, and for oneself. Some people self-disclose out of a desire to hurt the listener. Persons who tell their parents that they never loved them or that the parents hindered rather than helped their emotional development may be disclosing out of a desire to hurt and perhaps punish rather than to improve the relationship. Neither, of course, should self-disclosure be used to punish oneself, perhaps because of some guilt feeling or unresolved conflict. Self-disclosure should serve a useful and productive function for all persons involved.

Consider the Appropriateness of the Self-Disclosure   Self-disclosure should be appropriate to the context and to the relationship between you and your listener. Before making any significant self-disclosure, ask whether this is the right time and place. Could

Here is a parenting discussion group at a mother's center in New Paltz, New York. How would you expect the communication here to differ from one held at a "father's center"? Consider, for example, willingness to participate, topics discussed, and breadth and depth of self-disclosures.

a better time and place be arranged? Ask, too, whether this self-disclosure is appropriate to the relationship. Generally, the more intimate the disclosures, the closer the relationship should be. It is probably best to resist intimate disclosures (especially negative ones) with nonintimates or casual acquaintances, or in the early stages of a relationship.

Consider the Disclosures of the Other Person   During your disclosures, give the other person a chance to reciprocate with his or her own disclosures. If such reciprocal disclosures are not made, reassess your own self-disclosures. The lack of reciprocity may be a signal that for this person at this time and in this context, your disclosures are not welcome or appropriate.

Disclose gradually and in small increments. When disclosures are made too rapidly and all at once, it is impossible to monitor your listener's responses and to retreat if they are not positive enough. Further, you prevent the listener from responding with his or her own disclosures and thereby upset the natural balance that is so helpful in this kind of communication exchange.

Consider the Possible Burdens Self-Disclosure Might Entail   Carefully weigh the potential problems that you may incur as a result of your disclosure. Can you afford to lose your job if you disclose your prison record? Are you willing to risk relational difficulties if you disclose your infidelities? Ask yourself whether you are making unreasonable demands on the listener. For example, consider the person who swears his or her mother-in-law to secrecy and then self-discloses having an affair with a neighbor. This self-disclosure places an unfair burden on the mother-in-law, who is now torn between breaking her promise of secrecy or allowing her child to believe a lie. Parents often place unreasonable burdens on their children by self-disclosing marital problems, infidelities, or self-doubts without realizing that the children may be too young or too emotionally involved to deal effectively with this information.

GUIDELINES FOR RESPONDING TO SELF-DISCLOSURES

When someone discloses to you, it is usually a sign of trust and affection. In serving this most important receiver function, keep the following guidelines in mind. These guidelines will help you facilitate the disclosures of another person. An extended example of this important skill is provided in the box "The Art of Facilitating Self-Disclosure."

Practice the Skills of Effective and Active Listening The skills of effective listening (Unit 4) are especially important when listening to self-disclosures: listen actively, listen for different levels of meaning, listen with empathy, and listen with an open mind. Paraphrase the speaker so that you can be sure you understand both the thoughts and the feelings communicated. Express an understanding of the speaker's feelings to allow the speaker the opportunity to see them more objectively and through the eyes of another. Ask questions to ensure your own understanding and to signal your interest and attention.

Support and Reinforce the Discloser Express support for the person during and after the disclosures. Refrain from evaluation. For example, instead of saying, "You shouldn't have said that" or "You didn't cheat that often, did you?" concentrate on understanding and empathizing with the discloser. Allow the discloser to choose the pace; don't rush the discloser with the too-frequent "So how did it all end?" response. Make your supportiveness clear to the discloser through your verbal and nonverbal responses: maintain eye contact, lean toward the speaker, ask relevant questions, and echo the speaker's thoughts and feelings.

Keep the Disclosures Confidential When a person discloses to you, it is because she or he wants you to know the feelings and thoughts that are communicated. If you reveal these disclosures to others, negative effects are inevitable. Revealing what was said will probably inhibit future disclosures by this individual in general and to you in particular, and it is likely that your relationship will suffer considerably. But most important, betraying a confidence is unfair; it debases what could be and should be a meaningful interpersonal experience.

Don't Use the Disclosures Against the Person Many self-disclosures expose some kind of vulnerability or weakness. If you later turn around and use disclosures against the person, you betray the confidence and trust invested in you. Regardless of how angry you might get, resist the temptation to use the disclosures of others as weapons—the relationship is sure to suffer and may never fully recover.

The Art of Facilitating Self-Disclosure

Learning to facilitate the disclosures of others is a delicate art and one that is best explained by example. Consider, therefore, the first act of this dialogue, "Tommy's Family," which illustrates failure to facilitate another's disclosures. Note the specific ways in which Tommy's father, mother, and sister fail to help him share his feelings.

Tommy's Family

TOMMY: 12 years old and obviously troubled
FRANK: Tommy's father
MILLIE: Tommy's mother
SALLY: Tommy's teenage sister

ACT I. The Failure

[Tommy enters the living room, throws his books down on the coffee table, then goes to the refrigerator.]

FRANK: [To Millie] What's wrong with him?
MILLIE: I don't know. He's been acting strange the last few days.
SALLY: Acting strange? He is strange. Weird.

[Tommy comes back into the living room and sits down, looking into space.]

FRANK: Well, when your 12 years old, that's the way it is. I remember when I was 12. When I was your age, the big thing was girls. You got a girl, Tommy?
SALLY: Hey Mom, how about driving me to the mall? I gotta get a new dress for next week.
MILLIE: OK. I need a few things at K-Mart. You need anything, Tommy? You don't want to come with us, do you?
SALLY: Please say no. If people see us together, they'll think we're related. God! My life would be ruined. People would ignore me. No one would talk to me.
FRANK: You two go to the mall. I'm going bowling with Bill and Joe. Tommy will be OK home alone.
TOMMY: Yeah.
SALLY: Mom, let's go.
MILLIE: All right. I just have to call Grandma first and see if she's OK.
SALLY: Oh, that reminds me. I have to call Jack. Lori left him for a college guy, and he's really down in the dumps. I thought I'd call to cheer him up.
MILLIE: Can't you do that when we get back?
SALLY: Yeah, I guess.
FRANK: Well, you guys have fun. I'm off to bowl another 200 game. Joe is still bowling under 140, so Bill and I are going to try to give him a few tips.
MILLIE: [On the telephone] Hello, Mom? How are you doing? Is the arthritis acting up? I figure that with this weather, it must be really bad.
SALLY: Come on, Mom.
[Frank exits; Tommy turns on the TV.]

In Act I, Tommy's father, mother, and sister illustrate the typical failure to help another person share feelings. Although Tommy gave enough signals—throwing books down on the coffee table, saying nothing, staring into space—nobody showed any real concern, and nobody encouraged him to talk about what was on his mind. Note, too, that even though the father was aware that Tommy was disturbed, he directed his question to Millie instead of Tommy. Moreover, in his comment, Frank expressed a negative evaluation ("What's wrong with him?"). Even if Tommy had wanted to talk about his feelings, the father effectively closed the door to any empathic communication.

Note also that the few comments addressed to Tommy (for example, the father's "You got a girl, Tommy?" and the mother's "You don't want to come with us, do you?") fail to consider Tommy's *present* feelings. The father's comment is intimidating and seems more a reference to his own macho image than a question about Tommy. The mother's comment is negative and, in effect, asks Tommy not to join them.

But the most damaging part of this interaction occurs when father, mother, and sister not only ignore Tommy's feelings and problems but also express concern for someone else—sister for Jack, father for Joe, and mother for Grandma. Their comments tell Tommy that he is not worth their time and energy but that others are. When both the father and mother ignore Sally's put-downs of Tommy (normal as they may be among young children), they reinforce the idea that Tommy is unworthy. In their silence, they communicate agreement. In the language of transactional analysis, they tell Tommy that he is not OK but that these others are OK.

ACT II. The Success
[Frank, Millie, and Sally are sitting together. Tommy enters the living room, throws his books down on the coffee table, then goes to the refrigerator.]

FRANK: [Calling into the kitchen] Hey, Tommy, what's up? You look pretty angry.
TOMMY: It's nothing. Just school.
SALLY: He's just weird, Dad.
FRANK: You mean "weird" like the mad scientist in the old movies?
SALLY: No. You know what I mean—he's different.
FRANK: Oh, well that's something else. That's great. I'm glad Tommy is different. The world doesn't need another clone, and Tommy is certainly no clone. At 12 years old, it's not easy being unique. Right, Tommy?
TOMMY: [*To sister*] **Yeah, unique.**
FRANK: [To Millie and Sally] Are you still planning to go to the mall?
SALLY: Yeah, I have to get a new dress.
MILLIE: And I need some things at K-Mart. Are you going bowling?
FRANK: Well, I was planning on it, but I thought I might cancel and stay home. Tommy, you got any plans? If not, how about doing something together?
TOMMY: No. You want to go bowling.
FRANK: I can bowl anytime. After all, what's another 200 game? It's hardly a chal-

lenge. Come on. How about we take a drive to the lake and take a swim—
just the two of us. And I'd like to hear about what's going on in school.

TOMMY: OK, let's go. I need to put on my trunks. You know, I can swim four lengths without stopping.

FRANK: Four lengths? Well, I've got to see that. Get those trunks on and we're out of here.

SALLY: Mom, let's go-o-o-o.

MILLIE: OK. OK. OK. But I have to call Grandma first to see if she's all right.

FRANK: Let me say hello, too.

MILLIE: [To Tommy and Sally] Do you two want to talk to Grandma?

SALLY: Of course. I've got to tell her about this great new guy at school.

MILLIE: Oh, I want to hear about this, too. Well, we'll have plenty of time to talk in the car.

TOMMY: Hey, Mom, I gotta tell Grandma about my new bike. So let me talk first so Dad and I can get to the lake.

[Later, Tommy and Frank in car]

FRANK: [Puts arm on Tommy's shoulder] School got you down?

TOMMY: It's this new teacher. What a pain. I can't understand what he's talking about. Maybe I'm just stupid.

FRANK: What don't you understand?

TOMMY: I don't know. He calls it pregeometry. What's pregeometry?

Note that the interaction in Act II is drastically different from the interaction in Act I and illustrates how you can help someone self-disclose. Notice that Tommy's feelings are addressed immediately and directly by his father. Frank shows concern for Tommy's feelings by asking him about them and then about school. He shows that he cares for Tommy by defending him. For example, he turns Sally's negative comment into a positive one ("weird" becomes "unique") and also gives up bowling to be with Tommy. He continues to show caring and concern by putting Tommy first—ahead of his bowling and ahead of his friends Bill and Joe.

Frank further helps Tommy to disclose by being nonevaluative. Instead of asking Tommy indirectly, "What's wrong with him?" he talks to Tommy directly and asks about his feelings, using the information Tommy has already revealed ("School got you down?"). This is a good example of active listening (see Unit 4).

This dialogue is introductory; it merely sets the stage for meaningful self-disclosure. Both Tommy and his father are comfortable and are going to be away from any distractions. Tommy knows that his father is interested in him and that Frank is not going to find fault with him or otherwise give him a hard time. The atmosphere is supportive and nonthreatening.

SUMMARY: UNIT IN BRIEF

Self-Disclosure	Rewards and Dangers	Guidelines
Definition: revealing information about yourself to others, usually information you normally keep hidden **Influencing factors** • disclosures of others • audience size • topic • valence • gender • receiver relationship	**Rewards** • self-knowledge • ability to cope • communication effectiveness • meaningfulness of relationships • physiological health **Dangers** • personal risks • relational risks • professional risks • irreversibility	**Self-disclosing:** Consider motivation, appropriateness, the disclosures of others, and the possible burdens imposed. **Responding to disclosures of others:** Listen effectively, support and reinforce the discloser, keep disclosures confidential, and do not use disclosures as weapons.

THINKING CRITICALLY ABOUT SELF-DISCLOSURE

1. What general classes or types of information do you normally keep hidden? What types of information are you least likely to keep hidden?

2. How would you describe your tendency to self-disclose (a) your feelings of sadness or loneliness, (b) your past indiscretions, (c) your fantasies and dreams, and (d) your weaknesses?

3. When are you most likely to self-disclose? Least likely to self-disclose? What factors encourage you to self-disclose? What factors discourage your self-disclosing?

4. How would you describe your relationships (friendship, romantic, family) in terms of self-disclosure?

5. How satisfied are you with your current self-disclosing patterns? If you are dissatisfied, how might you go about repairing the situation?

6. Rosenfeld (1979) summarizes the results of his investigation of the reasons men and women give for avoiding self-disclosing by observing, "The stereotyped male role— independent, competitive, and unsympathetic—and the stereotyped female role—dependent, nonaggressive, and interpersonally oriented—were evident in the reasons indicated for avoiding self-disclosure. Seeking different rewards from their interpersonal relationships, many males and females go about the business of self-disclosing, and not self-disclosing, differently." Test some of these findings yourself by talking with your peers about the reasons why they avoid self-disclosure. Do men and women give different reasons for avoiding self-disclosure? What is there in the learning histories of the two sexes that might account for any observed differences? Do you think gender differences will increase or decrease over, say, the next ten years?

7. Do other people self-disclose to you? What types of people? On what topics?

8. How would you describe your self-disclosure response style? How would others describe it?
9. What kinds of self-disclosures are you likely to see on television talk shows? Why do these so engage audiences?
10. How would you go about seeking answers to the following questions?

   * What is the relationship between self-esteem and self-disclosure? For example, are high-self-esteem individuals likely to engage in more- or less-than-average self-disclosure? Are high-self-esteem individuals likely to engage in more positive or more negative disclosures than low-self-esteem individuals? How would you go about answering one or both of these questions?
   * Do men and women differ in the topics they self-disclose to their best friends? To their romantic partners?
   * Does the physical context influence self-disclosure?

Experiential Vehicles

8.1 DISCLOSING YOUR HIDDEN SELF

This experience is an extremely powerful one for exploring some of the dimensions of self-disclosure and is based on a suggestion by Gerard Egan (1970). The procedure is simple: Write on an index card a statement of information that is currently in your hidden self (that is, currently undisclosed to all or most of the others in the group). Do not put your name on the card. The statements are to be dealt with anonymously. The cards should be collected and read aloud to the entire group.

No comments should be made as the cards are read; no indication of evaluation should be made. The comments are to be dealt with in a totally supportive atmosphere. After the cards are read, you may wish to consider some or all of the following issues:

1. What topics did the statements deal with? Are they generally the topics about which you too keep information hidden?
2. Why do you suppose this type of information is kept in the hidden self? What advantages might there be in keeping it hidden? What disadvantages?
3. How would you react to people who disclosed such statements to you? For example, what difference, if any, would these types of disclosures make in your closest interpersonal relationships?

8.2 TO DISCLOSE OR NOT TO DISCLOSE?

Whether or not you should self-disclose is one of the most difficult decisions you have to make in interpersonal communication. Here are several instances of impending self-disclosure. For each, indicate whether you think the self-disclosure would be appropriate. Specify your reasons for each of your judgments. In making your decision, consider such questions as these: Will the self-disclosure help accomplish what the person wishes to accomplish? Is the self-disclosure appropriate? To the listener? To the speaker-listener relationship? (For example, in situation B, Tom wants to disclose on the telephone. Is this appropriate?)

A. A mother of two teenage children (one boy, one girl) has been feeling guilty for the past year over a romantic affair she had with her brother-in-law while her husband was in prison. She and her husband have been divorced for the last few months. She wants to self-disclose this affair and her guilt to her children.

B. Tom wants to break his engagement to Cathy. Tom has since fallen in love with another woman and wants to end his relationship with Cathy. Tom wants to call Cathy on the telephone, break his engagement, and disclose his new relationship.

C. Sam has been living in a romantic relationship with another man for the past several years. Sam wants to tell his parents, with whom he has been very close throughout his life, but can't seem to get up the courage to do so. He decides to tell them in a long letter.

D. Mary and Jim have been married for 12 years. Mary has been honest about most things and has self-disclosed a great deal to Jim—about her past romantic encounters, her fears, her insecurities, her ambitions, and so on. Yet Jim doesn't reciprocate. He almost never shares his feelings and has told Mary almost nothing about his life before they met. Mary wonders whether she should continue to self-disclose or whether she should begin to limit her disclosures.

E. Martin, a college student, recently found out he is HIV positive. Although he has sought the support of various groups, he wonders if he should tell his parents. His parents are in their 70s and relatively uneducated; they know little about the problems associated with HIV infection. He wants to tell them, but he fears that they will be unable to deal effectively with the news. He also fears that they will reject him, perhaps out of fear, perhaps out of their belief that AIDS is a disease that "good people" don't get.

UNIT 9

Apprehension and Assertiveness

Unit Objectives

After completing this unit, you should be able to:

1. Explain the theories of how apprehension and nonassertiveness develop
2. Define *communication apprehension*
3. Identify the causes of communication apprehension
4. Identify suggestions for managing communication apprehension
5. Define and distinguish among *assertiveness, non-assertiveness,* and *aggres-siveness*
6. Explain the principles for increasing assertiveness

Among the most important interpersonal communication skills are those of reducing communication apprehension and increasing assertiveness. Many of us are apprehensive (or shy or reticent) in different communication situations and to different degrees. Similarly, many of us are reluctant to assert ourselves, to speak up for our rights. In this unit, the related issues of apprehension and assertiveness are addressed with a view to increasing our understanding of these qualities and to enabling us to manage our own apprehension and assertiveness more effectively.

How Apprehension and Nonassertiveness Begin

There are a number of explanations for the origins of apprehension and nonassertiveness. Three of the most popular are the theories of innateness, personal inadequacy, and learned behavior.

The **innateness** theory holds that people are born apprehensive or nonassertive—that an innate factor determines whether a person will be apprehensive or nonapprehensive, assertive or nonassertive. If, as it seems, people are born with different sensitivities to sound or pain, it seems safe to argue that people are also born with different sensitivities to strangers, to new situations, or to interpersonal encounters that call for assertiveness. Recent research is adding support for this position (Richmond and McCroskey 1989).

There are probably hundreds of variations of the **personal inadequacy** theory, but all seem to agree that both nonassertive and apprehensive behaviors are symptoms of some personal problem or inadequacy. All the approaches also agree that the origin of apprehensive and nonassertive behavior is to be found in early experiences and in the problems and inadequacies they generated. According to this position, to reduce apprehension or increase assertiveness, one would need intensive therapy.

Another theory holds that apprehension and nonapprehension, assertiveness and nonassertiveness are **learned behaviors:** we have learned to act as we do. Some people, because of their unique set of experiences, learned assertive behaviors, while others, because of their unique set of experiences, learned nonassertive behaviors.

The important implication of this learning position is that if the behaviors were learned, they can be unlearned. This is not to say that such a change will be easy, but only that it is possible without rearranging our innate structure (even if that were possible) or solving all our early psychological problems (even if that were possible).

APPREHENSION

This discussion will prove more valuable to you if you first take the brief self-test titled "How Apprehensive Are You?" Developed by James McCroskey (1982), it is a measure of your apprehension in a variety of communication situations. Score the test according to the directions provided.

Now that you have a general idea of your own communication apprehension, it might be of interest to note that "communication apprehension is probably the most common handicap . . . suffered by people in contemporary American society" (McCroskey and Wheeless 1976). According to surveys of college students, between 10 percent and

TEST YOURSELF

HOW APPREHENSIVE ARE YOU?*

INSTRUCTIONS
This questionnaire is composed of 24 statements concerning your feelings about communication with other people. Please indicate in the space provided the degree to which each statement applies to you by marking whether you

    1 = strongly agree
    2 = agree
    3 = are undecided
    4 = disagree
    5 = strongly disagree

There are no right or wrong answers. Many of the statements are similar to other statements; do not be concerned about this. Work quickly; record your first impression.

    1. I dislike participating in group discussions.

    2. Generally, I am comfortable while participating in group discussions.

    3. I am tense and nervous while participating in group discussions.

    4. I like to get involved in group discussions.

    5. Engaging in a group discussion with new people makes me tense and nervous.

    6. I am calm and relaxed while participating in group discussions.

_____ 7. Generally, I am nervous when I have to participate in a meeting.

_____ 8. Usually, I am calm and relaxed while participating in meetings.

_____ 9. I am very calm and relaxed when I am called upon to express an opinion at a meeting.

_____ 10. I am afraid to express myself at meetings.

_____ 11. Communicating at meetings usually makes me uncomfortable.

_____ 12. I am very relaxed when answering questions at a meeting.

_____ 13. While participating in a conversation with a new acquaintance, I feel very nervous.

_____ 14. I have no fear of speaking up in conversations.

_____ 15. Ordinarily, I am very tense and nervous in conversations.

_____ 16. Ordinarily, I am very calm and relaxed in conversations.

_____ 17. While conversing with a new acquaintance, I feel very relaxed.

_____ 18. I'm afraid to speak up in conversations.

_____ 19. I have no fear of giving a speech.

_____ 20. Certain parts of my body feel very tense and rigid while I am giving a speech.

_____ 21. I feel relaxed while giving a speech.

_____ 22. My thoughts become confused and jumbled when I am giving a speech.

_____ 23. I face the prospect of giving a speech with confidence.

_____ 24. While giving a speech, I get so nervous that I forget facts I really know.

SCORING

The questionnaire gives you one total score and four subscores. The subscores relate to communication apprehension in each of four common communication contexts: group discussions, meetings, interpersonal conversations, and public speaking. To compute your scores, merely add or subtract your scores for each item as indicated below. (Note that a base of 18 is used in each of the formulas; this is done so that all scores come out as positive numbers.)

Subscore Desired	Scoring Formula
Group discussions	18 plus the scores for items 2, 4, and 6 and minus the scores for items 1, 3, and 5.
Meetings	18 plus the scores for items 8, 9, and 12 and minus the scores for items 7, 10, and 11.
Interpersonal	18 plus the scores for items 14, 16, and 17 conversations and minus the scores for items 13, 15, and 18.
Public speaking	18 plus the scores for items 19, 21, and 23 and minus the scores for items 20, 22, and 24.

To obtain your total score, simply add your four subscores together. Each subscore should range from 6 to 30; the higher the subscore, the greater your apprehension. Any score above 18 indicates some degree of apprehension. Most people score significantly higher for public speaking than for interpersonal conversations.

20 percent suffer "severe, debilitating communication apprehension," while another 20 percent suffer from "communication apprehension to a degree substantial enough to interfere to some extent with their normal functioning."

Apprehension, shyness, and the willingness to communicate generally varies from one culture to another. For example, in one study of shyness Israelis were found to be the least shy (only 24% reported they were currently experiencing shyness, compared to, for example, Mexicans (39%), Americans (42%), Germans (50%), Taiwanese (55%), and Japanese (60%) (Zimbardo 1977). In a study of the willingness to communicate, American college students indicated the highest willingness to communicate, whereas students from Micronesia indicated the lowest. Micronesian students also indicated the highest degree of shyness while, in this study, Puerto Ricans reported the lowest (McCroskey and Richmond 1990).

DEFINITION

The term *communication apprehension* (and shyness, unwillingness to communicate, stage fright, reticence) refers to a state of fear or anxiety about communication interaction. People develop negative feelings and predict negative results as a function of engaging in communication interactions. They feel that whatever gain would accrue from engaging in communication would be outweighed by the fear. To those with high communication apprehension, the communication interaction just isn't worth the fear it engenders.

Trait apprehension refers to fear of communication generally, regardless of the specific situation. It appears in dyadic, small-group, public speaking, and mass communication situations. **State apprehension,** in contrast, is specific to a given communication situation. For example, a speaker may fear public speaking but have no difficulty with dyadic communication, or a speaker may fear job interviews but have no fear of public speaking. State apprehension is extremely common; it is experienced by most people in some situations.

DIFFERENCES IN DEGREE

Speaker apprehension exists on a continuum. People are not either apprehensive or unapprehensive. We all experience some degree of apprehension. Some people are extremely apprehensive and become incapacitated in a communication situation. They suffer a great deal in a society oriented, as our is, around communication and in which one's success depends on the ability to communicate effectively. Others are so mildly apprehensive that they appear to experience no fear at all when confronted by communication situations; they actively seek out communication experiences and rarely feel any significant apprehension. Most of us fall between these two extremes.

APPREHENSIVE BEHAVIORS

Apprehension may also be examined in behavioral terms (Richmond and McCroskey 1989). Generally, apprehension leads to a decrease in the frequency, strength, and likelihood of engaging in communication transactions. High apprehensives avoid communication situations and, when forced to participate, do so as little as possible. This reluctance to communicate shows itself in a variety of forms. In small-group situations, apprehensives not only talk less but also avoid the seats of influence—for example, those in the group leader's direct line of sight. High apprehensives are less likely to be seen as leaders in small-group situations regardless of their actual behaviors. Even in classrooms, they avoid seats where they can be easily called on, and they maintain little direct eye contact with the instructor, especially when a question is likely to be asked. Probably related to this is the finding that apprehensives have more negative attitudes toward school, earn poorer grades, and are more likely to drop out of college (McCroskey, Booth-Butterfield, and Payne 1989).

High apprehensives are also considered less desirable social choices by both teachers and fellow students. Apprehensives disclose little and avoid occupations with heavy communication demands (for example, teaching or public relations). Within their occupation, they are less desirous of advancement, largely because of the associated increase in communication. High apprehensives are often less satisfied with their jobs, probably because they are less successful in advancing and in developing interpersonal relationships. High apprehensives are even less likely to get job interviews.

Apprehensives also engage more in steady dating, a finding that is not unexpected. One of the most difficult communication situations is asking for a date, especially a first date, and developing a new relationship. Consequently, once a dating relationship has been established, the apprehensive is reluctant to give it up and go through the anxiety of another first date and another get-acquainted period.

All this does not mean that apprehensives are ineffective or unhappy people. Most apprehensives have learned or can learn to deal with their communication anxiety.

INFLUENCES ON COMMUNICATION APPREHENSION

Research has identified several factors that increase communication apprehension (McCroskey and Daly 1987; Beatty 1988; Richmond and McCroskey 1989). A knowledge of these factors will help you to increase your understanding and control of your own apprehension.

Lack of Communication Skills and Experience   If you lack skills in typing, you can hardly expect to type very well. Yet you rarely assume that a lack of communication skills and experience can cause difficulty with communication and create apprehension. It can. If you have never asked for a date and have no idea how to go about doing it, for example, it is perfectly reasonable that you will feel apprehension.

Degree of Evaluation   The more you perceive the situation as one in which you will be evaluated, the greater your apprehension is likely to be. Employment interviews, for example, provoke anxiety largely because they are highly evaluative. Similarly, in asking for that first date, you are being evaluated and consequently experience apprehension.

Subordinate Status   When you feel that others are better communicators than you are or that they know more than you do, your apprehension increases. For example, shy students report particular difficulty in speaking with people who are authorities by virtue of what they know as well as by virtue of their roles in society (Zimbardo 1977). Thinking more positively about yourself and strengthening your own skills will help you feel more equal.

Degree of Conspicuousness   The more conspicuous you are, the more likely you are to feel apprehensive. This is why delivering a speech to a large audience is more anxiety provoking than speaking in a small-group situation; you are more conspicuous before the large group—you stand out, and all attention is on you. For example, in one survey, 73 percent of the shy students said they were especially shy while being the focus of attention in a large group (as in giving a speech), and 68 percent noted that they were shy in large groups generally (Zimbardo 1977). In small discussion groups, for example, attention is spread over a number of people, and the amount of time you are in focus is much less than it is when you are giving a public speech.

Degree of Unpredictability   The more unpredictable the situation, the greater your apprehension is likely to be. Ambiguous and new situations are unpredictable; you cannot know beforehand what they will be like, hence you become anxious. A similar condition seems to increase your shyness when interacting with strangers; 70 percent of shy students surveyed said they were especially shy with strangers (Zimbardo 1977). As the novelty of the situation or person is reduced, your apprehension is also reduced.

Degree of Dissimilarity   When you feel you have little in common with your listeners, you are likely to feel anxious. The more different you feel from your listeners, the more apt you are to experience fear in communicating. By stressing similarities, you will think less of your differences, and your apprehension should decrease.

Prior Successes and Failures   Your experience in similar situations greatly influences the way you respond to new ones. Prior success generally (though not always) reduces apprehension, whereas prior failure generally (though not always) increases apprehension. There is no mystery here: prior success says that you can succeed this time as well; prior failure warns that you may fail again.

MANAGING COMMUNICATION APPREHENSION

It is probably impossible to eliminate communication apprehension. However, we can manage apprehension effectively so that it does not debilitate us or prevent us from achieving goals that require us to communicate in a variety of situations.

ACQUIRE COMMUNICATION SKILLS AND EXPERIENCE

As already noted, one of the major causes of apprehension is lack of skills and experience. The remedy is to acquire the requisite skills and experience. In this course, you are acquiring the skills of effective interpersonal interaction. You should select additional courses and experiences that will enable you to acquire the skills you need most. Refer to your apprehension self-test scores to see in which areas you are most apprehensive, and then consider selecting courses and experiences to meet the most obvious needs.

Often the person who has trouble communicating effectively suffers from communication apprehension. Review the factors that influence communication apprehension. Which factors would be especially important in your asking someone for a date? In interviewing for an important job? In asking your boss for a substantial raise? In defending yourself to the police after being falsely accused of a crime? In criticizing a subordinate for not doing an effective job?

Prepare and Practice

The more preparation and practice you put into something, the more comfortable you feel with it and, consequently, the less apprehension you feel. For example, if you are apprehensive telling jokes, practice a joke you wish to tell. Rehearse it mentally and perhaps aloud in front of a mirror until you are comfortable with the material.

Focus on Success

Think positively. Concentrate your energies on doing the very best job you can in whatever situation you are in. Put negative thoughts and ideas of failure out of your mind. If you visualize yourself failing, you very likely will fail. Fortunately, the reverse also seems to be true: visualize yourself succeeding, and you stand a good chance of doing just that. Remember that having failed in the past does not mean that you must fail again in the future. You now have new skills and new experiences, and they increase your chances for success.

Familiarize Yourself with the Situation

The more you familiarize yourself with the situation, the better. The reason is simple: when you are familiar with the situation and with what will be expected of you, you are better able to predict what will happen. This will reduce ambiguity as well as the perceived newness of the situation.

PUT COMMUNICATION APPREHENSION IN PERSPECTIVE

When engaging in any communication experience, remember that the world will not cave in if you do not succeed. Also remember that other people are not able to perceive your apprehension in the same way you do. You may feel dryness in your throat and a rapid heartbeat, but no one knows this but you.

TRY TO RELAX

Apprehension is reduced when you are physically relaxed. Breathing deeply and engaging in some kind of physical activity (for example, walking or writing on a chalkboard) help reduce tension and lessen the apprehension and anxiety you feel.

Also relax mentally. For example, knowing that you have acquired new communication skills and that you have prepared yourself for the task should help alleviate your normal anxiety. Focusing on success and putting communication apprehension into perspective should help you feel more confident. This, too, will contribute to a more relaxed feeling.

ASSERTIVENESS

A number of interesting experiments illustrate just how passive many people have become (Moriarty 1975). In one experiment, subjects taking a psychological test were placed near a confederate of the experimenter's who played loud rock-and-roll music during the test. Of the 20 subjects, 16 made no comment at all. Even when the students were told they would receive mild electric shocks for wrong answers, 16 of the 20 subjects still said nothing to the music player. In one variation, experimenters approached people after they had left a phone booth; the experimenters claimed they had lost a ring and asked the people leaving the phone booth whether they would mind emptying their pockets to see if they had perhaps picked it up. Of the 20 adult males who were approached, 16 emptied their pockets (80 percent). When the experiment was repeated using graduate students, 20 of 24 men (83 percent) emptied their pockets. "I believe," concludes Moriarty, "that many of us have accepted the idea that few things are worth getting into a hassle about, especially with strangers. And I believe this is particularly true of younger people."

The importance of assertiveness in interpersonal communication is explained further by examining the distinctions among nonassertiveness, aggressiveness, and assertive communication.

NONASSERTIVENESS

Nonassertiveness comes in two forms: situational and generalized. **Situational nonassertiveness** refers to a lack of assertiveness only in certain kinds of situations—for example, those that create a great deal of anxiety or those in which authority must be exercised.

Generalized nonassertiveness, as the term implies, is nonassertive behavior that is typically demonstrated. People who exhibit this behavior are timid and reserved and are unable to assert their rights regardless of the situation. These people do what others tell them to do—parents, employers, and the like—without questioning and without concern for what is best for them. When these persons' rights are infringed upon, they do nothing about it and sometimes accuse themselves of being nonaccepting. Generalized nonassertive persons often ask permission from others to do what it is their perfect right to do.

AGGRESSIVENESS

Aggressiveness also comes in two forms. **Situationally aggressive** people are aggressive only under certain conditions or in certain situations. For example, they may become aggressive after being taken advantage of over a long period or by someone for whom they have done a great deal. These people are normally not aggressive; only in certain situations do they behave aggressively.

Generally aggressive people, however, meet all or at least most situations with aggressive behavior. These people seem in charge of almost all situations; regardless of what is going on, they take over. They appear to think little of the opinions, values, or beliefs of others, and yet they are extremely sensitive to criticisms of their own behavior. Consequently, they frequently get into arguments with others and find that they have few friends. They think little of others, and others think little of them.

ASSERTIVE COMMUNICATION

Assertive communication—communication that enables you to act in your own best interests without denying or infringing upon the rights of others—is the desired alternative. Assertive individuals are willing to assert their own rights, but unlike their aggressive counterparts, they do not hurt others in the process. Assertive individuals speak their minds and welcome others doing likewise. In *Your Perfect Right* (1970), the first book on assertiveness training, Robert Alberti and Michael Emmons note that "behavior which enables a person to act in his own best interest, to stand up for himself without undue anxiety, to express his honest feelings comfortably, or to exercise his own rights without denying the rights of others we call *assertive behavior.*" Furthermore, "the assertive individual is fully in charge of himself in interpersonal relationships, feels confident and capable without cockiness or hostility, is basically spontaneous in the expression of feelings and emotions, and is generally looked up to and admired by others." Surely, this is the picture of an effective individual. Not surprisingly, it is the picture of the person who experiences high job satisfaction (Rabin and Zelner 1992) and possesses greater dating skills (Prisbell 1986).

Four characteristics define assertiveness in interpersonal communication (Norton and Warnick 1976). Assertive individuals are:

open	They engage in frank expressions of their feelings.
not anxious	They readily volunteer opinions and beliefs, deal directly with stressful interpersonal communication situations, and question others without fear.

contentious	They stand up and argue for their rights, even if this entails unpleasantness with others.
not intimidated	They hold fast to their beliefs and are not easily persuaded.

Assertive people are assertive when they want to be, but they can be nonassertive if the situation seems to call for it. For example, we might wish to be nonassertive in a situation in which assertiveness might emotionally hurt the other person. Let us say that an older relative wishes us to do something for her or him. We could assert our rights and say no, but in doing so we would probably hurt this person; it might be better simply to do as asked. Of course, there are limits that should be observed. We should be careful, in such a situation, that we are not hurt instead. For example, the parents who want their child to continue to live at home until marriage may be hurt by the child's assertive behavior in refusing, yet the alternative is to hurt oneself.

PRINCIPLES FOR INCREASING ASSERTIVENESS

Most assertiveness trainers generally assume that most people are situationally nonassertive. Most people are able to modify their behavior, with a resulting increase in general interpersonal effectiveness and self-esteem. Those who are generally nonassertive, however, probably need extensive training with a therapist. Those who are only moderately nonassertive and wish to understand their lack of assertiveness—and perhaps behave differently in certain situations—should find the following principles of value.

ANALYZE THE ASSERTIVE COMMUNICATIONS OF OTHERS

The first step in increasing assertiveness is to understand the nature of assertive behaviors. This understanding should already have been achieved on an intellectual level. What is necessary and more important is to understand actual assertive behaviors, and the best way to start is to observe and analyze the behavior of others. Learn to distinguish the differences among assertive, aggressive, and nonassertive behaviors. Focus on what makes one behavior assertive and another behavior aggressive or nonassertive. Listen to what is said and how it is said.

ANALYZE YOUR OWN COMMUNICATIONS

After you have acquired some skills in observing the behaviors of others, turn your analysis to yourself. Analyze situations in which you are normally assertive, nonassertive, and aggressive. What characterizes these situations? What do the situations in which you are normally aggressive have in common? How do these situations differ from the ones in which you are normally nonassertive?

Analyze your own nonverbal behaviors. How do you stand when you are assertive? Aggressive? Nonassertive? What tone of voice do you use? What kind of eye contact do you maintain? What do you do with your hands? Your nonverbal behaviors are probably different for each type of behavior.

REHEARSE ASSERTIVE COMMUNICATIONS

Several systems are available for effective rehearsal of assertive behaviors. One of the most popular is to select a situation in which you are normally nonassertive and build a hierarchy that begins with a relatively nonthreatening behavior and ends with the desired behavior. For example, let us say that you have difficulty speaking in class and that the desired behavior is to speak your mind in class. You might construct a hierarchy of situations that lead up to speaking in class. It could begin with simply visualizing yourself sitting in class. You might then visualize yourself sitting in class in a state of relaxation. Once you have mastered this visualization, proceed to the next step, visualizing the instructor asking a question. Once you are able to visualize this situation and remain relaxed throughout, visualize the instructor asking you the question. Visualize this situation until you can do so while relaxed. Then try visualizing yourself answering the question. Again, repeat this until you can do it while fully relaxed. Next visualize volunteering your opinion in class—the desired behavior. Visualize this until you can do so while totally relaxed.

This is the mental rehearsal. You might add the vocal dimension by answering out loud the question you imagine the teacher asking you. Again, do this until you have no difficulty. Next try doing this in front of a supportive friend or group of friends. After this rehearsal, you are probably ready for the next step.

COMMUNICATE ASSERTIVELY

This step is naturally the most difficult but obviously the most important. You can increase assertiveness only by acting out assertive communications; you cannot become assertive by communicating nonassertively.

Again, do this in small steps. In keeping with the previous example, try to answer a question you are sure of before volunteering an opinion or arguing with the instructor.

Throughout this book, the specific skills that contribute to assertive communication are considered, for example:

- the characteristics of effective interpersonal interaction, especially confidence, expressiveness, and interaction management (Unit 6)
- powerful (and avoiding powerless) language (Unit 20)
- the skills of argumentativeness (Unit 21)
- appropriate conflict resolution strategies (Unit 21)

Once you have communicated assertively, *reward yourself.* Give yourself something you want—an ice-cream cone, a CD, a new jacket. The desired behavior will be more easily and permanently learned if you reward yourself immediately after engaging in the behavior. Try not to delay the reward too long: rewards work best when they are immediate.

After communicating, get feedback from others. Start with people who are generally supportive. They should provide you with the social reinforcement so helpful in learning new behaviorial patterns. This feedback is particularly important because your intention and the perception of your behavior by an observer may be totally different. For example, you may behave in certain ways with the intention of communicating confidence, but the observer may perceive arrogance. Thus, another person's perception of your behavior can often help you to see yourself as others do.

In all behaviors, but especially with new behaviors, recognize that you may initially fail in what you try to do. You may try to assert yourself, only to find that you have been unsuccessful. You might, for example, try to answer the teacher's question and find that not only do you have the wrong answer but you also do not even understand the question. You might raise your hand and find yourself at a loss for words when you are recognized. Such incidents should not discourage you; realize that in all attempts to change behaviors, you will experience both failure and success.

A note of caution should be added to this discussion. It is easy to visualize a situation in which people are talking behind us in a movie and, with our newfound enthusiasm for assertiveness, we tell these people to be quiet. It is also easy to visualize our getting smashed in the teeth as a result. It is equally easy to visualize asserting ourselves with someone we care for, only to find that as a result this person bursts into tears, unable to handle our new behavior. In applying these principles, be careful that you do not go beyond what you can handle, physically and emotionally. Do not, for example, assert yourself out of a job. It is wise to be careful when changing any behavior, especially assertiveness.

SUMMARY: UNIT IN BRIEF

Definitions	Management Principles
Apprehension: a state of fear or anxiety about communication situations	**Managing communication apprehension**
Trait apprehension: a fear of communication generally	1. Acquire communication skills and experience.
State apprehension: a fear of communication that is specific to a situation (for example, an interview or public speaking situation)	2. Prepare and practice.
	3. Focus on success.
	4. Familiarize yourself with the situation.
	5. Be aware that physical relaxation helps.
	6. Put communication apprehension in perspective.
Nonassertiveness: an inability to assert oneself or to stand up to defend one's rights	**Increasing assertiveness**
Situational nonassertiveness: inability to assert oneself in certain situations	1. Analyze the assertive communications of others.
Generalized nonassertiveness: inability to assert oneself in most or all situations	2. Analyze your own communications.
	3. Rehearse assertive communications.
Aggressiveness: behavior that serves self-interests without any consideration for the rights of others	4. Communicate assertively.
Assertive communication: communication that enables a person to act in his or her own best interests without denying the rights of others	

THINKING CRITICALLY ABOUT APPREHENSION AND ASSERTIVENESS

1. In what communication situations are you most apprehensive? Why do you suppose this is so?
2. Can you create a hierarchy of at least ten behaviors that vary in terms of your level of apprehension? Begin with behavior 1, identifying a situation in which you have little to no apprehension, and then work up to behavior 10, identifying a situation in which you have great apprehension. What distinguishes the situations with low numbers from situations with high numbers?
3. What do you think has contributed to your current level of communication apprehension? For example, can you identify early childhood influences?
4. In what communication situations are you likely to be evaluated during the next 12 months? Will you be apprehensive? What can you do about it at this point?
5. Read the following "Dear Abby" letter. Do the sentiments in this letter suggest any changes in your behaviors in dealing with shy people?

DEAR ABBY: Thank you for printing the letter from the teenage girl who was struggling with shyness.

I, too, am a very shy and quiet person. I've been this way all my life. I can't tell you how many people have said, "You sure are quiet." I can't imagine anyone going up to a person and saying, "You sure have a big mouth!"

I would like to reassure everyone that I know I am quiet, but I am a very well-adjusted, happy person who enjoys being quiet. I am quiet because I have nothing to say, and I don't want to fill the quietness with empty chatter. I would find it quite exhausting to make small talk, or worse yet, try to be the life of the party, or the center of attention.

In the past, I have tried to talk more and be more outgoing so people would like me better, but it did not become me . . . it was not natural.

It has taken me years to like myself just the way I am. I have many friends who like me just the way I am, so to the others who are disturbed by my quietness and shy personality, please leave me alone. Please don't try to make me feel that there is something wrong with me because I am different from you who feel compelled to talk all the time.

Abby, if you print this—and I hope you do—you will be doing an enormous favor to all the shy, quiet people who read your column. There are more of us than you could possibly imagine

—QUIET IN ATLANTA

DEAR QUIET: Here's your letter, which should make a highly audible statement, and will put an end to that question— "Why are you so quiet?"*

6. How will apprehension affect your professional life? Your relational life?
7. In what situations are you nonassertive? Aggressive? Assertive? What is it about these situations that leads you to behave differently?
8. Research shows that attitudes toward assertiveness are influenced by culture. For example, Caucasian-Americans endorsed the legitimacy of assertiveness more strongly than did Japanese-Americans (Johnson and Marsella 1978). Do you see cultural differences in attitudes toward assertiveness or in actual assertive behaviors?
9. Can you identify at least ten situations in which assertiveness would probably be the wrong mode of response?
10. How would you go about seeking answers to the following questions?

    *   Are shyness and apprehension hereditary?
    *   Do preteen boys or preteen girls experience greater apprehension?
    *   Are there points in a person's life when the level of apprehension significantly changes?
    *   Are assertive people happier than nonassertive or aggressive people?

---

*Small Talk a Big Problem for Shy People" taken from a *Dear Abby* column by Abigail Van Buren. Dist. by Universal Press Syndicate. Reprinted with permission. All rights reserved.

EXPERIENTIAL VEHICLES

9.1 ASSERTIVENESS QUESTIONNAIRE

Indicate how you would respond to each of the ten situations presented below. Use the following keys:

> AS = assertively
> AG = aggressively
> NA = nonassertively

Respond instinctively rather than in the way you feel you should respond. After each person has responded individually, discuss these situations and the responses in groups of five or six in any way you feel is meaningful.

_____ 1. Your meal in a restaurant arrives cold instead of hot.

_____ 2. A neighbor repeatedly drops by for coffee without being invited.

_____ 3. A fellow student does not work on a group project for which each member will receive the same grade.

_____ 4. You are attracted to someone in class and want to ask the person for a date.

_____ 5. A friend is continually late for appointments.

_____ 6. A group of students is speaking unfairly about someone you know.

_____ 7. A persistent salesperson keeps showing you merchandise you do not want to buy.

_____ 8. Your friend wants to borrow your expensive watch, and you are afraid it might be lost.

_____ 9. Your boss takes advantage of you by asking you to accept all sorts of extra responsibilities.

_____ 10. Someone asks you for a date, but you do not want to go.

9.2 ANALYZING ASSERTIVENESS

Read each of the following five situations. Consider all or some of the following questions, either individually, in small groups, or with the class as a whole:

1. How might an aggressive, a nonassertive, and an assertive person deal with each of these situations?
2. What obstacles might you anticipate if you chose to respond assertively?
3. What suggestions might you offer the person who wants to respond assertively but is having difficulty putting the principles into practice?

Cheating on an Examination. You and another student turn in examination papers that are too similar to be the result of mere coincidence. The instructor accuses you of cheating by allowing the student behind you to copy your answers. You were not aware that anyone saw your paper.

Decorating Your Apartment. You have just redecorated your apartment, expending considerable time and money in making it exactly as you want it. A good friend of yours brings you a house gift—the ugliest poster you have ever seen. Your friend insists that you hang it over your fireplace, the focal point of your living room.

Borrowing Money. A friend borrows $30 and promises to pay you back tomorrow. But tomorrow passes, as do 20 other tomorrows, and there is no sign of the money. You know that the person has not forgotten about it, and you also know that the person has more than enough money to pay you back.

Neighbor Intrusions. A neighbor has been playing a stereo at an extremely high volume late into the night. This makes it difficult for you to sleep.

Sexual Harassment. Your supervisor at work has been coming on to you and has asked repeatedly to go out with you. You have refused each time. Brushing up against you, touching you in passing, and staring at you in a sexual way are common occurrences. You have no romantic interest in your supervisor and simply want to do your job, free from this type of harassment.

Part

T W O

Messages: Verbal and Nonverbal

APPROACHING VERBAL AND NONVERBAL MESSAGES

In approaching your study of messages, keep the following in mind:

- In real communication, words are always accompanied by nonverbal messages. See messages, therefore, as combinations of verbal and nonverbal signals.
- Message systems, both verbal and nonverbal, are social and cultural institutions. They are part of the culture and reflect that culture. The rules of communication will thus differ from one culture to another; intercultural violations are created easily.
- Connect and relate the various aspects of nonverbal communication. Although each nonverbal code is discussed separately (for example, body, space, and time are considered separately), you communicate with different codes simultaneously. Therefore, remember that each code functions together with the other codes in actual interpersonal communication.
- Resist the temptation to draw conclusions about people on the basis of isolated bits of message behavior.
- Observe. Look at your own communications and interactions and notice the verbal and nonverbal messages discussed here and in class. See in practice what you read about in theory.

UNIT 10

Universals of Verbal and Nonverbal Messages

UNIT OBJECTIVES

AFTER COMPLETING THIS UNIT, YOU SHOULD BE ABLE TO:

1. Explain the major ways in which nonverbal and verbal messages interact
2. Explain these principles of meaning: meanings are in people, meanings are more than words, meanings are unique, meanings are denotative and connotative, and meanings are context-based

3. Explain these principles of messages: messages are packaged, messages are rule-governed, messages vary in directness, messages vary in believability, and messages may metacommunicate
4. Explain the structure and function of double-bind messages

You make yourself, your feelings, and your thoughts known to others by encoding your ideas and meanings into a code of verbal and nonverbal signals. The verbal portion is language—the words, phrases, and sentences you use. The nonverbal portion consists of a wide variety of elements—spatial relationships, time orientation, gestures, facial expressions, eye movements, touch, and variations in the rate, volume, and pitch of your speech.

THE INTERACTION OF VERBAL AND NONVERBAL MESSAGES

In face-to-face communication, you blend verbal and nonverbal messages to best convey your meanings. Enumerating the six major ways in which nonverbal messages are used with verbal messages helps to highlight this important verbal-nonverbal interaction.

TO ACCENT

Nonverbal communication is often used to emphasize some part of the verbal message. You might, for example, raise your voice to underscore a particular word or phrase, bang your fist on the desk to stress your commitment, or look longingly into someone's eyes when saying "I love you."

TO COMPLEMENT

Nonverbal communication may add nuances of meaning not communicated by your verbal message. Thus, you might smile when telling a story (to suggest that you find it humorous) or frown and shake your head when recounting someone's deceit (to suggest your disapproval).

TO CONTRADICT

You may deliberately contradict your verbal messages with nonverbal movements, for example, by crossing your fingers or winking to indicate that you are lying.

TO REGULATE

Nonverbal movements may be used to control, or to indicate your desire to control, the flow of verbal messages, as when you purse your lips, lean forward, or make hand movements to indicate that you want to speak. You might also put up your hand or vocalize your pauses (for example, with "um") to indicate that you have not finished and are not ready to relinquish the floor to the next speaker.

TO REPEAT

You can repeat or restate the verbal message nonverbally. You can, for example, follow your verbal "Is that all right?" with raised eyebrows and a questioning look, or you can motion with your head or hand to repeat your verbal "Let's go."

TO SUBSTITUTE

You may also use nonverbal communication to take the place of verbal messages. You can, for example, signal "OK" with a hand gesture. You can nod your head to indicate yes or shake your head to indicate no.

MEANINGS AND MESSAGES

Meaning is an active process created by cooperation between source and receiver, speaker and listener, writer and reader. Understanding what meanings are and how they are passed from one person to another is crucial to controlling the verbal and nonverbal message system.

MEANINGS ARE IN PEOPLE

Meaning depends not only on messages (whether verbal, nonverbal, or both) but also on the interaction of these messages and the receiver's own thoughts and feelings. You do not "receive" meaning; you create meaning. Words do not mean; people mean. Consequently, to uncover meaning, look into people, not just into words.

An example of the confusion that can result when this relatively simple fact is overlooked is provided by Ronald D. Laing, H. Phillipson, and A. Russell Lee in *Interpersonal Perception* (1966) and analyzed by Paul Watzlawick in *How Real Is Real?* (1977): A couple on the second night of their honeymoon are sitting at a hotel bar. The woman strikes up a conversation with the couple next to her. The husband refuses to communicate with the couple and becomes antagonistic toward his wife as well as the couple. The wife then grows angry because her husband has created such an awkward and unpleasant situation. Each becomes increasingly disturbed, and the evening ends in a bitter conflict in which each is convinced of the other's lack of consideration. Eight years later, they analyze this argument. Apparently, "honeymoon" had meant very different things to each of them. To the husband, it had meant a "golden opportunity to ignore the rest of the world and simply explore each other." He felt his wife's interaction with the other couple implied there was something lacking in him. To the wife, "honeymoon" had meant an opportunity to try out her new role as wife. "I had never had a conversation with another couple as a wife before," she said. "Previous to this I had always been a 'girlfriend' or 'fiancee' or 'daughter' or 'sister.'"

MEANINGS ARE MORE THAN WORDS AND GESTURES

When you want to communicate a thought or feeling to another person, you do so with relatively few symbols. These symbols represent just a small part of what you are thinking or feeling, much of which remains unspoken. If you were to try to describe every feeling in detail, you would never get on with the job of living. The meanings you seek to communicate are much more than the sum of the words and nonverbal behaviors you use to represent them.

Because of this, you can never fully know what another person is thinking or feeling. You can only approximate it on the basis of the meanings you receive, which, as already noted, are greatly influenced by who *you* are and what *you* are feeling. Conversely, others can never fully know you; they, too, can only approximate what you are feeling. Failure to understand another person or to be understood is not an abnormal situation. It is inevitable, although we should realize that we can always understand each other a little better than we now do.

MEANINGS ARE UNIQUE

Because meanings are derived from both the messages communicated and the receiver's own thoughts and feelings, no two people ever derive the same meanings. Similarly, because people change constantly, no one person can derive the same meanings on two separate occasions. Who you are can never be separated from the meanings you create. As a result, check your perceptions of another's meanings by asking questions, echoing what you perceive to be the other person's feelings or thoughts, seeking elaboration and clarification, and, in general, practicing the skills identified in the discussion on effective interpersonal perception and listening.

Also recognize that as you change, you also change the meanings you create out of past messages. Thus, although the message sent may not have changed, the meanings you created from it yesterday and the meanings you create today may be quite different. Yesterday, when a special someone said, "I love you," you created certain meanings. But today, when you learn that the same "I love you" was said to three other people or when you fall in love with someone else, you drastically change the meanings you perceive from these words.

MEANINGS ARE BOTH DENOTATIVE AND CONNOTATIVE

To explain denotative and connotative meaning, let us first take a word such as "death." To a doctor, this word might mean, or denote, simply the point at which the heart stops beating—that is, an objective description of a particular event. To a mother whose son has just died, however, the word means much more. It recalls the son's youth, his ambitions, his family, his illness, and so on. To her, the word is emotional, subjective, and highly personal. These emotional, subjective, and personal associations are the word's connotative meaning. The **denotation** of a word is its objective definition; the **connotation** is its subjective or emotional meaning.

Now consider a simple nod of the head in answer to the question, "Do you agree?" This gesture is largely denotative and simply says yes. What about a wink, a smile, or a vigorous nod of the head? These nonverbal expressions are more connotative; they express your feelings rather than communicate objective information.

The denotative meaning of a message is general or universal; most people would agree with the denotative meanings and would give similar definitions. Connotative meanings, however, are extremely personal, and few people would agree on the precise connotative meaning of a word or nonverbal behavior. Test this by trying to get a group of people to agree on the connotative meanings of such words as "religion," "God," "democracy," "wealth," and "freedom" or of such nonverbal behaviors as raised eyebrows, arms folded in front of one's chest, or legs crossed when one is seated. Chances are that it will be impossible to reach an agreement.

MEANINGS ARE CONTEXT-BASED

The same words or behaviors may have totally different meanings when they occur in different contexts. For example, the greeting "How are you?" means "Hello" to someone you pass regularly on the street but means "Is your health improving?" when said to a friend who is hospitalized. A wink to an attractive person on a bus means something completely different from a wink that signifies a put-on or a lie. Similarly, the meaning of a given signal depends on the other behavior it accompanies or is close to in time. Pounding a fist on the table during a speech in support of a politician means something quite different from that same gesture in response to news of a friend's death.

MESSAGE CHARACTERISTICS

Interpersonal communication messages occur in packages, are governed by rules, vary in directness, vary in believability, and may refer to objects and events in the real world as well as to other messages. Reviewing these five message characteristics enables us to understand better how interpersonal messages are transferred and how we can better control our own.

MESSAGES ARE PACKAGED

The sounds you make with your mouth or the gestures you make with your hands or eyes usually occur in packages or clusters in which the various verbal and nonverbal behaviors reinforce one another.

All parts of the message system usually work together to communicate a unified meaning. When you express anger verbally, your body and face also show anger by tensing, scowling, and perhaps assuming a fighting posture. You often fail to notice this because it seems so natural, so expected. But when the nonverbal messages of someone's posture or face contradict what is said verbally, you take special notice. For example, the person who says, "I'm so glad to see you," but avoids direct eye contact and looks around to see who else is present is sending contradictory messages. You see contradictory messages (also called "mixed messages" by some writers) when couples, whether newly dating or long married, say they love each other but seem to go out of their way to hurt each other nonverbally—for example, by being late for important dates, by flirting with others, or by not touching each other. In the classic film *The Graduate,* there is a particularly good example of a contradictory message. Benjamin Braddock, the graduate (played by Dustin Hoffman), and Mrs. Robinson (Anne Bancroft) are having an affair, which under normal circumstances would indicate a high degree of intimacy. But Benjamin repeatedly and consistently calls his partner "Mrs. Robinson," which shows that he is uncomfortable with the relationship and that he feels unequal in the partnership with a mature woman.

In the packaged nature of communication, then, is a warning against the too-easy interpretation of another's meaning, especially as revealed in nonverbal behaviors. Before you identify or guess the meaning of any bit of behavior, look at the entire package or cluster of which it is a part, the way in which the cluster is a response to its context, and the role of the specific nonverbal behavior within that cluster. That attractive person winking in your direction may be giving you the come-on; however, do not rule out the possibility of ill-fitting contact lenses.

Generally, you do not pay much attention to the packaged nature of communication unless there is an incongruity. When you spot a contradiction between the verbal and the nonverbal message, you begin to question the credibility and sincerity of the person.

Double-Bind Messages   A particular type of contradictory message that deserves special mention is the **double-bind** message, one whose verbal and nonverbal injunctions contradict each other. Consider the following interpersonal interaction:

> **PAT:** You're never affectionate anymore. You never hug me like you used to (that is, "love me").
> **CHRIS:** [*Makes advances of a loving nature.*]
> **PAT:** [*Tenses, fails to maintain eye contact, and, in general, sends nonverbal messages that say, "Don't love me."*]
> **CHRIS:** [*Withdraws.*]
> **PAT:** See? You don't love me.

The following factors must be involved for an interaction to constitute significant double-binding (Brommel 1990).

Intense Relationship. The two persons interacting must share a relatively intense relationship in which the messages and demands of one and the responses of the other are important. This kind of relationship can exist among various family members, between close friends and lovers, and, in some instances, between employer and employee.

Incompatible Responses. The two messages must demand different and incompatible responses. That is, the messages must be such that both cannot logically be verbalized. Usually, the positive message is communicated verbally—for example, "Love me." The accompanying negative message, usually communicated nonverbally, contradicts the first message—for example, withdrawal and a general tenseness that communicates "Stay away." Both parties in a double-bind relationship are likely to send such messages, either both in the same conversation or separately on different occasions.

Inability to Escape. One of the persons in a double-bind situation must be unable to escape from the contradictory messages. People in double-bind situations feel trapped. Preventing a person's escape from the contradictory message may be a legal commitment (such as a marriage license) or, in the case of lovers, an unwritten but understood agreement that each is responsible for meeting the needs of the other. No matter what response is made, the person receiving the message is failing to comply with at least one of the demands. If, for example, Chris makes loving advances, the nonverbal injunction "Don't love me" is violated. If Chris does not make any loving advances, the verbal injunction "Love me" is violated.

Threat of Punishment. There must be some threat of punishment for the receiver's failure to comply with the sender's verbal or nonverbal demands. In our example, there is an implied threat of punishment for the failure to make loving advances as well as for the failure to comply with the demand not to love. Regardless of how the lover responds, some form of punishment will follow. This is one reason why the relationship must be relatively intense; otherwise, the threat would not be significant.

Frequent Occurrences. For double-binding to be a serious communication problem, it must occur frequently. Frequent exposure to double-bind messages has the effect of setting up a response pattern in the person such that she or he comes to anticipate that whatever is done will be incorrect, that there is no escape from these confused and confusing communications, and that punishment will follow the inevitable noncompliance.

Double-bind messages are particularly damaging when children are involved. Children can neither escape from such situations nor communicate about the communications. They cannot talk about the lack of correspondence between the verbal and the nonverbal. They cannot ask their parents why they do not hold them or hug them when the parents say they love them.

Ernst Beier (1974) has argued that these double-bind messages are the result of the desire to communicate two different emotions or feelings. For example, you may like a person and want to communicate a positive feeling, but you may also feel resentment

In what ways does this photo illustrate the idea that meanings are packaged? Can you identify a verbal message that this father might be communicating that could be potentially double-binding (given his nonverbal messages)?

toward this person and want to communicate a negative feeling as well. The result is that you communicate both feelings, one verbally and one nonverbally.

MESSAGES ARE RULE-GOVERNED

The rule-governed nature of verbal communication is well-known. These are the rules of a language (the rules of grammar) that native speakers follow in producing and in understanding sentences, although they may be unable to state such rules explicitly.

You learned these rules from observing the behaviors of the adult community. For example, you learned how to express sympathy along with the rules that your culture has established for expressing it appropriately. You learned that touch is permissible under certain circumstances but not under others and which types of touching are permissible and which are not. You learned that women may touch each other in public; for example, they may hold hands, walk arm in arm, engage in prolonged hugging, and even dance together. You also learned that men may not do these things, at least not without inviting social criticism. Further, perhaps most obvious, you learned that certain parts of the body may not be touched and others may. As a relationship changes, so do the rules for touching. As you become more intimate, the rules for touching become less restrictive.

Nonverbal communication is also regulated by a system of rules or norms that state what is and what is not appropriate, expected, and permissible in specific social situations. Of course, these rules vary greatly from one culture to another. Rules are cultural (and relative) institutions; they are not universal laws (see "Communication Is Culture-Specific," in Unit 2).

In the United States, direct eye contact signals openness and honesty. Among some Latin Americans and Native Americans, however, direct eye contact between, say, a teacher and a student is considered inappropriate, perhaps aggressive; appropriate student behavior is to avoid eye contact with the teacher. From even this simple example it is easy to see how miscommunication can take place. To a teacher in the United States, avoidance of eye contact by a Latin American or Native American could signify guilt, lack of interest, or disrespect, when in fact the child was following her or his own culturally established rules. Table 10.1 gives you an idea of the problems that can arise when you assume that the rules governing message behavior in one culture are the same rules used in other cultures.

MESSAGES VARY IN DIRECTNESS

Consider the following sentence sets:

1. I'm so bored; I have nothing to do tonight.
2. I'd like to go to the movies. Would you like to come?

1. Do you feel like eating hamburgers tonight?
2. I'd like hamburgers tonight. How about you?

Table 10.1

A Few Nonverbals That Can Get You into Trouble*

Blinking your eyes is considered impolite in Taiwan.

Folding your arms over your chest is considered disrespectful in Fiji.

Waving your hand is insulting in Nigeria and Greece.

Gesturing with the thumb up is considered rude in Australia.

Tapping your two index fingers together means in Egypt either that a couple is sleeping together or that you are making a request to sleep with someone.

Pointing with the index finger is considered impolite in many Middle Eastern countries.

Bowing to a lesser degree than your host implies in Japan that you are superior.

With a clenched fist, inserting your thumb between your index and middle finger (called the *fig*) is considered obscene in some southern European countries.

Pointing at someone with your index and third fingers means in some African countries that you are wishing evil on the person.

Resting your feet on a table or chair is insulting in some Middle Eastern countries.

*These gestural taboos come from Axtell (1993).

The statements numbered 1 are indirect; they are attempts to get the listener to say or do something without committing the speaker. The number 2 statements are direct—they clearly identify the speaker's preferences and then ask the listeners if they agree. A more obvious example of an indirect message occurs when you glance at your watch to communicate that it is late and that you had better be going. Indirect messages serve at least two important functions.

Indirect messages allow you to express a desire without insulting or offending anyone; they allow you to observe the rules of polite interaction. So instead of saying, "I'm bored with this group," you say, "It's getting late and I have to get up early tomorrow," or you look at your watch and pretend to be surprised by the time. Instead of saying, "This food tastes like cardboard," you say, "I just started my diet" or "I'm stuffed."

Sometimes indirect messages allow you to ask for compliments in a socially acceptable manner; you might say, "I was thinking of getting a nose job," hoping to get the desired compliment, "A nose job? You? Your nose is perfect."

Problems with Indirect Messages Indirect messages, however, can also create problems. Consider the following dialogue in which an indirect request is made:

> **PAT:** You wouldn't like to have my parents over for dinner this weekend, would you?
> **CHRIS:** I really wanted to go to the shore and just relax.
> **PAT:** Well, if you feel you have to go to the shore, I'll make the dinner myself. You go to the shore. I really hate having them over and doing all the work myself. It's such a drag shopping, cooking, and cleaning all by myself.

Win-Lose and Win-Win Situations. Given this situation, Chris has two basic alternatives. One is to stick with the plans to go to the shore and relax. In this case, Pat is going to be upset, and Chris is likely to feel guilty for not helping with the dinner. A second alternative is to give in to Pat, help with the dinner, and not go to the shore. In this case, Chris has to give up much-desired plans and is sure to resent Pat's manipulative tactics. Regardless of the decision made, one person wins and one loses, a win-lose situation, which creates resentment, competition, and, often, an "I'll get even" mentality.

With direct requests, this type of situation is less likely to develop. Consider:

> **PAT:** I'd like to have my parents over for dinner this weekend. What do you think?
> **CHRIS:** Well, I really wanted to go to the shore and just relax.

Regardless of what develops next, both individuals are starting out on relatively equal footing. Each has clearly and directly stated a preference. In this case, these preferences seem mutually exclusive. But observe that there is the possibility of meeting both persons' needs. For example, Chris might say, "How about going to the shore this weekend and having your parents over next weekend? I'm really exhausted; I could use the rest." Here is a direct response to a direct request. Unless there is some pressing need to have Pat's parents over for dinner this weekend, this response may enable each to meet the other's needs.

With the use of indirect requests, win-win outcomes are difficult to see because, from the very beginning, there is an implied inequality and an attempt to manipulate the other person. With direct requests, in contrast, there is no manipulation. The result is that win-win solutions, where both parties can get what they want, readily suggest themselves. The win-win situation creates supportiveness and a willingness to cooperate.

Responsibility and Honesty.   Perhaps the most obvious difference between direct and indirect requests is that direct requests are honest and open; indirect requests are often, though not always, dishonest and manipulative. Direct questions encourage open, honest, and supportive responses; indirect questions encourage responses that are resentful, dishonest, and defensive.

For example, in saying "You don't really want to have my parents over for dinner this weekend," Pat tries to shift the responsibility for the decision to Chris. With a statement like "I'd like to have my parents over for dinner this weekend," the speaker owns his or her statements, thoughts, and feelings.

MESSAGES VARY IN BELIEVABILITY

For the most part, research shows that when verbal and nonverbal messages conflict, you are likely to believe the nonverbal. The nonverbal communication theorist Dale Leathers (1990), for example, reports that nonverbal cues are more than four times as effective as verbal cues in their impact on interpersonal impressions and ten times more important in expressing confidence. For most messages, a good guess is that approximately 60 percent to 65 percent of meaning is communicated nonverbally (Burgoon, Buller, and Woodall 1989).

Why do you believe the nonverbal message rather than the verbal one? It may be that you feel verbal messages are easier to fake. Consequently, when there is a contradiction, you are likely to distrust the verbal and accept the nonverbal. Or it may be that nonverbal messages often function below the level of conscious awareness. You learned and perceive them without conscious awareness. Thus, when a discrepancy between the verbal and the nonverbal messages arises, you may get a "feeling" from the nonverbal messages. Because you may not be able to isolate its source, you may assume that it is somehow correct.

Nonverbal cues help you to guess whether or not a person is lying. You also use them to help you discover the underlying truth a lie is meant to conceal. Interestingly enough, as you become more intimate, your ability to detect the underlying truth that your partner is trying to hide *declines*. Research also shows that women are better than men at discovering the underlying truth (McCornack and Parks 1990).

What nonverbal cues do you use in detecting whether someone is lying? Table 10.2 presents the findings from a wide variety of research studies on such cues. In reviewing this table, remember that it is important to interpret communication behaviors (verbal and nonverbal) within the context in which they occur. The examples cited should be used to suggest hypotheses, not firm conclusions, about possible deceit. After reviewing the extensive literature on deception, Paul Ekman in *Telling Lies* (1985) cautions: "Evaluating behavioral clues to deceit is hazardous. . . . The lie catcher must always estimate the *likelihood* that a gesture or expression indicates lying or truthfulness; rarely is it absolutely certain."

MESSAGES AND METACOMMUNICATION

Metacommunication is communication that refers to other communications; it is communication about communication (Unit 6). All behavior, verbal and nonverbal, can be metacommunicational. Verbally, you can say, for example, "This statement is false" or "Do you understand what I am trying to tell you?" Because these sentences refer to communication, they are called *metacommunicational statements.*

Nonverbal behavior may also be metacommunicational. Obvious examples include crossing one's fingers behind one's back or winking when telling a lie. But the more subtle instances of metacommunication are more interesting: as you say "I had a really nice time" to your blind date, the nonverbal messages—the lack of a smile, the failure to maintain eye contact, the extra-long pauses—contradict the verbal "really nice time" and tell your date that you did not enjoy the evening.

Nonverbal messages may also metacommunicate about other nonverbal messages. The individual who both smiles and avoids direct eye contact or extends a totally lifeless

---

Table 10.2

The Communication Behavior of Liars*

Liars:

1. Hesitate more and use more and longer pauses.
2. Make more speech errors.
3. Smile less.
4. Respond with shorter answers, often simple yes or no responses.
5. Use more "allness" terms: for example, "never," "always," "everyone."
6. Use fewer specifics (for example, references to verifiable people, places, and things) and more nonspecifics, such as "hung out" or "had fun."
7. Blink more and avert their gaze more often.
8. Use more adaptors (nervous-type self-touching movements)
9. Dilate their pupils.
10. Shift their posture more often.
11. Have a greater response latency (pause longer before responding to another's question or statement).
12. Use excessive gestures.
13. Spend more time looking away from the listener.
14. Use more generalizing phrases: for example, adding "stuff like that" and "you know" to the ends of sentences.
15. Appear less friendly and attentive.

*This table is based on the extensive research summaries of Knapp and Hall (1992), Miller and Burgoon (1990), O'Hair et al. (1988), Mehrabian (1978), and Leathers (1990). Note that not all studies find the same behaviors indicative of lying, largely because the situations are so different; for example, some situations involved the opportunity to rehearse the lie, whereas others did not. This table is intended to provide a broad overview of the cues that distinguish lying from truth-telling behavior, not to identify specific cues that should be used to distinguish a liar from a truth teller.

hand shows how one nonverbal behavior may contradict another.

But usually when nonverbal behavior is metacommunicational, it reinforces other verbal or nonverbal behavior. You smile when greeting someone, run to meet the person you say you are eager to see, or arrive early for a party you verbally express pleasure in attending. On the negative—though still consistent—side, you may arrive late for a dental appointment (presumably with a less-than-pleasant facial expression) or frown when telling off your boss.

SUMMARY: UNIT IN BRIEF

Verbal and Nonverbal Interaction	Meanings	Message Characteristics
To accent or emphasize **To complement** or add to or supplement **To contradict** or deny **To regulate** or control **To repeat** or restate **To substitute** or take the place of	**Meaning is** • an active process created by cooperation between source and receiver. • a function of the interaction of messages and the receiver's previous experiences, expectations, attitudes, and so forth. **Meanings are** • in people. • more than words and gestures. • unique. • both denotative and connotative. • context-based.	**Packaged:** Communication behaviors occur in clusters. **Rule-governed:** Both verbal and nonverbal messages follow rules. **Directness:** Messages may be direct or indirect. **Believability:** Messages vary in believability. **Metacommunication:** Messages may refer to events in the outside world (object communication) or to other messages (metacommunication).

THINKING CRITICALLY ABOUT VERBAL AND NONVERBAL MESSAGES

1. Observe someone communicate for 10 or 15 minutes, and record as many examples as you can find of the six ways in which verbal and nonverbal messages interact. What functions occur most often?
2. Can you supply a personal example of interpersonal miscommunication that occurred because of failure to recognize that meanings are in people, not in words?
3. Have your meanings changed for such terms as "success," "happiness," "love," and "friendship" over the last several years? In what ways?
4. The National Easter Seal Society offers a number of suggestions for communicating with people with disabilities. (Also see "Ten Commandments for Communicating

with People with Disabilities," in Unit 6.) Among their recommendations are:

- Don't use the word "handicapped"; instead, use the word "disability."
- Don't emphasize the disability; emphasize the person. For example, don't label a person as an epileptic; instead, refer to someone who has epilepsy.

How would you explain these suggestions in terms of denotation and connotation?

5. Have you ever experienced double-binding? How did you deal with it? What effects did it have on you and on your relationship?

6. How would you state the rules for such common nonverbal behaviors as (a) smiling, (b) winking, and (c) sitting? In your statement of rules, include at least the following two elements: when and how you should (and when and how you should not) use these behaviors, and the differences, if any, in the way women and men use them.

7. Identify at least one rule of verbal or nonverbal communication that differs from one culture to another. What are the consequences of using one culture's rule in the context of another culture?

8. How would you describe your own relational communication in terms of direct versus indirect messages? In what specific ways would you want your present communication patterns to change?

9. What cues to deception, in addition to those discussed in this unit, might prove useful in formulating hypotheses about whether a person is lying?

10. How would you go about finding answers to the following questions?

- Do people who engage in double-binding have less satisfying relationships than those who don't use double-binding?
- Are men or women more likely to use indirect speech?
- Are men or women more effective liars?
- Are children better lie detectors than adults?

EXPERIENTIAL VEHICLES

10.1 BREAKING NONVERBAL RULES*

The general objective of this exercise is to become better acquainted with some of the rules of nonverbal communication (in this case, rules from North American culture) and to analyze some of the effects of breaking these rules. Much as we learn verbal language without explicit instruction, we also learn nonverbal language—the rules for interacting nonverbally—in the same way. Among such rules might be the following:

- Upon entering an elevator, turn to face the door and stare either at it or at the numbers indicating which floor the elevator is on until your floor is reached.
- When sitting next to or near someone, do not invade the person's private space with your body or belongings.
- When strangers are talking, do not enter their group.
- When talking with someone, do not stand too close or too far away. You may move closer when talking about intimate topics. Never stand so close that you can smell

*The idea for this exercise was suggested by Professor Jean Civikly, University of New Mexico.

the other person's odor. This rule may be broken only under certain conditions: for example, when the individuals involved are physically attracted to each other, when one individual is consoling another, or when individuals are engaged in a game whose rules require this close contact.

- When talking in an otherwise occupied area, lower your voice so that other people are not disturbed by your conversation.

Form pairs, with one student in each pair designated as the rule breaker and the other the observer. The task of the rule breaker is simply to enter some campus situation in which one or more rules of nonverbal communication would normally be operative and to break one or more rules. The task of the observer is to record mentally (or in writing, if possible) what happens as a result of the rule breaking. Each pair should return after a specified amount of time and report to the entire class what happened.

Of course, no rules should be broken if it means infringing on the rights of others.

10.2 MEANINGS IN PEOPLE

To illustrate the implications of the principle that meanings are in people, record your meanings for the terms listed below in this "semantic differential." Write each term's first letter in the appropriate space for the various dimensions of meaning provided, depending on how close you feel the term's meaning is to the adjectives in the scale. Thus, if you feel that a concept is extremely good or extremely bad, then place the term's first letter on the space closest to good or bad. If you feel that the concept is quite good or quite bad, then place the first letter in the second or the seventh position. If you feel that the concept is fairly good or fairly bad, then place the first letter in the third or the fifth position. If you feel that the concept is neither good nor bad, then place the first letter in the middle position. Do likewise for all nine scales and for all five terms.

Terms: abortion, college, gun control, love, religion

good	____:____:____:____:____:____:____	bad
pleasant	____:____:____:____:____:____:____	unpleasant
ugly	____:____:____:____:____:____:____	beautiful
weak	____:____:____:____:____:____:____	strong
active	____:____:____:____:____:____:____	passive
sharp	____:____:____:____:____:____:____	dull
large	____:____:____:____:____:____:____	small
light	____:____:____:____:____:____:____	heavy
hot	____:____:____:____:____:____:____	cold

Compare your meanings with those of others in small groups or in the class as a whole.

1. Are there large differences between your meanings and those of others? How would you describe these differences in terms of connotation and denotation?
2. What accounts for the differences in meanings? That is, what factors contribute to your meanings for these terms? Put differently, how did you acquire the meanings you indicated on these scales?
3. What does this experience illustrate about the principle that meanings are in people?

UNIT 11

Verbal Messages: Principles and Pitfalls

<u>UNIT OBJECTIVES</u>

AFTER COMPLETING THIS UNIT, YOU SHOULD BE ABLE TO:

1. Define *talking down, talking up,* and the *principle* of equality and provide examples of each
2. Define *disconfirmation* and the *principle of confirmation*
3. Explain racism, sexism, and heterosexism as disconfirmation
4. Define *excluding talk* and the *principle of inclusion* and provide examples of each

5. Define *self-talk, other-talk,* and *the principle of balance* and provide examples of each
6. Explain how criticism and praise can cause difficulties and explain the principle of honesty

---

The effect that people have on you and that you have on them is due largely to the messages sent and received—the way you talk, the way you express your ideas and your feelings, the way you verbalize your relationship to the other person (and the way you communicate nonverbally, as discussed in Units 13 and 14). This unit explores five principles and their corresponding pitfalls—ways in which you may create negative effects. Applying these principles and avoiding the pitfalls should help create a more positive environment for all your communications. As you read this unit, you'll note that these principles deal more with relational than with content messages (Unit 2), further underscoring the importance of this level of interpersonal communication.

TALKING DOWN AND UP AND EQUALITY

In communication theory, particularly in the area concerned with organizations, downward communication and upward communication have very specific meanings. **Downward communication** refers to communication originating from a high-level source (for example, a manager or executive) directed at a lower-level receiver (for example, a line worker). **Upward communication** is the reverse: it is communication originating from an individual who is low in the organizational hierarchy and directed to someone higher. As used here, however (with somewhat similar meanings), the terms refer to the irksome habits of "talking down" or "talking up" to others.

TALKING DOWN

Here we are made to feel that the speaker, for some unknown reason, has "the word" and is passing it on to the masses. This speaker could be the doctor who talks to laypeople in "medicalese" or the so-called friend who puts himself or herself above others by using phrases such as "You probably didn't realize this but . . . " or "I know you don't keep up with the computer literature but . . ." Regardless of who is doing the talking, we get the distinct feeling that somehow the speaker feels that he or she is above us for any of a multitude of reasons—intelligence, experience, knowledge, position, wealth, whatever. We are put in the position of learner or subordinate.

Another way in which some people talk down is in telling others how to feel and how to act. You see this frequently when someone is feeling depressed or angry and another person says, "Ah, come on, don't feel like that" or in some other way tells the person how he or she should feel. This person no doubt means well but at the same time displays a lack of respect for the other person's behaviors and feelings.

People also talk down when they address someone else by his or her first name but expect to be addressed (and even refer to themselves) by a title with a last name. Doctors do this frequently: "Hi, Lou. I'm Dr. Gonzalez." Nonverbally, this same tendency is seen in people who place their hands on the shoulders of others to demonstrate their own "superior" position.

Talking down is also seen when an individual plays power games. Interruption, increasing one's vocal volume to overpower another, and verbal put-downs such as "You can't be serious" are popular forms of talking down. (These behaviors are covered in the discussion of power in Unit 20.)

Another popular type of talking down occurs in the making of "pronouncements" (Sanford 1982). Pronouncements are especially popular with persons in authority—teachers, religious leaders, doctors, and parents. It is easy for such people to assume a superior stance and to approach and "resolve" problems by making pronouncements rather than pursuing authentic communication: "Do it this way" or "You know what your problem is . . ." Differences of opinion or disagreements are "settled" by mandate rather than by compromise and cooperation.

Note that pronouncements not only "establish" the speaker as the authority but also put the listener in a childlike role in which he or she must be told what to do and how to do it. This usually results in resentment, defensiveness, and a general breakdown in meaningful and equal interaction.

A somewhat different form of talking down occurs when people use **gobbledygook**—language that is needlessly complex and confusing, double-talk (Rothwell 1982). Originally coined by Maury Maverick, a member of Congress from Texas, the term *"gobbledygook"* refers to much of the language around us, particularly in government documents, legal contracts, medical records, and, unfortunately, much academic writing.

TALKING UP

An equally problematic type of communication is that of the person who always approaches you as if you have the answer, as if you are the authority. As anyone who has been put in this position knows (and teachers, therapists, and doctors often are), it is tiresome and difficult. You have to be at your best at all times. In some Asian, Latin American, and African cultures, "talking up" is a sign of respect. If you are, for example, a teacher, a doctor, or perhaps a person of an advanced age, it is expected that you will be approached as an authority, sometimes on topics about which you may know very little. For someone to do otherwise would be considered insulting.

Sometimes talking upward is an attempt to manipulate, to flatter you into treating kindly what is to follow. In many instances, people who do this begin their communications with what are called disqualifiers: "I'm not sure of this but . . . " or "I'm probably wrong, but I was wondering . . . " or "You know this better than I do, but would it be possible to . . . ?" These disqualifiers appear to put the speaker one down and the listener one up (see Unit 2). At times, these disqualifiers express genuine doubt and uncertainty, in which case there is no problem. At other times, however, they are verbal tactics intended to throw the other person off guard or to create the impression that the speaker is powerless. At still other times, these disqualifiers reflect an inferiority complex that manifests itself in constant attempts to put oneself down.

THE PRINCIPLE OF EQUALITY

Both downward and upward talk, when used unfairly to intimidate or to manipulate, create problems for all involved. Although there are a number of ways of dealing with these kinds of talk, it is perhaps most helpful to keep in mind the principle of equality, the need to recognize that all parties in the communication act are equal in the sense that each person has something worthwhile to contribute. As receivers of messages that talk down to us or attempt to strip us of power, we are aware of the negative feelings they can engender. Some of you may be using these power plays and manipulations without even being aware of doing so (but, it is hoped, only until now). Perhaps keeping this principle of equality in mind will lessen the likelihood of your doing so in the future. As a receiver, recognize your own responsibility in these situations; when you allow people to interrupt you or to treat your communications as of lesser importance, for example, you are in effect encouraging and reinforcing downward-talking behavior.

Note, however, that even the principle of equality—seemingly so obvious to many readers—is not universal across all cultures. As mentioned earlier (Unit 6), in many cultures there is a rigid hierarchical structure that governs the way people are expected to talk. To violate this structure—and, say, talk with an older person as an equal—would be considered disrespectful.

DISCONFIRMATION AND CONFIRMATION

Before reading about these important concepts, take the self-test "How Confirming Are You?" to examine your own behavior.

Consider the following situation: Pat arrives home late one night. Chris is angry and complains about Pat's coming home so late. Consider some responses Pat might make:

1. Stop screaming. I'm not interested in what you're babbling about. I'll do what I want, when I want. I'm going to bed.
2. What are you so angry about? Didn't you get in three hours late last Thursday when you went to that office party? So knock it off.
3. You have a right to be angry. I should have called to tell you I was going to be late, but I got involved in an argument at work, and I couldn't leave until it was resolved.

In response 1, Pat dismisses Chris's anger and even indicates dismissal of Chris as a person. In response 2, Pat rejects the validity of Chris's reasons for being angry but does not dismiss either Chris's feelings of anger or Chris as a person. In response 3, Pat acknowledges Chris's anger and the reasons for being angry. In addition, Pat provides some kind

TEST YOURSELF

HOW CONFIRMING ARE YOU?

INSTRUCTIONS

In your typical communications, how likely are you to display the following behaviors? Use this scale in responding to each statement:

5 = always
4 = often
3 = sometimes
2 = rarely
1 = never

_____ 1. I acknowledge the presence of another person both verbally and nonverbally.

_____ 2. I acknowledge the contributions of the other person by, for example, supporting or taking issue with what the person says.

_____ 3. During the conversation, I sustain nonverbal connection by maintaining direct-eye contact, touching, hugging, kissing, and otherwise demonstrating acknowledgment of the other person.

_____ 4. I communicate, as both speaker and listener, with involvement and with concern and respect for the other person.

_____ 5. I signal my understanding of the other person both verbally and nonverbally.

_____ 6. I reflect back the other person's feelings as a way of showing that I understand them.

_____ 7. I ask questions as appropriate concerning the other person's thoughts and feelings.

_____ 8. I respond to the other person's requests by, for example, returning phone calls and answering letters within a reasonable time.

_____ 9. I encourage the other person to express his or her thoughts and feelings.

_____10. I respond directly and exclusively to what the other person says.

SCORING

All ten statements are phrased so that they express confirming behaviors. Therefore, high scores (say, above 35) reflect a strong tendency to engage in confirmation. Low scores (say, below 25) reflect a strong tendency to engage in disconfirmation.

of explanation and, in doing so, shows that both Chris's feelings and Chris as a person are important and that Chris deserves to know what happened. The first response is an example of disconfirmation, the second of rejection, and the third of confirmation.

The psychologist William James once observed that "no more fiendish punishment could be devised, even were such a thing physically possible, than that one should be turned loose in society and remain absolutely unnoticed by all the members thereof." In this often-quoted observation, James identifies the essence of disconfirmation (Watzlawick, Beavin, and Jackson 1967; Veenendall and Feinstein 1990).

Disconfirmation is a communication pattern in which you ignore a person's presence as well as that person's communications. You say, in effect, that the person and what she or he has to say are not worth serious attention or effort—that this person and her or his contributions are so unimportant or insignificant that there is no reason to be concerned with them. Disconfirming responses often lead to loss of self-esteem.

Note that disconfirmation is not the same as *rejection.* In rejection, you disagree with the person; you indicate your unwillingness to accept something the other person says or does. In disconfirming someone, however, you deny that person's significance; you claim that what this person says or does simply does not count.

Confirmation is the opposite communication pattern. In confirmation, we not only acknowledge the presence of the other person but also indicate our acceptance of this person, of this person's definition of self, and of our relationship as defined or viewed by this other person. Confirming responses often lead to gains in self-esteem.

Disconfirmation and confirmation may be communicated in a wide variety of ways. Table 11.1 shows just a few. It parallels the self-test presented earlier in this unit so that you can see clearly not only the confirming but also the opposite, disconfirming behaviors. As you review this table, try to imagine a specific illustration for each of the ways of communicating disconfirmation and confirmation (Pearson 1993; Galvin and Brommel 1991).

Talking with the Grief Stricken   Especially important implications of confirmation concern talking with the grief stricken. Grief is something everyone experiences at some time. It may be felt because of illness or death, the loss of a highly valued relationship (for example, a romantic breakup), the loss of certain physical or mental abilities, or the loss of material possessions (your house burning down or stock market losses). Here are a few suggestions for making this very difficult form of communication a bit easier:

- Confirm the other person and the person's feelings. "You must miss him a great deal" confirms the person's feelings, for example. Avoid expressions that are disconfirming: "You can't cry now; you have to set an example."

What do you think is the single most important principle for communicating with the grief stricken? Can you identify any typical comments that you find inappropriate?

Table 11.1
Disconfirmation and Confirmation

DISCONFIRMATION	CONFIRMATION
1. Ignore the presence of the other person.	1. Acknowledge the presence of the other verbally or nonverbally.
2. Ignore what the other says; express (nonverbally and verbally) indifference to anything the other says.	2. Acknowledge the contributions of the other by either supporting or taking issue with what the other says.
3. Make no nonverbal contact; avoid direct eye contact; avoid touching other person.	3. Make nonverbal contact by maintaining direct eye contact; touching, hugging, kissing, and otherwise demonstrating acknowledgment of the other.
4. Engage in monologue—communication in which one person speaks and one person listens,there is no real interaction, and there is no real concern or respect for each other.	4. Engage in dialogue—communication in which both persons are speakers and listeners, both are involved, and both are concerned with and have respect for each other.
5. Jump to interpretation or evaluation rather than work at understanding what the other means.	5. Demonstrate understanding of what the other says and means.
6. Express your own feelings, ignore the feelings of the other, or give abstract intellectualized responses.	6. Reflect back the other's feelings to demonstrate your understanding of these feelings.
7. Make statements about yourself; ignore any lack of clarity in the other's remarks.	7. Ask questions of the other concerning both thoughts and feelings.
8. Ignore the other's requests; fail to answer questions, return phone calls, and answer letters	8. Acknowledge the other's requests; answer the other's questions, return phone calls, and answer letters.
9. Interrupt or otherwise make it difficult for the other to express himself or herself.	9. Encourage the other to express thoughts and feelings.
10. Respond tangentially by acknowledging the other's comment but then shift the focus of the message in another direction.	10. Respond directly and exclusively to what the other says

- Give the grieving person permission to grieve. Let the person know that it is acceptable for him or her to grieve in the ways that feel most comfortable—for example, crying or talking about old times.
- Avoid trying to force the grief-stricken individual to focus on the bright side, because he or she may not be ready. Avoid expressions such as "You're so lucky you still have some vision left" or "It is better this way; Pat was suffering so much."
- Encourage the grieving person to express feelings and talk about the loss. Most people who experience grief welcome the opportunity to talk about it. However,

don't try to force the person to talk about experiences or feelings she or he may not be ready to share.

- Empathize with the grief-stricken person and communicate this empathic understanding. Let the person know that you can understand what he or she is going through. Do not assume, though, that your feelings (however empathic) are the same in depth or in kind. If, having never experienced this tragedy, you say to a parent who has lost a child, "I know exactly what you're feeling," you risk arousing resentment. (See Unit 6 for more on empathy.)
- Be especially sensitive to leave-taking cues. Don't try to force your presence on someone who is grief stricken or press the person to stay with you or a group of people. When in doubt, ask.

These concepts of confirmation and disconfirmation also give unique insight into a wide variety of offensive language practices, language that alienates and separates, language that disconfirms. The three obvious practices are racism, sexism, and heterosexism.

RACISM

According to Andrea Rich (1974), "any language that, through a conscious or unconscious attempt by the user, places a particular racial or ethnic group in an inferior position is racist." Racist language expresses racist attitudes. It also contributes to the development of racist attitudes in those who use or hear such language.

Racist terms are used by members of one culture to disparage members of other cultures—their customs or their accomplishments. Racist language emphasizes differences rather than similarities and separates rather than unites members of different cultures. Traditionally, racist language has been used by the dominant group to establish and maintain power over other groups. Today, however, it is used by racists (or the racist-talking) in all groups. The social consequences of racist language in terms of employment, education, housing opportunities, and general community acceptance are well known.

Many people feel that it is permissible for members of a culture to refer to themselves with racist terms. That is, Asians may use the negative terms referring to Asians, Italians may use the negative terms referring to Italians, and so on. This issue is currently being debated and in one case centers on the use of racial terms in rap music (*New York Times,* 24 January 1993, 1, 31). The reasoning seems to be that groups should be able to laugh at themselves.

It is interesting to note that the terms denoting some of the major movements in art—for example, "impressionism" and "cubism"—were originally applied negatively. The terms were adopted by the artists themselves and eventually became positive. A parallel can be seen in the use of the word "queer" by some lesbian and gay organizations. Their purpose in using the term is to cause it to lose its negative connotation.

One possible problem, though, is that such terms may not lose their negative connotations and may simply reinforce the negative stereotypes that society has already assigned to certain groups. By using these terms, members may come to accept the labels with their negative connotations and thus contribute to their own stereotyping.

It has often been pointed out (Davis 1973; Bosmajian 1974; Purnell 1982) that there are aspects of language that may be inherently racist. For example, Davis's examination of English found 134 synonyms for "white." Of these, 44 have positive connotations (for example, "clean," "chaste," and "unblemished") and only 10 have negative connotations (for example, "whitewash" and "pale"); the remaining synonyms are relatively neutral. Of the 120 synonyms for "black," 60 were found to have unfavorable connotations ("unclean," "foreboding," and "deadly") and none to have positive connotations.

Consider such phrases as the following:

- the Korean doctor
- the Latino prodigy
- the African-American mathematician
- the white nurse
- the Eskimo physicist

In some cases, of course, the racial identifier may be relevant, as in, say, "The Korean doctor argued for hours with the French doctor while the Swiss tried to secure a compromise." Here the aim might be to identify the nationality of the doctor as you would if you had forgotten her or his name.

Often, however, such identifiers are used to emphasize that the combination of race and occupation (or talent or accomplishment) is rare and unexpected, that this member of the race is an exception. It also implies that racial factors are somehow important in the context. As noted, there are times when this may be true, but most often race would be irrelevant.

SEXISM

Consider some of the language used to refer to women. A woman traditionally loses her maiden name when she marries and, in certain instances, loses her first name as well. She changes from "Ann Smith" to "Mrs. John Jones."

We say that a woman "marries into" a man's family and that a family "dies out" if there are no male children. In the United States, one does not usually speak of a man marrying into a woman's family (unless the family is extremely prestigious or wealthy), and a family can still "die out" even if there are ten female children. In some marriage ceremonies, you can still hear "I now pronounce you man and wife," not "man and woman" or "husband and wife." The man retains his status as man, but the woman changes hers from woman to wife. Barrie Thorne, Cheris Kramarae, and Nancy Henley, in *Language, Gender and Society* (1983), summarize this line of research by noting that "women tend to be defined by their relation to men. . . . The available and 'approved' titles, pronouns, lexicons, and labels," they note, "reflect the fact that women (as well as other subordinates) have been named by others."

Julia Stanley, for example, researched terms indicating sexual promiscuity, finding 220 terms referring to a sexually promiscuous woman but only 22 terms for a sexually promiscuous man (Thorne, Kramarae, and Henley 1983). Surely, there are as many promiscuous men as there are promiscuous women, yet the English language fails to reflect this. If the number of terms indicates the importance of a concept to a culture, then promiscuity among women is significant (that is, it is "abnormal" or "beyond the norm") and something to take special notice of, whereas promiscuity among men is not significant (that is, it is "normal"), and therefore no special notice need be taken of it.

The National Council of Teachers of English (NCTE) has proposed guidelines for nonsexist (gender-free, gender-neutral, or sex-fair) language. These guidelines concern the use of generic "man," "he," and "his" as well as sex role stereotyping (Penfield 1987).

Generic "Man."   The word "man" refers most clearly to an adult male. To use the term to refer to both men and women emphasizes "maleness" at the expense of "femaleness." Similarly, the terms "mankind," "the common man," or even "cavemen" imply a primary focus on adult males. Gender-neutral terms can easily be substituted. Instead of "mankind," you can say "humanity," "people," or "human beings." Instead of "the common man," you can say "the average person" or "ordinary people." Instead of "cavemen," you can say "prehistoric people" or "cave dwellers."

Similarly, the use of "policeman," "fireman," "salesman," "chairman," "mailman," and other terms that presume maleness as the norm and femaleness as a deviation from this norm are clear and common examples of sexist language. Consider using nonsexist alternatives for these and similar terms; make these alternatives (for example, "police officer," "mail carrier," and "firefighter") part of your active vocabulary.

Generic "He" and "His."   The use of the masculine pronoun to refer to any individual regardless of sex further illustrates the extent of linguistic sexism. There seems to be no legitimate reason why the feminine pronoun could not alternate with the masculine pronoun in referring to hypothetical individuals, or why such terms as "he and she" or "her and him" could not be used instead of just "he" or "him." Alternatively, we can restructure our sentences to eliminate any reference to gender. Here are a few examples from the NCTE Guidelines (Penfield 1987):

SEXIST	GENDER-FREE
The average student is worried about his grades.	The average student is worried about grades.
Ask the student to hand in his work as soon as he has finished.	Ask students to hand in their work as soon as they have finished.
When a teacher asks his students for an evaluation, he is putting himself on the spot.	When you ask your students for an evaluation, you are putting yourself on the spot.

Sex Role Stereotyping.   The words we use often reflect a sex role bias, the assumption that certain roles or professions belong to men and others belong to women. In eliminating sex role stereotyping, avoid, for example, making the hypothetical elementary school teacher female and the college professor male. Avoid referring to doctors as male and nurses as female. Avoid noting the sex of a professional with terms such as "female doctor" or "male nurse." When you are referring to a specific doctor or nurse, the person's sex will become clear when you use the appropriate pronoun: "Dr. Smith wrote the prescription for her new patient" or "The nurse recorded the patient's temperature himself."

How would you describe male-female work relationships in organizations with which you're familiar, for example, your college, supermarket, post office? How do male-female work relationships in the United States differ from those in other cultures with which you're familiar?

HETEROSEXISM

A close relative of sexism is heterosexism. The term is a relatively new addition to our list of linguistic prejudices. As the term implies, *heterosexism* refers to language used to disparage lesbians and gay men. As in the case of racist and sexist language, we see heterosexism in the derogatory terms used for lesbians and gay men.

As with racism and sexism, we also see the occurrence of heterosexism in more subtle forms of language usage. For example, when we qualify a description of a profession—as in "gay athlete" or "lesbian doctor"—we are in effect stating that athletes and doctors are not normally gay or lesbian. Further, we are highlighting the affectional orientation of the athlete and the doctor in a context in which it may have no relevance. This practice is, of course, the same as qualifying by race or gender, as already noted.

Still another instance of heterosexism—and perhaps the most difficult to deal with—is the presumption of heterosexuality. Usually, people assume that the person they are talking to or about is heterosexual. Usually, they are correct, because the majority of the population is heterosexual. At the same time, however, note that heterosexism denies lesbians and gay males their true identity. The practice of assuming that a person is heterosexual is very similar to the presumption of whiteness and maleness that we have made significant progress toward eliminating. Here are a few additional suggestions for avoiding heterosexist, or what some call "homophobic," language.

- Avoid offensive nonverbal mannerisms that parody stereotypes when talking about gays and lesbians.
- Avoid "complimenting" gay men and lesbians by saying they "don't look it." To gays and lesbians, that is not a compliment. Similarly, expressing disappointment

that a person is gay—for example, saying "What a waste!" and meaning it as a compliment—is not really a compliment.

* Avoid the assumption that every gay or lesbian knows what every other gay or lesbian is thinking. To do so is very similar to asking someone from Japan why Sony is investing heavily in the United States or, as one comic put it, asking an African-American, "What do you think Jesse Jackson meant by that last speech?"
* Avoid denying individual differences. Saying things like "Lesbians are so loyal" or "Gay men are so open with their feelings"—statements that ignore the reality of wide differences within any group—are potentially insulting to all groups.
* Avoid "overattribution," the tendency to attribute just about everything a person does, says, and believes to being gay or lesbian. This tendency helps to recall and perpetuate stereotypes.
* Remember that relationship milestones are important to all people. Ignoring the anniversaries or birthdays of partners is resented by everyone.

EXCLUDING TALK AND INCLUSION

One of the most annoying and destructive verbal habits is the use of in-group talk in the presence of someone who is not a member of the in-group. When doctors get together and discuss medicine, there is no problem. But when someone in the group is not a doctor, the doctors often fail to adjust to this person. Instead, they continue to discuss treatments, symptoms, medication, and other subjects that could interest only another doctor. Many professionals do the same thing: teachers talk teaching, lawyers talk law, and so on. In-grouping makes for pretty boring conversation, even among in-group members. But when nonmembers are involved, it makes for communication that is both ineffective and insulting.

A variant of this habit occurs when a group of people, most of whom belong to the same national group, talk together in their native language, sometimes just isolated words, sometimes sentences, sometimes even entire conversations in the presence of others who do not speak the language. This is not merely a question of comprehension; such use of a language in the presence of a nonspeaker emphasizes that person's outsider status. In almost every instance (assuming they all speak a common language), the foreign term could easily be translated.

When the use of the foreign expression aids communication and does not make others feel left out, it creates no problem. When, however, it does not aid communication and when it serves to mark the in-group members as united and the other person as an outsider, it is best omitted.

THE PRINCIPLE OF INCLUSION

Instead of trying to emphasize the exclusion of one or more members, consider the principle of inclusion. Regardless of the type of communication situation we are in, everyone needs to be included in the interaction. Even if job-related issues have to be discussed in the presence of a nonmember, that person can be included in a variety of ways, for example, by seeking the nonmember's perspective or drawing an analogy from his or her field.

Another way to practice inclusion is to fill in relevant details discussed by the group for those who may be unaware. For example, when people, places, or events are mentioned in a group discussion, briefly identify them for those to whom they may be unfamiliar. Brief parenthetical identifying phrases are usually sufficient: "Margo—she's Jeff's daughter—loved San Francisco State."

When someone asks a question or makes a comment requiring a response, be sure to respond in some way. Even if you are talking, attending to someone else, or otherwise engaged, respond in some way to indicate your acknowledgment of the comment—verbally, if possible, or nonverbally with a nod or smile, for example. Practicing inclusion is so easy that it is surprising that it is violated so blatantly and so often. When inclusion is practiced, everyone gains a great deal more satisfaction from the interaction.

TALKING ABOUT SELF OR OTHERS AND BALANCE

Many people—friends and family members are surely among them—act and talk as if they were the center of the universe. They talk constantly about themselves—about their jobs, their accomplishments, their plans, their families, their love lives, their problems, their successes, and sometimes even their failures. Rarely do they ask how we are, what we think (except perhaps about them), or what our plans are. Other people go to the other extreme and never talk about themselves. They are the underdisclosers we discussed in Unit 8, the people who want to learn everything about you but are not willing to share anything about themselves that might make them vulnerable. As a result, we come away from the interaction with the feeling that they either did not like us very much or did not trust us. Otherwise, we feel, they would have revealed something of themselves.

THE PRINCIPLE OF BALANCE

Admittedly, it is not easy to steer a comfortable course between too much and too little self-talk. Moreover, there are certainly times when we just cannot stop talking about a new job or new romantic partner. Under most circumstances, however, we should strive for interactions governed by the principle of balance—some self-talk, some other-talk, never all of either one. Communication is a two-way process: each person needs to function as source and as receiver, and each person should have a chance to function as subject. Balanced communication interactions are more satisfying and more interesting. We all get bored with too much talk about the other person, and, let's face it, others get bored with too much talk about us. The principle of balance is a guide to protect both us and others.

CRITICISM, PRAISE, AND HONEST APPRAISAL

Throughout our communication experiences, we are expected to criticize, to evaluate, and otherwise to render some kind of judgment. Especially in helping professions, such as teaching, nursing, or counseling, criticism is an important and frequently used skill. In short, criticism is a most useful and important part of our interactions and our communications generally. The problem arises when criticism is used outside of its helping function, when it is inappropriate or excessive. We need to develop a facility for detecting when a person is asking for our criticism and when that person is simply asking for a compliment. For example, when a friend asks how you like the new apartment, he or she may be searching for a compliment rather than wanting you to itemize all the things wrong with it. Often, too, we use such opportunities to hurt other people, sometimes even people we care for.

Sometimes the desire to be liked (or perhaps the need to be appreciated) is so strong that we go to the other extreme and paint everything with praise. The most ordinary jacket, the most common thought, the most average meal are given extraordinary praise, way beyond their merits. The overly critical and the overly complimentary soon find that their comments are no longer met with concern or interest.

The Principle of Honest Appraisal

As an alternative to excessive criticism or praise, consider the principle of honest appraisal. Tell the truth, but note that there is an art to truth telling, just as there is an art to all other forms of effective communication. First, distinguish between instances in which an honest appraisal is sought and those in which the individual needs a compliment. Respond to the appropriate level of meaning. Second, if an honest appraisal is desired and if yours is a negative one, give some consideration to how you should phrase your criticism. Here are a few suggestions on giving criticism:

- Focus on the event or the behavior rather than on personality; for example, say "This paper has four errors and needs retyping" rather than "You're a lousy typist; do this over."
- State criticism positively, if possible. Rather than saying "You look terrible in black," say "You look much better in bright colors."
- Own your thoughts and feelings. Instead of saying "Your report was unintelligible," say "I had difficulty following your ideas."
- State your concern for the other person along with your criticism, if appropriate. Instead of saying "The introduction to your speech is boring," say "I really want your speech to be great; I'd open with some humor to get the audience's attention." Say "I want you to make a good impression. I think the dark suit would work better."
- Avoid ordering or directing the other person to change; try identifying possible alternatives. Instead of saying "Don't be so forward when you're first introduced to someone," say "I think they might respond better to a less forward approach."
- Be specific. Instead of saying "This paper is weak," as some English teachers might, say "I think the introduction wasn't clear enough. Perhaps a more specific statement of purpose would have worked better."
- Avoid mind reading. Instead of saying "Don't you care about the impression you make? This report is terrible," say "I think I would use a stronger introduction and a friendlier writing style."

In expressing praise, keep the following in mind:

- Use I-messages. Instead of saying "That report was good," say "I thought that report was good" or "I liked your report."

- Make sure your affect communicates your positive feelings. Often when people praise others simply because it is the socially correct response, they may betray their lack of conviction with too little or inappropriate affect.
- Name the behavior you're praising. Instead of saying "That was good," say "I enjoyed your speech" or "I thought your introduction was great."

These principles will not correct all verbal message problems, but when conscientiously applied, they should go a long way toward both reducing the frequency of some annoying and destructive habits and making verbal interaction more pleasant and productive.

SUMMARY: UNIT IN BRIEF

Avoid These Patterns	Practice These Principles
Talking down and up	The principle of equality: address others on an equal level; demand communication equality.
Disconfirmation	The principle of confirmation: express acknowledgment and acceptance of others; avoid racist, sexist, and heterosexist expressions.
Excluding others; in-group talk	The principle of inclusion: include every one present in the interaction.
Excessive self-talk; excessive other-talk	The principle of balance: talk about yourself and about the other for balance.
Excessive criticism; undeserved praise	The principle of honest appraisal: say what you feel, but gently.

THINKING CRITICALLY ABOUT VERBAL MESSAGE PRINCIPLES

1. How would you describe the communication that takes place in this class with specific reference to the concepts of talking up and talking down?
2. How would you describe your own behavior in terms of confirmation and disconfirmation? Are you generally confirming? Disconfirming?
3. What other suggestions would you make for talking with those experiencing grief? What one commonly heard expression do you find the most troublesome?
4. What is the status of your language concerning racist, sexist, and heterosexist expressions? How do you feel about this?
5. Have you ever felt excluded from a particular interaction? What form did this exclusion take? What effects did it have on you?

6. If you asked your friends how often you talk about yourself versus how often you talk about them, what do you think they would say? Use a ten-point scale for "self-talk" and a ten-point scale for "other-talk." Now ask a few friends. How accurate were you?

7. Do you find that men and women differ in their use of racist, sexist, and heterosexist language? More specifically, would this type of language appear equally in all-female, all-male, and mixed groups? How does racist, sexist, and heterosexist language in interpersonal interactions differ from such language in more public situations (for example, in print, on television, or in public speeches)?

8. What other suggestions would you give for avoiding racist, sexist, and heterosexist talk?

9. What is your ethical obligation when it comes to racist, sexist, and heterosexist talk? For example, do you have an obligation to voice disapproval when others use such language?

10. How would you go about finding answers to the following questions?

    • Is disconfirmation related to self-esteem? For example, is it possible that people who frequently disconfirm others and use racist, sexist, and heterosexist language do so because of their level of self-esteem?
    • What are the effects of using racist, sexist, and heterosexist language on campus? At home? With your friends? With your colleagues at work?
    • Does using derogatory language about your own group influence your self-esteem?

EXPERIENTIAL VEHICLES

11.1 ANALYZING CONFIRMATION, REJECTION, AND DISCONFIRMATION

The purpose of this exercise is to increase your understanding of confirmation, rejection, and disconfirmation. Classify the following responses as confirmation, rejection, or disconfirmation:

Pat receives this semester's grades in the mail; they are better than the previous semesters' grades but are still not great. After opening the letter, Pat says, "I really tried hard to get my grades up this semester." Pat's parents reply:

_____ Going out every night hardly seems like trying very hard.
_____ What should we have for dinner?
_____ Keep up the good work.
_____ I can't believe you've really tried your best; how can you study with the stereo blasting in your ears?
_____ I'm sure you've tried real hard; next time you'll do better.
_____ That's great.
_____ What a rotten day I had at the office.
_____ I can remember when I was in school; I got all Bs without ever opening a book.

Chris, who has been out of work for the past several weeks, says, "I feel like such a failure. I just can't seem to find a job. I've been pounding the pavement for the last five weeks and still nothing." Chris's friend responds:

_____ I know you've been trying real hard.

_____ You really should get more training so you'd be able to sell yourself more effectively.

_____ I told you 100 times: you need that college degree.

_____ I've got to go to the dentist on Friday. Boy, do I hate that.

_____ The employment picture is real bleak this time of the year, but your qualifications are impressive. Something will come up soon.

_____ You are not a failure. You just can't find a job.

_____ What do you need a job for? Stay home and keep house. After all, Pat makes more than enough money to live in style.

_____ What's five weeks?

_____ Well, you'll just have to try harder.

11.2 EXPRESSING CONFIRMATION

For each of the following situations, provide examples of confirmatory, rejecting, and disconfirmatory responses.

Pat and the Elusive Date Pat: "I haven't had a date in the last four months. I'm getting very depressed over this." A friend responds:

Pat and Chris in Combat Pat and Chris have just had another fight. Pat tells a friend about what has been going on: "We just can't seem to get along anymore. Every day is a hassle. Every day, there's another conflict, another battle. I feel like walking away from the whole mess." The friend responds:

Relationship Problems Chris confides in a friend about some recent difficulties with Pat: "Pat wants me to quit trying to get a job acting and take that job in advertising so we'll be able to get a decent apartment and get out of debt. But acting is my whole life. I'm afraid if I give up doing what I really want, I'll come to resent Pat and our entire relationship will deteriorate." The friend responds:

11.3 TALKING WITH THE GRIEF STRICKEN

Here is an example of a message addressed to someone who has just lost a loved one. Analyze and evaluate this message. What problems do you see? How would you express your sympathy differently?

> I just heard that Harry died—I mean—passed away. I'm so sorry. I know exactly how you feel. But, you know, it's for the best. I mean the man was suffering. I remember seeing him last month; he was so weak he could hardly stand up. And he looked so sad. He must have been in constant pain. It's better this way. He's at peace. And you'll get over it. You'll see. Time heals all wounds. It was the same

way with me, and you know how close we were. I mean we were devoted to each other. Everyone said we were the closest pair they had ever seen. And I got over it. So how about we go to dinner tonight? We'll talk about old times. Come on. Come on. Don't be a spoilsport. I really need to get out. I've been in the house all week. Come on, do it for me. After all, you have to forget; you have to get on with your own life. I won't take no for an answer. I'll pick you up at seven.

UNIT 12

Verbal Messages: Barriers to Interaction

UNIT OBJECTIVES

AFTER COMPLETING THIS UNIT, YOU SHOULD BE ABLE TO:

1. Define *polarization* and identify specific examples
2. Define *intensional orientation* and *extensional orientation* and identify specific examples
3. Define *bypassing* and its two major correctives
4. Define *fact-inference confusion* and identify specific examples
5. Define *allness* and identify specific examples
6. Define *static evaluation* and specific examples
7. Define *indiscrimination* and specific examples
8. Define *ethnocentrism*

Interpersonal communication is fragile—in part because of its complexity and in part because it is a human process, subject to all the failings and problems of fallible people. Chief among these problems are what are called **barriers.**

The term "barriers" is used not to convey the idea that communicators function as machines or that communication is a mechanical process. Rather it emphasizes that meaningful interpersonal communication may lose some of its effectiveness when communicators think or behave in certain ways. Recognize that these barriers are of human origin and development; it is the communicators who, for one reason or another, create and maintain them.

All seven barriers discussed here—polarization, intensional orientation, bypassing, fact-inference confusion, allness, static evaluation, and indiscrimination—are ways in which your verbal messages describe the world in illogical, distorted, or unscientific ways. Some contemporary writers now refer to these barriers as "cognitive distortions" (Burns 1980; Beck 1988).

An analogy can be made between verbal messages and geographic maps: Maps that accurately portray the world assist you in getting from one place to another. To the extent that such maps inaccurately portray the world, they hinder you. Verbal messages are like maps. When they accurately represent reality, they aid effective and meaningful interpersonal communication; when they distort reality, they hinder effective and meaningful interpersonal communication.

POLARIZATION

Polarization, often referred to as the fallacy of "either-or," is the tendency to look at the world and to describe it in terms of extremes—good or bad, positive or negative, healthy or sick, brilliant or stupid, rich or poor, and so on. Polarized statements come in many forms, for example:

- After listening to the evidence, I'm still not clear who the good guys are and who the bad guys are.
- Well, are you for us or against us?
- College had better get me a good job. Otherwise, this has been a big waste of time.

Most people exist somewhere between the extremes of good and bad, healthy and sick, brilliant and stupid, rich and poor. Yet there seems to be a strong tendency to view only the extremes and to categorize people, objects, and events in terms of these polar opposites. You can easily demonstrate this tendency by filling in the opposites for each of the following words:

								Opposite
tall	___ :	*medium*	:	___ :	___			*short*
heavy	___ :	___ :	___ :	___ :	___ :	___		*light*
strong	___ :	___ :	___ :	___ :	___ :	___		*weak*
happy	___ :	___ :	___ :	___ :	___ :	___		*sad*
legal	___ :	___ :	___ :	___ :	___ :	___		*illegal*

Filling in the opposites should have been relatively easy and quick. The words should also have been fairly short. Further, if a number of people supplied opposites, there should be a high degree of agreement among them.

Now try to fill in the middle positions with words meaning, for example, "midway between tall and short," "midway between heavy and light," and so on. Do this before reading any further.

The midway responses (compared to the opposites) were probably more difficult to think of and took you more time. The responses should also have been either fairly long words or phrases of several words. Further, you would probably find little agreement among different people completing this same task.

Look at the familiar bell-shaped curve (Figure 12.1). If you selected 100 people at random, you would find that their intelligence, height, weight, income, age, health, and so on would fall into a bell-shaped or "normal" distribution. Few items exist at either of the two extremes, but as you move closer to the center, more and more items are included. This is true of any random sample. Yet many people tend to concentrate on the ends of this curve and ignore the middle, which contains the vast majority of cases.

It is legitimate to phrase certain statements in terms of two values. For example, this thing you are holding is either a book or it is not. Clearly, the classes "book" and "not-book" include all possibilities. There is no problem with this kind of statement. Similarly, you may say that a student will either pass this course or will not, as these two categories include all the possibilities.

CORRECTIVES

You create problems when you use this either-or form in situations where it is inappropriate: for example, "The politician is either for us or against us." Note that these two choices do not include all possibilities; the politician may be for us in some things and against us in others, or he or she may be neutral. During the Vietnam War, there was a tendency to categorize people as either "hawk" or "dove," but clearly many people were neither and many were probably both—hawks on certain issues and doves on others.

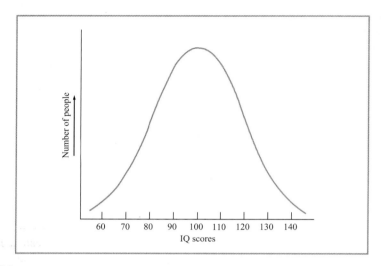

Figure 12.1
Bell-shaped curve.

Recognize that the vast majority of cases exist between extremes. Don't allow the ready availability of extreme terms to obscure the reality of what lies in between.

INTENSIONAL ORIENTATION

Intensional orientation refers to the tendency to view people, objects, and events in terms of how they are talked about or labeled rather than in terms of how they actually exist. **Extensional orientation** is the opposite, the tendency to look first at the actual people, objects, and events and only then at the labels. It is the tendency to be guided by what you see happening rather than by the way something or someone is talked about or labeled. Intensional orientation is seen in such statements as these:

- Rabbit! How could anyone eat rabbits? They're so cute and cuddly.
- But she's a lesbian (African-American, Italian, born-again Christian).
- It contains polyoxymorons, so it should work on this cough.

Intensional orientation occurs when you act as if the words and labels are more important than the things they represent—as if the map is more important than the territory. In its extreme form, intensional orientation is seen in the person who is afraid of dogs and who begins to sweat when shown a picture of a dog or when hearing people talk about dogs. Here the person is responding to a label as if it were the actual thing.

Intensional orientation is seen in the numerous studies on credibility (Riggio 1987). These studies demonstrate that you are influenced more when you assume that the message comes from a highly credible source than when you assume it comes from an average individual. Such studies have shown, for example, that you will evaluate a painting highly if you think it was painted by a famous artist, but you will give it a low evaluation if you think it was produced by a little-known artist. In all such credibility studies, the influencing factor was not the message itself—the painting or the speech, for example—

but the name attached to it. Advertisers have long known the value of this type of appeal and have capitalized on it by using popular figures from sports or music, for example, to endorse sneakers, soft drinks, and underwear.

CORRECTIVES

The corrective to intensional orientation is to focus first on the object, person, or event—the territory—and then on the way in which the object, person, or event is talked about—the map or label. Labels are certainly helpful guides, but don't allow them to obscure what they are meant to symbolize.

BYPASSING

Bypassing is a pattern of misevaluation in which people fail to communicate their intended meanings. It is "the miscommunication pattern which occurs when the sender (speaker, writer, and so on) and the receiver (listener, reader, and so forth) miss each other with their meanings" (Haney 1973).

Bypassing can take either of two forms. In one form, two people use different words but give them the same meaning. On the surface, there is apparent disagreement, but at the level of meaning there is agreement. Consider the following brief dialogue:

> **PAT:**   I want a permanent relationship. I'm not interested in one-night stands. [Meaning: I want to date you exclusively, and I want you to date me exclusively.]
> **CHRIS:**   I'm not ready for that. [Thinking and meaning: marriage.] Let's keep things the way they are. [Meaning: Let's continue dating only each other.]

Here we have a not-uncommon situation in which two people agree but assume, because they use different words (some of which may never actually be verbalized), that they disagree.

The second (and more common) form of bypassing occurs when two people use the same words but give them different meanings. Here there is apparent agreement but underlying disagreement.

Consider this brief dialogue:

> **PAT:**   I don't really believe in religion. [Meaning: I don't really believe in God.]
> **CHRIS:**   Neither do I. [Meaning: I don't really believe in organized religions.]

Here Pat and Chris assume they agree but actually disagree. At some later date, the implications of these differences may well become crucial.

Numerous other examples could be cited. Dating couples who say they are "in love" may mean very different things: one may mean "a permanent and exclusive emotional commitment," whereas the other may mean "a sexual involvement." "Come home early" may mean one thing to the anxious parent and quite another to the teenager.

Bypassing is especially significant in intercultural situations, say, between a native and nonnative speaker of English. Both may agree on the denotative meanings of the words used, but they may have very different connotative meanings. Consider, for example, the meanings for such terms as "democracy" or "family" to English speakers from Russia, Latin America, and the United States.

The underlying assumption in bypassing is that words have intrinsic meanings, so that when two people use the same word they mean the same thing, and when they use different words those words have different meanings. But words do not have meaning; meaning is in people.

CORRECTIVES

One obvious corrective for this misevaluation, as Haney (1973) points out, is to look for meaning in the person and not in the words. Remember, as we pointed out in the discussion of Johnson's model of meaning in Unit 9, that words may be assigned a wide variety of meanings by different people and, alternatively, people may assign different words the same meaning.

A second corrective is to use the active listening techniques discussed in Unit 4. By paraphrasing the speaker, you can check on whether there is agreement or disagreement, not in the words but in the communicators. By reflecting back the speaker's thoughts and feelings, you can see whether you understand the speaker, and you will also give the speaker an opportunity to clarify any misunderstanding or ambiguity. By asking questions, you can check on your perception of the speaker's meanings.

FACT-INFERENCE CONFUSION

You can make statements about the world that you observe, and you can make statements about what you have not observed. In form or structure, these statements are similar and cannot be distinguished from each other by any grammatical analysis. For example, you can say, "She is wearing a blue jacket" as well as, "She is harboring an illogical hatred." If you diagramed these sentences, they would yield identical structures, and yet you know that they are different types of statements. In the first one, you can observe the jacket and the blue color. But how do you observe "illogical hatred"? Obviously, this is not a descriptive statement but an **inferential statement,** a statement that you make not solely on the basis of what you observe but on the basis of what you observe plus your own conclusions.

There is no problem with making inferential statements; you must make them if you are to talk about much that is meaningful. The problem arises when you act as though those inferential statements were factual statements. Consider, for example, the following anecdote (Maynard 1963):

> A woman went for a walk one day and met her friend, whom she had not seen, heard from, or heard of in ten years. After an exchange of greetings, the woman said, "Is this your little boy?" and her friend replied, "Yes. I got married about six years ago." The woman then asked the child, "What is your name?" and the little boy replied, "Same as my father's." "Oh," said the woman, "then it must be Peter."

The question, of course, is how did the woman know the boy's father's name? The answer is obvious, but only after you recognize that in reading this short passage you

Most discussions we engage in involve listening without any serious critical analysis. How might the principles discussed in this unit serve as guidelines for critical listening and critical thinking?

have, quite unconsciously, made an inference that is preventing you from arriving at the answer. You have inferred that the woman's friend is a woman. Actually, the friend is a man named Peter.

Perhaps the classic example of this type of fact-inference confusion concerns the case of the "empty" gun that unfortunately proves to be loaded. With amazing frequency, we find in the newspapers examples of people being so sure that the guns are empty that they point them at someone else and fire. Often, of course, they are empty. But, unfortunately, often they are not. Here one draws the *inference* that the gun is empty, but acts as if it were a *fact* and fires the gun.

You may wish to test your ability to distinguish facts from inferences by taking the self-test "Can You Distinguish Facts from Inferences?"

CORRECTIVES

Some of the essential differences between factual and inferential statements are summarized in Table 12.1 (Haney 1973; Weinberg 1959). Distinguishing between these two types of statements does not imply that one type is better than the other. Both types of statements are useful; both are important. The problem arises when you treat an inferential statement as if it were fact. Phrase your inferential statements as tentative. Recognize that such statements may prove to be wrong. Leave open the possibility of other alternatives.

TEST YOURSELF

CAN YOU DISTINGUISH FACTS FROM INFERENCES?

INSTRUCTIONS
Carefully read the following report, modeled on that developed by William Haney (1973), and the observations based on it. Indicate whether you think the observations are true, false, or doubtful on the basis of the information presented in the report. Circle *T* if the observation is definitely true, *F* if the observation is definitely false, and *?* if the observation may be either true or false. Judge each observation in order. Do not reread the observations after you have indicated your judgment, and do not change any of your answers.

A well-liked college teacher had just completed making up the final examinations and had turned off the lights in the office. Just then a tall, broad figure appeared and demanded the examination. The professor opened the drawer. Everything in the drawer was picked up, and the individual ran down the corridor. The dean was notified immediately.

T F ?   **1.** The thief was tall and broad.
T F ?   **2.** The professor turned off the lights.
T F ?   **3.** A tall figure demanded the examination.
T F ?   **4.** The examination was picked up by someone.
T F ?   **5.** The examination was picked up by the professor.
T F ?   **6.** A tall figure appeared after the professor turned off the lights in the office.
T F ?   **7.** The man who opened the drawer was the professor.
T F ?   **8.** The professor ran down the corridor.
T F ?   **9.** The drawer was never actually opened.
T F ?   **10.** Three persons are referred to in this report.

SCORING
This test is designed to trap you into making inferences and treating them as facts. Statement 3 is true (it's in the report), statement 9 is false (the drawer was opened), but all the other statements are inferences and should have been marked *?*. Review these eight statements to see why you cannot be certain that any of them are either true or false.

ALLNESS

The world is infinitely complex, and because of this you can never say all there is to say about anything—at least not logically. This is particularly true in dealing with people. You may *think* you know all there is to know about certain individuals or about why they did what they did, yet clearly you do not know all. You can never know all the reasons you yourself do something, so there is no way you can know all the reasons why your parents or your friends or your enemies did something.

You may, for example, be assigned to read a textbook and, because previous texts have been dull and because perhaps the first chapter of this one is dull, you might infer

Table 12.1	
Differences Between Factual and Inferential Statements	
FACTUAL STATEMENTS	INFERENTIAL STATEMENTS
1. May be made only after observation	1. May be made at any time
2. Are limited to what has been observed	2. Go beyond what has been observed
3. May be made only by the observer	3. May be made by anyone
4. May be about only the past or the present	4. May be about any time—past, present, or future
5. Approach certainty	5. Involve varying degrees of probability
6. Are subject to verifiable standards	6. Are not subject to verifiable standards

that all the rest of the book will likewise be dull. Of course, the rest of a book is often even worse than its beginning. Yet it could be that the rest of the book would prove exciting were it read with an open mind. The problem here is that you run the risk of judging an entire text in such a way as to preclude any other possibilities. If you tell yourself that the book is dull, it will probably seem dull; if you say a required course will be useless, it will be extremely difficult for the instructor to make the course anything but what you have defined it to be. Only occasionally do people allow themselves to be proven wrong.

The parable of the six blind men and the elephant is an excellent example of an "allness orientation"—the tendency to judge the whole on the basis of experience with only some part of the whole—and its attendant problems. You may recall from elementary school the poem by John Saxe that concerns six blind men of Indostan who came to examine an elephant, an animal they had only heard about. The first blind man touched the elephant's side and concluded that the elephant was like a wall. The second felt the tusk and said the elephant must be like a spear. The third held the trunk and concluded that the elephant was much like a snake. The fourth touched the knee and knew the elephant was like a tree. The fifth felt the ear and said the elephant was like a fan. And the sixth grabbed the tail and concluded that the elephant was like a rope. Each of these learned men reached his own conclusion regarding what the elephant was really like. Each argued that he was correct and that the others were wrong.

Each, of course, was correct; at the same time, however, all were wrong. The point this parable illustrates is that everyone is in the position of the blind men. You can never see all of anything; you can never experience anything fully. You see part of an object, an event, or a person—and on that limited basis conclude what the whole is like. This procedure is universal, and you follow it because you cannot possibly observe everything. Yet recognize that when making judgments of the whole based on only a part, you are actually making inferences that can later be proven wrong. If you assume that you know everything there is to know about something or someone, you fall into the pattern of misevaluation called **allness.**

The famed British prime minister Disraeli once said that "to be conscious that you are ignorant is a great step toward knowledge." This observation is an excellent example of a *nonallness* attitude. If you recognize that there is more to learn, more to see, and more to hear, you leave yourself open to this additional information, and you are better prepared to assimilate it.

CORRECTIVES

A useful device to help remember to avoid allness is to end each statement, sometimes verbally but always mentally, with an *etc.* (et cetera), a reminder that there is more to learn, more to know, more to say—a reminder that every statement is inevitably incomplete.

STATIC EVALUATION

Static evaluation is the tendency to retain evaluations without change, while the reality to which they refer is constantly changing. A verbal statement about an event or person remains static and unchanging, while the object or person to whom it refers may change enormously. Alfred Korzybski (1933) used an interesting illustration in this connection: In a tank there is a large fish and many small fish that are its natural food source. Given freedom in the tank, the large fish will eat the small fish. After some time, the tank is partitioned, with the large fish on one side and the small fish on the other, divided only by a clear piece of glass. For a considerable time, the large fish will try to eat the small fish but will fail; each time it tries, it will knock into the glass partition. After some time, it will "learn" that trying to eat the small fish means difficulty, and it will no longer go after them. Now, however, the partition is removed and the small fish swim all around the big fish. But the big fish does not eat them and in fact will die of starvation while its natural food swims all around. The large fish has learned a pattern of behavior, and even though the actual territory has changed, the map remains static.

CORRECTIVES

To guard against static evaluation, date your statements and especially your evaluations. Remember that Gerry Smith $_{1984}$ is not Gerry Smith $_{1995}$; academic abilities $_{1995}$ are not academic abilities $_{1996}$. T. S. Eliot, in *The Cocktail Party,* said that "what we know of other people is only our memory of the moments during which we knew them. And they have changed since then . . . at every meeting we are meeting a stranger."

INDISCRIMINATION

Nature seems to abhor sameness at least as much as vacuums, for nowhere in the universe can you find identical entities. Everything is unique. Language, however, provides common nouns, such as "teacher," "student," "friend," "enemy," "war," "politician," "liberal," and the like, which may lead you to focus on similarities. Such nouns can lead you to group together all teachers, all students, and all friends and perhaps divert attention from the uniqueness of each individual, object, and event.

The misevaluation of **indiscrimination,** then, occurs when you focus on classes of individuals, objects, or events and fail to see that each is unique and needs to be looked at individually. Indiscrimination can be seen in such statements as these:

- He's just like the rest of them: lazy, stupid, a real slob.
- I really don't want another Martian on the board of directors. One is enough for me.
- Read a romance novel? I read one when I was 16. That was enough to convince me.

ETHNOCENTRISM

An interesting perspective can be gained on indiscrimination by looking briefly at ethnocentrism, the tendency to see others and their behaviors through your own cultural filters. **Ethnocentrism** is the tendency to evaluate the values, beliefs, and behaviors of your own culture as being more positive, logical, and natural than those of other cultures. Ideally, you would see both yourself and others as different but equal, with neither being inferior or superior. In ethnocentric thinking, there is no discrimination among the members of other groups; rather, there is discrimination against members of other groups.

Ethnocentrism exists on a continuum. People are not either ethnocentric or not-ethnocentric; rather, most are somewhere between these polar opposites. Of course, your degree of ethnocentrism varies, depending on the group on which you focus. For example, if you are Greek American, you may have a low degree of ethnocentrism when dealing with Italian Americans but a high degree when dealing with Turkish Americans or Japanese Americans. Most important for our purposes is that your degree of ethnocentrism (and we are all ethnocentric to at least some degree) will influence your interpersonal interactions.

Table 12.2, drawing from a number of researchers (Lukens 1978; Gudykunst and Kim 1984; Gudykunst 1991), summarizes some of the interconnections. In this table, five degrees of ethnocentrism are identified; in reality, of course, there are as many degrees as there are people. The "communication distances" are general terms that highlight the attitude that dominates that level of ethnocentrism. Under "communications" are some of the major ways people might interact given their particular degree of ethnocentrism.

Ethnocentric thinking is at the heart of the common practice of stereotyping national, sexual, racial, and religious groups. A **stereotype** is a relatively fixed mental picture

Here is a photo of the AIDS Quilt—each panel of which contains the name of a person who died of AIDS—on display in Washington, D.C. In what ways do you see the barriers to verbal interaction covered in this unit operate in popular discussions of AIDS and of people with AIDS?

Table 12.2
The Ethnocentrism Continuum

DEGREE OF ETHNOCENTRISM	COMMUNICATION DISTANCE	COMMUNICATIONS
Low	Equality	Treats others as equals; views different customs and ways of behaving as equal to one's own
Low-middle	Sensitivity	Wants to decrease distance between self and others
Middle	Indifference	Lacks concern for others; prefers to interact in a world of similar others
High-middle	Avoidance	Avoids and limits communications, especially intimate ones with interculturally different others
High	Disparagement	Engages in hostile behavior; belittles others; views different cultures and ways of behaving as inferior to one's own

of some group that is applied to each individual of the group without regard to his or her unique qualities. It is important to note that although stereotypes are usually thought of as negative, they may also be positive. You can, for example, consider certain national groups as lazy or superstitious or mercenary or criminal, but you can also consider them as intelligent, progressive, honest, hardworking, and so on. Regardless of whether such stereotypes are positive or negative, however, the problems they create are the same. They provide shortcuts that are usually inappropriate. For example, when you see someone through a stereotype, you invariably fail to devote sufficient attention to his or her unique characteristics.

There is nothing wrong with classifying. In fact, it is an extremely useful method of dealing with any complex matter; it puts order into thinking. The problem arises not from classification itself but from the application of an evaluative label to that class and the use of that label as an "adequate" map for each and every individual in the group.

CORRECTIVES

A useful antidote to indiscrimination is the **index,** a verbal or mental subscript that identifies each individual in a group as an individual even though all members of the group may be covered by the same label: $politician_1$ is not $politician_2$; $teacher_1$ is not $teacher_2$. The index helps us to discriminate *among* without discriminating *against*.

SUMMARY: UNIT IN BRIEF

Barrier	Communication Problem	Corrective
Polarization	Tendency to describe the world in terms of extremes or polar opposites	Use middle terms and. qualifiers
Intensional orientation	Tendency to view the world in the way it is talked about or labeled	Respond to things first; look for the labels second.
Bypassing	Tendency to assume that meanings are in words instead of in people	Look for meanings in people, not words; use the techniques of active listening.
Fact-inference confusion	Tendency to confuse factual and inferential statements and to respond to inferences as if they were facts	Distinguish facts from inferences, and respond to inferences as inferences, not as facts.
Allness	Tendency to describe the world in extreme terms that imply one knows all or is saying all there is to say	Avoid allness terms; recognize that one can never know all or say all about anything; use *etc.*
Static evaluation	Tendency to describe the world in static terms, denying constant change	Recognize the inevitability of change; date statements and especially evaluations.
Indiscrimination *Stereotyping*	Tendency to group unique individuals or items because they are covered by the same term or phrase	Recognize that sameness does not exist; index terms and statements.

THINKING CRITICALLY ABOUT MESSAGE BARRIERS

1. Do you select name-brand clothing because it is better or because of the name? Why? Are you willing to pay extra for a brand name of high status?
2. Do you ever confuse facts with inferences? What creates the confusion? What effects does the confusion have?
3. Do others commit the fallacy of indiscrimination in dealing with you? What problems does this cause? How might you prevent this from happening in the future?
4. Do you ever commit the fallacy of allness? Do you, for example, group all teachers together? All gay people? All politicians? All born-again Christians? All atheists? All African-Americans? All European-Americans? All Jews? All Hispanics?
5. In what ways do you respond intensionally? (Note that we make the assumption that most people respond intensionally at some times and in certain situations.) What con-

sequences does the intensional orientation have?

6. How many examples of the barriers to language and verbal interaction (polarization, intensional orientation, fact-inference confusion, bypassing, allness, static evaluation, and indiscrimination) can you find in one evening of television?

7. Visualize yourself seated with a packet of photographs before you, each showing a person you have never seen before. You are asked to scratch out the eyes in each photograph. You are further told that this is simply an experiment and that the individuals whose pictures you have will not be aware of anything that has happened here. As you progress through the pictures, scratching out the eyes, you come upon a photograph of your mother. What do you do? Are you able to scratch out the eyes as you have done with the pictures of the strangers? Or have you somehow lost your ability to scratch them out? Are you responding intensionally or extensionally?

8. Would it be possible to have ethnocentric thinking without indiscrimination? Does prejudice depend on indiscrimination?

9. In what ways can the barriers discussed in this unit create problems for relationships (friends, lovers, and families)?

10. How would you go about finding answers to the following questions?

   • Can corrective principles improve relationship communication or make it more satisfying?
   • Do people become less intensionally oriented with education?
   • What other qualities do ethnocentric individuals possess?

EXPERIENTIAL VEHICLES

12.1 E-PRIME

The expression *E-prime (E')* refers here to the mathematical equation $E - e = E'$, where E = the English language and e = the verb to be. E', therefore, stands for normal English without the verb *to be*. D. David Bourland, Jr. (1965–1966, 1992; Wilson 1989; Joyner 1993) suggests that if we wrote and spoke without the verb *to be,* we would describe events more accurately. The verb *to be* often suggests that qualities are in the person or thing rather than in the observer making the statement. We often forget that these statements are evaluative rather than purely descriptive. For example, we say, "Johnny is a failure," and imply that failure is somehow within Johnny instead of a part of someone's evaluation of Johnny. This type of thinking is especially important in making statements about ourselves. We say, for example, "I'm not good at mathematics" or "I'm unpopular" or "I'm lazy," and imply that these qualities are *in* us. But these are simply evaluations that may be incorrect or, if at least partly accurate, may change. The verb *to be* implies a permanence that is simply not true of the world in which we live.

To appreciate further the difference between statements that use the verb *to be* and those that do not, try to rewrite the following sentences without using the verb t*o be* in any of its forms—*is, are, am, was,* etc.

1. I'm a poor student.
2. They are inconsiderate.

3. What is meaningful communication?
4. Is this valuable?
5. Happiness is a dry nose.
6. Love is a useless abstraction.
7. Is this book meaningful?
8. Was the movie any good?
9. Dick and Jane are no longer children.
10. This class is boring.

12.2 BARRIERS IN RELATIONAL COMMUNICATION

Here is a brief dialogue written to illustrate the various barriers to communication discussed in this unit as they might apply to interpersonal relationships. Read over the dialogue and identify the barriers illustrated. Also consider why these statements establish barriers and how the people in the dialogue might have avoided the barriers.

PAT: Look, do you care about me or don't you? If you do, then you'll go away for the weekend with me as we planned originally.

CHRIS: I know we planned to go, but I got this opportunity to put in some overtime, and I really need the extra money.

PAT: Look, a deal is a deal. You said you'd go, and that's all that really matters.

CHRIS: Pat! You never give me a break, do you? I just can't go; I have to work.

PAT: All right, all right. I'll go alone.

CHRIS: Oh, no you don't. I know what will happen.

PAT: What will happen?

CHRIS: You'll go back to drinking again. I know you will.

PAT: I will not. I don't drink anymore.

CHRIS: Pat, you're an alcoholic and you know it.

PAT: I am not an alcoholic.

CHRIS: You drink, don't you?

PAT: Yes, occasionally.

CHRIS: Occasionally? Yeah, you mean two or three times a week, don't you?

PAT: That's occasionally. That's not being an alcoholic.

CHRIS: Well, I don't care how much you drink or how often you drink. You're still an alcoholic.

PAT: Anyway, what makes you think I'll drink if I go away for the weekend?

CHRIS: All those weekend ski trips are just excuses to drink. I've been on one of them—remember?

PAT: Well, see it your way, my dear. See it your way. I'll be gone right after I shower. [*Thinking: I can't wait to get away for the weekend.*]

CHRIS: [*Thinking: Now what have I done? Our relationship is finished.*]

UNIT 13

Nonverbal Messages: Body and Sound

AFTER COMPLETING THIS UNIT, YOU SHOULD BE ABLE TO:

1. Define and provide examples of *emblems, illustrators, affect displays, regulators,* and *adaptors*
2. Identify the types of information communicated by facial expressions
3. Describe the functions of eye contact and eye avoidance
4. Explain the types of information communicated by pupil dilation and constriction
5. Explain the meanings touch communicates
6. Define *paralanguage* and explain how it communicates
7. Identify the functions of silence

Of all the nonverbal communication systems, the body is surely the most important. With the body we communicate a wide variety of messages through gestures, facial expressions, eye movements, and touching behavior. We also communicate through sound and silence. Each of these major areas of nonverbal communication is examined in this unit.

COMMUNICATION THROUGH BODY MOVEMENT

Of course, the body communicates even without movement. For example, others may form impressions of you from your general body build, from your height and weight, and from your skin, eye, and hair color. Assessments of your power, your attractiveness, and your suitability as a friend or romantic partner are often made on the basis of your physical body (Sheppard and Strathman 1989).

However, it is body movements that we focus on here (Table 13.1). An especially useful classification of body movement (sometimes called **kinesics**) identifies five types: emblems, illustrators, affect displays, regulators, and adaptors (Ekman and Friesen 1969).

EMBLEMS

Emblems substitute for words. **Emblems** are body movements that have rather specific verbal translations. Emblems are nonverbal substitutes for specific words or phrases: for example, the nonverbal signs for "OK," "peace," "come here," "go away," "who me?" "be quiet," "I'm warning you," "I'm tired," and "it's cold." Emblems are as arbitrary as any words in any language. Consequently, your present culture's emblems are not necessarily the same as your culture's emblems of 300 years ago or the same as the emblems of other cultures. For example, the sign made by forming a circle with the thumb and index finger may mean "nothing" or "zero" in France, "money" in Japan, and something sexual in certain southern European cultures. But just as the English language is spreading throughout the world, so, too, is the English nonverbal language. The American use of this emblem to mean "OK" is spreading just as fast, for example, as English technical and scientific terms.

Table 13.1
The Five Body Movements

	NAME AND FUNCTION	EXAMPLES
	Emblems directly translate words or phrases.	"OK" sign, "come here" wave, hitch-hiker's sign
	Illustrators accompany and literally "illustrate" verbal messages.	Circular hand movements when talking of a circle; hands far apart when talking of something large
	Affect displays communicate emotional meaning.	Expressions of happiness, surprise, fear, anger, sadness, disgust/contempt
	Regulators monitor, maintain, or control the speaking of another.	Facial expressions and hand gestures indicating "keep going," "slow down," or "what else happened?"
	Adaptors satisfy some need.	Scratching one's head

ILLUSTRATORS

Illustrators accompany and literally illustrate the verbal messages. Illustrators make your communications more vivid and help to maintain your listener's attention. They also help to clarify and make more intense your verbal messages. In saying, "Let's go up," for example, you probably move your head and perhaps your finger in an upward direction. In describing a circle or a square, you more than likely make circular or square movements with your hands.

We are aware of illustrators only part of the time; at times, they may have to be brought to our attention. Illustrators are more universal than emblems; they are more common than emblems from one place to another and throughout time.

AFFECT DISPLAYS

Affect displays are the movements of the face that convey emotional meaning—the expressions that show anger and fear, happiness and surprise, eagerness and fatigue. They are the facial expressions that give you away when you try to present a false image and that lead people to say, "You look angry. What's wrong?" We can, however, consciously control affect displays, as actors do when they play a role. Affect displays may be unintentional (as when they give you away) or intentional (as when you want to show anger, love, or surprise).

REGULATORS

Regulators monitor, maintain, or control the speaking of another individual. When you listen to another, you are not passive; you nod your head, purse your lips, adjust your eye focus, and make various paralinguistic sounds such as "mm-mm" or "tsk." Regulators are culture-bound: each culture develops its own rules for the regulation of conversation. Regulators also include such broad movements as shaking your head to show disbelief or leaning forward in your chair to show that you want to hear more.

Regulators communicate what you expect or want speakers to do as they are talking: for example, "Keep going," "Tell me what else happened," "I don't believe that—are you sure?" "Speed up," and "Slow down." Speakers often receive these nonverbal signals without being consciously aware of them. Depending on their degree of sensitivity, they modify their speaking behavior in accordance with these regulators.

ADAPTORS

Adaptors are designed to satisfy some need. Sometimes the need is physical, as when you scratch to relieve an itch or push your hair out of your eyes. Sometimes the need is psychological, as when you bite your lip when anxious. Sometimes adaptors are directed at increasing comfort, as when you moisten dry lips. When these adaptors occur in private, they occur in their entirety: you scratch your head until the itch is gone. But in public, these adaptors usually occur in abbreviated form. For example, when people are watching us, we might put our fingers to our head and move them around a bit but probably not scratch with the same vigor as when in private. Because publicly emitted adaptors usually occur in abbreviated form, it is often difficult for an observer to tell what this partial behavior was intended to accomplish, as in seeing someone's fingers vaguely move about their head.

Adaptors usually occur without conscious awareness; they are unintentional movements that usually go unnoticed. Adaptors are usually signs of negative feelings; you emit more adaptors when feeling hostile than when feeling friendly. Further, as anxiety and uneasiness increase, so does the frequency of adaptors.

FACIAL COMMUNICATION

Throughout your interpersonal interactions, your face communicates, especially your emotions. In fact, facial movements alone seem to communicate the degree of pleasantness, agreement, and sympathy felt; the rest of the body doesn't provide any additional information. For other aspects, however—for example, the intensity with which an emotion is felt—both facial and bodily cues are used (Graham, Bitti, and Argyle 1975; Graham and Argyle 1975).

Some nonverbal communication researchers claim that facial movements may communicate at least the following eight emotions: happiness, surprise, fear, anger, sadness, disgust, contempt, and interest (Ekman, Friesen, and Ellsworth 1972). Others propose that in addition, facial movements may communicate bewilderment and determination (Leathers 1990).

Try to communicate surprise using only facial movements. Do this in front of a mirror, and try to describe in as much detail as possible the specific movements of the face that make up surprise. If you signal surprise as most people do, you probably exhibit raised and curved eyebrows, long horizontal forehead wrinkles, wide-open eyes, dropped-open mouth, and lips parted with no tension. Even if there were differences—and clearly there would be from one person to another—you could probably recognize the movements listed here as indicative of surprise. In FAST (*facial affect scoring*

How many of the five major body movements discussed here (emblems, illustrators, affect displays, regulators, and adapters) can you see in this photo? What meanings would you assign to each movement?

technique), the face is divided into three main parts: eyebrows and forehead, eyes and eyelids, and the lower face from the bridge of the nose down (Ekman, Friesen, and Tomkins 1971). Judges then try to identify various emotions by observing the different parts of the face and writing descriptions for the various emotions similar to the one just given for surprise. In this way, we can study more effectively just how the face communicates the various emotions.

Of course, some emotions are easier to communicate and to decode than others. For example, in one study, happiness was judged with an accuracy ranging from 55 percent to 100 percent, surprise from 38 percent to 86 percent, and sadness from 19 percent to 88 percent (Ekman, Friesen, and Ellsworth 1972). Research finds that women and girls are more accurate judges of facial emotional expression than men and boys (Hall 1984; Argyle 1988).

FACIAL MANAGEMENT TECHNIQUES

As you learned the nonverbal system of communication, you also learned certain facial management techniques: for example, to hide certain emotions and to emphasize others. Table 13.2 identifies four types of facial management techniques that you will quickly recognize as being frequently and widely used (Ekman and Friesen 1978; Malandro, Barker, and Barker 1989).

Table 13.1
Facial Management Techniques

TECHNIQUE	FUNCTION	EXAMPLE
Intensifying	To exaggerate a feeling	Exaggerating surprise when friends throw you a party to make your friends feel better
Deintensifying	To underplay a feeling	Moderating your own joy in the presence of a friend who, unlike you, didn't receive good news
Neutralizing	To hide a feeling	Covering up your sadness so as not to depress others
Masking	To replace or substitute the expression of one emotion with the expression of another	Expressing happiness to cover up your disappointment at not receiving the gift you had expected.

These facial management techniques are learned along with display rules, which tell you what emotions to express when; they are the rules of appropriateness. For example, when someone gets bad news in which you may secretly take pleasure, the display rule dictates that you frown and otherwise nonverbally signal your displeasure. If you violate these display rules, you will be judged insensitive.

THE FACIAL FEEDBACK HYPOTHESIS

According to the facial feedback hypothesis, your facial expression influences your level of physiological arousal. It has been found, for example, that subjects who exaggerated their facial expressions showed higher physiological arousal than subjects who suppressed these expressions. Those who neither exaggerated nor suppressed their expressions had arousal levels between these two extremes (Lanzetta, Cartwright-Smith, and Kleck 1976; Zuckerman et al. 1981; Cappella 1993). So not only does your facial expression influence the judgments and impressions that others have of you, but it also influences your own level of emotional arousal.

THE INFLUENCE OF CONTEXT AND CULTURE

The same facial expressions are perceived differently if people are supplied with different contexts. For example, when a smiling face was presented looking at a glum face, the smiling face was judged to be vicious and taunting. When the same smiling face was presented looking at a frowning face, however, it was judged to be peaceful and friendly (Cline 1956).

The wide variations in facial communication that we observe in different cultures seem to reflect which reactions are permissible and which are not, rather than a difference in the way emotions are facially expressed. For example, Japanese and American students watched a film of an operation (Ekman 1985). The students were videotaped in both an interview situation about the film and alone while watching the film. When alone, the students showed very similar reactions, but in the interview, the American students displayed facial expressions indicating displeasure, whereas the Japanese students did not show any great emotion. Thus, the difference may not be in the way different cultures express emotions but rather in the cultural rules for displaying emotions in public (cf. Matsumoto 1991).

EYE COMMUNICATION

From Ben Jonson's poetic observation "Drink to me only with thine eyes, and I will pledge with mine" to the scientific observations of contemporary researchers, the eyes have been regarded as the most important nonverbal message system.

EYE CONTACT FUNCTIONS

You use eye contact to serve several important functions (Knapp and Hall 1992; Malandro, Barker, and Barker 1989; Marshall 1983; Marsh 1988).

To Monitor Feedback   When you talk with someone, you look at the person intently, as if to say, "Well, what do you think?" or "React to what I've just said." You also look at speakers to let them know that you are listening. In studies conducted on gazing behavior and summarized by Knapp and Hall (1992), it has been found that listeners gaze at speakers more than speakers gaze at listeners. The percentage of interaction time spent gazing while listening, for example, has been found to range from 62 percent to 75 percent; the percentage of time spent gazing while talking, however, has been found to lie between 38 percent and 41 percent. When these percentages are reversed—when a speaker gazes at the listener for longer than "normal" periods or when a listener gazes at the speaker for shorter than "normal" periods—the conversational interaction becomes awkward. You may wish to try this with a friend. Even with mutual awareness, you will notice the discomfort caused by this seemingly minor communication change.

To Maintain Interest and Attention   When you speak with two or three other people, you maintain eye contact to secure the attention and interest of your listeners. When someone fails to pay the attention you want, you probably increase your eye contact, hoping your focus on this person will increase attention. When making an especially important point, you would look intently at your listeners—assuming what nonverbal researchers call "visual dominance behavior"—almost as a way of preventing them from devoting any attention to anything but what you are saying.

To Signal a Conversational Turn   Eye communication can also serve to inform the other person that the channel of communication is open and that she or he should now speak. A clear example of this occurs in the college classroom, where the instructor asks a question and then locks eyes with a student. Without any verbal message, it is assumed that the student should answer the question. Similarly, when you are nearing the end of what you want to say, you will probably focus eye contact on the person you think wants to speak next and then turn over the conversation to that person.

To Signal the Nature of the Relationship   Eye communication also helps signal the nature of the relationship between two people—for example, one of positive or negative regard. When you like someone, you increase your eye contact. The nonverbal communication researcher Michael Argyle (1988), for example, notes that when eye contact exceeds 60 percent in an interaction, the people are probably more interested in each other than in the verbal messages being exchanged.

People may signal power through **visual dominance behavior** (Exline, Ellyson, and Long 1975). The average person maintains a higher level of eye contact while listening and a lower level while speaking. When people want to signal dominance, they may reverse this pattern and maintain a high level of eye contact while talking but a much lower level while listening. Another way people try to signal dominance is to lower their eyebrows. Research does support this general interpretation of the behavior. For example, faces with lowered eyebrows, in both cartoons and photographs, were judged to communicate greater dominance than raised eyebrows (Keating, Mazur, and Segall 1977). Eye movements may also signal whether the relationship between two people is amorous, hostile, or indifferent.

To Compensate for Physical Distance   Eye movements are often used to compensate for increased physical distance. By making eye contact, we overcome psychologically the physical distance between us. When we catch someone's eye at a party, for example, we become psychologically close even though we may be separated by considerable physical distance. Eye contact and other expressions of psychological closeness, such as self-disclosure and intimacy, have been found to vary in proportion to each other.

We have already noted that women engage in more expressions of intimacy than men—for example, greater self-disclosure and greater use of affectional language. Women also engage in more eye contact than men (Argyle 1989; Mulac, Studley, Wiemann and Bradac 1987). Whether interacting with men or with other women, women maintain greater eye contact than men when listening as well as speaking.

EYE AVOIDANCE FUNCTIONS

The eyes, the sociologist Erving Goffman observed in *Interaction Ritual* (1967), are "great intruders." When you avoid eye contact or avert your glance, you allow others to maintain their privacy. You probably do this when you see a couple arguing, say, in the street or on a bus. You turn your eyes away as if to say, "I don't mean to intrude; I respect your privacy." Goffman refers to this behavior as **civil inattention.**

Eye avoidance can also signal lack of interest—in a person, a conversation, or some visual stimulus. At times, like the ostrich, we hide our eyes to try to cut off unpleasant stimuli. Notice, for example, how quickly people close their eyes in the face of some extreme unpleasantness. Interestingly enough, even if the unpleasantness is auditory, we tend to shut it out by closing our eyes. At other times, we close our eyes to block out visual stimuli and thus heighten our other senses; for example, we often listen to music with our eyes closed. Lovers often close their eyes while kissing, and many prefer to make love in a dark or dimly lit room.

PUPIL DILATION

In the fifteenth and sixteenth centuries, Italian women used to put drops of belladonna (which literally means "beautiful woman") into their eyes to enlarge the pupils so that they would look more attractive. Contemporary research supports the intuitive logic of these women: dilated pupils are in fact judged more attractive than constricted ones (Hess 1975; Marshall 1983).

In one study, photographs of women were retouched (Hess 1975). In one set of photographs, the pupils were enlarged, and in the other they were made smaller. Men were then asked to judge the women's personalities from the photographs. The photos of women with small pupils drew responses such as cold, hard, and selfish; those with dilated pupils drew responses such as feminine and soft. However, the male observers could not verbalize the reasons for the different perceptions. Pupil dilation and reactions to changes in the pupil size of others both seem to function below the level of awareness.

Although belladonna is no longer used, the cosmetics industry has made millions selling eye enhancers—eye shadow, eyeliner, false eyelashes, and tinted contact lenses that change eye color. These items function (ideally, at least) to draw attention to these most powerful communicators.

Pupil size also reveals your interest and level of emotional arousal. Your pupils enlarge when you are interested in something or when you are emotionally aroused. When homosexuals and heterosexuals were shown pictures of nude bodies, the homosexuals' pupils dilated more when viewing same-sex bodies, whereas the heterosexuals' pupils dilated more when viewing opposite-sex bodies (Hess, Seltzer, and Schlien 1965). Perhaps we judge dilated pupils more attractive because we judge them as indicative of a person's interest in us.

TOUCH COMMUNICATION

Touch communication, also referred to as **haptics,** is perhaps the most primitive form of communication. Developmentally, touch is probably the first sense to be used; even in the womb the child is stimulated by touch. Soon after birth, the child is fondled, caressed, patted, and stroked. In turn, the child explores its world through touch. In a very short time, the child learns to communicate a wide variety of meanings through touch.

THE MEANINGS OF TOUCH

Touch may communicate five major meanings (Jones and Yarbrough 1985). *Positive emotions* may be communicated by touch, mainly between intimates or others who have a relatively close relationship. Among the most important of these positive emotions are support, appreciation, inclusion, sexual interest or intent, and affection. It is interesting to note that people in relationships touch each other more during the intermediate stage than in either the beginning or firmly established relationship stages (Guerrero and Andersen 1991). Touch often communicates *playfulness,* either affectionately or aggressively. When touch is used in this manner, the playfulness deemphasizes the emotion and tells the other person that it is not to be taken seriously. Playful touches lighten an interaction.

Touch may also *control* the behaviors, attitudes, or feelings of the other person. Such control may communicate a number of messages. To ask for compliance, for example, we touch the other person to communicate, "Move over," "Hurry," "Stay here," or "Do it." Touching to control may also communicate dominance (Henley 1977). The higher-status and dominant person, for example, initiates touch. In fact, it would be a breach of etiquette for the lower-status person to touch the person of higher status.

The nonverbal communication researcher Nancy Henley (1977) argues that, in addition to indicating relative status, touching also demonstrates the assertion of male power and dominance over women. Men may, says Henley, touch women in the course of their daily routine—in the restaurant, office, and school, for example—and thus indicate their "superior status." However, because the interpretation of a female-dominant relationship would be unacceptable (to men), women's touching men is frequently interpreted as a sexual invitation.

Ritualistic touching centers on greetings and departures. Shaking hands to say "hello" or "goodbye" is perhaps the clearest example of ritualistic touching, but we might also hug, kiss, or put an arm around another's shoulder. *Task-related* touching is associated with the performance of some function. This ranges from removing a speck of dust from another person's face to helping someone out of a car or checking someone's forehead for fever. Task-related touching seems generally to be regarded positively. For example, book borrowers had a more positive attitude toward the library and the librarian when touched lightly, and customers gave larger tips when lightly touched by the waitress (Marsh 1988).

TOUCH AVOIDANCE

Much as we have a need and desire to touch and be touched by others, we also have a tendency to avoid touch from certain people or in certain circumstances (Andersen and Leibowitz 1978). Before reading about the research findings on touch avoidance, you may wish to take the touch avoidance self-test on page 232.

Among the important findings is the observation that touch avoidance is positively related to communication apprehension. Those who fear oral communication also seem to score high on touch avoidance. (You may wish to compare your scores on this touch avoidance test with your scores on the communication apprehension test presented in Unit 9.) Touch avoidance is also high among those who self-disclose little; both touch and self-disclosure are intimate forms of communication, and people who are reluctant to get close to another person by self-disclosure also seem reluctant to get close through touch. The tendency to avoid communication seems a general one that applies to all forms of communication.

Older people have higher touch avoidance scores for opposite-sex persons than do younger people. Apparently, as we get older we are touched less by members of the opposite sex, and this decreased frequency of touching may lead us to avoid touching. Males score higher than females on same-sex touch avoidance. This accords well with our stereotypes: men avoid touching other men, but women may and do touch other women. Women, it was also found, have higher touch avoidance scores for opposite-sex touching than do men.

DO YOU AVOID TOUCH?*

INSTRUCTIONS

This instrument is composed of 18 statements concerning how you feel about touching other people and being touched. Please indicate the degree to which each statement applies to you by indicating whether you

1 = strongly agree
2 = agree
3 = are undecided
4 = disagree
5 = strongly disagree

_____ 1. A hug from a same-sex friend is a true sign of friendship.
_____ 2. Opposite-sex friends enjoy it when I touch them.
_____ 3. I often put my arm around friends of the same sex.
_____ 4. When I see two friends of the same sex hugging, it revolts me.
_____ 5. I like it when members of the opposite sex touch me.
_____ 6. People shouldn't be so uptight about touching persons of the same sex.
_____ 7. I think it is vulgar when members of the opposite sex touch me.
_____ 8. When a member of the opposite sex touches me, I find it unpleasant.
_____ 9. I wish I were free to show emotions by touching members of the same sex.
_____ 10. I'd enjoy giving a massage to an opposite-sex friend.
_____ 11. I enjoy kissing a person of the same sex.
_____ 12. I like to touch friends who are the same sex as I am.
_____ 13. Touching a friend of the same sex does not make me uncomfortable.
_____ 14. I find it enjoyable when my date and I embrace.
_____ 15. I enjoy getting a back rub from a member of the opposite sex.
_____ 16. I dislike kissing relatives of the same sex.
_____ 17. Intimate touching with members of the opposite sex is pleasurable.
_____ 18. I find it difficult to be touched by a member of my own sex.

SCORING

1. Reverse your scores for items 4, 7, 8, 16, and 18 as follows: 5 becomes 1, 4 becomes 2, 3 remains 3, 2 becomes 4, and 1 becomes 5. Thus, for example, if you responded with 5 to question 4, you should reverse this to 1. Do these reversals only for Questions 4, 7, 8, 16, and 18. Use these reversed scores in all future calculations.
2. To obtain your same-sex touch avoidance score (the extent to which you avoid touching members of your sex), total the scores for items 1, 3, 4, 6, 9, 11, 12, 13, 16, and 18.
3. To obtain your opposite-sex touch avoidance score (the extent to which you avoid touching members of the opposite sex), total the scores for items 2, 5, 7, 8, 10, 14, 15, and 17.
4. To obtain your total touch avoidance score, add the subtotals from steps 2 and 3.

The higher the score, the higher the touch avoidance—that is, the greater your tendency to avoid touch. In studies by Andersen and Leibowitz (1978), who constructed this test, average opposite-sex touch avoidance scores were 12.9 for males and 14.85 for females. Average same-sex touch avoidance scores were 26.43 for males and 21.70 for females.

*From Andersen and Leibowitz (1978).

WHO TOUCHES WHOM WHERE: GENDER AND CULTURAL DIFFERENCES

A great deal of research has been directed at the question of who touches whom where. Most of it has attempted to address two basic questions: (1) Are there gender differences? Do men and women communicate through touch in the same way? Are men and women touched in the same way? (2) Are there cultural differences? Do people in widely different cultures communicate through touch in the same way?

Gender Differences   Sidney Jourard (1966) reported that touching and being touched differ little between men and women. Men touch and are touched as often and in the same places as women. The major exception to this is the touching behavior of mothers and fathers. Mothers touch children of both sexes and of all ages a great deal more than do fathers, who in many instances go no further than touching the hands of their children. The studies that have found differences between women's and men's touching behavior seem to indicate that women initiate touch and are touched more than men (Jones 1986).

A great deal more touching is reported among opposite-sex friends than among same-sex friends. Both male and female college students report that they touch and are touched more by their opposite-sex friends than by their same-sex friends (Jones 1986). No doubt the strong societal bias against same-sex touching accounts, at least in part, for the greater prevalence of opposite-sex touching that most studies report. A great deal of touching probably goes on among same-sex friends but goes unreported because many people are unaware of touching same-sex partners. When the Jourard (1966) study was replicated ten years later (Rosenfeld, Kartus, and Ray 1976), all of Jourard's earlier findings were confirmed, except that in the latter study both males and females were touched more by opposite-sex friends than in the earlier study.

Cultural Differences   Do recognize that the several functions and examples of touching discussed here have been based on studies in North America and that in other cultures these functions might not be served in the same way. In some cultures, for example, some task-related touching is viewed negatively and is to be avoided. Among Koreans, it is considered disrespectful for a store owner to touch a customer in, say, handing back change; it

The cultural differences in nonverbal communication discussed here center on touch. In what other areas of nonverbal communication covered in this unit might cultural differences be important?

is considered too intimate a gesture. Members of other cultures, expecting such touching, may consider the Korean's behavior cold and insulting.

For example, in one study on touch, college students in Japan and in the United States were surveyed (Barnlund 1975). Students from the United States reported being touched twice as much as did the Japanese students. In Japan, there is a strong taboo against strangers touching, and the Japanese are therefore especially careful to maintain sufficient distance.

Another obvious example of cross-cultural differences comes from the Middle East, where same-sex touching in public is extremely common. For example, men walk with their arms around each other's shoulders, a practice that would cause difficulty for many people raised in the United States. Middle Easterners, Latin Americans, and southern Europeans touch each other while talking a great deal more than do people from "noncontact cultures"—Asia and northern Europe, for example. As a result, northern Europeans and Japanese may be perceived as cold, distant, and uninvolved by southern Europeans, who may in turn be perceived as pushy, aggressive, and inappropriately intimate.

Another way to appreciate the influence of culture is to recognize that some cultures are contact cultures and others are noncontact cultures. Members of contact cultures maintain close distances, touch each other in conversation, face each other more directly, and maintain longer and more focused eye contact. Members of noncontact cultures maintain greater distance in their interactions, touch each other only rarely if at all, avoid facing each other directly, and maintain much less direct eye contact.

PARALANGUAGE

An old exercise used to increase a student's ability to express different emotions, feelings, and attitudes was to have the student say the following sentence while accenting or stressing different words: "Is this the face that launched a thousand ships?" Significant differences in meaning are easily communicated, depending on where the stress is placed. Consider, for example, the following variations:

1. *Is* this the face that launched a thousand ships?
2. Is *this* the face that launched a thousand ships?
3. Is this the *face* that launched a thousand ships?
4. Is this the face that *launched* a thousand ships?
5. Is this the face that launched a *thousand ships?*

Each of these five sentences communicates something different. Each, in fact, asks a totally different question, even though the words used are identical. All that distinguishes the sentences is stress, one of the aspects of what is called paralanguage. **Paralanguage** is the vocal (but nonverbal) dimension of speech. It refers to the *manner* in which you say something rather than to what you say.

In addition to stress, paralanguage includes such vocal characteristics as rate, volume, and rhythm. Paralanguage also includes the vocalizations we make when laughing, yelling, moaning, whining, and belching; vocal segregates—sound combinations that are not words—such as "uh-uh" and "shh"; and pitch, the highness or lowness of vocal tone (Argyle 1988; Trager 1958, 1961).

PARALANGUAGE AND PEOPLE PERCEPTION

It does seem that certain voices are symptomatic of certain personality types or certain problems and, specifically, that the personality orientation gives rise to the vocal qualities. When listening to people—regardless of what they are saying—we form impressions based on their paralanguage as to what kind of people they are. Our impressions from paralanguage cues span a broad range and consist of physical impressions (perhaps about body type and certainly about sex and age), personality impressions (they sound shy, they appear aggressive), and evaluative impressions (they sound like good people, they sound evil and menacing, they have vicious laughs).

One of the most interesting findings on voice and personal characteristics is that listeners can accurately judge the status (high, middle, or low) of speakers after hearing a 60-second voice sample. In fact, many listeners reported that they made their judgments in less than 15 seconds. It has also been found that the speakers judged to be of high status were rated as being of higher credibility than those rated of middle or low status.

It is interesting to note that listeners agree with each other about the personality of the speaker even when their judgments are in error. Listeners seem to have stereotyped ideas about the way vocal characteristics and personality characteristics are related, and they use these stereotypes in their judgments.

Testing Your Decoding Ability.   To test your ability to decode emotions on the basis of verbal descriptions, try to "hear" the following voices and to identify the emotions being communicated. Do you hear affection, anger, boredom, or joy?

1. This voice is soft, with a low pitch, a resonant quality, a slow rate, and a steady and slightly upward inflection. The rhythm is regular, and the enunciation is slurred.
2. This voice is loud, with a high pitch, a moderately blaring quality, a fast rate, an upward inflection, and a regular rhythm.
3. This voice is loud, with a high pitch, a blaring quality, a fast rate, and an irregular up-and-down inflection. The rhythm is irregular, and the enunciation is clipped.
4. This voice is moderate to low in volume, with a moderate-to-low pitch, a moderately resonant quality, a moderately slow rate, and a monotonous or gradually falling inflection. The enunciation is somewhat slurred.

According to research by Joel Davitz (1964), the first voice would communicate affection, the second joy, the third anger, and the fourth boredom.

PARALANGUAGE AND PERSUASION

The rate of speech is the aspect of paralanguage that has received the most attention. It is of interest to the advertiser, the politician, and, in fact, anyone who tries to convey information or to influence others orally, especially when time is limited or expensive. The research on rate of speech shows that in one-way communication situations, persons who talk fast are more persuasive and are evaluated more highly than those who talk at or below normal speeds (MacLachlan 1979). This greater persuasiveness and higher regard holds true whether the person talks fast naturally or the speech is sped up electronically (as in time-compressed speech).

In one experiment, subjects were asked to listen to taped messages and then to indicate both the degree to which they agreed with the message and their opinions as to how intelligent and objective they thought the speaker was (MacLachlan 1979). Rates of 111, 140, and 191 words per minute were used. (The average speaking rate is about 130 to 150 words per minute.) Subjects agreed most with the fastest speech and least with the slowest speech. Further, they rated the fastest speaker as the most intelligent and objective and the slowest speaker as the least intelligent and objective. Even in experiments in which the speaker was known to have something to gain personally from persuasion (as would, say, a used-car dealer), the speaker who spoke at the fastest rate was the most persuasive.

Rapid speech also has the advantage in comprehension. Subjects who listened to speeches at 201 words per minute (about 140 is average) comprehended 95 percent of the message, and those who listened to speeches at 282 words per minute (that is, double the normal rate) comprehended 90 percent. Even though the rates increased dramatically, the comprehension rates fell only slightly. These 5 percent and 10 percent losses are more than offset by the increased speed and thus make the faster rates much more efficient in communicating information. If the speech speeds are increased more than 100 percent, however, comprehension falls dramatically.

Exercise caution in applying this research to your own interpersonal interactions. As John MacLachlan (1979) points out, during the time the speaker is speaking, the listener is generating and framing a reply. If the speaker talks too rapidly, there may not be enough time to compose this reply, and resentment may therefore be generated. Furthermore, the increased rate may seem so unnatural that the listener may come to focus on the speed of speech rather than the thought expressed.

SILENCE

In one of the most often quoted observations on silence, Thomas Mann said, "Speech is civilization itself. The word, even the most contradictory word, preserves contact; it is silence which isolates." On the other hand, the philosopher Karl Jaspers observed that "the ultimate in thinking as in communication is silence," and the philosopher Max Picard noted that "silence is nothing merely negative; it is not the mere absence of speech. It is a positive, a complete world in itself." The one thing on which these contradictory observations agree is that silence communicates. Your silence communicates just as intensely as anything you verbalize (see Jaworski 1993).

FUNCTIONS OF SILENCE

Like words and gestures, silence, too, serves important communication functions. Silence allows the speaker *time to think,* time to formulate and organize his or her verbal communications. Before messages of intense conflict, as well as those confessing undying love, there is often silence. Again, silence seems to prepare the receiver for the importance of these future messages.

Some people use silence as a weapon *to hurt* others. We often speak of giving someone "the silent treatment." After a conflict, for example, one or both individuals might remain silent as a kind of punishment. Silence used to hurt others may also take the form of refusing to acknowledge the presence of another person, as in disconfirmation (see Unit 11); here silence is a dramatic demonstration of the total indifference one person feels toward the other.

Sometimes silence is used as a *response to personal anxiety,* shyness, or threats. You may feel anxious or shy among new people and prefer to remain silent. By remaining silent you preclude the chance of rejection. Only when the silence is broken and an attempt to communicate with another person is made do you risk rejection.

Silence may be used *to prevent communication* of certain messages. In conflict situations, silence is sometimes used to prevent certain topics from surfacing and to prevent one or both parties from saying things they may later regret. In such situations, silence often allows us time to cool off before expressing hatred, severe criticism, or personal attacks, which, we know, are irreversible.

Like the eyes, face, or hands, silence can also be used *to communicate emotional responses* (Ehrenhaus 1988). Sometimes silence communicates a determination to be uncooperative or defiant; by refusing to engage in verbal communication, you defy the authority or the legitimacy of the other person's position. Silence is often used to communicate annoyance, usually accompanied by a pouting expression, arms crossed in front of the chest, and nostrils flared. Silence may express affection or love, especially when coupled with long and longing stares into each other's eyes.

Of course, you may also use silence when you simply have *nothing to say,* when nothing occurs to you, or when you do not want to say anything. James Russell Lowell expressed this well: "Blessed are they who have nothing to say, and who cannot be persuaded to say it."

CULTURAL DIFFERENCES

The communicative functions of silence in the situations just cited are not universal. The traditional Apache, for example, regard silence very differently (Basso 1972). Among the Apache, mutual friends do not feel the need to introduce strangers who may be working in the same area or on the same project. The strangers may remain silent for several days. During this time, they are looking each other over, trying to determine if the other person is all right. Only after this period do the individuals talk. When courting, especially during the initial stages, the Apache remain silent for hours; if they do talk, they generally talk very little. Only after a couple has been dating for several months will they have lengthy conversations. These periods of silence are generally attributed to shyness or self-consciousness. The use of silence is explicitly taught to Apache women, who are especially discouraged from engaging in long discussions with their dates. Silence during courtship is a sign of modesty to many Apache.

SUMMARY: UNIT IN BRIEF

Body Movements (Types)	Facial Communication Functions	Eye Communication Functions	Touch Communication Functions	Paralanguage and Silence Functions
Emblems translate words and phrases rather directly. **Illustrators** accompany and literally illustrate the verbal messages. **Affect displays** convey emotional meaning. **Regulators** monitor or control the speaking of the other person. **Adaptors** serve some need and are usually performed only partially in public.	**To express emotions:** happiness, surprise, fear, anger, sadness, disgust/contempt, interest, bewilderment, determination **To manage the meanings communicated:** intensifying, deintensifying, neutralizing, masking	**Eye gaze:** monitor feedback, maintain interest/attention, signal conversational turns, signal the nature of the relationship, compensate for physical distance **Eye avoidance:** give others privacy, signal uninterest, cut off unpleasant stimuli, heighten other senses **Pupil dilation:** indicate interest/arousal, increase attractiveness	• positive affect • playfulness • control • ritual • task-relatedness	**Paralanguage functions:** provide cues for impression formation; provide cues for identifying emotional states; provide cues for judgments of credibility, intelligence, and objectivity **Silence functions:** provide thinking time, inflict hurt, hide anxiety, prevent communication, communicate feelings, communicate "nothing"

THINKING CRITICALLY ABOUT BODY AND SOUND

1. What messages does your general physical appearance communicate about you? Check your theories with those who know you. What general appearance factors do you use to make judgments about others? Can you state these judgments in terms of the principles that you used to make them, using the form, "People who are *green* are *clever*"?

2. Consider, as Nancy Henley suggests in her *Body Politics* (1977), who would touch whom—say, by putting an arm on the other person's shoulder or by putting a hand on the other person's back—in the following dyads: teacher and student, doctor and patient, master and servant, manager and worker, minister and parishioner, police officer and accused, business executive and secretary. Most people would say that the

first person in each dyad would be more likely to touch the second person than the other way around. It is the higher-status person who is permitted to touch the lower-status person. What implications does this have for your own touching and being touched?

3. Research shows that women initiate touching more often than men (Jones 1986). From your own experiences, what would you conclude about whether men or women initiate touching more often?

4. What nonverbal cues would you look for to discover whether someone was interested in you romantically? What nonverbal cues do you emit to show your own romantic interest?

5. Why do you suppose women touch each other more often and more intimately than do men?

6. On the basis of your observations for a period of one day (admittedly, much too short a time), what general conclusions can you draw about the following questions:

   • Whom do you touch the most?
   • Who touches you the most?
   • What meanings do you use touch to communicate?
   • What meanings do you derive from being touched by others?

7. What mistakes in nonverbal communication do men and women frequently make in their dating behavior? What advice would you give these people to eliminate these mistakes?

8. Research shows that women smile more than men, even when making negative comments or expressing negative feelings. What implications does this have for male-female communication? What implications might this have for child rearing? For teaching?

9. What meanings do you communicate with silence?

10. How would you go about finding answers to the following questions?

   • Do high-status people touch each other with the same frequency as lower-status people?
   • Do children who were born blind express emotions with the same facial expressions that sighted children use?
   • How do men and women in different cultures express romantic interest?

EXPERIENTIAL VEHICLES

13.1 FACIAL COMMUNICATION

Working in dyads or small groups, test the conclusion of Ekman, Friesen, and Ellsworth (1972) that the face is capable of communicating the following eight "emotion categories": happiness, surprise, fear, anger, sadness, disgust, contempt, and interest. Write the names of these emotion categories on index cards, one to a card. Place the cards facedown on the desk, and have one person select a card at random and attempt to communicate the emotion using only facial gestures. Keep a record of accurate and inaccurate guesses. Play until each emotion has been demonstrated at least twice. Then consider the following questions:

1. Do you agree with Ekman, Friesen, and Ellsworth that the face can communicate these eight emotion categories?
2. Are some emotions easier to communicate than others? Why do you suppose this is true?
3. Dale Leathers (1990) suggests that in addition to the eight emotions noted here, the face is also capable of communicating bewilderment and determination. Test this suggestion in any way that seems useful and valid to you.
4. Are some members of your small group better facial communicators (encoders) than others? Are some better decoders than others? How might you account for these differences in ability?

13.2 FACIAL EXPRESSIONS

The objective of this exercise is to gain a greater understanding of the role of facial features in communicating different emotions.

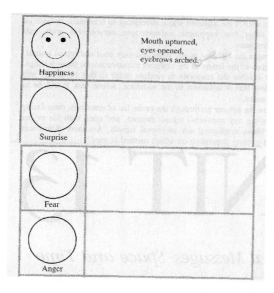

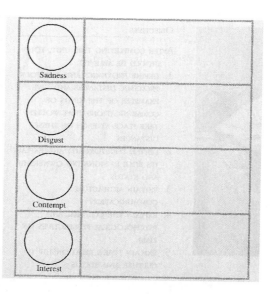

Draw faces, depicting only eyebrows, eyes, and mouth, to illustrate the primary emotions: happiness (provided as an example), surprise, fear, anger, sadness, disgust, contempt, and interest. In the space provided, write a verbal description of how one would facially express each of these emotions. Follow the format provided in the happiness example.

Compare your faces and descriptions with those done by others. What do the several faces for each emotion have in common? How do they differ? What do the verbal descriptions have in common? How do they differ?

13.3 EYE CONTACT

Form dyads and talk about any topic of mutual interest—sports, film, politics. For the first two minutes, the conversation should be conducted without any special rules. At an agreed-upon signal, eye-face contact is to cease. The conversation should continue for another two minutes, as before, ideally without interruption. At another signal, focused eye-to-eye contact is to be established. Each person is to maintain direct eye contact for two minutes and continue the conversation as usual. At another signal, the participants should return to their customary means of communication for the final two minutes. Each person should share her or his feelings during the four periods:

1. Normal interaction situation
2. No-eye-contact situation
3. Focused eye contact
4. Normal situation but with heightened awareness and perhaps some awkwardness carried over from the two periods of abnormal interaction

Specifically, members may address themselves to the influence of changes in eye contact on such variables as:

1. fluency, nonfluencies, and silences
2. general body movements, especially of the head, hands, and legs
3. comfort or discomfort
4. interest in the other person and in the conversation
5. time perception (did some eye-contact situations seem longer than others?)

What suggestions for effective interpersonal interaction might we derive from this brief experience?

13.4 COMMUNICATING THROUGH PARALANGUAGE

The aim of this exercise is to show that the same verbal statement can communicate praise and criticism, depending on the paralinguistic cues that accompany the statement. Read the ten statements first to communicate praise; read them a second time to communicate criticism. One procedure is to have the entire class sit in a circle and to go around the room, with the first student reading statement 1 with a praising meaning, the second student reading statement 1 with a criticizing meaning, and so on until all ten statements are read twice.

After all ten statements are read with both the praising and criticizing meaning, consider these questions:

1. What paralinguistic cues communicate praise? What paralinguistic cues communicate criticism?
2. What one paralinguistic cue was most helpful in enabling the speaker to communicate praise or criticism?
3. Most people would claim that it is easier to decode praise or criticism than to encode these meanings. Was this true in this experience? Why or why not?

4. Although this exercise focuses on paralanguage, the statements were probably read with different facial expressions, eye movements, and body postures. How would you describe these other nonverbals when communicating praise and criticism?

Statements

1. Now that looks good on you.
2. You lost weight.
3. You look younger than that.
4. You're gonna make it.
5. That was some meal.
6. You really know yourself.
7. You're an expert.
8. You're so sensitive. I'm amazed.
9. Your parents are really something.
10. Are you ready? Already?

UNIT 14

Nonverbal Messages: Space and Time

UNIT OBJECTIVES

AFTER COMPLETING THIS UNIT, YOU SHOULD BE ABLE TO:

1. Define *proxemics* and the four proxemic distances
2. Define *territoriality* and explain its role in signaling ownership and status
3. Explain artifactual communication
4. Explain the cultural and psychological perspectives of time
5. Explain time's relationship to culture and status

Like verbal behavior, spatial and temporal behaviors also communicate. In this unit, we explore several dimensions of space and time and the ways in which they communicate a variety of messages.

SPATIAL MESSAGES

Space is an especially important factor in interpersonal communication, although we seldom think about it. Edward T. Hall (1959, 1963, 1966), who has pioneered the study of spatial communication (sometimes called **proxemics**), distinguishes four distances that correspond closely to the major types of relationships: intimate, personal, social, and public (see Figure 14.1).

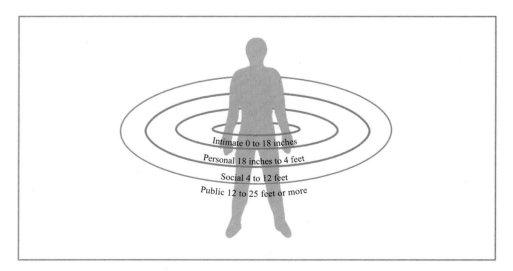

Figure 14.1
The four spatial distances.

Intimate Distance   Within **intimate distance,** ranging from the close phase of actual touching to the far phase of 6 to 18 inches, the presence of the other person is unmistakable. You experience the sound, smell, and feel of the other's breath. The close phase is used for lovemaking and wrestling, for comforting and protecting. In the close phase, the muscles and the skin communicate, while actual words play a minor role. The far phase allows people to touch each other by extending their hands. The individuals are so close that this distance is not considered proper for strangers in public. Because of the feeling of inappropriateness and discomfort (at least for some Americans) if strangers are this close (say, on a crowded bus), their eyes seldom meet but remain fixed on some remote object.

Personal Distance   You carry a protective bubble defining your **personal distance,** which allows you to stay protected and untouched by others and ranges from 18 inches to about 4 feet. In the close phase, people can still hold or grasp each other but only by extending their arms. You can then take into your protective bubble certain individuals—for example, loved ones. In the far phase, you can touch another person only if you both extend your arms. This far phase is the extent to which you can physically get your hands on things; hence, it defines, in one sense, the limits of your physical control over others. At times, you may detect breath odor, but generally at this distance etiquette demands that you direct your breath to some neutral area.

At this distance, you cannot perceive moderately applied cologne or perfume. Thus, it has been proposed that cologne has two functions: first, it disguises the body's odor, and second, it makes clear the limits of your protective bubble. The bubble, defined by the perfume, signals that you may not advance beyond the point at which you can smell the other person.

Social Distance   At the **social distance,** ranging from 4 to 12 feet, you lose the visual detail you had at the personal distance. The close phase is the distance at which you conduct impersonal business or interact at a social gathering. The far phase is the distance at which you stand when someone says, "Stand away so I can look at you." At this distance, business transactions have a more formal tone than they do when conducted in the close phase. In the offices of high officials, the desks are often positioned so that clients are kept at least this distance away. Unlike the intimate distance, where eye contact is awkward, the far phase of the social distance makes eye contact essential—otherwise, communication is lost. The voice is generally louder than normal at this level. This distance frees you from constant interaction with those with whom you work without seeming rude.

Public Distance   **Public distance** ranges from 12 to more than 25 feet. In the close phase, a person seems protected by space. At this distance, you are able to take defensive action should you feel threatened. On a public bus or train, for example, you might keep at least this distance from a drunkard. Although you lose the fine details of the face and eyes, you are still close enough to see what is happening.

At the far phase, you see others not as separate individuals but as part of the whole setting. People automatically set approximately 30 feet around important public figures, and they seem to do this whether or not there are guards preventing their coming closer. The far phase is the distance by which actors on stage are separated from their audience; consequently, their actions and voices have to be somewhat exaggerated.

The specific distances you would maintain between yourself and another person depend on a wide variety of factors. Some of the factors are presented in Table 14.1.

Table 14.1
Factors Influencing Dyadic Distance

INFLUENCING FACTORS	SAMPLE RESEARCH FINDINGS
Communicator characteristics:	
Gender	• Females sit and stand closer to each other than do males in same-sex dyads. • People approach women more closely than they approach men.
Age	• Distance increases with age. • People maintain closer distances with peers than with persons much older or younger.
Race/ethnicity	• Mexican-Americans maintain closer distances than do either African-Americans or whites.
Personality	• Introverts and highly anxious people maintain greater distances than do extroverts.
Relationship characteristics:	
Familiarity	• Persons familiar with each other maintain shorter distances.
Liking	• Persons maintain shorter distances with those they like.
Status	• The greater the status difference, the greater is the space maintained.
Context characteristics:	
Formality	• The more formal the situation, the greater is the space maintained.
Purpose of interaction	• Shorter distances are maintained for cooperative tasks than for competitive tasks.
Space availability	• The greater the space, the shorter is the distance

This table is based on the extensive research summary of Burgoon, Buller, and Woodall (1989), pp. 110–118.

THEORIES ABOUT SPACE

A number of nonverbal communication researchers have offered explanations as to why people maintain the distances they do. Prominent among these explanations are protection theory, equilibrium theory, and expectancy violation theory—rather complex names for simple and interesting concepts.

Protection Theory   **Protection theory** holds that you establish a body buffer zone around yourself as protection against unwanted touching or attack (Dosey and Meisels 1976). When you feel that you may be attacked, your body buffer zone increases; you want more space around you. For example, if you found yourself in a dangerous neighbor-hood at night, your body buffer zone would probably expand well beyond what it would be if you were in familiar and safe surroundings. If someone entered this buffer zone, you would probably feel threatened and seek to expand that distance by walking faster or crossing the street.

In contrast, when you are feeling secure and protected, your buffer zone becomes much smaller. For example, if you are with a group of close friends and feel secure, your buffer zone shrinks, and you may welcome the close proximity and mutual touching.

Equilibrium Theory   **Equilibrium theory** holds that intimacy and distance vary to-gether: the greater the intimacy, the closer the distance; the lower the intimacy, the greater the distance. This theory says that you maintain close distances with those with whom you have close interpersonal relationships and that you maintain greater distances with those with whom you do not have close relationships (Argyle and Dean 1965).

At times, of course, your interpersonal distance does not accurately reflect your level of intimacy. When this happens, you make adjustments. For example, let's say that you have an intimate relationship with someone, but for some reason you are separated—perhaps because you could not get concert seats next to each other or you are at a party and have each been led to different parts of a large banquet hall. When this happens, you probably try to preserve your psychological closeness by maintaining frequent eye con-tact or perhaps by facing each other.

At other times, however, you are forced into close distances with someone with whom you are not intimate (or may even dislike)—for example, on a crowded bus or per-haps in the dentist's chair. In these situations, you also compensate, but in such cases you seek to make the psychological distance greater. Consequently, you might avoid eye con-tact and turn in an opposite direction. In the dentist's chair, you probably close your eyes to decrease this normally intimate distance. If seated to the right of a stranger, you might cross your legs and turn your torso to the left.

Expectancy Violations Theory   **Expectancy violations theory** explains what hap-pens when you increase or decrease the distance between yourself and another in an inter-personal interaction (Burgoon and Hale 1988; Burgoon, Buller, and Woodall 1989). Each culture has certain expectancies for the distance people are to maintain in their conversa-tions. Of course, each person has certain idiosyncrasies. Together, these determine "ex-pected distance." What happens when these expectations are violated?

If you violate the expected distance to a great extent—small violations most often go unnoticed—then the relationship itself comes into focus. The other person begins to turn attention away from the topic of conversation and toward you and your relationship with him or her.

If this other person perceives you positively—for example, you are a high-status person or you are particularly attractive—then you will be perceived even more positive-ly if you violate the norm. If, however, you are perceived negatively and you violate the norm, you will be perceived even more negatively.

Thus, the positively evaluated person will be perceived more positively if he or she violates the norm, whereas the negatively evaluated person will be more positively per-ceived if the distance norm is not violated.

TERRITORIALITY

Another aspect of spatial communication is **territoriality,** the possessive reaction to an area or to particular objects. Through territorial behavior, you signal ownership and status. Of course, not all territories are the same (Altman 1975). **Primary territories** are yours and yours alone. **Secondary territories** are associated with you but are not owned by you. **Public territories** belong to or are used by all people. Table 14.2 summarizes these three types.

SIGNALING OWNERSHIP

Many male animals stake out a particular territory and signal their ownership to all others. They allow prospective mates to enter but defend the territory against other males of the same species. Among deer, for example, the size of the territory signifies the power of the buck, which in turn determines how many females he will mate with. Less powerful bucks will be able to control only small territories and consequently will mate with only one or two females. This adaptive measure ensures that the strongest members of the species produce most of the offspring.

These same general patterns are believed by many ethologists—scientists who study animal behavior in the animals' natural surroundings—to be integral to human behavior. Some researchers claim that this form of behavior is instinctive and is a symptom of the innate aggressiveness of humans. Others claim that territoriality is learned and is culturally based. Most, however, seem to agree that a great deal of human behavior can be understood and described as territoriality regardless of its possible origin or development (Ardrey 1966).

If you look around at your home, you will probably find certain territories that different people have staked out where invasions cause at least mild defensive action. This is perhaps seen most clearly in the case of siblings who each have or "own" a specific chair, room, stereo, and so on. Father has his chair and mother has hers. Territoriality can also be observed in a classroom where seats are not assigned. When a student sits in a seat that has normally been occupied by another student, the regular occupant will often become disturbed and resentful and may even claim the seat.

Table 14.2 Three Types of Territory		
TERRITORY	DEFINITION	EXAMPLES
Primary	Areas you might call your own; your exclusive preserve	Your room, your desk, your office
Secondary	Areas that do not belong to you but that you have occupied and with which you are associated	Table in the cafeteria that you sit at regularly, your neighborhood turf
Public	Areas that are open to all people	Movie theater, restaurant, shopping mall

The Home Field Advantage   When you operate in your own territory, you have an interpersonal advantage. In their own home or office, people take on a kind of leadership role: they initiate conversations, fill in silences, assume relaxed and comfortable postures, and maintain their positions with greater conviction. Because the territorial owner is dominant, you stand a better chance of getting your raise, your point accepted, and the contract resolved in your favor if you are in your territory (your office, your home) rather than in someone else's (your supervisor's office, for example) (Marsh 1988).

Markers   Like animals, humans mark their territory, using three types of markers: central, boundary, and ear markers (Goffman 1971). **Central markers** are items you place in a territory to reserve it for you—for example, a drink at the bar, books on your desk, or a sweater over a library chair.

    Boundary markers set boundaries that divide your territory from that of others. In the supermarket checkout line, the bar that is placed between your groceries and those of the person behind you is a boundary marker, as are a fence, the armrests separating your chair from those on either side, and the contours of the molded plastic seats on a bus or train.

    Ear markers—a term taken from the practice of branding animals on their ears—are identifying marks that indicate your possession of a territory or object. Trademarks, nameplates, and initials on a shirt or attaché case are all examples of ear markers.

    Markers are also important in giving you a feeling of belonging and ownership. For example, the interpersonal researcher Peter Marsh (1988) notes, for example, that students in college dormitories who marked their rooms by displaying personal items stayed in school longer than did those who did not personalize their spaces.

SIGNALING STATUS

Like animals' territory, the territory of humans communicates status. Clearly, the size and location of the territory indicates something about status. Status is also signaled by the unwritten law granting the right of invasion. Higher-status individuals have a "right" to invade the territory of lower-status persons, but the reverse is not true. The boss of a large company, for example, can barge into the office of a junior executive, but the reverse would be unthinkable. Similarly, a teacher may invade a student's personal space by looking over her or his shoulder as the student writes, but the student cannot do the same to the teacher.

TERRITORIAL ENCROACHMENT

When your "ownership" of a certain territory is challenged, this action constitutes **territorial encroachment.** Following Lyman and Scott (1967), we can distinguish three major types of territorial encroachment.

    Violation is the unwarranted use of another's territory, as when you enter another's office or home without permission or when you enter a place normally restricted to one group—for example, a rest room for the opposite sex.

    Invasion constitutes entering the territory of another and thereby changing the meaning of that territory. For example, if students entered a faculty meeting or if parents

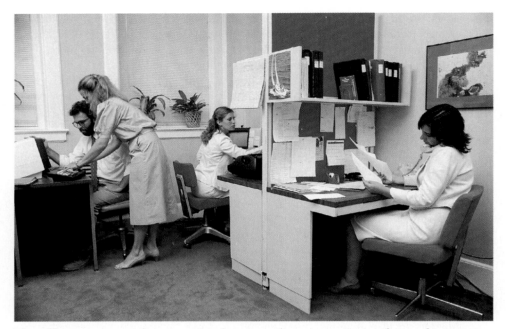

The office space a worker occupies, for example, communicates the worker's status in the organization. How would you describe the status of the people in this photo? What specific cues did you use to reach your conclusion? How does space communicate status differences at your school? For example, what specific features distinguish the office of the college president from that of an instructor?

entered their teenagers' hangout, it would change the meaning of the meeting and of the territory.

Contamination occurs when a territory is rendered impure. For example, a person who smokes a smelly cigar may contaminate an area. A couple's home or bed may be contaminated if an unfaithful spouse uses it for an extramarital affair. Obscenity may also contaminate a territory.

Reactions to Encroachment   You can react to encroachment in a number of ways. The most extreme form is **turf defense,** defending your territory against the intruders and expelling them. A less extreme form is **insulation**—erecting some sort of barrier between yourself and the invaders. In **linguistic collusion,** you would speak in a language unknown to the outsiders or perhaps use professional jargon to which they are not privy. Still another type of response is **withdrawal:** you can leave the territory. Table 14.3 summarizes these reactions to encroachment (Lyman and Scott 1967).

ARTIFACTUAL COMMUNICATION

Artifactual communication concerns the messages conveyed by objects that are made by human hands. Thus, aesthetics, color, clothing, jewelry, and even hairstyle are considered artifactual. We look at each of these briefly.

Table 14.3 Reactions to Encroachment		
REACTION	DEFINITION	EXAMPLES
Turf defense	Defending territory by fighting off invaders	International war, gang fights
Insulation	Setting up a barrier between ourselves and invaders	Great Wall of China, restricted communities or clubs, sunglasses, fences
Linguistic collusion	Speaking in a language unknown to invaders, uniting those who speak the language and excluding others	Speaking a foreign language or a sublanguage
Withdrawal	Leaving the territory	Moving to another country, moving out of your neighborhood, running away

SPACE DECORATION

That the decoration or surroundings of a place exert influence on perceptions should be obvious to anyone who has ever entered a hospital, with its sterile walls and furniture, or a museum, with its imposing columns, glass-encased exhibits, and brass plaques.

Even the way a room is furnished exerts influence on us. In a classic study, researchers attempted to determine if the aesthetic conditions of a room would influence the judgments people made in it (Maslow and Mintz, 1956). Three rooms were used: one was beautiful, one average, and one ugly. The beautiful room had large windows, beige walls, indirect lighting, and attractive, comfortable furnishings. The average room was a professor's office with mahogany desks and chairs, metal bookcases and filing cabinets, and window shades. The ugly room was painted battleship gray; lighting was provided by an overhead bulb with a dirty, torn shade. The room was furnished to give the impression of a janitor's storeroom in horrible condition. The ashtrays were filled and the window shades torn.

In the three different rooms, students rated art prints in terms of the fatigue/energy and displeasure/well-being depicted in them. As predicted, the students in the beautiful room rated the prints as more energetic and as displaying well-being; the prints judged in the ugly room were rated as displaying fatigue and displeasure, while those judged in the average room were perceived as somewhere between these two extremes.

In a follow-up study, two of the subjects from the previous experiment were used as "examiners" (Mintz 1956). For a period of three weeks, these two subjects tested other subjects for one hour per day, each alternating every day between the beautiful room and the ugly room. After each hour, the "examiners" rated the prints again, supposedly for measures of reliability. The subjects continued to rate the prints as displaying greater energy and well-being when judged in the beautiful room. Further, these results were consistent over the three weeks. The subjects did not adjust to the surroundings over time. Also, the "examiners" tested their subjects in the ugly room faster than they did in the beautiful room 27 out of 32 times. The "examiners" did not want to test in the ugly room, they became irritable and aggressive when they had to test in that room, and they felt that time there seemed to move more slowly.

The implications of this type of finding are extremely important. For example, does the ghetto child studying in a crowded tenement derive the same benefits as a middle-class child studying in her or his own room? Can workers in an unappealing factory ever enjoy their job as much as workers in a pleasant office? What about prisons? Is aggressive behavior in prisons influenced by the surroundings in which prisoners are forced to live? Does the ugliness of the surroundings influence the crime rate in a neighborhood?

The way your private spaces are decorated communicates something about who you are. The office with a mahogany desk, bookcases, and oriental rugs communicates importance and status within the organization, just as the metal desk and bare floors communicate a status much further down in the hierarchy.

Similarly, people will make inferences about you on the basis of the way you decorate your home. The cost of the furnishings may communicate your status and wealth, and their coordination may communicate your sense of style. The magazines may communicate your interests. The arrangement of chairs around a television set may reveal how important watching television is. Bookcases lining the walls reveal the importance of reading. In fact, there is probably little in your home that would not send messages to others and that others would not use for making inferences about you. Computers, wide-screen televisions, well-equipped kitchens, and oil paintings of great grandparents, for example, all say something about the people who own them.

Likewise, the lack of certain items will communicate something about you. Consider, for example, what messages you would get from a home in which there was no television, telephone, or books.

COLOR COMMUNICATION

When you are in debt, you speak of being "in the red"; when you make a profit, you are "in the black." When you are sad, you are "blue"; when you are healthy, you are "in the pink"; when you are jealous, you are "green with envy." To be a coward is to be "yellow" and to be inexperienced is to be "green." When you talk a great deal, you talk "a blue streak"; when you are angry, you "see red." As revealed through these time-worn cliches, language abounds in color symbolism.

In his *Symbol Sourcebook* (1971), Henry Dreyfuss reminds us of some of the positive and negative meanings associated with various colors. Some of these are presented in Table 14.4. Dreyfuss also notes some cultural comparisons for some of these colors. For example, in China red is used for joyous and festive occasions, whereas in Japan it signifies anger and danger. Blue signifies defeat for the Cherokee Indian but virtue and truth for the Egyptian. In the Japanese theater, blue is the color for villains. Yellow signifies happiness and prosperity in Egypt, but in tenth-century France yellow colored the doors of criminals. Green communicates femininity to certain American Indians, fertility and strength to Egyptians, and youth and energy to the Japanese. Purple signifies virtue and faith in Egypt, grace and nobility in Japan.

Table 14.4
Some Positive and Negative Messages of Color*

COLOR	POSITIVE MESSAGES	NEGATIVE MESSAGES
Red	warmth passion life liberty patriotism	death war revolution devil danger
Blue	religious feeling devotion truth justice	doubt discouragement
Yellow	intuition wisdom divinity	cowardice malevolence impure love
Green	nature hope freshness prosperity	envy jealousy opposition disgrace
Purple	power royalty love of truth nostalgia	mourning regret penitence resignation

*Adapted from *Symbol Sourcebook* by Henry Dreyfus, 1971. Reprinted by permission of McGraw-Hill, Inc.

There is some evidence that colors affect us physiologically. For example, respiratory movements increase in the presence of red light and decrease in the presence of blue light. Similarly, eye blinks increase in frequency when eyes are exposed to red light and decrease when exposed to blue. This seems consistent with our intuitive feelings that blue is more soothing and red more provocative. After changing a school's walls from orange and white to blue, the students' blood pressure decreased and their academic performance improved.

Colors surely influence our perceptions and behaviors (Kanner 1989). People's acceptance of a product, for example, is largely determined by its package. For example, the very same coffee taken from a yellow can was described as weak, from a dark brown can too strong, from a red can rich, and from a blue can mild. Even our acceptance of a person may depend on the colors worn. Consider, for example, the comments of one color expert (Kanner 1989): "If you have to pick the wardrobe for your defense lawyer heading into court and choose anything but blue, you deserve to lose the case. . . ." Black is so powerful that it can work against the lawyer with the jury. Brown lacks sufficient authority. Green will probably elicit a negative response.

CLOTHING AND BODY ADORNMENT

Clothing serves a variety of functions. It protects you from the weather and, in sports like football, from injury. It helps you conceal parts of your body and so serves a modesty function. Clothing also serves as a **cultural display** (Morris 1977). It communicates your cultural and subcultural affiliations. In the United States, where there are so many different ethnic groups, you regularly see examples of dress that tell you from what country the wearers have come.

The very poor and the very rich do not dress in the same way, nor do white- and blue-collar workers or the young and the old (Lurie 1983). People dress, in part at least, to identify with the groups of which they are or want to be members.

People infer who you are, in part, by the way you dress. Whether these inferences prove to be accurate or inaccurate, they will nevertheless influence what people think of you and how they react to you. Your social class, your seriousness, your attitudes (for example, whether you are conservative or liberal), your concern for convention, your sense of style, and perhaps even your creativity will all be judged—in part at least—from the way you dress. In fact, the very popular *Dress for Success* (1975) and *The Woman's Dress for Success Book* by John Molloy (1977) instructed men and women in how to dress so that they could communicate the image they wanted: for example, efficient, reliable, or authoritative.

Similarly, college students will perceive an instructor dressed informally as friendly, fair, enthusiastic, and flexible, and the same instructor dressed formally as prepared, knowledgeable, and organized (Malandro, Barker, and Barker 1989).

Your jewelry likewise communicates messages about you. Wedding and engagement rings are obvious examples of jewelry that communicates very specific messages. College rings and political buttons also communicate specific messages. If you wear a Rolex watch or large precious stones, others are likely to infer that you are rich. Men with earrings will be judged differently from men without earrings.

The way you wear your hair communicates who you are. Your hair may communicate a concern for being up-to-date, a desire to shock, or perhaps a lack of concern for appearances. Men with long hair will generally be judged as less conservative than men with shorter hair.

TEMPORAL COMMUNICATION

The study of temporal communication **(chronemics)** focuses on the use of time—how you organize it, how you react to it, and the messages it communicates. Time can be viewed from two major perspectives: cultural and psychological.

CULTURAL TIME

Generally, three types of cultural time are identified (Hall 1959). **Technical time** is precise, scientific time. Milliseconds and atomic years are examples of units of technical or scientific time. This time system is used only in the laboratory, so it seems to have little relevance to our daily lives.

Formal time refers to the manner in which a culture defines time. In the United States, time is divided into seconds, minutes, hours, days, weeks, months, and years.

Other cultures use phases of the moon or the seasons to delineate time periods. College courses are divided into 50- or 75-minute periods that meet at various times each week for 10- or 14-week periods called quarters or semesters. A certain number of quarters or semesters equal a college education. Formal time units are arbitrary and have been established by the culture for reasons of convenience.

Informal time refers to a rather loose use of time terms—for example, words such as "forever," "immediately," "soon," "right away," and "as soon as possible." This is the aspect of time that creates the most communication problems because the terms have different meanings for different people.

Displaced and Diffused Time Orientations   Another important distinction can be drawn between displaced and diffused time orientations (Hall 1959). In a **displaced time orientation,** time is viewed exactly. Persons with this orientation will be exactly on time. In a **diffused time orientation,** time is seen as approximate rather than exact. People with this orientation are usually late for appointments because they understand, for example, a scheduled time of 8:00 P.M. as meaning anywhere from 7:45 to 8:15 or 8:30.

Even the accuracy of clocks varies in different cultures and probably reflects each culture's time orientation. In one study (LeVine and Bartlett 1984), clocks in Japan were found to be the most accurate, while clocks in Indonesia were least accurate. Clocks in England, Italy, Taiwan, and the United States fell between these two extremes in accuracy. Not surprisingly, when the speed of pedestrians in these countries was measured, the Japanese were found to walk the fastest and the Indonesians the slowest. Such differences reflect the different ways in which cultures treat time and their general attitude toward the importance of time in everyday life.

PSYCHOLOGICAL TIME

Psychological time refers to the importance placed on the past, present, or future. In a **past orientation,** you give particular reverence to the past; you might relive old times and regard the old methods as the best. Events are seen as circular and recurring, so that the wisdom of yesterday is applicable also to today and tomorrow. In a **present orientation,** you live in the present for the present. Present activities command your attention; you engage in them not for their future rewards or their past significance but because they are happening now. In its extreme form, this orientation is hedonistic. In a **future orientation,** you give primary attention to the future. You save today, work hard in college, and deny yourself certain enjoyments and luxuries, all because you are preparing for the future.

Researchers have provided some interesting correlations to these different time orientations (Gonzalez and Zimbardo 1985). Before reading their conclusions, you may wish to take their time self-test "What Time Do You Have?"

One of the findings of the Gonzalez and Zimbardo time study is that future income is positively related to future orientation. The more future oriented a person is, the greater that person's income is likely to be. Present orientation is strongest among lowest-income males.

The time orientation that people develop depends a great deal on their socioeconomic class and personal experiences. Gonzalez and Zimbardo (1985) observe: "A child with parents in unskilled and semi-skilled occupations is usually socialized in a way that promotes a present-oriented fatalism and hedonism. A child of parents who are managers,

WHAT TIME DO YOU HAVE?

INSTRUCTIONS

Indicate whether each statement is true (*T*) of your general attitude and behavior or untrue (*F*) of your general attitude and behavior. (A few statements are purposely repeated to facilitate scoring and analyzing your responses.)

_____ 1. Meeting tomorrow's deadlines and doing other necessary work comes before tonight's partying.

_____ 2. I meet my obligations to friends and authorities on time.

_____ 3. I complete projects on time by making steady progress.

_____ 4. I am able to resist temptations when I know there is work to be done.

_____ 5. I keep wǏorking at a difficult, uninteresting task if it will help me get ahead.

_____ 6. If things don't get done on time, I don't worry about it.

_____ 7. I think that it's useless to plan too far ahead because things hardly ever come out the way you planned anyway.

_____ 8. I try to live one day at a time.

_____ 9. I live to make better what is rather than to be concerned about what will be.

_____ 10. It seems to me that it doesn't make sense to worry about the future, since fate determines that whatever will be, will be.

_____ 11. I believe that getting together with friends to party is one of life's important pleasures.

_____ 12. I do things impulsively, making decisions on the spur of the moment.

_____ 13. I take risks to put excitement in my life.

_____ 14. I get drunk at parties.

_____ 15. It's fun to gamble.

_____ 16. Thinking about the future is pleasant to me.

_____ 17. When I want to achieve something, I set subgoals and consider specific means for reaching these goals.

_____ 18. It seems to me that my career path is pretty well laid out.

_____ 19. It upsets me to be late for appointments.

_____ 20. I meet my obligations to friends and authorities on time.

_____ 21. I get irritated at people who keep me waiting when we've agreed to meet at a given time.

_____ 22. It makes sense to invest a substantial part of my income in insurance premiums.

_____ 23. I believe that "a stitch in time saves nine."

_____ 24. I believe that "a bird in the hand is worth two in the bush."

_____ 25. I believe it is important to save for a rainy day.

_____ 26. I believe a person's day should be planned each morning.

_____ 27. I make lists of things I must do.

_____ 28. When I want to achieve something, I set subgoals and consider specific means for reaching those goals.

_____ 29. I believe that "a stitch in time saves nine."

SCORING

This psychological time test measures seven different factors. If you scored *true* for all or most of the questions within any given factor, then you are probably high on that factor. If you scored *false* for all or most of the questions within any given factor, then you are probably low on that factor.

The first factor, measured by questions 1–5, is a future, work-motivation, perseverance orientation. People with this orientation have a strong work ethic and are committed to completing a task despite difficulties and temptations.

The second factor, measured by questions 6–10, is a present, fatalistic, worry-free orientation. People who score high on this factor live one day at a time, not necessarily to enjoy the day but to avoid both planning for the next day and worrying about a future that seems determined by fate rather than by anything they can do themselves.

The third factor, measured by questions 11–15, is a present, hedonistic, pleasure-seeking, partying orientation. People with this orientation seek to enjoy the present, take risks, and engage in a variety of impulsive actions. Teenagers score particularly high on this factor.

The fourth factor, measured by questions 16–18, is a future, goal-seeking, and planning orientation. People with this orientation derive special pleasure from planning and achieving a variety of goals.

The fifth factor, measured by questions 19–21, is a time-sensitivity orientation. People who score high on this factor are especially sensitive to time and its role in social obligations.

The sixth factor, measured by questions 22–25, is a future, pragmatic-action orientation. People with this orientation do what they have to do to achieve the future they want. They take practical actions for future gain.

The seventh factor, measured by questions 26–29, is a future, somewhat obsessive daily-planning orientation. People who score high on this factor make daily "to do" lists, and they devote great attention to specific details and subordinate goals.

teachers, or other professionals learns future-oriented values and strategies designed to promote achievement."

Different time perspectives also account for much intercultural misunderstanding, because different cultures often teach their members drastically different time orientations. The future-oriented person who works for tomorrow's goals will frequently look down on the present-oriented person who focuses on enjoying today as being lazy and poorly motivated. In turn, the present-oriented person may see those with strong future orientations as obsessed with accumulating wealth or rising in status.

TIME AND STATUS

Time is especially linked to status considerations. For example, the importance of being on time varies with the status of the individual you are visiting. If the person is extremely important, you had better be there on time or even early just in case he or she is able to see you before schedule. As the person's status decreases, so does the importance of being on time. Junior executives, for example, must be on time for conferences with senior executives, but it is even more important to be on time for the company president or the CEO. Senior executives, however, may be late for conferences with their juniors but not for conferences with the president. Within any hierarchy, similar unwritten rules are followed with respect to time. This is not to imply that these "rules" are just or fair; they simply exist.

Even the dinner hour and the period between a guest's arrival and the time when dinner is served varies according to status. Among lower-status individuals, dinner is served relatively early. If there are guests, they eat soon after they arrive. For higher-status people, dinner is relatively late, and a longer period elapses between arrival and eating—usually the time it takes to consume two cocktails.

SUMMARY: UNIT IN BRIEF

Proxemic Distance	Territoriality	Artifactual Communication	Temporal Communication
Types of distances • Intimate—touching to 18 inches • Personal—18 inches to 4 feet • Social—4 to 12 feet • Public—12 or more feet Theories about space • Protection • Equilibrium • Expectancy violations	Functions • signal ownership • signal status Markers • central • boundary • ear Types of encroachment • violation • invasion • contamination Reactions to encroachment • turf defense • insulation • linguistic collusion • withdrawal	Space decoration influences perceptions of energy, time, status, and personal characteristics. Colors communicate different meanings, depending on the culture. Clothing and body adornment serve especially as cultural display.	Cultural time: technical, formal, and informal Displaced and diffused time orientations: identify how accurately time is viewed Psychological time: past, present, and future orientation

THINKING CRITICALLY ABOUT SPACE AND TIME

1. Does protection theory explain any of your spatial behaviors? Does equilibrium theory? Expectancy violations theory? Can you give one example to illustrate each theory?
2. Why do you suppose people who are angry or tense need greater space around them? Do you find this true from your personal experience?
3. What factors other than those listed in Table 14.1 might influence the distances you maintain in your conversations?
4. What is your psychological time orientation? Will this orientation help you achieve the goals you've set for yourself?
5. Look carefully at the way you're dressed. What messages does your clothing (including your jewelry, hairstyle, makeup, and the colors you're wearing) communicate? Does it communicate different messages to different (types of) people? Are these the messages you want to communicate?
6. Can you recall a situation in which your territory was violated? Invaded? Contaminated? How did you respond to these encroachments?
7. Look around your home and at your belongings. Can you identify examples of central, boundary, and ear markers?
8. Have you seen any examples of territorial behavior today?
9. Have you seen any examples of marking behavior today?
10. How would you go about finding answers to the following questions?

   - What is the ideal outfit for a college teacher to wear on the first day of class?
   - What types of uniforms command the greatest respect? Have the highest credibility?
   - Do family photographs on an executive's desk contribute to the executive's credibility? Is the relationship between family photos and credibility the same for men and for women?
   - In the discussion of markers, it was noted that students in a college dorm who marked their territory with photographs and personal items stayed in school longer than those who did not personalize their spaces. Do these markers contribute to the students' staying in school, or are the students who are committed to stay in school more likely to personalize their spaces?

EXPERIENTIAL VEHICLES

14.1 INTERPERSONAL INTERACTIONS AND SPACE

Presented here are diagrams of tables and chairs. Imagine that the setting is the school cafeteria and that this is the only table not fully occupied. In the space marked *X* is seated the person described above the diagram. Place an *X* in the appropriate circle to indicate where you would sit.

1. A young man or woman to whom you are physically attracted and whom you would like to date but to whom you have never spoken

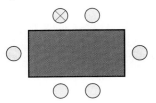

2. A person whom you find physically unattractive and to whom you have never spoken

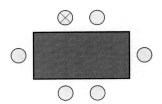

3. A person you dated once and had a miserable time with and whom you would never date again

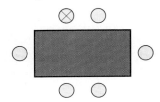

4. A person you have dated a few times and would like to date again

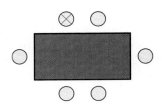

5. An instructor who gave you an undeserved F in a course last semester and whom you dislike intensely

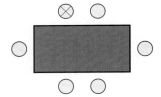

6. Your favorite instructor, whom you would like to get to know better

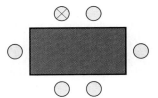

Questions for Discussion

1. Why did you select the positions you did? For example, how does the position you selected better enable you to achieve your purpose?
2. Assume that you were already seated in the position marked X. Do you think the person described would sit where you indicated you would (assuming that the feelings and motives are generally the same)? Why? Are there significant sex differences? Significant status differences? Explain.
3. What does the position you selected communicate to the person already seated? In what ways might this nonverbal message be misinterpreted? How would your subsequent nonverbal (and perhaps verbal) behavior reinforce your intended message? That is, what would you do to ensure that the message you intended to communicate is in fact the message communicated and received?

4. What is the relationship between distance and liking? What is the relationship between distance and status?

5. There is research evidence showing that seating arrangements are influenced by culture. For example, in the United States seating arrangements would unite men and women; in Taiwan, however, seating arrangements would separate the sexes (Cline and Puhl 1984). Do you notice cultural influences on seating arrangements?

14.2 WHO?

The purpose of this exercise is to explore some of the verbal and nonverbal cues that people give and that others receive and use in formulating assumptions about the knowledge, ability, and personality of another. The exercise should serve as a useful summary of the concepts and principles both of verbal and nonverbal communication and of perception.

The entire class should form a circle so that each member may see each other member without straining. If members do not know all the names of their classmates, some system of name tags should be used for this exercise.

Each student should examine the following list of phrases and should write in the column labeled *Who?* the name of one student to whom he or she feels each statement applies. Be certain to respond to all statements. Although one name may be used more than once, the experience will prove more effective if a wide variety of names are chosen. Unless the class is very small, no name should be used more than four times.

Next to each student's name, record a *certainty rating* in the column labeled *CR*, indicating how sure you are of your choice. Use a five-point scale, with 5 indicating great certainty and 1 indicating great uncertainty.

After the names and certainty ratings have been recorded for *each* statement by *each* student, the following procedure may prove useful. The instructor or group leader selects a statement and asks someone specifically, or the class generally, what names were written down. (There is no need to tackle the statements in the order they are given here.) Before the person whose name was selected is asked whether the phrase is correctly or incorrectly attributed to him or her, some or all of the following questions should be considered:

1. Why did you select the name you did? What was there about this person that led you to think that this phrase applied to him or her? What specific verbal or nonverbal cues led you to your conclusion?

2. What additional verbal and/or nonverbal cues would you need to raise your degree of certainty?

3. Is your response at all a function of a stereotype you might have of this individual's ethnic, religious, racial, or sexual identification? For example, how many women's names were written next to the questions or phrases about the saws or the pornographic movie? How many men's names were written for the statement pertaining to cooking?

4. Did anyone give off contradictory cues such that some cues were appropriate for a specific phrase and others were not? Explain the nature of these contradictory cues.

5. How pleased or disappointed are the people whose names have been proposed? Why? Were there any surprises? Why were some of these associations unexpected?

6. How do you communicate your "self" to others? How do you communicate what you know, think, feel, and do to your peers?

Who?   CR

1.____ ____ Goes to the professional theater a few times a year
2.____ ____ Has taken a vacation outside the country in the last 12 months
3.____ ____ Likes to cook
4.____ ____ Watches soap operas on a fairly regular basis
5.____ ____ Wants lots of children
6.____ ____ Has seen a pornographic (XXX-rated) movie within the last three months
7.____ ____ Has been to an opera
8.____ ____ Watches television for an average of at least three hours per day
9.____ ____ Has cried over a movie in the last few months
10.____ ____ Has many close friends
11.____ ____ Knows how potatoes should be planted
12.____ ____ Knows who Edward R. Murrow was
13.____ ____ Knows the differences among a hacksaw, a jigsaw, and a coping saw
14.____ ____ Knows the ingredients for a Bloody Mary
15.____ ____ Knows the function of the spleen
16.____ ____ Knows what an armoire is
17.____ ____ Can name all 12 signs of the zodiac
18.____ ____ Has a car in his or her immediate family costing over $40,000
19.____ ____ Is frequently infatuated (or in love)
20.____ ____ Would like, perhaps secretly, to be a movie star
21.____ ____ Knows the legal status of Puerto Rico
22.____ ____ Keeps a diary or a journal
23.____ ____ Knows what NAFTA stands for
24.____ ____ Knows what the prime rate means
25.____ ____ Is very religious
26.____ ____ Would describe himself or herself as a political activist
27.____ ____ Would vote in favor of gay rights legislation
28.____ ____ Is going to make a significant contribution to society
29.____ ____ Is going to be a millionaire
30.____ ____ Would emerge as a leader in a small-group situation

---

14.3 THE MEANINGS OF COLOR

This exercise is designed to raise questions about the meanings colors communicate and focuses on the ways advertisers and marketers use colors to influence our perceptions of a particular product. The color spectrum is presented on page 263, with numbers from 1 to 25 to help you identify the colors you select for the objects noted below.

Assume that you are working for an advertising agency and that your task is to select colors for the various objects in the following list on the next page. For each object, select the major color as well as the secondary colors you would use in its packaging. Record these choices in the spaces provided by selecting the numbers corresponding to the colors of the spectrum.

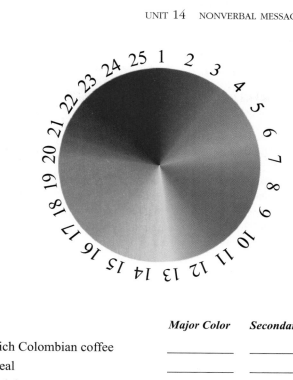

Objects	Major Color	Secondary Colors
Coffee can for rich Colombian coffee	_____	_____
A children's cereal	_____	_____
An especially rich ice cream	_____	_____
Expensive freshly squeezed orange juice	_____	_____
Packaging for upscale jewelry store	_____	_____
Dietetic TV dinners	_____	_____
Microwave popcorn	_____	_____
Shampoo for gray hair	_____	_____
Liquid detergent for heavy-duty washing	_____	_____
A textbook in interpersonal communication	_____	_____

After each person has recorded his or her decisions, discuss them in small groups of five or six or with the class as a whole. You may find it helpful to consider the following questions:

1. What meanings did you wish to communicate for each of the objects?
2. How much agreement is there among the group members that these meanings are the appropriate ones for these products?
3. How much agreement is there among the group members on the colors selected?
4. How effectively do the various colors communicate the desired meanings?
5. Pool the insights of all group members and recolor the products. Are these group designs superior to those developed individually? If a number of groups are working on this project at the same time, it may be interesting to compare the final group colors for each of the products.

14.4 SOME NONVERBAL SEX DIFFERENCES*

The following statements summarize some of the research findings on sex differences in nonverbal communication. For each statement, insert the word *men* or *women* (*man* or *woman* in item 11) in each blank space. After completing all 15 statements, consider the questions for discussion.

1. _____ seem to be slightly more accurate at judging emotions on the basis of facial expressions than _____.
2. _____ seem better able to communicate emotions by facial expressions than _____.
3. _____ smile more than _____.
4. _____ are generally approached more closely than _____.
5. _____ reveal their emotions facially more readily than _____.
6. _____ extend their bodies, taking up greater areas of space, than _____.
7. _____ maintain more eye contact than _____ in mixed-sex dyads.
8. Both men and women, when speaking, look at _____ more than at _____.
9. In mixed-sex dyads, _____ interrupt _____ more often.
10. Some research indicates that _____ speak with greater volume than _____.
11. If a man and a woman are walking toward each other, the _____ will be more apt to move out of the _____'s way.
12. Unattractive _____ seem to be less accepted than are unattractive _____.
13. _____ both touch and are touched more than _____.
14. _____ engage in greater mutual eye contact with a same-sex partner than _____.
15. Same-sex pairs of _____ sit more closely together than do same-sex pairs of _____.

Questions for Discussion

1. On what basis did you think that the nonverbal behavior was more accurately ascribed to one sex than the other?
2. What do you think might account for the differences in nonverbal behavior?
3. Are there types of women or men in which these differences are especially pronounced? Almost absent? Totally absent? On what basis do you make these predictions?
4. How would you go about testing one of these statements for accuracy?
5. After learning the answers given by research findings, do they seem to be consistent with your own observations? Note each that is not. How might you account for this discrepancy?

*Data for this exercise comes from the research reviews reported by Burgoon, Buller, and Woodall (1989); Eakins and Eakins (1978); Pearson, Turner, and Todd-Mancillas (1991); and Arliss (1991).

UNIT 15

Messages and Conversation

AFTER COMPLETING THIS UNIT, YOU SHOULD BE ABLE TO:

1. Explain the five-step model of conversation
2. Explain the cooperation principle, its conversational maxims, and how maxims differ culturally
3. Explain the processes of opening, maintaining, and closing conversations
4. Distinguish between monologue and dialogue
5. Explain the disclaimer and the excuse

Interpersonal researcher Margaret McLaughlin (1984) defines conversation as "relatively informal social interaction in which the roles of speaker and hearer are exchanged in a nonautomatic fashion under the collaborative management of all parties." Examining conversation provides an excellent opportunity to look at verbal and nonverbal messages as they are used in day-to-day communications and thus serves as a useful summary for this second part of the text.

   Before reading about the process of conversation, think of your own conversations, the ones that were satisfactory and the ones that were unsatisfactory. Think of a specific recent conversation as you respond to the accompanying self-test, "How Satisfactory Is Your Conversation?" Taking this test now will help highlight the characteristics of conversational behavior and what makes some conversations satisfying and others unsatisfying.

THE CONVERSATIONAL PROCESS

The process of conversation takes place in at least five steps: opening, feedforward, business, feedback, and closing (see Figure 15.1).

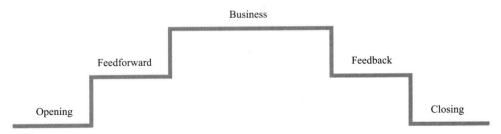

Figure 15.1
A five-step model of conversation.

TEST YOURSELF

HOW SATISFACTORY IS YOUR CONVERSATION?*

INSTRUCTIONS:
Respond to each of the following statements by recording the number that best represents your feelings. Use this scale:

1 = strongly agree
2 = moderately agree
3 = slightly agree
4 = neutral
5 = slightly disagree
6 = moderately disagree
7 = strongly disagree

_____   1.   The other person let me know that I was communicating effectively.

_____   2.   Nothing was accomplished.

_____   3.   I would like to have another conversation like this one.

_____   4.   The other person genuinely wanted to get to know me.

_____   5.   I was very *dis*satisfied with the conversation.

_____   6.   I felt that during the conversation I was able to present myself as I wanted the other person to view me.

_____   7.   I was very satisfied with the conversation.

_____   8.   The other person expressed a lot of interest in what I had to say.

_____   9.   I did NOT enjoy the conversation.

_____   10.   The other person did NOT provide support for what he/she was saying.

_____   11.   I felt I could talk about anything with the other person.

_____   12.   We each got to say what we wanted.

_____   13.   I felt that we could laugh easily together.

_____   14.   The conversation flowed smoothly.

_____   15.   The other person frequently said things which added little to the conversation.

_____   16.   We talked about something I was NOT interested in.

SCORING

1.   Add the scores for items 1, 3, 4, 6, 7, 8, 11, 12, 13, and 14.
2.   Reverse the scores for items 2, 5, 9, 10, 15, and 16 such that 7 (strongly disagree) becomes 1 (strongly agree), 6 becomes 2, 5 becomes 3, 4 remains 4, 3 becomes 5, 2 becomes 6, and 1 becomes 7.
3.   Add the reversed scores for items 2, 5, 9, 10, 15, and 16.
4.   Add the totals from steps 1 and 3 to yield your communication satisfaction score.

INTERPRETATION OF YOUR SCORE
You may interpret your score along the following scale:

16	32	48	64	80	96	112
Extremely satisfying	Quite satisfying	Fairly satisfying	Average	Fairly unsatisfying	Quite unsatisfying	Extremely unsatisfying

*This test was developed by Michael Hecht, "The Conceptualization and Measurement of Interpersonal Communication Satisfaction," *Human Communication Research* 4 (1978): 253–264. Reprinted by permission of Sage Publications.

OPENING

The first step is to open the conversation, usually with some kind of greeting: "Hi. How are you?" "Hello, this is Joe." The greeting is a good example of what we earlier called *phatic communication* (Unit 1). It is a message that establishes a connection between two people and opens up the channels for more meaningful interaction. Greetings, of course, may be nonverbal as well as verbal. A smile, kiss, or handshake may serve as an opening as clear as "Hello."

In normal conversation, the greeting is reciprocated with a greeting similar in degree of formality and intensity. When it isn't—when the other person turns away or responds coldly to your friendly "Good morning"—you know that something is wrong.

Openings are also generally consistent in tone with the main part of the conversation; a cheery "How ya doing today, big guy?" is not normally followed by news of a family death.

FEEDFORWARD

At the second step, you usually provide some kind of feedforward, which gives the other person a general idea of the conversation's focus: "I've got to tell you about Jack," "Did you hear what happened in class yesterday?" or "We need to talk about our vacation plans."

Feedforward may also identify the tone of the conversation ("I'm really depressed and need to talk with you") or the time required ("This will just take a minute") (Frentz 1976; Reardon 1987).

BUSINESS

At the third step, you talk "business," the substance or focus of the conversation. The term "business" is used to emphasize that most conversations are goal directed; you converse to fulfill one or several of the general purposes of interpersonal communication: to learn, relate, influence, play, or help (see Unit 1). The term is also sufficiently general to incorporate all kinds of interactions. The business is conducted through an exchange of speaker and listener roles. Brief, rather than long, speaking turns characterize most satisfying conversations.

Here you talk about Jack, what happened in class, or your vacation plans. This is obviously the longest part of the conversation and the reason for the opening and the feedforward.

Not surprisingly, each culture has its own conversational taboos, topics that should be avoided, especially by visitors from other cultures. Table 15.1 identifies several examples that Roger Axtell in *Do's and Taboos Around the World* (1993) recommends that visitors from the United States avoid. These examples are not intended to be exhaustive, but rather should serve as a reminder that each culture defines what is and what is not an appropriate topic of conversation.

FEEDBACK

The fourth step is the reverse of the second. Here you reflect back on the conversation to signal that as far as you're concerned the business is completed: "So you want to send Jack a get-well card," "Wasn't that the craziest class you ever heard of?" or "I'll call for reservations, and you'll shop for what we need."

Of course, the other person may not agree that the business has been completed and may therefore counter with, for example, "But what hospital is he in?" When this happens, you normally go back a step and continue the business.

Table 15.1 Conversational Taboos Around the World	
CULTURE	CONVERSATIONAL TABOOS
Belgium	Politics, language differences between French and Flemish, religion
Norway	Salaries, social status
Spain	Family, religion, jobs, negative comments on bullfighting
Egypt	Middle Eastern politics
Nigeria	Religion
Libya	Politics, religion
Iraq	Religion, Middle Eastern politics
Japan	World War II
Pakistan	Politics
Philippines	Politics, religion, corruption, foreign aid
South Korea	Internal politics, criticism of the government, socialism or communism
Bolivia	Politics, religion
Colombia	Politics, criticism of bullfighting
Mexico	Mexican-American war, illegal aliens
Caribbean nations	Race, local politics, religion

CLOSING

The fifth and last step, the opposite of the first step, is the closing, the good-bye, which often reveals how satisfied the persons are with the conversation: "I hope you'll call soon" or "Don't call us, we'll call you." The closing may also be used to schedule future conversations: "Give me a call tomorrow night" or "Let's meet for lunch at twelve."

REFLECTIONS ON THE MODEL

Not all conversations are easily divided into these five steps. Often the opening and the feedforward are combined, as when you see someone on campus, for example, and say, "Hey, listen to this" or when, in a work situation, someone says, "Well, folks, let's get the meeting going." In a similar way, the feedback and the closing might be combined: "Look, I've got to think more about this commitment, OK?"

As already noted, the business is the longest part of the conversation. The opening and the closing are usually about the same length, as are the feedforward and feedback. When these relative lengths are severely distorted, you quickly get the feeling that something is wrong. For example, when someone uses a long feedforward or too short an opening, you suspect that what is to follow is extremely serious.

This model may also help to identify conversation skill deficits and to distinguish effective and satisfying from ineffective and unsatisfying conversations. Consider, for example, the following violations and how they can damage an entire conversation:

- Using openings that are insensitive, for example, "Wow, you've gained a few pounds"
- Using overly long feedforwards that make you wonder whether the other person will ever get to the business
- Omitting feedforward before a truly shocking message (for example, the death or illness of a friend or relative), an omission that leads you to see the other person as insensitive or uncaring
- Doing business without the normally expected greeting, as when you go to a doctor who begins the conversation by saying, "Well, what's wrong?"
- Omitting feedback, which leads you to wonder whether the other person heard what you said or cared about it
- Omitting an appropriate closing, which makes you wonder whether the other person is disturbed or angry with you

Of course, each culture will alter these basic steps in different ways. In some cultures, the openings are especially short, whereas in others they are elaborate, lengthy, and sometimes highly ritualized. It is all too easy to violate another culture's conversational rules. Being overly friendly, too formal, or too forward may easily hinder the remainder of the conversation.

Such violations may have significant consequences if people are not mindful (see Unit 6) of these rules and hence do not see violations simply as cultural differences. Rather, we might see the rule violator as aggressive, stuffy, or pushy—and almost immediately dislike the person and put a negative cast on future conversation.

CONVERSATIONAL MAXIMS

During our conversations, we operate on the principle of cooperation (Grice 1975). That is, speaker and listener agree to cooperate in trying to understand what each is saying. If we didn't agree to cooperate, then communication would be extremely difficult, if not impossible. We cooperate largely by using four conversational maxims—principles that speakers and listeners follow in conversation. Although the names for these maxims may be new, the principles themselves will be easily recognized from your own experiences.

THE MAXIM OF QUANTITY

Speakers follow the maxim of **quantity:** they cooperate by being only as informative as necessary to communicate the intended meaning. Thus, speakers include information that makes the meaning clear but omit what does not. In following this principle, the speaker gives neither too little nor too much information. We see people violate this maxim when they try to relate an incident and digress to give us unnecessary information. We find ourselves thinking or saying, "Get to the point; so what happened?" Speakers also violate the maxim by omitting necessary information. In this situation, we find ourselves constantly interrupting to ask questions: "Where were they?" "When did this happen?" "Who else was there?"

THE MAXIM OF QUALITY

Speakers follow the maxim of **quality:** they cooperate by saying what they know or assume to be true and by not saying what they know to be false. When we are in conversation, we assume that the speaker's information is true—at least as far as the speaker knows. When we speak with people who frequently violate this principle by lying, exaggerating, or minimizing major problems, we come to distrust what the speaker is saying and wonder what is true and what is fabricated.

THE MAXIM OF RELATION

Speakers follow the maxim of **relation:** they cooperate by talking about what is relevant to the conversation. Thus, if a speaker is talking about Pat and Chris and says, for example, "Money causes all sorts of relationship problems," we assume—even without thinking about it—that the comment is somehow related to Pat and Chris. We see this principle violated by speakers who digress widely and frequently interject irrelevant comments.

THE MAXIM OF MANNER

Speakers follow the maxim of **manner:** they cooperate by being clear, by avoiding ambiguities, by being relatively brief, and by organizing their thoughts into a meaningful sequence. Thus, the speaker uses terms that the listener understands and omits or clarifies

This photo presents the popular stereotype of the expressive woman and the inexpressive man. Do you find this stereotype accurate? Look again at the photo. Why do you suppose that many people see the woman as more expressive nonverbally than the man? Can you make a case for the man being just as expressive as the woman?

terms that the listener will not understand. We see this maxim in clear operation when we adjust our speech on the basis of our listener. For example, when talking to a close friend we can refer to mutual acquaintances and to experiences we've shared. When talking to a stranger, however, we either omit such references or explain them. Similarly, when talking with a child, we simplify our vocabulary so that the child understands our meaning.

These maxims are, of course, quite simple. You follow them almost without thinking. When they are violated, however, communication is less meaningful. You go away frustrated rather than satisfied.

CONVERSATIONAL MAXIMS AND CULTURE

The four maxims are certainly accurate descriptions of most conversations as they take place in much of U.S. culture. Recognize, however, that these maxims may not apply in all cultures; for example, they do not seem to apply in Malagasy in Madagascar. Also, other cultures may have other maxims. These maxims, it is interesting to note, may contradict advice generally given to persons communicating in the United States or in other cultures (Keenan 1976). Here are a few maxims appropriate in cultures other than the culture of the United States.

The Maxim of Peaceful Relations   In research on Japanese conversations and group discussions, a maxim of preserving peaceful relationships with others may be noted (Midooka 1990). The ways in which such peaceful relationships may be maintained will vary with the person with whom you are interacting. For example, in Japan, your status or position in the hierarchy will influence the amount of self-expression you are expected to engage in. Similarly, there is a great distinction made between public and private conversations. This maxim is much more important in public than it is in private conversations, in which the maxim may be violated.

The Maxim of Politeness   In some Asian cultures, it is especially important to "save face," to avoid being embarrassed or embarrassing others. When this maxim operates, it may actually violate other maxims. For example, the maxim of politeness may require that you not tell the truth, a situation that would violate the maxim of quality (Fraser 1990).

The Maxim of Self-Denigration   This maxim, observed in the conversations of Chinese speakers, may require that a speaker avoid taking credit for some accomplishment or make less of some ability or talent (Gu 1990). To put oneself down in such a way is a form of politeness that seeks to elevate the person to whom you are speaking.

CONVERSATIONAL MANAGEMENT

Speakers and listeners have to work together to make conversation an effective and satisfying experience. They do so by managing conversations in terms of initiating, maintaining, and closing them.

INITIATING CONVERSATIONS

Opening a conversation is especially difficult. Often you may not be sure what to say or how to say it. You may fear being rejected or having someone misunderstand your meaning. Several approaches to opening a conversation can be derived from the elements of the interpersonal communication process discussed in Unit 1:

> *Self-references* say something about yourself. Such references may be of the name-rank-and-serial-number type—for example: "My name is Joe. I'm from Omaha." On the first day of class, students might say, "I'm worried about this class" or "I took this instructor last semester; she was excellent."
> *Other-references* say something about the other person or ask a question: "I like that sweater." "Didn't we meet at Charlie's?" Of course, there are pitfalls here as well. Generally, it is best not to comment on the person's race ("My uncle married a Korean"), the person's affectional orientation ("Nice to meet you; I have a gay brother"), or physical disability ("It must be awful to be confined to a wheelchair").
> *Relational references* say something about the two of you: for example, "May I buy you a drink?" "Would you like to dance?" or simply "May I join you?"
> *Context references* say something about the physical, social-psychological, cultural, or temporal context. The familiar "Do you have the time?" is a reference of this

type. But you can be more creative and say, for example, "This place seems very friendly" or "That painting is just great."

The Opening Line   Another way of looking at the process of initiating conversations is to examine the infamous "opening line," the opener designed to begin a romantic-type relationship. Interpersonal researcher Chris Kleinke (1986) finds that opening lines are of three basic types:

1. *Cute-flippant* openers are humorous, indirect, and ambiguous as to whether the one opening the conversation actually wants an extended encounter. Examples include "Is that really your hair?" "Bet I can outdrink you." "I bet the cherry jubilee isn't as sweet as you are."
2. *Innocuous* openers are highly ambiguous as to whether they are simple comments that might be made to just anyone or whether they are in fact openers designed to initiate an extended encounter. Examples include "What do you think of the band?" "I haven't been here before." "What's good on the menu?" "Could you show me how to work this machine?"
3. *Direct* openers clearly demonstrate the speaker's interest in meeting the other person. Examples include: "I feel a little embarrassed about this, but I'd like to meet you. Would you like to have a drink after dinner? Since we're both eating alone, would you like to join me?"

According to Kleinke (1986), the opening lines most preferred by both men and women are generally those that are direct or innocuous. The least preferred lines by both men and women are those that are cute-flippant; women dislike these openers even more than men do. Men generally underestimate how much women dislike the cute-flippant openers but probably continue to use them because they are indirect enough to cushion any rejection. Men also underestimate how much women actually like innocuous openers.

Women prefer men to use openers that are relatively modest and to avoid coming on too strong. Women generally underestimate how much men like direct openers. Most men prefer openers that are very clear in meaning, possibly because men are not used to having a woman initiate a meeting. Women also overestimate how much men like innocuous lines.

In Unit 17, initiating an interaction is again considered, but there it is examined in terms of establishing a relationship.

MAINTAINING CONVERSATIONS

In maintaining conversations, focus on at least two factors: the exchange of speaker and listener roles and the use of dialogue rather than monologue.

Conversational Turns   The defining feature of conversation is that the roles of speaker and listener are exchanged throughout the interaction. We accomplish this through a wide variety of verbal and nonverbal cues that signal conversational turns—the changing (or maintaining) of the speaker or listener role during the conversation. Combining the insights of a variety of communication researchers (Duncan 1972; Burgoon,

Most meals are in great part conversational experiences. Can you use the five-stage model of conversation presented here to describe the conversations that you have during meals? How do business lunches differ from family meals in terms of the conversation taking place?

Buller, and Woodall 1989; Pearson and Spitzberg 1990), we can look at conversational turns in terms of speaker cues and listener cues.

Speaker Cues.   Speakers regulate the conversation through two major types of cues: turn-maintaining cues and turn-yielding cues. As the term implies, **turn-maintaining cues** are designed to enable the speaker to maintain the speaker role. At least the following types of turn-maintaining cues may be identified (Duncan 1972; Burgoon, Buller, and Woodall 1989):

- audibly inhaling to show that the speaker has more to say
- continuing a gesture or gestures to show that the thought is not yet complete
- avoiding eye contact with the listener so there is no indication that the speaking turn is being passed
- sustaining the intonation pattern to indicate that more will be said
- vocalizing pauses ("er," "umm") to prevent the listener from speaking and to show that the speaker is still talking

In most cases, we expect the speaker to maintain relatively brief speaking turns and to turn over the speaking role willingly to the listener (when so signaled by the listener). Those who don't are generally perceived as egocentric bores.

Turn-yielding cues tell the listener that the speaker is finished and wishes to exchange the role of speaker for that of listener. These cues tell the listener (sometimes a specific listener) to take over the role of speaker. So, for example, at the end of a statement you might add some paralinguistic cue such as "eh?" which asks one of the listeners to assume the role of speaker. You can also indicate that you have finished speaking by dropping your intonation, by a prolonged silence, by making direct eye contact with a listener, by asking some general question, or by nodding in the direction of a particular listener.

In much the same way that we expect a speaker to yield the role of speaker, we also expect the listener to willingly assume the speaking role. Those who don't may be regarded as reticent or unwilling to involve themselves and take equal responsibility for the conversation. For example, in an analysis of turn-taking violations in the conversations of marrieds, the most common violation found was that of no response. Forty-five percent of the 540 violations identified involved a lack of response to an invitation to assume the speaker role (DeFrancisco 1991). Of these "no response" violations, 68 percent were committed by men and 32 percent by women. Other turn-taking violations include interruptions, delayed responses, and inappropriately brief responses. DeFrancisco argues that with these violations, all of which are committed more frequently by men, men silence women in marital interactions.

Listener Cues.   As a listener, you can regulate the conversation by using a variety of cues. **Turn-requesting cues** let the speaker know that you would like to take a turn as speaker. Sometimes you can do this by simply saying, "I would like to say something," but often you do it more subtly through some vocalized "er" or "um" that tells the speaker (at least the sensitive speaker) that you would now like to speak. This request to speak is also often made with facial and mouth gestures. Frequently, a listener will indicate a desire to speak by opening his or her eyes and mouth widely as if to say something, by beginning to gesture with a hand, or by leaning forward.

You can also indicate your reluctance to assume the role of speaker by using **turn-denying cues:** for example, intoning a slurred "I don't know" or a brief grunt that signals you have nothing to say. Turn-denying is often accomplished by avoiding eye contact with the speaker who wishes you to take on the role of speaker or by engaging in some behavior that is incompatible with speaking—for example, coughing or blowing your nose.

Back-channeling cues are used to communicate various types of information back to the speaker without one's assuming the role of speaker. Some researchers call these "acknowledgment tokens"—brief utterances such as "mm-hm," "uh-huh," and "yeah"— the three most often used such tokens—that tell the speaker you are listening (Schegloff 1982; Drummond and Hopper 1993). You can communicate at least four types of information with backchanneling cues (Burgoon, Buller, and Woodall 1989; Pearson and Spitzberg 1990).

First, you can indicate your agreement with the speaker through smiles; nods of approval; brief comments such as "Right," "Exactly," and "Of course"; or a vocalization like "hu-hah." Similarly, you can indicate your disagreement with the speaker through frowning, shaking your head, or making comments such as "No," "Not true," or "Never."

Second, you can indicate your degree of involvement or boredom with the speaker. Attentive posture, forward leaning, and focused eye contact tell the speaker that you are involved in the conversation, just as an inattentive posture, backward leaning, and avoidance of eye contact communicate your lack of involvement.

Third, you can give the speaker pacing cues. You can, for example, ask the speaker to slow down by raising your hand near your ear and leaning forward or to speed up by continued nodding of your head. You can also cue the speaker verbally by simply asking the speaker to slow down ("Slow down, I want to make sure I'm getting all this"). Similarly, you can tell the speaker to speed up by saying something like "and . . ." or "Go on, go on. . . ."

Fourth, you can ask for clarification. A puzzled facial expression, perhaps coupled with a forward lean, will probably tell most speakers that you want some clarification. Similarly, you can ask for clarification by interjecting an interrogative: Who? When? Where?

Some of these back-channeling cues are actually **interruptions.** These interruptions, however, are generally confirming rather than disconfirming. They tell the speaker that we are listening and involved (Kennedy and Camden 1988).

Other interruptions are not as confirming and simply take the speaking turn away from the speaker, either temporarily or permanently. Sometimes the interrupter may apologize for breaking in and at other times may not even seem aware of interrupting. Interruptions may serve a variety of specific functions:

- to change the topic ("I gotta tell you this story before I bust.")
- to correct the speaker ("You mean four months, not years, don't you?")
- to seek information, to ask a question of clarification ("Do you mean Jeff's cousin?")
- to better or top the speaker with a funnier story or a more extreme example ("If you think that's funny, wait till you hear this. . . .")
- to end the conversation ("I hate to interrupt, but I really have to get back to the office.")
- to introduce essential information ("Your car's on fire.")

One of the most often studied aspects of interruption is gender difference. Do men or women interrupt more? Research here is conflicting. These few research findings will give you an idea of the differing results (Pearson, Turner, and Todd-Mancillas 1991):

- The more malelike the person's gender identity—regardless of the person's biological sex—the more likely it is that the person will interrupt (Drass 1986).
- Men interrupt more than women do (Zimmerman and West 1975, West and Zimmerman 1977).
- There are no significant differences between boys and girls (ages 2–5) in interrupting behavior (Greif 1980).
- Fathers interrupt their children more than mothers do (Greif 1980).
- Men and women do not differ in their interrupting behavior (Roger and Nesshoever 1983).

The various turn-taking cues and how they correspond to the conversational wants of speaker and listener are summarized in Figure 15.2.

Monologue and Dialogue   Effective and satisfying conversation is based on interpersonal communication as dialogue rather than monologue (Buber 1958; Brown and Keller

1979; Thomlison 1982). **Monologue** refers to a form of communication in which one person speaks and others listen; there is no interaction among participants. The focus is solely on the one person speaking. The term **monologic communication,** or "communication as monologue," is an extension of this basic definition. It refers to communication in which there is no genuine interaction, in which one speaks without any real concern for the other person's feelings or attitudes. The monologic communicator is concerned only with his or her own goals and is interested in the other person only insofar as that person can be used to achieve those goals.

In **dialogue,** there is two-way interaction. Each person is both speaker and listener, sender and receiver. In **dialogic communication,** or "communication as dialogue," there is deep concern for the other person and for the relationship between the two people. The objective of dialogue is mutual understanding and empathy. There is respect for the other person, not because of what this person can do or give but simply because this person is a human being and therefore deserves to be treated honestly and sincerely.

In monologic interaction, you communicate what will advance your own goals, prove most persuasive, and benefit you. In a dialogic interaction, you respect the other person enough to allow that person the right to make his or her own choices without coercion, without the threat of punishment, without fear or social pressure. A dialogic communicator respects other people enough to believe that they can make decisions that are right for them and implicitly or explicitly lets them know that whatever choices they make, they will still be respected as people (Unit 5). In Carl Rogers's terms, the dialogic communicator gives unconditional positive regard to others, whether one agrees with their choices or not. When we feel that the choices other people make are illogical or

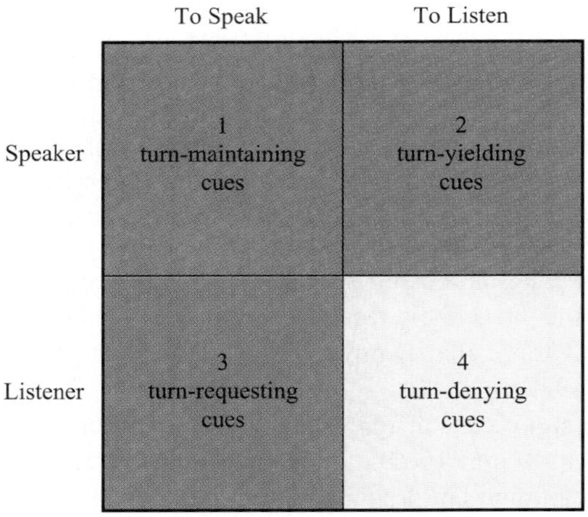

	To Speak	To Listen
Speaker	1 turn-maintaining cues	2 turn-yielding cues
Listener	3 turn-requesting cues	4 turn-denying cues

Figure 15.2
Quadrant 1 represents the speaker who wishes to continue to speak and uses turn-maintaining cues. Quadrant 2 represents the speaker who wishes to listen and uses turn-yielding cues. Quadrant 3 represents the listener who wishes to speak and uses turn-requesting cues. Quadrant 4 represents the listener who wishes to listen (continue listening) and uses turn-denying cues. Back-channeling cues would appear in quadrant 4, because they are cues that listeners use while they continue to listen. Interruptions would appear in quadrant 3, though they are not so much cues that request a turn as actual takeovers of the speaker's position.

unproductive, we may try to persuade them to do otherwise. But we do not withdraw (or threaten to withdraw) our positive regard for them as human beings who, as such, have the right to make their own choices—and mistakes. Table 15.2 presents a summary of the communication characteristics of both monologue and dialogue (Beatty 1986).

CLOSING CONVERSATIONS

Closing a conversation is almost as difficult as opening one. It is frequently an awkward and uncomfortable part of interpersonal interaction. Here are a few suggestions you might consider:

- Reflect back on the conversation and briefly summarize it so as to bring it to a close. For example: "I'm glad I ran into you and found out what happened at that union meeting. I'll probably be seeing you at the meetings next week."
- Directly state the desire to end the conversation and to get on with other things. For example: "I'd like to continue talking, but I really have to run. I'll see you around."

Table 15.2
Monologic and Dialogic Communicators

MONOLOGIC COMMUNICATOR	DIALOGIC COMMUNICATOR
1. Frequently uses negative criticism ("I didn't like that third explanation") and negative personal judgments ("You're not a very good listener, are you?")	1. Avoids negative criticism and negative personal judgments; practices using positive criticism ("I liked those first two explanations best; they were really well reasoned.")
2. Frequently uses dysfunctional communication such as expressing unwillingness to talk, or uses messages that are unrelated to the topic of discussion ("There's no sense discussing this; I can see you're not rational. Forget it.")	2. Keeps the channels of communication open ("I really don't know what I did that offended you, but tell me. I don't want to hurt you again.")
3. Rarely uses acknowledgment (demonstrations in the form of paraphrase or summary that you understand the other's meanings)	3. Frequently paraphrases or summarizes what the other person has said to ensure accurate understanding
4. Rarely requests clarification of the other's perspectives or ideas	4. Requests clarification as necessary and asks for the other person's point of view because of a genuine interest in the other person's perspective
5. Frequently requests personal positive statements or statements of approval ("How did you like the way I told that guy off? Clever, no?")	5. Avoids requesting personal positive statements

- Refer to future interaction. For example: "Why don't we get together next week sometime and continue this discussion?"
- Ask for closure. For example: "Have I explained what you wanted to know?"
- State that you enjoyed the interaction. For example: "I really enjoyed talking with you."

With any of these closings, it should be clear to the other person that you are attempting to end the conversation. Obviously, you will have to use more direct methods with those who don't take these subtle hints or don't realize that *both* persons are responsible for the interpersonal interaction and for bringing it to a satisfactory close.

CONVERSATIONAL PROBLEMS: PREVENTION AND REPAIR

In conversation, you may anticipate a problem and seek to prevent it. Or you may discover that you said or did something that will lead to disapproval, and you may seek to excuse yourself. Here we give just one example of a device to prevent potential conversational problems (the disclaimer) and one example of a device to repair conversational problems (the excuse). Our purpose is simply to illustrate the complexity of these processes, not to present you with an exhaustive list of the ways conversational problems may be prevented or repaired.

PREVENTING CONVERSATIONAL PROBLEMS: THE DISCLAIMER

Let us say, for example, that you fear your listeners will think your comment is inappropriate in the present context, that they may rush to judge you without hearing your full account, or will think that you are not in full possession of your faculties. In these cases, you may use some form of disclaimer. A **disclaimer** is a statement that aims to ensure that your message will be understood and will not reflect negatively on you.

Five types of disclaimers are usually identified (Hewitt and Stokes 1975; McLaughlin 1984). **Hedging** helps you to separate yourself from the message, so that if your listeners reject your message, they need not reject you (for example, "I may be wrong here, but. . . "). Hedges decrease the attractiveness of both women and men (Wright and Hosman 1983) if they are seen as indicating a lack of certainty or conviction because of some inadequacy. However, if the hedges are seen as indicating a lack of belief in allness (as indicating that no one can know all about any subject), as well as a belief that tentative statements are all one can reasonably make (Hosman 1989; Pearson, Turner, and Todd-Mancillas 1991), they will be more positively received.

Credentialing helps you to establish your special qualifications for saying what you are about to say (for example, "Don't get me wrong, I'm not homophobic"). **Sin licenses** ask listeners for permission to deviate in some way from some normally accepted convention (for example, "I know this may not be the place to discuss business, but . . . "). **Cognitive disclaimers** help you to make the case that you are in full possession of your faculties (for example, "I know you'll think I'm crazy, but let me explain the logic of the case"). **Appeals for the suspension of judgment** ask listeners to hear you out before making a judgment (for example, "Don't hang up on me until you hear my side of the story"). These disclaimers, along with their definitions and additional examples, are summarized in Table 15.3.

Table 15.3 Disclaimers		
DISCLAIMER	DEFINITION AND FUNCTION	EXAMPLES
Hedging	Speaker disclaims the importance of the message to his or her own identity; speaker makes it clear that listeners may reject the message without rejecting the speaker.	I didn't read the entire report, but . . . I'm no physiologist, but that irregularity seems . . .
Credentialing	Speaker tries to avoid undesirable inferences that may be drawn by listeners; speaker seeks to establish special qualifications.	Don't get the wrong idea; I'm not sexist, but . . . Some of my best friends are . . . I've lived with Martians all my life, so I know what they're like.
Sin licenses	Speaker announces that he or she will violate some social or cultural rule but should be "forgiven" in advance (a "license to sin").	I realize that this may not be the time to talk about money, but . . . I know you'll think this suggestion is out of order, but do consider . . .
Cognitive disclaimers	Speaker seeks to reaffirm his or her cognitive abilities in anticipation of listener doubts.	I know you think I'm drunk, but I'm as sober and as lucid as . . .
Appeals for the suspension of judgment	Speaker asks listeners to delay making judgments until a more complete account is presented.	Don't say anything until I explain the real story.If you promise not to laugh, I'll tell you exactly what happened.

REPAIRING CONVERSATIONAL PROBLEMS: THE EXCUSE

Earlier, we examined the concept of irreversibility, the idea that once something is said, it cannot be *un*communicated. In part because of this fact, we need at times to defend or justify messages that may be perceived negatively. Perhaps the most common method for doing so is the excuse. Excuses pervade all forms of communication and behavior. Although we emphasize their role in conversation, recognize that the excuse is applicable to all human behaviors, not just conversational ones.

You learn early in life that when you do something that will be perceived negatively, an excuse is in order to justify your poor performance. The excuse, as C. R. Snyder (1984) notes, "plays a central role in how we get along in life, both with yourself and with other people."

The excuse usually follows from three conditions:

1. You say something.
2. Your statement is viewed negatively; you desire to disassociate yourself from it.

3. Someone hears the message or the results of the message. (The "witness" may be an outsider, for example, a boss, a friend, or a colleague, but also could be yourself—you are a witness to your own messages.)

More formally, Snyder (1984; Snyder, Higgins, and Stucky 1983) defines **excuses** as "explanations or actions that lessen the negative implications of an actor's performance, thereby maintaining a positive image for oneself and others."

Excuses seem especially in order when we say or are accused of saying something that runs counter to what is expected, sanctioned, or considered "right" by the people involved or by society in general. The excuse, ideally, lessens the negative impact of the message.

Some Motives for Excuse Making The major motive for excuse making seems to be to maintain our self-esteem, to project a positive image to ourselves and to others. Excuses are also offered to reduce the stress that may be created by a bad performance. We feel that if we can offer an excuse—especially a good one that is accepted by those around us—it will reduce the negative reaction and the subsequent stress that accompanies a poor performance.

Excuses enable you to take risks and engage in behavior that may be unsuccessful; you may offer an anticipatory excuse: "My throat's a bit sore, but I'll give the speech a try." The excuse is designed to lessen the criticism should you fail to deliver an acceptable speech.

Excuses also enable us to maintain effective interpersonal relationships even after some negative behavior. For example, after criticizing a friend's behavior and observing the negative reaction to our criticism, we might offer an excuse such as, "Please forgive me; I'm really exhausted. I'm just not thinking straight." Excuses enable us to place our messages—even our possible failures—in a more favorable light.

Three Types of Excuses C. R. Snyder (1984; Snyder, Higgins, and Stucky 1983) identifies three classes of excuses. In the *I didn't do it* type, the excuse maker claims not to have done the behavior of which he or she is accused: "I didn't say that." "I wasn't even near the place when it happened." In the *it wasn't so bad* type, the excuse maker claims that the behavior was not really so bad, certainly not as bad as others may at first think: "I only copied one answer." "The fire was smoking, and your mink coat was the only thing I could find." "Sure, I punched him out; he asked for it." In the *yes, but* type, the excuse maker claims that extenuating circumstances accounted for the behavior: "It was the liquor talking." "I really tried to help him; I didn't mean to hurt his feelings." "It was just my jealousy making those accusations."

In his introduction to Margaret McLaughlin's insightful *Conversation* (1984), Mark Knapp observes, "While there is something inherently fascinating about discovering the anatomy of behaviors we habitually (and sometimes unthinkingly) perform, the real significance of understanding the structure of conversations is its centrality for understanding human interaction in general." The intention of this unit has been to help you approach this understanding.

Conversational Processes	Conversational Cooperation and Maxims	Conversational Management	Conversational Problems
Opening Feedforward Business Feedback Closing	**Cooperation:** speaker and listener agree to cooperate in conversation by following four maxims: 1. Quantity: Be as informative as necessary. 2. Quality: Be truthful. 3. Relation: Be relevant. 4. Manner: Be clear. Peaceful relations: keep peace Politeness: follow the rules of politeness Self-denigration: be modest	**Initiating** • Self-references • Other-references • Relational references • Context references **Managing conversational turns** • Speaker cues: turn-maintaining, turn-yielding • Listener cues: turn-requesting, turn-denying, back-channeling **Dialogue and monologue** • Dialogic conversation: two-way interaction, concern for each other and for the relationship • Monologic conversation: one-way interaction, concern only for oneself **Closing** • Reflect back on conversation as in summarizing. • Directly state desire to end conversation. • Refer to future interaction. • Ask for closure. • Express pleasure with interaction.	**Prevention:** the disclaimer, a statement that helps to ensure that your message will be understood and will not reflect negatively on the speaker: • Hedging • Credentialing • Sin licenses • Cognitive disclaimers • Appeals for the suspension of judgment **Repair:** the excuse, a statement of explanation designed to lessen the negative impact of a speaker's messages: • I didn't do it • It wasn't so bad • Yes, but . . .

THINKING CRITICALLY ABOUT CONVERSATION

1. How might you describe the process of conversation other than with the five-step model presented here?
2. Which conversational maxim do you think is the most important? Which do you think is the most frequently violated?
3. What methods other than those described in this unit seem to work for opening a conversation? Which openers do you especially resent? Why?
4. How would your conversational openers differ if you wanted to establish a romantic relationship?
5. Are there other conversational turns that might be identified? What additional verbal and nonverbal behaviors can you identify in describing conversational turns?
6. How would you describe the following interactions in terms of dialogue and monologue?
   a. you and your closest friend
   b. your family interaction
   c. you and a specific teacher
7. What ways, in addition to those noted in this unit, have you found for closing conversations?
8. How does closing a telephone conversation differ from closing a face-to-face conversation?
9. Have you heard (or used) any disclaimers over the last few days? How would you explain the functions they were designed to serve? Were they effective? Have you heard (or used) any excuses lately? How would you explain the functions that these excuses were designed to serve? Were they effective?
10. How would you go about finding answers to the following questions?

   - How do the stages in the conversational process identified here differ in other cultures?
   - Are people who violate the conversational maxims perceived negatively?
   - Are people who give lots of back-channeling cues perceived in the same way as people who give few or no back-channeling cues?
   - Do any disclaimers increase the perception of the user's credibility? Do any decrease it?
   - Do men and women use the same kinds of excuses?

EXPERIENTIAL VEHICLES

15.1 CONVERSATIONAL ANALYSIS: A CHANCE MEETING

Read the following dialogue, "A Chance Meeting."

1. Describe the conversational styles of each of the four participants. (For the purposes of this exercise, assume that each person speaks this way all the time. Although this assumption is certainly false—no one talks the same way all the time—most people do have a style of conversation that is consistent across a wide variety of situations.)

2. Which person do you think is, in general, the most effective communicator? Why?
3. Which person do you think is, in general, the least effective communicator? Why?

Then select one of the four participants, and analyze that person's conversational style in depth:

1. Describe the person's style, especially as it relates to appropriateness for this particular communication situation.
2. Describe the rules of conversation that this person is following. What specific lines of dialogue can you point to in support of your analysis?
3. Describe the rules of conversation that you feel this person should follow. On what basis do you make these recommendations?
4. Describe the ways in which you think this conversation would differ if this one person's style was changed in the ways you indicated in your answer to the preceding question (question 3).
5. Would this dialogue seem more realistic if you assumed that certain characters are men and others are women? If you assumed they are all men? All women? Why?

A Chance Meeting

PAT: Hi!

SMITTY: Hi, Pat.

CHRIS: What's up?

SMITTY: You look horrible. What's happened to you?

PAT: Nothing.

SMITTY: Oh, good. Just the day? I have days like that, too.

LEE: You make the day you have, you know. I mean, expect the worst and you'll get it. Cheer up, Pat. Things will change, once you change yourself, of course. You know: smile and the world smiles with you.

CHRIS: Nothing? You seem upset.

PAT: No, it's just my job. Kind of, but not exactly.

SMITTY: I wish I could forget my job, too. Now I gotta work Saturdays.

LEE: Try running an ice cream parlor. Seven days a week of pure torture.

CHRIS: You sound really disturbed, Pat. Are they cutting back? Is your job in danger?

PAT: In danger? No, it's not in danger. It's dead. I was let go three weeks ago.

SMITTY: Oh, bummer. Big bummer.

LEE: You screwed up again, didn't you?

CHRIS: And you didn't say anything? What's wrong with you? We talked three or four times since then, and you never said anything. Let's go for coffee.

PAT: No, I gotta get home.

SMITTY: Yeah, me too.

CHRIS: I know you do, Pat. But ten minutes for coffee won't hurt.

LEE: Okay. Ten minutes. Let's go.

[At coffee]

CHRIS: Now, what happened?

PAT: Nothing. I got fired. Cutbacks, same as everyone else. They let 35 of us go— all at once.

LEE: Thirty-five? Wow! Did Trainer get the ax, too?

PAT: I don't know. I think so.

LEE: Wow, I wonder what Trainer will do now.

CHRIS: What's your next step?

SMITTY: Unemployment! I've been on it more than off it.

PAT: Unfortunately, he's right. I'm on unemployment. I hate it.

SMITTY: I love it.

LEE: Yeah, that's because you try to avoid responsibilities. Pat is trying to face them, and I think that's good. If we don't face our problems, we'll never solve them.

CHRIS: Yeah, but you won't be for long. There are lots of places you could work.

SMITTY: That's not what the papers said. Everyone's cutting back.

LEE: I have the classified section right here. You can have it. It'll give you some leads.

PAT: I'd have to relocate to stay at my present job, and I really don't want to do that.

CHRIS: What do you mean?

PAT: I'm not qualified to do anything more than I'm doing. The market has changed; there's no place for my skills anymore.

LEE: Is that what happened to Tommy? No skills?

PAT: I don't know. I never hung out with Tommy.

SMITTY: That's what everybody's saying; computers can do it better. Soon they'll have robots, and we'll all be up the creek.

CHRIS: What about retraining?

PAT: Me? At 31?

SMITTY: Are you 31? I thought you were a lot older. Really? You look good.

LEE: Yeah, 31 is kind of old to start all over again.

CHRIS: Yes, you at 31. And 31 is not to old to retrain. And you might like it. You've got enough money to take a year off, retool, and get back in the game.

SMITTY: Back to school, like Rodney Dangerfield.

LEE: I'm not sure that's the answer. I think you gotta get your act together. You've got this defeatist attitude. You've got to get rid of that. You want the name of my shrink? He's great. Deals with all sorts of problems.

PAT: I don't really want to see your shrink, much as I should, I know. I guess with unemployment I can make it. Yeah, I could do it.

CHRIS: And you might even like it. You enjoyed college.

PAT: And I know exactly what I'd train for.

LEE: How can you know with such certainty? Have you looked at the predictions for the growth in different jobs?

SMITTY: Hey, how about getting out of here? I have to get home and take the kid to Little League. Talk about problems. Little League. That's a problem.

CHRIS: What would you train for?

PAT: What do you think of this idea?

15.2 GIVING AND TAKING DIRECTIONS

This exercise is designed to provide practice in the much needed skills of giving and taking directions. Presented below is a diagram of Commville. Each circle with a single letter is a starting point. Double- and triple-lettered circles are destinations. A much larger number of destinations than will be used in the exercise are included so that no one will be able to memorize the locations.

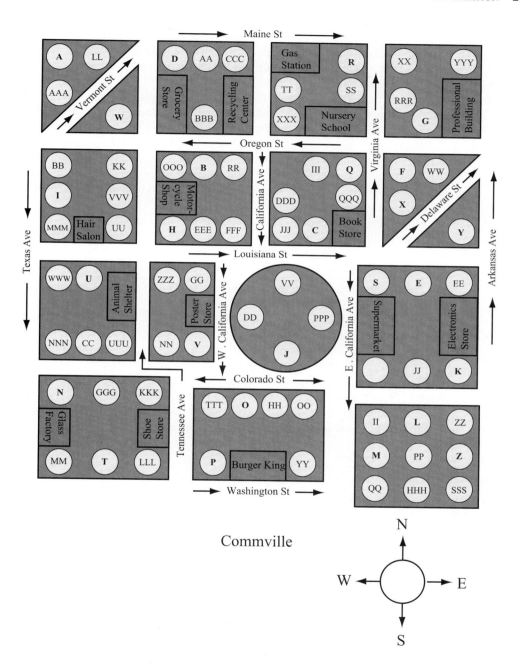

Commville

Procedures

1. The diagram of Commville with all the circles but without the double and triple letters should be put on the chalkboard or projected onto a screen. (A transparency master for this purpose is provided in the *Instructor's Manual.*)
2. Two students participate in each round; one is the direction giver and the other the direction taker. The direction giver should select one of the directions provided below and tell the direction taker how to get there. At this time, only the direction giver may look at the complete diagram in the text. Assume that the direction taker is driving and so must observe the one-way signs. The direction taker may ask any questions at this point (but only at this point) but may not take any notes. After the complete direction is given, the direction taker should follow the directions by tracing the path on the chalkboard or transparency.
3. This procedure should be continued for at least three to five rounds.
4. After each set of directions is given and taken, discussion may focus on some or all of the following issues. These issues identify the qualities of a good direction: easy to remember, specific, and efficient.

   - Were the directions easy to remember? In what ways might they have been made easier to remember?
   - Were the directions specific? Did the directions identify one and only one location?
   - Were the directions efficient? Did the directions enable the direction taker to get to the location with the least amount of effort, in this case, the least number of blocks traveled? Can you identify an easier way to get from the starting point to the location? Note that in some cases you may find that ease of remembering and maximum efficiency cannot both be achieved. It will then be necessary to sacrifice one of these qualities and give either a direction that is easy to remember but inefficient or a direction that is efficient but difficult to remember.

Guidelines in Giving Directions

You may find the following guidelines helpful in giving directions:

1. Use guide phrases such as "first" or "after you get to Maine Street" to help the listener follow your plan for directions.
2. Include internal summaries with complex directions: for example, "You should now be on East California Avenue in front of a supermarket."
3. Don't assume that the other person knows the area or its landmarks. "It's next to the recycling center" does not help the person who doesn't know where the recycling center is.
4. Include relevant details but, equally important, omit irrelevant details.
5. Ask the person if your directions are clear. Give the person an opportunity to ask questions or to confirm his or her understanding of your directions.

Sample Directions

Explain how to get from:

1. J to WW
2. T to YYY
3. U to MMM
4. G to SSS
5. C to UU
6. L to OOO
7. A to HHH
8. Y to CC
9. V to AA
10. F to GGG
11. B to EEE
12. M to LL
13. Z to ZZZ
14. D to PPP
15. H to YY
16. I to SS
17. E to LLL
18. K to AAA
19. N to VV
20. O to RRR

Part

THREE

Interpersonal Relationships

APPROACHING INTERPERSONAL RELATIONSHIPS

In approaching your study of interpersonal relationships, keep the following in mind:

- The research results and conclusions presented here are true in a statistical sense. They apply to the average person but not to everyone. Your task is to ask if they apply to you and to your relationships.
- Delay your conclusions until you have collected sufficient information. Avoid drawing conclusions about your friends, romantic partners, or, in fact, any of your relationships from isolated bits and pieces of information. Formulate hypotheses to be tested rather than hard-and-fast conclusions.
- Look for comparisons and analogies between the situations described here and those in which you find yourself. Ask yourself how your interpersonal life is similar to or different from the situations described here. Which of the skills covered in the following units can you apply to your life at home, at work, at school?
- Relationship change, should that be your goal, is not an easy process. And this is doubly true for dysfunctional relationships. Realize that change is often slow and that it may be facilitated with the help of others.

UNIT 16

Universals of Interpersonal Relationships

UNIT OBJECTIVES

AFTER COMPLETING THIS UNIT, YOU SHOULD BE ABLE TO:

1. Identify the functions interpersonal relationships serve
2. Explain the six-stage model of relationships
3. Define *breadth* and *depth* and illustrate how these concepts can be used to describe interpersonal relationships

There is probably nothing as important to you or me as our contact with other human beings. So important is this contact that, when we are deprived of it for prolonged periods, depression sets in, self-doubt surfaces, and we find it difficult to manage even the very basics of daily life. Research shows clearly that the most important contributor to happiness—outranking money, job, and sex—is a close relationship with one other person.

THE FUNCTIONS OF INTERPERSONAL RELATIONSHIPS

Although each relationship serves different functions for different people, four functions that most relationships serve can be identified. They may also be viewed as the reasons you seek out and develop relationships.

TO LESSEN LONELINESS

Contact with another human being helps alleviate loneliness. We want to feel that someone cares, that someone likes us, that someone will protect us, that someone ultimately will love us. Close relationships assure us that someone does care and will be there when we need human contact. Sometimes surrounding yourself with lots of people helps; often, however, a crowd only serves to underscore loneliness. One close relationship usually works a lot better.

TO SECURE STIMULATION

Human beings need stimulation; without it, they withdraw—sometimes they die. In *Intimate Relations* (1973), Murray Davis characterizes humans as *stimulotropic*. As plants are heliotropic and orient themselves to light, humans orient themselves to sources of stimulation. Human contact is one of the best ways to secure this stimulation. We have many needs and interests, all requiring different kinds of stimulation. We are intellectual, physical, and emotional creatures, so we need intellectual, physical, and emotional stimulation.

To Gain in Self-Knowledge and Self-Esteem

We need contact with other human beings because through them we learn about ourselves. Our self-perceptions are greatly influenced by what we think others think of us; if our friends see us as warm and generous, we probably will, too. Contact with others allows us to see ourselves from a different perspective. Thus, social comparison theory holds that we evaluate and assess ourselves—our attitudes, talents, values, accomplishments, abilities—primarily by comparing ourselves with others. These comparisons are, in large part, accomplished through our interpersonal relationships.

One of the major functions of interpersonal relationships is to enhance self-esteem and self-worth. Simply having a relational partner makes you feel desirable and worthy of love. When you are fortunate enough to have a supportive partner, the relationship can enhance self-esteem even more.

To Maximize Pleasure and Minimize Pain

The most general function served by interpersonal relationships, and one that could encompass all the others, is that of maximizing pleasure and minimizing pain. People have a need to share good fortune as well as their emotional and physical pain. Perhaps this goes back to childhood, when we ran to mother to have our wounds kissed or to be told everything is all right. We now find it difficult to run to mother, so we go to others, generally to friends who will provide the same consolation that mother did.

Stages in Interpersonal Relationships: Development to Dissolution

Relationships are established in stages. You and another person do not become intimate friends immediately upon meeting. Rather, you build an intimate relationship gradually, through a series of steps or stages. The same is probably also true of most other kinds of relationships. The "love at first sight" phenomenon creates a problem for a stage model of relationships, but rather than argue that such love cannot occur (my own feeling is that it can and frequently does), it seems wiser to claim that the stage model characterizes *most* relationships for *most* people *most* of the time.

Within each relationship and within each relationship stage, there are dynamic tensions between several opposites. The assumption made by this theory—called relational dialectics theory—is that all relationships can be defined by a series of opposites. For example, some research has found three such opposites (Baxter 1988, 1990; Baxter and Simon 1993). The tension between **autonomy and connection** expresses your desire to remain an individual but also to be intimately connected to another person and to a relationship. The tension between **novelty and predictability** centers on the dual desires for newness and adventure on the one hand and sameness and comfortableness on the other. The tension between **closedness and openness** relates to the desires to be in an exclusive relationship and one that is open to different people. The closedness-openness tension is more in evidence during the early stages of relationship development. Autonomy-connection and novelty-predictability are more a factor as the relationship progresses.

The six-stage model in Figure 16.1 describes the main stages in most relationships. For a particular relationship, you might wish to modify the basic model. But as a general

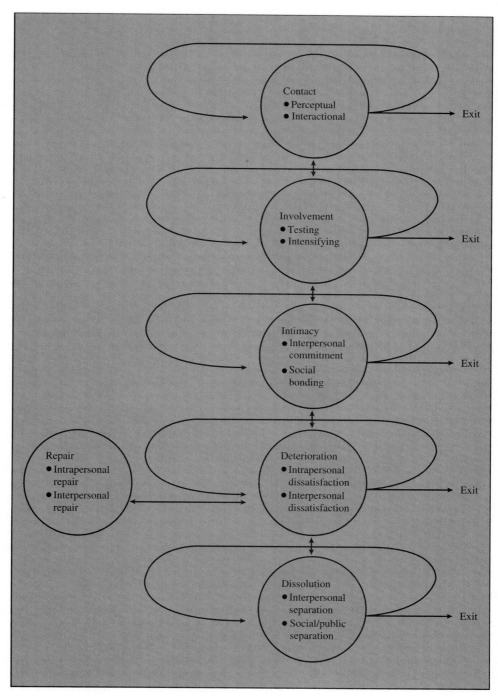

Figure 16.1
A six-stage model of interpersonal relationships.

description of relationship development, the stages seem fairly standard. Several additional attempts to identify relationship stages are presented in Table 16.1.

The six stages of relationships are contact, involvement, intimacy, deterioration, repair, and dissolution. These stages describe relationships as they are; they are not meant to evaluate or to prescribe how relationships should be.

CONTACT

At the initial phase of the contact stage, there is some kind of **perceptual contact**—you see, hear, and smell the person. From this you get a physical picture—sex, approximate age, height, and so on. After this perception, there is usually **interactional contact.** Here the contact is superficial and relatively impersonal. This is the stage at which you exchange basic information that is preliminary to any more intense involvement ("Hello, my name is Joe"). Here you initiate interaction ("May I join you?") and engage in invitational communication ("May I buy you a drink?"). According to some researchers, it is at this stage—within the first four minutes of initial interaction—that you decide whether you want to pursue the relationship (Zunin and Zunin 1972).

At the contact stage, physical appearance is especially important because it is the most readily seen. Yet through both verbal and nonverbal behaviors, qualities such as friendliness, warmth, openness, and dynamism are also revealed.

If you like the individual and want to pursue the relationship, you might use strategies to intensify your relationship, to move it to the next stage and perhaps to intimacy. The following are the five most popular types of strategies dating couples use to intensify their relationships, according to one research study (Tolhuizen 1989):

1. Increase contact with your partner.
2. Give your partner tokens of affection: for example, gifts, cards, or flowers.
3. Increase your own personal attractiveness to make yourself more desirable.
4. Do things that suggest intensifying the relationship: for example, flirting or making the partner jealous.
5. Become more sexually intimate.

INVOLVEMENT

At this stage, a sense of mutuality, of being connected develops. Here you experiment and try to learn more about the other person. At the initial phase of involvement, a kind of **testing** goes on. You want to see whether your initial judgment proves reasonable. And so you may ask questions: "Where do you work?" "What are you majoring in?" If you are committed to getting to know the person even better, you might continue your involvement by **intensifying** your interaction. Here you not only try to get to know the other person better but also begin to reveal yourself, though in a preliminary way.

Throughout the relationship process, but especially during the involvement and early intimacy stages, you test your partner, and you try to find out how your partner feels about the relationship. Among the strategies you might use are these (Bell and Buerkel-Rothfuss 1990; Baxter and Wilmot 1984):

- *Directness.* You ask your partner directly how he or she feels, or you disclose your own feelings on the assumption that your partner will also self-disclose.

Table 16.1
Models of Interpersonal Relationship Stages*

THE INTERPERSONAL COMMUNICATION BOOK	LEVINGER (1983)	KNAPP (1984)	WOOD (1982)	ALTMAN AND TAYLOR (1973)	KRUG (1982)	SWENSEN (1973)
Contact Perceptual Interactional	Zero contact Awareness Surface contact	Initiating	Individuals alone and receptive Invitational communication	Orientation	Initiation	Sampling
Involvement Testing Intensifying	Mutuality Moderate interaction	Experimenting Intensifying	Exploratory communication Intensifying Revising	Exploratory affective exchange	Experimentation Liking Trial	Bargaining
Intimacy Interpersonal commitment Social bonding	Major intersection	Integrating Bonding	Bonding Navigating	Affective exchange Stable exchange	Coupling Stabilization—nurturance	Commitment Institutionalization
Deterioration Intrapersonal dissatisfaction Interpersonal deterioration		Differentiating Circumscribing Stagnating Avoiding	Differentiating Disintegrating Stagnating		Stabilization—conflict development	
Repair Intrapersonal repair Interpersonal repair						
Dissolution Interpersonal separation Social public separation		Terminating	Terminating Individuals		Termination Avoidance Maintenance	

*Many writers on interpersonal communication have developed models of the stages in relationships. I present several of these here. My purpose is not to add complexity to an already complex area but rather to provide a sampling of additional perspectives and to enable you to see how any of the stages noted here could be differentiated further. For example, Levinger differentiates three levels of contact: zero or no contact, awareness, and surface contact. Knapp identifies two stages of involvement: experimenting and intensifying.

- *Endurance.* You subject your partner to various negative behaviors (for example, you behave badly or make inconvenient requests) on the assumption that if your partner endures them, he or she is serious about the relationship.
- *Indirect suggestion.* For example, you joke about a shared future together, touch more intimately, or hint that you are serious about the relationship. Similar responses from your partner will mean that he or she wishes to increase the intimacy of the relationship.
- *Public presentation.* For example, you introduce your partner as your "boyfriend" or "girlfriend" and see how your partner responds.
- *Separation.* You separate yourself physically to see how the other person responds. If your partner calls, then you know he or she is interested in the relationship.
- *Third party.* You ask mutual friends about your partner's feelings and intentions.
- *Triangle.* You set up a triangle and tell your partner that, for example, another person is interested in him or her; then you see how your partner reacts. If your partner shows no interest, it indicates a stronger commitment to you.

INTIMACY

At the intimacy stage, you commit yourself still further to the other person and establish a relationship in which this individual becomes your best or closest friend, lover, or companion. Not surprisingly, your relationship satisfaction also increases with the move to this stage (Siavelis and Lamke 1992). The intimacy stage usually divides itself into two phases: an **interpersonal commitment** phase, in which the two people commit themselves to each other in a private way, and a **social bonding** phase, in which the commitment is made public—perhaps to family and friends, perhaps to the public at large. Here you and your partner become a unit, an identifiable pair.

When the intimacy stage involves marriage, people are faced with three main premarital anxieties (Zimmer 1986):

1. *Security anxiety.* Will my mate leave me for someone else? Will my mate be sexually unfaithful?
2. *Fulfillment anxiety.* Will we be able to achieve a close, warm, and special rapport? Will we be able to have an equal relationship?
3. *Excitement anxiety.* Will boredom and routine set in? Will I lose my freedom and become trapped?

Of course, not everyone strives for intimacy (Bartholomew 1990). Some are so fearful of the consequences of intimacy that they actively avoid it. Others dismiss intimacy and defensively deny their need for more and deeper interpersonal contact.

To some people, relational intimacy is extremely risky. To others, it involves only low risk. For example, how true of your attitudes are the following statements?

- It is dangerous to get really close to people.
- I'm afraid to get really close to someone because I might get hurt.
- I find it difficult to trust other people.

• The most important thing to consider in a relationship is whether I might get hurt.

People who agree with these and similar statements perceive intimacy to involve great risk (Pilkington and Richardson 1988). Such people, it has been found, have fewer close friends, are less likely to be involved in a romantic relationship, have less trust in others, have a low level of dating assertiveness, and are generally less sociable than those who see intimacy as involving little risk.

DETERIORATION

This stage and the next (dissolution) are characterized by the weakening of bonds between the parties and represent the downside of the relationship progression.

The first phase of deterioration is usually **intrapersonal dissatisfaction:** you begin to feel that this relationship may not be as important as you previously thought. You experience personal dissatisfaction with everyday interactions and begin to view the future with your partner negatively. If this dissatisfaction continues or grows, you pass to the second phase, **interpersonal deterioration:** you withdraw and grow further and further apart. You share less of your free time; when you are together, there are awkward silences, fewer self-disclosures, less physical contact, and a lack of psychological closeness. Conflicts become more and more common and their resolution increasingly difficult.

REPAIR

The term "repair" can refer to "preventive maintenance": for example, to keeping the relationship as it is or in a satisfying condition. It can also refer to "corrective maintenance": for example, to correcting something that is not going well or to improving some unsatisfying aspect of the relationship (M. Davis 1973; Dindia and Canary 1993). As used here, the term "maintenance" means "preventive" care (considered in Unit 18), and the term "repair" means "corrective" care (considered in Unit 19).

The repair stage is optional and so is indicated in Figure 16.1 by a broken circle. Some relational partners may pause during deterioration and try to repair their relationship. Others, however, may progress—without stopping, without thinking—to dissolution.

The first phase of repair is *intrapersonal repair.* Here you analyze what has gone wrong and consider ways of solving your relational difficulties. You might at this stage consider changing your behaviors or perhaps changing your expectations of your partner. You might also evaluate the rewards of your relationship as it is now and the rewards to be gained if your relationship ended.

Should you decide that you want to repair your relationship, you might discuss this with your partner at the *interpersonal repair* level. You might discuss the problems in the relationship, the corrections you would want to see, and perhaps what you would be willing to do and what you would want the other person to do. This is the stage of negotiating new agreements, new behaviors. You and your partner might try to solve your problems yourselves, seek the advice of friends or family, or perhaps enter professional counseling.

DISSOLUTION

The dissolution stage is the cutting of the bonds between the individuals. In the beginning, it usually takes the form of **interpersonal separation,** in which you might move into separate apartments and begin to lead lives apart from each other. If this separation proves acceptable and if the original relationship is not repaired, you enter the phase of **social** or **public separation.** If the relationship is a marriage, this phase corresponds to divorce. In some cases, the former partners change the definition of their relationship, and, for example, the ex-lovers become friends or business partners. Avoidance of each other and a return to being "single" are among the primary characteristics of dissolution.

Dissolution is also the stage during which the ex-partners begin to look upon themselves as individuals rather than halves of a pair and seek the establishment of a new and different life, either alone or with another person. Some people, it is true, continue to live psychologically with a relationship that has already been dissolved: they frequent old meeting places, reread old love letters, daydream about all the good times, and fail to extricate themselves from a relationship that has died in every way except in their memory.

In cultures that emphasize continuity from one generation to the next and where being "old-fashioned" is evaluated positively—as in, say, China—interpersonal relationships are likely to be long-lasting and permanent. But, in cultures where change is seen as positive and being old-fashioned as negative—as in, say, the United States—interpersonal relationships are likely to be more temporary (Moghaddam, Taylor, and Wright 1993).

MOVEMENT AMONG THE STAGES

Figure 16.1 contains three types of arrows. The **exit arrows** indicate that each stage offers the opportunity to exit the relationship. After saying hello, you can say good-bye and exit. The vertical or **movement arrows** between stages represent the fact that we can move to another stage, either a more intense one (say, from involvement to intimacy) or a less intense one (say, from intimacy to deterioration). We can also go back to a previously established stage. For example, you may have established an intimate relationship with someone but do not want to maintain it at that level. You want it to be less intense. So you may go back to the involvement stage and reestablish the relationship at that more comfortable level. A married couple that divorces, for example, may move from the intimacy stage back to the involvement stage of friendship (Masheter and Harris 1986). The **self-reflexive arrows**—the arrows that loop back to the beginning of the same level or stage—signify that any relationship may become stabilized at any point. You may, for example, maintain a relationship at the intimate level without its deteriorating or returning to the less intense stage of involvement. Or you might remain at the "Hello, how are you?" stage—the contact stage—without ever getting any further involved.

Movement through the various stages is usually a gradual process; you don't jump from contact to involvement to intimacy. Rather, you progress gradually, a few degrees at a time. Yet there are leaps that must and do take place. For example, during the involvement stage of a romantic relationship, the first kiss or the first sexual encounter requires a leap; it requires a change in the kind of communication and in the kind of intimacy to be experienced by the two people. Before you take these leaps, you probably first test the waters. Before the first kiss, for example, you may hold each other, look longingly into

Table 16.2
Turning Points in Romantic Relationships*

TURNING POINTS	EXAMPLES
Getting-to-know time	first meeting, time spent together studying, first date
Quality time that enables the couple to appreciate one another and their relationship	meeting the family or getting away together
Physical separation	separations due to vacations or business trips (not to breakups)
External competition	presence of a new or old rival, demands that compete for relationship time
Reunion	getting back together after physical separation

*This table is based on research by Baxter and Bullis (1986).

each other's eyes, and perhaps caress each other's face. You might do this (in part) to discover if the leap—the kiss, for example—will be met with a favorable response. No one wants rejection—especially of romantic advances. These major jumps or turning points provide an interesting perspective on how relationships develop. Table 16.2 presents the five most frequently reported turning points in romantic relationships among college students (Baxter and Bullis 1986).

BREADTH AND DEPTH OF INTERPERSONAL RELATIONSHIPS

As you progress from contact through involvement to intimacy, you can see that the number of topics you talk about and the degree of "personalness" with which you pursue them increase (Altman and Taylor 1973). The number of topics communicated about is referred to as **breadth.** The degree to which the inner personalities, the inner cores, are penetrated is referred to as **depth.**

Let us represent an individual as a circle and divide that circle into various parts representing the topics of interpersonal communication, or breadth. Further, visualize the circle and its parts as consisting of concentric inner circles representing the different levels of communication, or depth. Representative examples are provided in Figure 16.2. Each circle is divided into eight topic areas (identified A through H) and five levels of intimacy (represented by the concentric circles). Note that in circle 1, only three of the topic areas are penetrated. Two of these are penetrated only to the first level and one to the second level. In this type of interaction, three topic areas are discussed, and only at rather superficial levels. This is the type of relationship you might have with an acquaintance. Circle 2 represents a more intense relationship, one that has greater breadth and in which the topics are discussed to a deeper level of penetration. This is the type of

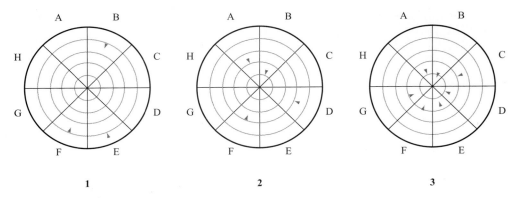

Figure 16.2
Social Penetration with (a) an acquaintance, (2) a friend, and (3) an intimate.

relationship you might have with a friend. Circle 3 represents a still more intense relationship. Here there is considerable breadth (seven of the eight areas are penetrated) and depth (note that most of the areas are penetrated to the deepest levels). This is the type of relationship you might have with a lover or a parent.

All relationships—friendships, loves, families—may be described in terms of breadth and depth, concepts that are central to the theory of **social penetration** (Altman and Taylor 1973). In its initial stage, a relationship is normally characterized by narrow breadth (few topics are discussed) and shallow depth (the topics are discussed only superficially). As the relationship grows in intensity and intimacy, both the breadth and the depth increase, and these increases are seen as comfortable, normal, and natural progressions.

DEPENETRATION

When a relationship begins to deteriorate, the breadth and depth will often reverse themselves—a process of **depenetration,** sometimes referred to as the **reversal hypothesis.** For example, in the process of terminating a relationship, you might eliminate certain topics from your interpersonal interactions and at the same time discuss acceptable topics in less depth. You might reduce the level of your self-disclosures and reveal less and less of your innermost feelings. This reversal does not always occur, of course (Baxter 1983). There is some evidence to show that, among friends for example, although depth decreases in the early stages of deterioration, it may later increase (Tolhuizen 1986).

Stage Talk

The table below gives examples of the kinds of messages you might compose at each of the six relationship stages. Notice that some messages ("How are you?" is an example) may be said at several stages. Although the words are the same, the meaning they communicate differs, depending on the stage. Thus, for example, at the contact stage "How are you?" may simply mean "Hello." At the involvement stage, it may mean "Tell me what has been going on." At the intimacy stage, it may be a request for highly personal information about the person's feelings.

Although the examples here are obviously incomplete, research finds that as the relationship becomes more intimate, messages communicating immediacy and affection, similarity and depth, trust, and composure also increase (Hale, Lundy, and Mongeau 1989).

CONTACT

Hello. Hi.	Surface-level messages we use with just about everyone to acknowledge them
How are you?	This is just another way of saying hello. We really don't want to hear about Sam's last operation.

Didn't I see you here last week?	Phatic communion, an indirect attempt to make contact
May I join you for coffee?	A direct statement expressing the desire to make contact

INVOLVEMENT

I like to cook, too.	Establishing and talking about common interests
How are you?	A request for some (mostly positive) information, but not in too much detail
I'm having some difficulties at home—nothing really serious.	Low- to mid-level self-disclosures are made. Nothing very serious will be discussed.
I'd like to take you to dinner. I'd like to get to know you.	Direct statements expressing the desire for involvement

INTIMACY

We might go dancing.	Expression of togetherness ("we-ness")
How are you?	A request for significant information about health or feelings, especially if there's reason to believe a recent change has occurred; a way of saying "I care"
I'm really depressed.	Significant self-disclosure
I love you.	A direct expression of intimacy

DETERIORATION

I can't stand . . .	Negative evaluations increase.
I'd like to start seeing others.	Direct statement expressing desire to reduce the present level of intimacy
Why don't you go to Kate and Allie's by yourself?	Expression of desire to separate in the eyes of others
You never listen to my needs. It was all your fault.	Faultfinding, criticism, and blaming

REPAIR

Is this relationship worth saving?	Self-analysis; assessing the value of repair
We need to talk; our lives are falling apart.	Opening the issue of repair

Will you give up seeing Pat?	Negotiation; identifying what you want if the relationship is to survive

DISSOLUTION

Good-bye.	The ultimate expression of dissolution
I want to end this relationship. I want a divorce.	A direct statement expressing the desire to dissolve the relationship formally
I tried, but I guess it wasn't enough.	Attempt to gain "social credit," approval from others

LEARNING TO HEAR STAGE TALK

Learning to hear stage-talk messages—messages that express a desire to move the relationship in a particular way or to stabilize the relationship at a particular stage—will help you understand and manage your own interpersonal relationships. Over the next few days, listen carefully to all stage-talk messages. Listen to the messages pertaining to your own interpersonal relationships as well as the messages friends or acquaintances disclose to you about theirs. Collect these messages and classify them into one of the following six categories:

1. **Contact messages** express a desire for contact: "Hi, my name is Joe."
2. **Closeness messages** express a desire for increased closeness, involvement, or intimacy: "I'd like to see you more often."
3. **Stabilizing messages** express a desire to stabilize the relationship at a particular stage: "Let's keep it this way for a while. I'm afraid to get more involved at this point in my life."
4. **Distancing messages** express a desire to distance oneself from a relationship. "I think we should spend a few weeks apart."
5. **Repair messages** express a desire to repair the relationship: "Couldn't we discuss this and work it out? I didn't mean to be so dogmatic."
6. **Dissolution messages** express a desire to break up or dissolve the existing relationship: "Look, it's just not working out as we planned; let's each go our own way."

Share these collected messages with others in small groups or with the class as a whole. Consider some or all of the following issues:

1. What types of messages are used to indicate the six different desires noted above?
2. Do people give reasons for their desire to move from one stage to another or to stabilize their relationship? If so, what types of reasons do they give?
3. Do men and women talk about relationship stages in the same way? In different ways? Explain.
4. Are there cultural differences in the way relationship desires are expressed?

SUMMARY: UNIT IN BRIEF

Functions of Interpersonal Relationships	Stages in Interpersonal Relationships	Breadth and Depth
To alleviate loneliness To secure stimulation To gain self-knowledge and self-esteem To maximize pleasure and minimize pain	**Contact** perceptual interactional **Involvement** testing intensification **Intimacy** interpersonal commitment social bonding **Deterioration** intrapersonal dissatisfaction interpersonal deterioration **Repair** intrapersonal repair interpersonal repair **Dissolution** interpersonal separation social/public separation	**Breadth:** the number of topics about which the individuals communicate; usually increases as the relationship develops and decreases as the relationship deteriorates **Depth:** the degree to which the inner personality is penetrated; usually increases as the relationship develops (*penetration*) and decreases as the relationship deteriorates (*depenetration*)

THINKING CRITICALLY ABOUT THE UNIVERSALS OF RELATIONSHIPS

1. Can you identify the major reasons you developed your three most important relationships? Do you maintain these relationships for the same reasons? If these reasons were no longer present, would you dissolve the relationships?

2. When do you experience loneliness most? How long do these feelings usually last? How do your interpersonal relationships help to lessen loneliness?

3. Do any of your relationships involve tension between such opposites as autonomy-connection, novelty-predictability, and closedness-openness? How are these tensions dealt with and reconciled?

4. With what relationship stage do you have the most difficulty? Why? Can you supply personal examples that illustrate the three types of movement among the relationship stages? That is, can you identify a personal relationship that moved from one stage to another? One that has remained at one stage for a relatively long period? One that has resulted in one person's exiting the relationship? Are there other types of movement that should be included in the model?

5. Can you identify any strategies that you have used in testing your friendship or romantic relationships? Can you identify strategies that others have used on you?

6. How would you describe "relational intimacy"? How do you know when you have reached this stage? Is this stage better defined by identifying "intimacy behaviors," "intimacy feelings," or some combination?

7. Security, fulfillment, and excitement anxieties were identified as the major premarital anxieties. Have you experienced these or other anxieties when you considered entering a relationship? What were the circumstances?

8. How would you distinguish between repair designed to maintain a relationship ("preventive maintenance," to keep the relationship satisfying and functioning smoothly) and repair designed to reverse deterioration ("corrective maintenance," to fix something that is broken or not functioning properly) (M. Davis 1973)? Do these two kinds of repair rely on different strategies?

9. How would you describe the stages of interpersonal relationships? Is the six-stage model presented here an adequate way to describe most interpersonal relationships as you understand them? Are the concepts of breadth and depth adequate in describing the development and deterioration of interpersonal relationships? What other concepts might prove helpful?

10. How would you design a research study to answer any one of the following questions?

    - Do all types of relationships follow the same pattern from development to dissolution?
    - Do men and women perceive their relationship stage similarly?
    - Can your relationship differences with an acquaintance, a friend, and an intimate be explained, in part, by the topics you discuss?

EXPERIENTIAL VEHICLES

16.1 EXTRAORDINARY PEOPLE: RELATIONAL ANALYSIS

The dialogue that follows is an abbreviated account of the development and dissolution of a relationship. Consequently, the six stages of relationships are easy to see and are quite clearly differentiated. In reality, these divisions would not be so obvious. The main purpose of this dialogue is to provide the focus for discussion and analysis of the universals of interpersonal relationships. Examine the dialogue, taking into consideration some or all of the following questions:

1. *Reasons for relational development.* Are there any indications why Chris and Pat sought a relationship with each other? What seems to account for the development of relationships among most college students?

2. *Stages in interpersonal relations.* Identify the stages in the dialogue. What specific phrases cue you to the stages of the relationship? What conversational cues signal movement from one stage to another?

3. *Breadth and depth of relationships.* What would you expect the breadth and depth of the relationship to be at each of the six stages? At what stage is there greatest breadth? Least breadth? At what stage is there greatest depth? Least depth? On what specific conversational cues do you base your responses? Draw diagrams similar to

those presented in Figure 16.2 to represent any two stages in the relationship. Explain these diagrams with reference to specific messages in the dialogue.

The Saga of Chris and Pat

PAT: Hi. Didn't I see you in English last semester?

CHRIS: Yeah. I'm surprised you noticed me. I cut that class more than I attended. I really hated it.

PAT: So did I. Higgins never did seem to care much about whether you learned anything or not.

CHRIS: That's why I think I cut so much. Your name's Pat, isn't it?

PAT: Yes. And you're Chris, right?

CHRIS: Right. What are you doing in interpersonal communication?

PAT: I'm majoring in communication. I want to go into television production— maybe editing or something like that. I'm not really sure. What about you?

CHRIS: It's required for engineering. I guess they figure engineers should learn to communicate.

PAT: You gonna have lunch after this class?

CHRIS: Yeah. You?

PAT: Yeah. How about going over to the Union for a burger?
[*At the Union cafeteria*]

CHRIS: I'm not only surprised you noticed me in English, I'm really flattered. Everyone in the class seemed to be interested in you.

PAT: Well, I doubt that, but it's nice to hear.

CHRIS: No, I mean it. Come on. You know you're popular.

PAT: Well, maybe . . . but it always seems to be with the wrong people. Today's the exception, of course.

CHRIS: You sure know the right things to say.

PAT: OK, then let me try another. What are you doing tonight? Want to go to a movie? I know it's late and all, but I thought just in case you had nothing to do. . . .

CHRIS: I'd love to. Even if I had something else planned, I'd break it.

PAT: That makes me feel good.

CHRIS: That makes me feel good, too.
[*Six months later*]

PAT: I hope that this doesn't cause problems, but I got you something.

CHRIS: What is it?

PAT: Take a look. I hope you like it.

CHRIS: [*Opens the package and finds a ring*] I love it. I can't believe it! You know, a few weeks ago when we had to write up a recent fantasy for class, I wrote one I didn't turn in. And this was it. My very own fantasy coming true. I love you.

PAT: I love you . . . very much.
[*Chris and Pat have now been living together for about two years.*]

PAT: It's me. I'm home.

CHRIS: So am I.

PAT: That's not hamburgers I smell, is it?

CHRIS: Yes, it is. I like hamburgers. We can afford hamburgers. And I know how to cook hamburgers. Make something else if you don't want to eat them.

PAT: Thanks. It's nice to know that you go to such trouble making something I like. I hate these damn hamburgers. And I especially hate them four times a week.

CHRIS: Eat out.

PAT: You know I have work to do tonight. I can't go out.

CHRIS: So shut up and eat the burgers. I love them.

PAT: That's good. It's you for you. Whatever happened to us and we?

CHRIS: They died when I found out about your little side trips upstate.

PAT: But I told you I was sorry about that. That was six months ago, anyway. I got involved, I know, but I'm sorry. What do you want to do, punish me for the rest of my life? I'm sorry, damn it. I'm sorry!

CHRIS: So am I. But I'm the one who was left at home alone while you were out fooling around.

PAT: Is that why you don't want to make love? You always have some kind of excuse.

CHRIS: It's not an excuse. It's a reason. And the reason is that I've been lied to and cheated on. How can I make love to someone who treats me like dirt?

PAT: But I don't. I love you.

CHRIS: But I don't love you. Maybe I never have.

PAT: I will eat out.

[*Two weeks later*]

PAT: Did you mean what you said when you said you didn't love me?

CHRIS: I think I did. I just lost my feelings. I can't explain it. When I learned about your upstate trips, I just couldn't deal with it. I guess I tried to protect myself and, in the process, lost my feelings for you.

PAT: Then why do you stay with me? Why don't you leave?

CHRIS: I don't know. Maybe I'm afraid to be alone. I'm not sure I can do it alone.

PAT: So you're going to stay with me because you're afraid to be alone? That's crazy. Crazy. I'd rather see us break up than live like this—a loveless relationship where you go out on Tuesdays and I go out on Wednesdays. What kind of life is that?

CHRIS: Not much.

PAT: Then let's separate. I can't live with someone who stays with me out of fear of being alone, who doesn't want to be touched, who doesn't want to love me. Let's try to live apart and see what happens. Maybe we need some distance. Maybe you'll want to try it again.

CHRIS: I won't, but I guess separation is the best thing.

PAT: Why don't you stay here and I'll go to my brother's place tonight. I'll pick up my things tomorrow when you're at work. I don't think I can bear to do it when you're here.

CHRIS: Good-bye.

16.2 INTERPERSONAL RELATIONSHIPS AND SONG

The objectives of this exercise are (1) to become familiar with some of the popular sentiments concerning interpersonal relationships as they are expressed in song and (2) to provide a stimulus for the consideration of significant concepts and theories of interpersonal relationships.

Bring to class a recording of one song that expresses a sentiment that is significant to the study of interpersonal relationships for any one of the following reasons:

- It expresses a sentiment that can assist us in understanding interpersonal relationships.
- It illustrates a concept or theory that is important in the study of interpersonal relationships.
- It suggests a useful question concerning interpersonal relationships.
- It illustrates a popular relational problem or difficulty.
- It illustrates a method for dealing with some kind of relationship problem or difficulty.

Be prepared to play this song for the class and to explain its relevance to the study of interpersonal relationships. Identify one principle of interpersonal communication that is expressed or suggested by this song.

UNIT 17

Relationship Development and Involvement

UNIT OBJECTIVES

AFTER COMPLETING THIS UNIT, YOU SHOULD BE ABLE TO:

1. Discuss the attraction, reinforcement, social exchange, and equity theories as explanations of relationship development
2. Explain the steps involved in initiating relationships
3. Provide at least eight suggestions for communicating in first encounters

Now that we have a general idea of the functions that relationships serve and the various stages of relationships, we can explore relationship development in greater detail. Later units cover relationships as they are maintained in friendship, love, and family situations, and relationships as they deteriorate.

THEORIES OF RELATIONSHIP DEVELOPMENT

A number of theories offer insight into why you develop your relationships. Several theories bearing directly on relationship development have already been discussed.

Uncertainty reduction theory (Unit 3) describes relationship development as a process of reducing uncertainty about one another. The theory makes a number of predictions about relationships and their development (Berger and Calabrese 1975). For example, the theory predicts that high uncertainty prevents intimacy, whereas low uncertainty creates intimacy. Similarly, high uncertainty decreases liking for another person, whereas low uncertainty increases liking.

Social penetration theory (Unit 16) describes the progression of a relationship along the communication dimensions of breadth and depth. As a relationship moves to greater intimacy, relationship depth and breadth increase; as a relationship moves away from intimacy, relationship depth and breadth decrease.

Relationship dialectics theory (Unit 16) describes relationships along a series of opposites representing competing desires or motivations, such as the desire for autonomy and the desire to belong to someone, for novelty and predictability, and for closedness and openness.

In this unit, four additional theories are singled out: attraction theory, reinforcement theory, social exchange theory, and equity theory. The theories offer unique perspectives and help explain what happens in interpersonal relationships (and in interpersonal communication generally) during the stages of development, maintenance, deterioration, and repair

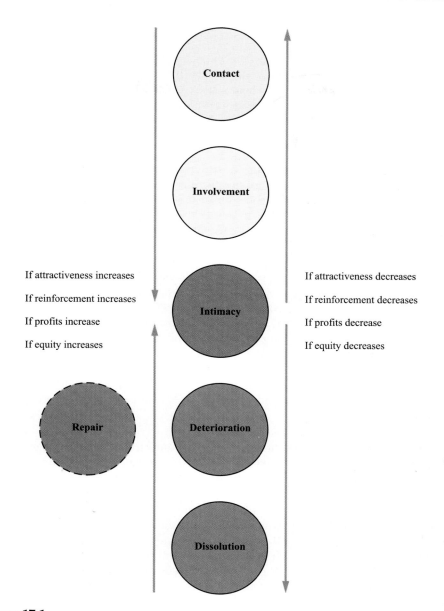

Figure 17.1
Relationship theories and the six-stage model. As illustrated in the model, movement toward greater intimacy occurs as attractiveness, reinforcement, profits, and equity increase. As attractiveness, reinforcement, profits, and equity decrease, there is a movement away from intimacy.

(Figure 17.1). They shed light on important interpersonal processes—for example, power and conflict—and on significant interpersonal relationships, such as friendship, love, and family.

ATTRACTION THEORY

You are no doubt attracted to some people and not attracted to others. In a similar way, some people are attracted to you and some are not. If you were to examine the people to whom you are attracted and those to whom you are not attracted, you would probably see patterns in your judgments, even though many of them seem subconsciously motivated.

Most people are attracted to others on the basis of three major factors: attractiveness (physical appearance and personality), proximity, and similarity.

Attractiveness: Physical Appearance and Personality   When you say, "I find that person attractive," you probably mean either that (1) you find that person physically attractive or that (2) you find that person's personality or behavior attractive. For the most part, you probably like physically attractive rather than physically unattractive people, and you probably like people who possess a pleasant rather than an unpleasant personality. Generally, you attribute positive characteristics to people you find attractive and negative characteristics to people you find unattractive.

Supporting the popular belief, research—in Bulgaria, Nigeria, Indonesia, Germany, and the United States—finds that men consider physical attractiveness in their partner more important than do women (Buss and Schmitt 1993). Similarly, in a study of gay male dating behavior, the physical attractiveness of the partner was the most important factor in influencing how much the person enjoyed his date and how much he wished to date that person again (Sergios and Cody 1985).

Those who are perceived as attractive are also perceived as competent. Interestingly enough, those who are perceived as more competent in communication—as a partner working on a joint task, socially and physically—are also perceived as more attractive (Duran and Kelly 1988).

Proximity   If you look around at people you find attractive, you will probably notice that they are the ones who live or work close to you. For example, in a study of friendships in a student housing development, researchers found that the closer the students' rooms were to each other, the better the chances that the occupants would become friends (Festinger, Schachter, and Back 1950). Also, the students who lived in units facing the courtyard had more friends than those who lived in units facing the street. The people who became friends were those who had the greatest opportunity to interact.

One reason why proximity influences attraction is that you probably have positive expectations of people who are near you and consequently fulfill these expectations by liking or being attracted to those people. Proximity also allows you to get to know the other person. You come to like people you know because you can better predict their behavior, and perhaps because of this they seem less frightening than complete strangers do (Berger and Bradac 1982).

Another approach argues that mere exposure to others leads us to develop positive feelings for them (Zajonc 1968). In one study (Saegert, Swap, and Zajonc 1973), women who were supposedly participating in a taste experiment were exposed throughout to other people—some ten times, others five times, others two times, others one time, and some not at all. The results showed that the subjects rated highest the persons they had seen ten times, next highest those they had seen five times, and so on down the line. How can we account for these results except by mere exposure? Mere exposure seems to

Research in interpersonal attractiveness shows that you become more attracted to people as a result of being physically close to one another. Can this factor of proximity help to explain the friendships that you have in college? Can it help explain the romantic relationships you have had?

increase attraction when the initial interaction is favorable or neutral. When the initial interaction is negative, repeated exposure may actually decrease attraction.

Similarity If you could construct your mate, he or she would probably look, act, and think very much like you. By being attracted to people like yourself, you validate yourself; you tell yourself that you are worthy of being liked. Although there are exceptions, you probably are attracted to your own mirror image, to people who are similar to you in nationality, race, ability, physical characteristics, intelligence, attitudes, and so on.

If you were to ask a group of friends, "To whom are you attracted?" they would probably name very attractive people; in fact, they would probably name the most attractive people they know. But if you were to observe these friends, you would find that they go out with and establish relationships with people who are quite similar to themselves in physical attractiveness. This tendency, known as the **matching hypothesis,** predicts that although you may be attracted to the most physically attractive people, you will date and mate with people who are similar to yourself in physical attractiveness (Walster, Walster, and Berscheid 1978). Intuitively, this seems satisfying. In some cases, however, you notice discrepancies: for example, an attractive person dating someone much less attractive. In cases such as these, you would probably look for compensating factors, for qualities that compensate for the lack of physical attractiveness: prestige, money, power, intelligence, and various personality characteristics are obvious examples.

Similarity in attitudes is especially important in attraction. Not surprisingly, people who are similar in attitudes grow in attraction for each other over time, whereas people who are dissimilar in attitudes grow less attracted to each other (Neimeyer and Mitchell 1988). Moreover, perceived attitudinal similarity seems related to marital happiness (Honeycutt 1986). We are particularly attracted to people who have attitudes similar to our own, who like what we like and dislike. The more significant the attitude, the more important the similarity. Marriages between people with great and salient dissimilarities are more likely to end in divorce than marriages between people who are very much alike (Blumstein and Schwartz 1983).

Attitude similarity is especially significant in initial attraction. It also seems to predict relationship success: People who are similar in attitude become more attracted to each other over time, whereas people who are dissimilar in attitude become less attracted to each other over time (Neimeyer and Mitchell 1988). Also, the more intellectually similar people are—the more they are alike in the way they perceive the world—the greater the interpersonal attraction (Neimeyer and Neimeyer 1983)

Although many people would argue that "birds of a feather flock together," others argue that "opposites attract." This latter concept is the principle of **complementarity.** People are attracted to dissimilar others only in certain situations. For example, the submissive student may get along especially well with an aggressive teacher but may not get along with an aggressive spouse. In *A Psychologist Looks at Love* (1944), Theodore Reik argues that we fall in love with people who possess characteristics that we do not possess and actually envy. The introvert, for example, if displeased with being shy, might be attracted to an extrovert.

Although intuitive support seems to exist for both complementarity and similarity, the research evidence favors similarity.

Affinity-Seeking Strategies   Attractiveness, proximity, and similarity are factors that influence interpersonal attraction apart from anything you may do or say. In addition, however, you can increase your attractiveness by using **affinity-seeking strategies,** which are listed in Table 17.1 (Bell and Daly 1984). These strategies were derived from studies in which people were asked to "produce a list of things people can say or do to get others to like them"; other subjects were asked to identify those things that lead others to dislike them. Thus, the strategies represent what people *think* makes us attractive to others, what people *think* makes people like us, what people *think* makes others feel positive toward us.

REINFORCEMENT THEORY

According to reinforcement theory, you develop relationships with those who reward you, and you avoid or break up relationships with those who do not reward you or who actually punish you.

Rewards or reinforcements may be social, such as compliments or praise, or they may be material, as in the case of the suitor whose gifts eventually win the hand of the beloved. But rewards can backfire. When overdone, rewards lose their effectiveness and may even lead to negative responses. The people who reward you constantly may become too sweet to tolerate, and you may come to discount whatever they say. Also, the reward must be perceived as genuine and not motivated by selfish concerns if it is to be successful.

You also tend to develop relationships with people *you* reward (Jecker and Landy 1969; Aronson 1980). You come to like people for whom you do favors. People need to justify going out of their way by convincing themselves that the person is worth the effort and is likable.

You may have noticed this phenomenon in your own interactions. You have probably increased your liking for persons after buying them an expensive present or going out

Table 17.1
Affinity-Seeking Strategies: How to Get People to Like Us and Feel Positive Toward Us

Altruism. Be of help to other.[*]

Assumption of control. Appear "in control," as a leader, as one who takes charge.

Assumption of equality. Present yourself as socially equal to Other.

Comfort. Present yourself as comfortable and relaxed when with Other.

Concession of control. Allow other to assume control over relational activities.

Conversational rule keeping. Follow the cultural rules for polite, cooperative conversation with Other.

Dynamism. Appear active, enthusiastic, and dynamic.

Drawing out Other's disclosures. Stimulate and encourage Other to talk about himself or herself; reinforce disclosures and contributions of Other.

Facilitation of enjoyment. Ensure that activities with Other are enjoyable and positive.

Inclusion of Other. Include Other in your social activities and groupings.

Perceptions of closeness. Create the impression that your relationship with Other is closer than it really is.

Listening. Listen to Other attentively and actively.

Nonverbal immediacy. Communicate interest in Other.

Openness. Engage in self-disclosure with Other.

Optimism. Appear optimistic and positive rather than pessimistic and negative.

Personal autonomy. Appear to Other as an independent and freethinking individual.

Physical attractiveness. Appear to Other as physically attractive as possible.

Presentation of interesting self. Appear to Other as an interesting person to get to know.

Reward association. Appear as one who is able to administer rewards to Other for associating with you.

Self-concept confirmation. Show respect for Other, and help Other to feel positively about himself or herself.

Self-inclusion. Arrange circumstances so that you and Other come into frequent contact.

Sensitivity. Communicate warmth and empathy to Other.

Similarity. Demonstrate that you share significant attitudes and values with Other.

Supportiveness. Communicate supportiveness in Other's interpersonal interactions.

Trustworthiness. Appear to Other as honest and reliable.

[*]In these definitions, the term "Other" is used as shorthand for "other person or persons."

of your way to do them a special favor. In these and similar instances, you justify your behavior by believing that the person is worth your efforts. Otherwise, you would have to admit to being a poor judge of character and to spending your money and effort on people who are not deserving.

SOCIAL EXCHANGE THEORY

Social exchange theory, based on an economic model of profits and losses, claims that you develop relationships that enable you to maximize your profits (Chadwick-Jones 1976; Gergen, Greenberg, and Willis 1980; Thibaut and Kelley 1959). The theory begins with the following equation:

$$\textbf{REWARDS} - \textbf{COSTS} = \textbf{PROFITS}$$

Rewards are anything that you incur costs to obtain. For example, to acquire the reward of financial gain, you might have to work rather than play. To earn an A in an interpersonal communication course, you might have to write a term paper or study more than you want to. To gain a promotion, you might have to do unpleasant tasks or work overtime. Love, affection, status, money, gifts, security, social acceptance, companionship, friendship, and intimacy are just a few examples of rewards for which you would be willing to work (that is, incur costs).

Costs are those things that you normally try to avoid—things you consider unpleasant or difficult. Working overtime, washing dishes and ironing clothes, watching a television show that your partner enjoys but you find boring, dressing in ways that are physically uncomfortable, and doing favors for people you dislike might all be considered costs.

Using this basic economic model, social exchange theory claims that you seek to develop relationships (friendly and romantic) that will give you the greatest profit: that is, relationships in which the rewards are greater than the costs. The preferred relationships, according to this theory, are those that give us the greatest rewards with the least costs.

Comparison Levels   You enter a relationship with a general idea of the kinds of rewards and profits you ought to get out of it. That is your **comparison level,** your realistic expectations of what you feel you deserve from a relationship. For example, in a study of married couples, it was found that most people expect reasonably high levels of trust, mutual respect, love, and commitment. Their expectations are significantly lower for time spent together, privacy, sexual activity, and communication (Sabatelli and Pearce 1986). When the rewards you get equal or surpass this comparison level, you feel satisfied with your relationship.

However, you also have a **comparison level for alternatives.** That is, you probably compare the profits you derive from your current relationships with the ones you think you can derive from alternative relationships. For example, if you believe you will not be able to find another suitable partner, you are more likely to stay in your relationship, even if it is an abusive one (Berscheid 1985; also see Unit 22). If you see that the profits from your present relationship are less than the profits you could get from an alternative relationship, you might decide to leave your current relationship and enter a new and potentially more profitable one.

EQUITY THEORY

Equity theory uses the concepts of social exchange but goes a step further; it claims that you develop and maintain relationships in which your ratio of rewards to costs is approximately equal to your partner's (Walster, Walster, and Berscheid 1978; Messick and Cook 1983). An equitable relationship, then, is one in which participants derive rewards that are proportional to their costs. If you work harder for the relationship than your partner does, then equity demands that you get greater rewards than your partner. If you work equally hard, then equity demands that each of you get approximately equal rewards. Not surprisingly, research finds that people want equity and feel that relationships should be characterized by equity (Ueleke et al. 1983).

Equity theory puts into clear focus the sources of relational dissatisfaction seen every day. For example, in a traditional marriage, both husband and wife may have full-time jobs, but the wife may also do the major share of the household chores. Thus, although both may be deriving equal rewards—they have equally good cars, they live in the same three-bedroom house, and so on—the wife is paying more of the costs. According to equity theory, she will be dissatisfied because of this lack of equity. In a work situation, we may see the same dynamic with two management trainees: each does an equal amount of work (that is, each has an equal amount of cost), but one of them gets a bonus (or reward) of $2000 and the other a bonus of $3000. Clearly, there is inequity, and there will be dissatisfaction.

Equity theory claims that you will develop, maintain, and be satisfied with relationships that are equitable. You will not develop, will be dissatisfied with, or will terminate relationships that are inequitable. The greater the inequity is, the greater the dissatisfaction and the greater the likelihood that the relationship will end.

Do note, however, that equity is consistent with the capitalistic orientation of Western culture, where each person is paid, for example, according to his or her contributions. The more you contribute to the organization or the relationship, the more rewards you should get out of it. In other cultures, a principle of equality or need might operate. Under equality, each person would get equal rewards, regardless of their own individual contribution. Under need, each person would get rewards according to his or her individual need (Moghaddam, Taylor, and Wright 1993). Thus, in the United States equity is found to be highly correlated with relationship satisfaction and with relationship endurance (Schafer and Keith 1980) but, in Europe equity seems to be unrelated to satisfaction or endurance (Lujansky and Mikula 1983).

In one study, for example, subjects in the United States and India were asked to read situations in which a bonus was to be distributed between a worker who contributed a great deal but who was economically well-off and a worker who contributed much less but who was economically needy. Their choices were to distribute the bonus equitably (on the basis of contribution), equally, or in terms of need (Berman, Murphy-Erman, and Singh 1985; Moghaddam, Taylor, and Wright 1993). The results are given in Table 17.2.

Table 17.2
Equity in Cultural Perspectives

METHOD FOR ALLOCATING BONUS	SUBJECTS FROM UNITED STATES	SUBJECTS FROM INDIA
Equity	49%	16%
Equality	34%	32%
Need	16%	51%

DEVELOPING RELATIONSHIPS: THE FIRST ENCOUNTER

Perhaps the most difficult and yet most important aspect of relationship development is the beginning—meeting the person, presenting yourself, and somehow generating movement, which, in our earlier model, would be to exit or to progress to a more intimate stage. In *Intimate Relations* (1973), Murray Davis notes that the first encounter consists of six steps. In addition to reviewing these steps, we consider some communication guidelines or principles (both for nonverbal and verbal interaction) that should help make the first encounter more effective.

Examine the Qualifiers   The first step is to examine the qualifiers, those qualities that make the person you wish to encounter an appropriate choice. Some qualifiers are open to easy inspection, such as beauty, style of clothes, jewelry, and the like. Other qualifiers are hidden from easy inspection, such as personality, health, wealth, talent, and intelligence. Qualifiers tell you something about who the person is and help you decide whether to pursue this initial encounter.

Determine Clearance   Try to discover if this person is available for an encounter. Is the person wearing a wedding ring? Does the person seem to be waiting for someone else?

Open the Encounter   Open the encounter, both nonverbally and verbally. Look for indications that the other person is ready to engage in a more extended encounter. If yes-no answers are given to your questions or if eye contact is not maintained, then you have a pretty good indication that this person is not open to a continued encounter with you at this time. If, however, the person responds at length or asks you questions in return, then you have some feedback that says, "Continue."

If you are perceived as being selective—neither hard to get nor easy to get—you will appear more desirable than people who are at the extremes, that is, who are nonselective or extremely selective (Wright and Contrada 1986).

Use an Integrating Topic   An integrating topic is one that will interest the other person and you and will integrate or unite the two of you. Look for **free information**—something about the person that you observe or that is dropped into the conversation—for example, a college ring or beeper. This will suggest a possible topic of conversation. Similarly, a casual remark may include the person's occupation, area of study, or sports interests, any of which can be used as a takeoff point for further interaction. Ask questions (none that are too prying, of course) to discover more about this person and to communicate your interest.

Create a Favorable Impression   Display what is called a "come-on self," a part of you that is inviting, engaging, and interesting to another person. Display a part of you that will make the other person want to continue the encounter.

Establish a Second Meeting   If you and your new friend or romantic partner seem to be getting along, then set up a second meeting. This may vary from a general type of meeting ("Do you always eat here on Fridays?") to a specific meeting ("How about going to the beach next Saturday?"). The box "How to Ask for a Date" discusses the process of setting up a special type of second meeting or any "date."

During the first encounter, put into operation all the interpersonal communication principles you have already learned. Here are a few additional suggestions geared specifically to the first encounter. Although they are discussed in terms of the nonverbal encounter and the verbal encounter, recognize that the two must be integrated in any effective initial meeting.

THE NONVERBAL ENCOUNTER

Nonverbal communication concerns every aspect of yourself that sends messages to another person. On the basis of these messages, the other person forms an impression of you—one that will be quickly and firmly established.

- *Establish eye contact.* Eye contact is the first nonverbal signal to send. The eyes communicate an awareness of and interest in the other person. While maintaining eye contact, smile and further signal your interest in and your positive response to the other person.
- *Concentrate your focus.* The rest of the room should be nonverbally shut off from awareness. Be careful, however, not to focus so directly that you make the person uncomfortable.
- *Decrease the physical distance between the two of you.* Approach (though not to the point of discomfort) so that your interest in making contact is obvious.
- *Maintain an open posture that communicates openness,* a willingness to interact with the other person. Hands crossed over the chest or clutched around the stomach are often taken to signal unwillingness to let others enter your space.
- *Reinforce positive behaviors.* Reinforce those behaviors of the other person that signal interest and a reciprocal willingness to make contact. Reinforce them by responding positively; again, nod, smile, or somehow indicate your favorable reaction.
- *Avoid overexposure.* Nonverbal communication works to make contact or to signal interest, but it can cause problems if it is excessive or if it is not followed by more direct communication. Consequently, if you intend to make verbal contact, do so after a relatively short time or wait until another time.

THE VERBAL ENCOUNTER

- *Introduce yourself.* Try to avoid trite opening lines. It is probably best simply to say, "Hi, my name is Pat."
- *Focus the conversation on the other person.* Get the other person involved in talking about himself or herself; few people enjoy talking about anything more.

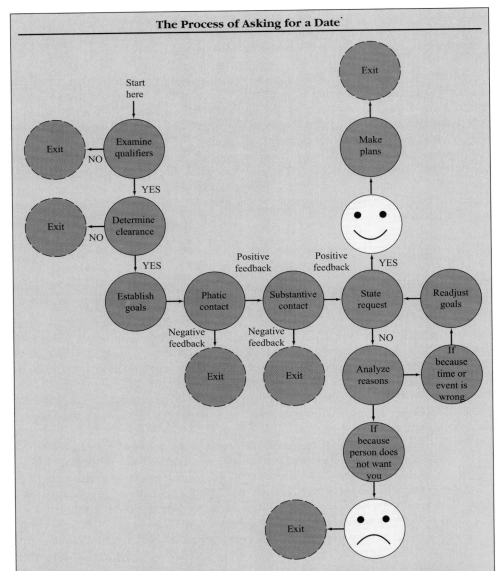

The Process of Asking for a Date

This flow diagram has been developed in an effort to summarize some of the ways of making contact and, at the same time, to answer a question students frequently ask. It is designed to identify some of the major steps or processes in asking for a date, not to specify an unvarying sequence of specifics that must occur. Begin at "Start here" and proceed through the diagram according to the answers and feedback you get from your prospective date.

How accurately does this diagram represent the process of asking for a date? What steps or processes would you add? Delete? Which steps are essential? Which steps are optional? What *one* factor do you feel best distinguishes effective from ineffective date asking?

- *Exchange favors/rewards.* Be sincere but complimentary and positive. Stress the positives. Such behavior contributes to a positive first impression simply because people are attracted more to a positive than to a negative person and like a positive person better.
- *Be energetic.* Demonstrate your high energy level by responding facially with appropriate affect, smiling, talking in a varied manner, being flexible with your body posture and gestures, asking questions as appropriate, and otherwise demonstrating your active involvement.
- *Avoid negative and too intimate self-disclosures.* Enter a relationship gradually and gracefully. Disclosures should come gradually and along with reciprocated disclosures. Anything too intimate or too negative early in the relationship will create a negative image.
- *Avoid yes-no questions, yes-no answers, and rapid-fire questions.* Ask open-ended questions that the receiver may answer at some length. Similarly, respond with answers more complete than simply yes or no. Be careful, too, that your questions don't appear to be an interrogation.

SUMMARY: UNIT IN BRIEF

Relationship Theories

Attraction theory

We develop relationships with those we consider attractive (physically and in personality), who are physically close to us, and who are similar to us.

Affinity-seeking strategies: a wide variety of behaviors designed to get people to like us and to think positively of us, for example:

- being altruistic
- appearing to be in control
- presenting oneself as socially equal
- presenting oneself as relaxed and comfortable

Reinforcement theory

We develop relationships with those who reinforce or reward us. We also come to like those we reward.

Social exchange theory

We develop relationships that enable us to maximize profits, relationships from which we derive more rewards than costs.

Equity theory

We develop and maintain relationships in which our ratio of rewards compared to costs is approximately equal to our partner's.

Steps in Initiating Relationships

- Examine the qualifiers
- Determine clearance.
- Open the encounter.
- Select and introduce into conversation an integrating topic.
- Create a favorable impression.
- Establish a second meeting.

Nonverbally, for example:

- Establish eye contact.
- Concentrate your focus.
- Maintain an open posture.

Verbally, for example:

- Introduce yourself.
- Focus conversation on the other person.
- Exchange favors/rewards.

THINKING CRITICALLY ABOUT RELATIONSHIP DEVELOPMENT AND INVOLVEMENT

1. In what ways can proximity account for your current relationships? Do you find the concept of "mere exposure" useful in explaining them?

2. Do you enter relationships with those who are similar to you or who complement you? What types of similarities do you find especially important to friendship relationships? To romantic relationships? How does complementarity figure into your relationships?

3. Examine the list of affinity-seeking strategies. Are there any strategies that are not included in Table 17.1? Are strategies included that you find ineffective? Which strategies work best *for* you? Which strategies work best *on* you? Do these strategies fit into the general categories of attractiveness, proximity, reinforcement, similarity, and complementarity? Which of these five categories is the most significant in terms of affinity-seeking strategies?

4. Research on affinity-seeking strategies shows that students feel more positive about their instructor when he or she uses certain affinity-seeking strategies (Roach 1991). What affinity-seeking strategies do you think would work best? Might some backfire? What suggestions would you offer your instructor about using or not using affinity-seeking strategies?

5. Are there ethical implications for the use of affinity-seeking strategies? When is the use of a given strategy ethical? When is it unethical? For example, is it bethical for you to use these strategies consciously to get someone to go on a date with you? To get someone to vote for you?

6. How does reinforcement theory work in your own relationships? Do you find that you develop relationships with those who reward you and avoid relationships with those who do not reward or who actually punish you? Do you find that you also come to like those you reward?

7. Select two friendship or romantic relationships, one that you value highly and one that has deteriorated and dissolved. For each, do a cost-benefit (rewards) analysis. In one column, identify all the costs, and in the other column identify all the benefits or rewards you derive from the highly valued relationship. Do the same cost-benefit analysis for the relationship that has dissolved. How do the benefits (their number and especially their importance) compare with the costs in both relationships?

8. Do you compare the rewards and costs of your current relationships with the potential rewards and costs you might derive from alternative relationships? Do you comparison shop in your relationships?

9. How equitable are your current relationships? Are you more satisfied with your equitable relationships than with your inequitable relationships?

10. How would you design a research study to seek answers to the following questions?

   - Do men and women find the same personality characteristics in friends and romantic partners attractive? If not, which personality characteristics are especially attractive to men and which are especially attractive to women?
   - Which affinity-seeking strategies are especially important during the early stages of a relationship, say, at the contact and the involvement stages?
   - What types of reinforcement would be especially powerful with students in this class? Would the reinforcements have the same influence in both friendship and romantic situations?

- Can social exchange theory account for the relationships (past and present) of those in this class?
- When a relationship is not equitable, which person is more likely to leave first—the one who is getting more profit than deserved or the one getting less profit?

EXPERIENTIAL VEHICLES

17.1 THE GREETING CARD

The objectives of this exercise are (1) to become familiar with some of the popular conceptions and sentiments concerning interpersonal relationships and (2) to review a wide variety of concepts important in the study of interpersonal relationships.

Bring to class one greeting card that expresses a sentiment that is significant for any one of the reasons listed below. This list is not exhaustive, and the items are not mutually exclusive. Remember that greeting card sentiments are communicated through a number of different channels. Therefore, consider the sentiments communicated through the verbal message, but also consider the messages communicated through the illustrations, the colors, the physical form of the card, the type of print, and so on.

- The card expresses a popular sentiment that is correct or true.
- The card expresses a popular sentiment that is incorrect or false.
- The card expresses a sentiment that incorporates a concept or theory that can assist us in understanding interpersonal relationships.
- The card illustrates a common problem in interpersonal relationships.
- The card illustrates a useful strategy for relationship development, maintenance, repair, or dissolution.
- The card suggests a useful question (or hypothesis for scientific investigation) that should be asked in the study of interpersonal relationships.
- The card supports or contradicts some currently accepted theory of interpersonal relationships.

Be prepared to give a brief (three-to-five-minute) discussion of the greeting card sentiment as it relates to the study of interpersonal relationships.

17.2 MATE PREFERENCES: I PREFER SOMEONE WHO. . .

This exercise is designed to stimulate a sharing of perspectives on what we want in a mate. Each of the choices here concerns issues considered throughout this text. In a gamelike setting, the importance of money, similarity, self-disclosure, and conflict strategies to relational desirability is explored.

"I Prefer Someone Who . . . " is played in a group of four to six people. The general procedure is as follows:

1. Each member individually ranks each of the three alternatives in the 15 groupings listed, using 1 for the most preferred and 3 for the least preferred choice.

2. Then the group considers each of the 15 categories, with each member giving her or his rank order.

3. Members may refuse to reveal their rankings for any category by saying "I pass." The group is not permitted to question the reasons for any member's passing.

4. When a member has revealed rankings for a category, the group members may ask questions relevant to that category. These questions may be asked after any individual member's response or may be reserved until all members have given their rankings for a particular category.

5. The group may establish any additional rules it wishes (for example, appointing a leader or establishing time limits).

I prefer someone who . . .

1. _____ is similar to me in race, religion, and nationality.
   _____ is similar to me in attitudes, values, and opinions.
   _____ is similar to me in personality.

2. _____ reduces my loneliness.
   _____ enhances my self-esteem.
   _____ increases my self-knowledge and self-growth.

3. _____ is deceptive.
   _____ is jealous.
   _____ is boring.

4. _____ reveals his or her innermost secrets to me.
   _____ reveals some secrets but keeps an equal number hidden from me.
   _____ reveals hardly anything about his or her innermost secrets.

5. _____ keeps confidences.
   _____ has a sense of humor.
   _____ is intelligent.

6. _____ thinks money is most important.
   _____ thinks friendship is most important.
   _____ thinks job satisfaction is most important.

7. _____ talks more than listens.
   _____ talks and listens about equally.
   _____ listens more than talks.

8. _____ dresses at the cutting edge of fashion.
   _____ dresses conventionally.
   _____ dresses very conservatively.

9. _____ is empathic.
   _____ is supportive.
   _____ is confident.

10. _____ wants to make most of the major decisions.
    _____ wants to share equally in making the major decisions.
    _____ wants me to make most of the major decisions.

11. _____ is unattractive.
    _____ is unemotional.
    _____ is uncommunicative.

12. _____ stands up for me in my absence.
    _____ trusts me.
    _____ tries to make me happy when I'm sad.

13. _____ views love as a game, as fun; focuses on entertainment and excitement.
    _____ views love as peaceful and slow; focuses on friendship and companionship.
    _____ views love as physical and erotic; focuses on beauty and sexuality.

14. _____ has great sex appeal.
    _____ has great intellectual appeal.
    _____ has lots of money

15. _____ is like a tiger.
    _____ is like a puppy dog.
    _____ is like a farm horse.

Questions for Discussion

In discussing the choices of the group members, consider some or all of the following issues:

1. What are the reasons for the choices? Where did these reasons come from? Were they acquired from parents, an older sibling, a teacher? Be sure to consider the reasons for the least preferred choices as well as the most preferred. Both are revealing.
2. Do men and women make similar choices? Explain.
3. Does an ideal man or an ideal woman emerge from the composite rankings? Does a least preferred man or a least preferred woman emerge? If so, describe these types as specifically as possible.
4. If the title of this exercise were "I am someone who. . . ," how similarly or differently would you respond to these choices? How close to yourself is your ideal mate?
5. Did some of the choices make you aware of preferences you didn't realize you had? If other people looked at your choices, what kind of person would they think you were?
6. Which are the three most important categories? Why are they so important to you?
7. In which of these categories do communication skills figure prominently? Explain.

UNIT 18

Relationship Deterioration and Dissolution

UNIT OBJECTIVES

AFTER COMPLETING THIS UNIT, YOU SHOULD BE ABLE TO:

1. Explain the nature of relationship deterioration
2. Explain at least six causes of relationship deterioration
3. Identify at least five patterns of communication that characterize relationship deterioration
4. Explain how the attraction, reinforcement, social exchange, and equity theories explain relationship deterioration
5. Explain the suggestions for dealing with the end of a relationship

Just as a relationship may grow and progress, becoming stronger and more meaningful, it can also wane and regress, becoming weaker and less meaningful. In this unit, we look at relationship deterioration and some of its causes. With this as a base, we then examine the communication patterns that characterize relationship deterioration. Last, we consider some suggestions that may prove useful if the relationship does end.

Even the consideration of dissolution as an important phase of interpersonal relationships implies that this is a viable option. But, in other cultures, relationships—such as marriage—are forever and cannot be dissolved if things begin to go wrong. More important to such cultures are such issues as "How do you maintain a relationship that has problems?" "What can you do to exist within an unpleasant relationship?" "How can you repair a relationship that is troubled?" (Moghaddam, Taylor, and Wright 1993).

THE NATURE OF RELATIONSHIP DETERIORATION

Relationship deterioration refers to the weakening of the bonds that hold people together. At one extreme, the relationship may become only slightly less intimate; at the other extreme, the parties separate and the relationship is completely dissolved. Between these two extremes lie infinite variations, which we group into stages for convenience.

The process of deterioration may be gradual or sudden. Gradual deterioration might occur in a situation in which one of the parties in a relationship develops close ties with a new intimate, and this new relationship gradually pushes out the old intimate. Sudden deterioration might occur when a rule that was essential to the relationship (for example, the rule of complete fidelity) is broken and both realize that the relationship cannot be sustained.

THE STAGES OF DETERIORATION

Interpersonal researcher Steve Duck (1986) proposes that you can best understand the process of deterioration by identifying the phases you might go through in passing from deterioration to dissolution. The first process begins at the **breakdown phase,** during which you experience dissatisfaction with the relationship and with each other.

During the **intrapsychic phase,** you brood privately about your dissatisfaction with the relationship and with each other. Gradually, you may share your feelings, initially with relative strangers and then eventually with close friends.

During the **dyadic phase,** you discuss your problems with your partner and perhaps attempt to correct the difficulties between you.

If the problems cannot be worked out, and if you decide to exit the relationship, you enter the **social phase,** during which you would share the dissatisfaction and the decision to exit the relationship with others. During this phase, you might try to enlist the support of others. You would seek understanding, empathy, and the social support that will help you through the breakup.

The fifth and final phase is the **grave-dressing phase,** during which you might create a kind of history of the relationship—its beginnings, its development, and its eventual dissolution. Your intention here is to distance yourself from the relationship at least a bit and to allow others to look at you favorably, or at least not too negatively.

THE STRATEGIES OF DISENGAGEMENT

When you wish to exit a relationship, you need some way of explaining this—to yourself as well as to your partner. That is, you must develop a strategy for getting out of a relationship that you no longer find satisfying or profitable. Table 18.1 identifies five major disengagement strategies (Cody 1982). As you read down the table, note that some strategies work better than others, depending on your ultimate aim. For example, the former partners are more likely to remain friends if de-escalation is used; they are not likely to remain friends after a strategy of justification or avoidance (Banks et al. 1987). You may also find it interesting to identify the disengagement strategies you have heard of or used yourself and see how they fit in with these five types.

THE NEGATIVES AND THE POSITIVES

When relationships deteriorate or break up, a variety of negative outcomes may occur. At the most obvious level, there is a loss of all the positives you enjoyed as a result of the relationship. Regardless of how unsatisfying the relationship might ultimately have been, it probably also had many good aspects, which are now lost.

There is also, generally, a loss of self-esteem. You may feel unworthy or perhaps guilty. You may blame yourself for doing the wrong things, not doing the right things, or being responsible for the loss you now confront. And, of course, there are likely to be friends and family members who will give you a hard time, perhaps implying that you are to blame.

Further, there are the practical issues. Most relationship breakups have financial implications, for example, and you may now encounter financial problems. Paying the rent, tuition, or outstanding loans by yourself may prove difficult. If the relationship is a marriage, then there are legal and perhaps religious implications of the breakup. If there are children, the situation becomes even more complicated.

Nevertheless, not all relationships should be sustained. Not all breakups are bad, and few, if any, bad breakups are entirely bad. In the midst of a breakup, this may be difficult to appreciate, but in retrospect it is almost always true.

Some relationships are unproductive for one or both parties, and a breakup is often the best alternative. A breakup may provide an opportunity for the individuals to regain their independence and to become self-reliant again. Some relationships are so absorbing that there is little time for reflection on oneself, on others, and on the relationship itself (see Unit 22). Sometimes distance helps. A breakup may also provide the opportunity to develop new associations and to explore different types of relationships with different types of people.

The major point to be made here is that relational deterioration need not have only negative consequences. For the most part, it is up to the individual to draw out of any decaying relationship some positive and productive lessons.

Table 18.1
Five Disengagement Strategies[*]

STRATEGY	FUNCTION	EXAMPLES
Positive tone	To maintain a positive relationship. To express positive feelings for the other person	"I really care for you a great deal but I'm not ready for such an intense relationship."
Negative identity management	To blame the other person for the breakup. To absolve oneself of the blame for the breakup	"I can't stand your jealousy, your constant suspicions, your checking up on me. I need my freedom."
Justification	To give reasons for the breakup	"I'm going away to college for four years; there's no point in not dating others."
Behavioral de-escalation	To reduce the intensity of the relationship	Avoidance; cutting down on phone calls; reducing time spent together, especially time alone
De-escalation	To reduce the exclusivity and hence the intensity of the relationship	"I'm just not ready for so exclusive a relationship. I think we should see other people."

[*]Based on Michael J. Cody, "A Typology of Disengagement Strategies and an Examination of the Role Intimacy, Reactions to Inequity and Relational Problems Play in Strategy Selection," *Communication Monographs* 49 (1982): 148–170.

SOME CAUSES OF RELATIONSHIP DETERIORATION

Because there are at least as many reasons for relationship deterioration as there are people in relationships, it is extremely difficult to identify specific causes for any specific relationship deterioration. Still, some general causes—applicable to a wide variety of relationship breakups—may be identified.

All these "causes" can also be *effects* of relationship deterioration. For example, when things start to go sour, the individuals may remove themselves physically from one another in response. This physical separation in turn causes further deterioration by driving the individuals further apart emotionally and psychologically. Similarly, the degree of mutual commitment between partners may lessen as other signs of deterioration appear. In turn, the lack of commitment may also cause further deterioration: for example, by lessening the individuals' need to resolve conflicts or to leave the channels of communication open.

In addition to considering the factors noted here, recall that the factors that are important in establishing relationships, discussed in Unit 16, may, when no longer present, be cause for relationship deterioration. For example, when loneliness is no longer reduced by the relationship, when one or both of the individuals feel lonely frequently or for prolonged periods, the relationship may well be on the road to decay because it is not serving a function it was created to serve.

EXCESSIVE INTIMACY CLAIMS

In most relationships—especially those of considerable intensity—the members make extensive intimacy claims on each other. Such claims may include expectations that the partner will sympathize and empathize, attend to self-disclosures with total absorption, or share the other's preferences with equal intensity. These intimacy claims often restrict personal freedom and may take the form of possessiveness. To be always responsive, always sympathetic, always loving, always attentive is more than many can manage. In some relationships, the intimacy claims and demands are so great that the partners' individual identities may be in danger of being absorbed or destroyed.

THIRD-PARTY RELATIONSHIPS

Some relationships are established and maintained to maximize pleasure and minimize pain. When this ceases to be the case, the relationship stands little chance of survival. These needs are so great that when they are not met within the existing relationship, their fulfillment will be sought elsewhere. When a new relationship serves these needs better, the old relationship may deteriorate. At times, this may be a romantic interest (discussed further under the heading "Sex-Related Problems"); at other times, the new relationship may be with a parent or, frequently, a child. When an individual's need for affection or attention, once supplied by the other party in the primary relationship, are now supplied by a friend or a child, the primary relationship may be in trouble.

RELATIONSHIP CHANGES

In addition to those factors that in one form help to establish a relationship and in another form help to dissolve it, there are a number of changes that might be mentioned as causes of relationship deterioration.

The development of incompatible attitudes, vastly different intellectual interests and abilities, and major goal changes may contribute to relationship deterioration. Similarly, changes in behavior may create difficulties; for example, the person who once devoted much time to the other person and to the development of the relationship and who then becomes totally absorbed in business or in school is going to face significant repercussions. The person who becomes addicted to drugs or alcohol will likewise present the relationship with a serious problem.

UNDEFINED EXPECTATIONS

"Unresolved disputes over 'who is in charge of what,'" notes William Lederer (1984), "[are] one of the most powerful and prevalent causes of conflicts and divorces." Often, conflicts over such trivial issues as who does the dishes or who walks the dog mask resentment and hostility concerning some more significant unresolved expectation.

At times, the expectations each person has of the other may be unrealistic, and when reality enters the relationship, conflict may ensue. This type of situation often occurs early in a relationship, when, for example, the individuals think they will want to spend all their time together. When it is discovered that neither one does, each resents this "lessening" of feeling in the other. The resolution of such conflicts lies in demonstrating that the original expectations are unrealistic and that realistic and satisfying ones can be substituted.

Another kind of undefined expectation may involve the traditional sex-role stereotypes. This finding surely contradicts the move toward equality verbally affirmed by most educated men and women. For example, according to Sara Yogev (1987):

> traditional sex-role stereotypes regarding the spouse are closely related to marital satisfaction and . . . deviations from the expected psychological characteristic in which the man is superior to his wife may reduce the level of marital satisfaction for both men and women but more so for women. Thus, while one sees behavioural-social changes (i.e., more women are employed, some even in male-dominated fields), psychological change does not follow immediately on the heels of the behavioural change for either sex.

SEX-RELATED PROBLEMS

Few relationships are free of sexual problems and differences that generate conflicts. In fact, sexual problems rank among the top three problems in almost all studies of newlyweds (Blumstein and Schwartz 1983). When these same couples are surveyed later in their relationship, the sexual problems have not gone away; they are just discussed less. Apparently, people resign themselves to living with the problems. In one survey, for example, 80 percent of the respondents identified their marriages as either "very happy" or "happy," but some 90 percent said they had sexual problems (Freedman 1978).

Although sexual frequency is not related to relationship breakdown, sexual satisfaction is. Research clearly shows that it is the quality, not the quantity, of a sexual relationship that is crucial (Blumstein and Schwartz 1983). When the quality is poor, outside affairs may be sought. Again, the research is clear: extrarelational affairs contribute significantly to breakups for all couples, whether married or cohabiting (Blumstein and Schwartz 1983).

Work-Related Problems

Problems associated with either partner's job often lead to difficulties within the relationship. This is true for all types of couples. With heterosexual couples (both marrieds and cohabitants), if the man is disturbed about the woman's job—for example, if she earns a great deal more than he does or devotes a great deal of time to the job—the relationship is in considerable trouble. This is true whether the relationship is in its early stages or is well established (Blumstein and Schwartz 1983).

A *New York Times* survey (24 February 1988), based on interviews with 1870 people throughout the United States, found that "even though more women are in the work force and have less time at home, they are still the primary care-givers and the people who pay attention to how, when, what, and where their families eat. . . . The idea of equality at home," the report concludes, "is an illusion." Too often the man expects the woman to work but neither reduces his expectations concerning her household responsibilities nor agrees to assume any of them himself. The man becomes resentful if the woman does not fulfill these expectations, and the woman becomes resentful if she takes on both outside work and full household duties. It is a no-win situation, and the relationship suffers as a result.

Financial Difficulties

In surveys of problems among couples, financial difficulties loom large. Money is a major taboo topic for couples beginning a relationship, yet it proves to be one of the causes of major problems they face as they settle into their relationship. One-fourth to one-third of all couples rank money as their primary problem; almost all rank it as one of their major problems.

Perhaps the main reason money is so important in relationships is its close connection with power. Money brings power in relationships, as it does in business. The person bringing in the most money wields the most power. This person has the final say, for example, on the purchase of expensive items as well as on decisions having nothing to do with money. The power that money brings quickly spreads to nonfinancial issues as well.

Money also creates problems by virtue of the fact that men and women view it differently (Blumstein and Schwartz 1983). To many men, money is power; to many women, it is security and independence. To men, money is accumulated to exert power and influence; to women, money is accumulated to achieve a sense of security and to reduce dependence on others. Conflicts over the way the couple's money is to be spent or invested can easily result from such different perceptions.

The most general equation to represent this difficulty is this:

DISSATISFACTION WITH MONEY = DISSATISFACTION WITH THE RELATIONSHIP

This is true for married and cohabiting couples and gay male couples but not for lesbian couples, who seem to care a great deal less about financial matters (Blumstein and Schwartz 1983). This difference has led some researchers to postulate (though without conclusive evidence) that the concern over money and its equation with power and relational satisfaction are largely male attitudes.

COMMUNICATION PATTERNS IN RELATIONSHIP DETERIORATION

Like relationship development, relationship deterioration involves special communication patterns. These patterns are in part a response to the deterioration; we communicate the way we do because we feel that our relationship is in trouble. However, these patterns are also causative: the communication patterns we use largely determine the fate of our relationship.

WITHDRAWAL

Perhaps the easiest communication pattern to see is that of withdrawal (Miller and Parks 1982). Nonverbally, this withdrawal is seen in the greater space each person requires and the speed with which tempers and other signs of disturbance are aroused when that space is invaded. Other nonverbal signs of withdrawal include a decrease in eye contact, touching, similarities in clothing, and display of items such as bracelets, photographs, and rings (Knapp and Vangelisti 1992).

Verbally, withdrawal is marked by decreased desire to talk and listen. At times, phatic communication (or something resembling it) is used not as a preliminary to serious conversation but as an alternative, perhaps to avoid confronting the serious issues.

DECLINE IN SELF-DISCLOSURE

Self-disclosing communications decline significantly. Self-disclosure may not be thought worth the effort if the relationship is dying. You might limit your self-disclosures because you feel that the other person may not accept them or can no longer be trusted to respond supportively and empathically.

DEFENSIVENESS

Where once supportiveness characterized the relationship, defensiveness is now more prevalent. In many deteriorating relationships, each party blames the other. We want to

Of all the communication patterns characteristic of relational deterioration, which do you think is the most damaging to the ultimate survival of the relationship? Do you observe differences in the communication patterns of men and women during relationship deterioration? Would your answers be different if you were describing a romantic relationship? a parent-child relationship?

protect our egos; we want to continue believing that we are not to blame, that it is not our fault. Perhaps you want especially to believe that you are not the cause of another person's and your own pain.

DECEPTION

Deception increases as relationships break down. Sometimes this takes the form of clear-cut lies that may be used to avoid arguments over such things as staying out all night, not calling, or being seen in the wrong place with the wrong person. At other times, lies may be used because of a feeling of shame; you might not want the other person to think less of you. Perhaps you want to save the relationship and do not want to add another obstacle. One of the problems with deception is that it has a way of escalating. Eventually, a climate of distrust and disbelief comes to characterize the relationship.

EVALUATIVE BEHAVIORS

During deterioration, there is likely to be an increase in negative and a decrease in positive evaluation. Where once you may have praised the other's behaviors or ideas, you now criticize them. Often the behaviors have not changed significantly; what has changed is your way of looking at them. What was once a cute habit now becomes annoying; what was once seen as "different" now becomes inconsiderate. This negative evaluation frequently leads to outright fighting and conflict; although conflict is not necessarily bad, in deteriorating relationships the conflict is often left unresolved.

During relational deterioration, there is also a marked change in the types of requests made (Lederer 1984). When a relationship is deteriorating, requests for pleasurable behaviors decrease ("Will you fix me my favorite dessert?"). At the same time, requests to stop unpleasant or negative behaviors increase ("Will you stop monopolizing the phone every evening?").

Another symptom is the sometimes gradual, sometimes sudden decrease in the social niceties that accompany requests, a progression from "Would you please make me a cup of coffee, honey?" to "Get me some coffee, will you?" to "Where's my coffee?"

Figure 18.1 summarizes the changes in communication (discussed in this unit and the previous two) that take place as we move toward or away from intimacy. The general and most important point this figure makes is that communication effectiveness and satisfaction increase as we move toward intimacy and decrease as we move away from intimacy.

WHAT THE THEORIES SAY ABOUT RELATIONSHIP DETERIORATION AND DISSOLUTION

Attraction theory holds that relationships deteriorate and may perhaps dissolve when the attraction the individuals felt for each other, which is still important to them, has faded to some significant degree. When relationships break up, it is the more attractive person who leaves (Blumstein and Schwartz 1983). There is no denying the power of attractiveness in the development of relationships and the influence of its loss to the deterioration of relationships.

Reinforcement theory holds that relationships deteriorate when the relationship is no longer seen as rewarding and may dissolve if the relationship becomes more punishing than rewarding.

According to social exchange theory, your relationship will deteriorate if the costs exceed the rewards. When this happens, there is a tendency to reduce the rewards. For example, compliments, once given frequently and sincerely, are now rare; positive stroking is minimal; there is little eye contact and few smiles. This reduction in rewards further tips the scales toward deterioration.

The relationship will also become unstable and may begin to deteriorate if the alternatives (your available options) are seen as more rewarding than your current relationship. However, even if your relationship is less than you expected it to be, it will probably not be dissolved unless you perceive that another relationship (or being alone) will provide a greater profit.

According to equity theory, you stay in relationships in which you receive rewards in proportion to your costs; a person who pays more of the costs should obtain more of the rewards. When a relationship becomes inequitable, that is, when one person derives a disproportionate share of the rewards or suffers an excessive share of the costs, the relationship suffers.

According to some research, women are more likely to engage in extramarital affairs when they perceive their relationship as inequitable (Prins, Buunk, and

THE MOVEMENT IS TOWARD INTIMACY WHEN:

attractiveness of alternatives decreases

other-orientation increases

withdrawal decreases

empathy expressions increase

positive exchanges increase

loving/liking becomes less conditional

interpersonal breadth increases

interpersonal depth increases

uncertainty decreases

self-disclosure and openness increase

use of private language increases

defensiveness decreases and supportiveness increases

behavioral synchrony increases

deception decreases

negative request behaviors decrease and positive request behaviors increase

power to punish and reward increases

immediacy increases

cherishing behaviors increase

nonverbal communication carries more meaning

commitment increases

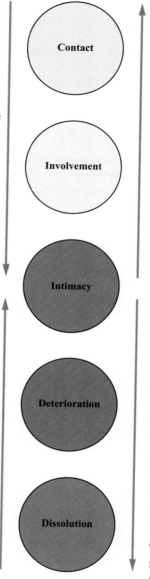

Contact

Involvement

Intimacy

Deterioration

Dissolution

THE MOVEMENT IS AWAY FROM INTIMACY WHEN:

attractiveness of alternatives increases

other-orientation decreases

withdrawal increases

empathy expressions decrease

negative exchanges increase

loving/liking becomes more conditional

interpersonal breadth decreases

interpersonal depth decreases

uncertainty increases

self-disclosure and openness decrease

use of private language decreases

defensiveness increases and supportiveness decreases

behavioral synchrony decreases

deception increases

negative request behaviors increase and positive request behaviors decrease

power to punish and reward decreases

immediacy decreases

cherishing behaviors decrease

nonverbal communication carries less meaning

commitment decreases

Figure 18.1
Communication in relationships.

Van Yperen 1994). Perceptions of inequity by men, however, did not influence their likelihood of engaging in extramarital affairs. Further, women are more likely than men to break up a relationship as a result of their own extrarelational affair (Janus and Janus 1993).

When partners perceive their relationship to be equitable, they will continue to date, live together, or marry. When the relationship is not perceived to be equitable, the relationship suffers, and it may well deteriorate.

IF THE RELATIONSHIP ENDS

Some relationships, of course, do end. Sometimes there is simply not enough to hold the couple together. Sometimes there are problems that cannot be resolved. Sometimes the costs are too high and the rewards too few, or the relationship is recognized as destructive and escape seems the only alternative. Regardless of the specific reason, relationship breakups are difficult to deal with and cause considerable stress. You are likely to experience high levels of distress over the breakup of a relationship in which you were satisfied, were close to your partner, had dated your partner for a long time, and felt it would not be easy to replace the relationship with another one (Simpson 1987). Not surprisingly, marriages are more complex and more difficult to dissolve than simple dating relationships (Cupach and Metts 1986).

Given both the inevitability that some relationships will break up and the importance of such breakups, here are some suggestions to ease the difficulty that is sure to be experienced. These suggestions apply to the termination of any type of relationship— between friends or lovers, through death, separation, or breakup.

BREAK THE LONELINESS-DEPRESSION CYCLE

The two most common feelings following the end of a relationship are loneliness and depression. These feelings are significant; treat them seriously. Realize that depression often leads to serious illness. In most cases, fortunately, loneliness and depression are temporary. Depression, for example, usually does not last longer than three or four days. Similarly, the loneliness that follows a breakup is generally linked to this specific situation and will fade when the situation changes. When depression does last, is especially deep, or disturbs your normal functioning, it is time for professional help.

TAKE TIME OUT

Resist the temptation to jump into a new relationship while the old one is still warm or before a new one can be assessed with some objectivity. At the same time, resist swearing off all relationships. Neither extreme works well.

Take time out for yourself. Renew your relationship with yourself. If you were in a long-term relationship, you probably saw yourself as part of a team, as part of a couple. Now get to know yourself as a unique individual, standing alone at present but fully capable of entering a meaningful relationship in the near future.

BOLSTER SELF-ESTEEM

When relationships fail, self-esteem often declines. You may feel guilty for having caused the breakup or inadequate for not holding on to the relationship. You may feel unwanted and unloved. Your task is to regain the positive self-image needed to function effectively (see Unit 7).

Recognize, too, that having been in a relationship that failed—even if you view yourself as the primary cause of the breakup—does not mean that you are a failure. Neither does it mean that you cannot succeed in a new and different relationship. It does mean that something went wrong with this one relationship. And (ideally) it was a failure from which you have learned something important about yourself and about your relationship behavior.

REMOVE OR AVOID UNCOMFORTABLE SYMBOLS

After any breakup, there are a variety of reminders—photographs, gifts, and letters, for example. Resist the temptation to burn all the old photographs and love letters; instead, remove them. Give them to a friend to hold or put them in a closet where you will not see them. If possible, avoid places you frequented together. These symbols will bring back uncomfortable memories. After you have achieved some emotional distance, you can go back and enjoy these as reminders of a once-pleasant relationship. Support for this suggestion comes from research showing that the more vivid your memory of a broken love

If you were ever in a relationship that eventually dissolved, did you learn anything that might prove helpful to others? In hindsight—which is always 20/20—would you have done anything differently?

affair—a memory greatly aided by these relationship symbols—the greater your depression is likely to be (Harvey, Flanary, and Morgan 1986).

SEEK SUPPORT

Although many people feel they should bear their burdens alone (men, in particular, have been taught that this is the only "manly" way to handle things), seeking the support of others is one of the best antidotes to the unhappiness caused when a relationship ends. Tell your friends and family of your situation—in only general terms, if you prefer—and make it clear that you need support right now. Seek out people who are positive and nurturing while avoiding negative individuals who will paint the world in even darker tones. Make the distinction between seeking support and seeking advice. If you feel you need advice, seek out a professional.

AVOID REPEATING NEGATIVE PATTERNS

Many people repeat their mistakes. They enter second and third relationships with the same blinders, faulty preconceptions, and unrealistic expectations with which they entered earlier relationships. The knowledge gained from failed relationships may prevent repetition of the same patterns.

At the same time, do not become a prophet of doom. Do not see in every relationship vestiges of the old. Do not jump at the first conflict and say, "Here it goes all over again." Treat the new relationship as the unique relationship it is, and do not evaluate it through past experiences. Use past relationships and experiences as guides, not filters.

SUMMARY: UNIT IN BRIEF

Stages of Deterioration	Causes of Relationship Deterioration	Communication Patterns in Deteriorating Relationships	Management Guidelines for Relationship Dissolution
Breakdown phase	Excessive intimacy claims	Withdrawal	Break the loneliness-depression cycle.
Intrapsychic phase		Decline in self-disclosure	
Dyadic phase	Third-party relationships		Take time out.
Social phase		Increased defensiveness	Bolster self-esteem.
Grave-dressing phase	Relational changes		Remove or avoid uncomfortable symbols.
	Undefined expectations	Increased deception	
		Change in evaluations	
	Sex-related problems		Seek support.
	Work-related problems		Avoid repeating negative patterns.
	Financial difficulties		
	Inequity		

THINKING CRITICALLY ABOUT RELATIONSHIP DETERIORATION AND DISSOLUTION

1. At what point would you describe a relationship as "deteriorating"? That is, what has to be going on for you to say that this is happening?

2. Let us say that you were dating someone for the last six months but met someone else with whom you wanted to get serious. What disengagement strategy would you be most likely to use? Why?

3. What are (were) your expectations for a primary romantic relationship? Are these expectations realistic? Might these expectations cause problems?

4. How important is money to your relational decisions and relational happiness? That is, do you make any relational decisions on the basis of money? To what extent—if any—does your relational happiness depend on money?

5. Would you be unhappy in a relationship in which you and your partner contributed an equal share of the costs (that is, you each worked equally hard) but your partner derived significantly greater rewards? Why?

6. How do your communication patterns change during relational deterioration? Do these changed patterns also create additional problems for your relationship? In what way?

7. Can you explain each of the rules for maintaining a relationship discussed in Unit 19 as a cause of deterioration when it is broken?

8. What other predictions do the four theories of interpersonal relationships (attraction, reinforcement, social exchange, and equity) make about relationship deterioration and dissolution? Do they offer any practical suggestions for dealing with relationship deterioration and dissolution?

9. Consider the research finding of Yogev discussed in the section "Undefined Expectations." Why do you think this was found? Is this changing? What evidence do you have that would support or contradict Yogev's findings?

10. How would you go about researching answers to the following questions?

   - In the discussion of financial difficulties, it was noted that concern over money in a relationship and money's equation with power may be largely attitudes of men. Is this true of, say, students in this class?

   - Do excessive intimacy claims create difficulties for romantic relationships? For friendship relationships? What kinds of excessive intimacy claims are especially dangerous?

   - Do relationships going from deterioration to dissolution follow the five stages noted in this unit: breakdown, intrapsychic, dyadic, social, and grave-dressing? Is this equally true for men and women? Is it equally true for heterosexual and homosexual relationships?

   - Research shows that when relationships break up, it is the more attractive person who leaves first. What other factors might account for who leaves first?

18.1 BELIEFS ABOUT YOUR RELATIONSHIPS*

Instructions: For each of the following statements, select the number (1 to 7) of the category that best fits how much you agree or disagree. Enter that number on the line next to each statement.

7 = agree completely
6 = agree a good deal
5 = agree somewhat
4 = neither agree nor disagree
3 = disagree somewhat
2 = disagree a good deal
1 = disagree completely

_____ 1. If a person has any questions about the relationship, then it means there is something wrong with it.

_____ 2. If my partner truly loved me, we would not have any quarrels.

_____ 3. If my partner really cared, he or she would always feel affection for me.

_____ 4. If my partner gets angry at me or is critical of me in public, this indicates he or she doesn't really love me.

_____ 5. My partner should know what is important to me without my having to tell him or her.

_____ 6. If I have to ask for something that I really want, it spoils it.

_____ 7. If my partner really cared, he or she would do what I ask.

_____ 8. A good relationship should not have any problems.

_____ 9. If people really love each other, they should not have to work on their relationship.

_____ 10. If my partner does something that upsets me, I think it is because he or she deliberately wants to hurt me.

*This test was taken from *Love Is Never Enough* by Aaron T. Beck. Copyright © 1988 by Aaron T. Beck. Reprinted by permission of HarperCollins Publishers and Arthur Pine Associates, Inc. Beck notes that this test was adapted in part from the Relationship Belief Inventory of N. Epstein, J. L. Pretzer, and B. Fleming, "The Role of Cognitive Appraisal in Self-Reports of Marital Communication," *Behavior Therapy* 18 (1987): 51–69.

_____ 11. When my partner disagrees with me in public, I think it is a sign that he or she doesn't care for me very much.

_____ 12. If my partner contradicts me, I think that he or she doesn't have much respect for me.

_____ 13. If my partner hurts my feelings, I think it is because he or she is mean.

_____ 14. My partner always tries to get his or her own way.

_____ 15. My partner doesn't listen to what I have to say.

Aaron Beck, one of the leading theorists on cognitive therapy and the author of the popular *Love Is Never Enough,* claims that all these beliefs are unrealistic and may well create problems in your interpersonal relationships. The test was developed to help people identify potential sources of difficulty for relationship development and maintenance. The more statements that you indicated you believe in, the more unrealistic your expectations are.

Do you agree with Beck that these beliefs are unrealistic and that they will cause problems? Which belief is the most dangerous to the development and maintenance of an interpersonal relationship?

Review the list—individually or in small groups—and identify with hypothetical or real examples why each belief is unrealistic (or realistic).

18.2 MALE AND FEMALE

This exercise is designed to increase your awareness of matters that may prevent meaningful interpersonal communication between the sexes. It is also designed to encourage meaningful dialogue among class members.

The women and the men are separated, and one group goes into another classroom. The task of each group is to write on the chalkboard all the things that members of the opposite sex think, believe, say, or do in reference to them that they dislike and that prevent meaningful interpersonal communication from taking place.

After this is done, the groups should change rooms. The men discuss what the women have written, and the women discuss what the men have written. After satisfactory discussion has taken place, the groups should get together in the original room.

Discussion might center on the following questions:

1. Were there any surprises?
2. Were there any disagreements? That is, did the members of one sex write anything that the members of the other sex argued they do not believe, think, do, or say?
3. How do you suppose the ideas about the other sex got started?
4. Is there any reliable evidence in support of the men's beliefs about the women or the women's about the men?
5. What kind of education or training program (if any) do you feel is needed to eliminate these problems?
6. In what specific ways do these beliefs, thoughts, actions, and statements prevent meaningful interpersonal communication?
7. How do you feel now that these matters have been discussed?

UNIT 19

Relationship Maintenance and Repair

Unit Objectives

AFTER COMPLETING THIS UNIT, YOU SHOULD BE ABLE TO:

1. Explain the reasons for relationship maintenance
2. Explain how rules may be used to explain relationship maintenance
3. Identify at least five maintenance strategies
4. Describe how the attraction, reinforcement, social exchange, and equity theories explain relationship maintenance
5. Explain the repair wheel
6. Explain how relationships may be repaired by only one person

Relationships are not static; they are constantly changing, constantly evolving, constantly becoming something different. After a relationship is established, it needs to be maintained and sometimes repaired—two topics we cover in this unit.

Relationship Maintenance

Relationship maintenance concerns that part of the relationship process in which you act to continue (maintain, retain) the relationship. Of course, maintenance behaviors can serve a variety of functions, for example:

- to keep the relationship intact, to retain the semblance of a relationship, to prevent dissolution of the relationship
- to keep the relationship at its present stage, to prevent it from moving too far toward either less or greater intimacy
- to keep the relationship satisfying, to maintain an appropriate balance between rewards and penalties

Some people, after entering a relationship, assume that it will continue unless something catastrophic happens. Consequently, while they may seek to prevent any major mishaps, they are unlikely to engage in much maintenance behavior. Others will be ever on the lookout for something wrong and will seek to patch it up as quickly and as effectively as possible. In between lie most people, who will engage in maintenance behaviors when things are going wrong and when there is the possibility that the relationship can be improved. Behaviors directed at improving badly damaged or even broken relationships are considered under the topic of repair, in the second half of this unit.

REASONS FOR MAINTAINING RELATIONSHIPS

The reasons for maintaining relationships are as numerous and varied as the reasons for beginning them. Some of the more popular and frequently cited reasons are mentioned here.

Emotional Attachment   The most obvious reason is that the individuals love each other and want to preserve their relationship. They do not find alternative couplings as inviting or as potentially enjoyable—the individuals' needs are being satisfied, and so the relationship is maintained. In some cases, these needs are predominantly for love and mutual caring, but in other cases, the needs being met may not be quite so positive. For example, one individual may maintain a relationship because it provides a means of exercising control over another. Someone else might continue a relationship because it provides ego gratification, each according to his or her specific need.

Convenience   Often the relationship involves neither great love nor great need satisfaction but is maintained for reasons of convenience. Perhaps both partners may jointly own a business or have mutual friends who are important to them. In these cases, it may be more convenient to stay together than to break up and go through the difficulties involved in finding another person to live with, another business partner, or another social escort. At times, both feel the same way about the relationship, and in such cases there is seldom any difficulty; neither person is "fooling" the other. At other times, the relationship is one of great love for one partner and one of convenience for the other.

Children   Relationships are often maintained because there are children involved. Children are sometimes (fortunately or unfortunately) brought into the world to save a relationship. In some cases they do. The parents stay together because they feel, rightly or wrongly, that it is in the best interests of the children. In other instances, the children provide a socially acceptable excuse to mask the real reason—convenience, financial advantage, fear of being alone, and so on. In childless relationships, both parties can be more independent and can make life choices based more on individual needs and wants. These individuals, therefore, are less likely to remain in relationships they may find unpleasant or uncomfortable.

Fear   Fear motivates many couples to stay together. The individuals may fear the outside world; they may be fearful of being alone and of facing others as "singles." They may remember the horrors of the singles bars, the one-night stands, and the lonely weekends. As a result, they may elect to preserve their current relationship as the better alternative. Sometimes the fear may be of social criticism: "What will our friends say? They'll think I'm a failure because I can't hold on to another person." Sometimes the fear concerns the consequences of violating a religious or parental tenet.

Financial Considerations   Financial advantages motivate many couples to stick it out. Divorces and separations are both emotionally and financially expensive. Some people fear a breakup that may cost them half their wealth or even more. Moreover, depending on where the individuals live and their preferred lifestyle, being single can be expensive. The cost of living in New York, Philadelphia, Chicago, San Francisco, Boston, and many other cities is almost prohibitive for single people. Many couples stay together to avoid facing additional economic problems.

Inertia A major reason for the preservation of many relationships is inertia, the tendency for a body at rest to remain at rest and a body in motion to remain in motion. Many people simply go along with the program, and it hardly occurs to them to consider changing their status; change seems too much trouble. Inertia is greatly aided by the media. It is easier for many individuals to remain in their present relationship and to seek vicarious satisfactions from situation comedies, dramas, and especially soap operas, wherein the actors do all the things the viewer would do if he or she were not so resistant to change.

Commitment An important factor influencing the course of relationship maintenance is the degree of commitment the individuals have toward each other and toward the relationship. All relationships are held together, in part, by our degree of commitment. Furthermore, the strength of the relationship, including its resistance to possible deterioration, is often directly related to this degree of commitment.

When a relationship shows signs of deterioration and yet there is a strong commitment to preserving it, the individuals may well surmount the obstacles and reverse the process. When commitment is weak and the individuals doubt that there are good reasons for staying together, the relationship deteriorates faster and more intensely.

Financial Commitment. One significant type of commitment is financial. On the one hand, it is only after a couple develops a strong commitment to each other and to the relationship that they pool their financial resources. "Failure to pool," note Blumstein and Schwartz (1983), "often indicates that couples have not given up their independence and may never have visualized the relationship as lasting into the indefinite future." The fact that cohabitants, who have few legal constraints, pool their finances only after a strong commitment has been made clearly illustrates this natural sequence of events. On the other hand, the pooling of finances often increases the commitment of the individuals to each other and to the relationship.

Temporal Commitment. The commitment may be based on time considerations. People may feel that because they have lived together for the past 10 or 15 years, all that time would be lost if the relationship were terminated. College students who have dated the same person for three or four years often feel that the time investment has been so great that they might as well continue the relationship. Often they allow it to progress into a permanent one. However, time spent in a relationship is not wasted if something has been learned from it and, more importantly, if the relationship has been enjoyed for its day-to-day value rather than for what it will mean 10 or 20 years from now. It is far better to terminate a four-year-old unsatisfactory relationship than to continue to be dissatisfied for the rest of one's life. Unfortunately, this seems obvious only to those who have never been in such a relationship.

Emotional Commitment. Sometimes commitment is based on emotional investment; so much emotional energy may have been spent on the relationship that the individuals find it difficult even to consider dissolving it. Or people may feel committed because they care for each other and for the relationship and feel that despite all its problems and difficulties, the relationship is more good than bad, more productive than destructive, more pleasurable than painful. This is the kind of commitment that will stem and perhaps reverse relational deterioration. Other bases for commitment (for example, materialism or time spent) may preserve the outward appearance of the relationship but do little to preserve or reclaim its meaning and intimacy.

Few couples stay together for a single reason. Rather, there is usually a multiplicity of reasons that vary in intensity and differ from one relationship to another. Obviously, the more urgent the reason, the more likely it is that the relationship will be preserved. Because so many of the reasons for relational preservation are subconscious, however, it is difficult to discover why a particular couple stays together or breaks up or to predict which relationships will last and which will not.

MAINTENANCE BEHAVIORS

One reason why relationships last is that people try to make them work. A number of researchers have focused on the maintenance strategies people use in their various relationships (Ayres 1983; Canary and Stafford 1994; Dindia and Baxter 1987; Dainton and

What behaviors do you engage in to maintain your friendship relationships? Your romantic relationships? Your family relationships? Can you identify behaviors that would help maintain these relationships but in which you do not engage? Why?

Stafford 1993; Guerrero, Eloy, and Wabnik 1993). Here, for example, are four general types (Dindia and Baxter 1987):

1. **Prosocial behaviors** include being polite, cheerful, and friendly; avoiding criticism; and compromising even when it involves self-sacrifice. Prosocial behaviors also include talking about a shared future: for example, talking about a future vacation or buying a house together.
2. **Ceremonial behaviors** include celebrating birthdays and anniversaries, discussing past pleasurable times, and eating at a favorite restaurant.
3. **Communication behaviors** include calling just to say, "How are you?" They also include talking about the honesty and openness in the relationship and talking about shared feelings. Responding constructively in a conflict (even when your partner may act in ways harmful to the relationship) is another type of communicative maintenance strategy (Rusbult and Buunk 1993).
4. **Togetherness behaviors** include spending time together visiting mutual friends, doing specific things as a couple, and sometimes just being together with no concern for what is done. Controlling extrarelational activities would be another type of togetherness behavior (Rusbult and Buunk 1993).

The following are some specific maintenance strategies identified in two recent studies (Canary et al. 1993; Dainton and Stafford 1993):

- **Openness.** The person engages in direct discussion and listens to the other—for example, self-disclosing, talking about what the person wants from the relationship, giving advice, and expressing empathy (rather than judgment).
- **Assurances.** The person assures the other of the significance of the relationship—for example, comforting the other, putting the partner first, and expressing love.
- **Sharing joint activities.** The person spends time with the other—for example, playing ball together, going to events together, or simply talking.
- **Positivity.** The person tries to make interactions pleasant and upbeat—for example, holding hands, giving in to make the other person happy, and doing favors for the other person.
- **Cards, letters, and calls.** The person sends cards or letters or calls the other.
- **Avoidance.** The person stays away from the other or from certain issues—for example, doing some things with third parties or not talking about potentially sensitive issues.
- **Sharing tasks.** The person performs various tasks with the other—for example, cleaning the house together.
- **Antisocial behavior.** The person behaves in unfriendly or coercive ways—for example, acting moody or being rude.
- **Social networks.** The person relies on friends and relatives for support and to help with various problems.

Also found were such strategies as **humor** (making jokes or teasing the other); **talk** (engaging in small talk and establishing specific times for talking); **affection, including sexual intimacy** (acting affectionately and romantically); and **focus on self** (making oneself look good) (Canary et al. 1993; Dainton and Stafford 1993).

INTERPERSONAL MAINTENANCE AND RULES

An interesting perspective may be gained by looking at interpersonal relationships in terms of the rules that govern them. The general assumption of this perspective is that relationships—friendship and love in particular—are held together by mutual adherence to certain rules. When those rules are broken, the relationships may deteriorate and eventually dissolve.

Discovering relationship rules serves several functions. Ideally, these rules help identify successful versus destructive relationship behavior. In addition, they help pinpoint why relationships break up and how they may be repaired. Further, if we know what the rules are, we will be better able to teach the social skills involved in relationship development and maintenance. Because these rules vary from one culture to another, it is necessary to identify those unique to each culture so that intercultural relationships may be more effectively developed and maintained.

Friendship Rules   Table 19.1 presents some of the most important rules of friendship (Argyle and Henderson 1984). When these rules are followed, the friendship is strong and mutually satisfying. When these rules are broken, the friendship suffers and may die.

Table 19.2 presents the abuses that are most significant in breaking up a friendship (Argyle and Henderson 1984). Note that some of the rules for maintaining a friendship directly correspond to the abuses that break up friendships. For example, it is important to demonstrate emotional support to maintain a friendship; when emotional support is not shown, the friendship will prove less satisfying and may well break up. The general assumption here is that friendships break down when a significant friendship rule is violated. The maintenance strategy depends on your knowing the rules and having the ability to apply the appropriate skills (Trower 1981; Blieszner and Adams 1992).

Romantic Rules   Other research has identified the rules that romantic relationships establish and follow. Leslie Baxter (1986), for example, has identified eight major rules. Baxter argues that these rules both keep the relationship together and, when broken, lead to deterioration and eventually to dissolution.

Table 19.1

Six Rules for Maintaining a Friendship

1. Stand up for the friend in his or her absence.

2. Share information and feelings about successes.

3. Demonstrate emotional support.

4. Trust each other; confide in each other.

5. Offer to help the friend in time of need.

6. Try to make the friend happy when the two of you are together.

Table 19.2
How to Break Up a Friendship

1. Be intolerant of the friend's friends.
2. Criticize the friend in public.
3. Discuss confidences between yourself and the friend with others.
4. Don't display any positive regard for the friend.
5. Don't demonstrate any positive support for the friend.
6. Nag the friend.
7. Don't trust or confide in the friend.
8. Don't volunteer to help the friend in time of need.
9. Be jealous or critical of the friend's other relationships.

The general form for each rule, as Baxter phrases it, is "If parties are in a close relationship, they should . . . "

1. acknowledge one another's individual identities and lives beyond the relationship.
2. express similar attitudes, beliefs, values, and interests.
3. enhance one another's self-worth and self-esteem.
4. be open, genuine, and authentic with one another.
5. remain loyal and faithful to one another.
6. have substantial shared time together.
7. reap rewards commensurate with their investments relative to the other party.
8. experience a mysterious and inexplicable "magic" in one another's presence.

WHAT THE THEORIES SAY ABOUT MAINTENANCE

What predictions do the theories of interpersonal relationships make about relationship maintenance? Attraction theory holds that relationships are maintained when there is significant attraction, generally of the kind that led to the development of the relationship. Although both individuals, as well as their definitions of what constitutes attractiveness, may have changed, the importance of attraction—however defined—is likely to continue throughout the life of the relationship.

Reinforcement theory holds that relationships are maintained when the individuals feel rewarded. Note, however, that this theory's predictions may not be intuitively obvious. For example, when a person gives many rewards, the power of future rewards to increase positive feelings actually decreases. However, the punishments given out by this (normally rewarding) person are likely to be extremely influential because of their infrequency. According to reinforcement theory, rewards should be somewhat unpredictable. Predictable rewards are less likely to influence a person than are unpredictable rewards.

Can you identify any rules that help maintain one or more of your friendships? Your romantic relationships? How would you react if your friend or romantic partner broke these rules? How would your friend or romantic partner react if you broke these rules? What would happen to these relationships as a result of such rule-breaking?

Reinforcement theory has the following practical implications:

- Give rewards that are at times unpredictable; surprise your partner.
- Recognize that because you are liked or loved, your power to punish is considerable; limit it.

Social exchange theory holds that relationships will be maintained as long as the rewards are greater than the costs, as long as the relationship is profitable. Note, of course, that what constitutes a reward and how significant that reward is can only be defined by the individual.

More specifically, a relationship is likely to be maintained when it is more rewarding than what you expected (your comparison level) or what you feel you could get (your comparison level for alternatives). Your relationship is also likely to be maintained when your present relationship falls short of your comparison level but is still higher than your comparison level for alternatives. Maintenance is likely to be in jeopardy when your comparison level for alternatives is greater than your present level of rewards.

Equity theory, similar to social exchange theory, holds that a relationship is maintained when the individuals perceive relative equity. If each person feels that he or she is getting rewards from the relationship proportional to the costs paid, then the relationship is likely to be maintained. If either person—but especially the person who is being short-changed—perceives a lack of equity, the relationship may experience difficulty.

RELATIONSHIP REPAIR

If you wish to salvage a relationship, you may try to do so by changing your communication patterns and, in effect, putting into practice the insights and skills learned in this course. First, let's look at some general ways to repair a relationship, and then we can examine ways to deal with repair when you are the only one who wants to change the relationship.

GENERAL RELATIONSHIP REPAIR STRATEGIES

We can look at the strategies for repairing a relationship in terms of the following six suggestions, which conveniently spell out the word REPAIR, a useful reminder that repair is not a one-step but a multistep process (Figure 19.1):

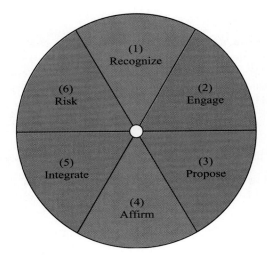

Figure 19.1
The relationship repair wheel. The wheel seems an apt metaphor for the repair process; the specific repair strategies—the spokes—all work together in constant process. The wheel is difficult to get moving, but once in motion it becomes easier to turn, and, of course, it is easier to start when two people are pushing.

1. **R**ecognize the problem.
2. **E**ngage in productive conflict resolution.
3. **P**ose possible solutions.
4. **A**ffirm each other.
5. **I**ntegrate solutions into normal behavior.
6. **R**isk.

Recognize the Problem   Your first step is to identify the problem and to recognize it both intellectually and emotionally. Specify what is wrong with your present relationship (in concrete terms) and what changes would be needed to make it better (again, in specific terms). Create a picture of your relationship as you would want it to be, and compare that picture to the way the relationship looks now. Specify the changes that would have to take place if the ideal picture were to replace the present picture.

If the relationship is to be repaired and become rewarding once again, then the withdrawal and deception that characterize communication during the stage of deterioration must give way to open and honest communication. As with alcohol or drug addiction, we have to admit we have a problem before we can work on a cure. And we have to be honest about what the problem is.

Try to see the problem from your partner's point of view and to have your partner see the problem from yours. Exchange these perspectives, empathically and with open minds. Try, too, to be descriptive when discussing grievances, taking special care to avoid such troublesome terms as "always" and "never." Own your feelings and thoughts; use I-messages and take responsibility for your feelings instead of blaming your partner.

Engage in Productive Conflict Resolution   Interpersonal conflict is an inevitable part of relationship life. It is not so much the conflict that causes relationship difficulties as the way the conflict is approached. If it is confronted with productive strategies, the conflict may be resolved, and the relationship may actually emerge stronger and healthier. If, however, unproductive and destructive strategies are used, then the relationship may well deteriorate further. Because this topic is so crucial, Unit 21 is devoted exclusively to the process of interpersonal conflict and especially to ways to engage in it productively.

Pose Possible Solutions   After the problem is identified, you need to discuss solutions, the ways to lessen or eliminate the difficulty. Look for solutions that will enable both of you to win. Try to avoid "solutions" in which one person wins and the other loses. With such win-lose solutions, resentment and hostility are likely to fester. For example, financial problems were earlier noted as one of the factors that may lead to relational deterioration. In dealing with such an issue, possible solutions, according to *Money* magazine (Cook 1993), are these:

* Have a meeting about finances, and review the way your joint money is being spent.
* Agree on a budget.
* Discuss your investments in light of your goals: for example, to send the children to college or to retire.
* Consult your partner before buying something or borrowing money.
* Plan investments to make the more anxious partner comfortable.

Affirm Each Other   Any strategy of relationship repair should incorporate supportiveness and positive evaluations. For example, it has been found that happily married couples engage in greater positive behavior exchange; they communicate more agreement, approval, and positive affect than do unhappily married couples (Dindia and Fitzpatrick 1985). Clearly, these behaviors result from the positive feelings the spouses have for each other. However, it can also be argued that these expressions help to increase the positive regard each person has for his or her partner.

One obvious way to affirm another is to talk positively. Reverse negative communication patterns. For example, instead of withdrawing, talk about the causes of and the possible cures for your disagreements and problems. Reverse the tendency to hide your inner self. Disclose your feelings.

Another way to affirm another is to tell the truth and avoid deception. Be honest with yourself, about yourself, and about the relationship. Ask yourself how your own behavior has contributed to the deterioration. Is there justice in your partner's criticisms? Be honest with your partner and about your partner. Most important, be honest about the problems facing the relationship. As with alcoholism, before you can work on a cure, you have to admit you have a problem.

Increasing the expression of positive evaluations and decreasing the expression of negative evaluations will help to further affirm your partner. Positive expressions and behaviors help to increase the positive regard each person has for his or her partner. Compliments, positive stroking, and all the nonverbals that say "I care" are especially important when you wish to reverse negative communication patterns.

Cherishing behaviors are an especially insightful way to affirm another person and to increase favor exchange (Lederer 1984). Cherishing behaviors are those small gestures you enjoy receiving from your relational partner (a smile, a wink, a squeeze, a kiss). Cherishing behaviors should be (1) specific and positive, (2) focused on the present and future rather than related to issues about which the partners have argued in the past, (3) capable of being performed daily, and (4) easily executed. People can make a list of the cherishing behaviors they each wish to receive and then exchange lists. Each person then performs the cherishing behaviors desired by the partner. At first, these behaviors may seem self-conscious and awkward. In time, however, they will become a normal part of interaction.

Integrate Solutions into Normal Behavior   Often solutions that are reached after an argument are followed for only a very short time; then the couple goes back to their previous and unproductive behavior patterns. Instead, integrate the solutions into your normal behavior; they need to become integral to your everyday relationship behavior. Exchanging favors, compliments, and cherishing behaviors, for example, needs to become a part of your relational behavior.

Risk   Take risks in trying to improve any relationship. Risk giving favors without any certainty of reciprocity. Risk rejection by making the first move to make up or say you are sorry. Be willing to change, to adapt, to take on new tasks and responsibilities.

Interpersonal Skill Application.   Throughout this process of repair, apply your interpersonal communication skills. Make them a normal part of your interactions. Here is just a handful of suggestions designed to refresh your memory:

- Look closely for relational messages that will help clarify motivations and needs. Respond to these messages as well as to the content messages.

- Exchange perspectives with your partner, and see the situation as your partner does.

- Practice empathic and positive responses, even in conflict situations.

- Own your feelings and thoughts. Use I-messages and take responsibility for these feelings.

- Use active listening techniques to help your partner explore and express relevant thoughts and feelings.

- Remember the principle of irreversibility. Think carefully before saying things you may later regret.

- Keep the channels of communication open. Be available to discuss problems, to negotiate solutions, and to practice new and more productive communication patterns.

Reconciliation Strategies.   Still more insight into repairing a relationship comes from research on reconciliation strategies. These strategies focus on reestablishing a relationship *after* it has broken up. There is some overlap between these strategies and the maintenance strategies discussed earlier, which are designed to strengthen a relationship that still exists. Here is one set of *reconciliation* strategies (Patterson and O'Hair 1992).

In **spontaneous development,** subjects report that reconciliation just seemed to happen without their doing anything specific. In **third-party mediation,** some outside person perhaps suggested reconciliation or served as a go-between.

High affect/ultimatum strategies involve accusations or threats—for example, pointing to the other person's fear of commitment. **Tacit/persistence** involves asking the person to do something without mentioning reconciliation specifically—for example, to take a walk in the park. **Mutual interaction** involves having long talks and engaging in open communication.

In **avoidance,** a partner makes special efforts to avoid the issues that led to the relationship breakup. In **vulnerable appeal,** a partner makes direct appeals to get back together again, confessing, for example, that he or she still cares for or loves the other person or wants the relationship to work.

SOLO RELATIONSHIP REPAIR

One of the most important implications for repair comes from the principle of punctuation (see Unit 2) and the idea that communication is circular rather than linear (see Unit 1; Duncan and Rock 1991). Let's consider an example involving Pat and Chris: Pat is highly critical of Chris; Chris is defensive and attacks Pat for being insensitive, overly negative, and unsupportive. If you view the communication process as beginning with Pat's being critical (that is, the stimulus) and with Chris's attacks being the response, you have a pattern such as occurs in Figure 19.2.

With this view, the only way to stop the unproductive communication pattern is for Pat to stop criticizing. But what if you are Chris and can't get Pat to stop being critical? What if Pat doesn't want to stop being critical?

Figure 19.2
A stimulus-response view of relationship problems.

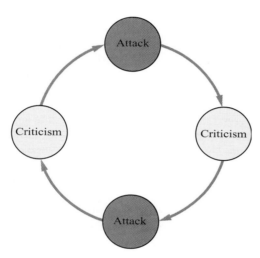

Figure 19.3
A circular view of relationship problems.

You get a different view of the problem when you see communication as circular and invoke the principle of punctuation. The result is a pattern such as appears in Figure 19.3.

Note that no assumptions are made about causes. Instead, the only assumption is that each response triggers another response—each response depends in part on the previous response. Therefore, the pattern can be broken at any point: Pat's criticism, for example, may be stopped by Chris's not responding with attacks. Similarly, Pat can stop Chris's attacks by not responding to them with criticism.

In this view, either person can break an unproductive and damaging circle. Clearly, relationship communication can be most effectively improved when both parties change their unproductive patterns. Nevertheless, communication can be improved even if only one person changes and begins to use a more productive pattern. This is true to the extent that Pat's criticism depends on Chris's attacks and to the extent that Chris's attacks depend on Pat's criticism.

SUMMARY: UNIT IN BRIEF

Relationship Maintenance: The Process of Preventive Care	Relationship Repair: The Process of Corrective Care
Reasons for maintaining a relationship	**General repair strategies**

• emotional attachment
 • convenience
 • children
 • fear
 • financial considerations
 • inertia
 • commitment
 • maintenance behaviors
	1. Recognize the problem.
	 2. Engage in productive conflict resolution.
	 3. Pose possible solutions.
	 4. Affirm each other.
	 5. Integrate solutions into normal behavior.
	 6. Risk.
	    • Apply interpersonal skills.
	    • Consider specific reconciliation strategies.

Relationship maintenance can be characterized by adherence to a set of mutually agreed-upon rules that when broken will lead to deterioration.	Repair is not necessarily a two-person process.

THINKING CRITICALLY ABOUT RELATIONSHIP MAINTENANCE AND REPAIR

1. What general factors are currently maintaining your own friendship or romantic relationships? What is the most important factor?

2. Can you describe your current friendship or romantic relationships in terms of need satisfaction? Can you distinguish close friends and acquaintances on the basis of need satisfaction?

3. Are financial commitment, temporal commitment, and emotional commitment the major types you have encountered? Are there other types of commitment you would identify?

4. Would you be more comfortable using some maintenance strategies rather than others? If so, which strategies would you find it easy to use? Hard to use?

5. Can you describe a current or past friendship or romantic relationship in terms of the rules discussed in this unit? What three rules are most important to your current relationship?

6. Are the descriptions of the verbal and nonverbal indicators of love given here generally accurate in representing what you have observed? How would you modify these descriptions?

7. What other predictions about relationship maintenance do the four theories of interpersonal relationships make? Do they offer any additional practical advice for effectively maintaining relationships? Do they make any predictions or offer any advice on relationship repair?

8. Can you identify additional general repair strategies? What other suggestions for repairing a relationship by yourself might you offer?

9. What interpersonal communication skill do you think is most important to relationship repair? Why?

10. How would you go about researching answers to the following questions?

* Does a knowledge of interpersonal communication really help in dealing with relationship problems?
* Do men and women use the same or different reconciliation strategies?
* Are certain reconciliation strategies more effective than others?

EXPERIENTIAL VEHICLES

19.1 THEORIES AND PROBLEMS

Read each of the following letters and describe each of the problems in terms of the (1) attraction, (2) reinforcement, (3) social exchange, and (4) equity theories. Do the theories make any predictions about how these situations are likely to be resolved? Do they offer any suggestions as to what the individuals should do?

Love and Age Difference

I'm in love with an older woman. She's 51, and I'm 22 but very mature; in fact, I'm a lot more mature than she is. I want to get married but she doesn't; she says she doesn't love me, but I know she does. She wants to break up our romance and "become friends." How can I win her over?

22 and Determined

Love and the Best Friend

Chris and I have been best friends for the last ten years. Now Chris has fallen in love and is moving to California. I became angry and hurt at the idea of losing my best friend, and I said things I shouldn't have. Although we still talk, things aren't the same ever since I opened my big mouth. What should I do?

Big Mouth

Love and Sports

My relationship of the last 20 years has been great—except for one thing: I can't watch sports on television. If I turn on the game, Pat moans and groans until I turn it off. Pat wants to talk; I want to watch the game. I work hard during the week, and on the weekend I want to watch sports, drink beer, and fall asleep on the couch. This problem has gotten so bad that I'm seriously considering separating. What should I do?

Sports Lover

Love and the Dilemma

I'm 29 and have been dating two really great people fairly steadily. Each knows about my relationship with the other, and for a while they went along with it and tolerated what they felt was an unpleasant situation. They now threaten to break up with me if I don't make a decision. To be perfectly honest, I like both of them a great deal; I simply need more time before I can make the decision and ask one to be my life mate. How can I get them to stay with the status quo for maybe another year or so?

Simply Undecided

19.2 RELATIONAL REPAIR FROM ADVICE COLUMNISTS

Select a specific question and answer from an advice column in a newspaper or magazine. Be sure the question refers to a relationship. Bring this column to class and be prepared to discuss it, covering at least the following issues:

1. Is the advice generally good? Bad? Is there any evidence to support the usefulness or validity of the answer given?
2. What relational rule is the advice columnist using in answering this question?
3. To what other situations might this relational rule apply? That is, what other applications might we find for this specific rule?
4. What are the limitations of this rule? That is, specify the parameters for the application of this relational rule.
5. Is there a more appropriate relational rule that might have been used to answer this question? State this rule and its limitations.
6. What difficulties can you foresee in applying the advice offered by the columnist? What additional advice do you feel should have accompanied the columnist's response?

UNIT 20

Power in Interpersonal Relationships

UNIT OBJECTIVES

AFTER COMPLETING THIS UNIT, YOU SHOULD BE ABLE TO:

1. Define *power* and explain its general principles
2. Define the six bases of power
3. Discuss at least six suggestions for making your speech more powerful
4. Explain the ways in which the following power games are played and how you can effectively manage them: *nobody upstairs, you owe me, metaphor, yougottobekidding,* and *thought stoppers*
5. Explain compliance-gaining and compliance-resisting strategies

Power permeates all interpersonal relationships and interactions. It influences what you do, when you do it, and with whom. It influences your choice of friends, your romantic and your family relationships—and how successful you feel they are. Interpersonal power is what enables one person to control the behavior of the other. Thus, if A has power over B, then A, by virtue of this power—through either its exercise or the threat of its being exercised—can control B's behaviors.

PRINCIPLES OF POWER

Power in interpersonal relationships may best be introduced by a discussion of some of its most important principles, which help to explain how power operates interpersonally and how you may effectively manage its use.

SOME PEOPLE ARE MORE POWERFUL THAN OTHERS

In the United States, all people are considered equal under the law and therefore equal in their entitlement to education, legal protection, and freedom of speech. But all people are not equal when it comes to just about everything else. Some are born into wealth, others into poverty. Some are born physically strong, good-looking, and healthy; others are born weak, less attractive, and with a variety of inherited illnesses.

Most important for our purposes here, some people are born powerful. And some of those who are not born powerful learn to be so. In short, some people control and others are controlled. Of course, the world is not quite that simple; some exert power in certain areas, some in others. Some exert their power in many areas, some in just a few.

POWER CAN BE INCREASED OR DECREASED

Although we differ greatly in the amount of power we wield at any time and in any specific area, all of us can increase our power in some ways. You can lift weights and increase your physical power. You can learn the techniques of negotiation and increase your power in group situations. You can learn the principles of communication and increase your persuasive power. Power can also be decreased. Probably the most common way we lose power is by unsuccessfully attempting to control another's behavior. For example, the person who threatens you with punishment and then fails to carry out the threat loses power. A dating partner who tries to dictate religious principles may lose power through an ineffective attempt to influence or control your behavior.

POWER FOLLOWS THE PRINCIPLE OF LEAST INTEREST

In any interpersonal relationship, the person who holds the power is the one least interested in and least dependent on the rewards and punishments controlled by the other person. If, for example, Pat can walk away from the rewards Chris controls or can suffer the punishments Chris can mete out, Pat controls the relationship. If, on the other hand, Pat needs the rewards Chris controls or is unable or unwilling to suffer the punishments Chris can administer, Chris maintains the power and controls the relationship. Put differently, Chris holds the relationship power to the degree that Chris is not dependent upon the rewards and punishments under Pat's control.

The more a person needs a relationship, the less power that person has in it. The less a person needs a relationship, the greater the power possessed. In a love relationship, for example, the person who maintains greater power is the one who would find it easier to break up the relationship. The person who is unwilling (or unable) to break up has little power, precisely because he or she is dependent upon the relationship and the rewards provided by the other person.

Another way of looking at this principle is in terms of social exchange theory (see Unit 17). From this perspective, power may be viewed as control of the significant rewards and costs in the relationship. The person who controls the rewards and punishments controls the relationship. The person who needs to receive the rewards and to avoid the costs or punishments controlled by the other person is less powerful. Alternatively, the person who can effectively ignore both the rewards and the costs is the less interested party and therefore possesses the controlling power in the relationship.

BASES OF POWER

Power is present in all relationships and in all communication interchanges. But the type of power varies greatly from one situation to another and from one person to another. Here we identify six types of power (French and Raven 1968; Raven, Centers, and Rodrigues 1975).

REFERENT POWER

Person A has **referent power** over person B when B wishes to be like A or to be identified with A. For example, an older brother may have power over a younger brother because the younger brother wants to be like the older one. The assumption made by the younger brother is that he will be more like his older brother if he behaves and believes as his brother does. Once he decides to do so, it takes little effort for the older brother to exert influence or power over the younger. Referent power depends greatly on attractiveness and prestige; as they increase, so does identification and consequently power. When person A is well liked and well respected, is of the same sex as B, and has the same attitudes and experiences as B, A's referent power over B is even greater.

Referent power is also seen in a person's tendency to conform with rather than contradict another. For example, a teenager will be more likely to try drugs if he or she sees others in the peer group doing it.

LEGITIMATE POWER

Person A has **legitimate power** over person B when B believes A has a right—by virtue of A's position—to influence or control B's behavior. Legitimate power stems from our belief that certain people should have power over us, that they have a right to influence us because of who they are. Legitimate power usually derives from the roles people occupy. Teachers are often perceived to have legitimate power, and this is doubly true for religious teachers. Parents are seen as having legitimate power over their children. Employers, judges, managers, doctors, and police officers are others who may hold legitimate power.

REWARD POWER

Person A has **reward power** over person B if A has the ability to reward B. Rewards may be material (money, promotion, jewelry) or social (love, friendship, respect). If I am in a position to grant you some kind of reward, I have control over you to the extent that you want what I can give you. The degree of power wielded by A is directly related to the desirability of the reward as seen by B. Teachers have reward power over students because they control grades, letters of recommendation, social approval, and so on. Students, in turn, have reward power over teachers because they control social approval, student evaluations of faculty, and various other rewards. Parents control rewards for children—food, television privileges, rights to the car, curfew times, and the like—and thus possess reward power.

COERCIVE POWER

Person A has **coercive power** over person B when A has the ability to administer punishments to or remove rewards from B should B not yield to A's influence. Usually, people

What type of power are these police officers exercising in writing a ticket to this young driver? What nonverbal symbols of power are illustrated in this photo?

who have reward power also have coercive power. Teachers not only may reward with high grades, favorable letters of recommendation, and social approval but also may punish with low grades, unfavorable letters, and social disapproval. Parents may deny as well as grant privileges to their children, and hence they possess coercive as well as reward power.

The strength of coercive power depends on two factors: (1) the magnitude of the punishment that can be administered and (2) the likelihood that it will be administered as a result of noncompliance. When threatened by mild punishment or by punishment we think will not be administered, we are not as likely to do as directed as we would be if the threatened punishment were severe and likely to be administered.

Reward Versus Coercive Power: Some Consequences Consider a few consequences of using reward and coercive power. First, reward power seems to increase one's attractiveness; we like people who have the power to reward us and who do in fact reward us. But coercive power decreases attractiveness; we dislike those who have the power to punish us and who threaten us with punishment, whether they actually follow through or not.

Second, those who use rewards to exert power do not incur the same costs as those who use punishment. When we exert reward power, we deal with a contented and happy individual. When we use coercive punishments, however, we must be prepared to incur anger and hostility, which may well be turned against us as heavy costs in the future.

Third, when a reward is given, it signals effectively exercised power and compliance. That is, we reward the individual for doing as we wish. But note that in the exercise of coercive power, the reverse is true. When punishment is given, it is a sign that the coercive power has been ineffective and that there has been no compliance.

Fourth, when coercive power is exerted, other bases of power frequently are diminished. There seems to be a kind of boomerang effect in operation. We tend to see a person who exercises coercive power as possessing less expert, legitimate, and referent power. (Expert power is discussed in the following section.) Alternatively, when reward power is exerted, other bases of power increase.

Fifth, the use of coercive power in the classroom leads to a decrease in cognitive learning and hinders effective learning generally (Richmond and McCroskey 1984; Kearney et al. 1984, 1985). In classrooms where the teacher is seen by the students to exercise coercive (and legitimate) power, students learn less effectively; have more negative attitudes toward the course, the course content, and the teacher; are less likely to take similar courses; and are less likely to perform the behaviors taught in the course. Coercive power and legitimate power also have a negative impact when used by supervisors on subordinates in business settings (Richmond et al. 1984). All in all, coercive power seems a last resort, one whose potential negative consequences should be carefully weighed before it is used.

EXPERT POWER

Person A has **expert power** over person B if B regards A as having expertise or knowledge; the knowledge that A has gives A expert power. Persons with expert power influence us in ways that persons without such power do not. Further, that power is usually subject-specific. For example, when we are ill, we are influenced by the recommendation of someone with expert power related to our illness—say, a doctor. But we would not be influenced by the recommendation of someone to whom we do not attribute illness-related expert power—say, the mail carrier or a plumber. We give the lawyer expert power in matters of law and psychiatrists expert power in matters of the mind, but, ideally, we do not interchange them. We are not influenced by the lawyer's recommendations on depression or anxiety or the psychiatrist's recommendations as to the legal process of filing for divorce or writing a will.

Expert power increases when the source (expert) is seen as unbiased, with nothing to gain personally from influencing us. It decreases if the expert is seen as biased and as having something to gain from our compliance.

INFORMATION OR PERSUASION POWER

Person A has **information** or **persuasion power** over person B when B attributes to A the ability to communicate logically and persuasively. I give another person information power by believing that he or she has the ability to persuade me. We generally attribute persuasion power to someone we see as possessing significant information and the ability to use that information in presenting a well-reasoned argument. Information or persuasion power is also enhanced by the use of powerful speech. A summary of some of the major characteristics of powerful and powerless speech is presented in Table 20.1 (Molloy 1981; Kleinke 1986; Johnson 1987).

Table 20.1
Toward More Powerful Speech

SUGGESTIONS	EXAMPLES	REASONS
Avoid hesitations.	"I *er* want to say that *ah* this one is *er* the best, *you know.*"	Hesitations cause one to sound unprepared and uncertain.
Avoid too many intensifiers.	"*Really,* this was *the greatest;* it was *truly phenomenal.*"	Too many intensifiers make speech sound the same and do not allow for intensifying what should be emphasized.
Avoid disqualifiers.	"*I didn't read the entire article,* but. . . ." "*I didn't actually see the accident,* but. . . ."	Disqualifiers signal a lack of competence and a feeling of uncertainty.
Avoid tag questions.	"That was a great movie, *wasn't it?*" "She's brilliant, *don't you think?*"	Tag questions ask for another's agreement and therefore signal both need for agreement and uncertainty.
Avoid self-critical statements.	"*I'm not very good at this.*" "*This is my first public speech.*"	Self-critical statements signal a lack of confidence and make public one's inadequacies.
Avoid slang and vulgar expressions.	"##!!!///****!" "*No problem!*"	Slang and vulgarity signal low social class and hence little power.

In the first five bases of power, the personal qualities of the power holder are significant. In information power, however, the content of the communication is the important element, not the influencing agent's personal qualities. Thus, for example, the speaker who presents a convincing argument or the teacher who explains a logical problem will exert influence over the listener regardless of the speaker's or teacher's personal qualities.

In any given situation, you rarely find only one base of power used to influence another individual; usually, a number of power bases are used in concert. If you possess expert power, it is likely that you also possess information power and perhaps legitimate power as well. If you want to control the behavior of another person, you would probably use all three bases of power rather than rely on just one. As can be appreciated from this discussion, certain individuals have a number of power bases at their disposal, whereas others seem to have none. This point brings us back to our first principle: some people are more powerful than others.

A Note on Negative Power   We normally think of attempts to influence others as having some desirable effect. At times, however, negative power operates; here the attempt to influence backfires, widening the differences between the agent and the individual influenced. Each of the six power bases may, at times, have such negative influence.

For example, negative referent power occurs when a son rejects his father and wants to be his exact opposite. Negative coercive power may be seen when a child is warned against doing something under threat of punishment and then does exactly what he or she was told not to do; the threat of punishment may have made the forbidden behavior seem exciting or challenging.

POWER PLAYS

Because no interpersonal relationship exists without a power dimension, all interactions invariably involve power maneuvers and consequences. A number of researchers have identified some of the power plays or games that occur in interpersonal interactions. Here are five discussed by Claude Steiner in *The Other Side of Power* (1981).

NOBODY UPSTAIRS

In this power play, the individual refuses to acknowledge your request. The game takes the form of not listening to what you are saying, regardless of how or how many times you say it. One common form is the refusal to take no for an answer, clearly seen in the stereotypical man who persists in making advances to a woman despite her repeated refusals.

Sometimes "nobody upstairs" takes the form of ignoring common socially accepted (but unspoken) rules, such as knocking when you enter someone's room or refraining from opening another person's mail or wallet. The power play takes the form of expressing ignorance of the rules: "I didn't know you didn't want me to look in your wallet" or "Do you want me to knock the next time I come into your room?"

Management Strategies   What do you do when confronted by such a power play? One commonly employed response is to ignore the power play and allow the other person to control the conversation and us. Some people ignore power plays because they don't recognize them as consistent patterns of behavior. They don't realize that this other person behaves this way repeatedly to maintain power. Others ignore this behavior for fear that any objection might start an argument. They therefore elect the lesser of the two evils and ignore the power play.

Another response is what Steiner calls neutralizing the power play. In this type of response, you treat the power play as an isolated instance (rather than as a pattern of behavior) and object to it. For example, you might say quite simply, "Please don't come into my room without knocking first" or "Please don't look in my wallet without permission."

A third response is what Steiner calls a cooperative response. In this response, you seek to accomplish the following:

- *Express your feelings.* Tell the person that you are angry, annoyed, or disturbed by his or her behavior.
- *Describe the behavior to which you object.* Tell the person—in language that describes rather than evaluates—the specific behavior you object to: for example,

reading your mail, coming into your room without knocking, persisting in trying to hug you.

• *State a cooperative response you both can live with comfortably.* Tell the person—in a cooperative tone—what you want: for example: "I want you to knock before coming into my room." "I want you to stop reading my mail." "I want you to stop trying to hug me when I tell you to stop."

A cooperative response to "nobody upstairs" might go something like this: "I'm angry (*statement of feelings*) that you persist in opening my mail. You have opened my mail four times this past week alone (*description of the behavior to which you object*). I want you to allow me to open my own mail. If there is anything in it that concerns you, I will let you know immediately" (*statement of cooperative response*).

In considering the management strategies for the remaining four power plays, we provide examples of the cooperative response because they are the most difficult to formulate, and the examples should make both the power play and the nature of cooperative responses clearer. Steiner advocates the cooperative response because it has the potential both to put an end to the power play and to restructure the interaction into a more equal one. Realize, however, that in some instances, for some people, and for some relationships, it may be wiser to ignore the power play or perhaps simply to neutralize it, treating it as an isolated instance. You have a choice as to how to respond; only you can make that choice after weighing the other variables at play.

You Owe Me

In this power play, an individual does something for you and then demands something in return. This game is played frequently by men who take women on expensive dates and then act as though the woman owes something, usually sex, in return. It is also seen in the woman who gives a man a great deal—sexually, emotionally, financially—and then demands something in return, for example, marriage. These two examples are, of course, stereotypes; they occur a great deal in the movies, in popular fiction, and on television, but they have their basis in real life as well.

Another common example is the parents who sacrifice for their child but expect repayment. Whenever the child wants to do something against the parents' wishes, they remind the child that they are owed something: "How can you quit college after all we sacrificed?" or "How can you get such low grades when we worked so hard for your education?" or "Why don't you want to wear that jacket? I spent two hours fixing it."

Management Strategy   The cooperative response involves confronting the game player with our three-part strategy: statement of feelings, description of the behavior you object to, and statement of a cooperative response.

One such response might be, "I'm angry that you're doing this to me (*statement of feelings*). I'm angry that when you want me to do something, you start by reminding me of my obligations to you. You tell me all you did for me and then claim that I should therefore do what you want me to do (*description of the behavior to which you object*). Please don't do things for me because you want something in return. I don't want to feel obligated. I want to do what I do because I think it is best for me and not because I would feel guilty about not paying you back for what you have done for me" (*statement of cooperative response*).

METAPHOR

Metaphor is an interesting power play that is at times difficult to identify as a power maneuver. For example, consider the situation in which one member of a group is going out with someone the other members do not like, and they respond with such comments as "How can you go out with her? She's a real dog" or "How can you date him? He's such a pig." "Dog" and "pig" are metaphors. Metaphors are figures of speech in which one word is used in the place of another. In these examples, "dog" and "pig" are used in place of the persons referred to, with the intention of associating the most obvious characteristics of these animals (ugliness and sloppiness, for example) with the people. The object here is to put the individual down and not allow you a chance to defend him or her. After all, it is difficult to defend dating a dog or a pig!

Management Strategy   The three-part cooperative strategy to deal with metaphor might go something like this: "I resent your calling Jane a dog. I'm very attached to her and she to me. I feel like a real loser (*statement of feelings*) when you refer to my dates as pigs or dogs. You've called the last three women I've dated these insulting names (*description of the behavior to which you object*). If you don't like the women I'm dating, please tell me. But please don't insult them or me by using terms like 'pig' or 'dog'" (*statement of cooperative response*).

YOUGOTTOBEKIDDING

In this power play, one person attacks the other by saying "yougottobekidding" or some similar phrase: "You can't be serious." "You can't mean that." "You didn't say what I thought you said, did you?" The intention here is to express utter disbelief in the other's statement so as to make the statement and the person seem inadequate or stupid.

This power play is frequently used when one person says something outside his or her usual and perhaps stereotypical role. For example, if Pat is generally regarded as mechanically minded and Chris as artistic, Pat might use this power play to counter Chris's suggestion as to why the car isn't starting. Alternatively, it may be used by Chris if, for example, Pat offers an opinion on a work of fine art or a play.

Management Strategy   Applying the three-part cooperative strategy to yougottobekidding, you might say, "I'm angry and annoyed; I feel like an idiot (*statement of feelings*) when you say, 'You can't be serious' or 'yougottobekidding' when I offer an opinion in an area you may know more about than I do (*statement of behavior to which you object*). I'd much prefer that you take issue with what I say—tell me why you disagree with me—than simply to dismiss it by telling me I have to be kidding" (*statement of cooperative response*).

Thought Stoppers

A thought stopper is a power play that is designed to literally stop your thinking and especially to stop you from expressing your thoughts. Thought stoppers may take a number of forms. Perhaps the most common is the interruption. Before you can finish your thought, the other person interrupts you and either completes it or goes off on another topic. Other thought stoppers include the use of profanity and raising one's voice to drown you out. Regardless of the specific form, it shifts the speaker role from you to the other person.

Management Strategy   The cooperative strategy might go something like this: "I get frustrated (*statement of feelings*) when you interrupt me before I've had a chance to complete my thoughts. You've done this three times in the last ten minutes (*description of the behavior to which you object*). I don't interrupt you, and I'd appreciate your not interrupting me. Please let me complete my thoughts, and I'll let you complete yours. OK?" (*statement of cooperative response*).

Compliance Gaining and Compliance Resisting

The use of compliance strategies clearly illustrates the way power is exercised. *Compliance-gaining strategies* are the tactics that influence others to do what you want them to do. *Compliance-resisting strategies* are the tactics that enable you to say no and to resist another person's attempts to influence you.

Compliance-Gaining Strategies

Sixteen compliance-gaining strategies, from the research of Gerald Marwell and David Schmitt (1967, 1990), are presented in Table 20.2 (also see Miller and Parks 1982, Dillard 1990). In reviewing these strategies, keep in mind that compliance gaining, like all interpersonal processes, involves two people in a transaction. Reading down the list may give the impression that these strategies are one-shot affairs, with one person using the strategy and the other person complying. Actually, compliance gaining is best viewed as a transactional, back-and-forth process. That is, conflict, compromise, renegotiation of the goal, rejection of the strategy, and a host of other responses—in addition to simple compliance—are possible.

For example, when two friends are involved in a conflict, compliance gaining by appeals to altruism are more effective than appeals to guilt, which may lead the other person to feel angry (Rubin and Shaffer 1987).

Also, note that these strategies and the responses to them depend both on the personalities of the individuals and on the individuals' unique relationship. Which strategies you use, which strategies will work for you, and which strategies will backfire all depend on who you are, on who the other people are, and on the interpersonal relationship among you.

Table 20.2
Compliance-Gaining Strategies

1. **PREGIVING.** Pat rewards Chris and then requests compliance.

   Pat: I'm glad you enjoyed dinner. This really is the best restaurant in the city. How about going back to my place for a nightcap and whatever?

2. **LIKING.** Pat is helpful and friendly in order to get Chris in a good mood so that Chris will be more likely to comply with Pat's request.

   Pat: [After cleaning up the living room and bedroom] I'd really like to relax and bowl a few games with Terry. OK?

3. **PROMISE.** Pat promises to reward Chris if Chris complies with Pat's request.

   Pat: I'll give you anything you want if you will just give me a divorce. You can have the house, the car, the stocks, the three kids; just give me my freedom.

4. **THREAT.** Pat threatens to punish Chris for noncompliance.

   Pat: If you don't give me a divorce, you'll never see the kids again.

5. **AVERSIVE STIMULATION.** Pat continuously punishes Chris and makes cessation of the punishment contingent upon compliance. Pat demonstrates hysterical reactions (for example, screaming and crying) and stops only when Chris agrees to comply.

6. **POSITIVE EXPERTISE.** Pat promises that Chris will be rewarded for compliance because of "the nature of things."

   Pat: It will be a lot easier for everyone involved if you don't contest the divorce.

7. **NEGATIVE EXPERTISE.** Pat promises that Chris will be punished for noncompliance because of "the nature of things."

   Pat: If you don't listen to the doctor, you're going to wind up back in the hospital.

8. **POSITIVE SELF-FEELINGS.** Pat promises that Chris will feel better if Chris complies with Pat's request.

   Pat: You'll see. You'll be a lot better off without me; you'll feel a lot better after the divorce.

9. **NEGATIVE SELF-FEELINGS.** Pat promises that Chris will feel worse if Chris does not comply with Pat's request.

   Pat: Only a selfish creep would force another person to stay in a relationship. You'll hate yourself if you don't give me this divorce.

10. **POSITIVE ALTERCASTING.** Pat casts Chris in the role of the "good" person and argues that Chris should comply because a person with "good" qualities would comply.

   PAT: Any intelligent person would grant their partner a divorce when the relationship had died.

11. **NEGATIVE ALTERCASTING.** Pat casts Chris in the role of the "bad" person and argues that Chris should comply because only a person with "bad" qualities would not comply.

   PAT: Only a cruel and selfish neurotic could stand in the way of another's happiness.

12. **POSITIVE ESTEEM.** Pat tells Chris that people will think more highly of Chris (relying on our need for the approval of others) if Chris complies with Pat's request.

   PAT: Everyone will respect your decision to grant me a divorce.

13. **NEGATIVE ESTEEM.** Pat tells Chris that people will think poorly of Chris if Chris does not comply with Pat's request.

   PAT: Everyone will think you're paranoid if you don't join the club.

14. **MORAL APPEALS.** Pat argues that Chris should comply because it is moral to comply and immoral not to comply.

   PAT: An ethical individual would never stand in the way of their partner's freedom and sanity.

15. **ALTRUISM.** Pat asks Chris to comply because Pat needs this compliance (relying on Chris's desire to help and be of assistance).

   PAT: I would feel so disappointed if you quit college now. Don't hurt me by quitting.

16. **DEBT.** Pat asks Chris to comply because of the past favors given to Chris.

   PAT: Look at how we sacrificed to send you to college. How can you quit now?

COMPLIANCE-RESISTING STRATEGIES

Let's say that someone you know asks you to do something you do not want to do: for example, lend your term paper so this person can copy it and turn it in to another teacher. Research with college students shows that there are four principal ways of responding (McLaughlin, Cody, and Robey 1980; O'Hair, Cody, and O'Hair 1991).

   In **identity management,** you resist by trying to manipulate the image of the person making the request. You might do this negatively or positively. In negative identity management, you might picture the requesting agent as unreasonable or unfair and say, for example, "That's really unfair of you to ask me to compromise my ethics." Or you might tell the person that it hurts that he or she would even think you would do such a thing.

You might also use positive identity management. Here you resist complying by making the requesting agent feel good about himself or herself. For example, you might say, "You know this material much better than I do; you can easily do a much better paper yourself."

Another way to resist compliance is to use **nonnegotiation,** a direct refusal to do as requested. You might simply say, "No, I don't lend my papers out."

In **negotiation,** you resist compliance by, for example, offering a compromise ("I'll let you read my paper but not copy it") or by offering to help the person in some other way ("If you write a first draft, I'll go over it and try to make some comments"). If the request is a romantic one—for example, a request to go away for a ski weekend—you might resist by discussing your feelings and proposing an alternative: for example, "Let's double date first."

Another way to resist compliance is through **justification.** Here you justify your refusal by citing possible consequences of compliance or noncompliance. For example, you might cite a negative consequence if you complied ("I'm afraid that I'd get caught, and then I'd fail the course"), or you might cite a positive consequence of your not complying ("You'll really enjoy writing this paper; it's a lot of fun").

Remember that compliance gaining and resisting—like all interpersonal communication—are transactional processes in which all elements are interdependent; each element influences each other. Your attempts to gain compliance, for example, will be influenced by the responses of the person you wish to influence. These responses in turn will influence your responses, and so on. Also, just as your relationship (its type, length, intimacy, for example) will influence the strategies you use, so will the strageties you use influence your relationship. Inappropriate strategies will effect the relationship negatively, just as appropriate strageties will effect the relationship positively.

SUMMARY: UNIT IN BRIEF

Principles of Power	Bases of Power	Compliance Gaining and Compliance Resisting	Power Plays
Some people are more powerful than others. Power can be increased or decreased. Power follows the principle of least interest.	**Referent:** B wants to be like A. **Legitimate:** B believes A has a right to influence or control B's behavior. **Reward:** A has the ability to reward B. **Coercive:** A has the ability to punish B. **Expert:** B regards A as having knowledge. **Information or persuasion:** B attributes to A the ability to communicate effectively.	Tactics that influence others to do as you want (for example, liking, promise, threat) or that enable you to resist compliance (for example, identity management, negotiation)	•Nobody upstairs •You owe me •Metaphor •Yougottobekidding •Thought stoppers **Management strategy** •Statement of feelings •Statement of behavior to which you object •Statement of cooperative response

THINKING CRITICALLY ABOUT POWER IN AN INTERPERSONAL RELATIONSHIPS

1. Whom do you consider the three most interpersonally powerful people you have ever known? Why were these people so powerful? Which types of power did they possess? What types of power do you wield?

2. Does the statement that power follows the principle of least interest explain the balance of power as you see it at work in interpersonal relationships? Test this principle by examining your own interpersonal relationships to determine if the power is in fact held by the less interested party. Consider, too, the implications of such power on your interpersonal interactions.

3. Will the discussion of the consequences of reward versus coercive power influence your own exercise of these two types of power? In what ways?

4. At times, the "sleeper effect" operates in expert power. It goes something like this: a person with little or no expert power says X is Y. Because of the person's lack of expert power, we think we discount the information. Actually, we don't discount it; it is only "sleeping." At a later time, we remember the information but forget its source. The nonexpert source is no longer associated with the information, and so we believe it. Thus, we frequently give expert power to nonexperts because we dissociate the content of a message from its source. This sleeper effect seems to be the major reason why many people who verbally dismiss the "information" in advertisements and in

many newspapers (such as the *Enquirer*) later quote statistics and "facts" from these very sources. Quite likely, these people have retained the message but forgotten the source. His this ever happened to you? Have you ever heard others do this?

5. Which—if any—of the 16 compliance-gaining strategies have you used? Which—if any—have been used on you? How effective were these attempts?

6. Have you ever either been a party to or witnessed any of the power plays discussed in this unit (nobody upstairs, you owe me, metaphor, yougottobekidding, and thought stoppers)? What led to their use? What effects did these power plays have on the people involved?

7. In what kinds of situations do you think it might be best simply to ignore the power play? In what situations might it be best to neutralize the power play (treat it as an isolated instance)? In what situations might it be best to employ a cooperative response to the power play?

8. Examine the strategies for compliance gaining. Which of these strategies do you find most effective? Which strategies work best on you? What other strategies can you identify? Note that these strategies are regarded as generally effective though not necessarily moral or ethical. Which strategies would you consider ethical? Which would you consider unethical?

9. How would you use compliance-gaining strategies to say no to someone's romantic advances? How would you use compliance-gaining strategies to specify that there must be a particular condition for a romantic involvement?

10. How would you go about designing a study to investigate each of the following questions?

- What bases of power work best in the elementary or high school classroom? Which work best in the college classroom? Which work best in your own interpersonal relationships?
- What effects does the recommended management strategy for power plays have on friendship relationships? On romantic relationships?
- Which compliance-gaining strategies work best in same-sex and opposite-sex interactions? Which are least effective?
- Which compliance-resisting strategies work best for teenagers resisting drugs? Which are least effective?
- Which compliance-gaining and which compliance-resisting strategies create the most goodwill? The most ill will?

EXPERIENTIAL VEHICLES

20.1 THE EXERCISE OF POWER

Examine your most important interpersonal relationships in terms of (1) the power that you exert and (2) the power that is exerted on you.

Select one significant other and state the amount of power you exert over her or him and the amount that she or he exerts over you. Express the amount of power in terms of percentages; the total should add up to 100 percent for each column.

You exert over other	*Power*	*Other exerts over you*
_____	Referent	_____
_____	Legitimate	_____
_____	Reward	_____
_____	Coercive	_____
_____	Expert	_____
_____	Information	_____
100%		100%

Consider the following questions:

1. One of the assumptions made in this unit is that power is a factor in all relationships. Do you agree with this? Can you identify a relationship that does not have a power dimension?
2. Research suggests that we like the person who has reward power over us and dislike the person who has coercive power over us. Is this true in your situation? Explain why you think the relationships prevail in your case.
3. On what bases do most people attribute expert power to you? That is, in what fields or areas do you have expert power? How might you increase your expert power?
4. What type of power seems to work best when exerted on you? That is, what type of power best enables people to control your behavior? Explain. What power is least effective when exerted on you? Explain.
5. In what ways are reward and coercive power exerted over you? In what ways do you exert reward and coercive power over others?
6. To whom do you attribute legitimate power? Why?
7. Do you exercise legitimate power? Who attributes legitimate power to you? Explain.
8. In what ways might you increase your interpersonal power?
9. Are you satisfied or dissatisfied with your responses to power and with your use of power? How would you like to change? What might you do to effect these changes?

20.2 MANAGING POWER PLAYS

Here are some examples of the five power plays we have just considered. For each one, identify the power play, and provide an appropriate three-part management strategy as identified in the text:

- State your feelings (remember to use I-messages).
- Describe the other person's behavior that you object to.
- State a cooperative response.

1. Fred continually interrupts you. Whenever you want to say something, Fred breaks in, finishes what he thinks you were saying, and then says what he wants to say.
2. One of your coworkers responds to your ideas, plans, and suggestions with statements like "yougottobekidding," "you can't mean that," and "you can't possibly be serious." So when you say you are going to date Harry, she says, "You can't be serious! Harry!" When you say you are going to apply for a promotion, she says, "Promotion! You got to be kidding! You've only been with the company six months."
3. Your close friend has helped you get a job in his company. Now, whenever he wants you to do something, he reminds you that he got you the job. Whenever you object

that you have your own work to do, he reminds you that you wouldn't have any work to do if it wasn't for his getting you the job in the first place.

4. Your supervisor is compulsive about neatness and frequently goes around telling the workers to clean up their areas. Frequently, this supervisor uses the power play of metaphor: "Clean up this crap before you leave tonight" or "Make sure this junk is put away."

5. Your friend Amida sits next to you in class but rarely listens to the instructor. Instead, she waits until you copy something down in your notes, and then she copies what you have written. In doing this, she frequently distracts you, and you miss a great deal of what the instructor has said. You have told her repeatedly that you object to this, but she acts as though she doesn't hear you.

UNIT 21

Conflict in Interpersonal Relationships

UNIT OBJECTIVES

AFTER COMPLETING THIS UNIT, YOU SHOULD BE ABLE TO:

1. Define Interpersonal conflict
2. Distinguish between content and relationship conflict
3. Identify potentially negative and positive aspects of conflict
4. Explain the model of conflict resolution

5. Identify and explain at least six conflict strategies
6. Explain verbal aggressiveness and argumentativeness

In its most basic form, conflict refers to a disagreement. Interpersonal conflict, then, refers to a disagreement between or among connected individuals: for example, close friends, lovers, or family members. The word "connected" emphasizes the transactional nature of interpersonal conflict, the fact that each person's position affects the other person. The positions in conflict are to some degree interrelated and incompatible.

THE NATURE OF CONFLICT

Conflicts can center on:

- goals to be pursued ("We want you to go to college and become a teacher or a doctor, not a disco dancer").
- allocation of resources, such as money or time ("I want to spend the tax refund on a car, not on new furniture").
- decisions to be made ("I refuse to have the Jeffersons over to dinner").
- behaviors that are considered appropriate or desirable by one person and inappropriate or undesirable by the other ("I hate it when you get drunk, pinch me, ridicule me in front of others, flirt with others, dress provocatively, and so on").

MYTHS ABOUT CONFLICT

One of the problems in studying and in dealing with interpersonal conflict is that we may be operating with false assumptions about what conflict is and what it means. For example, do you think the following statements are true or false?

- If two people engage in relationship conflict, it means their relationship is a bad one.
- Conflict hurts an interpersonal relationship.
- Conflict is bad because it reveals our negative selves—for example, our pettiness, our need to be in control, our unreasonable expectations.

As with most things, simple answers are usually wrong. The three assumptions above may all be true or may all be false. It depends. Conflict is a part of every interpersonal relationship, between parents and children, brothers and sisters, friends, lovers, coworkers.

It is not so much the conflict that creates the problem as the way in which you approach and deal with the conflict. Some ways of approaching conflict can resolve difficulties and actually improve the relationship. Other ways can hurt the relationship; they can destroy self-esteem, create bitterness, and foster suspicion.

Similarly, it is not the conflict that reveals your negative side but the fight strategies you use. Thus, if you attack the other person personally or use force, you reveal your negative side. But you can also reveal your positive self—your willingness to listen to opposing points of view, to change unpleasant behaviors, and to accept imperfection in others.

THE NEGATIVES AND POSITIVES OF CONFLICT

Interpersonal conflict is inevitable because people are different and will necessarily see things differently. But it is neither good nor bad in itself. Rather, there are both negative and positive aspects to interpersonal conflict.

Negative Aspects   Conflict often leads to increased negative regard for the opponent, and when this opponent is someone you love or care for, it can create serious problems. One problem is that many conflicts involve unfair fighting methods and focus largely on hurting the other person. If this happens, negative feelings are sure to increase. Conflict may also deplete energy better spent on other areas, especially when unproductive conflict strategies are used.

At times, conflict may lead you to close yourself off from the other individual. When you do this and hide your true feelings from an intimate, you prevent meaningful communication. Because the need for intimacy is so strong, one possible outcome is that one or both parties may seek this intimacy elsewhere. This often leads to further conflict, mutual hurt, and resentment—qualities that add heavily to the costs carried by the relationship. As these costs increase, the rewards may become more difficult to exchange. Here, then, is a situation in which costs increase and rewards decrease—a situation that often results in relationship deterioration and eventual dissolution.

Positive Aspects   The major advantage of interpersonal conflict is that it forces you to examine a problem and work toward a potential solution. If productive conflict strategies are used, your relationship may well emerge from the encounter stronger, healthier, and more satisfying than before.

Conflict enables you to state what you each want and—if the conflict is resolved effectively—perhaps to get it. For example, let's say that I want to spend our money on a new car (my old one is unreliable), and you want to spend it on a vacation (you feel the need for a change of pace). Through our conflict and its resolution, we can learn what each genuinely wants: in this case, a reliable car and a break from routine. We may then be able to figure out a way for us each to get what we want. I might accept a good used car or a less expensive new car, and you might accept a shorter or less expensive vacation. Or we might buy a used car and take an inexpensive motor trip. Each of these solutions will satisfy both of us; they are win-win solutions—each of us wins, and each of us gets what we wanted.

Conflict also prevents hostilities and resentments from festering. Say I'm annoyed at your talking with your colleague from work for two hours on the phone instead of giving that time to me. If I say nothing, my annoyance and resentment are likely to grow. Further, by saying nothing I have implicitly approved of such behavior, and so it is likely that such phone calls will be repeated.

Through our conflict and its resolution, we stop resentment from increasing. In the process, we also let our own needs be known—that I need lots of attention when I come home from work and that you need to review the day's work and gain the assurance that it has been properly completed. If we both can appreciate the legitimacy of these needs, then solutions may be identified. Perhaps the phone call can be made after my attention needs are met, or perhaps I can delay my need for attention until you get closure about work. Or perhaps I can learn to provide for your closure needs and in doing so get my attention needs met. Again, we have win-win solutions; each of us gets our needs met.

Consider, too, that when we try to resolve conflict within an interpersonal relationship, we are saying in effect that the relationship is worth the effort; otherwise, we would walk away from such a conflict. Although there may be exceptions—as when we confront conflict to save face or to gratify some ego need—confronting a conflict usually indicates concern, commitment, and a desire to preserve the relationship.

CONTENT AND RELATIONSHIP CONFLICTS

Using concepts developed earlier, we can make a distinction between content and relationship conflict. **Content conflict** centers on objects, events, and persons that are usually, but not always, external to the parties involved in the conflict. They include the many issues we argue and fight about every day—the value of a particular movie, what to watch on television, the fairness of the last examination or job promotion, and the way to spend our savings.

Relationship conflicts are seen in situations like these: a younger brother does not obey his older brother, two partners each want an equal say about vacation plans, and a mother and daughter each want the final word about the daughter's lifestyle. Here the conflicts are concerned not so much with external objects as with the relationships between the individuals, with such issues as who is in charge, the equality of a primary relationship, and who has the right to establish rules of behavior.

Content and relationship conflicts are always easier to separate in a textbook than they are in real life, where many conflicts contain elements of both. But if we can recognize which issues pertain to content and which to relationship, we will better understand the conflict and thus be able to manage it more effectively.

A MODEL OF CONFLICT RESOLUTION

We can explain conflict more fully and provide guidance for dealing with it effectively by referring to the model in Figure 21.1.

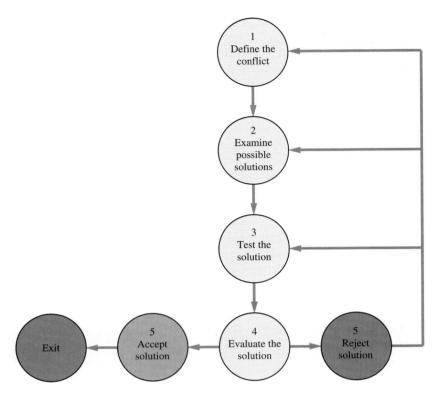

Figure 21.1
Stages in conflict resolution.

DEFINE THE CONFLICT

Define the obvious content issues (who should do the dishes, who should take the kids to school, who should take out the dog) as well as the underlying relationship issues (who has been avoiding household responsibilities, who has been neglecting responsibility toward the kids, whose time is more valuable).

Define the problem in specific terms. Conflict defined in the abstract is difficult to deal with and resolve. It is one thing for a husband to say that his wife is "cold and unfeeling" and quite another to say that she does not call him at the office, kiss him when he comes home, or hold his hand when they are at a party. These behaviors can be agreed upon and dealt with, but the abstract "cold and unfeeling" remains elusive.

Throughout this process, try to understand the nature of the conflict from the other person's point of view. Use your perspective-taking skills. Why is your partner disturbed that you are not doing the dishes? Why is your neighbor complaining about taking the kids to school? Why is your mother insisting you take out the dog?

Don't try to read the other person's mind. Ask questions to make sure you see the problem from the other person's point of view. Ask directly and simply: for example, "Why are you insisting that I take the dog out now when I have to call three clients before nine o'clock?"

Let us select an example and work it through the remaining steps. This conflict revolves around Pat's not wanting to socialize with Chris's friends. Chris is devoted to them, but Pat actively dislikes them. Chris thinks they are wonderful and exciting; Pat thinks they are unpleasant and boring.

EXAMINE POSSIBLE SOLUTIONS

Most conflicts can probably be resolved through a variety of solutions. At this stage, try to identify as many solutions as possible.

Look for solutions that will enable both parties to win—to get something each wants. Avoid win-lose solutions, in which one wins and one loses. They will cause difficulty for the relationship by engendering frustration and resentment.

In examining these potential solutions, carefully weigh the costs and the rewards that each solution entails. Most solutions will involve costs to one or both parties (after all, *someone* has to take the dog out). Seek solutions in which the costs and the rewards will be evenly shared.

Once you have examined all possible solutions, select one and test it out. Among the solutions that Pat and Chris might identify are these:

1. Chris should not interact with these friends anymore.
2. Pat should interact with Chris's friends.
3. Chris should see these friends without Pat.

Clearly solutions 1 and 2 are win-lose solutions. In solution 1, Pat wins and Chris loses; in 2, Chris wins and Pat loses. Solution 3 has some possibilities. Both might win and neither must necessarily lose. Let's examine this solution more closely.

An especially interesting way to examine the solutions is to apply the critical-thinking hats technique, developed by the critical-thinking theorist Edward deBono (1987). The technique, applicable to defining, analyzing, and evaluating problems and solutions, involves six "thinking hats." With each hat, you look at the problem from a different perspective.

- The **fact hat** focuses attention on the data, the facts and figures that bear on the problem. For example: *What are the relevant data in this conflict? How can Pat get more information on the rewards that Chris gets from these friends? How can Chris find out exactly what Pat doesn't like about these friends?*
- The **feeling hat** focuses attention on feelings, emotions, and intuitions concerning the problem. For example: *How do we feel about the problem? How does Pat feel when Chris goes out with these friends? How does Chris feel when Pat refuses to meet with them?*
- The **negative argument hat** puts you in the position of devil's advocate. For example: *How might this relationship deteriorate if Chris continues seeing these friends without Pat? How might the relationship deteriorate if Pat resists interacting with Chris's friends?*
- The **positive benefits hat** asks that you look at the upside. For example: *What opportunities might be gained if Chris sees these friends without Pat? What benefits might Pat and Chris derive from this new arrangement? What would be the best thing that could happen?*

- The **creative new idea hat** focuses attention on new ways of looking at the problem. For example: *In what other ways can you look at this problem? What other possible solutions might you consider?*
- The **control of thinking hat** helps you analyze what you have done and are doing. It asks you to reflect on your own thinking processes and to synthesize the results of your thinking. For example: *Have you adequately defined the problem? Are you focusing too much on insignificant issues? Have you given enough attention to the possible negative effects?*

TEST THE SOLUTION

Test the solution mentally. How does it feel now? How will it feel tomorrow? Are you comfortable with it? Would Pat be comfortable with Chris's socializing with these friends alone? Some of Chris's friends are attractive; would this cause difficulty for Pat and Chris's relationship? Will Chris give people too much to gossip about? Will Chris feel guilty? Will Chris enjoy these friends without Pat?

Test the solution in practice. Put the solution into operation. How does it work? If it doesn't work, then discard it and try another solution. Give each solution a fair chance, but don't hang on to a solution when it is clear that it won't resolve the conflict.

Perhaps Chris might go out without Pat once to test this solution. How was it? Did these friends think there was something wrong with Chris's relationship with Pat? Did Chris feel guilty? Did Chris enjoy this new experience? How did Pat feel? Did Pat feel jealous? Lonely? Abandoned?

EVALUATE THE SOLUTION

Did the solution help resolve the conflict? Is the situation better now than it was before the solution was tried? Share your feelings and evaluations of the solution.

Pat and Chris now need to share their perceptions of this possible solution. Would they be comfortable with this solution on a monthly basis? Is the solution worth the costs each will pay? Are the costs and rewards evenly distributed? Might other solutions be more effective?

ACCEPT OR REJECT THE SOLUTION

If you accept the solution, you are ready to put it into more permanent operation. If you decide that this is not the right solution for the conflict, then you might test another solution or perhaps go back to redefine the conflict.

Let us say that Pat is actually quite happy with the solution. Pat was able to use that time to visit college friends. The next time Chris goes out with friends, Pat intends to go to wrestling with these people from college. Chris feels pretty good about seeing friends without Pat. Chris explains that they have both decided to see their friends separately and both are comfortable with this decision.

If, however, Pat or Chris was unhappy with this solution, they would have to try out another one or perhaps go back and redefine the problem and seek other ways to resolve it.

Throughout this process, avoid the common but damaging conflict strategies that can destroy a relationship. At the same time, use those strategies that will help to resolve the conflict and even improve the relationship.

CONFLICT MANAGEMENT STRATEGIES

We have already covered a wide variety of conflict resolution skills. For example, active listening is a skill that has wide application in conflict situations (see Unit 4). Similarly, using I-messages (rather than accusatory you-messages; see Unit 6) will contribute to effective interpersonal conflict resolution (Noller and Fitzpatrick 1993). And, of course, the characteristics of interpersonal competence (Unit 6) are clear and effective conflict resolution techniques.

The following discussion focuses on unproductive strategies that should be avoided, as well as their productive counterparts.

AVOIDANCE AND FIGHTING ACTIVELY

Avoidance may involve actual physical flight: for example, leaving the scene of the conflict (walking out of the apartment or going to another part of the office), falling asleep, or blasting the stereo to drown out all conversation. It may also take the form of emotional or intellectual avoidance, whereby you leave the conflict psychologically by not dealing with the issues raised. Men are more likely to use this strategy, coupled with denial that anything is wrong (Haferkamp 1991–92).

Nonnegotiation is a special type of avoidance. Here you refuse to discuss the conflict or to listen to the other person's argument. At times, this nonnegotiation takes the form of hammering away at one's own point of view until the other person gives in.

Instead of avoiding the issues, take an active role in your interpersonal conflicts. This is not to say that a cooling-off period is not at times desirable. It is to say, instead, that if you wish to resolve conflicts, you need to confront them actively.

Involve yourself on both sides of the communication exchange. Be an active participant as a speaker and as a listener; voice your own feelings and listen carefully to your partner's feelings.

Another part of active fighting involves taking responsibility for your thoughts and feelings. For example, when you disagree with your partner or find fault with her or his behavior, take responsibility for these feelings. Say, for example, "I disagree with . . . " or "I don't like it when you. . . ." Avoid statements that deny your responsibility: for example, "Everybody thinks you're wrong about . . . " or "Chris thinks you shouldn't. . . ."

FORCE AND TALK

When confronted with conflict, many people prefer not to deal with the issues but rather to force their position on the other person. The force may be emotional or physical. In either case, however, the issues are avoided, and the person who "wins" is the one who exerts the most force. This is the technique of warring nations, children, and even some normally sensible adults.

More than 50 percent of both single and married couples reported that they had experienced physical violence in their relationship. If we add symbolic violence (for example, threatening to hit the other person or throwing something), the percentages are above 60 percent for singles and above 70 percent for marrieds (Marshall and Rose 1987). In another study, 47 percent of a sample of 410 college students reported some experience with violence in a dating relationship (Deal and Wampler 1986). In most cases, the violence was reciprocal—each person in the relationship used violence.

In cases in which only one person was violent, the research results are conflicting. For example, the study involving the college students found that in cases in which one partner was violent, the aggressor was significantly more often the female (Deal and Wampler 1986). Earlier research found similar sex differences (for example, Cate et al. 1982). These findings contradict the popular belief that males are more violent in heterosexual partnerships. One possible explanation for this is that in our society women are more likely to accept victimization as "normal," the implication being that they are therefore less likely to report it. . . . Aggression by women on the other hand, being "unnatural," would stand out more and be remembered more. Since women are stereotypically seen as less aggressive than men, it may take less aggression on the part of a woman for her to be labelled aggressive. This may then lead to an overreporting of the woman's aggressive acts. (Deal and Wampler 1986; also see Gelles 1981). Other research, however, has found that the popular conception of men being more likely than women to use force to achieve compliance is indeed true (Deturck 1987).

One form of relational force is, of course, rape. The studies in this area show alarming findings. According to Karen Kersten and Lawrence Kersten (1988), "forced sex on a date is probably one of the most common forms of all types of rape." In a study of force and violence on one college campus, more than half of the women students reported that they were verbally threatened, physically coerced, or physically abused; more than 12 percent indicated they had been raped (Barrett 1982; Kersten and Kersten 1988). In another investigation of sexual assault on college campuses, 45 percent of the women surveyed reported being victims of criminal sexual assault, criminal sexual abuse, and battery-intimidation (Illinois Coalition 1990). In yet another study, 42 percent of the men surveyed indicated they had engaged in coercive sexual relationships in which they were the coercing partners (Craig, Kalichman, and Follingstad 1989).

One of the most puzzling findings is that many victims of violence interpret it as a sign of love. For some reason, they see being beaten, verbally abused, or raped as a sign that their partner is fully in love with them (see Unit 22). Many victims, in fact, accept the blame for contributing to the violence instead of blaming their partners (Gelles and Cornell 1985).

Equally puzzling but more frightening is the finding—from at least one study—that of the college-age men surveyed, 51 percent said they would rape a woman if they knew they would never get caught (Illinois Coalition 1990).

Findings such as these point to problems well beyond the prevalence of unproductive conflict strategies that we want to identify and avoid. They demonstrate the existence of underlying pathologies, which we are discovering are a lot more common than we previously thought when issues like these were never mentioned in college textbooks or lectures. Awareness is, of course, only the first step in understanding and eventually combating such problems.

The only real alternative to force is talk. Instead of using force, talk and listen. The qualities of openness, empathy, and positiveness (see Unit 6), for example, are suitable starting points.

BLAME AND EMPATHY

Because most relationship conflicts are caused by a wide variety of factors, any attempt to single out one or two for *blame* is sure to fail. Yet a frequently used fight strategy is to blame someone. Consider, for example, the couple who fight over their child's getting into trouble with the police. The parents may—instead of dealing with the conflict itself—blame each other for the child's troubles. Such blaming, of course, does nothing to resolve the problem or to help the child.

Often when you blame someone you attribute motives to the person. Thus, if the person forgot your birthday and this oversight disturbs you, fight about the forgetting of the birthday (the actual behavior). Try not to mind read the motives of another person: "Well, it's obvious you just don't care about me. If you really cared, you could never have forgotten my birthday!"

Perhaps the best alternative to blame is empathy. Try to feel what the other person is feeling and to see the situation as the other person does. Try to see the situation as punctuated by the other person and how this punctuation may differ from your own.

Demonstrate empathic understanding. Once you have empathically understood your opponent's feelings, validate those feelings when appropriate. If your partner is hurt or angry and you believe such feelings are legitimate and justified, say so: "You have a right to be angry; I shouldn't have called your mother a slob. I'm sorry. But I still don't want to go on vacation with her." In expressing validation, you are not necessarily expressing agreement on the issue in conflict; you are merely stating that your partner has feelings that you recognize as legitimate.

SILENCERS AND FACILITATING OPEN EXPRESSION

Silencers are conflict techniques that literally silence the other individual. Among the wide variety that exists, one frequently used silencer is crying. When a person is unable to deal with a conflict or when winning seems unlikely, he or she may cry and thus silence the other person.

Another silencer is to feign extreme emotionalism—to yell and scream and pretend to be losing control of oneself. Still another is to develop some "physical" reaction—headaches and shortness of breath are probably the most popular. One of the major problems with silencers is that you can never be certain whether they are strategies to win the argument or real physical reactions to which you should pay attention. Regardless of what we do, however, the conflict remains unexamined and unresolved.

Grant the other person permission to express himself or herself freely and openly; grant permission to be oneself. Avoid power tactics that suppress or inhibit freedom of expression. Avoid, for example, tactics such as "nobody upstairs" or "you owe me," identified in Unit 20. These tactics are designed to put the other person down and to subvert true interpersonal equality.

One consistent recommendation made by interpersonal theorists is that if conflict is to be resolved and if it is not to seriously damage the relationship, it needs to be discussed. Do you agree with this recommendation? What positive and negative consequences might result from openly discussing your relational conflicts? Would theorists in other cultures make the same recommendation?

GUNNYSACKING AND PRESENT FOCUS

Gunnysacking—a term derived from the large burlap bag called a gunnysack—refers to the practice of storing up grievances so they may be unloaded at another time. The immediate occasion may be relatively simple (or so it might seem at first), such as someone's coming home late without calling. Instead of arguing about this, the gunnysacker unloads all past grievances. The birthday you forgot, the time you arrived late for dinner, the hotel reservations you forgot to make are all thrown at you. As you may know from experience, gunnysacking begets gunnysacking. When one person gunnysacks, the other person gunnysacks. The result is two people dumping their stored-up grievances on one another. Frequently, the original problem never gets addressed. Instead, resentment and hostility escalate.

Focus your conflict on the here-and-now rather than on issues that occurred two months ago (as in gunnysacking). Similarly, focus your conflict on the person with whom you are fighting and not on the person's mother, child, or friends.

MANIPULATION AND SPONTANEITY

In *manipulation,* there is avoidance of open conflict. The individual attempts to divert the conflict by being especially charming (disarming, actually). The manipulator gets the other person into a receptive and noncombative frame of mind. Then the manipulator presents his or her demands to a weakened opponent. The manipulator relies on the tendency to give in to people who act especially nice.

Instead, try expressing your feelings with spontaneity. Remember that in interpersonal conflict there is no need to win a war. The objective is not to win but to increase mutual understanding and to reach a decision that both parties can accept.

PERSONAL REJECTION AND ACCEPTANCE

In *personal rejection,* one person withholds love and affection. He or she seeks to win the argument by getting the other person to break down in the face of this withdrawal. The individual acts cold and uncaring in an effort to demoralize the other person. In withdrawing affection, for example, the individual hopes to make the other person question his or her own self-worth. Once the other is demoralized and feels less than worthy, it is relatively easy for the "rejector" to get his or her way.

Instead, express positive feelings for the other person and for the relationship between the two of you. Throughout any conflict, many harsh words will probably be exchanged, later to be regretted. The words cannot be unsaid or uncommunicated, but they can be partially offset by the expression of positive statements. If you are engaged in combat with someone you love, remember that you are fighting with a loved one and express that feeling: "I love you very much, but I still don't want your mother on vacation with us. I want to be alone with you."

FIGHTING BELOW AND ABOVE THE BELT

Much like prize fighters in a ring, each of us has a "belt line." When you hit someone below it, you can inflict serious injury. When you hit above the belt, however, the person is able to absorb the blow. With most interpersonal relationships, especially those of long standing, you know where the belt line is. You know, for example, that to hit Pat with the inability to have children is to hit below the belt. You know that to hit Chris with the failure to get a permanent job is to hit below the belt. Hitting below the belt line causes all persons involved added problems. Keep blows to areas your opponent can absorb and handle.

The aim of relationship conflict is not to win and have your opponent lose. Rather, it is to resolve a problem and strengthen the relationship. Keep this ultimate goal always in clear focus, especially when you are angry or hurt.

VERBAL AGGRESSIVENESS AND ARGUMENTATIVENESS

An especially interesting perspective on conflict is emerging from the work on verbal aggressiveness and argumentativeness (Infante and Rancer 1982; Infante and Wigley 1986; Infante 1988). Understanding these two concepts will help in understanding some of the reasons why things go wrong and some of the ways in which you can use conflict to actually improve your relationships.

VERBAL AGGRESSIVENESS

Verbal aggressiveness is a method of winning an argument by inflicting psychological pain, by attacking the other person's self-concept. It is a type of disconfirmation (and the opposite of confirmation) in that it seeks to discredit the individual's view of self (see Unit 11). To explore this tendency further, take the accompanying self-test of verbal aggressiveness.

TEST YOURSELF

HOW VERBALLY AGGRESSIVE ARE YOU?*

INSTRUCTIONS
This scale is designed to measure how people try to obtain compliance from others. For each statement, indicate the extent to which you feel it is true for you in your attempts to influence others. Use the following scale:

1 = almost never true
2 = rarely true
3 = occasionally true
4 = often true
5 = almost always true

_____ 1. I am extremely careful to avoid attacking individuals' intelligence when I attack their ideas.

_____ 2. When individuals are very stubborn, I use insults to soften the stubbornness.

_____ 3. I try very hard to avoid having other people feel bad about themselves when I try to influence them.

_____ 4. When people refuse to do a task I know is important, without good reason, I tell them they are unreasonable.

_____ 5. When others do things I regard as stupid, I try to be extremely gentle with them.

_____ 6. If individuals I am trying to influence really deserve it, I attack their character.

_____ 7. When people behave in ways that are in very poor taste, I insult them in order to shock them into proper behavior.

_____ 8. I try to make people feel good about themselves even when their ideas are stupid.

_____ 9. When people simply will not budge on a matter of importance, I lose my temper and say rather strong things to them.

_____10. When people criticize my shortcomings, I take it in good humor and do not try to get back at them.

_____11. When individuals insult me, I get a lot of pleasure out of really telling them off.

_____12. When I dislike individuals greatly, I try not to show it in what I say or how I say it.

_____13. I like poking fun at people who do things which are very stupid in order to stimulate their intelligence.

_____14. When I attack a person's ideas, I try not to damage their self-concepts.

_____15. When I try to influence people, I make a great effort not to offend them.

_____16. When people do things which are mean or cruel, I attack their character in order to help correct their behavior.

_____17. I refuse to participate in arguments when they involve personal attacks.

_____18. When nothing seems to work in trying to influence others, I yell and scream in order to get some movement from them.

_____19. When I am not able to refute others' positions, I try to make them feel defensive in order to weaken their positions.

_____20. When an argument shifts to personal attacks, I try very hard to change the subject.

SCORING
To compute your verbal aggressiveness score, follow these steps:

1. Add the scores on items 2, 4, 6, 7, 9, 11, 13, 16, 18, 19.
2. Add the scores on items 1, 3, 5, 8, 10, 12, 14, 15, 17, 20.
3. Subtract the sum obtained in step 2 from 60.
4. To compute your verbal aggressiveness score, add the total obtained in step 1 to the result obtained in step 3.

If you scored between 59 and 100, you are high in verbal aggressiveness; if you scored between 39 and 58, you are moderate in verbal aggressiveness; if you scored between 20 and 38, you are low in verbal aggressiveness.

In computing your score, make special note of the characteristics the statements identify in connection with the tendency to act verbally aggressive. Note those inappropriate behaviors you are especially prone to commit. High agreement (4 or 5 on the scale) with statements 2, 4, 6, 7, 9, 11, 13, 16, 18, and 19 and low agreement (1 and 2 on the scale) with statements 1, 3, 5, 8, 10, 12, 14, 15, 17, and 20 will help you highlight any significant verbal aggressiveness you might have. Review previous encounters when you acted verbally aggressive. What effect did such action have on your subsequent interaction? What effect did it have on your relationship with the other person? What alternative ways of getting your point across might you have used? Might these have proved more effective?

*From "Verbal Aggressiveness: An Interpersonal Model and Measure" by Dominic Infante and C.J. Wrigley, *Communication Monographs* 53, 1986, pp. 61–69. Reprinted by permission of the Speech Communication Association.

Character attack, perhaps because it is extremely effective in inflicting psychological pain, is the most popular tactic of verbal aggressiveness. Other tactics include attacking the person's abilities, background, and physical appearance; cursing; teasing; ridiculing; threatening; swearing; and using various nonverbal emblems (Infante et al. 1990).

Some researchers have argued that "unless aroused by verbal aggression, a hostile disposition remains latent in the form of unexpressed anger" (Infante, Chandler, and Rudd 1989). There is some evidence to show that people in violent marriages are more often verbally aggressive than people in nonviolent marriages.

Because verbal aggressiveness does not help to resolve conflicts, results in loss of credibility for the person using it, and increases the credibility of the target of the aggressiveness (Infante, Hartley, Martin, Higgins, Bruning, and Hur 1992), you may wonder why people act verbally aggressive. What, if anything, would lead you to act in a verbally aggressive manner? Acting verbally aggressive as a response to the other person's aggressiveness is the most frequently cited reason. Other reasons are dislike for the other person, anger, feeling unable to argue effectively, responding to a degenerating discussion, being taught to respond this way, being reminded of being hurt, and being in a bad mood (Infante, Riddle, Horvath, and Tumlin 1992).

ARGUMENTATIVENESS

Contrary to popular usage, the term "argumentativeness" refers to a quality to be cultivated rather than avoided. Argumentativeness is your willingness to argue for a point of view, your tendency to speak your mind on significant issues. It is the mode of dealing with disagreements that is the preferred alternative to verbal aggressiveness. Before reading about ways to increase your argumentativeness, take the accompanying self-test, "How Argumentative Are You?"

Generally, those who score high in argumentativeness have a strong tendency to state their position on controversial issues and argue against the positions of others. A high scorer sees arguing both as exciting and intellectually challenging and as an opportunity to win a kind of contest. Not surprisingly, high argumentatives also have greater resistance to persuasion and can generate a greater number of counterarguments to a persuasive appeal of another (Kazoleas 1993).

The person who scores low in argumentativeness tries to prevent arguments. This person experiences satisfaction not from arguing but from avoiding arguments. The low argumentative sees arguing as unpleasant and unsatisfying. Not surprisingly, this person has little confidence in his or her ability to argue effectively. The moderately argumentative person possesses some of the qualities of both the high argumentative and the low argumentative.

The researchers who developed this test note that both high and low argumentatives may experience communication difficulties. The high argumentative, for example, may argue needlessly, too often, and too forcefully. The low argumentative, in contrast, may avoid taking a stand even when it is necessary. Persons scoring somewhere in the middle are probably the more interpersonally skilled and adaptable, arguing when it is necessary but avoiding the many arguments that are needless and repetitive. People skilled in argumentativeness are also less likely than both low argumentatives and verbally aggressive people to experience marital violence (Infante, Chandler, and Rudd 1989).

TEST YOURSELF

HOW ARGUMENTATIVE ARE YOU?*

INSTRUCTIONS
This questionnaire contains statements about controversial issues. Indicate how often each statement is true for you personally according to the following scale:

1 = almost never true
2 = rarely true
3 = occasionally true
4 = often true
5 = almost always true

_____ 1. While in an argument, I worry that the person I am arguing with will form a negative impression of me.

_____ 2. Arguing over controversial issues improves my intelligence.

_____ 3. I enjoy avoiding arguments.

_____ 4. I am energetic and enthusiastic when I argue.

_____ 5. Once I finish an argument, I promise myself that I will not get into another.

_____ 6. Arguing with a person creates more problems for me than it solves.

_____ 7. I have a pleasant, good feeling when I win a point in an argument.

_____ 8. When I finish arguing with someone, I feel nervous and upset.

_____ 9. I enjoy a good argument over a controversial issue.

_____ 10. I get an unpleasant feeling when I realize I am about to get into an argument.

_____ 11. I enjoy defending my point of view on an issue.

_____ 12. I am happy when I keep an argument from happening.

_____ 13. I do not like to miss the opportunity to argue a controversial issue.

_____ 14. I prefer being with people who rarely disagree with me.

_____ 15. I consider an argument an exciting intellectual challenge.

_____ 16. I find myself unable to think of effective points during an argument.

_____ 17. I feel refreshed and satisfied after an argument on a controversial issue.

_____ 18. I have the ability to do well in an argument.

_____ 19. I try to avoid getting into arguments.

_____ 20. I feel excitement when I expect that a conversation I am in is leading to an argument.

SCORING
1. Add your scores on items 2, 4, 7, 9, 11, 13, 15, 17, 18, and 20.
2. Add 60 to the sum obtained in step 1.
3. Add your scores on items 1, 3, 5, 6, 8, 10, 12, 14, 16, and 19.
4. To compute your argumentativeness score, subtract the total obtained in step 3 from the total obtained in step 2.

Here are some suggestions for cultivating argumentativeness and for preventing it from degenerating into aggressiveness (Infante 1988):

- Treat disagreements as objectively as possible; avoid assuming that because someone takes issue with your position or interpretation, they are attacking you as a person.
- Avoid attacking the other person (rather than the person's arguments), even if the attack would give you a tactical advantage; center your arguments on issues rather than personalities.
- Reaffirm the other person's sense of competence; compliment the other person as appropriate.
- Avoid interrupting; allow the other person to state her or his position fully before you respond.
- Stress equality (see Unit 6), and stress the similarities you have with the other person; emphasize areas of agreement before attacking the disagreements.
- Express interest in the other person's position, attitude, and point of view.
- Avoid presenting your arguments too emotionally; using an overly loud voice or interjecting vulgar expressions will prove offensive and eventually ineffective.
- Allow the other person to save face; never humiliate the other person.

BEFORE AND AFTER THE CONFLICT

If you are to make conflict truly productive, consider a few suggestions for preparing for conflict and for using it for relational growth.

BEFORE THE CONFLICT

Try to fight in private. When you air your conflicts in front of others, you create a variety of other problems. You may not be willing to be totally honest when third parties are present; you may feel you have to save face and therefore must win the fight at all costs. This may lead you to use strategies to win the argument rather than to resolve the conflict. You may become so absorbed by the image that others will have of you that you forget you have a relationship problem that needs to be resolved. Also, you run the risk of embarrassing your partner in front of others, and this embarrassment may create resentment and hostility.

Be sure you are each ready to fight. Although conflicts arise at the most inopportune times, you can choose the time to resolve them. Confronting your partner when she or he comes home after a hard day of work may not be the right time for resolving a conflict. Make sure you are both relatively free of other problems and ready to deal with the conflict at hand.

Know what you're fighting about. Sometimes people in a relationship become so hurt and angry that they lash out at the other person just to vent their own frustration. The problem at the center of the conflict (for example, the uncapped toothpaste tube) is merely an excuse to express anger. Any attempt to resolve this "problem" will be doomed to failure because the problem addressed is not what is causing the conflict. Instead, it is the underlying hostility, anger, and frustration that needs to be addressed.

Fight about problems that can be solved. Fighting about past behaviors or about family members or situations over which you have no control solves nothing; instead, it creates additional difficulties. Any attempt at resolution will fail because the problems are incapable of being solved. Often such conflicts are concealed attempts at expressing one's frustration or dissatisfaction.

AFTER THE CONFLICT

After the conflict is resolved, there is still work to be done. Learn from the conflict and from the process you went through in trying to resolve it. For example, can you identify the fight strategies that merely aggravated the situation? Do you or your partner need a cooling-off period? Can you tell when minor issues are going to escalate into major arguments? Does avoidance make matters worse? What issues are particularly disturbing and likely to cause difficulties? Can they be avoided?

Keep the conflict in perspective. Be careful not to blow it out of proportion to the extent that you begin to define your relationship in terms of conflict. Avoid the tendency to see disagreement as inevitably leading to major blowups. Conflicts in most relationships actually occupy a very small percentage of the couple's time, and yet, in recollection, they often loom extremely large. Also, don't allow the conflict to undermine your own or your partner's self-esteem. Don't view yourself, your partner, or your relationship as failures just because you had an argument or even lots of arguments.

Attack your negative feelings. Negative feelings frequently arise after an interpersonal conflict. Most often they arise because unfair fight strategies were used to undermine the other person—for example, personal rejection, manipulation, or force. Resolve to avoid such unfair tactics in the future, but at the same time let go of guilt, of blame, for yourself and your partner. If you think it would help, discuss these feelings with your partner or even a therapist.

Increase the exchange of rewards and cherishing behaviors to demonstrate your positive feelings and to show you are over the conflict and want the relationship to survive and flourish.

SUMMARY: UNIT IN BRIEF

Nature of Conflict	Conflict Resolution Model	Conflict Strategies	Verbal Aggressiveness and Argumentativeness
Content and/or **relationship:** disagreement between or among connected individuals resulting in negative or positive consequences and centering on content (issues external to the individuals) or relationship (issues concerning the relationship between the individuals)	Define the conflict. Examine possible solutions. Test the solution. Evaluate the solution. Accept or reject the solution.	• avoidance and active fighting • force and talk • blame and empathy • gunnysacking and present focus • personal rejection and acceptance • fighting below and above the belt	**Verbal aggressiveness:** a strategy to win an argument by inflicting psychological pain **Argumentativeness:** a willingness to argue for a point of view, to speak your mind on significant issues

THINKING CRITICALLY ABOUT INTERPERSONAL CONFLICT

1. How would you describe interpersonal conflict? How does conflict with a close friend or romantic partner differ from conflict with, say, a stranger on a bus?
2. Do you have any personal conflict myths? That is, do you entertain any beliefs about interpersonal conflict that might be untrue and self-defeating?
3. What, if any, positive outcomes emerged from your previous interpersonal conflicts? What negative outcomes?
4. How do you think your closest friend or romantic partner would score on the conflict test used in this unit? What are the implications of differences in conflict strategies for your interpersonal relationships?
5. Do you generally follow the pattern of conflict resolution identified in the five-step model? Can you trace a recent conflict resolution through the model? What additional suggestions can you offer for dealing with any of the five stages?
6. Which unproductive conflict strategy do you resent the most? Which unproductive conflict strategy—if any—are you most ashamed of using? Why? Which of the unproductive conflict strategies, if any, have you used in the last two or three months? What effects—both immediate and long-term—did your use of these strategies have?
7. Can you identify a character in a television series who demonstrates verbal aggressiveness? One who demonstrates argumentativeness? What distinguishes these two characters? What can you do to more effectively regulate your own tendencies toward verbal aggressiveness and argumentativeness?
8. Do you agree with the before and after suggestions made for dealing with conflict? Which do you find most useful? Would some suggestions be more useful for certain conflicts? What other suggestions would you offer?

9. What do you feel is the single most important interpersonal conflict principle?
10. How would you go about finding answers to the following questions?

   • Are men or women more likely to use avoidance (or blame, force, manipulation, ridicule, silencers, beltlining, gunnysacking, or personal rejection) as a romantic conflict strategy?
   • Are there certain kinds of conflicts that are better resolved in public than in private?
   • Are people with high self-esteem likely to have more or fewer interpersonal conflicts than those with low self-esteem?

EXPERIENTIAL VEHICLES

21.1 DEALING WITH CONFLICT STARTERS

The purpose of this exercise is to give you some practice in responding productively to potential interpersonal conflicts. For each of the numbered conflict starters:

   • Write an unproductive response, that is, a response that will aggravate the potential conflict.
   • Write a productive response, that is, a response that will lessen the potential conflict.
   • Identify the implicit rule for productive and unproductive conflict management that your responses assume.

1. You're late again. You're always late. Your lateness is so inconsiderate of my time and my interests.
2. I can't bear another weekend of sitting home watching television. I'm just not going to do that again.
3. Who forgot to phone for reservations?
4. Well, there goes another anniversary—another anniversary you forgot.
5. You think I'm fat, don't you?
6. Just leave me alone.
7. Did I hear you say that your mother knows how to dress?
8. We should have been more available when he needed us. I was always at work.
9. Where's the pepper? Is there no pepper in this house?
10. The Romeros think we should spend our money and start enjoying life.

21.2 ANALYZING A CONFLICT EPISODE

Here is a brief dialogue centering on interpersonal conflict. It was written to illustrate the various unproductive conflict strategies discussed in the text (avoidance, force, blame, gunnysacking, personal rejection, and fighting below the belt) as well as the failure to use their more productive counterparts (active fighting, talk, empathy, present focus, acceptance, and fighting above the belt). The dialogue should provide a stimulus for the consideration of alternative and more productive methods of conflict management.

Identify the conflict strategies used by Pat and Chris so you can see the strategies as they operate in an interactional context.

You may also find it profitable to write a continuation of the dialogue. Assume, for example, that Pat and Chris meet a few weeks later and wish to patch things up. How might the dialogue go if they used the principles of effective interpersonal communication and conflict management?

PAT: It's me. Just came in to get my papers for the meeting tonight.

CHRIS: You're not going to another meeting, are you?

PAT: I told you last month that I had to give a lecture to the new managers on how to use some new research methods. What do you think I've been working on for the past two weeks? If you cared about what I do, you'd know that I was working on this lecture and that it was especially important that it go well.

CHRIS: What about shopping? We always do the shopping on Friday night.

PAT: The shopping will have to wait; this lecture is important.

CHRIS: Shopping is important, too, and so are the children and so is my job and so is the leak in the basement that's been driving me crazy for the past week and that I've asked you to look at every day since I found it.

PAT: Get off it. We can do the shopping anytime. Your job is fine and the children are fine and we'll get a plumber just as soon as I get the name from the Johnsons.

CHRIS: You always do that. You always think only you count, only you matter. Even when we were in school, your classes were the important ones, your papers, your tests were the important ones. Remember when I had that chemistry final and you had to have your history paper typed? We stayed up all night typing *your* paper. I failed chemistry, remember? That's not so good when you're pre-med! I suppose I should thank you for my not being a doctor? But you got your A in history. It's always been that way. You never give a damn about what's important in my life.

PAT: I really don't want to talk about it. I'll only get upset and bomb out with the lecture. Forget it. I don't want to hear any more about it. So just shut up before I do something I should do more often.

CHRIS: You hit me and I'll call the cops. I'm not putting up with another black eye or another fat lip—never, never again.

PAT: Well, then, just shut up. I just don't want to talk about it anymore. Forget it. I have to give the lecture and that's that.

CHRIS: The children were looking forward to going shopping. Johnny wanted to get a new record, and Jennifer needed to get a book for school. You promised them.

PAT: I didn't promise anyone anything. You promised them, and now you want me to take the blame. You know, you promise too much. You should only promise what you can deliver—like fidelity. Remember you promised to be faithful? Or did you forget that promise? Why don't you tell the kids that? Or do they already know? Were they here when you had your sordid affair? Did they see their loving parent loving some stranger?

CHRIS: I thought we agreed not to talk about that. You know how bad I feel about what happened. And anyway, that was six months ago. What has that to do with tonight?

PAT: You're the one who brought up promises, not me. You're always bringing up the past. You live in the past.

CHRIS: Well, at least the kids would have seen me enjoying myself—one enjoyable experience in eight years isn't too much, is it?

PAT: I'm leaving. Don't wait up.

UNIT 22

*Dysfunctional Relationships and
Interpersonal Communication*

UNIT TOPICS

Verbally Abusive Relationships

> *The Characteristics and Effects of
> Verbal Abuse*
> *Problems in Recognizing and
> Combating Verbal Abuse*
> *Dealing with Verbal Abuse*

Addictive Relationships

> *Dealing with Addictive
> Relationships*

UNIT OBJECTIVES

AFTER COMPLETING THIS UNIT, YOU SHOULD BE ABLE TO:

1. Define *verbal abuse* and identify its major characteristics
2. Identify the problems in recognizing and combating verbal abuse
3. Identify the suggestions for dealing with verbal abuse
4. Define *Addictive relationships*
5. Identify the suggestions for dealing with addictive relationships

Throughout this book, the qualities that make for effective and satisfying relationships have been emphasized. Yet it helps also to see relationships at the opposite end of the spectrum so that we might compare the qualities that make for productive and healthy relationships with those that make for destructive and unhealthy ones. To this end, two dysfunctional relationships are looked at: the verbally abusive relationship and the addictive relationship.

Although these two relationship types are different from each other, they are not mutually exclusive. They have, in fact, much in common. As you read this unit, remember that labeling the relationship as abusive or addictive may be an important (and difficult) first step because such labeling may directly confront a person's long history of denial. However, such labeling may also obscure the uniqueness of your own situation, the nuances that characterize your situation that are not captured in the textbook definitions. Do not let the map (the label) obscure the territory (the actual behavior patterns). Note, too, that there is a tendency (as we noted in our discussion of polarization in Unit 12) to look at such issues as all-or-none—either the relationship is abusive or it is not; either the relationship is addictive or it is not. Relationships are not so simple; they resist such easy either-or classifications. Abusiveness and addictiveness exist in degrees. Although some relationships are extremely abusive and others are totally unabusive, there are many relationships in between.

In reading about these communication patterns, examine your own relationships and communications as both a sender (for example, one who may be verbally abusive) and a receiver (for example, one who may be verbally abused).

VERBALLY ABUSIVE RELATIONSHIPS

Before reading further, take the accompanying self-test, "Are You Verbally Abusive." It will help you to examine your own behavior and that of any partner on whom you might wish to focus. This self-test is presented before any discussion of verbal abuse so you can look at your relationship more objectively.

The interpersonal patterns in verbal abuse may be spelled out more completely as follows. The first two items listed for each of the five qualities are included in the self-test.

TEST YOURSELF

ARE YOU VERBALLY ABUSIVE?

INSTRUCTIONS:

Respond to each of the following questions by indicating whether your relationship behavior is more likely to resemble the *A* or *B* responses. In reading these questions, visualize a specific relationship partner—for example, a friend, a romantic partner, or a family member—and respond in terms of your relationship with this person. The general term "partner" is used as shorthand for any participant in a relationship.

In interacting with my partner, I am generally likely to:

1A. reveal my feelings.
1B. conceal my feelings.

2A. listen to and encourage my partner to express his or her feelings.
2B. discourage the expression of feelings.

3A. become disturbed when my partner's feelings, attitudes, or beliefs about important issues differ from mine.
3B. try to understand my partner's feelings, attitudes, or beliefs about important issues when they differ from mine.

4A. assume that my partner knows that I understand what he or she is saying.
4B. tell my partner that I understand what he or she is saying from his or her point of view.

5A. evaluate and possibly criticize my partner's failures or unsatisfactory performance.
5B. express support for my partner when he or she fails or does something poorly.

6A. state my position or my interpretation of some issue with certainty.
6B. state my position or my interpretation of some issue tentatively.

7A. emphasize the positives of our relationship or our interactions.
7B. emphasize the negatives of our relationship or our interactions.

8A. compliment my partner rarely (once a day at most).
8B. compliment my partner frequently (at least three or four times a day).

9A. stress my own superior knowledge or abilities.
9B. stress my partner's and my equality.

10A. talk a great deal more than I listen.
10B. talk and listen about equally.

SCORING

The characteristics of verbal abuse used in developing this test are derived from the five qualities of interpersonal effectiveness—openness, empathy, supportiveness, positiveness, and equality—identified in the humanistic model in Unit 6. Responses considered verbally abusive are *A* responses to items 3, 4, 5, 6, 9, and 10 and *B* responses to items 1, 2, 7, and 8. Give yourself 1 point for each verbally abusive response. A score of 5 or higher probably indicates that your communications have the potential to prove verbally abusive to at least some reasonable people.

If you wish to discuss potential verbal abuse with your partner, you might ask your partner to respond to the same test. You and your partner might then discuss each response to see whether you both agree on the way you are most likely to respond in each situation. You might also consider the extent to which you both feel the responses might constitute verbal abuse. Obviously, the next step is to think about how such behaviors may be changed. Do realize the potential dangers of making others aware of their abusive patterns. Awareness, in some cases, may stimulate increased abuse, perhaps even violence. So, discuss such issues cautiously and in a secure context.

Verbal Abusers

lack openness.

1. refuse to reveal their feelings
2. refuse to admit there is a problem when their silence is questioned ("Nothing's wrong; I'm just quiet.")
3. discourage their partners from revealing feelings ("Let's not get morbid"; "Why must you always talk about feelings? Can't you just keep them to yourself?"); discourage the mutual sharing of thoughts and feelings ("I'm really not in the mood to talk; watch the game.")
4. avoid reacting openly and honestly to the feelings expressed by the partners
5. avoid taking responsibility for their own thoughts and feelings and instead attribute them to others; nothing seems to be their fault ("Everyone thinks you should ask for a raise"; "No one likes the way you dress"; "Well, it was your decision that got us into this mess.")

lack empathy.

6. become disturbed by their partners' disagreements or holding attitudes and beliefs different from their own ("How can you possibly say that?" "You've got to be kidding.")
7. refuse to acknowledge any understanding of their partners' communications
8. refuse to grant their partners' feelings any validity ("You're being silly"; "You're always complaining.")
9. focus solely on what is said and ignore mixed messages
10. avoid checking or verifying their perceptions of their partners' feelings

lack supportiveness.

11. judge their partners' accomplishments ("Now that was fine—much better than last time.")
12. criticize their partners' shortcomings ("You never could fix the plumbing"; "You're afraid to try anything new, aren't you?")
13. state their own position as final, definitive, and unalterable ("Harrington is the best person for the job and that's it; there's no question about it.")
14. assume their partners are at fault when something goes wrong ("What did you do wrong now?")
15. assume their partners will fail even before they try ("Why bother? You know you'll never finish.")

lack positiveness.
16. emphasize the negatives in their relationship and in their partners' behaviors
17. refuse to compliment their partners regardless of their accomplishments
18. blame their partners for difficulties ("How can I accomplish anything with you always nagging me?")
19. use derogatory names to describe their partners or their partners' ways of behaving (often their children) ("Hey, big ears, come here a minute"; "Clumsy must be your middle name.")
20. act indifferently to their partners and their partners' thoughts and feelings
lack equality.
21. emphasize their own superiority over their partners ("Look, I studied accounting; you can't even balance a checkbook.")
22. talk a great deal more than listen and interrupt their partners' talk to interject their own thoughts
23. refuse to grant their partners' thoughts any credibility or value ("That's ridiculous"; "You're talking about economics?")
24. give ultimatums to get their way ("If you don't want to go to London, then let's forget about a vacation altogether.")
25. give orders rather than make requests ("Get me coffee before you go out"; "Buy butter pecan; I hate that vanilla you always buy.")

THE CHARACTERISTICS AND EFFECTS OF VERBAL ABUSE

Verbal abuse may be defined as a consistent pattern of attacking another person's self-concept and self-esteem through communication that is closed, nonempathic, unsupportive, negative, and unequal. It is in many ways similar to the concept of verbal aggressiveness, described in Unit 21. Verbal aggressiveness, according to Infante (1988), is "the inclination to attack the self-concepts of individuals instead of, or in addition to, their positions on particular issues." Verbal aggressiveness is thus a way of approaching an argument or conflict; verbal abusiveness is a way of relating to another person, a way of treating another person. Both concepts highlight attacking the other person's self-concept.

Three essential characteristics are identified in this definition. First, to constitute verbal abuse, the behavior must be relatively *consistent.* Although isolated statements may prove abusive (cursing at someone, for example), verbal abuse as an interpersonal relationship problem is a repeated pattern: it is the consistency of such behavior that makes it so debilitating. (Verbal aggressiveness, in contrast, centers on the *specific message*—for example, a specific attack on a person's character or physical appearance [Infante 1993].)

Second, verbal abuse *attacks the person's concept of self.* It is not, for example, merely negative behaviors but negative behaviors that are directed at the self-image of the other person. It is not simply critical and evaluative behaviors but behaviors directed at another's self-concept. Verbally abusive statements are relational rather than content oriented. It is relatively unimportant what content they address, and, in fact, they may frequently address quite trivial issues. Their defining characteristic is that they comment on the person's self-image (attacking and lowering it) and on the way the person is defined in the relationship (as of little competence, importance, or consequence, for example).

Sexual Harassment

Sexual harassment is not a single act but rather a series of communicative acts that come to characterize a relationship; therefore, it is useful to place sexual harassment in the context of dysfunctional relationships.

WHAT IS SEXUAL HARASSMENT?

Ellen Bravo and Ellen Cassedy (1992) define sexual harassment as "bothering someone in a sexual way. The harasser offers sexual attention to someone who didn't ask for it and doesn't welcome it. The unwelcome behavior might or might not involve touching. It could just as well be spoken words, graphics, gestures or even looks (not any look—but the kind of leer or stare that says, 'I want to undress you.'"

Other researchers say "sexual harassment refers to conduct, typically experienced as offensive in nature, in which unwanted sexual advances are made in the context of a relationship of unequal power or authority. The victims are subjected to verbal comments of a sexual nature, unconsented touching and requests for sexual favors" (Friedman, Boumil, and Taylor 1992).

Attorneys note that under the law "sexual harassment is any unwelcome sexual advance or conduct on the job that creates an intimidating, hostile or offensive working environment" (Petrocelli and Repa 1992).

The Equal Employment Opportunity Commission (EEOC) has defined sexual harassment as follows:

> Unwelcome sexual advances, requests for sexual favors and other verbal or physical conduct of a sexual nature constitute sexual harassment when (1) submission to such conduct is made either explicitly or implicitly a term or condition of an individual's employment, (2) submission to or rejection of such conduct by an individual is used as the basis for employment decisions affecting such individual, or (3) such conduct has the purpose or effect of unreasonably interfering with an individual's work performance or creating an intimidating, hostile, or offensive working environment. (Friedman, Boumil, and Taylor 1992)

Following Petrocelli and Repa (1992), we can say that behavior constitutes sexual harassment when it is:

1. sexual in nature—for example, sexual advances, showing pornographic pictures, telling jokes that revolve around sex, comments on anatomy.
2. unreasonable—for example, behavior that a reasonable person would object to.
3. severe or pervasive—for example, physical molestation or creating an intimidating environment.

4. unwelcome and offensive—for example, behavior that you let others know offends you and that you want stopped.

In a recent Harris poll (*New York Times,* 2 June 1993) concerning sexual harassment in junior and senior high school, 56 percent of the boys and 75 percent of the girls said they were the target of some form of sexual harassment consisting of sexually explicit comments, jokes, or gestures. Forty-two percent of the boys and 66 percent of the girls said they were the victims of sexual touching, grabbing, or pinching.

The following table presents the major behaviors and the percentage of students reporting that they were victims of such behaviors. All the behaviors are sexual in nature.

BEHAVIOR	BOYS	GIRLS
Sexual comments or looks	56%	76%
Touched, grabbed, or pinched	42	65
Intentionally pushed up against	36	57
Sexual rumors spread about them	34	42
Clothing pulled at	28	38
Shown, given, or left sexual materials	34	31
Had sexual messages written about them in public areas	16	20

Source: American Association of University Women. From *The New York Times,* 6/2/93.
Copyright © 1993 by The New York Times. Reprinted by permission.

The students noted that among the effects of sexual harassment were not wanting to go to school, reluctance to talk in class, finding it difficult to pay attention or to study, getting lower grades, and even considering changing schools. This is especially true for gay and lesbian youth. In fact, in New York City, a special high school has been established—the Harvey Milk School—to accommodate gay and lesbian teens who have been sexually harassed to the point where they cannot function effectively in the school environment.

SOME MYTHS OF SEXUAL HARASSMENT

Myth: Some people invite sexual harassment.

Reality: Even if this were true, it would not mean that others do not invite such behavior and yet are subjected to it anyway.

Myth: Technically, only women can be sexually harassed.

Reality: Although most cases involve sexual harassment against women, it can be directed against men by both men and women and against women by other women. Sexual harassment is frequently directed against gay men and lesbians—often beginning in elementary school—because of their affectional orientation.

Myth: Sexual harassment is harmless fun.

Reality: Empathically, placing yourself into the position of the sexually harassed person should quickly put this myth to rest.

Myth: The best way to deal with sexual harassment is to ignore it.

Reality: This doesn't seem to be the case; sexual harassment doesn't seem to go away when ignored. In many cases, ignoring harassment may appear to the other person as acceptance of it.

Myth: For the behavior to be considered sexual harassment, it must be intentional.

Reality: Interpersonally and legally, this is not true. Whether an act constitutes sexual harassment is a judgment made on the basis of behavior, not intention, by the person being harassed. For example, Fred may think his sexual jokes are very funny and that everyone in the office enjoys them, so he continues to tell such jokes. But if Maria finds this repeated behavior offensive (and, legal experts like to add, if Maria is a reasonable person or represents the judgment of reasonable people), it constitutes sexual harassment.

Myth: Sexual harassment isn't technically illegal.

Reality: Actually, it is. The Civil Rights Act of 1964 made sexual harassment illegal through its prohibition of discrimination on the basis of religion, color, race, national origin, or sex. The Civil Rights Act of 1991 made harassment victims eligible to collect damages.

To determine whether behavior constitutes sexual harassment, Memory VanHyning (1993) suggests that you ask the following four questions to help you assess your own situation objectively rather than emotionally:

1. Is it real? Does this behavior have the meaning it seems to have?
2. Is it job related? Does this behavior have something to do with or will it influence the way you do your job?
3. Did you reject this behavior? Did you make your rejection of unwanted messages clear to the other person?
4. Have these types of messages persisted? Is there a pattern, a consistency to these messages?

AVOIDING SEXUAL HARASSMENT BEHAVIORS

Three suggestions for avoiding behaviors that might be considered sexual harassment will help to clarify the concept further and to prevent the occurrence of harassment (Bravo and Cassedy 1992):

1. Begin with the assumption that others at work are not interested in your sexual advances, sexual stories and jokes, or sexual gestures.
2. Listen and watch for negative reactions to any sex-related discussion. Use the suggestions and techniques discussed throughout this book to become aware of such reactions (for example, Unit 6). Of course, when in doubt, ask questions. Use your perception-checking skills (Unit 3).
3. Av oid saying or doing what you think your parent, partner, or child would find offensive in the behavior of someone with whom she or he worked.

WHAT TO DO ABOUT SEXUAL HARASSMENT

What should you do if you believe you are being sexually harassed and feel a need to do something about it? Here are a few suggestions recommended by workers in the field (Petrocelli and Repa 1992; Bravo and Cassedy 1992; Rubenstein 1993):

1. Talk to the harasser. Tell this person, assertively, that you do not welcome the behavior in question and that you find it offensive. Simply informing Fred that his sexual jokes are not appreciated and are seen as offensive may be sufficient to make him stop this joke telling. Unfortunately, in some instances such criticism goes unheeded, and the offensive behavior continues.
2. Collect evidence—perhaps corroboration from others who have experienced similar harassment at the hands of the same individual, perhaps a log of the offensive behaviors.
3. Use appropriate channels within the organization. Most organizations have established channels to deal with such grievances. This step will in most cases eliminate any further harassment. In the event that it doesn't, you may consider going further.
4. File a complaint with an organization or governmental agency or perhaps take legal action.
5. Don't blame yourself. Like many who are abused, you may tend to blame yourself, to feel that you are somehow responsible for being harassed. You aren't; however, you may need to secure emotional support from friends or perhaps from trained professionals.

Third, verbal abuse consists of a *variety of communication patterns* that can be grouped conveniently as violations of the five qualities of interpersonal effectiveness. This is not to imply that other patterns could not be identified. The five qualities focused on here are offered as an introductory description of this type of interpersonal behavior.

Just as physical abuse attacks and weakens the body, verbal abuse attacks and weakens self-image. In fact, many would argue that verbal abuse is more damaging and more destructive than physical abuse. Physical abuse is, in many cases, relatively easy to recover from; verbal abuse is likely to leave scars for long periods, sometimes throughout one's life. In a study of 234 battered women aged 19 through 64, 159 reported that the verbal abuse (defined in this study as ridicule, jealousy, threats of abuse, threats to change the marriage, the imposing of restrictions, and the damaging of property) had a greater impact than the actual physical abuse (Follingstad et al. 1990).

Research finds, moreover, that wives who engage in verbal abuse—especially swearing and attacking the other's character and competency—also experience greater relationship violence (Infante, Sabourin, Rudd, and Shannon 1990).

If you are in a verbally abusive relationship, it is difficult to feel good about yourself, to maintain a positive self-image, or to feel competent, successful, or worthwhile. Whether it is your physical appearance, intellectual abilities, relational expertise, or emotional stability that is being undermined, it is difficult to maintain a positive self-image when you are subjected to verbal abuse.

PROBLEMS IN RECOGNIZING AND COMBATING VERBAL ABUSE

Verbal abuse is difficult to recognize and equally difficult to combat. People may be in a verbally abusive relationship and never realize it; a person may simply feel inadequate without realizing that this feeling has been brought on by the partner's constant barrage of criticism and negativity. Or, to take a different example, the partner who refuses to reveal his or her feelings or says "nothing's wrong" while maintaining long periods of silence can easily make the other partner feel at fault or inadequate. Yet on the surface, "nothing's wrong." In fact, repeated inquiries as to what is wrong often intensify the underlying—and slowly surfacing—hostility: "NOTHING'S WRONG, DAMN IT!" The conclusion that the questioning partner may easily reach is "I'm creating problems where none exist."

Similarly, the partner who is evaluated and criticized rather than supported may easily come to believe that he or she is deserving of such criticism. This is more likely to occur in romantic relationships in which such criticism is often interpreted against a backdrop of love and sexual attraction. Here the conclusion is likely to be, "I must really deserve such criticism; after all, she (he) loves me and wouldn't say critical things if they weren't true."

Another problem is that any accusation of verbal abuse is likely to be denied and may result in an even more pointed attack: "Just because I want to be quiet, I'm being abusive? Are you crazy? Are you paranoid?" Accusations that you are somehow psychologically unbalanced simply because you raise the issue are often enough to keep you quiet.

Still another problem, as some of the preceding examples indicate, is that verbally abusive statements may deal with trivial issues: for example, the kind of ice cream to buy, being silly, or completing a task that may actually seem quite unimportant. One

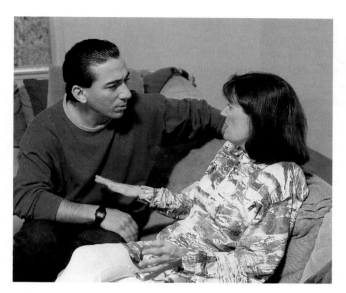

Do men and women use different verbally abusive messages? Do they respond differently to verbal abuse? To what do you attribute these differences?

abused woman, for example, gave this example: "If he saw that I put the roll of toilet paper on the holder with the paper going under instead of over, he'd lose it. It was always silly things (*Newsweek,* 12 October 1992, 92). Because you conclude that the issues are trivial, the verbally abusive experiences themselves may come to be labeled "trivial." As a result, there may be a tendency to attribute little importance to them. The implications, however, as already noted, go far beyond the specific content: the attack is on the person's self-concept, and therein lies the importance of recognizing the seriousness of verbal abuse. It is the relational rather than the content implications that make verbally abusive experiences significant and potentially damaging.

Dealing with Verbal Abuse

Perhaps the first step in dealing with any troublesome interpersonal behavior is awareness: you first have to recognize it; you have to be able to see it in your own interpersonal interactions. In the case of verbal abuse, it is necessary that it be identified by both individuals, the abuser and the one abused. Often, of course, both parties may function as both abuser and abused. George and Martha in Edward Albee's *Who's Afraid of Virginia Woolf?* are perfect examples of a couple who are equally abusive and equally abused. There is nothing in the definition of verbal abuse that excludes mutuality.

Verbal abuse, as already noted, is frequently denied by the abuser. This need not be because the abuser is particularly adept at defense and denial (although it may be), but rather because it is simply difficult to recognize in oneself behaviors that are so ingrained. Distinguishing between criticizing because your partner made an important mistake and criticizing because your normal tendency is to look for things to criticize is not always easy. A useful guide is to look at the interpretation of the behavior by the other person. If the behavior is interpreted as abusive, then perhaps it is and bears inspection.

The second step is to recognize the significant consequences of verbally abusive behavior in your own interpersonal relationships. For example, does frequent criticism lead you to withdraw and fail to express yourself? Does it make you unhappy? Does it prevent you from trying new things or expanding your talents and competencies? Does lack of empathy create self-doubt? Does negativity lead you to feel depressed? These are not simple matters to discuss openly, but discussion is essential if the effects of verbal abuse are to be identified and ultimately combated.

Do recognize that there are potential dangers. Bringing abusive behavior to the attention of an abusive partner may itself lead not to rational discussion but to more abusive behavior, perhaps even physical abuse. You may wish to choose a safe place for such discussion—for example, one in which supportive others are nearby.

The third step is to change the behaviors. Assuming that the verbally abusive patterns are not the product of a severely disturbed psyche, changing these behaviors should prove no more difficult than changing any other behaviors. The techniques for creating and increasing openness, empathy, supportiveness, positiveness, and equality, identified throughout this text (and especially in Unit 6), are especially relevant tools. Similarly, the skills of effective conflict resolution (Unit 21) and the suggestions for dealing with power games (Unit 20) will prove helpful in confronting and eventually changing the destructive behavior patterns.

If the verbal abuse continues, if you continue to suffer, and if you are unable to change the behavior, you may wish to consider seeking professional help. College student-services personnel will prove a useful source of information on available local facilities. Of course, another alternative is to end the relationship, a topic considered in depth in Unit 18.

Many people, of course, stay in abusive relationships, and to outsiders this may appear incomprehensible. Yet there are many reasons why people remain in such relationships (Johnson 1993). For example, the person may believe that he or she can change the abuser's behavior or that such abuse is normal. The person may fear for his or her own safety or the safety of children. The person may not have a suitable support system or may not know where to seek help. Moreover, abusers are not abusive all the time; during many of their relationship interactions, they may be loving, empathic, and supportive.

ADDICTIVE RELATIONSHIPS

As in the case of verbal abuse, it will help if you first examine, with the accompanying self-test, your own behaviors concerning addictive relationships. The characteristics of addictive relationships and some suggestions for dealing with such relationships are then considered.

Addictive relationships make up an extremely broad relationship category that encompasses a wide variety of specific interpersonal behaviors and addictions. Addiction, notes one researcher, is "any compulsive, habitual behavior that limits the freedom of human desire. It is caused by the attachment, or nailing, of desire to specific objects" (May 1988). Note that addiction is not the same as strong desire for or feelings about something. The major factor distinguishing the two situations is freedom. With strong desires and feelings, you retain freedom of expression and involvement. With addiction, you lose this freedom or control of yourself (May 1988).

TEST YOURSELF

ARE YOU IN AN ADDICTIVE RELATIONSHIP?

INSTRUCTIONS:

Respond to each of the following items by indicating whether your relationship behavior is more likely to be characterized by the *A* or the *B* statement. Visualize a specific relationship partner—for example, a friend, romantic partner, or family member—and respond to each item in terms of your relationship with this person. The general term "partner" is used as shorthand for any participant in a relationship.

1. When I am honest about myself and my relationship, I would be more apt to believe that
    A I would be unable to survive without it.
    B I would be fine (after a reasonable recovery time) if this relationship broke up.
2. When I am honest about myself and my relationship, I would be more apt to believe that
    A I am not a valuable person, and I sometimes wonder why my partner remains with me.
    B I am a valuable person, and my partner is lucky to have me.
3. Generally, I would consider my relationship as
    A appearing intimate but actually lacking in intimacy.
    B consisting of a true and deep intimacy.
4. I sometimes feel that my relationship is
    A an escape from intimacy.
    B a means for intimacy.
5. Generally, I would say that
    A I am independent of my relationship.
    B I am dependent on my relationship.
6. Generally, I tend to feel
    A clearheaded and right on target.
    B confused and lacking in focus and clear thinking.
7. Generally, my relationship communications (about who I am, what I like, and what I want in a relationship) are
    A too often dishonest.
    B only very rarely dishonest.
8. In my relationship, I
    A carefully monitor the impression I give to my partner.
    B act spontaneously; what I feel, I reveal.
9. Over time, I have become
    A less demanding and more willing to be supportive of my partner.
    B more demanding and less willing to be supportive of my partner.
10. I would generally characterize my relationship behavior as
    A other-oriented (focused on the other person).
    B self-centered (focused on myself)

SCORING

The qualities tested here are derived from the literature of addiction and addictive relationships (Schaef 1986, 1990; Beattie 1987) and are organized under the qualities of interpersonal effectiveness—confidence, immediacy, expressiveness, interaction management, and other-orientation—identified in the pragmatic model (Spitzberg and Hecht 1984) discussed in detail in Unit 6. Responses that *may* indicate an addictive relationship are as follows:

A RESPONSES TO:

1. items 1 and 2 (showing a lack of *confidence* or self-esteem)
2. items 3 and 4 (showing a lack of real intimacy or *immediacy,* although an image of intimacy may be projected)
3. items 7 and 8 (showing a lack of *expressiveness,* an inability, unwillingness, or even fear to express yourself openly and honestly)

B RESPONSES TO:

4. items 5 and 6 (showing a lack of skill in *interaction management*—inability to manage the relationship to mutual satisfaction; development of dependency on the relationship)
5. items 9 and 10 (these responses show a lack of *other-orientation,* an almost exclusive concern with self, though the reverse may also be indicative of an addictive relationship when, for example, the person focuses total attention on the partner and none on the self. It is the exclusive or total concern with oneself or with one's partner that distinguishes this relationship from a healthy relationship in which there is concern and focus on both the self and the other.)

As in the case of the verbal abuse self-test, it may prove helpful to discuss these statements with your relationship partner. You might, for example, ask your partner to respond to the same statements. Again, however, recognize that there may be dangers in discussing such topics. If, for example, your partner is prone to reacting violently when confronted with this type of information, you may choose not to discuss it, at least not without the protection of other people.

According to Anne Wilson Schaef (1990), whose *Addictive Relationships* brought this concept to wide attention and whose theoretical model is used here, addictive relationships are the result of one or more of three specific addictions: sexual, romantic, and relationship.

Like drug addicts, sexual addicts need a fix. For the sexual addict, the fix is sex; the sexual addict is obsessed with getting a sexual high and generally conducts his or her life to make sure that this fix is always and readily available. Real intimacy is not desired and will not prove satisfying. Again, as with drugs, the pursuit of the sexual high comes to dominate one's life. In healthy relationships, it is the quality of one's sexual relationship that contributes to satisfaction (Unit 18); in addictive relationships, it is the quantity of sexual relations that makes for at least temporary satisfaction.

Romantic addicts live in a world of make-believe, a world of fantasy rather than reality. Some romantic addicts go further and act out their romantic fantasies. To the romantic addict, "the fun is in the wooing," in the flowers, the candlelight dinners, the romantic trips. In normal, nonaddictive relationships, these romantic experiences are considered preliminary to real intimacy. In romantic addiction, they are ends in themselves.

Many relationship addicts are addicted to the idea of a relationship—like so many who are in love with the idea of being in love—and to being in a relationship. They become obsessed with having a relationship, with having a steady partner or lover, or with being married or even being a parent. Other relationship addicts are addicted to a specific relationship and relationship partner. Everything they think or do revolves around this person, and they will do just about anything to maintain this relationship.

Addictive relationships, then, may be of any or all of these types. Basically, they are relationships in which you are so absorbed, so obsessed, by sex, romance, or the relationship itself that you lose your own independence. You become so totally absorbed with your addiction that you forget your own self-growth and self-development. Your addiction becomes more important than you are.

If you looked carefully at the behaviors of people in addictive relationships, you would find that they lack the five qualities of interpersonal effectiveness identified in the pragmatic or behavioral model (Unit 6): confidence, immediacy, interaction management, expressiveness, and other-orientation.

DEALING WITH ADDICTIVE RELATIONSHIPS

According to Schaef (1990), addictive relationships are "the norm in our society. We have confused true love with the cling-clung behavior of an addictive relationship." If your relationship seems addictive and if you are unhappy about it, here are several steps you can take to strengthen the characteristics identified in our model of interpersonal effectiveness. All of them work together; changes in any one will influence the others. Thus, for example, as you develop self-confidence, you will probably reduce your need to control and monitor the impression you make on others; you will be more confident to let others see the real you.

These suggestions—if they were to be actualized fully—might well require one to undertake extensive retraining, perhaps with the assistance of a professional counselor or therapist. Do not assume, therefore, that a few pages in a textbook will prove sufficient to change lifelong patterns of behavior. This discussion is simply a way of gaining a different perspective on behavior, a way of understanding your relationship behaviors and their influence on you.

First, develop your own self-confidence and self-esteem. Most people in addictive relationships lack self-confidence, and it is essential that confidence be built up. "In order to feel good," notes one researcher, "we must all learn how to love ourselves and to hold ourselves in high esteem. This feeling of contentment is the by-product of *self-respect* and *self-acceptance*" (Peabody 1989). Engaging in self-affirmation, seeking out nourishing people, working on projects that will result in success, and understanding and truly believing that you do not have to be loved or be successful in everything you do—recommendations covered in the discussion of self-esteem (Unit 7)—are good starting places.

Second, distinguish between pseudo-intimacy and real intimacy and try to understand why pseudo-intimacy may make you more comfortable than true intimacy.

Pseudo-intimacy is intimacy in appearance only; it looks like intimacy, but there is no genuine exchange of feelings, no real love of self and other that characterizes true intimacy. Sex, romantic fantasy, and relationship addiction are quite different from love and intimacy. The fear of intimacy so many people have is likely to decline as you develop greater self-confidence.

Third, structure your relationship behavior so that both you and your partner achieve satisfaction. If you repeatedly and consistently give up your own needs in order to satisfy your partner's needs, then you are not managing your interaction to mutual benefit. Instead, you are creating a relationship in which you try to control your partner's behaviors (albeit through happiness and satisfaction) and ensure the maintenance of your relationship. But you are doing this at your own expense. In this situation, two things are likely to happen. First, you are training your partner to achieve satisfaction only through you and to put his or her own needs ahead of yours. Second, you are likely to become resentful because your own needs are not being met.

Fourth, cultivate a balance between other-orientation and self-orientation. Truly satisfying relationships are mutually satisfying. Other-orientation is especially important because so many people are egocentric, and it is useful to counteract this tendency by focusing more on the other person. Clearly, your major task is to take care of yourself; your second task is to take care of your relationship and your partner.

Fifth, cultivate expressiveness; talk about it with yourself and with your relationship partner. Melody Beattie (1987), one of the leading voices in the field of co-dependency and addictive relationships, advises that you "feel your own feelings." Your feelings are important to understanding yourself in general and any addictive tendencies in particular. Again, confidence will help you face your own feelings and develop the strength to reveal these feelings to your partner.

One of the major problems with addictive relationships is that the relationship and its problems are never discussed. (The same is true in co-dependency; communication about the illness, the alcoholism or drug addiction, for example, is not allowed. "We all knew that Daddy drank too much, but no one talked about it" is a commonly heard reaction.) If your addictive relationship is to change, however, then it must be talked about. But again, keep in mind the potential dangers that open discussion may create if your partner is not psychologically ready to consider such issues.

Recognize that there are many obstacles in the way of accurate communication of your feelings: Here are a few that you might recognize:

- *Societal rules.* If you grew up in the United States, then you probably learned that many people frown on emotional expression. This is especially true for men. Contemporary communication research shows clearly that men are verbally and nonverbally less expressive of emotions than women are (Dosser, Balswick, and Halverson 1986). Do realize, however, that many in our culture negatively evaluate men who express emotions openly.
- *Fear of making yourself vulnerable.* Emotional expression exposes a part of you that makes you vulnerable to attack from others. You reveal a part of yourself that can now be hurt by the uncaring and the insensitive. Fear of vulnerability (whether realistic or imagined) often prevents emotional expression.
- *Denial.* Denying to yourself and others that you have emotions is one of the ways culture teaches us to deal with them. But they do exist and refuse to go away even when ignored.

How can you distinguish between a productive romantic relationship and one that is addictive? Can you identify addictive relationships from literature or from recent newspaper accounts?

• *Inadequate communication abilities.* Perhaps the most important obstacle to effective communication of emotions is lack of communication competence, a condition that should be remedied with the insights and skills gained from this course.

In communicating your feelings, consider including the following elements, in whatever order seems appropriate:

1. Describe your feelings; don't evaluate them: "I feel angry." "I feel hurt." "I feel scared."
2. Describe the intensity of your feelings: "I feel so hurt I want to cry."
3. Own your feelings. Take responsibility for your feelings. Use I-messages and avoid you-messages, especially those that blame others for your feelings.
4. Describe whatever influenced or stimulated you to feel as you do: "I feel so angry when I think that I really have no friends of my own." "I feel hurt when you don't touch me when we're alone."
5. Describe what, if anything, you want the listener to do: "I want to have a night out, too." "I need your support to go back to school and get my degree."

SUMMARY: UNIT IN BRIEF		
Dysfunctional Relationships	**Verbal Abuse**	**Addictive Relationships**
Relationships that are destructive to one or both individuals	A relationship dysfunction characterized by a consistent pattern of attacking another person's self-concept and self-esteem through communication that is • closed • nonempathic • unsupportive • negative • unequal	Dysfunctional relationships in which one becomes so obsessed with sex, romance, or the relationship itself that the individuals become unimportant; characterized by communication that is • lacking in confidence • lacking in immediacy • lacking in expressiveness • not managed to mutual satisfaction • almost exclusively concerned with oneself

THINKING CRITICALLY ABOUT DYSFUNCTIONAL RELATIONSHIPS

1. Can you identify any abusive tendencies you may have? How do they manifest themselves?
2. What communication patterns other than those discussed here might you find in verbal abuse?
3. Do you agree that verbal abuse can often be more dangerous than physical abuse? Why is it so difficult to recognize verbal abuse?
4. What other specific recommendations would you offer for talking about abusive relationships?
5. Can you identify any addictive tendencies in people you know?
6. What other suggestions would you offer for communicating your feelings?
7. What would the theories of attraction, reinforcement, social exchange, and equity say about abusive or addictive relationships? For example, how would the theories account for the maintenance of such relationships? What predictions would the theories make as to the eventual course of these relationships?
8. What other dysfunctional relationships can you identify? What kinds of communication patterns do they involve?
9. Although most sexual harassment is committed by men against women, can you think of specific ways in which men can be sexually harassed? Can you think of specific situations in which women may be sexually harassed by other women? What would you advise someone to do who has been sexually harassed?
10. How would you go about discovering answers to the following questions?

    • Does verbal abuse have any influence on physical violence? For example, does verbal abuse lead to or deter physical violence?

- What are the major consequences of verbal abuse for children? For teens? For adult women? For adult men?
- What verbal and nonverbal messages constitute sexual harassment? How do these messages vary from one culture to another?
- What happens to a person's self-esteem when he or she is in an addictive relationship?

EXPERIENTIAL VEHICLES

22.1 RESPONDING TO VERBAL ABUSE

Here are a few specific instances of verbal abuse that call for some response. How would you respond?

1. *Your friend* frequently belittles anything you say, do, or try to do. Comments such as "You can't be serious about that" or "That's just plain stupid" or "You won't be able to do that" have become so debilitating that you decide to tell him or her to stop.
2. *Your mother* criticizes the way you dress: "You always dress like a slob, like you just got out of bed. Why don't you dress like your brother?" You know your mother loves you, but her behavior makes you feel inadequate.
3. *Your boyfriend (or girlfriend)* constantly interrupts you, never allowing you to finish a thought. When you object, s/he says s/he knows you so well, s/he knows just what you're going to say. You're tired of this and want it to stop.
4. *Your boss* is a blamer; whenever things go wrong, the boss blames you for not following the rules, reading the directions, or exercising caution. This constant blaming undermines your confidence, and you want it to stop.

22.2 ADDICTIVE RELATIONSHIPS

Here are a few letters to our fictional advice columnist. For each letter, describe the situation in terms of addiction and offer any advice you think might prove useful, based on the principles discussed in this unit and throughout the text. What explanations other than addiction might be reasonable?

Dear Doc:

I'm a young woman about to be married. My fiancé, I'll call him Tom, insists that I not work. He's a multimillionaire and wants me to assume my role in the community, doing volunteer projects and the like. I really was looking forward to teaching (I just graduated from the state university), but I'm wondering whether I should give in and simply learn to enjoy driving my Jaguar to the mall.

Twenty-two and Wondering

Dear Doc:

I'm going out with a beautiful woman; she's cultured, well-educated, and has a great sense of humor. She goes out with me every time I call and has never given me cause to doubt her feelings. Yet I'm worried that some day she'll leave me. It's gotten so bad that I can't sleep because I'm so worried that she'll wake up the next day and decide to break it off. Even my job is suffering; I can't concentrate the way I used to. I'm twenty-seven and a little less than average in looks, I guess.

Average in Peoria

Dear Doc:

I may have a problem. My friend says that I'm afraid to express myself with my husband. I say it's just to avoid arguments. I find it easier to agree with him than to get into a long political discussion in which he will only "prove" me wrong. So I tell him what he wants to hear. I do this a lot. I even let him think everything is fine when I'm worried about something or when I'm feeling bad. He's easy to fool, and this way he doesn't get upset with me. Do you think I'm wrong, or is my girlfriend just jealous because she's not married?

Jane Plaine

Dear Doc:

I'm a well-off, good-looking Wall Street type ($250,000 income, condo, BMW, you know, the works) in my early thirties and interested in having fun. I have been dating a gorgeous woman for the last six months. We do the very things other people envy: we eat at the best restaurants, go to the Italian Riviera for vacations, and go to all the right parties. I've given her expensive jewelry and never show up without flowers or some other gift. In short, I've done everything I could. Now, she says she wants to break off with me if I don't commit myself. She wants to be engaged by the end of the year and to start planning the wedding. Otherwise, she says, it's all off. I'm happy with the way things are, and you'd think she would be, too. Should I dump her and find someone else, or should I try to change her mind?

Feeling Concerned

UNIT 23

Friends and Lovers

UNIT OBJECTIVES

UNIT OBJECTIVES

AFTER COMPLETING THIS UNIT, YOU SHOULD BE ABLE TO:

1. Define *friendship* and its three types
2. Identify the three stages of friendship development and characterize the communications at each stage
3. Describe the gender differences in friendship
4. Identify the major elements that make up love
5. Define *ludus, storge, mania, pragma, eros,* and *agape*
6. Describe the gender differences in loving

Of all the interpersonal relationships you have, no doubt the most important are those with your friends, lovers, and family. In this unit, we cover friends and lovers and in the next, family. The combination of friends and lovers in one unit seems especially appropriate because many people see love as a natural progression from friendship. Both relationships also serve many of the same functions: for example, lessening loneliness and providing excitement and security.

FRIENDS

Friendship has engaged the attention and imagination of poets, novelists, and artists of all kinds. In television, our most influential mass medium, friendships have become almost as important as romantic pairings. Friendship now engages the attention of a range of interpersonal communication researchers. Table 23.1 presents a selection of findings to illustrate the range of topics addressed. In reviewing the table, consider why the results were obtained and what implications they may have for developing, maintaining, and repairing friendship relationships.

Throughout your life, you will meet many people, but out of this wide array you'll develop relatively few relationships you would call friendships. Yet despite the low number of friendships you may form, their importance is great.

THE NATURE OF FRIENDSHIP

Friendship is an interpersonal relationship between two persons that is mutually productive and characterized by mutual positive regard.

Friendship is an interpersonal relationship; communication interactions must have taken place between the people. Further, the interpersonal relationship involves a "personalistic focus" (Wright 1978, 1984). Friends react to each other as complete persons, as unique, genuine, and irreplaceable individuals.

Friendships must be mutually productive; this qualifier emphasizes that, by definition, they cannot be destructive either to oneself or to the other person. Once destructive-

Table 23.1

A Selection of Research Findings on Friendship*

1. Young single men see their friends more often than young married men do (Farrell and Rosenberg 1981).

2. Women are more expressive in their friendships than are men. Men talk about business, politics, and sports, whereas women talk about feelings and relationship issues (Fox, Gibbs, and Auerbach 1985).

3. When women were asked about the most important benefit they derive from their friendships, conversation was highlighted and included listening in a supportive way, enhancing feelings of self-esteem, and validating their experiences (Johnson and Aries 1983).

4. Men and women did not differ in their rankings of the characteristics of personal relationships with friends (Albert and Moss 1990).

5. Similarity in personality was not found to be a strong basis for selecting friends, but similarity of needs and beliefs was (Henderson and Furnhan 1982). Friends with dissimilar attitudes were preferred in recent friendships, whereas in established friendships similar attitudes were preferred (McCarthy and Duck 1976).

6. The average number of friends of college students varies from 2.88 to 9.1 (Blieszner and Adams 1992); for older persons, the average varies between 1 and 12.2 (Adams 1987).

*These findings were taken from the extensive literature review in Blieszner and Adams (1992).

ness enters into a relationship, it can no longer be characterized as friendship. Lover relationships, marriage relationships, parent-child relationships, and just about any other possible relationship can be either destructive or productive. But friendship must enhance the potential of each person and can only be productive.

Friendships are characterized by mutual positive regard. Liking people is essential if we are to call them friends. Three major characteristics of friends—trust, emotional support, and sharing of interests (Blieszner and Adams 1992)—testify to this positive regard.

In North America friendships clearly are a matter of choice; you choose—within limits—who your friends will be. The density of the cities and the ease of communication and relocation makes friendships voluntary, a matter of choice. But, in many parts of the world—small villages miles away from urban centers, where people are born, live, and die without venturing much beyond this small village, for example—relationships are not voluntary. In these cases, you simply form relationships with those in your village. Here you do not have the luxury of selecting certain people to interact with and others to ignore. You must interact with and form relationships with members of the community simply because these people are the only ones you come into contact with on a regular basis (Moghaddam, Taylor, and Wright 1993).

A Friendship Profile   Friendship can be further defined by identifying the essential characteristics of any friendship relationship (Davis 1985):

- **Enjoyment.** Friends enjoy each other's company.
- **Acceptance.** Friends accept each other as each is now; a friend does not attempt to change a friend into another person.
- **Mutual assistance.** Friends can count on each other for assistance and support.
- **Confiding.** Friends share feelings and experiences with each other.
- **Understanding.** Friends understand what is important and why friends behave as they do. Friends are good predictors of their friends' behaviors and feelings.
- **Trust.** Friends trust each other to act in the other's best interest.
- **Respect.** Friends respect each other; each assumes that the other will demonstrate good judgment in making choices.
- **Spontaneity.** Friends do not have to engage in self-monitoring; friends can express their feelings spontaneously, without worrying that these expressions will create difficulties for the friendship.

Goethe defined friendship more poetically:

> *The world is so empty*
> *if one thinks only*
> *of mountains, rivers, and*
> *cities; but to know someone*
> *who thinks and feels with me,*
> *and who, though distant,*
> *is close to me in spirit,*
> *this makes the earth for me*
> *an inhabited garden.*

Three Types of Friendships   Not all friendships are the same. But how do they differ? One way of answering this question is by distinguishing among the three major types of friendship: reciprocity, receptivity, and association (Reisman 1979, 1981).

The friendship of **reciprocity** is the ideal type, characterized by loyalty, self-sacrifice, mutual affection, and generosity. A friendship of reciprocity is based on equality: each individual shares equally in giving and receiving the benefits and rewards of the relationship. In the friendship of **receptivity,** in contrast, there is an imbalance in giving and receiving; one person is the primary giver and one the primary receiver. This imbalance, however, is a positive one because each person gains something from the relationship. The different needs of both the person who receives and the person who gives affection are satisfied. This is the friendship that may develop between a teacher and a student or between a doctor and a patient. In fact, a difference in status is essential for the friendship of receptivity to develop.

The friendship of **association** is a transitory one. It might be described as a friendly relationship rather than a true friendship. Associative friendships are the kind we often have with classmates, neighbors, or coworkers. There is no great loyalty, no great trust, no great giving or receiving. The association is cordial but not intense.

The definition and types of friendships may be seen in the responses of people who were asked to identify the qualities they felt were most important in a friend. The responses, presented in Table 23.2, are derived from a *Psychology Today* survey of 40,000 respondents (Parlee 1979). As you examine the list, you will find it easy to match each of these qualities to one of the types of friendship just described.

Table 23.2
The Most Frequently Mentioned Qualities of a Friend

FRIENDSHIP QUALITIES	PERCENTAGE OF RESPONDENTS
Keep confidences	89%
Loyalty	88
Warmth, affection	82
Supportiveness	76
Frankness	75
Sense of humor	74
Willingness to make time for me	62
Independence	61
Good conversationalist	59
Intelligence	57

THE NEEDS OF FRIENDSHIP

In the *Psychology Today* survey, the 40,000 respondents selected from a wide number of activities the ones they had shared with friends over the previous month. Table 23.3 presents the ten activities most frequently noted by these respondents. As can be appreciated from this list, friendship seems to serve the same needs that all relationships serve (lessening loneliness, providing stimulation, and encouraging self-knowledge).

You develop and maintain friendships to satisfy those needs that can only be satisfied by certain people. On the basis of your experiences or your predictions, you select as friends those who will help to satisfy your basic growth needs. Selecting friends on the basis of need satisfaction is similar to choosing a marriage partner, an employee, or any person who may be in a position to satisfy your needs. Thus, for example, if you need to be the center of attention or to be popular, you might select friends who allow you, and even encourage you, to be the center of attention or who tell you, verbally and nonverbally, that you are popular.

As your needs change, the qualities you look for in friendships also change. In many instances, old friends are dropped from your close circle to be replaced by new friends who better serve these new needs.

We can also look at needs in terms of the five values or rewards we seek to gain through our friendships (Wright 1978, 1984). First, friends have a **utility value.** A friend may have special talents, skills, or resources that prove useful to us in achieving our specific goals and needs. We may, for example, become friends with someone who is particularly bright because such a person might assist us in getting better grades, in solving our personal problems, or in getting a better job.

Second, friends have an **affirmation value.** A friend's behavior toward us acts as a mirror that affirms our personal value and helps us to recognize our attributes. A friend

Table 23.3
The Ten Most Frequently Identified Activities Shared with Friends

1. Had an intimate talk
2. Had a friend ask you to do something for him or her
3. Went to dinner in a restaurant
4. Asked your friend to do something for you
5. Had a meal together at home or at your friend's home
6. Went to a movie, play, or concert
7. Went drinking together
8. Went shopping
9. Participated in sports
10. Watched a sporting event

may, for example, help us to see more clearly our leadership abilities, athletic prowess, or sense of humor.

Third, friends have an **ego-support value.** By behaving in a supportive, encouraging, and helpful manner, friends help us to view ourselves as worthy and competent individuals.

Fourth, friends have a **stimulation value.** A friend introduces us to new ideas and new ways of seeing the world and helps us to expand our worldview. A friend brings us into contact with previously unfamiliar issues, concepts, and experiences—for example, modern art, foreign cultures, new foods.

Fifth, friends have a **security value.** A friend does nothing to hurt the other person or to emphasize or call attention to the other person's inadequacies or weaknesses. Because of this security value, friends can interact freely and openly without having to worry about betrayal or negative responses.

STAGES AND COMMUNICATION IN FRIENDSHIP DEVELOPMENT

Friendships develop over time in stages. At one end of the friendship continuum are strangers, or two persons who have just met, and at the other end are intimate friends. What happens between these two extremes?

As you progress from the initial contact stage to intimate friendship, the depth and breadth of communications increase (see Unit 17). You talk about issues that are closer and closer to your inner core. Similarly, the number of communication topics increases as your friendship becomes closer. As depth and breadth increase, so does the satisfaction you derive from the friendship.

Earlier (Unit 16), the concept of dynamic tension in relationships was discussed. It was pointed out that there is a tension between, for example, autonomy and connection—the desire to be an individual but also to be connected to another person. The interpersonal researcher William Rawlins (1983) argues that friendships are also defined by dynamic tensions. One tension is between, for example, the impulse to be open and to reveal personal thoughts and feelings on the one hand and the impulse to protect oneself by not revealing personal information on the other. Also, there is the tension between being open and candid with your friend and being discreet. These contradictory impulses make it clear that friendships do not follow a straight path of, say, ever increasing openness or candor. This is not to say that openness and candor do not increase as you progress from initial to casual to close friendships; they do. But the pattern does not follow a straight line; throughout the friendship development process, there are tensions that periodically restrict openness and candor.

Three stages of friendship development are discussed next, along with the ten characteristics of effective interpersonal communication identified earlier (Unit 6). The assumption made here is that as the friendship progresses from initial contact and acquaintanceship through casual friendship to close and intimate friendship, the qualities of effective interpersonal communication increase. However, there is no assumption made that close relationships are necessarily the preferred type or that they are better than casual or temporary relationships. We need all types.

Initial Contact and Acquaintanceship   The first stage of friendship development is obviously an initial meeting of some kind. This does not mean that what has happened prior to the encounter is unimportant—quite the contrary. In fact, your prior history of friendships, your personal needs, and your readiness for friendship development are extremely important in determining whether the relationship will develop.

At the initial stage, the characteristics of effective interpersonal communication are usually present to only a small degree. You are guarded rather than open or expressive, lest you reveal aspects of yourself that might be viewed negatively. Because you do not yet know the other person, your ability to empathize with or to orient yourself significantly to the other is limited, and the "relationship"—at this stage, at least—is probably viewed as too temporary to be worth the effort. Because the other person is not well-known to you, supportiveness, positiveness, and equality would all be difficult to manifest in any meaningful sense. The characteristics demonstrated are probably more the result of politeness than any genuine expression of positive regard.

At this stage, there is little genuine immediacy; the people see themselves as separate and distinct rather than as a unit. The confidence that is demonstrated is probably more a function of the individual personalities than of the relationship. Because the relationship is so new and because the people do not know each other very well, the interaction is often characterized by awkwardness—for example, overlong pauses, uncertainty over the topics to be discussed, and ineffective exchanges of speaker and listener roles.

Casual Friendship   In this second stage, there is a dyadic consciousness, a clear sense of "we-ness," of togetherness; communication demonstrates a sense of immediacy. At this stage, you participate in activities as a unit rather than as separate individuals. A casual friend is one we would go with to the movies, sit with in the cafeteria or in class, or ride home with from school.

At this casual-friendship stage, the qualities of effective interpersonal interaction begin to be seen more clearly. You start to express yourself openly and become interested in the other person's disclosures. You begin to own your feelings and thoughts and respond openly to his or her communications. Because you are beginning to understand this person, you empathize and demonstrate significant other-orientation. You also demonstrate supportiveness and develop a genuinely positive attitude toward both the other person and mutual communication situations. As you learn this person's needs and wants, you can stroke more effectively.

There is an ease at this stage, a coordination in the interaction between the two persons. You communicate with confidence, maintain appropriate eye contact and flexibility in body posture and gesturing, and use few adaptors signaling discomfort.

Close and Intimate Friendship   At the stage of close and intimate friendship, there is an intensification of the casual friendship; you and your friend see yourselves more as an exclusive unit, and each of you derives greater benefits (for example, emotional support) from intimate friendship than from casual friendship (Hays 1989).

Because you know each other well (for example, you know one another's values, opinions, attitudes), your uncertainty about each other has been significantly reduced—you are able to predict each other's behaviors with considerable accuracy. This knowledge makes possible significant interaction management. Similarly, you can read the other's nonverbal signals more accurately and can use these signals as guides to your interactions—avoiding certain topics at certain times or offering consolation on the basis of facial expressions.

At this stage, you exchange significant messages of affection, messages that express fondness, liking, loving, and caring for the other person. Openness and expressiveness are more clearly in evidence.

You become more other-oriented and willing to make significant sacrifices for the other person. You will go far out of your way for the benefit of this friend, and the friend in turn does the same for you.

You empathize and exchange perspectives a great deal more, and you expect in return that your friend will also empathize with you. With a genuinely positive feeling for this individual, your supportiveness and positive stroking become spontaneous. Because you see yourselves as an exclusive unit, both equality and immediacy are in clear evidence. You view this friend as one who is important in your life; as a result, conflicts—inevitable in all close relationships—become important to work out and resolve through compromise and empathic understanding rather than through, for example, refusal to negotiate or a show of force.

You are willing to respond openly, confidently, and expressively to this person and to own your feelings and thoughts. Your supportiveness and positiveness are genuine expressions of the closeness you feel for this person. Each person in an intimate friendship is truly equal; each can initiate and each can respond; each can be active and each can be passive; each speaks and each listens.

GENDER DIFFERENCES IN FRIENDSHIP

Perhaps the best-documented finding—already noted in our discussion of self-disclosure—is that women self-disclose more than do men. This difference holds throughout male and female friendships. Male friends self-disclose less often and with less intimate details than female friends do.

Women engage in significantly more affectional behaviors with their friends than do males (Hays 1989). This difference, Hays notes, may account for the greater difficulty men experience in beginning and maintaining close friendships. Women engage in more casual communication; they also share greater intimacy and more confidences with their friends than do men. Communication, in all its forms and functions, seems a much more important dimension of women's friendships.

When women and men were asked to evaluate their friendships, women rated their same-sex friendships higher in general quality, intimacy, enjoyment, and nurturance than did men (Sapadin 1988). Men, in contrast, rated their opposite-sex friendships higher in quality, enjoyment, and nurturance than did women. Both men and women rate their opposite-sex friendships similarly in intimacy. These differences may be due, in part, to our society's suspicion of male friendships; as a result, a man may be reluctant to admit to having close relationship bonds with another man.

Men's friendships are often built around shared activities—attending a ball game, playing cards, working on a project at the office. Women's friendships, on the other hand, are built more around a sharing of feelings, support, and "personalism." Similarity in status, in willingness to protect one's friend in uncomfortable situations, in academic major, and even in proficiency in playing Password were significantly related to the relationship closeness of male-male friends but not of female-female or female-male friends (Griffin and Sparks 1990). Perhaps similarity is a criterion for male friendships but not for female or mixed-sex friendships.

The ways in which men and women develop and maintain their friendships will undoubtedly change considerably—as will all sex-related variables—in the next several years. Perhaps there will be a further differentiation or perhaps an increase in similarities. In the meantime, given the present state of research in gender differences, we need to be careful not to exaggerate and to treat small differences as if they were highly significant. "Let us," warns the friendship researcher Paul Wright (1988), "avoid stereotypes or, worse yet, caricatures."

Further, friendship researchers warn that even when we find differences, the reasons for them are not always clear (Blieszner and Adams 1992). An interesting example is the finding that middle-aged men have more friends than middle-aged women and that women have more intimate friendships (Fischer and Oliker 1983). But why is this so? Do men have more friends because they are friendlier than women or because they have more opportunities to develop such friendships? Do women have more intimate friends because they have more opportunities to pursue such friendships or because they have a greater psychological capacity for intimacy?

LOVERS

Of all the qualities of interpersonal relationships, none seems as important as love. "We are all born for love," noted the famed British prime minister Disraeli; "It is the principle of existence and its only end." It is also an interpersonal relationship developed, maintained, and sometimes destroyed through communication.

THE NATURE OF LOVE

Much research is currently devoted to identifying the ingredients of love. What makes up the love experience? What are its major parts? Here are two well-reasoned explanations. As a preface, it should be noted that in the United States it is expected that you fall in love with and perhaps marry someone of your own choosing. In other parts of the world, however, romantic relationships and marriages are still arranged. In some parts of India, for example, children are frequently wed as early as 6 or 7 as, perhaps, a way of cementing ties between families or making an extended family more powerful. It's interesting to note that when people in arranged marriages in India were compared with people in self-chosen marriages—after 5 years—those in arranged marriages indicated a greater intensity of love (Gupta and Singh 1982; Moghaddam, Taylor, Wright, 1993).

Passion and Caring   Keith Davis (1985) identifies two clusters of behaviors that characterize love: the passion cluster and the caring cluster:

1. The **passion cluster** consists of *fascination* (seen in the lovers' preoccupation with each other), *exclusiveness* (seen in their mutual commitment), and *sexual desire* (seen in their desire to touch).
2. The **caring cluster** consists of *giving the utmost* (seen in sacrifice for the lover) and *serving as the lover's champion* or advocate (seen in support for the lover's interest and success).

Intimacy, Passion, and Commitment   Robert Sternberg (1986, 1988) proposes three ingredients: intimacy, passion, and commitment.

1. **Intimacy** (corresponding to part of Davis's caring cluster) is the emotional aspect of love and includes sharing, communicating, and mutual support; it is a sense of closeness and connection.
2. **Passion** is the motivational aspect (corresponding to the passion cluster) and consists of physical attraction and romantic passion.
3. **Commitment** (corresponding to part of the caring cluster) is the cognitive aspect and consists of the decisions you make concerning your lover.

When you have a relationship characterized by intimacy only, you have essentially a **liking** relationship. When you have only passion, you have a relationship of **infatuation.** When you have only commitment, you have **empty love.** When you have all three components to about equal degrees, you have **complete** or **consummate love.**

TYPES OF LOVE

As a preface to our consideration of the types of love, you may wish to respond to the self-test "What Kind of Lover Are You?"

TEST YOURSELF

WHAT KIND OF LOVER ARE YOU?*

INSTRUCTIONS
Respond to each of the following statements with *true* if you believe the statement to be a generally accurate representation of your attitudes about love or *false* if you believe the statement does not accurately represent your attitudes about love.

_____ 1. My lover and I have the right physical "chemistry" between us.

_____ 2. I feel that my lover and I were meant for each other.

_____ 3. My lover and I really understand each other.

_____ 4. My lover fits my ideal standards of physical beauty/handsomeness.

_____ 5. I try to keep my lover a little uncertain about my commitment to him/her.

_____ 6. I believe that what my lover doesn't know about me won't hurt him/her.

_____ 7. My lover would get upset if he/she knew of some of the things I've done with other people.

_____ 8. When my lover gets too dependent on me, I want to back off a little.

_____ 9. To be genuine, our love first required _caring_ for a while.

_____ 10. I expect to always be friends with my lover.

_____ 11. Our love is really a deep friendship, not a mysterious, mystical emotion.

_____ 12. Our love relationship is the most satisfying because it developed from a good friendship.

_____ 13. In choosing my lover, I believed it was best to love someone with a similar background.

_____ 14. A main consideration in choosing my lover was how he/she would reflect on my family.

_____ 15. An important factor in choosing a partner is whether or not he/she would be a good parent.

_____ 16. One consideration in choosing my lover was how he/she would reflect on my career.

_____ 17. When things aren't right with my lover and me, my stomach gets upset.

_____ 18. Sometimes I get so excited about being in love with my lover that I can't sleep.

_____ 19. When my lover doesn't pay attention to me, I feel sick all over.

_____ 20. I cannot relax if I suspect that my lover is with someone else.

_____ 21. I try to always help my lover through difficult times.

_____ 22. I would rather suffer myself than let my lover suffer.

_____ 23. When my lover gets angry with me, I still love him/her fully and unconditionally.

_____ 24. I would endure all things for the sake of my lover.

Scoring

This scale is designed to enable you to identify those styles that best reflect your own beliefs about love. The statements refer to the six types of love we discuss in this unit: eros, ludus, storge, pragma, mania, and agape. _True_ answers represent your affinity and _false_ answers represent your lack of affinity with the type of love to which the statements refer. Statements 1–4 are characteristic of the eros lover. If you answered _true_ to these statements, you have a strong eros component to your love style; if you answered _false,_ you have a weak eros component. Statements 5–8 refer to ludus love, 9–12 to storge love, 13–16 to pragma love, 17–20 to manic love, and 21–24 to agapic love.

*Adapted from "A Relationship: Specific Version of the Love Attitudes Scale" by C. Hendrick and S. Hendrick from _Journal of Social Behavior and Personality,_ 1990, 5, pp. 239-254. Reprinted by permission of Select Press, Inc. Based on the work of Lee (1976), as is our discussion of the six types of love.

Eros: Beauty and Sexuality   Like Narcissus, who fell in love with the beauty of his own image, the **erotic** lover focuses on beauty and physical attractiveness, sometimes to the exclusion of qualities we might consider more important and more lasting. Also like Narcissus, the erotic lover has an idealized image of beauty that is unattainable in reality. Consequently, the erotic lover often feels unfulfilled.

Erotic lovers are particularly sensitive to physical imperfections in their beloveds— a nose that is too long, a complexion that is blemished, a figure that is too full. This is one reason why the erotic lover wants to experience (emotionally and physically) the entire person as quickly in the relationship as possible.

Ludus: Entertainment and Excitement   **Ludus** love is experienced as a game. The ludic lover sees love as fun, as a game to be played. The better he or she can play the game, the more the love is enjoyed. To the ludic lover, love is not to be taken too seriously; emotions are to be held in check lest they get out of hand and make trouble; passions never rise to the point where they get out of control. A ludic lover is self-controlled; this lover is consciously aware of the need to manage love rather than allow it to control him or her.

The ludic lover retains a partner only as long as he or she is interesting and amusing. When the interest fades, it is time to change partners. Ludic lovers change partners frequently. Perhaps because love is a game, sexual fidelity is not of major importance in ludic love. The ludic lover expects his or her partner to have had (and probably to have in the future) other partners and does not get upset if this happens occasionally during their relationship.

Storge: Peaceful and Slow   Like ludus, **storge** lacks passion and intensity. Storgic lovers do not set out to find lovers but to establish a companionable relationship with someone they know and with whom they can share interests and activities. Storgic love develops over time rather than in one mad burst of passion. Sex in storgic relationships comes late, and when it comes it assumes no great importance. One advantage of this is that storgic lovers are not plagued by sexual difficulties, as are so many other types of lovers.

Storgic lovers rarely say "I love you" or even remember what many would consider romantic milestones, such as the first date, the first weekend alone, the first verbalization of feelings of love, and so on. Storgic love is a gradual process of unfolding thoughts and feelings; the changes seem to come so slowly and so gradually that it is often difficult to define exactly where the relationship is at any point in time.

Pragma: Practical and Traditional   The **pragma** lover is practical and seeks a relationship that will work. Pragma lovers want compatibility and a relationship in which their important needs and desires will be satisfied. In its extreme, pragma may be seen in the person who writes down the qualities wanted in a mate and actively goes about seeking someone who matches up. The pragma lover is concerned with the social qualifications of a potential mate even more than with personal qualities; family and background are extremely important to the pragma lover, who relies not so much on feelings as on logic. The pragma lover wants to marry, settle down, and get on with the business of living. The pragma lover views love as a useful relationship, one that makes the rest of life easier. So the pragma lover asks such questions of a potential mate as "Will this person earn a good living?" "Can this person cook?" "Will this person help me advance in my career?"

Not surprisingly, pragma lovers' relationships rarely deteriorate. This is partly because pragma lovers choose their mates carefully and emphasize similarities. Perhaps they intuitively discovered what experimental research has confirmed, namely, that relationships between similar people are much less likely to break up than those between people who are very different. Another reason for the less frequent breakups seems to be that pragma lovers have realistic romantic expectations.

Mania: Elation and Depression   The quality of **mania** that separates it from other types of love is the extremes of its highs and lows, its ups and downs. The manic lover loves intensely and at the same time intensely worries about and fears the loss of the love. This fear often prevents the manic lover from deriving as much pleasure as possible from the relationship. With little provocation, the manic lover may experience extreme jealousy. Manic love is obsessive; the manic lover has to possess the beloved completely. In return, the manic lover wishes to be possessed, to be loved intensely. The manic lover's poor self-image seems capable of being improved only by being loved; self-worth comes from being loved rather than from any sense of inner satisfaction. Because love is so important, danger signs in a relationship are often ignored; the manic lover genuinely believes that if there is love, then nothing else matters.

Agape: Compassionate and Selfless   Agape (ah-guh-pay) is a compassionate, egoless, self-giving love. Agape is nonrational and nondiscriminatory. The agapic lover loves even people with whom he or she has no close ties. This lover loves the stranger on the road, and the fact that they will probably never meet again has nothing to do with it. Agape is a spiritual love, offered without concern for personal reward or gain. The agapic lover loves without expecting that the love will be reciprocated. Jesus, Buddha, and Gandhi practiced and preached this unqualified love, agape (Lee 1976).

The agapic lover gives to the other person the kind of love that person needs, even though there may be difficulties or personal hardships involved. For example, if one person in a love relationship would prefer to be free or to live with someone else, the true agapic lover will leave the relationship for the sake of the beloved without being concerned about whether this altruistic act will result in the return of his or her love. Furthermore, the true agapic lover will want this new relationship to succeed and will be unhappy if it brings unpleasantness or pain to the beloved.

In one sense, agape is more a philosophical kind of love than a love that most of us have the strength to achieve. In fact, John Alan Lee (1973) notes: "Unfortunately, I have yet to interview any respondent involved in even a relatively short-term affiliative love relationship which I could classify without qualification as an example of agape. I *have* encountered brief agapic episodes in continuing love relationships."

Each of these varieties of love can combine with others to form new and different patterns. These six, however, identify the major types of love and illustrate the complexity of any love relationship. The six styles should also make it clear that different people want different things, that each person seeks satisfaction in a unique way. The love that may seem lifeless or crazy or boring to you may be ideal for someone else. At the same time, another person may see these very same negative qualities in the love you are seeking.

Loving and Communication

Herbert A. Otto, one of the leaders of the human potential movement, notes in *Love Today* (1972) the paradoxical conclusions made about communication in love. Communication in love, says Otto, is characterized by two features: (1) confusion and lack of clarity and (2) increased clarity and comprehension. Whereas some lovers note the extreme difficulty of understanding what the other person means, many others note the exceptional ability they now seem to possess to understand their partner.

VERBAL INDICATORS OF LOVE

Verbally, we tend to exaggerate our beloved's virtues and minimize his or her faults. We share emotions and experiences and speak tenderly, with an extra degree of courtesy, to each other; "please," "thank you," and similar politenesses abound. We frequently use "personalized communication." This type of communication includes secrets we keep from other people and messages that have meaning only within this specific relationship (Knapp, Ellis, and Williams 1980). Researchers have studied examples of relationship-specific messages, calling them personal idioms—those words, phrases, and gestures that carry meaning only for the particular relationship (Hopper, Knapp, and Scott 1981). When outsiders try to use personal idioms—as they sometimes do—the expressions seem inappropriate, at times even an invasion of privacy.

Researchers offer some interesting predictions on the basis of their analysis of personal idioms (Hopper, Knapp, and Scott 1981). They predict that personal idioms will occur more frequently when the couple wishes to emphasize relational commitment and to create a bond between themselves. After the relationship has existed for a time, the use of personal idioms will probably decrease. Last, the researchers note that these idioms may appear deceitful when used during times of relationship difficulty.

Lovers engage in significant self-disclosure (Unit 8). There is more confirmation and less disconfirmation among lovers than among either nonlovers or those who are going through romantic breakups. Lovers are also highly aware of what is and is not appropriate to the loved one. They know how to reward but also how to punish each other. In short, lovers know what to do to obtain the desired response.

NONVERBAL INDICATORS OF LOVE

We have all seen moonstruck lovers staring into each other's eyes in the movies. This prolonged and focused eye contact is perhaps the clearest nonverbal indicator of love. Lovers lean toward each other in an attempt, it would seem, to minimize physical distance and keep any possible intruders outside the privacy of the relationship. The physical closeness (even a spatial overlap) echoes the emotional closeness.

Lovers grow more aware not only of their loved one but also of their own physical selves. Muscle tone is heightened, for example. People in love tend to engage in preening gestures, especially immediately prior to meeting the loved one, and to position the body attractively—stomach pulled in, shoulders square, legs arranged in masculine or feminine positions.

Lovers' speech may even have a somewhat different vocal quality. There is some evidence to show that sexual excitement enlarges the nasal membranes, which introduces a certain nasal quality into the voice (M. Davis 1973).

Perhaps the most obvious nonverbal behavior of all is the elimination of socially taboo adaptors, at least in the presence of the loved one: scratching one's head, picking one's teeth, cleaning one's ears, and passing wind are avoided. Interestingly enough, these adaptors often return after the lovers have achieved a permanent relationship.

Lovers touch more frequently and more intimately. There is also greater use of "tie signs," nonverbal gestures that indicate that people are together, such as holding hands, walking with arms entwined, kissing, and the like. Lovers also dress alike. The styles of clothes and even the colors selected by lovers are more similar than those worn by nonlovers.

How do lovers communicate their love? Here are the six most frequently mentioned ways, along with the percentage of respondents who mentioned each, put in a "how-to" form (Marston, Hecht, and Robers, 1987).

HOW TO COMMUNICATE LOVE

LOVE MESSAGE	PERCENTAGE OF RESPONDENTS USING THE MESSAGE
Tell the person "I love you" face-to-face or by telephone	79%
Do special (or traditional) things for the other person —for example, send a card or flowers	49
Be supportive, understanding, and attentive to the loved one	43
Touch the loved one—for example, hold hands or hug	42
Be together	31
Negotiate, talk things out, cooperate	13

Love changes. A relationship that began as pragma may develop into ludus or eros. A relationship that began as erotic may develop into mania or storge. The interpersonal researcher Steve Duck (1986) sees love as a developmental process having three major stages:

1. Initial attraction: eros, mania, and ludus
2. Storge (as the relationship develops)
3. Pragma (as relationship bonds develop)

GENDER DIFFERENCES IN LOVING

In our culture, the differences between men and women in love are considered great. In poetry, novels, and the mass media, women and men are depicted as acting very differently when falling in love, being in love, and ending a love relationship. Women are seen as totally absorbed in love, whereas men are said to relegate love to one part of their lives. As Lord Byron put it in *Don Juan,* "Man's love is of man's life a thing apart, / 'Tis woman's whole existence." Women are portrayed as emotional, men as logical. Women are supposed to love intensely; men are supposed to love with detachment.

Degrees of Love   Through the use of a questionnaire designed to investigate love, the social psychologist Zick Rubin (1973) found that men and women seem to experience love to a similar degree. However, women indicate greater love than men do for their same-sex friends. This may reflect a real difference between the sexes, or it may be a function of the greater social restrictions on men. A man is not supposed to admit his love for another man, lest he be thought homosexual or somehow different from his fellows. Women are permitted greater freedom to communicate their love for other women.

Men and women also differ in the types of love they prefer (Hendrick et al. 1984). For example, on the love self-test presented earlier, men have been found to score higher on erotic and ludic love, whereas women score higher on manic, pragmatic, and storgic love. No difference has been found for agapic love.

Romantic Experiences and Attitudes   Women have their first romantic experiences earlier than men. The median age of first infatuation for women was 13 and for men 13.6; the median age for first time in love for women was 17.1 and for men 17.6 (Kirkpatrick and Caplow 1945; Hendrick et al. 1984).

Contrary to popular myth, men were found to place more emphasis on romance than women (Kirkpatrick and Caplow 1945). For example, college students were asked the following question: "If a boy (girl) had all the other qualities you desired, would you marry this person if you were not in love with him (her)?" Approximately two-thirds of the men responded no, which seems to indicate that a high percentage were concerned with love and romance. However, less than one-third of the women responded no. Further, when men and women were surveyed concerning their view on love—whether it is basically realistic or basically romantic—it was found that married women had a more realistic (less romantic) conception of love than did married men (Knapp 1984).

More recent research confirms this view that men are more romantic. For example, "Men are more likely than women to believe in love at first sight, in love as the basis for marriage and for overcoming obstacles, and to believe that their partner and relationship

Expressions of love vary greatly from one culture to another, from one relationship to another, and, of course, from one person to another. If you had to leave your romantic partner for an extended period of time (say, an entire year), what would you say? What would you do? What would you want your partner to say to you?

will be perfect" (Sprecher and Metts 1989). This difference seems to increase as the romantic relationship develops: men become more romantic and women less romantic (Fengler 1974).

Romantic Breakups   Popular myth would have us believe that love affairs break up as a result of the man's outside affair. But the research does not support this. When surveyed as to the reason for breaking up, only 15 percent of the men indicated that it was their interest in another partner, whereas 32 percent of the women noted this as a cause of the breakup. These findings are consistent with their partners' perceptions as well: 30 percent of the men but only 15 percent of the women noted that their partner's interest in another person was the reason for the breakup. The most common reason reported was a mutual loss of interest: 47 percent of the men and 38 percent of the women noted this as a reason for breaking up (Blumstein and Schwartz 1983).

In their reactions to broken romantic affairs, women and men exhibit both similarities and differences. For example, the tendency for women and men to recall only pleasant memories and to revisit places with past associations was about equal. However, men engaged in more dreaming about the lost partner and in more daydreaming generally as a reaction to the breakup.

SUMMARY: UNIT IN BRIEF

Friendship	Love
Definition: an interpersonal relationship (rule-governed?) between two persons that is mutually productive and characterized by mutual positive regard	**Definition:** a feeling characterized by passion and caring (K. Davis) and by intimacy, passion, and commitment (Sternberg)

Friendship

Types and purposes

Types:
• reciprocity
• receptivity
• association

Purposes:
• utility value
• affirmation value
• ego-support value
• stimulation value
• security value

Gender differences

• Women share more and are more intimate with same-sex friends.
• Men's friendships are built around shared activities.

Love

Types of love

• eros: love as sensuous and erotic
• ludus: love as a game
• storge: love as companionship
• pragma: love as a practical relationship
• mania: love as obsession and possession
• agape: love as self-giving, altruistic

Gender differences

• Men score higher on erotic and ludic love; women score higher on manic, pragmatic, and storgic love.
• Men score higher than women on romanticism.

THINKING CRITICALLY ABOUT FRIENDS AND LOVERS

1. What are the five most important qualities of your best friend? How would your best friend answer this question about you? Which of these qualities is the most important in maintaining your friendship?
2. Of the three types of friendship identified in this unit—reciprocity, receptivity, and association—which type characterizes most of your friendships? Which type characterizes your closest friendships?
3. After meeting someone for the first time, how long (on average) does it take you to decide whether this person will become a friend? What specific qualities do you look for?
4. Do you find significant sex differences in your own friendships with men and women? In what ways are men and women different in their friendship behaviors?
5. Review the friendship behaviors in Experiential Vehicle 23.1. How would an acquaintance, a casual friend, and an intimate friend respond to each situation?
6. What type of lover are you, according to the love-style test on page 430? Does this correspond to (or contradict) your self-image? Which type of love relationship (ludus, storge, mania, pragma, eros, or agape) do you think stands the best chance for survival? What type do you consider the most satisfying?

7. Do you think that the love in a man and in a woman develop in essentially the same way? In a heterosexual relationship and in a homosexual relationship? How would you go about finding evidence to help answer these questions?

8. Do you have difficulty saying "I love you" to a romantic partner? To a family member? To a same-sex friend? To an opposite-sex friend? Do you find that one sex has greater difficulty saying "I love you," or are men and women equally willing or unwilling?

9. The psychotherapist Albert Ellis has argued that love and infatuation are actually the same emotion; he claims that we use the term "infatuation" to describe relationships that did not work out and "love" to describe our current romantic relationships. Do you agree that infatuation and love are essentially the same emotion? If you disagree, in what specific ways are they different?

10. How would you go about finding answers to the following questions?

   • Why are women's friendships considered more intimate than men's?
   • Why do men's friendships seem to revolve around doing something while women's friendships seem to revolve around talking and relating?
   • How is friendship related to loneliness? To self-esteem? To having successful romantic relationships?
   • What types of lovers (eros, ludus, storge, pragma, mania, agape) were the great lovers of history and literature?

EXPERIENTIAL VEHICLES

23.1 FRIENDSHIP BEHAVIORS

Three specific situations are presented here. For each situation indicate (1) how you, as a friend, would respond, by writing the word "would" in the appropriate space; (2) how you think a good friend should respond, by writing "should" in the appropriate space; and (3) the qualities or characteristics you feel a good friend should have relevant to the situation, by completing the sentence "because a good friend should. . . ."

After completing your responses for all three situations, answer the questions presented at the end of this exercise—alone, in dyads, or in small groups of five, six, or seven persons.

Friendship and Money

Your closest friend has just gotten into serious debt through some misjudgment. You have saved $5000 over the past few years and plan to buy a car upon being graduated from college. Your friend asks to borrow the money, which could not be repaid for at least four or possibly five years. Although you do not need the car for work or for any other necessity, you have been looking forward to the day when you could get one. You've worked hard for it and feel you deserve the car, but you are also concerned about the plight of your friend, who would be in serious trouble without the $5000 loan. You wonder what you should do.

_____ 1. Lend your friend the money.

_____ 2. Tell your friend that you have been planning to buy the car for the last few years and that you cannot lend him or her the money.

_____ 3. Give your friend the money and tell your friend that there is no need to pay it back; after all, your friend already has enough problems without having to worry about paying money back.

_____ 4. Tell your friend that you already gave the $5000 to your brother but that you would certainly have lent him or her the money if you still had it.

_____ 5. (Other—you suggest an alternative.)
because a good friend should _____

Friendship and Advice

Two friends, Pat and Chris, have been dating for the past several months. They will soon enter into a more permanent relationship after graduation from college. Pat is now having second thoughts and is currently having an affair with another friend, Lee. Chris tells you that there is probably an affair going on (which you know to be true) and seeks your advice. You are the only one who is friendly with all three parties. You wonder what you should do.

_____ 1. Tell Chris everything you know.

_____ 2. Tell Pat to be honest with Chris.

_____ 3. Say nothing; don't get involved.

_____ 4. Suggest to Chris that the more permanent relationship plan should be reconsidered, but don't be specific.

_____ 5. (Other—you suggest an alternative.)
because a good friend should _____

Friendship and Cheating

Your anthropology instructor is giving a midterm and is grading it on a curve. Your close friend somehow manages to secure a copy of the examination a few days before it is scheduled to be given. Because you are a close friend, the examination is offered to you as well. You refuse to look at it.

The examination turns out to be even more difficult than you had anticipated, the highest grade being a 68 (except for your friend's, which was a 96). According to the system of curving used by this instructor, each grade will be raised by 4 points. But this means that the highest grade (aside from your friend's) will be only a 72, or a C-. A few students will receive C-, about 30 percent to 40 percent will receive D, and the rest (more than 50 percent) will receive F. Although only you and your friend know what happened, you know that the instructor and the entire class are wondering why this one student, never particularly outstanding, did so well. After curving, your grade is 70 (C-). You wonder what you should do.

_____ 1. Tell your friend to confess or you will tell the instructor yourself.

_____ 2. Tell the instructor what happened.

_____ 3. Say nothing; don't get involved.

_____ 4. (Other—you suggest an alternative.)
because a good friend should _____

Questions for Discussion

1. Were there significant differences between the "would" and the "should" responses? How do you account for these differences?
2. What values, standards, or models did you use in making the "should" responses? Why did you choose them?
3. With which situation did you experience the greatest difficulty deciding what you would do? Can you explain why?
4. Does friendship necessarily entail the willingness to make sacrifices?
5. How would you define "friend"?

23.2 EXPLORING ROMANTICISM*

Indicate the extent to which you agree or disagree with each of the following beliefs. Use the following scale:

7 = agree strongly
6 = agree a good deal
5 = agree somewhat
4 = neither agree nor disagree
3 = disagree somewhat
2 = disagree a good deal
1 = disagree strongly

_____ 1. I don't need to know someone for a time before I fall in love with him or her.

_____ 2. If I were in love with someone, I would commit myself to him or her even if my parents and friends disapproved of the relationship.

_____ 3. Once I experienced "true love," I could never experience it again, to the same degree, with another person.

_____ 4. I believe that to be truly in love is to be in love forever.

_____ 5. If I love someone, I know I can make the relationship work, despite any obstacles.

_____ 6. When I find my "true love" I will probably know it soon after we meet.

_____ 7. I'm sure that every new thing I learn about the person I choose for a long-term commitment will please me.

_____ 8. The relationship I will have with my "true love" will be nearly perfect.

_____ 9. If I love someone, I will find a way for us to be together regardless of the opposition to the relationship, physical distance between us, or any other barrier.

_____ 10. There will be only one real love for me.

_____ 11. If a relationship I have was meant to be, any obstacles (for example, lack of money, physical distance, career conflicts) can be overcome.

_____ 12. I am likely to fall in love almost immediately if I meet the right person.

_____ 13. I expect that in my relationship, romantic love will really last; it won't fade with time.

_____ 14. The person I love will make a perfect romantic partner; for example, he/she will be completely accepting, loving, and understanding.

_____ 15. I believe if another person and I love each other we can overcome any differences and problems that may arise.

To compute your romanticism score, add your scores for all 15 items. The higher your score, the stronger your romantic beliefs are. In research by Sprecher and Metts (1989), the mean score for this test was 60.45 for males and females taken together. The mean score for males was 62.55 and for females 59.10. How romantic are your beliefs compared to this research sample?

In the discussion of gender differences, research was cited showing that men are more romantic than women. The test presented above was developed for and used in that research (Sprecher and Metts 1989). Do you think the test adequately measures "romantic belief"? What items in the test do you find particularly important? Do you find any items that you consider irrelevant to romanticism? What other items would you include if you were devising a test of romantic belief?

Test the finding that men are more romantic than women by asking at least ten men and ten women to complete the scale. Compare the two groups. Are men more romantic than women? Would the finding from the Sprecher and Metts study and your findings be the same for all age groups? For example, would the same findings be obtained if you surveyed elementary school children? Senior citizens? Would there be cross-cultural differences? Test one of your theories by surveying members of different age groups or different cultures.

UNIT 24

Primary and Family Relationships

Unit Objectives

After completing this unit, you should be able to:

1. Define *family* and *primary relationship*
2. Identify five characteristics common to all primary relationships
3. Define and distinguish among *traditionals, independents,* and *separates*
4. Explain the four communication patterns that characterize primary relationships
5. Describe the five suggestions for improving communication within the primary relationship and the family

All of us are now or were at one time part of a family. Some of our experiences have been pleasant and positive and are recalled with considerable pleasure. Other experiences have been unpleasant and negative and are recalled only with considerable pain. Part of the reason for this lies in the interpersonal communication patterns that operate within the family. This unit is designed to provide a better understanding of these patterns as well as insight into how family interactions can be made more effective, more productive, and more pleasant.

Primary Relationships and Families: Nature and Characteristics

If you had to define "family," you would probably note that a family consists of a husband, a wife, and one or more children. When pressed, you might add that some of these families also consist of other relatives-in-law, brothers and sisters, grandparents, aunts and uncles, and so on. But there are other types of relationships that are, to its own members, "families."

One obvious example is the family with one parent. Statistics from 1991 indicate that out of 67 million households in the United States, 52.5 million are headed by two adults, 11.7 million by a woman, and 3.0 million by a man (Johnson 1994).

Another obvious example is people living together in an exclusive relationship who are not married. For the most part, these cohabitants live as if they were married: there is an exclusive sexual commitment; there may be children; there are shared financial responsibilities, shared time, and shared space; and so on. These relationships mirror traditional marriages, except that in marriage the union is recognized by a religious body, the state, or both and in a relationship of cohabitants it generally is not. In their comprehensive study *American Couples* (1983), sociologists Philip Blumstein and Pepper Schwartz report that although cohabiting couples represent only about 2 percent to 3.8

percent of all couples, their number is increasing: one bit of supporting evidence for increase is that among couples in which the male is under age 25, the percentage of cohabiting couples is 7.4 percent. In Sweden, a country that often leads in sexual trends, 12 percent of all couples are cohabitants.

Another example is the gay male or lesbian couple who live together as "domestic partners"—a relatively new term needed to designate nonmarrieds living together—and have all the other characteristics of a "family." Many of these couples have children from previous heterosexual unions, through artificial insemination, or by adoption. Although accurate statistics are difficult to secure, primary relationships among gays and lesbians seem more common than the popular media leads us to believe. Research estimates the number of gay and lesbian couples to be 70 percent to more than 80 percent of the gay population (itself estimated variously at between 4 percent and 16 percent of the total population, depending on the definitions used and the studies cited). In summarizing these previous studies and their own research, Blumstein and Schwartz (1983) conclude, "'Couplehood,' either as a reality or as an aspiration, is as strong among gay people as it is among heterosexuals."

The communication principles that apply to the traditional nuclear family (the mother-father-child family) also apply to these relationships. In the following discussion, the term **primary relationship** denotes the relationship between the two principal parties—the husband and wife, the lovers, the domestic partners, for example—and the term **family** denotes the broader constellation that includes children, relatives, and assorted significant others. Table 24.1 provides a variety of definitions of "family" by the authors of works on family communication. All primary relationships and families have several characteristics that further define this relationship type.

DEFINED ROLES

Primary relationship partners have a relatively clear perception of the roles each person is expected to play in relation to the other and to the relationship as a whole. Each acquired the rules of the culture and social group; each knows approximately what his or her obligations, duties, privileges, and responsibilities are. The partners' roles might include wage earner, cook, house cleaner, child care giver, social secretary, home decorator, plumber, carpenter, food shopper, money manager, and so on. At times, the roles may be shared, but even then it is generally assumed that one person has primary responsibility for certain tasks and the other person for others.

Most heterosexual couples divide the roles rather traditionally, with the man as primary wage earner and maintenance person and the woman as primary cook, child rearer, and housekeeper. This is less true among the more highly educated and those in the higher socioeconomic classes, where changes in traditional role assignments are first seen. However, among gay male and lesbian couples, clear-cut, stereotypical male and female roles are not found. In her review of the research literature, the psychologist Letitia Anne Peplau (1988) notes that scientific studies "have consistently debunked this myth. Most contemporary gay relationships do not conform to traditional 'masculine' and 'feminine' roles; instead, role flexibility and turn-taking are more common patterns. . . . In this sense, traditional heterosexual marriage is not the predominant model or script for current homosexual couples."

Table 24.1
Definitions of Family

Here are several definitions of family that researchers in family communication use. You may find it interesting to formulate your own definition first and then compare it with those presented here. What relationships does your definition include that these definitions exclude? What relationships does your definition exclude that these definitions include?

"Any number of persons who live in relationship with one another and are usually, but not always, united by marriage and kinship"

—*Family Talk: Interpersonal Communication in the Family* (Beebe and Masterson 1986)

"Networks of people who share their lives over long periods of time; who are bound by ties of marriage, blood, or commitment, legal or otherwise; who consider themselves as family; and who share future expectations of connected relationship"

—*Family Communication: Cohesion and Change* (Galvin and Brommel 1991)

"A group of intimates, who generate a sense of home and group identity, complete with strong ties of loyalty and emotion, and an experience of a history and a future."

—*Communication in Family Relationships* (Noller and Fitzpatrick 1993)

"An organized, relational transaction group, usually occupying a common living space over an extended time period, and possessing a confluence of interpersonal images that evolve through the exchange of meaning over time"

—*Communication in the Family* (Pearson 1993)

"A multigenerational social system consisting of at least two interdependent people bound together by a common living space (at one time or another) and a common history, and who share some degree of emotional attachment to or involvement with one another"

—*Understanding Family Communication* (Yerby, Buerkel-Rothfuss, and Bochner 1990)

RECOGNITION OF RESPONSIBILITIES

The parties see themselves as having certain obligations and responsibilities to each other. A person in the single state does not have the same kinds of obligations to another as someone in a primary relationship. For example, individuals have an obligation to help each other financially. There are also emotional responsibilities: to offer comfort when our partners are distressed, to take pleasure in their pleasures, to feel their pain, to raise their spirits. Each person also has a temporal obligation to reserve some large block of time for the other. Time sharing seems important to all relationships, although each couple will define it differently.

SHARED HISTORY AND FUTURE

Primary relationships have a shared history and the prospect of a shared future. For a relationship to become a primary one, there must be some history, some significant past interaction. This interaction enables the members to get to know each other, to understand each other a little better, and ideally to like and even love each other. Similarly, the individuals view the relationship as having a potential future.

Despite researchers' prediction that 50 percent of those couples now entering first marriages will divorce (the rate is higher for second marriages) and that 41 percent of all persons of marriageable age will experience divorce, most couples entering a relationship such as marriage view it—ideally, at least—as permanent.

SHARED LIVING SPACE

In our culture, persons in primary interpersonal relationships usually share the same living space. When living space is not shared, the situation is generally seen as an "abnormal" or temporary one both by the culture as a whole and by the individuals involved in the relationship. Even those who live apart for significant periods probably perceive a shared space as the ideal and, in fact, usually do share some special space at least part of the time. In some cultures, men and women do not share the same living space; the women may live with the children while the men live together in a communal arrangement.

TYPES OF RELATIONSHIPS

Although each relationship is unique, a few basic types of primary relationships can be identified (Fitzpatrick 1983, 1988; Noller and Fitzpatrick 1993). This typology was derived from a series of studies, including cross-cultural ones (for example, Noller and Hiscock 1989), that investigated eight significant aspects of relational life:

1. **ideology of traditionalism,** the extent to which the individuals believe in the traditional sex roles for couples
2. **ideology of uncertainty and change,** the extent to which unpredictability and change are tolerated or welcomed
3. **sharing,** the extent to which the individuals share their feelings for each other and engage in significant self-disclosure
4. **autonomy,** the extent to which each retains his or her own identity and autonomy
5. **undifferentiated space,** the extent to which the individuals have their own space and privacy
6. **temporal regularity,** the extent to which the individuals spend time together
7. **conflict avoidance,** the extent to which the individuals seek to avoid conflict and confrontation
8. **assertiveness,** the extent to which each asserts his or her own rights

At this point, you may wish to examine your own relational attitudes and style by taking the "Perceptions of Relationships" self-test. If you have a relational partner, you might wish to have him or her also complete the test and then compare your results.

Based on responses from more than 1000 couples to questions covering these eight dimensions, three major types of primary relationships were identified: traditionals, separates, and independents.

TEST YOURSELF

PERCEPTIONS OF RELATIONSHIPS[*]

INSTRUCTIONS

Respond to each of the following 24 statements by indicating the degree to which you agree with each. Encircle *high* if you agree strongly, *med* if you agree moderately (medium), and *low* if you feel little agreement. For now, do not be concerned with the fact that these terms appear in different positions in the columns to the right. Note that in some cases there are only two alternatives. When you agree with an alternative that appears twice, circle it both times.

IDEOLOGY OF TRADITIONALISM

1. A woman should take her husband's last name when she marries.	High	Low	Med
2. Our wedding ceremony was (will be) very important to us.	High	Low	Med
3. Our society, as we see it, needs to regain faith in the law and in our institutions.	High	Low	Med

Ideology of Uncertainty and Change

4. In marriage/close relationships, there should be no constraints or restrictions on individual freedom.	Low	High	Med
5. The ideal relationship is one marked by novelty, humor, and spontaneity.	Low	High	Med
6. In a relationship, each individual should be permitted to establish the daily rhythm and time schedule that suits him/her best.	Low	High	Med

Sharing

7. We tell each other how much we love or care about each other.	High	Med	Low
8. My spouse/mate reassures and comforts me when I am feeling low.	High	Med	Low
9. I think that we joke around and have more fun than most couples.	High	Med	Low

Autonomy

10. I have my own private work space (study, workshop, utility room, etc.).	Low	High	High
11. My spouse has his/her own private work space (workshop, utility, etc.).	Low	High	High
12. I think it is important for one to have some private space which is all his/her own and separate.	Low	High	High

Undifferentiated Space

13. I feel free to interrupt my spouse/mate when he/she is concentrating on something if he/she is in my presence.	High	High	Low
14. I open my spouse/mate's personal mail without asking permission.	High	Med	Low
15. I feel free to invite guests home without informing my spouse/mate.	High	High	Low

Temporal Regularity

16. We eat our meals (i.e., the ones at home) at the same time every day.	High	Low	High
17. In our house, we keep a fairly regular daily time schedule.	High	Low	High
18. We serve the main meal at the same time every day.	High	Low	High

Conflict Avoidance

19. If I can avoid arguing about some problems, they will disappear.	Med	Low	High
20. In our relationships, we feel it is better to engage in conflicts than to avoid them.	Med	Low	High
21. It is better to hide one's true feelings in order to avoid hurting your spouse/mate.	Med	Low	High

Assertiveness

22. My spouse/mate forces me to do things I do not want to do.	Low	Med	Med
23. We are likely to argue in front of friends or in public places.	Low	Med	Med
24. My spouse/mate tries to persuade me to do something I do not want to do.	Low	Med	Med

SCORING

The responses noted in column 1 are characteristic of traditionals. The number of circled items in this column, then, indicates your agreement with and similarity to those considered "traditionals." Responses noted in column 2 are characteristic of independents; those noted in column 3 are characteristic of separates.

*These statements are from Mary Anne Fitzpatrick's *Relational Dimensions Instrument* and are reprinted by permission of Mary Anne Fitzpatrick.

TRADITIONALS

Traditional couples are, as the term implies, traditional in several ways. For example, they share a basic belief system and philosophy of life. They see themselves as a blending of two persons into a single couple rather than as two separate individuals. They are

interdependent and believe that an individual's independence must be sacrificed for the good of the relationship.

Traditionals believe in mutual sharing and do little separately. For example, they spend a lot of time together, eat their meals together, place considerable emphasis on the home, and, perhaps most important, present themselves to others as a unified couple. This couple holds to the traditional sex roles, and there are seldom any role conflicts. There are few power struggles and few conflicts because each person knows and adheres to a specified role within the relationship. Perhaps as a result of the relative serenity of their lives, traditionals view their relationship as well-adjusted and permanent. Traditionals rarely even think of separation or divorce.

In their communications, traditionals are highly responsive to each other. Traditionals lean toward each other, smile, talk a lot, interrupt each other, and finish each other's sentences. Although they claim to be open with each other and free to express their vulnerabilities and weaknesses, in actual fact their self-disclosures involve relatively low-risk rather than high-risk, and positive rather than negative, items.

INDEPENDENTS

In contrast to traditionals, independents stress their individuality. The relationship is important but never more important than each person's individual identity—identities they frequently discuss. A strong sense of self is essential to independents. The relationship exists to provide satisfaction for each individual. Although independents spend a great deal of time together, they do not ritualize it, for example, with schedules. Each individual spends time with outside friends.

Independents see themselves as relatively androgynous, as individuals who combine the traditionally feminine and the traditionally masculine roles and qualities. The communication between independents is responsive. Although they do not finish each other's sentences, they do interrupt with questions. They engage in conflict openly and without fear. Their disclosures are quite extensive and include high-risk and negative disclosures that are typically absent among traditionals. This couple sees their relationship as relatively well-adjusted.

SEPARATES

Separates live together but view their relationship as more a matter of convenience than a result of their mutual love or closeness. They seem to have little desire to be together and, in fact, usually are so only at ritual functions, such as mealtime or holiday get-togethers. It is important to these separates that each has his or her own physical as well as psychological space. Separates share little; each seems to prefer to go his or her own way. They try to avoid conflict and the expression of negative feelings, but when conflict does emerge, it frequently takes the form of personal attack.

Separates hold relatively traditional values and beliefs about sex roles, and each person tries to follow the behaviors normally assigned to each role. They see their relationship as a part of normal life rather than as created out of a strong emotional attachment or love. What best characterizes this type, however, is that each person sees himself or herself as a separate individual and not as a part of a "we."

In addition to these three pure types, we also find combinations: for example, the separate-traditional couple, in which one individual is a separate and one a traditional.

Another common pattern is the traditional-independent, in which one individual believes in the traditional view of relationships and one in autonomy and independence.

COMMUNICATION PATTERNS IN PRIMARY RELATIONSHIPS AND FAMILIES

Another way to gain insight into primary relationships is to focus on communication patterns rather than on attitudes and beliefs, as in the previous discussion. Four general communication patterns are identified here; each interpersonal relationship may then be viewed as a variation on one of these basic patterns.

THE EQUALITY PATTERN

The equality pattern probably exists more in theory than in practice, but it is a good starting point for examining communication in primary relationships. In the **equality pattern,** each person shares equally in the communication transactions; the roles played by each are equal. Thus, each person is accorded a similar degree of credibility; each is equally open to the ideas, opinions, and beliefs of the other; each engages in self-disclosure on a more or less equal basis. The communication is open, honest, direct, and free of the power plays that characterize so many other interpersonal relationships. There is no leader or follower, no opinion giver or opinion seeker; rather, both parties play these roles equally. Because of this basic equality, the communication exchanges themselves, over a substantial period, are equal. For example, the number of questions asked, the depth and frequency of self-disclosures, and the nonverbal behaviors of touching and eye gaze would all be about the same for both people.

Both parties share equally in the decision-making processes—the insignificant ones, such as which movie to attend, as well as the significant ones, such as where to send the child to school, whether to attend church, what house to buy, and so on. Conflicts in equality relationships may occur with some frequency, but they are not seen as threatening to the individuals or to the relationship. They are viewed, rather, as exchanges of ideas, opinions, and values. These conflicts are content rather than relational in nature (Unit 21), and the couple has few power struggles within the relationship domain.

If a communication model of this relationship were drawn and arrows were used to signify individual messages, there would be an equal number of arrows emanating from each person. Further, if the arrows were classified into different types, they would likewise be similar. A representation of this is given in Figure 24.1(A).

THE BALANCED SPLIT PATTERN

In the **balanced split pattern,** represented in Figure 24.1(B), an equality relationship is maintained, but here each person has authority over different domains. Each person is seen as an expert in different areas. For example, in the traditional nuclear family, the husband maintains high credibility in business matters and perhaps in politics. The wife maintains high credibility in such matters as child care and cooking. Although these patterns are changing, they can still be seen clearly in numerous traditional families.

Conflict is generally viewed as nonthreatening by these individuals because each has specified areas of expertise; consequently, the win-lose patterns are more or less determined before the conflict begins.

THE UNBALANCED SPLIT PATTERN

In the **unbalanced split relationship,** represented in Figure 24.1(C), one person dominates; one person is seen as an expert in more than half the areas of mutual communication. In many unions, this expertise takes the form of control. Thus, in the unbalanced split, one person is more or less regularly in control of the relationship. In some cases, this person is the more intelligent or more knowledgeable, but in many cases he or she is the more physically attractive or the higher wage earner. The less attractive or lower-income partner compensates by giving in to the other person, allowing the other to win the arguments or to have his or her way in decision making.

The person in control makes more assertions, tells the other person what should or will be done, gives opinions freely, plays power games to maintain control, and seldom asks for opinions in return. The noncontrolling person, conversely, asks questions, seeks opinions, and looks to the other person for decision-making leadership.

THE MONOPOLY PATTERN

In a **monopoly relationship,** represented in Figure 24.1(D), one person is seen as the authority. This person lectures rather than communicates. Rarely does this person ask questions to seek advice, and he or she always reserves the right to have the final say. In this type of couple, the arguments are few because both individuals already know who is boss and who will win the argument should one arise. When the authority is challenged, there are arguments and bitter conflicts. One reason the conflicts are so bitter is that these individuals have had no rehearsal for adequate conflict resolution. They do not know how to argue or how to disagree agreeably, so their arguments frequently take the form of hurting the other person.

The controlling person tells the partner what is and what is not to be. The controlling person talks more and talks more about matters independent of the other person's remarks than does the noncontrolling partner (Palmer 1989). The noncontrolling person looks to the other to give permission, to voice opinion leadership, and to make decisions, almost as a child looks to an all-knowing, all-powerful parent.

REFLECTIONS ON TYPES AND PATTERNS OF PRIMARY RELATIONSHIPS

In thinking about the three types and four patterns of primary relationships, it is easy to identify with, say, those who are independents or those in the equality pattern. But many of our decisions are based on subconscious factors, and our motivations are not always "logical" and "mature." What makes for happiness, satisfaction, and productivity in a relationship varies with the individuals involved. For example, an equality pattern that might give satisfaction in one relationship may lead to dissatisfaction among individuals who need either to control another person or to be controlled. The type and pattern of

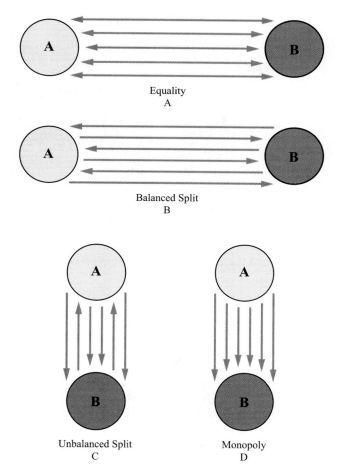

Figure 24.1
Communication patterns in primary relationships.

relationship that makes you happy might make your father and mother or your son and daughter unhappy. A clear recognition of this factor of relativity is essential to understanding and appreciating your own and other people's relationships.

IMPROVING COMMUNICATION WITHIN PRIMARY RELATIONSHIPS AND FAMILIES

Communication in primary interpersonal relationships can be improved by applying the same principles that improve communication in any other context. To be most effective, however, these principles need to be adapted to the unique context of the primary relationship. The purpose of this section is to suggest how the general principles of effective communication may be best applied to primary relationships. Additional suggestions for

How would you define "family"? How does your definition compare with those presented in Table 24.1? Would the people in these photos constitute a family by your

improving communication within relationships are presented in Unit 18 (see the section "Communication Patterns in Relational Deterioration").

EMPATHIC UNDERSTANDING

If meaningful communication is to be established, we must learn to see the world from the other person's point of view, to feel that person's pain and insecurity, to experience the other person's love and fear. Empathy is an essential ingredient if a primary relationship or a family is to survive as a meaningful and productive union. It is essential, for example, that the individuals be allowed—and in fact encouraged—to explain how and why they see the world, their relationship, and their problems as they do.

SELF-DISCLOSURES

The importance of self-disclosure in the development and maintenance of a meaningful interpersonal relationship has been noted repeatedly. Recall that total self-disclosure may not always be effective (Noller and Fitzpatrick 1993). At times, it may be expedient to omit, for example, past indiscretions, certain fears, and perceived personal inadequacies if these disclosures may lead to negative perceptions or damage the relationship in some way. In any decision concerning self-disclosure, the possible effects on the relationship should be considered. But it is also necessary to consider the ethical issues involved, specifically the other person's right to know about behaviors and thoughts that may influence the choices he or she will make. Most relationships would profit from greater self-disclosure of present feelings rather than details of past sexual experiences or past psychological problems. The sharing of present feelings also helps a great deal in enabling each person to empathize with the other; each comes to understand better the other's point of view when these self-disclosures are made.

OPENNESS TO CHANGE

Throughout any significant relationship, there will be numerous and significant changes in each of the individuals and in the relationship. Because persons in relationships are interconnected, with each having an impact on the other, changes in one person may demand changes in the other person. Frequently asked-for changes include, for example, giving more attention, complimenting more often, and expressing feelings more openly (Noller 1982). Willingness to be responsive to such changes, to be adaptable and flexible, is likely to enhance relationship satisfaction (Noller and Fitzpatrick 1993).

FAIR FIGHTING

Conflict, we know, is inevitable; it is an essential part of every meaningful interpersonal relationship. Perhaps the most general rule to follow is to fight fair. Winning at all costs, beating down the other person, getting one's own way, and the like have little use in a primary relationship or family. Instead, cooperation, compromise, and mutual understanding must be substituted. If we enter into conflict with a person we love with the idea that we must win and the other must lose, the conflict has to hurt at least one partner, very often both. In these situations, the loser gets hurt and frequently retaliates, so no one truly wins in any meaningful sense. However, if we enter a conflict with the aim of resolving it by reaching some kind of mutual understanding, neither party need be hurt, and both parties may benefit from the clash of ideas or desires and from the airing of differences.

REASONABLENESS

Some people expect their relationship to be perfect. Whether influenced by the media, by a self-commitment to have a relationship better than one's parents', or by a mistaken belief that other relationships are a lot better than one's own, many people expect and look for perfection. Of course, this quest is likely to result in disappointment and dissatisfaction with existing relationships. Psychologist John DeCecco (1988) argues that relationships should be characterized by reasonableness: "*reasonableness* of need and expectation, avoiding the wasteful pursuit of the extravagant fantasy that *every* desire will be fulfilled, so that the relationship does not consume its partners or leave them chronically dissatisfied."

SUMMARY: UNIT IN BRIEF

Characteristics of Primary Relationships	Types of Primary Relationships	Communication Patterns	Communication Improvement
Defined roles	Traditionals	Equality	Empathy
Recognition of responsibilities	Independents	Balanced split	Self-disclosure
Shared history and future	Separates	Unbalanced split	Openness to change
Shared living space		Monopoly	Fair fighting
			Reasonableness

THINKING CRITICALLY ABOUT PRIMARY AND FAMILY RELATIONSHIPS

1. How would you define "family"? What types of relationships would be included in your definition? What types would be excluded? What advantages does your definition have?
2. Of the characteristics of primary relationships and families discussed in this unit (defined roles, recognition of responsibilities, shared history and future, and shared living space), which is the most important in keeping a relationship or family together? Which one—when absent—will contribute most to the breakup of the relationship?
3. Can you describe couples you know as being traditionals, independents, or separates? With what type of relationship (traditional, independent, or separate) do you most identify?
4. What communication pattern (equality, balanced split, unbalanced split, or monopoly) characterizes your primary relationship? How effective is it in keeping the relationship together? How personally satisfying is it?
5. Although studies show there is no disadvantage in a child's growing up in a gay home (Goleman 1992), the major argument made against granting adoption rights to gay men and lesbians is that the child will suffer. How do you account for this?
6. What roles do you play in your family system? If you are in a primary relationship, what roles do you play in it? What roles do you play in your friendship relationships? How satisfied are you with these roles? What roles do you like or would you like to serve?
7. What single rule of communication is most often abused in primary relationships and families? What one suggestion would you give your best friend for improving his or her relationship communication?
8. Can you describe your family communication in terms of the rules operating when family members talk? What is the single most important family communication rule? What happens when this rule is broken?
9. What would you want to know about the research that reports the conclusion that "men disclose less than women"?
10. How would you go about finding answers to the following questions?

12. What meaning is and how it is transferred from one person to another (Unit 11)

13. The role of racism, sexism, and heterosexism in interpersonal communication: causes, effects, and remedies (Unit 11)

14. The major barriers to interpersonal understanding (Unit 12)

15. How the nonverbal messages of the body and of sound, space, time, and touch communicate (Units 13 and 14)

16. How conversation works, the rules it follows, and the qualities that make it effective (Unit 15)

17. The functions and stages of interpersonal relationships—from development through maintenance, deterioration, and repair to dissolution (Unit 16)

18. Why relationships develop and how relationship involvement is regulated (Unit 17)

19. How and why relationships deteriorate and dissolve (Unit 18)

20. How relationships are maintained and repaired (Unit 19)

21. The role of power in interpersonal communication and relationships (Unit 20)

22. The role of conflict in interpersonal communication and relationships (Unit 21)

23. What verbally abusive and addictive relationships look like and what communications are common in such relationships (Unit 22)

24. The role of communication in developing and maintaining friendship and love (Unit 23)

25. The role of interpersonal communication in primary and family relationships (Unit 24)

12. Avoid the pitfalls of verbal communication and talking with equality, inclusion, balance, and honest appraisal as appropriate (Unit 11).

13. Speak without racist, sexist, or heterosexist language and respond appropriately when hearing such language (Unit 11)

14. Use language to accurately reflect reality, avoiding such barriers as polarization, intensional confusion, allness, static evaluation, and indiscrimination (Unit 12)

15. Use nonverbal messages to accent, complement, contradict, regulate, repeat, and substitute for verbal messages as appropriate and regulate the messages of body, sound, space, time, and touch (Units 13 and 14)

16. Manage conversations effectively by, for example, opening and closing conversations effectively, giving appropriate feedback to others, and smoothly exchanging the roles of speaker and listener (Unit 15)

17. Use interpersonal communication strategies as appropriate to the relationship functions and stages (Unit 16)

18. Regulate the communications and the course of relationships as desired (Unit 17)

19. Controlling relationship deterioration and dealing productively with the ending of relationships (Unit 18)

20. Use appropriate strategies for maintaining and repairing relationships (Unit 19)

21. Speak with power as appropriate and productively combat unfair power strategies (Unit 20)

22. Problem-solve relationship conflicts and engage in interpersonal conflict fairly and productively (Unit 21)

23. Use appropriate interpersonal strategies to discuss and change dysfunctional relationships (Unit 22)

24. Use communication to more effectively develop and maintain important interpersonal relationships such as friendship and love (Unit 23)

25. Use interpersonal communication to improve understanding in primary and family relationships (Unit 24)

25 THINGS EVERY INTERPERSONAL COMMUNICATION STUDENT SHOULD UNDERSTAND

1. How interpersonal communication works and what purposes it serves (Unit 1)

2. Why interpersonal communication is transactional, inevitable, and irreversible, and how messages can refer to both content and to the relationships between people (Unit 2)

3. How culture influences interpersonal communication (Unit 2)

4. How people perception works and how it influences interpersonal communication (Unit 3)

5. How listening works, its stages, and the various modes of listening available; the functions and techniques of active listening (Unit 4)

6. The role of ethics in interpersonal communication and the ethical implications of lying, using fear and emotion, censoring messages, and gossiping (Unit 5)

7. What makes interpersonal communication effective (Unit 6)

8. How self-concept, self-awareness, and self-esteem influence what you say and what you hear (Unit 7)

9. What self-disclosure is, the factors that influence it, and the potential rewards and dangers of self-disclosing (Unit 8)

10. How fear of communication and the lack of assertiveness develop and the factors that influence these tendencies (Unit 9)

11. How verbal and nonverbal messages work together in communication (Unit 10)

25 THINGS EVERY INTERPERSONAL COMMUNICATOR SHOULD KNOW HOW TO DO

1. Regulate and adjust interpersonal communications to the desired purposes and contexts (Unit 1)

2. Interact simultaneously as both speaker and listener and avoid the problems caused by the failure to recognize that messages cannot be taken back, and recognize and respond appropriately to both content and relationship messages (Unit 2)

3. Communicate with people from other cultures effectively, without ethnocentrism and stereotyping, for example (Units 2 and 3)

4. Increase accuracy in people perception, avoid common perceptual biases, and critically evaluate the perceptions of self and others (Unit 3)

5. Listen effectively by regulating participatory and passive, empathic and objective, nonjudgmental and critically, and surface and depth listening; listen actively as appropriate (Unit 4)

6. Use interpersonal communication ethically; respond appropriately to unethical communications (Unit 5)

7. Become a more effective interpersonal communicator by using such regulating skills as mindfulness, flexibility, cultural sensitivity, and metacommunications and such expressive skills as openness, empathy, supportiveness, positiveness, equality, confidence, immediacy, interactive management, expressiveness, and other-orientation (Unit 6)

8. Increase self-awareness and self-esteem for greater interpersonal effectiveness (Unit 7)

9. Self-disclose appropriately and respond appropriately to the self-disclosures of others (Unit 8)

10. Manage the fear of interpersonal communication and communicate assertively as appropriate (Unit 9)

11. Use verbal and nonverbal messages to reinforce each other (Unit 10)

- Do persons who are high in self-disclosure make better primary relationship partners than those who are low in self-disclosure?
- Are couples with children happier than couples without children?
- Will primary relationships involving people who entered with unrealistically low expectations last longer than those involving people with realistic or unrealistically high expectations?
- In what ways are primary relationships among heterosexuals and homosexuals different? In what ways are they the same?

EXPERIENTIAL VEHICLES

24.1 PRIMARY RELATIONSHIP COMMUNICATION

This exercise is designed to encourage you to examine more closely the communication patterns operative in your own primary relationship(s). The exercise is divided into a number of related phases.

1. Select the relationship on which you wish to focus for this experience. It may be the one shared by you and your closest intimate, you and your husband or wife, you and one or more members of your immediate or extended family, or any other relationship. Before progressing further, it will help if you record the name(s) of the individual(s) you've selected and the relationship to you.
2. For each of the ten communication characteristics listed in the following Primary Relationship Communication Questionnaire, indicate the member of the primary relationship to whom this characteristic applies most closely. Do this for all ten characteristics before reading further.

Primary Relationship Communication Questionnaire

For each characteristic, indicate the name of the member of the relationship to whom it most closely applies.

1. Has the greatest general credibility
2. Self-discloses the most; self-discloses the least
3. Is the most supportive
4. Is the most open-minded; is the most closed-minded
5. Needs the relationship more than the others
6. Has the final say in making the important decisions
7. Is the most apt to avoid conflict rather than confront it
8. Is the most empathic
9. Is the most apt to use unfair methods in conflict
10. Has the greatest commitment to the relationship

3. After all ten statements have been responded to, write one or more implications of your responses for the relationship as a whole or for the other members of the relationship as individuals. For example, let us assume that you are concentrating on your immediate family (you, your mother, and your father). For "has the greatest general

credibility," you might note that this characteristic applies most to your father. This attribution of credibility to your father has various implications. One might be that your father is the one who is looked to for information or advice and the one who is expected to make most of the decisions. Another implication might be that you resent this unchallenged credibility that your mother attributes to him, and this in turn causes you purposely to avoid asking his advice.

4. After each person has completed the questionnaire, discuss your responses in groups of five or six. In the discussion, try to develop hypotheses that might be applicable to relationship communication in general. From this example, you might formulate the hypothesis that "in a nuclear family, it is the father who has the greatest credibility." Another hypothesis might be, "The most credible person is resented the most by the second most credible person or by the person who is growing intellectually at the most rapid rate."

5. After all groups have discussed the characteristics and developed a set of hypotheses, share them with the entire class and consider.

24.2 THE TELEVISION RELATIONSHIP

This exercise is designed to enable you to gain some insight and experience in the difficult task of analyzing family communication. The class should be separated into several small groups, each of which should select a different television program that centers on a family.

Each member should watch the assigned television show and respond to the questions in this exercise. Then members should meet in their groups and discuss their responses, working toward consensus in their answers. After recording the group's responses (noting any significant differences of opinion), each group should report the results of its discussion to the entire class. A general class discussion should then follow and might concentrate on the implications of the responses to question 8.

1. Who constitutes the "family"? List the members of the family or primary relationship, and identify their major roles within the family structure. Are there some persons in the show whose status in the family is not clear?

2. In the text, we identified several characteristics that all primary relationships or families have in common: relatively clear definition of roles, a recognition of responsibilities to each other, a shared history and future, and a shared living space. Are these characteristics evident in the family portrayed in the program you viewed? Are there other characteristics that might be offered to define their relationships?

3. What factors seem to hold this family together? Identify specific elements of plot or dialogue that demonstrate these factors.

4. Can you classify the primary relationship as traditional, independent, or separate?

5. What type of communication pattern best describes this particular family? Diagram the communication pattern(s). Can you identify specific elements of dialogue that led to your conclusions? Do the communication patterns cause any difficulties?

6. If the characters on this television show wished to improve their family communication, what suggestions would you make?

7. Assume that a Martian has come to earth and has no information other than that gained from this television series. What conclusions might this Martian make about earth families and primary relationships?

Postscript

These twenty-four units introduced the study of interpersonal communication—its concepts, principles, and theories—and identified its skills and practical applications. These principles and skills will always play a significant part in your life—in social and intimate situations with friends, family, and lovers; in professional settings with colleagues; and, of course, in intercultural exchanges in which you will increasingly find yourself.

Clearly, you've covered a great deal. At the same time, however, a great deal of material was necessarily omitted or touched on very briefly. There is certainly more to learn and more to experience about every topic we've explored in these pages.

If you are to take interpersonal communication from this text and from this class into your own world, you have to begin to:

- understand yourself as an interpersonal communicator, the ways you interact, the perceptual errors you are prone to make, the barriers to verbal interaction you are likely to run into, the relationship rules you may break, the ways you listen, and the ways you fail to listen
- understand the interpersonal message systems, how they operate, how messages may be communicated or not communicated, how emotions figure into your own interpersonal interactions, how cultural rules influence our communications and relationships, and how the process of conversation can be managed with greater effectiveness
- understand your interpersonal relationships, the functions they serve and fail to serve, and the conflicts and conflict strategies that are a part of your interactions; how power figures into your relationships; the role of friendship, love, and family; and how your own relationships may break down and be repaired
- become especially sensitive to those relationships that may be self-destructive and to communications that are personal attacks; because of its importance, this topic was focused on in several places and from varied perspectives: verbal aggressiveness (Unit 21), verbally abusive and addictive relationships and sexual harassment (Unit 22), power plays to control behavior (Unit 20), and unproductive conflict strategies, such as force and threat (Unit 21).
- use the skills discussed here to strengthen your ability to communicate and to relate to others more effectively, more empathically, and in ways that are more satisfying

Learning to communicate interpersonally and to establish and maintain meaningful relationships is a lifelong process that I have only—but with great pleasure—introduced here. If interpersonal communication is to make a difference in your personal, social, and professional life, then continue its study. Fortunately, many popular books on the topic are currently available in most bookstores, and your college catalogue undoubtedly contains a variety of follow-up courses. And as already demonstrated (I hope), the field of interpersonal communication is a rapidly growing one with many new and exciting areas to pursue.

Glossary of Interpersonal Communication Concepts

Listed here are definitions of the technical terms of interpersonal communication—the words that are peculiar or unique to this discipline. These definitions should make new or difficult terms a bit easier to understand. For the most part, the words included here are used in this text. Also included are other terms that may be used in the conduct of a course in interpersonal communication. All boldface terms within the definitions appear as separate entries in the glossary.

active listening. A process of putting together into some meaningful whole the listener's understanding of the speaker's total message—the verbal and the nonverbal, the content and the feelings.

adaptors. Nonverbal behaviors that, when engaged in either in private or in public without being seen, serve some kind of need and occur in their entirety—for example, scratching one's head until the itch is relieved.

adjustment (principle of). The principle of verbal interaction that claims that communication may take place only to the extent that the parties communicating share the same system of signals.

affect displays. Movements of the facial area that convey emotional meaning—for example, anger, fear, and surprise.

affinity-seeking strategies. Behaviors designed to increase our interpersonal attractiveness.

agapic love. Compassionate love; self-giving love; spiritual love; altruistic love.

allness. The assumption that all can be known or is known about a given person, issue, object, or event.

altercasting. Placing the listener in a specific role for a specific purpose and asking that the listener approach the question or problem from the perspective of this specific role.

ambiguity. The condition in which a message may be interpreted as having more than one meaning.

appeals for the suspension of judgment. A type of **disclaimer** in which the speaker asks the listeners to delay their judgments.

arbitrariness. The feature of human language that reflects the absence of a real or inherent relationship between the form of a word and its meaning. If we do not know anything of a particular language, we cannot examine the form of a word and thereby discover its meaning.

argot. A kind of sublanguage; cant and **jargon** of a particular class, generally an underworld or a criminal class, which is difficult and sometimes impossible for outsiders to understand.

argumentativeness. A willingness to argue for a point of view, to speak one's mind.

assertiveness. A willingness to stand up for one's rights but with respect for the rights of others.

assimilation. A process of message distortion in which messages are reworked to conform to our own attitudes, prejudices, needs, and values.

attention. The process of responding to a stimulus or stimuli; usually some consciousness of responding is implied.

attitude. A predisposition to respond for or against an object, person, or position.

attraction. The state or process by which one individual is drawn to another, by having a highly positive evaluation of that other person.

attractiveness. The degree to which one is perceived to be physically attractive and to possess a pleasing personality.

attribution theory. A theory concerned with the processes involved in attributing causation or motivation to a person's behavior.

avoidance. An unproductive **conflict** strategy in which a person takes mental or physical flight from the actual conflict.

barriers to communication. Those factors (physical or psychological) that prevent or hinder effective communication.

behavioral synchrony. The similarity in the behavior, usually nonverbal, of two persons. Generally, it is taken as an index of mutual liking.

belief. Confidence in the existence or truth of something; conviction.

beltlining. An unproductive **conflict** strategy in which one hits at the level at which the other person cannot withstand the blow.

blame. An unproductive **conflict** strategy in which we attribute the cause of the conflict to the other person or devote our energies to discovering who is the cause and avoid talking about the issues causing the conflict.

blindering. A misevaluation in which a label prevents us from seeing as much of the object as we might see; a process of concentrating on the verbal level while neglecting the nonverbal levels; a form of **intensional orientation.**

blind self. The part of the self that contains information about the self that is known to others but unknown to oneself.

boundary marker. A marker that sets boundaries that divide one person's territory from another's—for example, a fence.

breadth. The number of topics about which individuals in a relationship communicate.

bypassing. A misevaluation caused when individuals each give the same word a different meaning.

cant. A kind of **sublanguage;** the conversational language of a special group (usually, a lower-social-class group), generally understood only by members of the subculture.

censorship. Legal restriction imposed on one's right to produce, distribute, or receive various communications.

central marker. A marker or item that is placed in a territory to reserve it for a specific person—for example, the sweater thrown over a library chair to signal that the chair is taken.

certainty. An attitude of closed-mindedness that creates a defensiveness among communication participants; opposed to **provisionalism.**

channel. The vehicle or medium through which signals are sent.

cherishing behaviors. Small behaviors we enjoy receiving from others, especially from our relational partner—for example, a kiss before leaving for work.

chronemics. The study of the communicative nature of time—the way you treat time and use it to communicate. Two general areas of chronemics are cultural and psychological time.

civil inattention. Polite ignoring of others so as not to invade their privacy.

cliché. An expression whose overuse calls attention to itself; "tall, dark, and handsome" as a description of a man would be considered a cliché.

closed-mindedness. An unwillingness to receive certain communication messages.

code. A set of symbols used to translate a message from one form to another.

coercive power. Power dependent on one's ability to punish or to remove rewards from another person.

cognitive disclaimer. A **disclaimer** in which the speaker seeks to confirm his or her own cognitive capacity—for example, "You may think I'm drunk, but I'm as sober as anyone here."

communication. (1) The process or act of communicating; (2) the actual message or messages sent and received; (3) the study of the processes involved in the sending and receiving of messages. (The term **communicology** is suggested for the third definition.)

communication apprehension. Fear or anxiety over communicating; "trait apprehension" refers to fear of communication generally, regardless of the specific situation; "state apprehension" refers to fear that is specific to a given communication situation.

communicology. The study of communication, particularly the subsection concerned with human communication.

competence. "Language competence" is a speaker's ability to use the language; it is a knowledge of the elements and rules of the language. "Communication competence" refers to the rules of the social or interpersonal dimensions of communication and is often used to denote the qualities that make for effectiveness in interpersonal communication.

complementarity. A principle of **attraction** holding that one is attracted by qualities one does not possess or one wishes to possess and to people who are opposite or different from oneself; opposed to **similarity.**

complementary relationship. A relationship in which the behavior of one person serves as the stimulus for the complementary behavior of the other; in complementary relationships, behavioral differences are maximized.

compliance-gaining   strategies. Behaviors that are directed toward gaining the agreement of others; behaviors designed to persuade others to do as we wish.

compliance-resisting   strategies. Behaviors directed at resisting the persuasive attempts of others.

confidence. A quality of interpersonal effectiveness; a comfortable, at-ease feeling in interpersonal communication situations.

confirmation. A communication pattern that acknowledges another person's presence and also indicates an acceptance of this person, this person's definition of self, and the relationship as defined or viewed by this other person; opposed to **disconfirmation.**

conflict. An extreme form of competition in which a person attempts to bring a rival to surrender; a situation in which one person's behaviors are directed at preventing something or at interfering with or harming another individual. *See also* **interpersonal conflict.**

congruence. A condition in which both verbal and nonverbal behaviors reinforce each other.

connotation. The feeling or emotional aspect of meaning, generally viewed as consisting of the evaluative (for example, good-bad), potency (strong-weak), and activity (fast-slow) dimensions; the associations of a term. *see also* **denotation.**

consensus. A principle of attribution through which we attempt to establish whether other people react or behave in the same way as the person on whom we are now focusing; if the person is acting in accordance with the consensus, we seek reasons for the behavior outside the individual; if the person is not acting in accordance with the consensus, we seek reasons that are internal to the individual.

consistency. (1) A perceptual process that influences us to maintain balance among our perceptions; a process that makes us tend to see what we expect to see and to be uncomfortable when our perceptions run contrary to our expectations. (2) A principle of attribution through which we attempt to establish whether a person behaves the same way in similar situations; if there is consistency, then we are likely to attribute the behavior to the person, to some internal motivation; if there is no consistency, then we are likely to attribute the behavior to some external factor.

contamination. A form of **territorial encroachment** that renders another's territory impure.

content and relationship dimensions. A principle of communication that messages refer both to content (the world external to both speaker and listener) and to the relationship existing between the individuals who are interacting.

context of communication. The physical, psychological, social, and temporal environment in which communication takes place.

controllability. The extent to which a person is in control of his or her own behavior; one of the factors that influence our judgments of others.

conversation. Two-person communication usually possessing an opening, feedforward, a business stage, feedback, and a closing.

conversational turns. The process of passing the speaker and listener roles during conversation.

cooperation. An interpersonal process by which individuals work together for a common end; the pooling of efforts to produce a mutually desired outcome.

cooperation principle. An implicit agreement between speaker and listener to cooperate in trying to understand what each is communicating.

credentialing. A type of disclaimer in which speakers acknowledge that what is about to be said may reflect poorly on them but that they will say it nevertheless (usually for quite positive reasons).

credibility. The degree to which a receiver perceives the speaker to be believable; competence, character, and charisma (dynamism) are its major dimensions.

critical thinking. The process of logically evaluating reasons and evidence and reaching a judgment on the basis of this analysis.

cultural time. The meanings given to time communication by a particular culture.

date. An **extensional device** used to emphasize the notion of constant change and symbolized by a subscript: for example, John Smith$_{1986}$ is not John Smith$_{1996}$.

decoder. Something that takes a message in one form (for example, sound waves) and translates it into another form (for example, nerve impulses) from which meaning can be formulated (for example, in vocal-auditory communication). In human communication, the decoder is the auditory mechanism; in electronic communication, the decoder is, for example, the telephone earpiece. Decoding is the process of extracting a message from a code—for example, translating speech sounds into nerve impulses. *See also* **encoder.**

defensiveness. An attitude of an individual or an atmosphere in a group characterized by threats, fear, and domination; messages evidencing evaluation, control, strategy, neutrality, superiority, and certainty are assumed to lead to defensiveness; opposed to **supportiveness.**

delayed reactions. Reactions that are consciously delayed while a situation is analyzed.

denial. One of the obstacles to the expression of emotion; the process by which we deny our emotions to ourselves or to others.

denotation. Referential meaning; the objective or descriptive meaning of a word. *See also* **connotation.**

depenetration. A reversal of penetration; a condition in which the **breadth** and **depth** of a relationship decrease.

depth. The degree to which the inner personality—the inner core of an individual—is penetrated in interpersonal interaction.

determinism (principle of). The principle of verbal interaction that holds that all verbalizations are to some extent purposeful, that there is a reason for every verbalization.

dialogue. A form of **communication** in which each person is both speaker and listener; communication characterized by involvement, concern, and respect for the other person; opposed to **monologue.**

direct speech. Speech in which the speaker's intentions are stated clearly and directly.

disclaimer. Statement that asks the listener to receive what the speaker says as intended without its reflecting negatively on the image of the speaker.

disconfirmation. The process by which one ignores or denies the right of the individual even to define himself or herself; opposed to **confirmation.**

distinctiveness. A principle of attribution in which we ask whether a person reacts in similar ways in different situations; if the person does, then there is low distinctiveness, and we are likely to conclude that there is an internal cause or motivation for the behavior; if there is high distinctiveness, we are likely to seek the cause in external factors.

dogmatism. Closed-mindedness in dealing with communications.

double-bind message. A particular kind of contradictory message possessing the following characteristics: (1) the persons interacting share a relatively intense relationship; (2) two messages are communicated by one person at the same time, demanding different and incompatible responses; (3) at least one person in the double-bind cannot escape from the contradictory messages; and (4) there is a threat of punishment for noncompliance.

downward communication. Communication in which the messages originate at the higher levels of an organization or hierarchy and are sent to lower levels—for example, management to line worker; more generally, the habit of some people to address others as if these listeners were subordinate or ignorant; opposed to **upward communication.**

dyadic coalition. A two-person group formed from some larger group to achieve a particular goal.

dyadic communication. Two-person communication.

dyadic consciousness. An awareness of an interpersonal relationship or pairing of two individuals; distinguished from situations in which two individuals are together but do not perceive themselves as being a unit or twosome.

dyadic effect. The tendency for the behaviors of one person to stimulate behaviors in the other interactant; usually used to refer to the tendency of one person's self-disclosures to prompt the other to self-disclose, also.

ear marker. A marker that identifies an item as belonging to a specific person—for example, a nameplate on a desk or initials on an attaché case.

effect. The outcome or consequence of an action or behavior; communication is assumed always to have some effect.

emblems. Nonverbal behaviors that directly translate words or phrases—for example, the signs for "OK" and "peace."

emotion. The feelings we have—for example, our feelings of guilt, anger, or sorrow.

empathy. The feeling of another person's feeling; feeling or perceiving something as does another person.

encoder. Something that takes a message in one form (for example, nerve impulses) and translates it into another form (for example, sound waves). In human communication, the encoder is the speaking mechanism; in electronic communication, the encoder is, for example, the telephone mouthpiece. Encoding is the process of putting a message into a code—for example, translating nerve impulses into speech sounds. *See also* **decoder.**

E-prime. A form of the language that omits the verb "to be" except when used as an auxiliary or in statements of existence. Designed to eliminate the tendency toward **projection.**

equality. An attitude that recognizes that each individual in a communication interaction is equal, that no one is superior to any other; encourages supportiveness; opposed to **superiority.**

equity theory. A theory claiming that relational satisfaction depends on the rewards being distributed in proportion to the costs paid by each individual.

erotic love. A sexual, physical love; a love that is ego centered and given because of an anticipated return.

etc. (et cetera). An **extensional device** used to emphasize the notion of infinite complexity; because one can never know all about anything, any statement about the world or an event must end with an explicit or implicit "etc."

ethics. The branch of philosophy that deals with the rightness or wrongness of actions; the study of moral values.

ethnocentrism. The tendency to see others and their behaviors through our own cultural filters, often as distortions of our own behaviors; the tendency to evaluate the values and beliefs of one's own culture more positively than those of another culture.

euphemism. A polite word or phrase used to substitute for some taboo or otherwise offensive term.

evaluation. A process whereby a value is placed on some person, object, or event.

excuse. An explanation designed to lessen the negative consequences of something done or said.

experiential limitation. The limit of an individual's ability to communicate, as set by the nature and extent of that individual's experiences.

expert power. Power dependent on a person's expertise or knowledge; knowledge gives an individual expert power.

expressiveness. A quality of interpersonal effectiveness; genuine involvement in speaking and listening, conveyed verbally and nonverbally.

extensional devices. Linguistic devices proposed by Alfred Korzybski to keep language a more accurate means for talking about the world. The extensional devices include **etc., date,** and **index** (the working devices) and the **hyphen** and **quotes** (the safety devices).

extensional orientation. A point of view in which the primary consideration is given to the world of experience and only secondary consideration is given to labels. *See also* **intensional orientation.**

facial feedback hypothesis. The hypothesis or theory that your facial expressions can produce physiological and emotional effects.

facial management techniques. Techniques used to mask certain emotions and to emphasize others, for example, intensifying your expression of happiness to make a friend feel good about a promotion.

fact-inference confusion. A misevaluation in which one makes an inference, regards it as a fact, and acts upon it as if it were a fact.

factual statement. A statement made by the observer after observation and limited to what is observed. *See also* **inferential statement.**

fear appeal. The appeal to fear to persuade an individual or group of individuals to believe or to act in a certain way.

feedback. Information that is given back to the source. Feedback may come from the source's own messages (as when we hear what we are saying) or from the receiver(s) in the form of applause, yawning, puzzled looks, questions, letters to the editor of a newspaper, increased or decreased subscriptions to a magazine, and so forth. *See also* **negative feedback, positive feedback.**

feedforward. Information that is sent prior to the regular messages telling the listener something about what is to follow.

force. An unproductive **conflict** strategy in which you try to win an argument by physically overpowering the other person either by threat or by actual behavior.

free information. Information that is revealed implicitly and that may be used as a basis for opening or pursuing conversations.

friendship. An interpersonal relationship between two persons that is mutually productive, established and maintained through perceived mutual free choice, and characterized by mutual positive regard.

game. A simulation of some situation with rules governing the behaviors of the participants and with some payoff for winning; in transactional analysis, "game" refers to a series of ulterior transactions that lead to a payoff; the term also refers to a basically dishonest kind of transaction in which participants hide their true feelings.

general semantics. The study of the relationships among language, thought, and behavior.

gossip. Communication about someone not present, some third party, usually about matters that are private to this third party.

gunnysacking. An unproductive **conflict** strategy of storing up grievances—as if in a gunnysack—and holding them in readiness to dump on the person with whom one is in conflict.

halo effect. The tendency to generalize an individual's virtue or expertise from one area to another.

haptics. Technical term for the study of touch communication.

hedge. A type of **disclaimer** in which the speaker discounts the importance to his or her own identity of what is about to be said.

heterosexist language. Language that assumes all people are heterosexual and thereby denigrates lesbians and gay men.

hidden self. The part of the self that contains information about the self known to oneself but unknown to (hidden from) others.

home field advantage. The increased power that comes from being in your own territory.

home territories. Territories for which individuals have a sense of intimacy and over which they exercise control—for example, a teacher's office.

hyphen. An **extensional device** used to illustrate that what may be separated verbally may not be separable on the event level or on the nonverbal level; although one may talk about body and mind as if they were separable, in reality they are better referred to as body-mind.

illustrators. Nonverbal behaviors that accompany and literally illustrate verbal messages—for example, upward movements that accompany the verbalization "It's up there."

I-messages. Messages in which the speaker accepts responsibility for personal thoughts and behaviors; messages in which the speaker's point of view is stated explicitly; opposed to **you-messages.**

immediacy. A quality of interpersonal effectiveness; a sense of contact and togetherness; a feeling of interest and liking for the other person.

implicit personality theory. A theory of personality that each individual maintains, complete with rules or systems, through which others are perceived.

inclusion principle. In verbal interaction, the principle that all members should be a part of (included in) the interaction.

index. An **extensional device** used to emphasize the notion of nonidentity (no two things are the same) and symbolized by a subscript—for example, politician$_1$ is not politician$_2$.

indirect speech. Speech that hides the speaker's true intentions; speech in which requests and observations are made indirectly.

indiscrimination. A misevaluation caused by categorizing people, events, or objects into a particular class and responding to them only as members of the class; a failure to recognize that each individual is unique; a failure to apply the **index.**

inevitability. A principle of communication holding that communication cannot be avoided; all behavior in an interactional setting is communication.

inferential statement. A statement that can be made by anyone, is not limited to what is observed, and can be made at any time. *See also* **factual statement.**

information overload. A condition in which the amount of information is too great to be dealt with effectively or the number or complexity of messages is so great that the individual or organization is not able to deal with them.

information power. Power dependent on one's ability to communicate logically and persuasively. Also called persuasion power.

in-group talk. Talk about a subject or in a vocabulary that only certain people understand; such talk often occurs in the presence of someone who does not belong to the group and therefore does not understand.

insulation. A reaction to **territorial encroachment** in which you erect some sort of barrier between yourself and the invaders.

intensional orientation. A point of view in which primary consideration is given to the way things are labeled and only secondary consideration (if any) to the world of experience. *See also* **extensional orientation.**

interaction management. A quality of interpersonal effectiveness; the control of interaction to the satisfaction of both parties; managing conversational turns, fluency, and message consistency.

intercultural communication. Communication that takes place between persons of different cultures or persons who have different cultural beliefs, values, or ways of behaving.

interethnic communication. Communication between members of different ethnic groups.

international communication. Communication between nations.

interpersonal communication. Communication between two persons or among a small group of persons and distinguished from public or mass communication; communication of a personal nature and distinguished from impersonal communication; communication between or among connected persons or those involved in a close relationship.

interpersonal conflict. A disagreement between two connected persons.

interpersonal perception. The perception of people; the processes through which we interpret and evaluate people and their behavior.

interracial communication. Communication between members of different races.

intimate distance. The closest proxemic distance, ranging from touching to 18 inches. *See also* **proxemics.**

intrapersonal communication. Communication with oneself.

invasion. A form of **territorial encroachment** consisting of one's entering a territory and thereby changing its meaning.

irreversibility. A principle of communication holding that communication cannot be reversed; once something has been communicated, it cannot be uncommunicated.

jargon. A kind of **sublanguage;** the language of any special group, often a professional class, which is unintelligible to individuals not belonging to the group; "shop talk."

Johari window. A diagram of the four selves: **open, blind, hidden,** and **unknown.**

kinesics. The study of the communicative dimensions of facial and bodily movements.

language relativity hypothesis. The theory that the language we speak influences our

behaviors and our perceptions of the world and that therefore persons speaking widely differing languages will perceive and behave differently as a result of the language differences. Also referred to as the Sapir-Whorf hypothesis and the Whorfian hypothesis.

legitimate power. Power dependent on the belief that a person has a right, by virtue of position, to influence or control the behavior of another.

leveling. A process of message distortion in which a message is repeated but the number of details is reduced, some details are omitted entirely, and some details lose their complexity.

linguistic collusion. A reaction to **territorial encroachment** in which you speak in a language unknown to the intruders and thus separate yourself from them.

listening. An active process of receiving aural stimuli; this process consists of five stages: receiving, understanding, remembering, evaluating, and responding.

loving. An interpersonal process in which one feels a closeness, a caring, a warmth, and an excitement for another person.

ludus love. Love as a game, as fun; the position that love is not to be taken seriously and is to be maintained only as long as it remains interesting and enjoyable.

maintenance. A stage of relationship stability at which the relationship does not progress or deteriorate significantly; a continuation as opposed to a dissolution of a relationship.

maintenance strategies. Specific behaviors designed to preserve an interpersonal relationship. *See also* **repair strategies.**

manic love. Love characterized by extreme highs and extreme lows; obsessive love.

manipulation. An unproductive **conflict** strategy that avoids open conflict; instead, attempts are made to divert the conflict by being especially charming and getting the other person into a noncombative frame of mind.

manner maxim. A principle of conversation that holds that speakers cooperate by being clear and by organizing their thoughts into some meaningful and coherent pattern.

markers. Devices that signify that a certain territory belongs to a particular person. *See also* **boundary marker, central marker,** and **ear marker.**

matching hypothesis. An assumption that we date and mate with people who are similar to ourselves—who match us—in physical attractiveness.

meaningfulness. A principle of perception holding that we assume that the behavior of people is sensible, stems from some logical antecedent, and is consequently meaningful rather than meaningless.

mere exposure hypothesis. The theory that repeated or prolonged exposure to a stimulus may result in a change in attitude toward the stimulus object, generally in the direction of increased positiveness.

message. Any signal or combination of signals that serves as a **stimulus** for a receiver.

metacommunication. Communication about communication.

metalanguage. Language used to talk about language.

micromomentary expressions. Extremely brief movements that are not consciously controlled or recognized and that are thought to be indicative of an individual's true emotional state.

mindfulness and mindlessness. States of relative awareness. In a mindful state, we are aware of the logic and rationality of our behaviors and the logical connections existing among elements. In a mindless state, we are unaware of this logic and rationality.

minimization. An unproductive **conflict** strategy in which one makes light of the objections or complaints of another person, stating that the conflict, its causes, and its consequences are insignificant.

model. A representation of an object or process.

monologue. A form of **communication** in which one person speaks and the other listens; there is no real interaction among participants; opposed to **dialogue.**

negative feedback. Feedback that serves a corrective function by informing the source that his or her message is not being received in the way intended. Negative feedback serves to redirect the source's behavior. Looks of boredom, shouts of disagreement, letters critical of newspaper policy, and teachers' instructions on how better to approach a problem would be examples of negative feedback.

neutrality. A response pattern lacking in personal involvement; encourages defensiveness; opposed to **empathy.**

noise. Anything that interferes with a person's receiving a message as the source intended the message to be received. Noise is present in a communication system to the extent that the message received is not the message sent.

nonallness. An attitude or point of view in which it is recognized that one can never know all about anything and that what we know, say, or hear is only a part of what there is to know, say, or hear.

nondirective language. Language that does not direct or focus our attention on certain aspects; neutral language.

nonnegotiation. An unproductive **conflict** strategy in which the individual refuses to discuss the conflict or to listen to the other person.

nonverbal communication. Communication without words; communication by means of space, gestures, facial expressions, touching, vocal variation, and silence, for example.

object language. Language used to communicate about objects, events, and relations in the world; the structure of the object language is described in a **metalanguage;** the display of physical objects—for example, flower arranging and the colors of the clothes we wear.

olfactory communication. Communication by smell.

openness. A quality of interpersonal effectiveness encompassing (1) a willingness to interact openly with others, to self-disclose as appropriate; (2) a willingness to react honestly to incoming stimuli; and (3) a willingness to own one's feelings and thoughts.

open self. The part of the self that contains information about the self that is known both to oneself and to others.

opinion. A tentative conclusion concerning some object, person, or event.

other-orientation. A quality of interpersonal effectiveness involving attentiveness, interest, and concern for the other person.

other talk. Talk about the listener or some third party.

owning feelings. The process by which we take responsibility for our own feelings instead of attributing them to others.

packaging. *See* **reinforcement.**

paralanguage. The vocal (but nonverbal) aspect of speech. Paralanguage consists of voice qualities (for example, pitch range, resonance, tempo), vocal characterizers (laughing or crying, yelling or whispering), vocal qualifiers (intensity, pitch height), and vocal segregates ("uh-uh," meaning "no," or "sh" meaning "silence").

passive listening. Listening that is attentive and supportive but occurs without talking and without directing the speaker in any nonverbal way; also used negatively to refer to inattentive and uninvolved listening.

pauses. Silent periods in the normally fluent stream of speech. Pauses are of two major types: filled pauses (interruptions in speech that are filled with such vocalizations as "er" or "um") and unfilled pauses (silences of unusually long duration).

perception. The process of becoming aware of objects and events through the senses.

perceptual accentuation. A process that leads us to see what we expect to see and what we want to see—for example, we see people we like as better looking and smarter than people we do not like.

personal distance. The second-closest proxemic distance, ranging from 18 inches to 4 feet. *See also* **proxemics.**

personal rejection. An unproductive **conflict** strategy in which the individual withholds love and affection and seeks to win the ar-

gument by getting the other person to break down under this withdrawal.

persuasion. The process of influencing attitudes and behavior.

persuasion power. *See* **information power.**

phatic communication. Communication that is primarily social; communication designed to open the channels of communication rather than to communicate something about the external world; "Hello" and "How are you?" in everyday interaction are examples.

pitch. The highness or lowness of the vocal tone.

polarization. A form of fallacious reasoning by which only two extremes are considered; also referred to as "black-or-white" and "either-or" thinking or two-valued orientation.

positive feedback. Feedback that supports or reinforces the continuation of behavior along the same lines in which it is already proceeding—for example, applause during a speech.

positiveness. A characteristic of effective communication involving positive attitudes toward oneself and toward the interpersonal interaction. Also used to refer to positively **stroking** another person through compliments and expressions of acceptance and approval.

power. The ability to control the behaviors of others.

pragmatic love. Practical love; love based on compatibility; love that seeks a relationship in which each person's important needs and desires will be satisfied.

pragmatics. In communication, an approach that focuses on behaviors, especially on the effects or consequences of communication.

primacy effect. The condition by which what comes first exerts greater influence than what comes later. *See also* **recency effect.**

primary affect displays. The communication of the six primary emotions: happiness, surprise, fear, anger, sadness, and disgust/contempt.

primary territory. Areas that one can consider one's exclusive preserve—for example, one's room or office.

process. Ongoing or nonstatic activity; communication is referred to as a process to emphasize that it is always changing, always in motion.

progressive differentiation. A relational problem caused by the exaggeration or intensification of differences or similarities between individuals.

projection. A psychological process whereby we attribute characteristics or feelings of our own to others; often used to refer to the process whereby we attribute our own faults to others.

pronouncements. Authoritative statements that imply that the speaker is in a position of authority and that the listener is in a childlike or learner role.

provisionalism. An attitude of open-mindedness that leads to the creation of supportiveness; opposed to **certainty.**

proxemics. The study of the communicative function of space; the study of how people unconsciously structure their space—the distance between people in their interactions, the organization of space in homes and offices, and even the design of cities.

proximity. As a principle of perception, the tendency to perceive people or events that are physically close as belonging together or representing some unit; physical closeness; one of the qualities influencing interpersonal **attraction.**

psychological time. The importance you place on past, present, or future time.

public distance. The farthest proxemic distance, ranging from 12 feet to more than 25 feet.

public territory. Areas that are open to all people—for example, restaurants or parks.

punctuation of communication. The breaking up of continuous communication sequences into short sequences with identifiable beginnings and endings or stimuli and responses.

punishment. Noxious or aversive stimulation.

pupillometrics. The study of communication through changes in the size of the pupils of the eyes.

Pygmalion effect. The condition in which one makes a prediction and then proceeds to fulfill it; a type of self-fulfilling prophecy but one that refers to others and to our evaluation of others rather than to ourselves.

quality maxim. A principle of **conversation** that holds that speakers cooperate by saying what they know or think is true and by not saying what they know or think is false.

quantity maxim. A principle of **conversation** that holds that speakers cooperate by being only as informative as necessary to communicate their intended meanings.

quotes. An **extensional device** to emphasize that a word or phrase is being used in a special sense and should therefore be given special attention.

racist language. Language that denigrates a particular race.

rate. The speed with which we speak, generally measured in words per minute.

receiver. Any person or thing that takes in messages. Receivers may be individuals listening to or reading a message, a group of persons hearing a speech, a scattered television audience, or machines that store information.

recency effect. The condition in which what comes last (that is, most recently) exerts greater influence than what comes first. *See also* **primacy effect.**

reconciliation strategies. Behaviors designed to re-create a broken relationship.

redundancy. The quality of a message that makes it totally predictable and therefore lacking in information. A message of zero redundancy would be completely unpredictable; a message of 100 percent redundancy would be completely predictable. All human languages contain some degree of built-in redundancy, generally estimated to be about 50 percent.

referent power. Power dependent on one's desire to identify with or to be like another person.

reflexiveness. The feature of human language that makes it possible for that language to be used to refer to itself; that is, we can talk about our talk and create a **metalanguage,** a language for talking about language.

regulators. Nonverbal behaviors that regulate, monitor, or control the communications of another person.

reinforcement or packaging (principle of). The principle of verbal interaction that holds that in most interactions, messages are transmitted simultaneously through a number of different channels that normally reinforce each other; messages come in packages.

reinforcement theory. A theory of behavior that when applied to relationships would hold (essentially) that relationships develop because they are rewarding and end because they are punishing.

rejection. A response to an individual that rejects or denies the validity of that individual's self-view.

relational communication. Communication between or among intimates or those in close relationships; used by some theorists as synonymous with interpersonal communication.

relation maxim. A principle of **conversation** that holds that speakers cooperate by talking about what is relevant to the conversation and by not talking about what is not relevant.

relationship deterioration. The stage of a relationship during which the connecting bonds between the partners weaken and the partners begin drifting apart.

repair. A relationship stage in which one or both parties seek to improve the relationship.

repair strategies. Behaviors designed to improve a deteriorating relationship. See *also* **maintenance strategies.**

resemblance. As a principle of perception, the tendency to perceive people or events that are similar in appearance as belonging together.

response. Any bit of overt or covert behavior.

reward power. Power dependent on one's ability to reward another person.

rigid complementarity. The inability to break away from the complementary type of relationship that was once appropriate and now is no longer.

role. The part an individual plays in a group; an individual's function or expected behavior.

secondary territory. Areas that do not belong to a particular person but have been occupied by that person and are therefore associated with her or him—for example, the seat you normally take in class.

selective exposure (principle of). A principle of persuasion that states that listeners actively seek out information that supports their opinions and actively avoid information that contradicts their existing opinions, beliefs, attitudes, and values.

self-acceptance. Being satisfied with ourselves, our virtues and vices, and our abilities and limitations.

self-attribution. A process through which we seek to account for and understand the reasons and motivations for our own behaviors.

self-concept. An individual's self-evaluation; an individual's self-appraisal.

self-disclosure. The process of revealing something about ourselves to another, usually used to refer to information that would normally be kept hidden.

self-fulfilling prophecy. The situation in which we make a prediction or prophecy and fulfill it ourselves—for example, expecting a class to be boring and then fulfilling this expectation by perceiving it as boring.

self-monitoring. The manipulation of the image one presents to others in interpersonal interactions so as to give the most favorable impression of oneself.

self-serving bias. A bias that operates in the self-attribution process and leads us to take credit for the positive consequences and to deny responsibility for the negative consequences of our behaviors.

self-talk. Talk about oneself.

semantics. The area of language study concerned with meaning.

sexist language. Language derogatory to one sex, generally women.

sharpening. A process of message distortion in which the details of messages, when repeated, are crystallized and heightened.

shyness. The condition of discomfort and uneasiness in interpersonal situations.

signal and noise (relativity of). The principle of verbal interaction that holds that what is signal (meaningful) and what is noise (interference) is relative to the communication analyst, the participants, and the context.

signal reaction. A conditioned response to a signal; a response to some signal that is immediate rather than delayed.

silence. The absence of vocal communication; often misunderstood to refer to the absence of any and all communication.

silencers. A tactic (such as crying) that literally silences one's opponent—an unproductive **conflict** strategy.

similarity. A principle of **attraction** holding that one is attracted to qualities similar to those possessed by oneself and to people who are similar to oneself; opposed to **complementarity.**

sin licenses. A type of **disclaimer** in which the speaker acknowledges that he or she is about to break some normally operative rule; the speaker asks for a license to sin (that is, to break a social or interpersonal rule).

slang. The language used by special groups that is not considered proper by the general society; language made up of the **argot, cant,** and **jargon** of various subcultures and known by the general public.

social comparison processes. The processes by which you compare yourself (for example, your abilities, opinions, and values) with others and then assess and evaluate yourself; one of the sources of self-concept.

social distance. The third proxemic distance, ranging from 4 feet to 12 feet; the distance at which business is usually conducted. *See also* **proxemics.**

social exchange theory. A theory hypothesizing that we develop relationships in which our rewards or profits will be greater than our costs and that we avoid or terminate relationships in which the costs exceed the rewards.

social penetration theory. A theory concerned with relationship development from the superficial to the intimate levels and from few to many areas of interpersonal interaction.

source. Any person or thing that creates messages. A source may be an individual speaking, writing, or gesturing or a computer solving a problem.

speaker apprehension. A fear of engaging in communication transactions; a decrease in the frequency, strength, and likelihood of engaging in communication transactions.

speech. Messages conveyed via a vocal-auditory channel.

spontaneity. The communication pattern in which one verbalizes what one is thinking without attempting to develop strategies for control; encourages **supportiveness;** opposed to **strategy.**

stability. The principle of perception that refers to the fact that our perceptions of things and of people are relatively consistent with our previous conceptions.

state apprehension. Speaker apprehension for specific types of communication situations—for example, public speaking or interview situations.

static evaluation. An orientation that fails to recognize that the world is characterized by constant change; an attitude that sees people and events as fixed rather than as constantly changing.

status. The relative level one occupies in a hierarchy; status always involves a comparison, and thus one's status is only relative to the status of another. In our culture, occupation, financial position, age, and educational level are significant determinants of status.

stereotype. In communication, a fixed impression of a group of people through which we then perceive specific individuals; stereotypes are most often negative (Martians are stupid, uneducated, and dirty) but may also be positive (Venusians are scientific, industrious, and helpful).

stimulus. Any external or internal change that impinges on or arouses an organism.

stimulus-response models of communication. Models of communication that assume that the process of communication is linear, beginning with a stimulus that then leads to a response.

storge love. Love based on companionship, similar interests, and mutual respect; love that is lacking in great emotional intensity.

strategy. The use of some plan for control of other members of a communication interaction that guides one's own communications; encourages **defensiveness;** opposed to **spontaneity.**

stroking. Verbal or nonverbal acknowledgment of another person; positive stroking consists of compliments, rewards, and, in general, behaviors we look forward to or take pride in receiving; negative stroking is punishing and would consist of criticisms, expressions of disapproval, or even physical punishment.

subjectivity. The principle of perception that refers to the fact that one's perceptions are not objective but are influenced by one's wants and needs and one's expectations and predictions.

sublanguage. A variation from the general language, one used by a particular subculture; **argot, cant,** and **jargon** are particular kinds of sublanguages.

superiority. A point of view or attitude that assumes that others are not equal to oneself; encourages **defensiveness;** opposed to **equality.**

supportiveness. An attitude of an individual or an atmosphere in a group that is characterized by openness, absence of fear, and a genuine feeling of equality.

symmetrical relationship. A relation between two or more persons in which one person's behavior serves as a stimulus for the same type of behavior in the other person(s). Examples of such relationships include those in which anger in one person encourages or serves as a stimulus for anger in another person or in which a critical comment by the person leads the other person to respond in like manner.

taboo. Forbidden; culturally censored. Taboo language is language that is frowned upon by "polite society." Topics and specific words may be considered taboo—for example, death, sex, certain forms of illness, and various words denoting sexual activities and excretory functions.

tactile communication. Communication by touch; communication received by the skin.

territorial encroachment. A challenge to one's ownership or occupation of some space or object.

territoriality. A possessive or ownership reaction to an area of space or to particular objects.

theory. A general statement or principle applicable to a number of related phenomena.

touch avoidance. The tendency to avoid touching and being touched by others.

trait apprehension. Speaker apprehension for communication generally; a fear of communication situations regardless of their context.

transactional. Characterizing the relationship among elements whereby each influences and is influenced by each other element; communication is a transactional process because no element is independent of any other element.

trust. Faith in the behavior of another person; confidence in another person that leads us to feel that whatever we risk will not be lost.

turf defense. The most extreme reaction to **territorial enroachment,** in which you defend your territory and expel intruders.

universal of interpersonal communication. A feature of communication common to all interpersonal communication acts.

unknown self. The part of the self that contains information about the self that is unknown to oneself and to others but is inferred to exist on the basis of various projective tests, slips of the tongue, dream analyses, and the like.

upward communication. In organizational communication, communication that originates from an individual who is low on the organizational hierarchy and is directed to someone higher up; more generally, the habit of some people to address others as if these listeners were superiors or authorities; opposed to **downward communication.**

value. Relative worth of an object; a quality that makes something desirable or undesirable; ideals or customs about which we have emotional responses, whether positive or negative.

verbal aggressiveness. A method of winning an argument by attacking the other person's **self-concept.**

violation. A form of **territorial encroachment** consisting of the unwarranted use of another's territory.

voice qualities. Aspects of **paralanguage**—specifically, pitch range, vocal lip control, glottis control, pitch control, articulation control, rhythm control, resonance, and tempo.

volume. The relative loudness of the voice.

withdrawal. A reaction to **territorial encroachment** in which you leave the territory; a tendency to close yourself off from conflicts rather than confront them.

you-messages. Messages in which the speaker denies responsibility for his or her own thoughts and behaviors; messages that attribute the speaker's perception to another person; messages of blame; opposed to **I-messages.**

Glossary of Interpersonal Communication Skills

active listening. Listen actively by paraphrasing the speaker's meanings, expressing an understanding of the speaker's feelings, and asking questions to enable you to check the accuracy of your understanding of the speaker. Express acceptance of the speaker's feelings, and encourage the speaker to explore further his or her feelings and thoughts and thereby increase meaningful sharing.

active listening and self-disclosure. In responding to the disclosures of others, listen actively: paraphrase the speaker's thoughts and feelings, express understanding of the speaker's feelings, and ask relevant questions to ensure understanding and to signal attention and interest.

adaptor interference. Avoid adaptors that interfere with effective communication and reveal your discomfort or anxiety.

addictive relationships. If you are in an addictive relationship, consider developing your own self-confidence, distinguish between pseudo-intimacy and real intimacy, structure your relationship behavior so that both you and your partner achieve satisfaction, cultivate other-orientation, and talk about the relationship and the possibility of addiction *intra*personally and *inter*personally.

adjustment. Expand the common areas between you and significant others; learn each other's system of communication signals and meanings in order to increase understanding and interpersonal communication effectiveness.

aesthetics. Make the physical context of communication as aesthetically pleasing as possible in order to make interpersonal interactions more effective and satisfying.

affinity-seeking strategies. Use the various affinity-seeking strategies (for example, listening, openness, and dynamism), as appropriate to the interpersonal relationship and the situation, to increase your own interpersonal attractiveness.

affirm. Use affirmation to express your supportiveness and to raise esteem.

allness. End statements with an implicit "etc." ("et cetera") to indicate that more could be known and said; avoid allness terms and statements.

apprehension causes. Identify the causes of your own apprehension, considering, for example, lack of communication skills and experience, fear of evaluation, conspicuousness, unpredictability of the situation (ambiguity, newness), and your history of prior successes or failures in similar and related situations.

apprehension management. Manage your own communication apprehension by acquiring the necessary communication skills and experience, preparing and practicing for relevant communication situations, focusing on success, familiarizing yourself with the communication situations important to you, using physical activity and deep breathing to relax, and putting communication apprehension in perspective. In cases of extreme communication apprehension, seek professional help.

argumentativeness. Cultivate your argumentativeness, your willingness to argue for what you believe, by, for example, treating disagreements as objectively as possible, reaffirming the other, stressing equality, expressing interest in the other's position, and allowing the other person to save face.

arrangement of physical setting. Arrange the physical setting of communication to stimulate effective and satisfying interactions; avoid creating spaces that make communication difficult and tedious (for example, seats that are too far apart or awkwardly aligned); arrange seating positions that are most conducive to the task at hand.

assertiveness. Increase assertiveness (if desired) by analyzing the assertive and nonassertive behaviors of others, analyzing your own behaviors in terms of assertiveness, recording your behaviors, rehearsing assertive behaviors, and acting assertively in appropriate situations. Secure feedback from others for further guidance in increasing assertiveness.

attitudinal similarity. Identify those attitudes for which you feel similarity is important and those for which it is unimportant.

attractiveness. Use physical proximity to increase interpersonal attractiveness.

attribution. In attempting to identify the motivation for behaviors, examine consensus, consistency, and distinctiveness. Generally, low consensus, high consistency, and low distinctiveness identify internally motivated behavior; high consensus, low consistency, and high distinctiveness identify externally motivated behavior. Also inquire into controllability and stability judgments.

back-channeling cues. Respond to back-channeling cues as appropriate to the conversation. Use back-channeling cues to let the speaker know you are listening.

barriers to intercultural communication. Avoid the major barriers to intercultural communication: ignoring differences between yourself and the culturally different, ignoring differences among the culturally different, ignoring differences in meaning, violating cultural rules and customs, and evaluating differences negatively.

believability judgments. Weigh both verbal and nonverbal messages before making believability judgments; increase sensitivity to cues to nonverbal (and verbal) deception— for example, too little movement, long pauses, slow speech, increased speech errors, mouth guard, nose touching, eye rubbing, or the use of few words, especially monosyllabic answers. Use such cues to formulate hypotheses rather than conclusions concerning deception.

bypassing. Recognize that the same word may be given different meanings by different people and that different words may be used to mean the same thing. Look for meaning in the person, and use active listening techniques to combat possible bypassing.

color communication. Use colors (in clothing and in room decor, for example) to convey desired meanings.

communication adjustment. Adjust your communications as appropriate to the stage of your interpersonal relationship.

complementarity. Identify the characteristics that you do not find in yourself but admire in others and that therefore might be important in influencing your perception of complementarity.

complementary and symmetrical relationships. Use complementary and symmetrical messages to best communicate your meanings and to achieve your goals.

compliance-gaining strategies. Use the various compliance-gaining strategies to increase your own persuasive power.

compliance-resisting strategies. Use such strategies as identity management, nonnegotiation, negotiation, and justification as appropriate in resisting compliance.

confidence. Communicate a feeling of being comfortable and at ease with the interaction through appropriate verbal and nonverbal signals.

confidentiality. Keep the disclosures of others confidential.

confirmation and disconfirmation. Avoid those verbal and nonverbal behaviors that disconfirm another person. Substitute confirming behaviors, behaviors that acknowledge the presence and the contributions of the other person.

consistency. Recognize the human tendency to seek and to see consistency even where it does not exist—to see our friends as all positive and our enemies as all negative, for example.

context. Assess the context in which messages are communicated and interpret that communication behavior accordingly; avoid seeing messages as independent of context.

conversational management. Respond to conversational turn cues from the other person, and use conversational cues to signal your own desire to exchange (or maintain) speaker or listener roles.

conversational processes. Use the general five-step process in conversation, and avoid the several barriers that can be created when the normal process is distorted.

conversational turn cues. Become sensitive to and respond appropriately to conversational turn cues, such as turn-maintaining, turn-yielding, turn-requesting, and turn-denying cues.

cultural maxims. Discover, try not to violate, and, if appropriate, follow the conversational maxims of the culture in which you are communicating.

cultural rules. Respond to messages according to the cultural rules of the sender; avoid interpreting the messages of others exclusively through the perspective of your own culture in order to prevent misinterpretation of the intended meanings.

culture-specific nature of interpersonal communication. Recognize that the rules of interpersonal interaction vary from one culture to another.

dealing with the end of a relationship. If the relationship ends: (1) break the loneliness-depression cycle, (2) take time out to get to know yourself as an individual, (3) bolster your self-esteem, (4) remove or avoid uncomfortable symbols that may remind you of your past relationship and may make you uncomfortable, (5) seek the support of friends and relatives, and (6) avoid repeating negative patterns.

dialogic conversation. Treat conversation as a dialogue rather than a monologue; show concern for the other person, and for the relationship between you, with other-orientation.

direct speech. Use direct requests and responses (1) to encourage compromise, (2) to acknowledge responsibility for your own feelings and desires, and (3) to state your own desires honestly so as to encourage honesty, openness, and supportiveness in others.

disclaimers. Avoid using disclaimers that may not be accepted by your listeners (they may raise the very doubts you wish to put to rest), but do use disclaimers when you think your future messages might offend your listeners.

disclosure responses. In responding to the disclosures of others, demonstrate the skills of effective listening, express support for the discloser (but resist evaluation), reinforce the disclosing behavior, keep the disclosures confidential, and avoid using the disclosures against the person.

discriminating. Being sensitive to differences *among* individuals prevents discrimination against individuals.

dyadic effect. Be responsive to the dyadic effect; if it is not operating, consider why.

effectiveness characteristics. Use the characteristics of interpersonal effectiveness as general guidelines, and modify them as the different cultural orientations warrant.

emotional expression. Before expressing your emotions, understand them, decide whether you wish to express them, and assess your communication options. In expressing your emotions, describe your feelings as accurately as possible, identify the reasons for them, anchor your feelings and their expression to the present time, and own your feelings.

empathic understanding. Increase empathic understanding for your primary partner by sharing experiences, role-playing, and seeing the world from his or her perspective.

empathy. Empathize with others, and express this empathic understanding verbally and nonverbally.

equal communication. Talk neither down nor up to others but communicate as an equal to increase interpersonal satisfaction and efficiency.

equality. Share the speaking and the listening; recognize that all parties in communication have something to contribute.

evaluating cultural differences. Avoid evaluating your own cultural values, beliefs, and ways of behaving more positively than others.

excuses. Avoid excessive excuse making. Too many excuses may backfire and create image problems for the excuse maker.

expectations. Define and discuss the expectations each relationship partner has of the other, the nature of sexual satisfaction as each sees it, and the role and function of work and money in the relationship as a way of preventing unrealistic and unfulfilled expectations from creating conflicts.

expressiveness. Communicate involvement and interest in the interaction by providing appropriate feedback, by assuming responsibility for your thoughts and feelings and your role as speaker and listener, and by appropriate expressiveness, variety, and flexibility in voice and bodily action.

eye gaze. Use eye contact effectively to monitor feedback, to signal conversational turns, to signal the nature of a relationship, and to compensate for physical distance.

fact-inference differentiation. Distinguish facts from inferences; respond to inferences as inferences and not as facts.

feedback. Give clear and immediate feedback to others, and respond to others' feedback, either through corrective measures or by continuing current performance, to increase communication efficiency and satisfaction.

feedforward appropriately. When appropriate, preface your messages in order to open the channels of communication, to preview the messages to be sent, to disclaim, and to altercast.

feedforward effectively. In your use of feedforward, be brief, use feedforward sparingly, and follow through on your feedforward promises. Also, be sure to respond to the feedforward as well as the content messages of others.

flexibility. Apply the principles of interpersonal communication with flexibility; remember that each situation calls for somewhat different skills.

friendship. Adjust your verbal and nonverbal communication as appropriate to the stages of your various friendships.

friendship rules. Learn the rules that govern your friendships; follow them or risk damaging the relationship.

gossip. Avoid gossip that breaches confidentiality, is known to be false, and is unnecessarily invasive.

immediacy. Communicate immediacy through appropriate word choice, feedback, eye contact, body posture, and physical closeness.

implicit personality theory. Be conscious of your implicit personality theories; avoid drawing firm conclusions about other people on the basis of these theories.

inclusion. Include everyone present in the interaction (both verbally and nonverbally) so you do not exclude or offend others or fail to profit from their contributions.

increasing accuracy in perception. Increase your accuracy in interpersonal perception by looking for a variety of cues that point in the same direction, formulating hypotheses (not conclusions), being especially alert to contradictory cues that may refute your initial hypotheses, avoiding the assumption that others will respond as you would, and being careful not to perceive only the positive in those you like and the negative in those you dislike.

indirect speech. Use indirect speech (1) to express a desire without insulting or offending anyone, (2) to ask for compliments in a socially acceptable manner, and (3) to disagree without being disagreeable.

indiscrimination. Index your terms and statements to emphasize that each person and event is unique; avoid treating all individuals the same way because they are covered by the same label or term.

inevitability. Remember that all behavior in an interactional situation communicates; seek out nonobvious messages and meanings.

informal time. Recognize that informal-time terms are often the cause of interpersonal difficulties. When misunderstanding is likely, use more precise terms.

initiating relationships. In initiating relationships, remember the following steps: examine the qualifiers, determine clearance, open the encounter, select and put into operation an integrating topic, create a favorable impression, and establish a second meeting.

integrating topics. In selecting an integrating topic, look for free information and ask relevant (but not prying) questions.

intensional orientation. Respond first to things; avoid responding to labels as if they were things; do not let labels distort your perception of the world.

interaction management. Manage the interaction to the satisfaction of both parties by sharing the roles of speaker and listener, avoiding long and awkward silences, and being consistent in your verbal and nonverbal messages.

interest. Demonstrate interest in and acceptance of another person through appropriate verbal and nonverbal means.

interpersonal needs. Identify the needs that led you to seek your interpersonal relationships and those that led others to seek relationships with you; do this to understand and deal with the nature and function of these relationships.

interpreting time cues. Interpret time cues from the point of view of the other's culture rather than your own.

intimacy claims. Reduce the intensity of intimacy claims when things get rough; give each other space as appropriate.

invasive behaviors. Recognize that your own behaviors can be considered invasive by others; be careful of violating, invading, or contaminating the territories of others.

irreversibility. Avoid saying things (for example, in anger) or making commitments that you may wish to retract (but will not be able to) in order to prevent resentment and ill feeling.

language fairness. Use language fairly; avoid language that offends or demeans.

leave-taking cues. Increase your sensitivity to leave-taking cues; pick up on the leave-taking cues of others, and communicate such cues tactfully so as not to insult or offend others.

listening. Adjust your listening perspective, as the situation warrants, between active and passive, judgmental and nonjudgmental, surface and depth, and empathic and objective listening.

listening and self-disclosure. Demonstrate the skills of effective listening by listening for different levels of meaning; do so with empathy, empathic responses, and an openness to the other person.

love. Share meaningful emotions and experiences with a significant other.

maintenance strategies. Use appropriate maintenance strategies (for example, openness, sharing joint activities, and acting positively) to preserve a valued relationship.

markers. Become sensitive to the markers (central, boundary, and ear) of others, and learn to use these markers to define your own territories and to communicate the desired impression.

meaning interpretation. Assess meaning as a function of both the messages sent and the speaker's (and your own) attitudes and values to account for the influence of personality, past experiences, attitudes, and the like.

metacommunication. Metacommunicate to ensure understanding of the other person's thoughts and feelings: give clear feedforward, explain feelings as well as thoughts, paraphrase your own complex thoughts, and ask questions.

mindfulness. Apply the principles of interpersonal communication mindfully rather than mindlessly. Increase mindfulness by creating and re-creating categories, being open to new information and points of view, and being careful of relying too heavily on first impressions.

mirroring destructive behavior. Beware of

mirroring destructive behavior and creating a spiral wherein the unproductive behavior of one person stimulates similarly unproductive behavior in the other; the result of such a pattern is that conflict and differences are maximized and agreements and similarities are minimized.

mixed-message detection. Detect mixed messages in other people's communications and avoid being placed in double-bind situations by seeking clarification from the sender.

mixed-message sending. Avoid emitting mixed messages by focusing clearly on your purposes when communicating and by increasing conscious control over your verbal and nonverbal behaviors.

negative allness and conflict. Avoid negative allness terms and statements in conflict situations.

noise. Combat the effects of physical, semantic, and psychological noise by eliminating or lessening the sources of physical noise, securing agreement on meanings, and interacting with an open mind in order to increase communication accuracy.

nonverbal dominance. Resist (as sender and receiver) nonverbal expressions of dominance when they are inappropriate—for example, when they are sexist.

nonverbal encounter. In initiating relationships, keep the following nonverbal guidelines in mind: establish eye contact, signal interest and positive responses, concentrate your focus, establish physical closeness, maintain an open posture, respond visibly, reinforce positive behaviors, and avoid overexposure.

open self. Adjust your open self in light of the total context, disclosing or not disclosing yourself to others as appropriate.

other-orientation. Convey concern for and interest in the other person by means of empathic responses, appropriate feedback, and attentive listening responses.

ownership of feelings. Own your feelings; use I-messages; acknowledge responsibility for your own thoughts and feelings to increase honest sharing.

packages or clusters. Assess the entire package or cluster of message behaviors, and interpret any message as part of the cluster; avoid interpreting messages in isolation.

paralanguage. Vary paralinguistic elements, such as rate, volume, and stress, to add variety and emphasis to your communications, and be responsive to the meanings communicated by others' variation of paralanguage features.

perception checking. Use perception checking to get more information about your impressions: (1) describe what you think is happening, and (2) ask whether this is correct or in error.

perceptual accentuation. Be aware of the influence your own needs, wants, and expectations have on your perceptions. Recognize that what you perceive is a function both of what exists in reality *and* what is going on inside your own head.

polarization. Use middle terms and qualifiers when describing the world; avoid talking in terms of polar opposites (black and white, good and bad) in order to describe reality more accurately.

positiveness. Verbally and nonverbally communicate a positive attitude toward yourself, others, and the situation with smiles, positive facial expressions, attentive gestures, positive verbal expressions, and the elimination or reduction of negative appraisals.

power bases. Increase your sources or bases of power (referent, legitimate, reward, coercive, expert, and information).

power communication. Communicate power through forceful speech, avoidance of weak modifiers and excessive body movement, and demonstration of your knowledge, preparation, and organization in the matters at hand.

power play management strategy. Try managing power plays cooperatively by expressing your feelings, describing the behavior you object to, and stating a cooperative response.

power plays. Identify the power plays people

owe me, metaphor, yougottobekidding, and thought stoppers, and respond to these power plays so as to stop them.

pragmatic and logical implication. Distinguish between pragmatic and logical implications, and recognize that memory often confuses the two. In recalling situations and events, ask yourself whether your conclusions are based on pragmatic or logical implications.

praise and criticism. Say what you feel without excessive and unjustified praise or criticism.

premature self-disclosures. Resist too intimate or too negative self-disclosures early in the development of a relationship.

primacy and recency. Be aware that first impressions can serve as filters that prevent you from perceiving others, perhaps contradictory behaviors as well as changes in situations and, especially, changes in people. Recognize the normal tendency for first impressions to leave lasting impressions and to color both what we see later and the conclusions we draw. Be at your very best in first encounters. Also, take the time and effort to revise your impressions of others on the basis of new information.

productive conflict. Follow these guidelines to fight more productively: (1) state your position directly and honestly; (2) react openly to the messages of your combatant; (3) own your thoughts and feelings; (4) address the real issues causing the conflict; (5) listen with and demonstrate empathic understanding; (6) validate the feelings of your interactant; (7) describe the behaviors causing the conflict; (8) express your feelings spontaneously rather than strategically; (9) state your position tentatively; (10) capitalize on agreements; (11) view conflict in positive terms to the extent possible; (12) express positive feelings for the other person; (13) be positive about the prospects of conflict resolution; (14) treat your combatant as an equal, avoiding ridicule or sarcasm, for example; (15) involve yourself in the conflict; play an active role as both sender and receiver; (16) grant the other person permission to express himself or her-

self freely; and (17) avoid power tactics that may inhibit freedom of expression.

proxemic distances. Adjust spatial (proxemic) distances as appropriate to the specific interaction; avoid distances that are too far, too close, or otherwise inappropriate, as they might falsely convey, for example, aloofness or aggression.

psychological time. Recognize the significance of your own time orientation to your ultimate success, and make whatever adjustments you think desirable.

punctuation. See the sequence of events punctuated from perspectives other than your own in order to increase empathy and mutual understanding.

pupil dilation. Detect pupil dilation and constriction, and formulate hypotheses concerning their possible meanings.

racist language. Avoid racist language—any language that demeans or is derogatory toward members of a particular race—so as not to offend or alienate others or reinforce stereotypes.

reconciliation strategies. Consider using such reconciliation strategies as third-party intervention, tacit persistence, and mutual interaction to patch up a broken relationship.

reinforcement. Reinforce others as a way to increase interpersonal attractiveness and general interpersonal satisfaction.

relationship improvement. If you wish to preserve or repair a deteriorating relationship, take positive action by specifying what is wrong with the relationship, applying the skills and insights you have acquired to the task of relationship improvement, and taking risks in attempting to find a satisfactory solution to the relationship difficulty.

relationship messages. Recognize and respond to relationship as well as content messages in order to ensure a more complete understanding of the messages intended.

relationship repair. Consider the following steps when you wish to repair a relationship: (1) avoid withdrawal, keep the channels of communication open at all times, (2) avoid the sudden decrease in self-disclosure that often signals distrust, (3) increase supportiveness, (4) avoid deception, (5) avoid excessive negative responses, and (6) increase cherishing behaviors to create an environment conducive to compromise and rebuilding.

relationship stimulation. Keep a relationship stimulating by changing routines and exposing yourselves to new experiences.

repair strategies. Relationship repair may be accomplished by recognizing the problem, engaging in productive conflict resolution, posing possible solutions, affirming each other, integrating solutions into everyday behavior, and taking relational risks.

romantic rules. Learn the romantic rules that govern your relationship, and follow them or risk damaging the relationship.

self-appreciation. Appreciate yourself; identify your positive qualities; think positively about yourself.

self-awareness. Increase self-awareness by asking yourself about yourself and listening to others; actively seek information about yourself from others by carefully observing their interactions with you and by asking relevant questions. See yourself from different perspectives (see your different selves), and increase your open self.

self-disclosure   conditions. Self-disclose when the motivation is to improve the relationship, when the context and the relationship are appropriate for the self-disclosure, when there is an opportunity for open and honest responses, when the self-disclosures will be clear and direct, when there are appropriate reciprocal disclosures, and when you have examined and are willing to risk the possible burdens that self-disclosure might entail.

self-disclosure regulation. Self-disclose selectively; regulate your self-disclosures as appropriate to the context, topic, audience, and potential rewards and risks to secure the maximum advantage and reduce the possibility of negative effects.

self-esteem. Increase your self-esteem by at-

tacking destructive beliefs, engaging in self-affirmation, seeking out nourishing people, and working on projects that will result in success.

self-fulfilling prophecy. Avoid fulfilling your own negative prophecies and seeing only what you want to see. Be especially careful to examine your perceptions when they conform too closely to your expectations; check to make sure that you are seeing what exists in real life, not just in your expectations or predictions.

self-monitoring. Monitor your verbal and nonverbal behavior as appropriate to communicate the desired impression.

self-serving bias. In examining the causes of your own behavior, beware of the tendency to attribute negative behaviors to external factors and positive behaviors to internal factors. In self-examinations, ask whether and how the self-serving bias might be operating.

self-talk and other-talk. Balance talk about yourself with talk about the other; avoid excessive self-talk or extreme avoidance of self-talk to encourage equal sharing and interpersonal satisfaction.

sexist language. Whether man or woman, avoid sexist language—for example, terms that presume maleness as the norm ("police*man*" or "mail*man*"); avoid masculine pronouns when referring to both sexes.

sexual harassment action. If confronted with sexual harassment, consider talking to the harasser, collecting evidence, using appropriate channels within the organization, or filing a complaint.

sexual harassment avoidance. Avoid any indication of sexual harassment by beginning with the assumption that others at work are not interested in sexual advances and stories; listen for negative reactions to any sexually explicit discussions, and avoid behaviors you think might prove offensive.

silence. Use silence to communicate feelings or to prevent communication about certain topics.

silence interpretation. Interpret silences of

others through their culturally determined rules rather than your own.

spatial distance. Use spatial distance to signal the type of relationship you are in: intimate, personal, social, or public. Let your spatial relationships reflect your interpersonal relationships.

speech rate. Use variations in rate to increase communication efficiency and persuasiveness as appropriate.

static evaluation. Date your statements to emphasize constant change; avoid the tendency to think of and describe things as static and unchanging.

status differences. Avoid inappropriate use of time cues in establishing and maintaining status differences.

stereotyping. Avoid stereotyping others; instead, see and respond to each individual as a unique individual.

stroking. Stroke, or positively reinforce, others to express acknowledgment and validation and thus encourage increased positiveness and interpersonal satisfaction.

supportiveness. Exhibit supportiveness to others by being descriptive rather than evaluative, spontaneous rather than strategic, and provisional rather than certain.

supportiveness in self-disclosure. Express support for the discloser. Resist evaluation. Do not rush the discloser. Express support verbally and nonverbally: nod in agreement, maintain appropriate eye contact, smile, ask for relevant elaboration, and maintain physical closeness and directness.

taboo. Avoid taboo expressions so that others do not make negative evaluations; substitute more socially acceptable expressions or euphemisms where and when appropriate.

territorial invasion. Give others the space they need. Remember, for example, that people who are angry or disturbed need more space than usual.

territoriality. Establish and maintain territory nonverbally by marking or otherwise indicating temporary or permanent ownership. Become sensitive to the territorial behavior of others.

touch. Use touch when appropriate to express positive effect, playfulness, control, and ritualistic meanings and to serve task-related functions.

touch avoidance. Recognize that some people may prefer to avoid touching and being touched. Avoid drawing too many conclusions about people from the way they treat interpersonal touching.

touch rules. Respond to the touch patterns of others in light of their gender and culture and not exclusively on the basis of your own.

truth and deception. State the truth as you know it with gentleness.

uncertainty reduction strategies. Increase your accuracy in interpersonal perception by using all three uncertainty reduction strategies: passive, active, and interactive strategies.

unproductive conflict strategies. Avoid unproductive conflict strategies such as avoidance, force, blame, silencers, gunnysacking, manipulation, personal rejection, and fighting below the belt.

using time cues. Use time cues to signal your degree of interest or uninterest, willingness or unwillingness to communicate and socialize, and concern or lack of concern—for example, by arriving on time or by asking whether it is an appropriate time to discuss an issue.

verbal abuse. In dealing with verbal abuse, first recognize it for what it is; second, recognize the significant consequences, and try to change the behavior.

verbal aggressiveness. Avoid inflicting psychological pain on the other person to win an argument.

verbal encounter. In initiating relationships, keep the following verbal guidelines in mind: introduce yourself, focus the conversation on the other person, exchange favors-rewards, be energetic, stress the positives, avoid negative and too intimate self-disclosures, establish commonalities, avoid yes-no questions and answers, and avoid rapid-fire questions.

Bibliography

Adams, Linda, with Elinor Lenz (1989). *Be Your Best.* New York: Putnam.

Adams, R. G. (1987). Patterns of Network Change: A Longitudinal Study of Friendships of Elderly Women. *The Gerontologist* 27:222–227.

Addeo, Edmond G., and Robert E. Burger (1973). *Egospeak: Why No One Listens to You.* New York: Bantam.

Adler, Mortimer J. (1983). *How to Speak, How to Listen.* New York: Macmillan.

Adler, Ronald B. (1977). *Confidence in Communication: A Guide to Assertive and Social Skills.* New York: Holt, Rinehart & Winston.

Adler, Ronald B., Lawrence B. Rosenfeld, and Neil Towne (1989). *Interplay: The Process of Interpersonal Communication.* 4th ed. New York: Holt, Rinehart & Winston.

Akmajian, A., R. A. Demers, and R. M. Harnish (1979). *Linguistics: An Introduction to Language and Communication.* Cambridge, Mass.: MIT Press.

Albert, S. M., and M. Moss (1990). Consensus and the Domain of Personal Relationships Among Older Adults. *Journal of Social and Personal Relationships* 7:353–369.

Alberti, Robert E., ed. (1977). *Assertiveness: Innovations, Applications, Issues.* San Luis Obispo, Calif.: Impact.

Alberti, Robert E., and Michael L. Emmons (1970). *Your Perfect Right: A Guide to Assertive Behavior.* San Luis Obispo, Calif.: Impact.

Alberts, J. K. (1988). An Analysis of Couples' Conversational Complaints. *Communication Monographs* 55:184–197.

Altman, Irwin (1975). *The Environment and Social Behavior.* Monterey, Calif.: Brooks/Cole.

Altman, Irwin, and Dalmas Taylor (1973). *Social Penetration: The Development of Interpersonal Relationships.* New York: Holt, Rinehart & Winston.

Andersen, Peter A., and Ken Leibowitz (1978). The Development and Nature of the Construct Touch Avoidance. *Environmental Psychology and Nonverbal Behavior* 3:89–106. Reprinted in DeVito and Hecht (1990).

Ardrey, Robert (1966). *The Territorial Imperative.* New York: Atheneum.

Argyle, Michael (1983). *The Psychology of Interpersonal Behavior.* 4th ed. New York: Penguin.

Argyle, Michael (1988). *Bodily Communication.* 2d ed. New York: Methuen.

Argyle, Michael and J. Dean (1965). Eye Contact, Distance and Affiliation. *Sociometry* 28:289–304.

Argyle, Michael and Monika Henderson (1984). The Rules of Friendship. *Journal of Social and Personal Relationships* 1 (June):211–237.

Argyle, Michael and Monika Henderson (1985). *The Anatomy of Relationships: And the Rules and Skills Needed to Manage Them Successfully.* London: Heinemann.

Argyle, Michael, and R. Ingham (1972). Gaze, Mutual Gaze, and Distance. *Semiotica* 1:32–49.

Arliss, Laurie P. (1991). *Gender Communication.* Englewood Cliffs, N.J.: Prentice-Hall.

Arnold, Carroll C., and John Waite Bowers, eds. (1984). *Handbook of Rhetorical and Communication Theory.* Boston: Allyn & Bacon.

Aronson, Elliot (1980). *The Social Animal.* 3d ed. San Francisco: W. H. Freeman.

Asch, Solomon (1946). Forming Impressions of Personality. *Journal of Abnormal and Social Psychology* 41:258–290.

Authier, Jerry, and Kay Gustafson (1982). Microtraining: Focusing on Specific Skills. In *Interpersonal Helping Skills: A Guide to Training Methods, Programs, and Resources,* edited by Eldon K. Marshall, P. David Kurtz, and Associates, 93–130. San Francisco: Jossey-Bass.

Axtell, Roger (1993). *Do's and Taboos Around the World.* 3d ed. New York Wiley.

Aylesworth, Thomas G., and Virginia L. Aylesworth (1978). *If You Don't Invade My Intimate Zone or Clean Up My Water Hole, I'll Breathe in Your Face, Blow on Your Neck, and Be Late for Your Party.* New York: Condor.

Ayres, J. (1983). Strategies to Maintain Relationships: Their Identification and Perceived Usage. *Communication Quarterly* 31:62–67.

Ayres, Joe (1986). Perceptions of Speaking Ability: An Explanation for Stage Fright. *Communication Education* 35:275–287.

Bach, George R., and Peter Wyden (1968). *The Intimacy Enemy.* New York: Avon.

Bach, George R., and Ronald M. Deutsch (1979). *Stop! You're Driving Me Crazy.* New York: Berkeley.

Backrack, Henry M. (1976). Empathy. *Archives of General Psychiatry* 33:35–38.

Balswick, J. O., and C. Peck (1971). The Inexpressive Male: A Tragedy of American Society? *The Family Coordinator* 20:363–368.

Banks, Stephen P., Dayle M. Altendorf, John O. Greene, and Michael J. Cody (1987). An Examination of Relationship Disengagement: Perceptions, Breakup Strategies, and Outcomes. *Western Journal of Speech Communication* 51 (winter): 19–41.

Bavelas, Janet Beavin (1990). Can One Not Communicate? Behaving and Communicating: A Reply to Motley. *Western Journal of Speech Communication* 54 (Fall):593–602.

Barker, Larry, R. Edwards, C. Gaines, K. Gladney, and F. Holley (1980). An Investigation of Proportional Time Spent in Various Communication Activities by College Students. *Journal of Applied Communication Research* 8:101–109.

Barna, LaRay M. (1985). Stumbling Blocks in Intercultural Communication. In Samovar and Porter (1985), 330–338.

Barnlund, Dean C. (1970). A Transactional Model of Communication. In *Language Behavior: A Book of Readings in Communication,* compiled by J. Akin, A. Goldberg, G. Myers, and J. Stewart. The Hague: Mouton.

Barnlund, Dean C. (1975). Communicative Styles in Two Cultures: Japan and the United States. In *Organization of Behavior in Face-to-Face Interaction,* edited by A. Kendon, R. M. Harris, and M. R. Key. The Hague: Mouton.

Baron, Robert A., and Donn Byrne (1984). *Social Psychology: Understanding Human Interaction.* 4th ed. Boston: Allyn & Bacon.

Barrett, Karen (1982). Date Rape. *Ms.,* September, 48–51.

Bartholomew, Kim (1990). Avoidance of Intimacy: An Attachment Perspective. *Journal of Social and Personal Relationships* 7:147–178.

Basso, K. H. (1972). To Give Up on Words: Silence in Apache Culture. In *Language and Social Context,* edited by Pier Paolo Giglioli. New York: Penguin.

Bate, Barbara (1988). *Communication and the Sexes.* New York: Harper & Row.

Bateson, Gregory (1972). *Steps to an Ecology of Mind.* New York: Ballantine.

Baxter, Leslie A. (1983). Relationship Disengagement: An Examination of the Reversal Hypothesis. *Western Journal of Speech Communication* 47:85–98.

Baxter, Leslie A. (1986). Gender Differences in the Heterosexual Relationship Rules Embedded in Break-up Accounts. *Journal of Social and Personal Relationships* 3:289–306.

Baxter, Leslie A. (1988). A Dialectical Perspective on Communication Strategies in Relationship Development. In *Handbook of Personal Relationships,* ed. Steve W. Duck. New York: Wiley.

Baxter, Leslie A. (1990). Dialectical Contradictions in Relationship Development. *Journal of Social and Personal Relationships* 7 (February): 69–88.

Baxter, Leslie A. (1992). Root Metaphors in Accounts of Developing Romantic Relationships. *Journal of Social and Personal Relationships* 9 (May): 253–275.

Baxter, Leslie A. and C. Bullis (1986). Turning Points in Developing Romantic Relationships. *Human Communication Research* 12 (Summer):469–493.

Baxter, Leslie A. and Eric P. Simon (1993). Relationship Maintenance Strategies and Dialectical Contradictions in Personal Relationships. *Journal of Social and Personal Relationships* 10 (May):225–242.

Baxter, Leslie A., and W. W. Wilmot (1984). "Secret Tests": Social Strategies for Acquiring Information About the State of the Relationship. *Human Communication Research* 11:171–201.

Beach, Wayne A. (1990). On (Not) Observing Behavior Interactionally. *Western Journal of Speech Communication* 54 (Fall):603–612.

Beattie, Melody (1987). *Co-Dependent No More.* New York: HarperCollins.

Beatty, Michael J. (1986). *Romantic Dialogue: Communication in Dating and Marriage.* Englewood, Colo.: Morton Publishing Co.

Beatty, M. (1988). Situational and Predispositional Correlates of Public Speaking Anxiety. *Communication Education* 37:28–39.

Beck, A. T. (1988). *Love Is Never Enough.* New York: Harper & Row.

Beebe, Steven A. and John T. Masterson (1986). *Family Talk: Interpersonal Communication in the Family.* New York: Random House.

Beier, Ernst (1974). How We Send Emotional Messages. *Psychology Today* 8:53–56.

Bell, Robert A., and John A. Daly (1984). The Affinity-Seeking Function of Communication. *Communication Monographs* 51:91–115.

Bell, Robert A., and N. L. Buerkel-Rothfuss (1990). S(he) Loves Me, S(he) Loves Me Not: Predictors of Relational Information-Seeking in Courtship and Beyond. *Communication Quarterly* 38:64–82.

Berg, John H., and Richard L. Archer (1983). The Disclosure-Liking Relationship. *Human Communication Research* 10:269–281.

Berger, Charles R., and James J. Bradac (1982). *Language and Social Knowledge: Uncertainty in Interpersonal Relations.* London: Edward Arnold.

Berger, Charles R. and Richard J. Calabrese (1975). Some Explorations in Initial Interaction and Beyond: Toward a Theory of Interpersonal Communication. *Human Communication Research* 1 (Winter):99–112.

Berger, Charles R., and Steven H. Chaffee, eds. (1987). *Handbook of Communication Science.* Newbury Park, Calif.: Sage.

Berman, J. J., V. Murphy-Berman, and P. Singh (1985). Cross-Cultural Similarities and Differences in Perceptions of Fairness. *Journal of Cross-Cultural Psychology* 16:55–67.

Bernstein, W. M., W. G. Stephan, and M. H. Davis (1979). Explaining Attributions for Achievement: A Path Analytic Approach. *Journal of Personality and Social Psychology* 37:1810–1821.

Berscheid, Ellen (1985). Interpersonal Attraction. In *Handbook of Social Psychology,* edited by G. Lindzey and E. Aronson, 413–484. New York: Random House.

Berscheid, Ellen, and Elaine Hatfield Walster (1974). A Little Bit About Love. In *Foundations of Interpersonal Attraction,* edited by T. L. Huston. New York: Academic Press.

Berscheid, Ellen, and Elaine Hatfield Walster (1978). *Interpersonal Attraction.* 2d ed. Reading, Mass.: Addison-Wesley.

Bibby, Cyril (1967). The Art of Love. In *The Encyclopedia of Sexual Behavior,* edited by Albert Ellis and Albert Abarbanel. New York: Hawthorn.

Birdwhistell, Ray L. (1970). *Kinesics and Context: Essays on Body Motion Communication.* New York: Ballantine.

Blieszner, Rosemary, and Rebecca G. Adams (1992). *Adult Friendship.* Newbury Park, Calif.: Sage.

Blumstein, Philip, and Pepper Schwartz (1983). *American Couples: Money, Work, Sex.* New York: Morrow.

Bochner, Arthur (1978). On Taking Ourselves Seriously: An Analysis of Some Persistent Problems and Promising Directions in Interpersonal Research. *Human Communication Research* 4:179–191.

Bochner, Arthur (1984). The Functions of Human Communication in Interpersonal Bonding. In Arnold and Bowers (1984).

Bochner, Arthur, and Clifford Kelly (1974). Interpersonal Competence: Rationale, Philosophy, and Implementation of a Conceptual Framework. *Communication Education* 23:279–301.

Bochner, Arthur, and Janet Yerby (1977). Factors Affecting Instruction in Interpersonal Competence. *Communication Education* 26:91–103.

Bok, Sissela (1978). *Lying: Moral Choice in Public and Private Life.* New York: Pantheon.

Bok, Sissela (1983). *Secrets.* New York: Vintage.

Borisoff, Deborah, and Lisa Merrill (1985). *The Power to Communicate: Gender Differences as Barriers.* Prospect Heights, Ill.: Waveland Press.

Bourland, D. D., Jr. (1965–66). A Linguistic Note: Writing in E-prime. *General Semantics Bulletin* 32–33:111–114.

Bourland, D. David, Jr. (1992). E-Prime and Un-Sanity. *Etc.: A Review of General Semantics* 49 (Summer):213–223.

Bradac, James J., John Waite Bowers, and John A. Courtright (1979). Three Language Variables in Communication Research: Intensity, Immediacy, and Diversity. *Human Communication Research* 5:256–269.

Bravo, Ellen and Ellen Cassedy (1992). *The 9 to 5 Guide to Combating Sexual Harassment.* New York: Wiley.

Brecher, Edward M. (1969). *The Sex Researchers.* Boston: Little, Brown.

Brommel, Bernard (1990). Personal Communication.

Brougher, Toni (1982). *A Way with Words.* Chicago: Nelson-Hall.

Brown, Charles T., and Paul W. Keller (1979). *Monologue to Dialogue: An Exploration of Interpersonal Communication.* 2d ed. Englewood Cliffs, N.J.: Prentice Hall.

Bruneau, Tom (1985). The Time Dimension in Intercultural Communication. In Samovar and Porter (1985), 280–289.

Bruneau, Tom (1990). Chronemics: The Study of Time in Human Interaction. In DeVito and Hecht (1990), 301–311.

Buber, Martin (1958). *I and Thou.* 2d ed. New York: Scribner's.

Bugental, J., and S. Zelen (1950). Investigations into the "Self-Concept." I. The W-A-Y Technique. *Journal of Personality* 18:483–498.

Bull, Peter (1983). *Body Movement and Interpersonal Communication.* New York: Wiley.

Burgoon, Judee and Jerold L. Hale (1988). Nonverbal Expectancy Violations: Model Elaboration and Application to Immediacy Behaviors. *Communication Monographs* 55:58–79.

Burgoon, Judee K., David B. Buller, and W. Gill Woodall (1989). *Nonverbal Communication: The Unspoken Dialogue.* New York: Harper & Row.

Burns, D. D. (1980). *Feeling Good.* New York: New American Library.

Burns, D. D. (1985). *Intimate Connections.* New York: Morrow.

Buss, David (1989). Sex Differences in Human Mate Preferences: Evolutionary Hypotheses Tested in 37 Cultures. *Behavioral and Brain Sciences* 12:1–49.

Buss, David M., and David P. Schmitt (1993). Sexual Strategies Theory: An Evolutionary Perspective on Human Mating. *Psychological Review* 100 (April): 204–232.

Butler, Pamela E. (1981). *Talking to Yourself: Learning the Language of Self-Support.* New York: Harper & Row.

Camden, Carl, Michael T. Motley, and Ann Wilson (1984). White Lies in Interpersonal Communication: A Taxonomy and Preliminary Investigation of Social Motivations. *Western Journal of Speech Communication* 48:309–325.

Canary, Daniel J. and Laura Stafford (1994). *Communication and Relational Maintenance.* Orlando, Fla.: Academic Press.

Canary, Daniel J., Laura Stafford, Kimberley S. Hause, and Lise A. Wallace (1993). An Inductive Analysis of Relational Maintenance Strategies: Comparisons Among Lovers, Relatives, Friends, and Others. *Communication Research Reports* 10 (June): 5–14.

Canary, D. J., and L. Stafford (1994). Maintaining Relationships Through Strategic and Routine Interaction. In *Communication and Relational Maintenance,* edited by D. J. Canary and L. Stafford. New York: Academic Press.

Cappella, Joseph N. (1987). Interpersonal Communication: Definitions and Fundamental Questions. In Berger and Chaffee (1987), 184–238.

Cappella, Joseph N. (1993). The Facial Feedback Hypothesis in Human Interaction: Review and Speculation. *Journal of Language and Social Psychology* 12 (March–June): 13–29.

Carpenter, David, and David Knox (1986). Relationship Maintenance of College Students Separated During Courtship. *College Student Journal* 20 (spring): 86–88.

Cate, R., J. Henton, J. Koval, R. Christopher, and S. Lloyd (1982). Premarital Abuse: A Social Psychological Perspective. *Journal of Family Issues* 3:79–90.

Cegala, Donald J., Grant T. Savage, Claire C. Brunner, and Anne B. Conrad (1982). An Elaboration of the Meaning of Interaction Involvement. *Communication Monographs* 49:229–248.

Chadwick-Jones, J. K. (1976). *Social Exchange Theory: Its Structure and Influence in Social Psychology.* New York: Academic Press.

Chaikin, A. L., and V. J. Derlega (1974). Variables Affecting the Appropriateness of Self-Disclosure. *Journal of Consulting and Clinical Psychology* 42:588–628.

Chanowitz, B. and E. Langer (1981). Premature Cognitive Commitment. *Journal of Personality and Social Psychology* 41:1051–1063.

Cherry, Kittredge (1991). *Hide and Speak: How to Free Ourselves from Our Secrets.* San Francisco, Calif.: HarperSanFrancisco.

Chesebro, James, ed. (1981). *Gayspeak.* New York: Pilgrim Press.

Cialdini, Robert T. (1984). *Influence: How and Why People Agree to Things.* New York: Morrow.

Clark, Herbert (1974). The Power of Positive Speaking. *Psychology Today* 8:102, 108–111.

Clement, Donald A., and Kenneth D. Frandsen (1976). On Conceptual and Empirical Treatments of Feedback in Human Communication. *Communication Monographs* 43:11–28.

Cline, M. G. (1956). The Influence of Social Context on the Perception of Faces. *Journal of Personality* 2:142–185.

Cline, Rebecca J. and Carol A. Puhl (1984). Culture and Geography: A Comparison of Seating Arrangements in the United States and Taiwan. *Journal of International Relations* 8:199–219.

Cody, Michael J. (1982). A Typology of Disengagement Strategies and an Examination of the Role Intimacy, Reactions to Inequity, and Relational Problems Play in Strategy Selection. *Communication Monographs* 49:148–170.

Cody, Michael J., P. J. Marston, and M. Foster (1984). Deception: Paralinguistic and Verbal Leakage. In *Communication Yearbook 7,* edited by R. N. Bostrom, 464–490. Newbury Park, Calif.: Sage.

Collins, B. E., and B. H. Raven (1969). Group Structure: Attraction, Coalitions, Communication, and Power. In *The Handbook of Social Psychology,* 2d ed., edited by Gardner Lindzey and Elliot Aronson, 102–204. Reading, Mass.: Addison-Wesley.

Condon, John C. (1974). *Semantics and Communication.* 2d ed. New York: Macmillan.

Condon, John C., and Yousef Fathi (1975). *An Introduction to Intercultural Communication.* Indianapolis, Ind.: Bobbs-Merrill.

Cook, Anthony (1993). How Couples Can Avoid Money Misunderstandings. *Money* (July): 92.

Cook, Mark (1971). *Interpersonal Perception.* Baltimore: Penguin.

Cook, Mark, ed. (1984). *Issues in Person Perception.* New York: Methuen.

Cooley, Charles Horton (1922). *Human Nature and the Social Order,* rev. ed. New York: Scribner's.

Cozby, Paul (1973). Self-Disclosure: A Literature Review. *Psychological Bulletin* 79:73–91.

Craig, Mary E., Seth C. Kalichman, and Diane R. Follingstad (1989). Verbal Coercive Sexual Behavior Among College Students. *Archives of Sexual Behavior* 18 (October): 421–434.

Cupach, William R., and Sandra Metts (1986). Accounts of Relational Dissolution: A Comparison of Marital and Non-Marital Relationships. *Communication Monographs* 53 (December): 311–334.

Dainton, M., and L. Stafford (1993). Routine Maintenance Behaviors: A Comparison of Relationship Type, Partner Similarity, and Sex Differences. *Journal of Social and Personal Relationships* 10:255–272.

Daly, John A., and James C. McCroskey, eds. (1984). *Avoiding Communication: Shyness, Reticence, and Communication Apprehension.* Newbury Park: Calif.: Sage.

Davis, Flora (1973). *Inside Intuition.* New York: New American Library.

Davis, Keith E. (1985). Near and Dear: Friendship and Love Compared. *Psychology Today* 19:22–30.

Davis, Murray S. (1973). *Intimate Relations.* New York: Free Press.

Davis, Ossie (1973). The English Language Is My Enemy. In *Language: Concepts and Processes,* ed., Joseph A. DeVito. Englewood Cliffs, N.J.: Prentice-Hall, pp. 164–170.

Davitz, Joel R., ed. (1964). *The Communication of Emotional Meaning.* New York: McGraw-Hill.

Deal, James E., and Karen Smith Wampler (1986). Dating Violence: The Primacy of Previous Experience. *Journal of Social and Personal Relationships* 3:457–471.

deBono, Edward (1987). *The Six Thinking Hats.* New York: Penguin.

DeCecco, John (1988). Obligation versus Aspiration. In *Gay Relationships,* John DeCecco, ed., New York: Harrington Park Press.

Deetz, Stanley, and Sheryl Stevenson (1986). *Managing Interpersonal Communication.* New York: Harper & Row.

DeFrancisco, Victoria (1991). The Sound of Silence: How Men Silence Women in Marital Relations. *Discourse and Society* 2: 413–423.

Derlega, Valerian J., and J. H. Berg, eds. (1987). *Self-Disclosure: Theory, Research, and Therapy.* New York: Plenum Press.

Derlega, Valerian J., Barbara A. Winstead, Paul T. P. Wong, and Michael Greenspan (1987). Self-Disclosure and Relationship Development: An Attributional Analysis. In *Interpersonal Processes: New Directions in Communication Research,* edited by Michael E. Roloff and Gerald R. Miller, 172–187. Newbury Park, Calif.: Sage.

Derlega, Valerian J., Stephen T. Margulis, and Barbara A. Winstead (1987). A Social-Psychological Analysis of Self-Disclosure in Psychotherapy. *Journal of Social and Clinical Psychology* 5:205–215.

Deturck, Mark A. (1987). When Communication Fails: Physical Aggression as a Compliance-Gaining Strategy. *Communication Monographs* 54:106–112.

DeVito, Joseph A. (1970). *The Psychology of Speech and Language: An Introduction to the Study of Psycholinguistics.* New York: Random House.

DeVito, Joseph A. (1974). *General Semantics: Guide and Workbook.* Rev. ed. DeLand, Fla.: Everett/Edwards.

DeVito, Joseph A. (1986a). *The Communication Handbook: A Dictionary.* New York: Harper & Row.

DeVito, Joseph A. (1986b). Teaching as Relational Development. In *Communicating in College Classrooms,* edited by Jean Civikly, 51–60. New Directions for Teaching and Learning, no. 26. San Francisco: Jossey-Bass.

DeVito, Joseph A. (1989). *The Nonverbal Communication Workbook.* Prospect Heights, Ill.: Waveland Press.

DeVito, Joseph A. (1990). *Messages: Building Interpersonal Communication Skills.* New York: Harper & Row.

DeVito, Joseph A., ed. (1973). *Language: Concepts and Processes.* Englewood Cliffs, N.J.: Prentice Hall.

DeVito, Joseph A., ed. (1981). *Communication: Concepts and Processes.* 3d ed. Englewood Cliffs, N.J.: Prentice Hall.

DeVito, Joseph A., and Michael L. Hecht, eds. (1990). *The Nonverbal Communication Reader.* Prospect Heights, Ill.: Waveland Press.

Dickson-Markman, Fran (1984). How Important Is Self-Disclosure in Marriage? *Communication Research Reports* 1:7–14.

Dillard, James Price (1988). Compliance-Gaining Message-Selection: What Is Our Dependent Variable? *Communication Monographs* 55:162–183.

Dillard, James Price, ed. (1990). *Seeking*

Compliance: The Production of Interpersonal Influence Messages. Scottsdale, Ariz.: Gorsuch Scarisbrick.

Dindia, Kathryn (1987). The Effects of Sex of Subject and Partner on Interruptions. *Human Communication Research* 13:345–371.

Dindia, Kathryn and Daniel J. Canary (1993). Definitions and Theoretical Perspectives on Maintaining Relationships. *Journal of Social and Personal Relationships* 10 (May): 163–174.

Dindia, Kathryn, and Mary Anne Fitzpatrick (1985). Marital Communication: Three Approaches Compared. In *Understanding Personal Relationships: An Interdisciplinary Approach,* edited by Steve Duck and Daniel Perlman, 137–158. Newbury Park, Calif.: Sage.

Dindia, Kathryn, and Leslie A. Baxter (1987). Strategies for Maintaining and Repairing Marital Relationships. *Journal of Social and Personal Relationships* 4:143–158.

Dion, K., E. Berscheid, and E. Walster (1972). What Is Beautiful Is Good. *Journal of Personality and Social Psychology* 24:285–290.

Dodd, Carley H. (1982). *Dynamics of Intercultural Communication.* Dubuque, Iowa: William C. Brown.

Dodd, David H., and Raymond M. White, Jr. (1980). *Cognition: Mental Structures and Processes.* Boston: Allyn & Bacon.

Dosey, M. and M. Meisels (1976). Personal Space and Self-Protection. *Journal of Personality and Social Psychology* 38:959–965.

Dosser, David A., Jr., Jack O. Balswick, and Charles F. Halverson, Jr. (1986). Male Inexpressiveness and Relationships. *Journal of Social and Personal Relationships* 3:241–258.

Drass, Kriss A. (1986). The Effect of Gender Identity on Conversation. *Social Psychology Quarterly* 49 (December):294–301.

Dreyfuss, Henry (1971). *Symbol Sourcebook.* New York: McGraw-Hill.

Driscoll, R., K. E. Davis, and M. E. Lipetz (1972). Parental Interference and Romantic Love: The Romeo and Juliet Effect. *Journal of Personality and Social Psychology* 24:1–10.

Drummond, Kent and Robert Hopper (1993). Acknowledgment Tokens in Series. *Communication Reports* 6 (Winter):47–53.

Dubois, Betty Lou, and Isabel Crouch (1975). The Question of Tag Questions in Women's Speech: They Don't Really Use More of Them, Do They? *Language and Society* 4:289–294.

Duck, Steve (1986). *Human Relationships.* Newbury Park, Calif.: Sage.

Duck, Steve (1988). *Relating to Others.* Milton Keynes, England: Open University Press.

Duck, Steve, ed. (1982). *Personal Relationships. 4: Dissolving Personal Relationships.* New York: Academic Press.

Duck, Steve, and Robin Gilmour, eds. (1981). *Personal Relationships. 1: Studying Personal Relationships.* New York: Academic Press.

Dullea, Georgia (1981). Presents: Hidden Messages. *New York Times,* 14 December, D12.

Duncan, Barry L. and Joseph W. Rock (1991). *Overcoming Relationship Impasses: Ways to Initiate Change When Your Partner Won't Help.* New York: Plenum Press/Insight Books.

Duncan, S. D., Jr. (1972). Some Signals and Rules for Taking Speaking Turns in Conversation. *Journal of Personality and Social Psychology* 23:283–292.

Duran, R. L., and L. Kelly (1988). The Influence of Communicative Competence on Perceived Task, Social, and Physical Attraction. *Communication Quarterly* 36:41–49.

Eakins, Barbara, and R. Gene Eakins (1978). *Sex Differences in Communication.* Boston: Houghton Mifflin.

Edgar, T., and M. A. Fitzpatrick (1988). Compliance-Gaining in Relational Interactions: When Your Life Depends on It. *Southern Speech Communication Journal* 53 (summer): 385–405.

Egan, Gerard (1970). *Encounter: Group Processes for Interpersonal Growth.* Belmont, Calif.: Brooks/Cole.

Ehrenhaus, Peter (1988). Silence and Symbolic Expression. *Communication Monographs* 55 (March): 41–57.

Ekman, Paul (1965). Communication Through Nonverbal Behavior: A Source of Information About an Interpersonal Relationship. In *Affect, Cognition and Personality,* edited by S. S. Tomkins and C. E. Izard. New York: Springer.

Ekman, Paul (1985). *Telling Lies: Clues to Deceit in the Marketplace, Politics, and Marriage.* New York: W. W. Norton.

Ekman, Paul, and Wallace V. Friesen (1969). The Repertoire of Nonverbal Behavior: Categories, Origins, Usage, and Coding. *Semiotica* 1:49–98.

Ekman, Paul and Wallace V. Friesen (1978). *The Facial Action Coding System.* Palo Alto, Calif.: Consulting Psychologists Press.

Ekman, Paul, Wallace V. Friesen, and S. S. Tomkins (1971). Facial Affect Scoring Technique: A First Validity Study. *Semiotica* 3:37–58.

Ekman, Paul, Wallace V. Friesen, and Phoebe Ellsworth (1972). *Emotion in the Human Face: Guidelines for Research and an Integration of Findings.* New York: Pergamon Press.

Ellis, Albert (1988). *How to Stubbornly Refuse to Make Yourself Miserable About Anything, Yes Anything.* Secaucus, N.J.: Lyle Stuart.

Ellis, Albert, and Robert A. Harper (1975). *A New Guide to Rational Living.* Hollywood, Calif.: Wilshire Books.

Elmes, Michael B., and Gary Gemmill (1990). The Psychodynamics of Mindlessness and Dissent in Small Groups. *Small Group Research* 21 (February): 28–44.

Epstein, N., J. L. Pretzer, and B. Fleming (1987). The Role of Cognitive Appraisal in Self-Reports of Marital Communication. *Behavior Therapy* 18:51–69.

Exline, R. V., S. L. Ellyson, and B. Long (1975). Visual Behavior as an Aspect of Power Role Relationships. In *Nonverbal Communication of Aggression,* edited by P. Pliner, L. Krames, and T. Alloway. New York: Plenum Press.

Faber, Adele, and Elaine Mazlish (1980). *How to Talk so Kids Will Listen and Listen so Kids Will Talk.* New York: Avon.

Falk, Dennis R., and Pat N. Wagner (1985). Intimacy of Self-Disclosure and Response Processes as Factors Affecting the Development of Interpersonal Relationships. *Journal of Social Psychology* 125:557–570.

Farrell, M. P., and S. D. Rosenberg (1981). *Men at Midlife.* Westport, Conn.: Auburn House.

Fengler, A. P. (1974). Romantic Love in Courtship: Divergent Paths of Male and Female Students. *Journal of Comparative Family Studies* 5:134–139.

Festinger, L., S. Schachter, and K. W. Back (1950). *Social Pressures in Informal Groups: A Study of Human Factors in Housing.* New York: Harper & Row.

Filley, Alan C. (1975). *Interpersonal Conflict Resolution.* Glenview, Ill.: Scott, Foresman.

Fischer, C. S., and S. J. Oliker (1983). A Research Note on Friendship, Gender, and the Life Cycle. *Social Forces* 62:124–133.

Fishman, Joshua A. (1972). *The Sociology of Language.* Rowley, Mass.: Newbury House.

Fiske, Susan T., and Shelley E. Taylor (1984). *Social Cognition.* Reading, Mass.: Addison-Wesley.

Fitzpatrick, Mary Anne (1983). Predicting Couples' Communication from Couples' Self-Reports. In *Communication Yearbook 7,* edited by R. N. Bostrom, 49–82. Newbury Park, Calif.: Sage.

Fitzpatrick, Mary Anne (1988). *Between Husbands and Wives: Communication in Marriage.* Newbury Park, Calif.: Sage.

Floyd, James J. (1985). *Listening: A Practical Approach.* Glenview, Ill.: Scott, Foresman.

Folger, Joseph P., and Marshall Scott Poole (1984). *Working Through Conflict: A Communication Perspective.* Glenview, Ill.: Scott, Foresman.

Follingstad, Diane R., et al. (1990). The Role of Emotional Abuse in Physically Abusive Relationships. *Journal of Family Violence* 5 (June): 107–120.

Fox, M., M. Gibbs, and D. Auerbach (1985). Age and Gender Dimensions of Friendship. *Psychology of Women Quarterly* 9:489–501.

Fraser, Bruce (1990). Perspectives on Politeness. *Journal of Pragmatics* 14 (April):219–236.

Freedman, Jonathan (1978). *Happy People: What Happiness Is, Who Has It, and Why.* New York: Ballantine.

French, J. R. P., Jr., and B. Raven (1968). The Bases of Social Power. In *Group Dynamics: Research and Theory,* 3d ed., edited by Dorwin Cartwright and Alvin Zander, 259–269. New York: Harper & Row.

Frentz, Thomas (1976). A General Approach to Episodic Structure. Paper presented at the Western Speech Association Convention, San Francisco. Cited in Reardon (1987).

Friedman, Joel, Marcia Mobilia Boumil, and Barbara Ewert Taylor (1992). *Sexual Harassment.* Deerfield Beach, Fla.: Health Communications, Inc.

Friedman, Meyer, and Ray Rosenman (1974). *Type A Behavior and Your Heart.* New York: Fawcett Crest.

Frye, Jerry K. (1980). *FIND: Frye's Index to Nonverbal Data.* Duluth: University of Minnesota Computer Center.

Furnham, Adrian, and Stephen Bochner (1986). *Culture Shock: Psychological Reactions to Unfamiliar Environments.* New York: Methuen.

Gabor, Don (1989). *How to Talk to the People You Love.* New York: Simon & Schuster.

Gabrenya, W. K., Jr., Y. E. Wang, and B. Latane (1985). Social Loafing on an Optimizing Task: Cross-Cultural Differences among Chinese and Americans. *Journal of Cross-Cultural Psychology* 16:223–242.

Galbraith, J. K. (1983). *The Anatomy of Power.* Boston: Houghton Mifflin.

Galvin, Kathleen, and Bernard J. Brommel (1991). *Family Communication: Cohesion and Change.* 3d ed. Glenview, Ill.: Scott, Foresman.

Gangestad, S. and M. Snyder (1985). To Carve Nature at Its Joints: On the Existence of Discrete Classes in Personality. *Psychological Review* 92:317–349.

Garner, Alan (1981). *Conversationally Speaking.* New York: McGraw-Hill.

Gelles, R. (1981). The Myth of the Battered Husband. In *Marriage and Family 81/82,* edited by R. Walsh and O. Pocs. Guildford: Dushkin.

Gelles, R., and C. Cornell (1985). *Intimate Violence in Families.* Newbury Park, Calif.: Sage.

Gergen, K. J., M. S. Greenberg, and R. H. Willis (1980). *Social Exchange: Advances in Theory and Research.* New York: Plenum Press.

Gibb, Jack (1961). Defensive Communication. *Journal of Communication* 11:141–148.

Gilmour, Robin, and Steve Duck, eds. (1986). *The Emerging Field of Personal Relationships.* Hillsdale, N.J.: Lawrence Erlbaum.

Gladstein, Gerald A., et al. (1987). *Empathy and Counseling: Explorations in Theory and Research.* New York: Springer-Verlag.

Glucksberg, Sam and Joseph H. Danks (1975). *Experimental Psycholinguistics: An Introduction.* Hillsdale, N.J.: Lawrence Erlbaum.

Goffman, Erving (1967). *Interaction Ritual: Essays on Face-to-Face Behavior.* New York: Pantheon.

Goffman, Erving (1971). *Relations in Public: Microstudies of the Public Order.* New York: Harper Colophon.

Goldberg, Philip (1968). Are Women Prejudiced Against Women? *Trans-action* 6:528–530.

Goleman, Daniel (1992). Studies Find No Disadvantage in Growing Up in a Gay Home. *New York Times,* 2 December, C14.

Gonzalez, Alexander, and Philip G. Zimbardo (1985). Time in Perspective. *Psychology Today* 19:20–26. Reprinted in DeVito and Hecht (1990).

Gordon, Thomas (1975). *P.E.T.: Parent Effectiveness Training.* New York: New American Library.

Goss, Blaine (1985). *The Psychology of Communication.* Prospect Heights, Ill.: Waveland Press.

Goss, Blaine, M. Thompson, and S. Olds (1978). Behavioral Support for Systematic Desensitization for Communication Apprehension. *Human Communication Research* 4:158–163.

Graham, Jean Ann, and Michael Argyle

(1975). The Effects of Different Patterns of Gaze, Combined with Different Facial Expressions, on Impression Formation. *Journal of Movement Studies* 1 (December): 178–182.

Graham, Jean Ann, Pio Ricci Bitti, and Michael Argyle (1975). A Cross-Cultural Study of the Communication of Emotion by Facial and Gestural Cues. *Journal of Human Movement Studies* 1 (June): 68–77.

Greif, Esther Blank (1980). Sex Differences in Parent-Child Conversations. *Women's Studies International Quarterly* 3:253–258.

Grice, H. P. (1975). Logic and Conversation. In *Syntax and Semantics.* Vol. 3, *Speech Acts,* edited by P. Cole and J. L. Morgan, 41–58. New York: Seminar Press.

Griffin, Em, and Glenn G. Sparks (1990). Friends Forever: A Longitudinal Exploration of Intimacy in Same-Sex Friends and Platonic Pairs. *Journal of Social and Personal Relationships* 7:29–46.

Gu, Yueguo (1990). Polite Phenomena in Modern Chinese. *Journal of Pragmatics* 14 (April):237–257.

Gudykunst, W. B. (1989). Culture and the Development of Interpersonal Relationships. In *Communication Yearbook 12,* edited by J. A. Anderson, 315–354. Newbury Park, Calif.: Sage.

Gudykunst, W. B., ed. (1983). *Intercultural Communication Theory: Current Perspectives.* Newbury Park, Calif.: Sage.

Gudykunst, William B. (1991). *Bridging Differences: Effective Intergroup Communication.* Newbury Park, Calif.: Sage.

Gudykunst, W. B., and Y. Y. Kim (1984). *Communicating with Strangers: An Approach to Intercultural Communication.* New York: Random House.

Gudykunst, William B. and Stella Ting-Toomey with Elizabeth Chua (1988). *Culture and Interpersonal Communication.* Newbury Park, Calif.: Sage.

Guerrero, Laura K. and Peter A. Andersen (1991). The Waxing and Waning of Relational Intimacy: Touch as a Function of Relational Stage, Gender and Touch Avoidance. *Journal of Social and Personal Relationships* 8 (May):147–165.

Guerrero, L. K., S. V. Eloy, and A. I. Wabnik

(1993). Linking Maintenance Strategies to Relationship Development and Disengagement: A Reconceptualization. *Journal of Social and Personal Relationships* 10:273–282.

Gupta, U., and P. Singh (1982). Exploratory Studies in Love and Liking and Types of Marriages. *Indian Journal of Applied Psychology* 19:92–97.

Haferkamp, Claudia J. (1991–92). Orientations to Conflict: Gender, Attributes, Resolution Strategies, and Self-Monitoring. *Current Psychology: Research and Reviews* 10 (winter): 227–240.

Haggard, E. A., and K. S. Isaacs (1966). Micromomentary Facial Expressions as Indicators of Ego Mechanisms in Psychotherapy. In *Methods of Research in Psychotherapy,* edited by L. A. Gottschalk and A. H. Auerbach. Englewood Cliffs, N.J.: Prentice Hall.

Hale, Jerold, James C. Lundy, Paul A. Mongeau (1989). Perceived Relational Intimacy and Relational Message Content. *Communication Research Reports* 6 (December): 94–99.

Hall, Edward T. (1959). *The Silent Language.* Garden City, N.Y.: Doubleday.

Hall, Edward T. (1963). System for the Notation of Proxemic Behavior. *American Anthropologist* 65:1003–1026.

Hall, Edward T. (1966). *The Hidden Dimension.* Garden City, N.Y.: Doubleday.

Hall, Edward T. (1976). *Beyond Culture.* Garden City, N.Y.: Anchor Press.

Hall, Edward T., and Mildred Reed Hall (1987). *Hidden Differences: Doing Business with the Japanese.* New York: Anchor Books.

Hall, Edward T. (1983). *The Dance of Life: The Other Dimension of Time.* New York: Anchor Books/Doubleday.

Hall, J. A. (1984). *Nonverbal Sex Differences.* Baltimore: Johns Hopkins University Press.

Hamachek, Don E. (1982). *Encounters with Others: Interpersonal Relationships and You.* New York: Holt, Rinehart & Winston.

Haney, William (1973). *Communication and Organizational Behavior: Text and Cases.* 3d ed. Homewood, Ill.: Irwin.

Haney, William (1981). Serial Communication of Information in Organizations. In De-Vito (1981), 169–182.

Hart, R. P., and D. M. Burks (1972). Rhetorical Sensitivity and Social Interaction. *Communication Monographs* 39:75–91.

Hart, R. P., R. E. Carlson, and W. F. Eadie (1980). Attitudes Toward Communication and the Assessment of Rhetorical Sensitivity. *Communication Monographs* 47:1–22.

Harvey, John H., Rodney Flanary, and Melinda Morgan (1986). Vivid Memories of Vivid Loves Gone By. *Journal of Social and Personal Relationships* 3:359–373.

Hastorf, Albert, David Schneider, and Judith Polefka (1970). *Person Perception.* Reading, Mass.: Addison-Wesley.

Hatfield, Elaine, and Jane Traupman (1981). Intimate Relationships: A Perspective from Equity Theory. In Duck and Gilmour (1981), 165–178.

Hayakawa, S. I., and A. R. Hayakawa (1989). *Language in Thought and Action.* 5th ed. New York: Harcourt Brace Jovanovich.

Hays, Robert B. (1989). The Day-to-Day Functioning of Close Versus Casual Friendships. *Journal of Social and Personal Relationships* 6:21–37.

Hecht, Michael (1978a). The Conceptualization and Measurement of Interpersonal Communication Satisfaction. *Human Communication Research* 4:253–264.

Hecht, Michael (1978b). Toward a Conceptualization of Communication Satisfaction. *Quarterly Journal of Speech* 64:47–62.

Hecht, Michael, and Sidney Ribeau (1984). Ethnic Communication: A Comparative Analysis of Satisfying Communication. *International Journal of Intercultural Relations* 8:135–151.

Hegstrom, Timothy (1979). Message Impact: What Percentage Is Nonverbal? *Western Journal of Speech Communication* 43:134–142.

Heiskell, Thomas L., and Joseph F. Rychlak (1986). The Therapeutic Relationship: Inexperienced Therapists' Affective Preference and Empathic Communication. *Journal of Social and Personal Relationships* 3:267–274.

Henderson, M., and A. Furnham (1982). Similarity and Attraction: The Relationship Between Personality, Beliefs, Skills, Needs, and Friendship Choice. *Journal of Adolescence* 5:111–123.

Hendrick, Clyde, Susan Hendrick, Franklin H. Foote, and Michelle J. Slapion-Foote (1984). Do Men and Women Love Differently? *Journal of Social and Personal Relationships* 1:177–195.

Hendrick, Clyde, and Susan Hendrick (1990). A Relationship-Specific Version of the Love Attitudes Scale. In *Handbook of Replication Research in the Behavioral and Social Sciences* (special issue), edited by J. W. Heulip, *Journal of Social Behavior and Personality* 5:239–254.

Henley, Nancy M. (1977). *Body Politics: Power, Sex, and Nonverbal Communication.* Englewood Cliffs, N.J.: Prentice Hall.

Hertzler, J. O. (1965). *A Sociology of Language.* New York: Random House.

Heseltine, Olive (1927). *Conversation.* London: Methuen.

Hess, Eckhard H. (1975). *The Tell-Tale Eye.* New York: Van Nostrand Reinhold.

Hess, Eckhard H., Allan L. Seltzer, and John M. Schlien (1965). Pupil Response of Hetero- and Homosexual Males to Pictures of Men and Women: A Pilot Study. *Journal of Abnormal Psychology* 70:165–168.

Hewitt, John, and Randall Stokes (1975). Disclaimers. *American Sociological Review* 40:1–11.

Hickson, Mark L., and Don W. Stacks (1989). *NVC: Nonverbal Communication: Studies and Applications.* 2d ed. Dubuque, Iowa: William. C. Brown.

Hocker, Joyce L., and William W. Wilmot (1985). *Interpersonal Conflict.* 2nd ed. Dubuque, Iowa: William C. Brown.

Hockett, Charles F. (1977). *The View from Language: Selected Essays, 1948–1974.* Athens: University of Georgia Press.

Hoijer, Harry, ed. (1954). *Language in Culture.* Chicago: University of Chicago Press.

Hollender, Marc, and Alexander Mercer (1976). Wish to Be Held and Wish to Hold in Men and Women. *Archives of General Psychiatry* 33:49–51.

Honeycutt, James (1986). A Model of Marital Functioning Based on an Attraction Paradigm and Social Penetration Dimensions.

Journal of Marriage and the Family 48 (August): 51–59.

Hopper, Robert, Mark L. Knapp, and Lorel Scott (1981). Couples' Personal Idioms: Exploring Intimate Talk. *Journal of Communication* 31:23–33.

Hosman, Lawrence A. (1989). The Evaluative Consequences of Hedges, Hesitations, and Intensifiers: Powerful and Powerless Speech Styles. *Human Communication Research* 15:383–406.

Huffines, LaUna (1986). *Connecting with All the People in Your Life.* New York: Harper & Row.

Hymes, Dell (1974). *Foundations in Sociolinguistics: An Ethnographic Approach.* Philadelphia: University of Pennsylvania Press.

Illinois Coalition Against Sexual Assault (spring 1990). *Coalition Commentary.* Urbana: Illinois Coalition Against Sexual Assault.

Infante, Dominic A. (1988). *Arguing Constructively.* Prospect Heights, Ill.: Waveland Press.

Infante, Dominic (1993). Personal Communication.

Infante, Dominic and Andrew Rancer (1982). A Conceptualization and Measure of Argumentativeness. *Journal of Personality Assessment* 46:72–80.

Infante, Dominic and C. J. Wigley (1986). Verbal Aggressiveness: An Interpersonal Model and Measure. *Communication Monographs* 53:61–69.

Infante, Dominic A., Teresa A. Chandler, and Jill E. Rudd (1989). Test of an Argumentative Skill Deficiency Model of Interspousal Violence. *Communication Monographs* 56 (June): 163–177.

Infante, Dominic A., Andrew S. Rancer, and Deanna F. Womack (1990). *Building Communication Theory.* Prospect Heights, Ill.: Waveland Press.

Infante, Dominic A., Teresa Chandler Sabourin, Jill E. Rudd, and Elizabeth A. Shannon (1990). Verbal Aggression in Violent and Nonviolent Marital Disputes. *Communication Quarterly* 38 (fall): 361–371.

Infante, Dominic A., Bruce L. Riddle, Cary L. Horvath, and S. A. Tumlin (1992). Verbal Aggressiveness: Messages and Reasons. *Communication Quarterly* 40 (spring): 116–126.

Infante, Dominic A., Karen C. Hartley, Matthew M. Martin, Mary Anne Higgins, Stephen D. Bruning, and Gyeongho Hur (1992). Initiating and Reciprocating Verbal Aggression: Effects on Credibility and Credited Valid Arguments. *Communication Studies* 43 (fall): 182–190.

Infante, Dominic A., Teresa Chandler Sabourin, Jill E. Rudd, and Elizabeth A. Shannon (1990). Verbal Aggression in Violent and Nonviolent Marital Disputes. *Communication Quarterly* 38 (fall): 361–371.

Insel, Paul M., and Lenore F. Jacobson, eds. (1975). *What Do You Expect? An Inquiry into Self-Fulfilling Prophecies.* Menlo Park, Calif.: Cummings.

Jacobson, W. D. (1972). *Power and Interpersonal Relations.* Belmont, Calif.: Wadsworth.

Jaksa, James A., and Michael S. Pritchard (1988). *Communication Ethics: Methods of Analysis.* Belmont, Calif.: Wadsworth.

Janus, Samuel S., and Cynthia L. Janus (1993). *The Janus Report on Sexual Behavior.* New York: Wiley.

Jaworski, Adam (1993). *The Power of Silence: Social and Pragmatic Perspectives.* Newbury Park, Calif.: Sage.

Jecker, Jon, and David Landy (1969). Liking a Person as a Function of Doing Him a Favor. *Human Relations* 22:371–378.

Jensen, J. Vernon (1985). Perspectives on Nonverbal Intercultural Communication. In Samovar and Porter (1985), 256–272.

Johannesen, Richard L. (1971). The Emerging Concept of Communication as Dialogue. *Quarterly Journal of Speech* 57:373–382.

Johannesen, Richard L. (1990). *Ethics in Human Communication.* 4th ed. Prospect Heights, Ill.: Waveland Press.

Johnson, C. E. (1987). An Introduction to Powerful and Powerless Talk in the Classroom. *Communication Education* 36:167–172.

Johnson, F. L., and E. J. Aries (1983). The Talk of Women Friends. *Women's Studies International Forum* 6:353–361.

Johnson, Otto, ed. (1994). *The 1994 Informa-*

tion Please Almanac, New York: Houghton Mifflin.

Johnson, Frank A. and Anthony J. Marsella (1976). Differential Attitudes toward Verbal Behavior in Students of Japanese and European Ancestry. *Genetic Psychology Monographs* 97 (February): 43–76.

Johnson, Scott, A. (1993). *When "I Love You" Turns Violent: Emotional and Physical Abuse in Dating Relationships.* Far Hills, N.J.: New Horizon Press.

Johnson, Wendell (1951). The Spoken Word and the Great Unsaid. *Quarterly Journal of Speech* 37:419–429.

Jones, E. E., et al. (1964). *Social Stigma: The Psychology of Marked Relationships.* New York: W. H. Freeman.

Jones, E. E., and K. E. Davis (1965). From Acts to Dispositions: The Attribution Process in Person Perception. In *Advances in Experimental Social Psychology,* edited by L. Berkowitz, vol. 2, 219–266. New York: Academic Press.

Jones, E. E., Leslie Rock, Kelley G. Sharver, and Lawrence M. Wad (1968). Pattern of Performance and Ability Attribution: An Unexpected Primacy Effect. *Journal of Personality and Social Psychology* 10:317–340.

Jones, Stanley (1986). Sex Differences in Touch Communication. *Western Journal of Speech Communication* 50:227–241.

Jones, Stanley, and A. Elaine Yarbrough (1985). A Naturalistic Study of the Meanings of Touch. *Communication Monographs* 52:19–56. A version of this paper appears in DeVito and Hecht (1990).

Jourard, Sidney M. (1966). An Exploratory Study of Body-Accessibility. *British Journal of Social and Clinical Psychology* 5:221–231.

Jourard, Sidney M. (1968). *Disclosing Man to Himself.* New York: Van Nostrand Reinhold.

Jourard, Sidney M. (1971a). *Self-Disclosure.* New York: Wiley.

Jourard, Sidney M. (1971b). *The Transparent Self.* Rev. ed. New York: Van Nostrand Reinhold.

Joyner, Russell (1993). An Auto-Interview on the Need for E-Prime. *Etc.: A Review of General Semantics* 50 (Fall): 317–325.

Kanner, Bernice (1989). Color Schemes. *New York Magazine,* 3 April, 22–23.

Kazoleas, Dean (1993). The Impact of Argumentativeness on Resistance to Persuasion. *Human Communication Research* 20 (September): 118–137.

Kearney, P., T. G. Plax, V. P. Richmond, and J. C. McCroskey (1984). Power in the Classroom IV: Alternatives to Discipline. In *Communication Yearbook 8,* edited by R. N. Bostrom, 724–746. Newbury Park, Calif.: Sage.

Kearney, P., T. G. Plax, V. P. Richmond, and J. C. McCroskey (1985). Power in the Classroom III: Teacher Communication Techniques and Messages. *Communication Education* 34:19–28.

Keating, Caroline F., Alan Mazur, and Marshall H. Segall (1977). Facial Gestures Which Influence the Perception of Status. *Sociometry* 40 (December): 374–378.

Keenan, Elinor Ochs (1976). The Universality of Conversational Postulates. *Language in Society* 5 (April): 67–80.

Kelley, H. H. (1967). Attribution Theory in Social Psychology. In *Nebraska Symposium on Motivation,* edited by D. Levine, 192–240. Lincoln: University of Nebraska Press.

Kelley, H. H. (1973). The Process of Causal Attribution. *American Psychologist* 28:107–128.

Kelley, H. H. (1979). *Personal Relationships: Their Structures and Processes.* Hillsdale, N.J.: Lawrence Erlbaum.

Kelley, H. H., and J. W. Thibaut (1978). *Interpersonal Relations: A Theory of Interdependence.* New York: Wiley/Interscience.

Kennedy, C. W., and C. T. Camden (1988). A New Look at Interruptions. *Western Journal of Speech Communication* 47:45–58.

Kersten, K., and L. Kersten (1988). *Marriage and the Family: Studying Close Relationships.* New York: Harper & Row.

Keyes, Ken, Jr., and Penny Keyes (1987). *Gathering Power Through Insight and Love.* St. Mary, Ky.: Living Love.

Kim, Young Yun (1988). Communication and

Acculturation. In Samovar and Porter (1988), 344–354.

Kim, Young Yun, ed. (1986). *Interethnic Communication: Current Research.* Newbury Park, Calif.: Sage.

Kim, Young Yun (1991). Intercultural Communication Competence. In *Cross-Cultural Interpersonal Communication,* ed., Stella Ting-Toomey and Felipe Korzenny. Newbury Park, Calif.: Sage, pp. 259–275.

Kim, Young Yun, and William B. Gudykunst, eds. (1988). *Theories in Intercultural Communication.* Newbury Park, Calif.: Sage.

Kirkpatrick, C., and T. Caplow (1945). Courtship in a Group of Minnesota Students. *American Journal of Sociology* 51:114–125.

Kleinke, Chris L. (1978). *Self-Perception: The Psychology of Personal Awareness.* San Francisco: W. H. Freeman.

Kleinke, Chris L. (1986). *Meeting and Understanding People.* New York: W. H. Freeman.

Knapp, Mark L. (1984). *Interpersonal Communication and Human Relationships.* Boston: Allyn & Bacon.

Knapp, Mark L., and Mark Comadena (1979). Telling It Like It Isn't: A Review of Theory and Research on Deceptive Communication. *Human Communication Research* 5:270–285.

Knapp, Mark L., Donald Ellis, and Barbara A. Williams (1980). Perceptions of Communication Behavior Associated with Relationship Terms. *Communication Monographs* 47:262–278.

Knapp, Mark L., and Judith Hall (1992). *Nonverbal Behavior in Human Interaction.* 3d ed. New York: Holt, Rinehart & Winston.

Knapp, Mark L., and Anita Vangelisti (1992). *Interpersonal Communication and Human Relationships.* 2d ed. Boston: Allyn & Bacon.

Knapp, Mark L., and G. R. Miller, eds. (1985). *Handbook of Interpersonal Communication.* Newbury Park, Calif.: Sage.

Kochman, Thomas (1981). *Black and White: Styles in Conflict.* Chicago: University of Chicago Press.

Komarovsky, M. (1964). *Blue Collar Marriage* (New York: Random House).

Korda, M. (1975). *Power! How to Get It, How to Use It.* New York: Ballantine.

Korzybski, A. (1933). *Science and Sanity.* Lakeville, Conn.: The International Non-Aristotelian Library.

Kramarae, Cheris (1981). *Women and Men Speaking.* Rowley, Mass.: Newbury House.

Kramer, Ernest (1963). Judgment of Personal Characteristics and Emotions from Nonverbal Properties. *Psychological Bulletin* 60:408–420.

Krug, Linda (1982). Alternative Lifestyle Dyads: An Alternative Relationship Paradigm. *Alternative Communications* 4:32–52.

LaBarre, W. (1964). Paralinguistics, Kinesics, and Cultural Anthropology. In *Approaches to Semiotics,* edited by T. A. Sebeok, A. S. Hayes, and M. C. Bateson, 191–220. The Hague: Mouton.

LaFrance, M., and C. Mayo (1978). *Moving Bodies: Nonverbal Communication in Social Relationships.* Monterey, Calif.: Brooks/Cole.

Lahey, B. B. (1989). *Psychology.* Dubuque, Iowa: William C. Brown.

Laing, Ronald D., H. Phillipson, and A. Russell Lee (1966). *Interpersonal Perception.* New York: Springer.

Lakoff, Robin (1975). *Language and Woman's Place.* New York: Harper & Row.

Lambdin, William (1981). *Doublespeak Dictionary.* Los Angeles: Pinnacle Books.

Langer, Ellen J. (1978). Rethinking the Role of Thought in Social Interaction. In *New Directions in Attribution Research,* vol. 2, edited by J. H. Harvey, W. J. Ickes, and R. F. Kidd, 35–58. Hillsdale, N.J.: Lawrence Erlbaum.

Langer, Ellen J. (1989). *Mindfulness.* Reading, Mass.: Addison-Wesley.

Lanzetta, J. T., J. Cartwright-Smith, and R. E. Kleck (1976). Effects of Nonverbal Dissimulations on Emotional Experience and Autonomic Arousal. *Journal of Personality and Social Psychology* 33:354–370.

Latane, B., K. Williams, and S. Harkins (1979). Many Hands Make Light the Work: Causes and Consequences of Social Loafing. *Journal of Personality and Social Psychology* 37:822–832.

Leathers, Dale G. (1986). *Successful Nonverbal Communication: Principles and Applications.* New York: Macmillan.

Lederer, William J. (1984). *Creating a Good Relationship.* New York: W. W. Norton.

Lederer, William J., and D. D. Jackson (1968). *The Mirages of Marriage.* New York: W. W. Norton.

Lee, John Alan (1973). Styles of Loving. *Psychology Today* 8:43–51.

Lee, John Alan (1976). *The Colors of Love.* New York: Bantam.

LeVine, R., and K. Bartlett (1984). Pace of Life, Punctuality, and Coronary Heart Disease in Six Countries. *Journal of Cross-Cultural Psychology* 15:233–255.

Levinger, George (1983). The Embrace of Lives: Changing and Unchanging. In *Close Relationships: Perspectives on the Meaning of Intimacy,* edited by George Levinger and Harold L. Raush, 1–16. Amherst: University of Massachusetts Press.

Lips, H. M. (1981). *Women, Men, and the Psychology of Power.* Englewood Cliffs, N.J.: Prentice Hall.

Littlejohn, Stephen W. (1989). *Theories of Human Communication.* 3d ed. Belmont, Calif.: Wadsworth.

Loftus, Elizabeth F. (1979). *Eyewitness Testimony.* Cambridge, Mass.: Harvard University Press.

Loftus, Elizabeth F., and J. C. Palmer (1974). Reconstruction of Automobile Destruction: An Example of the Interaction Between Language and Memory. *Journal of Verbal Learning and Verbal Behavior* 13:585–589.

Loftus, Elizabeth F., and J. Monahan (1980). Trial by Data: Psychological Research as Legal Evidence. *American Psychologist* 35:270–283.

Lorenz, Konrad (1937). Imprinting. *The Auk* 54:245–273.

Luft, Joseph (1969). *Of Human Interaction.* Palo Alto, Calif.: Mayfield.

Luft, Joseph (1970). *Group Processes: An Introduction to Group Dynamics.* 2d ed. Palo Alto, Calif.: Mayfield.

Lujansky, H. and G. Mikula (1983). Can Equity Theory Explain the Quality and Stability of Romantic Relationships? *British Journal of Social Psychology* 22:101–112.

Lukens, J. (1978). Ethnocentric Speech. *Ethnic Groups* 2:35–53.

Lurie, Alison (1983). *The Language of Clothes.* New York: Vintage.

Lyman, Stanford M., and Marvin B. Scott (1967). Territoriality: A Neglected Sociological Dimension. *Social Problems* 15:236–249.

McCarthy, B., and S. W. Duck (1976). Friendship Duration and Responses to Attitudinal Agreement-Disagreement. *British Journal of Clinical and Social Psychology* 15:377–386.

McCornack, Steven A., and Malcolm R. Parks (1990). What Women Know That Men Don't: Sex Differences in Determining the Truth Behind Deceptive Messages. *Journal of Social and Personal Relationships* 7:107–118.

McCroskey, James C. (1982). *Introduction to Rhetorical Communication.* 4th ed. Englewood Cliffs, N.J.: Prentice Hall.

McCroskey, James, and Lawrence Wheeless (1976). *Introduction to Human Communication.* Boston: Allyn & Bacon.

McCroskey, James C., and Virginia P. Richmond (1983). Power in the Classroom I: Teacher and Student Perceptions. *Communication Education* 32:175–184.

McCroskey, James C. and Virginia P. Richmond (1990). Willingness to Communicate: Differing Cultural Perspectives. *Southern Communication Journal* 56 (Fall): 72–77.

McCroskey, James, Virginia P. Richmond, and Robert A. Stewart (1986). *One on One: The Foundations of Interpersonal Communication.* Englewood Cliffs, N.J.: Prentice Hall.

McCroskey, James C., S. Booth-Butterfield, and S. K. Payne (1989). The Impact of Communication Apprehension on College Student Retention and Success. *Communication Quarterly* 37:100–107.

McCroskey, James C., and John Daly, eds. (1987). *Personality and Interpersonal Communication.* Newbury Park, Calif.: Sage.

McGill, Michael E. (1985). *The McGill Report on Male Intimacy.* New York: Harper & Row.

MacLachlan, John (1979). What People Really Think of Fast Talkers. *Psychology Today* 13:113–117.

McLaughlin, Margaret L. (1984). *Conversation: How Talk Is Organized.* Newbury Park, Calif.: Sage.

McLaughlin, Margaret L., Michael L. Cody, and C. S. Robey (1980). Situational Influences on the Selection of Strategies to Resist Compliance-Gaining Attempts. *Human Communication Research* 1:14–36.

Mahl, George F., and Gene Schulze (1964). Psychological Research in the Extralinguistic Area. In *Approaches to Semiotics,* edited by T. A. Sebeok, A. S. Hayes, and M. C. Bateson. The Hague: Mouton.

Majeski, William J. (1988). *The Lie Detection Book.* New York: Ballantine.

Malandro, Loretta A., Larry Barker, and Deborah Ann Barker (1989). *Nonverbal Communication.* 2d ed. New York: Random House.

Malinowski, Bronislaw (1923). The Problem of Meaning in Primitive Languages. In *The Meaning of Meaning,* edited by C. K. Ogden and I. A. Richards, 296–336. New York: Harcourt Brace Jovanovich.

Marsh, Peter (1988). *Eye to Eye: How People Interact.* Topside, Mass.: Salem House.

Marshall, Evan (1983). *Eye Language: Understanding the Eloquent Eye.* New York: New Trend.

Marshall, Linda L., and Patricia Rose (1987). Gender, Stress, and Violence in the Adult Relationships of a Sample of College Students. *Journal of Social and Personal Relationships* 4:229–316.

Marston, Peter J., Michael L. Hecht, and Tia Robers (1987). True Love Ways: The Subjective Experience and Communication of Romantic Love. *Journal of Personal and Social Relationships* 4:387–407.

Martel, Myles (1989). *The Persuasive Edge.* New York: Fawcett.

Marwell, G., and D. R. Schmitt (1967). Dimensions of Compliance-Gaining Behavior: An Empirical Analysis. *Sociometry* 39:350–364.

Marwell, Gerald and David R. Schmitt (1990). An Introduction. In *Seeking Compliance: The Production of Interpersonal Influence Messages,* ed. James Price Dillard. Scottsdale, Ariz.: Gorsuch Scarisbrick, pp. 3–5.

Masheter, Carol, and Linda M. Harris (1986). From Divorce to Friendship: A Study of Dialective Relationship Development. *Journal of Social and Personal Relationships* 3:177–189.

Maslow, Abraham, and N. L. Mintz (1956). Effects of Esthetic Surroundings: I. Initial Effects of Three Esthetic Conditions upon Perceiving "Energy" and "Well-Being" in Faces. *Journal of Psychology* 41:247–254.

Matsumoto, David (1991). Cultural Influences on Facial Expressions of Emotion. *Southern Communication Journal* 56 (Winter): 128–137.

May, Gerald G. (1988). *Addiction and Grace.* San Francisco: HarperSanFrancisco.

Maynard, Harry E. (1963). How to Become a Better Premise Detective. *Public Relations Journal* 19:20–22.

Mehrabian, Albert (1968). Communication Without Words. *Psychology Today* 2:53–55.

Mehrabian, Albert (1976). *Public Places and Private Spaces.* New York: Basic Books.

Mehrabian, Albert (1978). *How We Communicate Feelings Nonverbally.* A *Psychology Today* cassette. New York: Ziff-Davis.

Mencken, H. L. (1971). *The American Language.* New York: Knopf.

Merton, Robert K. (1957). *Social Theory and Social Structure.* New York: Free Press.

Messick, R. M., and K. S. Cook, eds. (1983). *Equity Theory: Psychological and Sociological Perspectives.* New York: Praeger.

Midooka, Kiyoshi (1990). Characteristics of Japanese Style Communication. *Media, Culture and Society* 12 (October):477–489.

Millar, Frank E. and L. E. Rogers (1987). Relational Dimensions of Interpersonal Dynamics. In *Interpersonal Processes: New Directions in Communication Research,* ed. Michael E. Roloff and Gerald R. Millar, eds. Newbury Park, Calif.: Sage, pp. 117–139.

Miller, Casey, and Kate Swift (1976). *Words and Women: New Language in New Times.* Garden City, N.Y.: Doubleday.

Miller, Gerald R. (1978). The Current State of Theory and Research in Interpersonal Communication. *Human Communication Research* 4:164–178.

Miller, Gerald R. (1990). Interpersonal Communication. In *Human Communication:*

Theory and Research, edited by G. L. Dahnke and G. W. Clatterbuck, 91–122. Belmont, Calif.: Wadsworth.

Miller, Gerald R. and Judee Burgoon (1990). In DeVito and Hecht (1990), pp. 340–357.

Miller, Gerald R., and Malcolm R. Parks (1982). Communication in Dissolving Relationships. In Duck (1982), 127–154.

Miller, Mark J. and Charles T. Wilcox (1986). Measuring Perceived Hassles and Uplifts among the Elderly. *Journal of Human Behavior and Learning* 3:38–46.

Miller, Rodney, A. Reynolds, and Ronald E. Cambra (1987). The Influence of Gender and Culture on Language Intensity. *Communication Monographs* 54:101–105.

Miller, Sherod, Daniel Wackman, Elam Nunnally, and Carol Saline (1982). *Straight Talk.* New York: New American Library.

Miner, Horace (1956). Body Ritual Among the Nacierma. *American Anthropologist* 58:503–507.

Mintz, N. L. (1956). Effects of Esthetic Surroundings: II. Prolonged and Repeated Experience in a "Beautiful" and "Ugly" Room. *Journal of Psychology* 41:459–466.

Moghaddam, Fathali M., Donald M. Taylor, and Stephen C. Wright (1993). *Social Psychology in Cross-Cultural Perspective.* New York: W. H. Freeman.

Molloy, John (1975). *Dress for Success.* New York: P. H. Wyden.

Molloy, John (1977). *The Woman's Dress for Success Book.* Chicago: Follet.

Molloy, John (1981). *Molloy's Live for Success.* New York: Bantam.

Montague, Ashley (1971). *Touching: The Human Significance of the Skin.* New York: Harper & Row.

Montgomery, Barbara M. (1981). The Form and Function of Quality Communication in Marriage. *Family Relations* 30:21–30.

Montgomery, M. (1986). *An Introduction to Language and Society.* New York: Methuen.

Moriarty, Thomas (1975). A Nation of Willing Victims. *Psychology Today* 8:43–50.

Morris, Desmond (1967). *The Naked Ape.* London: Jonathan Cape.

Morris, Desmond (1972). *Intimate Behavior.* New York: Bantam.

Morris, Desmond (1977). *Manwatching: A Field Guide to Human Behavior.* New York: Abrams.

Morris, Desmond (1985). *Bodywatching.* New York: Crown.

Morris, Desmond, Peter Collett, Peter Marsh, and Marie O'Shaughnessy (1979). *Gestures: Their Origins and Distribution.* New York: Stein & Day.

Motley, Michael (1988). Taking the Terror Out of Talk. *Psychology Today* 22:46–49.

Motley, Michael T. (1990a). On Whether One Can(not) not Communicate: An Examination via traditional communication postulates. *Western Journal of Speech Communication* 54 (winter):1–20.

Motley, Michael T. (1990b). Communication as Interaction: A Reply to Beach and Bavelas. *Western Journal of Speech Communication* 54 (fall):613–623.

Mulac, Anthony, Lisa B. Studley, John W. Wiemann, and James J. Bradac (1987). Male/Female Gaze in Same-Sex and Mixed-Sex Dyads: Gender-Linked Differences and Mutual Influence. *Human Communication Research* 13 (Spring):323–344.

Mulac, A., J. M. Wiemann, S. J. Widenmann, and T. W. Gibson (1988). Male/Female Language Differences and Effects in Same-Sex and Mixed-Sex Dyads: The Gender-Linked Language Effect. *Communication Monographs* 55:315–335.

Naifeh, Steven, and Gregory White Smith (1984). *Why Can't Men Open Up? Overcoming Men's Fear of Intimacy.* New York: Clarkson N. Potter.

Naisbitt, John (1984). *Megatrends: Ten New Directions Transforming Our Lives.* New York: Warner.

Neimeyer, Robert A., and Greg J. Neimeyer (1983). Structural Similarity in the Acquaintance Process. *Journal of Social and Clinical Psychology* 1:146–154.

Neimeyer, Robert A., and Kelly A. Mitchell (1988). Similarity and Attraction: A Longitudinal Study. *Journal of Social and Personal Relationships* 5 May: 131–148.

Newsweek (1992). The Wounds of Words: When Verbal Abuse Is as Scary as Physical Abuse. 12 October, 90–92.

Nichols, Ralph (1961). Do We Know How to

Listen? Practical Helps in a Modern Age. *Communication Education* 10:118–124.

Nichols, Ralph, and Leonard Stevens (1957). *Are You Listening?* New York: McGraw-Hill.

Nierenberg, Gerald, and Henry Calero (1971). *How to Read a Person Like a Book.* New York: Pocket Books.

Nierenberg, Gerald, and Henry Calero (1973). *Metatalk.* New York: Simon & Schuster.

Noller, Patricia (1982). Couple Communication and Marital Satisfaction. *Australian Journal of Sex, Marriage, and Family* 3:69–75.

Noller, Patricia, and Harley Hiscock (1989). Fitzpatrick's Typology: An Australian Replication. *Journal of Social and Personal Relationships* 6:87–92.

Noller, Patricia, and Mary Anne Fitzpatrick (1993). *Communication in Family Relationships.* Englewood Cliffs, N.J.: Prentice Hall.

Norton, Robert, and Barbara Warnick (1976). Assertiveness as a Communication Construct. *Human Communication Research* 3:62–66.

Notarius, Clifford I., and Lisa R. Herrick (1988). Listener Response Strategies to a Distressed Other. *Journal of Social and Personal Relationships* 5:97–108.

Oberg, K. (1960). Cultural Shock: Adjustment to New Cultural Environments. *Practical Anthropology* 7:177–182.

O'Hair, D., M. J. Cody, and M. L. McLaughlin (1981). Prepared Lies, Spontaneous Lies, Machiavellianism, and Nonverbal Communication. *Human Communication Research* 7:325–339.

O'Hair, D., M. J. Cody, B. Goss, and K. J. Krayer (1988). The Effect of Gender, Deceit Orientation, and Communicator Style on Macro-Assessments of Honesty. *Communication Quarterly* 36:77–93.

O'Hair, Mary John, Michael J. Cody, and Dan O'Hair (1991). The Impact of Situational Dimensions on Compliance-Resisting Strategies: A Comparison of Methods. *Communication Quarterly* 39 (summer):226–240.

Otto, Herbert A., ed. (1972). *Love Today: A New Exploration.* New York: Delta.

Palmer, M. T. (1989). Controlling Conversations: Turns, Topics, and Interpersonal Control. *Communication Monographs* 56:1–18.

Parlee, Mary Brown (1979). The Friendship Bond. *Psychology Today* 13 (October):43–54, 113.

Patterson, Brian, and Dan O'Hair (1992). Relational Reconciliation: Toward a More Comprehensive Model of Relational Development. *Communication Research Reports* 9 (December): 119–130.

Peabody, Susan (1989). *Addiction to Love: Overcoming Obsession and Dependency in Relationships.* Berkeley, Calif.: Ten Speed Press.

Pearce, W. Barnett, and Steward M. Sharp (1973). Self-Disclosing Communication. *Journal of Communication* 23:409–425.

Pearson, Judy C. (1980). Sex Roles and Self-Disclosure. *Psychological Reports* 47:640.

Pearson, Judy C. (1993). *Communication in the Family,* 2d ed. New York: Harper-Collins.

Pearson, Judy C., and Brian H. Spitzberg (1990). *Interpersonal Communication: Concepts, Components, and Contexts,* 2d ed. Dubuque, Iowa: William C. Brown.

Pearson, Judy C., Lynn H. Turner, and William Todd-Mancillas (1991). *Gender and Communication.* 2d ed. Dubuque, Iowa: William C. Brown.

Pease, Allen (1984). *Signals: How to Use Body Language for Power, Success, and Love.* New York: Bantam.

Penfield, Joyce, ed. (1987). *Women and Language in Transition.* Albany: State University of New York Press.

Pennebacker, James W. (1991). *Opening Up: The Healing Power of Confiding in Others.* New York: Morrow.

Peplau, Letitia Anne (1988). Research on Homosexual Couples: An Overview. In *Gay Relationships,* edited by John DeCecco, 33–40. New York: Harrington Park Press.

Peplau, Letitia Anne, and Daniel Perlman, eds. (1982). *Loneliness: A Sourcebook of Current Theory, Research, and Therapy.* New York: Wiley/Interscience.

Perlman, Daniel, and Letitia Anne Peplau (1981). Toward a Social Psychology of Loneliness. In *Personal Relationships. 3: Personal Relationships in Disorder,* edited by Steve Duck and Robin Gilmour, 31–56. New York: Academic Press.

Petrocelli, William and Barbara Kate Repa (1992). *Sexual Harassment on the Job.* Berkeley, Calif.: Nolo Press.

Pilkington, Constance J., and Deborah R. Richardson (1988). Perceptions of Risk in Intimacy. *Journal of Social and Personal Relationships* 5:503–508.

Pittenger, R. E., C. F. Hockett, and J. J. Danehy (1960). *The First Five Minutes.* Ithaca, N.Y.: Paul Martineau.

Plutchik, R. (1980). *Emotions: A Psycho-Evolutionary Synthesis.* New York: Harper & Row.

Prather, H., and G. Prather (1988). *A Book for Couples.* New York: Doubleday.

Prins, K. S., B. P. Buunk, and N. W. Van Yperen (1994). Equity, Normative Disapproval, and Extramarital Sex. *Journal of Social and Personal Relationships* 50, in press.

Prisbell, Marshall (1986). The Relationship Between Assertiveness and Dating Behavior Among College Students. *Communication Research Reports* 3 (December): 9–12.

Purnell, Rosentene B. (1982). Teaching Them to Curse: A Study of Certain Types of Inherent Racial Bias in Language Pedagogy and Practices. *Phylon* 43 (September): 231–241.

Rabin, Claire, and Dvora Zelner (1992). The Role of Assertiveness in Clarifying Roles and Strengthening Job Satisfaction of Social Workers in Multidisciplinary Mental Health Settings. *British Journal of Social Work* 22 (February): 17–32.

Rank, H. (1984). *The PEP Talk: How to Analyze Political Language.* Park Forest, Ill.: Counter Propaganda Press.

Rankin, Paul (1929). Listening Ability. *Proceedings of the Ohio State Educational Conference's Ninth Annual Session.*

Raven, B., C. Centers, and A. Rodrigues (1975). The Bases of Conjugal Power. In *Power in Families,* edited by R. E. Cromwell and D. H. Olson, 217–234. New York: Halsted Press.

Rawlins, William K. (1983). Negotiating Close Friendship: The Dialectic of Conjunctive Freedoms. *Human Communication Research* 9 (spring): 255–266.

Rawlins, William K. (1989). A Dialectical Analysis of the Tensions, Functions, and Strategic Challenges of Communication in Young Adult Friendships. *Communication Yearbook/12,* edited by James A. Anderson, 157–189. Newbury Park, Calif.: Sage.

Reardon, Kathleen K. (1987). *Where Minds Meet: Interpersonal Communication.* Belmont, Calif.: Wadsworth.

Reed, Warren H. (1985). *Positive Listening: Learning to Hear What People Are Really Saying.* New York: Franklin Watts.

Reik, Theodore (1944). *A Psychologist Looks at Love.* New York: Rinehart.

Reisman, John (1979). *Anatomy of Friendship.* Lexington, Mass.: Lewis.

Reisman, John M. (1981). Adult Friendships. In *Personal Relationships. 2: Developing Personal Relationships,* eds. Steve Duck and Robin Gilmour. New York: Academic Press, pp. 205–230.

Rich, Andrea L. (1974). *Interracial Communication.* New York: Harper & Row.

Richards, I. A. (1951). Communication Between Men: The Meaning of Language. In *Cybernetics, Transactions of the Eighth Conference,* edited by Heinz von Foerster.

Richmond, Virginia P., and J. C. McCroskey (1984). Power in the Classroom II: Power and Learning. *Communication Education* 33:125–136.

Richmond, Virginia P., L. M. Davis, K. Saylor, and J. C. McCroskey (1984). Power Strategies in Organizations: Communication Techniques and Messages. *Human Communication Research* 11:85–108.

Richmond, Virginia P., J. C. McCroskey, and Steven Payne (1987). *Nonverbal Behavior in Interpersonal Relationships.* Englewood Cliffs, N.J.: Prentice Hall.

Richmond, Virginia P., and J. C. McCroskey (1989). *Communication: Apprehension, Avoidance, and Effectiveness.* 2d ed. Scottsdale, Ariz.: Gorsuch Scarisbrick.

Riggio, Ronald E. (1987). *The Charisma Quotient.* New York: Dodd, Mead.

Roach, K. David (1991). The Influence and Effects of Gender and Status on University

Instructor Affinity-Seeking Behavior. *Southern Communication Journal* 57 (fall): 73–80.

Robinson, W. P. (1972). *Language and Social Behavior.* Baltimore: Penguin.

Rodriguez, Maria (1988). Do Blacks and Hispanics Evaluate Assertive Male and Female Characters Differently? *Howard Journal of Communication* 1:101–107.

Roger, Derek and Willfried Nesshoever (1987). Individual Differences in Dyadic Conversational Strategies: A Further Study. *British Journal of Social Psychology* 26 (September):247–255.

Rogers, Carl (1970). *Carl Rogers on Encounter Groups.* New York: Harrow Books.

Rogers, Carl, and Richard Farson (1981). Active Listening. In DeVito (1981), 137–147.

Rogers, Everett M. (1983). *Diffusion of Innovations.* 3d ed. New York: Free Press.

Rogers, Everett M., and Rekha Agarwala-Rogers (1976). *Communication in Organizations.* New York: Free Press.

Rogers, L. E., and R. V. Farace (1975). Analysis of Relational Communication in Dyads: New Measurement Procedures. *Human Communication Research* 1:222–239.

Rogers-Millar, Edna and Frank E. Millar (1979). Domineeringness and Dominance: A Transactional View. *Human Communication Research* (spring):238–246.

Rosenfeld, Lawrence (1979). Self-Disclosure Avoidance: Why I Am Afraid to Tell You Who I Am. *Communication Monographs* 46:63–74.

Rosenfeld, Lawrence, Sallie Kartus, and Chett Ray (1976). Body Accessibility Revisited. *Journal of Communication* 26:27–30.

Rosenthal, Peggy (1984). *Words and Values: Some Leading Words and Where They Lead Us.* New York: Oxford University Press.

Rosenthal, Robert, and L. Jacobson (1968). *Pygmalion in the Classroom.* New York: Holt, Rinehart & Winston.

Rosnow, Ralph L. (1977). Gossip and Marketplace Psychology. *Journal of Communication* 27 (winter):158–163.

Rossiter, Charles M., Jr. (1975). Defining "Therapeutic Communication." *Journal of Communication* 25:127–130.

Rothwell, J. Dan (1982). *Telling It Like It Isn't: Language Misuse and Malpractice/What We Can Do About It.* Englewood Cliffs, N.J.: Prentice Hall.

Rowland-Morin, Pamela A., and J. Gregory Carroll (1990). Verbal Communication Skills and Patient Satisfaction: A Study of Doctor-Patient Interviews. *Evaluation and the Health Professions* 13:168–185.

Ruben, Brent D. (1985). Human Communication and Cross-Cultural Effectiveness. In Samovar and Porter (1985), 338–346.

Ruben, Brent D. (1988). *Communication and Human Behavior.* 2d ed. New York: Macmillan.

Rubenstein, Carin (1993). Fighting Sexual Harassment in Schools. *New York Times,* 10 June, C8.

Rubenstein, Carin, and Philip Shaver (1982). *In Search of Intimacy.* New York: Delacorte.

Rubin, Jeffrey, and Warren F. Shaffer (1987). Some Interpersonal Effects of Imposing Guilt Versus Eliciting Altruism. *Counseling and Values* 31 (April): 190–193.

Rubin, Rebecca B., and Elizabeth E. Graham. (1988). Communication Correlates of College Success: An Exploratory Investigation. *Communication Education* 37:14–27.

Rubin, Rebecca B. and Randi J. Nevins (1988). *The Road Trip: An Interpersonal Adventure.* Prospect Heights, Ill.: Waveland Press.

Rubin, Theodore Isaac (1983). *One to One: Understanding Personal Relationships.* New York: Viking.

Rubin, Zick (1973). *Liking and Loving: An Invitation to Social Psychology.* New York: Holt, Rinehart & Winston.

Rubin, Zick, and Elton B. McNeil (1985). *Psychology: Being Human.* 4th ed. New York: Harper & Row.

Ruesch, Jurgen, and Gregory Bateson (1951). *Communication: The Social Matrix of Psychiatry.* New York: W. W. Norton.

Rusbult, Caryl E. and Bram P. Buunk (1993). Commitment Processes in Close Relationships: An Interdependence Analysis. *Journal of Social and Personal Relationships* 10 (May):175–204.

Sabatelli, Ronald M., and John Pearce (1986). Exploring Marital Expectations. *Journal of*

Social and Personal Relationships 3:307–321.

Saegert, Susan, Walter Swap, and Robert B. Zajonc (1973). Exposure, Context, and Interpersonal Attraction. *Journal of Personality and Social Psychology* 25:234–242.

Samovar, Larry A., Richard E. Porter, and Nemi C. Jain (1981). *Understanding Intercultural Communication.* Belmont, Calif.: Wadsworth.

Samovar, Larry A., and Richard E. Porter, eds. (1985). *Intercultural Communication: A Reader,* 4th ed. Belmont, Calif.: Wadsworth.

Samovar, Larry A., and Richard E. Porter, eds. (1988). *Intercultural Communication: A Reader.* 5th ed. Belmont, Calif.: Wadsworth.

Sanders, Judith A., Richard L. Wiseman, and S. Irene Matz (1991). Uncertainty Reduction in Acquaintance Relationships in Ghana and the United States. In *Cross-Cultural Interpersonal,* ed., Stella Ting-Toomey and Felipe Korzenny. Newbury Park, Calif.: Sage, pp. 79–98.

Sanford, John A. (1982). *Between People.* New York: Paulist Press.

Sapadin, Linda A. (1988). Friendship and Gender: Perspectives of Professional Men and Women. *Journal of Social and Personal Relationships* 5:387–403.

Sargent, J. F., and Gerald R. Miller (1971). Some Differences in Certain Communication Behaviors of Autocratic and Democratic Leaders. *Journal of Communication* 21:233–252.

Sashkin, Marshall, and William C. Morris (1984). *Organizational Behavior: Concepts and Experiences.* Reston, Va.: Prentice Hall, Reston Publishing.

Satir, Virginia (1972). *Peoplemaking.* Palo Alto, Calif.: Science and Behavior Books.

Satir, Virginia (1983). *Conjoint Family Therapy.* 3d ed. Palo Alto, Calif.: Science and Behavior Books.

Schachter, Stanley (1964). The Interaction of Cognitive and Physiological Determinants of Emotional State. In *Advances in Experimental Social Psychology,* vol. 1, edited by Leonard Berkowitz. New York: Academic Press.

Schaef, Anne Wilson (1986). *Co-Dependence.* New York: HarperCollins.

Schaef, Anne Wilson (1990). *Addictive Relationships.* New York: HarperCollins.

Schaefer, Charles E. (1984). *How to Talk to Children About Really Important Things.* New York: Harper & Row.

Schafer, R. B. and P. M. Keith (1980). Equity and Depression Among Married Couples. *Social Psychology Quarterly* 43:430–435.

Schatski, Michael (1981). *Negotiation: The Art of Getting What You Want.* New York: New American Library.

Schegloff, E. (1982). Discourses as an Interactional Achievement: Some Uses of "uh huh" and Other Things that Come Between Sentences. In *Georgetown University Roundtable on Language and Linguistics,* edited by Deborah Tannen. Washington, D.C.: Georgetown University Press, pp. 71–93.

Scherer, K. R. (1986). Vocal Affect Expression. *Psychological Bulletin* 99:143–165.

Schmidt, Tracy O., and Randolph R. Cornelius (1987). Self-Disclosure in Everyday Life. *Journal of Social and Personal Relationships* 4:365–373.

Schramm, Wilbur (1988). *The Story of Human Communication: Cave Painting to Microchip.* New York: Harper & Row.

Seaver, W. B. (1973). Effects of Naturally Induced Teacher Expectancies. *Journal of Personality and Social Psychology* 28:333–342.

Sergios, Paul A., and James Cody (1985). Physical Attractiveness and Social Assertiveness Skills in Male Homosexual Dating Behavior and Partner Selection. *Journal of Social Psychology* 125 (August): 505–514.

Shannon, J. (1987). Don't Smile When You Say That. *Executive Female* 10:33, 43. Reprinted in DeVito and Hecht (1990), 115–117.

Sheppard, James A. and Alan J. Strathman (1989). Attractiveness and Height: The Role of Stature in Dating Preferences, Frequency of Dating, and Perceptions of Attractiveness. *Personality and Social Psychology* 15 (December): 617–627.

Shimanoff, Susan (1980). *Communication*

Rules: Theory and Research. Newbury Park, Calif.: Sage.

Shuter, Robert (1990). The Centrality of Culture. *Southern Communication Journal* 55 (spring): 237–249.

Siavelis, Rita L., and Leanne K. Lamke (1992). Instrumentalness and Expressiveness: Predictors of Heterosexual Relationship Satisfaction. *Sex Roles* 26 (February): 149–159.

Sillars, Alan L., and Michael D. Scott (1983). Interpersonal Perception Between Intimates: An Integrative Review. *Human Communication Research* 10:153–176.

Simpson, Jeffry A. (1987). The Dissolution of Romantic Relationships: Factors Involved in Relationship Stability and Emotional Distress. *Journal of Personality and Social Psychology* 53 (October): 683–692.

Singer, Marshall R. (1987). *Intercultural Communication: A Perceptual Approach.* Englewood Cliffs, N.J.: Prentice Hall.

Siu, R. G. H. (1984). *The Craft of Power.* New York: Quill.

Small, Jacquelyn (1990). *Becoming Naturally Therapeutic.* New York: Bantam.

Smith, L. J., and L. A. Malandro (1985). *Courtroom Communication Strategies.* New York: Kluwer Law Book Publishers.

Snyder, C. R. (1984). Excuses, Excuses. *Psychology Today* 18:50–55.

Snyder, C. R., Raymond L. Higgins, and Rita J. Stucky (1983). *Excuses: Masquerades in Search of Grace.* New York: Wiley.

Snyder, Mark (1986). *Public Appearances, Private Realities.* New York: W. H. Freeman.

Snyder, Mark (1987). *Public Appearances/ Private Realities: The Psychology of Self-Monitoring.* New York: W. H. Freeman & Co.

Solomon, Michael R. (1986). Dress for Effect. *Psychology Today* 20:20–28.

Sommer, Robert (1969). *Personal Space: The Behavioral Basis of Design.* Englewood Cliffs, N.J.: Prentice Hall, Spectrum.

Sommer, Robert (1972). *Design Awareness.* Englewood Cliffs, N.J.: Prentice Hall.

Spencer, Ted (1993). A New Approach to Assessing Self-Disclosure in Conversation.

Paper presented at the Annual Convention of the Western Speech Communication Association, Albuquerque, New Mexico.

Spencer, Ted (1994). Transforming Relationships Through Everyday Talk. In *The Dynamics of Relationships,* Vol. 4, *Understanding Relationships,* edited by Steve Duck. Newbury Park, Calif.: Sage.

Spitzberg, Brian H., and Michael L. Hecht (1984). A Component Model of Relational Competence. *Human Communication Research* 10:575–599.

Spitzberg, Brian H., and William R. Cupach (1984). *Interpersonal Communication Competence.* Newbury Park, Calif.: Sage.

Spitzberg, Brian H., and William R. Cupach (1989). *Handbook of Interpersonal Competence Research.* New York: Springer-Verlag.

Sprecher, Susan (1987). The Effects of Self-Disclosure Given and Received on Affection for an Intimate Partner and Stability of the Relationship. *Journal of Social and Personal Relationships* 4:115–127.

Sprecher, Susan, and Sandra Metts (1989). Development of the "Romantic Beliefs Scale" and Examination of the Effects of Gender and Gender-Role Orientation. *Journal of Social and Personal Relationships* 6:387–411.

Stafford, L., and D. J. Canary (1991). Maintenance Strategies and Romantic Relationship Type, Gender, and Relational Characteristics. *Journal of Social and Personal Relationships* 8:217–242.

Staines, Graham L., Kathleen J. Pottick, and Deborah A. Fudge (1986). Wives' Employment and Husbands' Attitudes Toward Work and Life. *Journal of Applied Psychology* 71:118–128.

Steil, Lyman K., Larry L. Barker, and Kittie W. Watson (1983). *Effective Listening: Key to Your Success.* Reading, Mass.: Addison-Wesley.

Steiner, Claude (1981). *The Other Side of Power.* New York: Grove.

Sternberg, Robert J. (1986). A Triangular Theory of Love. *Psychological Review* 93:119–135.

Sternberg, Robert J. (1988). *The Triangle of Love: Intimacy, Passion, Commitment.* New York: Basic Books.

Stillings, Neil A., et al. (1987). *Cognitive Science: An Introduction.* Cambridge, Mass.: MIT Press.

Sunnafrank, Michael (1989). Uncertainty in Interpersonal Relationships: A Predicted Outcome Value Interpretation of Gudykunst's Research Program. In *Communication Yearbook 12,* edited by J. A. Anderson, 355–370. Newbury Park, Calif.: Sage.

Swensen, C. H. (1973). *Introduction to Interpersonal Relations.* Glenview, Ill.: Scott, Foresman.

Swets, Paul W. (1983). *The Art of Talking so That People Will Listen.* Englewood Cliffs, N.J.: Prentice Hall, Spectrum.

Taylor, Dalmas A., and Irwin Altman (1987). Communication in Interpersonal Relationships: Social Penetration Processes. In *Interpersonal Processes: New Directions in Communication Research,* edited by M. E. Roloff and G. R. Miller, 257–277. Newbury Park, Calif.: Sage.

Tersine, Richard J., and Walter E. Riggs (1980). The Delphi Technique: A Long-Range Planning Tool. In *Intercom: Readings in Organizational Communication,* edited by Stewart Ferguson and Sherry Devereaux Ferguson, 363–373. Rochelle Park, N.J.: Hayden Books.

Thayer, Stephen (1988). Close Encounters. *Psychology Today* 22:31–36. Reprinted in DeVito and Hecht (1990), 217–225.

Thibaut, J. W., and H. H. Kelley (1959). *The Social Psychology of Groups.* New York: Wiley. Reissued (1986). New Brunswick, N.J.: Transaction Books.

Thomlison, Dean (1982). *Toward Interpersonal Dialogue.* New York: Longman.

Thompson, S. C., and H. H. Kelley (1981). Judgments of Responsibility for Activities in Close Relationships. *Journal of Personality and Social Psychology* 41:469–477.

Thorne, Barrie, Cheris Kramarae, and Nancy Henley, eds. (1983). *Language, Gender, and Society.* Rowley, Mass.: Newbury House.

Tolhuizen, James H. (1986). Perceiving Communication Indicators of Evolutionary Changes in Friendship. *Southern Speech Communication Journal* 52:69–91.

Tolhuizen, James H. (1989). Communication Strategies for Intensifying Dating Relationships: Identification, Use, and Structure. *Journal of Social and Personal Relationships* 6 (November): 413–434.

Trager, George L. (1958). Paralanguage: A First Approximation. *Studies in Linguistics* 13:1–12.

Trager, George L. (1961). The Typology of Paralanguage. *Anthropological Linguistics* 3:17–21.

Trenholm, Sarah (1986). *Human Communication Theory.* Englewood Cliffs, N.J.: Prentice Hall.

Trower, P. (1981). Social Skill Disorder. In *Personal Relationships* 3, edited by S. Duck and R. Gilmour, 97–110. New York: Academic Press.

Truax, C. (1961). A Scale for the Measurement of Accurate Empathy. Wisconsin Psychiatric Institute Discussion Paper no. 20, Madison.

Tschann, J. M. (1988). Self-Disclosure in Adult Friendship: Gender and Marital Status Differences. *Journal of Social and Personal Relationships* 5:65–81.

Tubbs, Stewart L. (1988). *A Systems Approach to Small Group Interaction.* 3d ed. New York: Random House.

Ueleke, William, et al. (1983). Inequity Resolving Behavior as a Response to Inequity in a Hypothetical Marital Relationship. *A Quarterly Journal of Human Behavior* 20:4–8.

Ullmann, Stephen (1962). *Semantics: An Introduction to the Science of Meaning.* New York: Barnes & Noble.

VandeCreek, Leon, and Lori Angstadt (1985). Client Preferences and Anticipations About Counselor Self-Disclosure. *Journal of Counseling Psychology* 32:206–214.

VanHyning, Memory (1993). *Crossed Signals: How to Say No to Sexual Harassment.* Los Angeles: Infotrends Press.

Veenendall, Thomas L., and Marjorie C. Feinstein (1990). *Let's Talk About Relationships: Cases in Study.* Prospect Heights, Ill.: Waveland Press.

Verderber, Rudolph F., and Verderber, Kathleen S. (1989). *Inter-Act: Using Interpersonal Communication Skills.* Belmont, Calif.: Wadsworth.

Victor, David (1992). *International Business Communication.* New York: HarperCollins.

Walster, E., and G. W. Walster (1978). *A New Look at Love.* Reading, Mass.: Addison-Wesley.

Walster, E., G. W. Walster, and E. Berscheid (1978). *Equity: Theory and Research.* Boston: Allyn & Bacon.

Wardhaugh, R. (1985). *How Conversation Works.* New York: Basil Blackwell.

Watson, Arden K., and Carley H. Dodd (1984). Alleviating Communication Apprehension Through Rational Emotive Therapy: A Comparative Evaluation. *Communication Education* 33:257–266.

Watson, Kittie W., and Larry L. Barker (1984). Listening Behavior: Definition and Measurement. In *Communication Yearbook 8,* edited by Robert N. Bostrom, 178–197. Newbury Park, Calif.: Sage.

Watzlawick, Paul (1977). *How Real Is Real? Confusion, Disinformation, Communication: An Anecdotal Introduction to Communications Theory.* New York: Vintage.

Watzlawick, Paul (1978). *The Language of Change: Elements of Therapeutic Communication.* New York: Basic Books.

Watzlawick, Paul, Janet Helmick Beavin, and Don D. Jackson (1967). *Pragmatics of Human Communication: A Study of Interactional Patterns, Pathologies, and Paradoxes.* New York: W. W. Norton.

Webster, E. (1988). The Power of Negative Thinking: Twenty-two Convenient Ways to Bury an Idea. *Etc.: A Review of General Semantics* 45:246–249.

Weinberg, Harry L. (1959). *Levels of Knowing and Existence.* New York: Harper & Row.

Weiner, Bernard (1985). An Attributional Theory of Achievement, Motivation, and Emotion. *Psychological Review* 92:548–573.

Weiner, Bernard, J. Amirkhan, V. S. Folkes, and J. A. Verette (1987). An Attributional Analysis of Excuse Giving: Studies of a Naive Theory of Emotion. *Journal of Personality and Social Psychology* 52:316–324.

Weinstein, Eugene A., and Paul Deutschberger (1963). Some Dimensions of Altercasting. *Sociometry* 26:454–466.

Wells, Theodora (1980). *Keeping Your Cool under Fire: Communicating Non-Defensively.* New York: McGraw-Hill.

Wertz, Dorothy C., James R. Sorenson, and Timothy C. Heeren (1988). "Can't Get No (Dis) Satisfaction": Professional Satisfaction with Professional-Client Encounters. *Work and Occupations* 15 (February):36–54.

Wessells, Michael G. (1982). *Cognitive Psychology.* New York: Harper & Row.

West, Candace and Don H. Zimmerman (1977). Women's Place in Everyday Talk: Reflections on Parent-Child Interaction. *Social Problems* 24 (June):521–529.

Wheeless, Lawrence R., and Janis Grotz (1977). The Measurement of Trust and Its Relationship to Self-Disclosure. *Human Communication Research* 3:250–257.

Wiemann, John M. (1977). Explication and Test of a Model of Communicative Competence. *Human Communication Research* 3:195–213.

Wiemann, John M., and P. Backlund (1980). Current Theory and Research in Communicative Competence. *Review of Educational Research* 50:185–199.

Wiemann, John M., A. Mulac, D. Zimmerman, and S. K. Mann (1987). Interruption Patterns in Same-Gender and Mixed-Gender Dyadic Conversations. Paper presented at the Third International Conference on Social Psychology and Language, Bristol, England. Cited in Mulac, Wiemann, Widenmann, and Gibson (1988).

Williams, Andrea (1985). *Making Decisions.* New York: Zebra.

Wilmot, William W. (1987). *Dyadic Communication.* 3d ed. New York: Random House.

Wilson, Glenn, and David Nias (1976). *The Mystery of Love.* New York: Quadrangle/New York Times.

Wilson, R. A. (1989). Toward Understanding E-prime. *Etc.: A Review of General Semantics* 46:316–319.

Wolf, Florence I., Nadine C. Marsnik,

William S. Tacey, and Ralph G. Nichols (1983). *Perceptive Listening.* New York: Holt, Rinehart & Winston.

Won-Doornink, Myong-Jin (1985). Self-Disclosure and Reciprocity in Conversation: A Cross-National Study. *Social Psychology Quarterly* 48:97–107.

Wood, John, ed. (1974). *How Do You Feel?* Englewood Cliffs, N.J.: Prentice Hall.

Wood, Julia T. (1982). Communication and Relational Culture: Bases for the Study of Human Relationships. *Communication Quarterly* 30:75–83.

Wright, John, ed. (1990). *The Universal Almanac.* New York: Andrews & McMeel.

Wright, J. W. and L. A. Hosman (1983). Language Style and Sex Bias in the Courtroom: The Effects of Male and Female Use of Hedges and Intensifiers on Impression Formation. *Southern Speech Communication Journal* 48:137–152.

Wright, Paul H. (1978). Toward a Theory of Friendship Based on a Conception of Self. *Human Communication Research* 4:196–207.

Wright, Paul H. (1984). Self-Referent Motivation and the Intrinsic Quality of Friendship. *Journal of Social and Personal Relationships* 1:115–130.

Wright, Paul H. (1988). Interpreting Research on Gender Differences in Friendship: A Case for Moderation and a Plea for Caution. *Journal of Social and Personal Relationships* 5:367–373.

Wright, Rex A., and Richard J. Contrada (1986). Dating Selectivity and Interpersonal Attraction: Toward a Better Understanding of the "Elusive Phenomenon." *Journal of*

Social and Personal Relationships 3:131–148.

Yerby, Janet, Nancy Buerkel-Rothfuss, and Arthur P. Bochner (1990). *Understanding Family Communication.* Scottsdale, Ariz.: Gorsuch Scarisbrick.

Yogev, Sara (1987). Marital Satisfaction and Sex Role Perceptions Among Dual-Earner Couples. *Journal of Social and Personal Relationships* 4:35–45.

Yun, Hum (1976). The Korean Personality and Treatment Considerations. *Social Casework* 57:173–178.

Zajonc, Robert B. (1968). Attitudinal Effects of Mere Exposure. *Journal of Personality and Social Psychology Monograph* Suppl. 9, no. 2, pt. 2.

Zanden, James W. Vander (1984). *Social Psychology.* 3d ed. New York: Random House.

Zimbardo, Philip A. (1977). *Shyness: What It Is and What to Do About It.* Reading, Mass.: Addison-Wesley.

Zimmer, Troy A. (1986). Premarital Anxieties. *Journal of Social and Personal Relationships* 3:149–159.

Zimmerman, Don H. and Candace West (1975). Sex Roles, Interruptions and Silences in Conversations. In *Language and Sex: Differences and Dominance,* eds. B. Thorne and N. Henley. Rowley, Mass: Newbury House.

Zuckerman, M., R. Klorman, D. T. Larrance, and N. H. Spiegel (1981). Facial, Autonomic, and Subjective Components of Emotion: The Facial Feedback Hypothesis Versus the Externalizer-Internalizer Distinction. *Journal of Personality and Social Psychology* 41:929–944.

Zunin, Leonard M., and Natalie B. Zunin (1972). *Contact: The First Four Minutes.* Los Angeles: Nash.

Credits

Index

Note: Page numbers in italics indicate where terms are defined